SYNTAX

SYNTAX

Theory and Problems

Donna Jo Napoli

New York   Oxford
OXFORD UNIVERSITY PRESS
1993

Oxford University Press

Oxford   New York   Toronto
Delhi   Bombay   Calcutta   Madras   Karachi
Kuala Lumpur   Singapore   Hong Kong   Tokyo
Nairobi   Dar es Salaam   Cape Town
Melbourne   Auckland   Madrid

and associated companies in
Berlin   Ibadan

Copyright © 1993 by Donna Jo Napoli

Published by Oxford University Press, Inc.
200 Madison Avenue, New York, New York 10016

Oxford is a registered trademark of Oxford University Press, Inc.

Library of Congress Cataloging-in-Publication Data
Napoli, Donna Jo, 1948–
Syntax : theory and problems / Donna Jo Napoli.
p. cm.   Includes bibliographical references and index.
ISBN 0-19-507946-9
1. Grammar, Comparative and general—Syntax.
2. Linguistics-Methodology—Problems, exercises, etc.   I. Title.
P291.N27   1993
415—dc20   92-27413

1 3 5 7 9 8 6 4 2

Printed in the United States of America
on acid free paper

Acknowledgments

I am deeply grateful to Jennifer Arnold, Virginia Brennan, Nell Duke, and Mika Hoffman for discussing with me an earlier draft of this book, and to Noriko Nagai, Mutsuko Endo Hudson, and Natsuko Tsujimura for comments on the Japanese problem sets. This work was partially supported by the National Endowment for the Humanities Fellowship for College Teachers and Independent Scholars, number FB-27947-90, from May 1990 to May 1991. I hereby thank the NEH, which in no way endorses or is to be held responsible for the contents of this text. I also thank Swarthmore College, which gave me a sabbatical in 1990–1991 so that I could write this book. My greatest debt is to all of the students I've ever taught.

Contents

6. Empty Categories and Movement   256

7. Control Theory, NP-Trace, and Governing Categories   320

9. Accessibility, the Empty-Category Principle, and Crossover   474

10. Residual Issues in Binding Theory   512

SYNTAX

Introduction

This book is intended to get the reader started doing linguistic analysis of sentences and phrases (that is, syntactic analysis) within a Government and Binding (GB) framework. This text can be used in a classroom or at home. However, it is organized and designed in a nonstandard way.

Linguistics, like other sciences, proceeds deductively. One forms hypotheses and then considers data that confirm or deny those hypotheses. Teachers of syntax, therefore, often present their students with a theoretical model before turning to the data. I do not do that in this book. I have found that students faced with the intricacies of a theory may be tempted to memorize without understanding. Also, when faced with a completed theory, a student, overwhelmed, may simply accept the theory as gospel. So, instead, I have adopted an inductive approach in this book. The reader is faced with data right from the start and is led to considerations of the data that allow the reader to develop a theory of grammar. If you become a syntactician and do original research, you will probably proceed in the reverse—deductive— logical direction. Still, the skills taught here do apply to syntactic research. It is my hope that the present organization will allow you easy access to an intricate theory (known as GB) without mindless memorization and without the inappropriate feeling that the theory is unassailable.

An additional result of the data-oriented approach adopted here is that a range of phenomena are handled, some of which would otherwise have been left out since they are not crucial to understanding the theory. Thus you are offered a richer discussion of data than might be found in other modern syntax texts. Given that as theories change the types of phenomena that are interesting from a theoretical perspective also change, in the long run, covering a wider range of phenomena can also be beneficial from a theoretical perspective.

I have used this inductive method of teaching syntax at Smith College, the University of North Carolina at Chapel Hill, Georgetown University, the University of Michigan, and Swarthmore College. It is a time-tested method. Students from a variety of backgrounds have used it and learned to do syntactic analysis successfully.

3

Since the reader is developing a theory, and since the particular theory the reader is led to develop is complex, the various elements of the grammar are not introduced as nicely rounded, self-contained wholes. Instead, you will gain some knowledge about several modules of the grammar in any given chapter. You will add more information as you read later chapters until, by the end of the book, a coherent picture of the theory will have emerged. Often you will be referred to future problem sets or later chapters, where a more complete handling of the issues can be found. An inductive discussion is by nature almost always incomplete. The overviews at the end of each chapter are designed to summarize the theoretical conclusions reached thus far in the book and supply a sense of closure.

The overviews are not chapter reviews. They state in brief terms the final theoretical positions arrived at in the chapter. They pull the reader back from various tangents and numerous details to the focus of the book. They often supply the motive for the next chapter. The overviews integrate the theoretical material thus far, allowing you to get a firm handle on exactly how much you now know about each part of the grammar. The overviews are therefore essential parts of each chapter.

In this book inadequacies and uncertainties of the theory are presented at the same time that the theory is being developed, so you may at times get the false impression that this theory has little to recommend it. Again, my hope is that by facing problems even as the theory is being developed, you will maintain a healthy openness toward alternatives—an openness that will help you to become the kind of syntactician who is open-minded and takes nothing for granted.

This book also differs from many others in that it begins with syntax from the first page, rather than discussing the general philosophical, theoretical, and methodological underpinnings of the contemporary study of natural-language syntax or of linguistics in general. Thus, nowhere is the logical problem of language acquisition addressed. I direct the reader to the introduction or the first chapter of virtually any other introductory syntax textbook. The purpose of the present book is to give you the ability to work within GB, assuming that you have already decided that syntactic analysis is worth doing.

The data base drawn on consistently and heavily is English. Particular attention is paid to the language of American native speakers in linguistically unselfconscious contexts (such as ordinary daily speech). The aim is to describe and account for a range of syntactic phenomena that occur in language. Our goals are explanatory and descriptive, rather than prescriptive. Thus normative language (that is, careful language, or language that one might be told should be used but, in fact, is not produced without conscious decision to use it) will only rarely be mentioned. If we study unselfconscious language usage, we are presumably studying the patterns produced by the natural-language mechanism in our brains. Whatever principles emerge from this study, then, can be viewed as a reflection of how the human mind thinks. This book takes the position (dominant today) that linguistics is a branch of cognitive psychology. Texts that prescribe rather than describe language certainly have their place. This book, however, is not among them.

American English is most heavily studied here, but reference is made to other languages of the world. The problem sets use a variety of languages, most often English, Japanese, and Romance languages. The principles developed in this book are taken to be universals of human language unless there is an explicit statement to the contrary.

There are two caveats to be kept in mind while doing the Japanese problem sets. First, various parts of Japanese words are said to be "accented" or not. This means that some parts are phonetically prominent, primarily because they have a higher pitch, but also partially because they are stressed (that is, louder). No accents will be marked on any Japanese examples in this book because none of our problem sets will involve the sounds of Japanese.

Second, the sources from which I have drawn Japanese examples (given in the bibliography for each problem set) employ differing Romanization systems (that is, differing transliteration systems). Thus a comparison between words in various problem sets may reveal discrepancies. These differences should not lead to confusion, however, since you are never asked to consider information from other problem sets in doing the Japanese problem sets.

This book assumes no prior knowledge of linguistics. The issues covered are basic. However, many issues are covered and they are often intricate. Thus the book could easily take two or even three semesters to cover in a classroom setting.

Given the fundamental nature of the issues discussed, this book can serve as an introduction to the field regardless of the theoretical orientation that you eventually assume. That is, this book can be used by people who wind up opting for a grammar that has no syntactic movement rules in it as well as by people who choose a grammar that allows an elaborate set of permutations. That does not mean the book has no theoretical bias; it certainly does. But the organization of the material and its range are such that the book can be useful for many different types of courses on syntactic analysis. With the background here, you will be able to approach linguistic literature framed in any of the modern theories of today, and be able to understand the issues discussed in that literature. The particular picture of syntax developed here closely resembles that of Noam Chomsky's Theory of Government and Binding as I currently understand it. However, that theory is not treated dogmatically; rather, you are encouraged to challenge each step of its presentation.

If the description and caveats above put you off, this book may still be useful to you: there are multiple problem sets that can be good pedogogical tools, with or without the text.

Caveats aside, let me describe the more mechanical aspects of the book's structure.

The book is organized into chapters, and each chapter has four parts: the main narrative, the tangents, the problem sets, and the overview.

The main narrative is straightforward, and technical terms that are introduced for the first time are set in small capitals. They are usually followed immediately by a definition or demonstration of their significance for this book. (I try to present definitions that are generally accepted by the wider linguistics community.)

The narratives are divided into sections. The sections, however, are not organized to contain discrete material. Instead, the section headings are really just interruptions to the flow of the narrative. These headings are placed where they are as reference aids to the reader who may wish to go back later to find a particular discussion.

As you read the narrative, you will come to sections called "tangents" in some chapters. Tangents deal with side issues that are complex enough to warrant extended discussion. They are noted in the narrative and are located at the end of the narrative, preceding the problem sets. Placement of material in a tangent does not mean that it is theoretically tangential. In fact, the tangents often contain material that is crucial to the understanding of the theory.

I suggest that you read the narrative of each chapter from beginning to end and then return to the tangents when you have finished, unless the text specifically recommends otherwise. If, however, the topic of a particular tangent is of special and immediate interest to you, you might want to read it at the point where it keys into the narrative. Be forewarned, however, that tangents sometimes make use of terms that are not introduced until later in the chapter narrative.

All tangents should be read. Their topics (which are sometimes tangential to the particular matter handled at that point in the chapter and at other times are fundamental to the matter but just too complex to be handled within the text without interrupting the flow of the text) are all important, and knowledge of the material presented in them will be assumed in later chapters. Furthermore, the issues of theoretical methodology brought out in the tangents are central to the goals of this book. I should warn you, however, that the tangents sometimes briefly describe interesting facts about various languages that are not alluded to again. This sort of exotica is included simply to give you an inkling of the range of systems (such as gender systems and number systems) that can be found in language. My choice of languages used in these examples is largely arbitrary.

At the end of every chapter you will find problem sets that are designed to be done by anyone who has read and understood the chapter. Problem sets marked with an asterisk include material whose mastery will be assumed in later chapters. *All asterisked problem sets should be done.* In general, if there is no direction to the contrary, you will probably benefit from reading an entire problem set before starting to answer any part of it.

Every chapter has problem sets that use English as a data base. Every chapter also has at least one problem set that uses Japanese and one problem set that uses a modern Romance language as a data base. You are not expected to have familiarity with any of the languages used in these problem sets other than English. However, with respect to the Japanese problem sets, it may be difficult to do one in a later chapter if you have not done those in earlier chapters. Relevant background information about Japanese is explained only the first time the information becomes important.

In some of the later chapters there are many problem sets. This is a consequence of my belief that in order to truly understand syntactic analysis one must do syntactic analysis. Later chapters assume that students have done the asterisked earlier problem sets. The sorts of problem sets in this book might be found in any syntax class. I am grateful and indebted to all the teachers I have studied with, all the students and colleagues I have worked with, and all the articles and books concerning syntax that I have read over the past twenty years: each has contributed to these exercises.

When problem sets draw heavily on a particular piece of linguistic literature, that work is listed in the bibliography at the end of the book. Often the problem sets are written to steer the reader toward conclusions that differ from those reached in the cited works in the bibliography. Thus the authors of the works in the bibliography should in no way be held responsible for what I have done with their data and arguments in these problem sets.

The problem sets are followed by a list of suggested questions and problems for the advanced and/or more interested reader. I call these the "star" problem sets. Some of these questions are not particularly difficult and can be answered briefly. They are set aside from the regular problem sets because they call for a more sophisticated approach to syntax than one might expect the reader to have at this point in the book. Others of the star problem sets are quite difficult and could be used as a starting point for a research paper or even a monograph.

Each chapter concludes with an overview. These overviews are not chapter summaries; rather, they are theory summaries that bring you up to date on the theoretical conclusions arrived at up to that point which will factor into our final model of syntax. They incorporate findings from the problem sets as well as from the chapters. And, as I said above, they often supply motivation for the next chapter. They cannot be skipped.

The bibliography at the end of this book covers the topics handled in the narrative and tangents of each chapter as well as ones from the problem sets. I urge the reader not to make use of these bibliographies until after completing the book. This is no casual advice. After teaching linguistics for twenty years, I firmly believe that the starting student, particularly the undergraduate, can be too vulnerable to persuasion to read syntax articles. That is, articles in linguistics are meant to persuade the reader of a particular point. And linguists, in my opinion, are generally good at argumentation. The starting student who picks up a linguistics article is bombarded with what look like invincible arguments in favor of a particular analysis of a particular construction. Such a student will often be unable to uncover the assumptions of the article and test them. This student is also typically unable to attack the argumentation form of the article. And, finally, this student is usually at a loss to figure out the predictions of the article and test them. The student, then, is most likely to simply be "wowed" by the article—and to adopt the blinders of the linguist who wrote it.

My advice is this: Finish the book (including the asterisked problem sets) without reading other works on syntax. By that point you will be able to do all the things listed in the previous paragraph that the starting student typically cannot do. You can then face the great mass of linguistic articles with the skills necessary to glean from them what is valuable and to challenge what is weak (or even clearly untenable). In fact, I advise you, as you go on in linguistics, to work on a given topic at length before you start to read other articles about that topic. Every article you read about a given construction—before you yourself have thought about that construction—robs you of the opportunity to come up with the relevant questions and some of the major arguments for the analysis of that construction on your own. Furthermore, if you start out with a clean slate, you are more likely to come up with a new approach to the problem, and you may avoid pitfalls that have troubled others before you. Be fair to yourself. Take yourself seriously, from the first page of this book on. Some of the most important breakthroughs in linguistics have been made by novice linguists. I hope you join those ranks.

1

Reflexives,
Features of Nouns,
Reference

Reflexives and Gender

Many sentences sound just fine. For example, no one would blink their eyes at:

    (1)   Jack saved himself.

But not all sentences sound great. A native speaker of English might at first feel uncomfortable with

    (2)   Jack saved herself.

The choice between *himself* and *herself* is the only difference between 1 and 2. And the only difference between these two *self* words is GENDER: *himself* is masculine; *herself* is feminine. So we are led to attribute the strangeness of 2 to the fact that *herself* is feminine (Tangent 1.1).

Why should gender matter here? To answer that we need to reconsider 2.

Notice that 2 need not be taken as a bad sentence. It only seems strange at first because it is out of context. If we assumed Jack were female, we could easily accept 2.

It appears, then, that the *self* word in 1 and 2 must be understood to have the same gender that Jack has. The typical term for these *self* words is REFLEXIVES. The other reflexives are *myself, ourselves, yourself, yourselves, itself, oneself,* and *themselves.*

We can say, then, that there is a compatibility requirement involving gender in 1 and 2. (And we will not state precisely at this point what this compatibility requirement is.)

Now the question is whether such a compatibility requirement is manifested in all sentences of English. But, surely, the answer is no. There are many sentences in which the words for two elements that have real-world and/or linguistic gender appear in which no compatibility requirement is exhibited:

(3) Jack found {my/our/your/her/his/its/their} lunch.

So something is triggering the compatibility requirement in 1 and 2. Is it *Jack* or the reflexive? We can quickly answer that this compatiblity requirement is not a property of sentences about Jack, simply by pointing to 3, where no compatibility requirement is present. Furthermore, if we substitute *Ralph* for *Jack* in 1 and 2, we find the same possible readings:

(4) Ralph saved himself.
Ralph saved herself.

Which reflexive we feel comfortable with in 4 depends on our understanding of the gender of the person named Ralph. Names like *Jack* and *Ralph* are typically men's. And our first reaction is to expect *himself.* We therefore expect that if we took a name that is typically a woman's, we would get the opposite first reactions. And we do.

(5) Sue saved himself.
Sue saved herself.

Here our first reaction is to blink twice (or several times) at *himself,* but to accept *herself* without question. If someone utters the first sentence of 5, we are led to the conclusion that Sue is male.

Notice that *Jack, Ralph,* and *Sue,* being PROPER NOUNS (this term is explored in Star Problem 1.2), can conceivably bring to mind either males or females, since parents are free to name their children whatever they like (at least in those societies in which *Jack, Ralph,* and *Sue* are likely to be ordinary names). If the above account of the first reactions to the sentences in 1, 2, 4, and 5 is correct, then we predict that if, instead of *Jack, Ralph,* or *Sue,* we have a word or words that are not a proper name and if that word or those words have a gender LEXICALLY (that is, by the very meaning of the word as an item in our vocabulary) associated with it, then the compatibility requirement will make the wrong choice of reflexive yield a bad sentence. This prediction holds:

(6) The boy saved himself.
*The boy saved herself.

(7) *The girl saved himself.
The girl saved herself.

(The ASTERISK before one of the sentences in both 6 and 7 indicates that these sentences are strange to a native speaker of English regardless of context.) The word *boy* has masculine gender lexically associated with it. And, as we predicted, *himself* is the only acceptable choice in 6. Likewise, the word *girl* forces the feminine gender, and *herself* is the only acceptable choice in 7. Examples 6 and 7 are important confirmation that a gender compatibility requirement exists and that it is triggered by the use of the reflexive.

Why should there be such a requirement on the gender of the reflexive in all the sentences above? To answer that question, we need to play with these examples a little more.

Reflexives and Number

Let us assume that Jack is male. Now compare 1 to 8:

(8)   *Jack saved themselves.

What can account for the failure of 8? If *themselves* were incompatible with *Jack* for gender here, we could see 8 as being in violation of the compatibility requirement that we have just been discussing above. But this is, in fact, not so: the reflexive *themselves* can easily be understood as masculine in other sentences, as in:

(9)   The boys saved themselves.

We know from 6 above that only a masculine reflexive can be associated with the word *boy*, and by extension we know that only a masculine reflexive can be associated with the word *boys*. So *themselves* in 9 is open to a masculine interpretation. Therefore, the failure of 8 is not due to gender incompatibility.

The relevant incompatibility in 8, as you may have recognized, is NUMBER: *themselves* is plural, but *Jack* is singular (Tangent 1.2). We might, then, jump immediately to the claim that there is a compatibility requirement on the number of the reflexive in all the sentences we have seen (parallel to the claim we made above that there is a compatibility requirement on the gender). In support of this claim, we can note that *themselves* is not acceptable in place of the reflexive in examples 1, 2, and 4–6:

(10)   *Ralph saved themselves.
        *Sue saved themselves.
        *The boy saved themselves.
        *The girl saved themselves.

And we predict that only *themselves* and not *himself* or *herself* will be acceptable in sentences parallel to those above with a plural word or words in place of *Jack*, *Ralph*, *Sue*, *the boy*, and *the girl*. This prediction holds:

(11)   *Jessie and Pete saved himself.
        Jessie and Pete saved themselves.

        *Sally and Maria saved herself.
        Sally and Maria saved themselves.

        *People will always save himself/herself.
        People will always save themselves.

        *All the children saved himself/herself.
        All the children saved themselves.

Why should there be such a requirement on the number of the reflexive in all the sentences above? Again, we need to delay trying to answer that question (just as we delayed trying to answer why the gender compatibility requirement should exist) until we look a little further.

Reflexives and Person

Let us take the following sentence spoken by a male:

(12)   *I saved himself.

Contrast 12 to 1, repeated here for convenience:

(13)   Jack saved himself.

Something is blocking 12, but it can be neither a compatibility requirement of gender nor one of number, since both *I* and *himself* are masculine and singular here. We find that we must talk about yet another feature in language: PERSON. (Please read Tangent 1.3 before continuing with the main text narrative.) In 12 *I* is first person, but *himself* is third person. So it looks like we have a compatibility requirement on person this time. And we want to ask why.

Features, Agreement, Sense, and Reference

But first let us consider what we know about FEATURES (this term is introduced in Tangent 1.1) at this point.

The three features of gender, number, and person are found in the PRONOMINAL system of English and, as you have learned or will learn by reading Tangents 1.1–1.3, they are determined by the relevant characteristics of the REFERENT (defined below) of the PRONOUN. For example, if the referent (the person spoken about) is a female, we will use *she, her,* or *hers,* and not *he* or *us* or *yours* or any other personal pronoun.

The PERSONAL PRONOUNS of English, then, have at least three features: person, number, and gender. In fact, one could argue that a pronoun such as *he* is a FEATURE BUNDLE containing at least three features (masculine, singular, third person). So what we have found out is that these three features of the feature bundle of the reflexive in the sentences we have looked at so far must be compatible with the feature bundle of some other item in the sentence.

Why? There are at least two possibilities. One is that this compatibility is the result of an obligatory linguistic process of matching or AGREEMENT. The other possibility is that this compatibility is due to something that the reflexive and the relevant other item in the sentence have in common.

The other relevant item in all the sentences above has been a NOUN PHRASE (hereafter NP). We categorize words grammatically according to whether they are NOUNS (hereafter N, such as *dog*), VERBS (hereafter V, such as *eat*), ADJECTIVES (such as *true*), ADVERBS (such as *quickly*), or PREPOSITIONS (hereafter P, such as *into*). And we categorize STRINGS OF WORDS according to whether they are or are not PHRASAL LEVELS of any of these categories. (You will gain a working knowledge of categories and phrases by doing Problem Set 1.2, and a full discussion of these concepts is found in chapters 2 and 4.) For now let us say that an NP is a string of words made up of an N and all its paraphernalia. For example, *girl* is an N. But *the nice girl I met yesterday* is an NP. In Problem Set 1.1 you will find ways to distinguish between Ns and NPs SYNTACTICALLY and MORPHOLOGICALLY. The syntactic distinctions have to do with the distribution of Ns and NPs in larger phrases. The morphological distinctions have to do with word-formation processes (specifically, where certain prefixes, suffixes, and, in general, AFFIXES can attach; see Tangent 1.4). The SEMANTIC (or meaning) difference between Ns and NPs, however, is not as cleanly delineated, although it is certainly just as crucial for your understanding of linguistics. Consider the N *dog* in:

(14)   [A dog] came in.
        [Dogs] came in.
        [The dog] came in.
        [A dog] wouldn't ever come in.
        [No dog] would come in.
        [Those big dogs] came in.
        [Dogs] wouldn't ever come in.
        [Big dogs] came in.
        [No dogs] would come in.

All of these sentences have something in common. They are assigning the PROPERTY of coming in (or not coming in, or having already come in, etc.) to a set whose members are a certain kind of entity: that entity we call a dog. That is, the word *dog* carries a SENSE—animal, four-legged, hairy—and that sense is present in all sentences that make use of this word as an N. This is true even if in a particular sentence we negate part of the sense of the N:

(15)   That dog has only three legs.

The other words that belong to (or are paraphernalia of) the N, however, help us to pick out the particular set of entities with the sense of *dog* that we happen to be talking about in each sentence. When we hear *the dog*, we know that either a dog that is OLD INFORMATION to the discourse is being talked about or the class of all dogs (the GENERIC set) is being talked about. We see the old information use in 16 and the generic use in 17:

(16)   I saw a huge hound the other day. It was sniffing its way along the gutter. Suddenly *the dog* lunged. I ran, of course.

(17)   *The dog* is a four-legged mammal that has been around since prehistoric time.

We cannot use *the dog* to talk about a specific dog that is not old information to the discourse. That is, we cannot say something like:

(18)   The dog smells yucky today.

unless we are assuming that the listener will know which dog we are talking about.

Similar remarks can be made about the other NPs above. For example, *no dog* in:

(19)   No dog came in.

tells us that, of creatures with the sense of *dog*, we are saying none of them has the property of having come in.

The N, then, carries a sense, but it is the NP that has REFERENCE; it is the NP that picks out the entity being talked about. And the entity being talked about is called the REFERENT of the NP.

The notion of *reference* is not a simple one and there is much more that could be said about it. However, an in-depth study of semantic notions such as this one will not be found in this book, since our primary interest is syntax, and we are aiming to develop a theory of syntax in a reasonable number of pages.

Back to Agreement versus Reference as an Account of Our Compatibility Requirement

Returning to the fact that the features of person, number, and gender of a reflexive must be the same as those features of some other NP in the sentence, we can now restate the two possible explanations that we mentioned above for this fact.

First, there could be an agreement process between the relevant NP and the reflexive.

Second, the NP and the reflexive might be required to have the same referent. That is, a reflexive's features of person, number, and gender are determined by characteristics of its referent. Therefore, if these features of the reflexive are required to be the same as these features of some other NP, it is possible that this requirement reflects a more basic requirement: that the reflexive and the relevant other NP must have the same referent.

The first HYPOTHESIS amounts to saying that in a sentence like:

(20)   Ralph likes himself.

an agreement process assures us that the features of gender, number, and person will be identical for *Ralph* and *himself.* This process could be one of COPYING these features from *Ralph* onto the feature bundle for the reflexive. Alternatively, the agreement process could be one of FILTERING out (that is, discarding) any reflexive with a feature bundle for person, number, and gender that does not match that of *Ralph*'s. And there are still other alternative ways this process might work.

The second hypothesis amounts to saying that in a sentence like 20, *Ralph* and *himself* are COREFERENTIAL (that is, they have the same referent): therefore they have the same features of person, number, and gender. To decide between these two possibilities, we need more information.

Case

There is one other feature found in the pronominal system of English: CASE. (Please read Tangent 1.5 before continuing with the main text narrative. You will not be able to follow the narrative without reading the tangent now.)

The form *he* can appear only in Subject position of TENSED CLAUSES. (You will study Subjects and clauses in Chapter 2 and you will look at tensed versus non-tensed clauses in chapter 3.) But the form *his* is used in other places, and *him* is used in still others:

> (21) He is nice. (cf. *Him is nice.)
> His father is nice. (cf. *Him father is nice.)
> I like him. (cf. *I like he.)

(Sentences like *His is nice* and *I like his* are good also. These are called ELLIPTICAL sentences; see Star Problem 1.5.) Unlike the other features of pronouns, however, the feature of Case is not determined by characteristics of the referent. Instead, Case is determined by syntactic factors that you will study in chapter 5.

Looking at sentences with reflexives, we find that the Case of the reflexive and the Case of the relevant other NP is not the same:

> (22) I like myself.

Here *I* is in the SUBJECTIVE or NOMINATIVE Case. But Subjective Case can occur only in the Subject position of tensed clauses, so *myself* is not in the Subjective Case in 22 since it is occurring in a position other than Subject of a tensed clause.

That the relevant NP and the reflexive in 22 do not have the same Case may not come as a surprise to you. You may have enough previous experience with grammar studies to expect that Subjects and Direct Objects of tensed clauses will not have the same Case. But, in fact, the simple fact that the revelant NP and the reflexive do not have the same Case is revealing and will help us to determine which of the hypotheses above is correct.

First, if the identity of the features of person, number, and gender between the reflexive and some other NP were the result of an agreement process, we might have expected the feature of Case to be identical also. In order to account for this lack of identity, we must put a stipulation on our agreement process excluding Case (either from the copying process or from the filtering process). This stipulation begs for a motivated explanation.

But if the identity of the features of person, number, and gender between the reflexive and some other NP is the result of coreference, we can have no expectation about the feature of Case. That is, the features of person, number, and gender are determined by characteristics of the referent, so coreferential items should have the same features of person, number, and gender. The feature of Case, on the other hand, is determined not by the referent but by syntactic factors pertinent to each particular NP in a particular sentence. Therefore we have no expectation that the Case of coreferential NPs should be the same. Their Case is totally independent of their reference.

Thus we will opt for the second hypothesis: the reflexive and the relevant other

NP have the same features of person, number, and gender because they are coreferential.

Notice that our conclusion has some welcome results. For one, we now have a truly explanatory account of the identity of these features, whereas with an agreement account we would be left with the question of why agreement should take place with reflexives but not with all pronominals.

Second, with our account we can see reflexives as having a referent and a bundle of features, some of which are dependent upon that referent. In this way, reflexives are similar to the personal pronouns, whose features of person, number, and gender are dependent upon their referent. For surely, it would be impossible to account for these features of personal pronouns by way of an agreement process. To see this, consider the situation in which you and I are looking out a window. We see a little girl on the curb of a busy street. You turn to me and say:

(23)   She's going to get hit by a car.

Here there is no linguistic entity that the pronoun *she* might possibly be agreeing with: neither you nor I have said the word *girl*. Instead, the situation is such that you are sure I will be able to figure out who *she* refers to when you say it. The PRAGMATIC context (that is, the real-world situation in which the utterance takes place) is helping us here. But, let me repeat, there is no linguistic entity that the *she* could possibly be agreeing with. Thus agreement processes are not responsible for the features on NOMINALS (that is, noun-type things—you will learn more about them in Problem Set 1.1) in English, in general.

Anaphors and Binding

To this point we have learned that a reflexive must be coreferential with some other NP in the sentence, whereas pronouns need not be. This generalization predicts that reflexives cannot occur as the only nominal in a sentence, and, in fact, they usually cannot. (But we will look at some unusual uses of reflexives in Chapter 10.):

(24)   *Himself left quickly.

We will call the required other NP the ANTECEDENT. And we will call items like reflexives, that require a LINGUISTIC ANTECEDENT (as opposed to a PRAGMATIC ANTECEDENT, as in the context for 24 above), ANAPHORS.

Actually, while we have just worked hard to establish that the notion of coreference is the key here, in fact coreference is only one of the various concrete examples (instantiations) of the relationship that must hold between an anaphor and its antecedent. Consider:

(25)   Nobody truly hates himself.

The nominal *nobody* (like the NPs *no dog, nothing*, etc.) is not referential in any ordinary sense. Hence it may not make sense to speak of any forced coreference in 25.

Likewise, we find reflexive anaphors in examples like:

(26)   Jack repeats himself.
        Amoebae reproduce themselves continually.

Again, the semantic relationship between the reflexive and its antecedent is not one of coreference. In fact, it is difficult to state precisely what the semantic relationship is between the reflexive and its antecedent in the two examples in 26.

However, there is a generalization we can make for the anaphors in 25 and 26 and all other instances of anaphors above: their interpretation must be determined through association with a linguistic antecedent. We call this necessary dependence in interpretation a BINDING relationship, and we say that the antecedent BINDS the anaphor.

This is certainly not the whole story. We have recognized the existence of anaphors, a type of nominal that requires a linguistic antecedent. And we have recognized that this antecedent must be located somewhere in the same overall sentence that contains the anaphor. But we have not yet even approached the question of whether there are restrictions on where the anaphor and its antecedent may occur within the sentence with respect to each other. In fact, the data relevant to this question have been interpreted and analyzed in numerous ways, and the puzzle is still one of the more compelling issues in linguistic theory. This puzzle is the driving force behind this entire book, and piece by piece we will try to put the puzzle together.

Tangent 1.1: Gender

This tangent is best read after you have completed reading the main text narrative, since it uses terminology that is introduced in that narrative.

How do we know there is a gender difference between *himself* and *herself*? The difference between these words is in the first syllable, and this difference is paralleled by the fact that we have personal pronouns corresponding to these first syllables: *him* and *her*. *Him* is a MASCULINE pronoun; *her* is a FEMININE one. The question arises as to whether it would be sensible to internally analyze pronouns like *him* and *her* with respect to gender. That is, should we simply say that *him* is masculine, while *her* is feminine, or should we look inside these two words for some smaller part of each one that signals gender? (In technical terms, should we analyze them MORPHOLOGICALLY?)

Nouns can be classified as proper (that is, names, such as *Marion, Paul*, etc.) or COMMON (the run-of-the-mill noun which has a lexical sense, such as *cow, anger*, etc.). If we look at common nouns in English, we find that their morphological form does not usually distinguish them for gender. For example, there is no particular ending or beginning or middle to *mother* that tells us that this noun is feminine (compare to *father, brother, grocer*). However, there are a few handfuls of common nouns that are distinguished morphologically for gender. Included here are pairs like *steward/stewardess, lion/lioness*, and *duke/duchess*, which are witness to the fact that the suffix *-ess* carries feminine gender. (And pairs of this sort may well be witness to a history of sexism in the English language and the societies in which it is spoken: consider who governs whom in the pair *governor/governess*, for example.)

In general, then, only third-person singular personal pronouns (number is discussed in Tangent 1.2 and person is discussed in Tangent 1.3) are lexically MARKED for gender. Other pronouns are not and most nouns are not.

Now the question is whether there is any motivation to analyze some subpart of *him* and *her* as carrying gender. For example, we might take the initial *h* to be a marker of something else and the final *-im* and *-er* to be markers of gender. The alternative would be to say that *him* is simply lexically marked as masculine, while *her* is lexically feminine. Which is the correct approach? The answer lies in how useful each analysis would be. Let us consider the other personal pronouns. In tables A–C the lexical items are arranged by number (singular versus plural; you will read about number in Tangent 1.2) and person (first, second, and third; you will read about person in Tangent 1.3).

A. (Partial) System of personal pronouns

	Singular	Plural
first person:	I, me	we, us
second person:	you	you (all)
third person:	he, she, it	they, them

There are other sets of pronominal elements, one of which is the POSSESSIVES. Some of these occur only with another nominal that they act as the genitive to

B. Possessives that occur with nominals

	Singular	Plural
first person:	my	our
second person:	your	our
third person:	his, her, its	their

Others occur without another nominal:

C. Isolated possessives

	Singular	Plural
first person:	mine	ours
second person:	yours	yours
third person:	his, hers, its	theirs

Here again, we see lexical gender marking, but only in *his*, *her*, *its*, and *hers*.

It is important to recognize that while the forms in Tables B and C are typically called possessives, they are not uniformly to be associated with a possessive sense. You will explore this question in part of Problem Set 1.1.

Now that we have seen these three sets of pronominals, we can return to the question of whether or not -*im* (in *him*) and -*er* (in *her*) are markers of gender. Nowhere else in this system do we find a final -*im* or -*er* acting as a gender marker. And nowhere else in this system do we find an initial *h* acting as a marker of something else. Thus the internal analysis of *him* and *her* does not productively carry over to the analysis of other personal pronouns. And, in fact, nowhere in the lexical system of English do we find such a correlation between these endings and gender.

Instead, if we were to claim that the -*im* of *him* was a masculine marker and the -*er* of *her* was a feminine marker, we would have a totally ad hoc analysis of these words. And this ad hoc analysis sheds no more light on the grammatical system as a whole than the analysis which takes the whole pronoun *him* to be masculine (without any specific internal part taken to carry the gender) and the whole pronoun *her* to be feminine.

We will analyze grammatical entities into smaller units only insofar as such analyses will prove perspicuous. That is, if an analysis offers insight into the grammatical system, it is worth considering. If two analyses are equally perspicuous (or not), we will choose the one that calls for less internal analysis. For this reason, we will not internally analyze *him* and *her* with respect to gender, but simply take *him* as a masculine pronoun and *her* as a feminine pronoun, where the entire word in each case tells us the gender.

The assumption that we just made is important. We said that if two analyses are equally perspicuous, we will choose the one that calls for less internal analysis. We will recognize subparts and classifications within groups only if there are data in the language whose analysis demands such recognition.

If we were looking at a language as it changes across time (in a DIACHRONIC study), we would consider a wider set of data than if we were looking at a language in a given time period (in a SYNCHRONIC study). This book uses a synchronic analysis of English syntax to teach linguistic methodology. For this reason, it is irrelevant to the present study whether or not -*im* signaled masculine and -*er* signaled feminine at some earlier stage of English. The relevant question for a synchronic study is whether -*im*, for example, carries such a message now. And, from our look at the rest of the pronominal system and at the LEXICON (the vocabulary) as a whole, we can say it does not.

Notice further that by requiring that there be linguistic data to justify every refinement of an analysis, we have taken a highly restrictive approach to the study of language. A philosopher might set up classifications of verbs, for example, based on any number of imaginable factors—such as whether the verbs deal with matters of theology or epistemology or any other field of study. But we could not do that unless verbs that deal with matters of theology, for example, exhibited some special linguistic behavior that justifies the classification. For instance, if all verbs that dealt with matters of theology were limited to appearing in the present tense, then there would be linguistic grounds upon which to set them up as a verb class. Or if all verbs that dealt with matters of theology had three syllables, we would have linguistic grounds upon which to set them up as a verb class. (So far as I know, of course, there are no linguistic grounds for setting up these verbs as a special class.)

Let us return to the matter of gender.

There is another gender represented on our list of the personal pronouns: NEU-TER, as in *it*. But most of the pronouns are not lexically marked for gender: *I* can be understood as feminine or masculine, depending on the speaker; *you* can be understood as feminine or masculine, depending on the person spoken to; and so forth.

The fact that there is a correlation between gender and the object that the pronoun is referring to is evidence of the larger fact that in English gender is related to semantics in a rather straightforward way, which I will state below. Objects in the world are either male or female or neither. Language, however, does not necessarily use linguistic gender in a one-to-one correlation to real-world gender. In fact, I know of no language that has such a correlation. So, for example, in English the referent of *I* is definitely going to have a real-world gender, since (in normal situations) only people talk and people have gender. But *I* in English is not lexically marked for gender: it can be used to refer both to males and females. What we can see about English then is that if a given lexical item is marked for linguistic gender (such as the Ns *girl* and *stewardess* or the pronoun *it*), its gender will typically match real-world gender. (I say typically, because some speakers of English can use gender-marked pronouns to refer to entities that do not have a real-world gender, such as referring to a ship as *she*.) But linguistic gender in English need not be marked on every lexical item (such as the Ns *teacher* and *cook* or the pronoun *we*).

The only personal pronouns that are marked for gender are the third-person ones. That means that our personal-pronoun system is rather POOR (as opposed to RICH) in gender-marking.

The above comments are particular to English. There are other languages in which many words are lexically marked as having a given gender. For example, in Italian every N is either feminine or masculine. Often this gender corresponds to the real-world gender of the referent of the NP. Here are some examples using the masculine and feminine counterparts of the N meaning 'friend':

Carlo ha un amico.   'Carlo has a male friend.'
Carlo ha un'amica.   'Carlo has a female friend.'

But even objects that have no real-world gender are referred to by NPs that have a morphological gender:

Carlo ha il libro.   'Carlo has the book.'
Carlo ha la tavola.   'Carlo has the table.'

In these examples the NP *il libro* is morphologically marked as having masculine gender (by the -*o* ending) and the NP *la tavola* is morphologically marked (by the -*a* ending) as having feminine gender. And sometimes the morphological gender of an N will not necessarily match its real-world gender:

L'Italia ha la spia.   'Italy has the spy.'

Here the word *spia* is morphologically feminine whether we are using it to talk about a male or female spy.

Many languages linguistically mark their nouns and pronouns for gender, like Italian (and most of the languages of Europe). Some of them make use of just masculine and feminine (like Italian), while some also use the neuter (like German, Latin, and Ancient Greek). Other languages either do not mark them or mark only a small subset of them, like English (and Japanese, Chinese, and many other languages). In the Bantu language family of southern Africa there may be as many as ten "genders"; nouns have different prefixes according to a variety of semantic and morphological factors, and the actual physiological gender of the referents of the animate NPs is often irrelevant.

If languages mark words in the lexicon for gender, the words most commonly marked are nominals (like nouns and pronouns). This fact, of course, suggests a fundamental relationship between linguistic gender and real-world gender, since it is nominals that have referents. However, as we have seen, no simple correlation between the two is apparent.

In sentences and phrases other words may be marked for gender, but typically this occurs by a process of agreement. For example, verbs can agree with other items. In some varieties of Arabic and other Semitic languages verbs in certain persons are distinguished for masculine versus feminine with regard to their Subject. In Nimboran (a language of New Guinea) a third-person verb is distinguished for masculine versus feminine with regard to the ACTOR. (Terms like *actor* and *agent* are discussed fully in chapter 3.) In Basque (spoken in the western Pyrenees of southern France and northern Spain) the verb is sometimes morphologically marked for the gender of the person addressed.

A much more common agreement process for gender is that between nominals and MODIFYING or PREDICATIVE adjectives. (We will be discussing modification and predication in chapter 3). For example, in Italian the word-root *alt-* means 'tall,' and it is not lexically marked for gender. But when it is used in a sentence or phrase it will have the morphological gender-marking appropriate for whatever nominal it modifies (that is, describes) or is predicated of (that is, assigns a property to):

Il mio amico è alto.   'My male friend is tall.'
La mia amica è alta.   'My female friend is tall.'

Even adjectives that in some sense have a real-world gender (such as *incinto* "pregnant") undergo agreement processes:

Il sorcio è incinto.   'The mouse is pregnant.'
La mia sorella è incinta.   'My sister is pregnant.'

The N *sorcio* is masculine whether the mouse we're talking about is male or female. And the adjective here agrees with the NP for gender.

While nominals are the typical types of words that bring to mind a real-world gender, we can see that some adjectives can do that, as well (as in the examples immediately above). Even some predicates do that (such as *partorire*—'give birth to'), simply by virtue of their meaning and our knowledge of how the world works. (That is, only female creatures typically give birth.) Furthermore, there are languages in which some words or morphological forms bring to mind a given real-world gender not because of what they mean, but because of restrictions on or tendencies in their usage. Thus, for example, the use of the so-called beautification honorific in Japanese, the *o*-prefix, suggests that the speaker is female simply by virtue of the fact that women use this prefix more often than men.

We say that gender is a feature that some words have. Features are gross (as opposed to refined or detailed) bits of information that are common to many words. For example, in the word *hag* we have the gross bit of information that the feature of feminine gender supplies us—that bit of information that is common to *girl* and *waitress* and *schoolmarm* and many other words. But we also have very detailed lexical information. That is, the word *hag* is used to describe an ugly female who is perhaps skinny with hanging skin and a long nose. A hag is worn out, maybe with discolored or missing teeth. A hag is not likely to burst into song.

Words can vary on how much information they give us. *Hag* is a HIGH-INFOR-MATION WORD. *Female* is a LOW-INFORMATION WORD. (In fact, it seems to contain no information other than the feature of gender.) And this range of information is common to words other than nominals, too. Thus *skip* is a high-information verb; *move* is a low-information verb.

When talking about features, then, we are talking about information that even our low-information Ns or NPs might carry.

Tangent 1.2: Number

Number is the term we use to talk about linguistic distinctions in quantity. Number in English is a distinction between one and more than one. We label one SINGULAR, and more than one PLURAL. Unlike gender, however, our number distinction is morphologically apparent on most pronominal elements. The chart below contains the personal pronouns and possessives (found in tables A–C of Tangent 1.1):

	Singular	*Plural*
first person:	I, me, my, mine	we, us, our, ours
second person:	you, your, yours	you, your, yours
third person:	he, him, his she, her, hers it, its	they, them, their, theirs

The only pronominals that are not lexically marked for number are *you*, *your*, and *yours*, the second person pronouns. (In Tangent 1.3 we discuss person.)

Actually, the situation is a bit more complex than that in ordinary usage today. Thus we find the pronouns *they*, *them*, *their*, and *theirs* used not just for plural, but for singular when their antecedent is an INDEFINITE:

Anybody who wants their paper back should tell me.

and in other situations in which the gender of the referent is unknown or varying and a speaker wants to avoid applying our rather uncomfortable prescriptivist rule of using *he*, *him*, and *his* for animate individuals:

If a person comes in and they want to see me, please tell them I've left for Panama.

It would be more accurate to say, then, that *they, them, their,* and *theirs* in ordinary speech are not marked for number. The choice of these pronouns in the instances described in this paragraph is undoubtedly related to the fact that they are also not marked for gender.

Like most pronouns, nouns are distinguished for number. An easily identifiable morphological ending is regularly employed:

> I saw the boy.
> versus: I saw the boys.

While the sounds /z/ (as in *boys*), /s/ (as in *cats*), and /əz/ (as in *glasses*) are the most common and the productive endings for plural nouns in English, we have small groups of nouns that exemplify patterns for plural formation that have been lost from English as PRODUCTIVE patterns:

> foot : feet   goose : geese

(A productive pattern is one that would be produced on newly coined words. In English if the new N *bloot* came into the language, we would make its plural be *bloots* not *bleet*. At an earlier stage of English, however, we might have chosen *bleet* as the plural.) We also have small groups of Ns that exhibit singular/plural pairs which have been borrowed in relative isolation from other languages:

> cherub : cherubim   phenomenon : phenomena

Cherub/cherubim is a Hebrew borrowing; *phenomenon/phenomena* is a Greek borrowing. Furthermore, we have some Ns that are lexically marked as having a given number. Thus *scissors* is always plural, whether we are referring to one pair or many. Again, as with gender, we find that there is no one-to-one correspondence between linguistic number and real-world number (although the correlation here is a lot cleaner in general than with gender).

Many languages mark number with some sort of morphological ending or set of endings, like English. Italian is one:

> Ecco i miei amici.   'Here are my friends.'
> Ecco il mio amico.   'Here is my male friend.'
> Ecco le mie amiche.   'Here are my female friends.'
> Ecco la mia amica.   'Here is my female friend.'

(In the plural if anyone in the group is a male, the masculine ending will be chosen.)

Number, like gender, is a feature—it is a gross bit of information. And, like gender, it can be realized on words other than nominals. Once more, however, this realization is typically due to agreement processes. For example, in Italian, adjectives are marked for number, but not lexically. So *american-* means 'American' and it can be used with a singular or plural nominal, where its ending will match that of the nominal:

> Ecco il ragazzo americano.   'Here is the American boy.'
> Ecco i ragazzi americani.   'Here are the American boys.'

Ecco la ragazza americana.   'Here is the American girl.'
Ecco le ragazze americane.   'Here are the American girls.'

Above we see that Italian adjectives can have two plural forms, differentiated by the feature of gender. (*Americani* is plural masculine; *americane* is plural feminine.)

Tensed verbs in Italian are also marked for number, in agreement with their Subject:

Il   ragazzo parla   lentamente.
'The boy   speaks slowly.'

I   ragazzi parlano lentamente.
'The boys   speak   slowly.'

In English we also have agreement between a tensed verb and its Subject (which we will explore in chapter 2), but it is phonetically distinct only in the simple present-tense third-person singular, regardless of aspect (and please wait until chapter 2 Tangent 2.1 for a discussion of tense and aspect):

The boy *leaves* his things all over the floor.
*The boy *leave* his things all over the floor.

The boys *leave* their things all over the floor.
*The boys *leaves* their things all over the floor.

The boy *has* left a mess.
*The boy *have* left a mess.

The boys *have* left a mess.
*The boys *has* left a mess.

Most languages use the singular-versus-plural distinction for their number feature on nominals. And many of these languages mark number morphologically on nominals, like Italian and English do. Most of the languages of Europe pattern this way.

Other languages use a different distinction. Ancient Greek and Sanskrit, for example, mark nominals (including pronouns) for the number distinctions of one, two, or more than two. The three classes are called singular, dual, and plural. While dual was used in the most ancient texts we have of Greek (including Homer), it is only rarely used in classical Greek, being limited for the most part to common pairs (such as yoked oxen or hands). Adjectives and verbs that agree with a dual nominal in these languages also have a dual form (although in Attic Greek we sometimes find plural adjectives agreeing with dual nominals). Furthermore, in some languages which distinguish only singular and plural in the nominal system, the three-way distinction of singular, dual, and plural shows up when a verb agrees with its Subject (as in Old English and residually in Russian). And there are even languages which have a four-way distinction in verbal agreement, adding in the trial (for precisely three) number (such as Kiwai, a language of New Guinea).

Tangent 1.3: Person

There are three persons in English. One is called *first person,* and it refers to the
SPEAKER. It is seen in the pronominals here:

Singular: I, me, my, mine

Plural: we, us, our, ours

The next person is called *second,* and it refers to the person spoken to (often
called the HEARER):

you, your, yours

In English the second person is not phonetically distinct for number. Some tables
may represent the plural by having *you all* as the personal pronoun (as in table A
of tangent 1.1). But there are two problems with this. One is that the possessives
have no corresponding special forms for the plural. The other is that in some varieties of English *you all* can be used to refer to a singular hearer (as in those varieties
of North Carolina speech that I am familiar with).

The last person is called *third,* and it refers to the person spoken about:

Singular: she, her, hers / he, him, his / it, its

Plural: they, them, their, theirs

The first row here is distinguished for both singular number and all three genders.
In prescriptivist speech and in writing the second row is third-person plural with no
gender distinction. But in much ordinary speech (see Tangent 1.2) the second row
is third person with neither number nor gender distinction.

The full nouns of English, as contrasted to the pronominal system, are not morphologically distinguished for person (just as they are typically not morphologically
distinguished for gender). Instead, every noun phrase that is not pronominal is
treated by the grammar as being third person. For example, Subject-Verb Agreement (which we will discuss in chapter 2) with a full NP is always third person in
English:

I love cotton candy.
*This woman love cotton candy.
This woman loves cotton candy.

The above fact points out that verbs, like pronominals, are marked for person in
English. However, just as we saw (in Tangent 1.2) that number distinction on verbs
is heard only in the third person of present tense verbs, we find that person distinction on verbs is heard only in the third person of present-tense verbs.

The number system of English is a simple one and is typical of many languages
of the world. More elaborate systems are possible, however. For example, languages
can morphologically distinguish a first person exclusive (where only the speaker or
speakers are included) from a first-person inclusive (where both the speaker and the
person spoken to are included).

Tangent 1.4: Affixes

The term *affix* may well be new to you, but the concept is not. Anyone who is reading this book has surely been told that the ending -*s* on:

cats

is the plural SUFFIX (as in Tangent 1.2, for example). And you are familiar with a wide range of other suffixes in English:

progressive -*ing*: walk*ing*
perfective -*ed*: walk*ed*
comparative -*er*: tall*er*
superlative -*est*: tall*est*
diminutives: Ann*ie*, Jimm*y*, duck*ling*, book*let*

Suffixes are endings added onto a word. They are a type of MORPHEME, where morphemes are, generally speaking, the meaning-bearing building blocks of words. They are often classified as GRAMMATICAL or LEXICAL in nature. The grammatical affixes can be INFLECTIONAL or DERIVATIONAL. Inflectional affixes do not change the category of a word (an N stays an N; a V stays a V; etc.) but do make the form of the word appropriate to the context. Thus, if we have an NP with the quantifier *five*, the plural suffix will appear on the N:

I saw five cat*s*.

Derivational affixes can change the category of a word. For example, there is a use of -*er* that can be added to a V to derive an N:

sleep, sleeper
walk, walker

Lexical affixes do not change the category of a word, nor do they make the form of the word appropriate to the context. Instead, they add some meaning to the word. Examples are the diminutives seen above. Another is -*ish*, meaning "sort of," as in:

blue, bluish
tall, tallish

Affixes added to the beginning of the word are called PREFIXES, as in:

kind, unkind

Many languages allow an affix internal to the ROOT of the word. These are called INFIXES. In English we do not have any widely productive infixes. However, in casual speech certain words (typically obscene) can be infixed into other words, as in:

fanfreakingtastic

(to use a milder variant of the more commonly found expression). Here *freaking* is infixed, rather than prefixed or suffixed, since it occurs internally to the root *fantastic. Freaking* is not restricted to being only an infix; it can be a word all alone, or it can be prefixed to a root so long as another prefix precedes it:

That is absolutely freaking!
unfreakingbelievable

And some languages allow affixes that connect two words or other meaning-bearing units: INTERFIXES. Again in English it is difficult to find clear examples, although the *-o-* of words like the following may be one:

thermometer, speedometer, barometer

Suffixes, prefixes, infixes, and interfixes are lumped together into the group of morphemes called AFFIXES.

Words can consist of a single morpheme that is monosyllabic or polysyllabic:

dog
tomato

(If a word consists of a single morpheme, that morpheme cannot be an affix, by definition. It is a root.) Or words can be made of multiple morphemes, where at least one morpheme is considered a root:

unreasonableness
noncomplementary
son-in-law

The study of affixation is usually considered part of the study of word formation, which is also called MORPHOLOGY. Of course, there is more to morphology than just affixation. We can form words by adding roots together (as above in *son-in-law*, and in COMPOUND words like *teakettle*), as well as by adding affixes to roots. We can pile on multiple affixes and we can pile on multiple roots. And there are rules governing all the various combinations. One of the important points of debate in the literature concerns whether all word formation takes place in the lexicon or whether some is the result of syntactic processes. We will not enter into this debate in this book, however, since the reader needs to be familiar with both syntax and morphology in order to approach the debate intelligently.

Tangent 1.5: Case

English lexically marks its personal pronoun system for Case, where Case is associated with structural position. (We will follow modern convention and write *Case*, with a capital *C*, to distinguish it from other uses of the word *case* that do not pertain to linguistic terminology, as in: *In case he comes, please give him this note.*) Certain structural positions, called the GRAMMATICAL FUNCTIONS (GFs), have names. For now we can say in rough terms that Case correlates loosely to the Grammatical Function of the NP in the sentence. The GFs include SUBJECT, DIRECT OBJECT (DO), INDIRECT OBJECT (ID), and OBJECT OF A PREPOSITION (OP). In chapters 2 and 3 we will go into a discussion of GFs. For now, use whatever working definition you have from your grade-school classes in English grammar. (The linguistic terms *Subject* and *Object*, like the linguistic term *Case*, will be captalized in this book to distinguish them from their nonlinguistic-terminology counterparts—as in: *I enjoyed the subject of his lecture* and *The object of my affection is Jim*.) Here we will discuss Case in terms of the GFs. In chapter 5, however, you will learn a way to discuss Case matters without making reference to GFs.

We find that Subject position of tensed clauses is singled out and only the personal pronouns *I, we, you, she, he, it,* and *they* can occur here:

I'm leaving for Italy on the fifth.
*Me am leaving for Italy on the fifth.

The grammatical functions of DO, IO, and OP, however, if pronominal, are typically filled with the personal pronouns *me, us, you, her, him, it,* and *them*:

Ralph saw me.
*Ralph saw I.

Ralph gave a book to me./Ralph gave me a book.
*Ralph gave a book to I./*Ralph gave I a book.

Ralph went there with me.
*Ralph went there with I.

Because the grammatical functions split with regard to Case into Subject of tensed clauses versus all others (DO, IO, and OP), some people call the Case of the Subject SUBJECTIVE (hereafter *Subjective*, with a capital *S*, in contrast to the nontechnical term *subjective*) and the Case of all the others OBJECTIVE (hereafter *Objective*, with a capital *O*, in contrast to the nontechnical term *objective*).

Full NPs, as opposed to pronominals, are not distinguished for Subjective-versus-Objective Case in English. That is, we have no Ns or forms of any Ns that occur only in certain structural positions. Thus, regardless of the grammatical function of the NP *the dog*, for example, its morphological form does not change:

The dog barks.
I saw the dog.
I gave food to the dog./I gave the dog food.
I took a walk with the dog.

There is a third Case, however, that is morphologically distinguished for both pronominals and full NPs. That is called the GENITIVE. In Problem Set 1.1 below, you will consider certain properties of the genitive and you will learn there that no single semantic value can be assigned to the genitive, despite the fact that you have probably been told that the genitive expresses possession. For full NPs, it is regularly realized as *'s*, as in:

Sally's brother is nice.
I like *Sally's* brother.
This book is *Sally's*.

For pronominals, the form found in Table B of Tangent 1.1 occurs when it precedes other material within an NP:

{My/your/ her/his/ our/their} book isn't written yet.

And the form found in Table C of Tangent 1.1 occurs when the genitive pronominal stands in isolation:

That book is mine/yours/ hers/his/ ours/theirs.

Many languages are like English in having more audible Case distinctions on pronominals than on full NPs, including the Romance languages (that is, the languages descended from Latin, where full NPs exhibit no audible Case distinctions whatsoever, not even genitive). Other languages have an audibly rich Case system that extends over both pronominals and full NPs. For example, in Latin there are several audible Cases. Nominative is the Case for Subject. ACCUSATIVE is typically the Case for DO, although certain verbs may require a genitive or dative DO. DATIVE is typically the Case for IO. And OPs often have the ABLATIVE Case, although certain Ps may call for other Cases (such as accusative), sometimes with semantic distinctions attached to the Case choice. Furthermore, some Ns have a morphologically distinct Case for VOCATIVE uses (that is, direct address, as in the famous Latin line *Et tu, Brute*—'You, too, Brutus,' where *Brute* is the vocative form of *Brutus*). And Ns also have a genitive form. If you read that English has "nominative" Case, as well as "accusative" and "dative," you can be pretty sure that the labels here are simply borrowed from Latin and applied to mean the Case of the Subject, the Case of the DO, and the Case of the IO, respectively. But, in fact, there is no phonetic or morphological evidence that English distinguishes between the Cases of DO and IO (and OP, for that matter). Thus the Latin model is not a completely appropriate one for the English system. We will not adopt the Latin model in this book, but instead use only the terms *Subjective* (which is equivalent to *nominative*), *Objective* (which covers roughly *accusative, dative*, and *ablative*), and *genitive*.

While English, Latin, Greek, German, and many other languages give the Subject of tensed clauses one Case and assign another Case (or other Cases) to NPs in other positions, there are many languages that make a different split. They assign one Case to the Subjects of transitive verbs, and a different Case to the Subjects of intransitive verbs and the DOs of transitive verbs. Languages with this sort of Case system are called ERGATIVE and include Basque (spoken in the Pyrenees of Spain and southern France) and many native languages of Australia, New Zealand, and New Guinea, as well as North America.

Some languages have no audible Case system whatsoever, neither on the pronominals nor on the full NPs. Chinese is such a language. Some languages have no audible affixal Case system, but have a set of particles that in many ways give information similar to that supplied by Case endings in Indo-European languages (and some have argued that such particles are, in fact, Case-markers). Japanese is such a language.

We can now return to the text with some basic knowledge about Case systems.

*Problem Set 1.1: English Ns and NPs

Later chapters assume that you will have done this problem set.

In the text we find the terms Noun (N) and Noun Phrase (NP), where an NP is an N (called the HEAD of the NP) and all its paraphernalia. (In chapter 4 we will look more closely at the various types of paraphernalia that can accompany an N within an NP. In this problem set and in Problem Set 1.2 you can gain a rudimentary knowledge of phrases in general.) An example of an N is:

dog

An example of an NP is:

a dog

or:

a large dog

where *dog* is the head of the NP *a dog* and of the NP *a large dog*.

Part 1

In the following sentences underline all the Ns once and all the NPs (the entire NPs) two times:

(1)   Colorless green ideas sleep furiously.

(2)   The people who left without helping have to be sick.

(3)   That boy's sister isn't telling the truth.

Part 2

Consider the morpheme (here the suffix) *s* in:

dogs (as in: I like dogs.)
some big dogs (as in: Some big dogs are friendly.)
scary dogs with big teeth (as in: I try to avoid scary dogs with big teeth.)

(a) Does this morpheme attach to the end of the head N or to the end of an NP? Justify your answer. (Be careful. If an NP ends in the head N and the *s* appears at the end, we cannot determine whether the *s* is attaching to the end of the head N or to the end of the entire NP. But, in fact, the *s* is attached to the end of only one of them. So make sure you look at examples where the end of the N and the end of the NP do not coincide.)

(b) Recall that the term "nominal" means a noun-type thing (either N or NP). I will use this term in this question so I will not give away the answer to (a) above.

What does this morpheme add to the semantics of a nominal? Give examples to support your answer. (This should be brief—a couple of sentences.)

(c) Do any categories other than nominal use this same morpheme (that is, the *s* of *cats*, for example) to mean the same thing as it does with a nominal? If so, which categories? (Consider only the categories of verb [such as *implicate*], adjective [such as *beautiful*], adverb [such as *contrapuntally*], and preposition [such as *under*], please.)

(d) Instead of *s* some nominals have an irregular form to get across the meaning that this morpheme *s* adds to the regular nominals we have seen above. For example, we find the pair:

goose geese

List at least five other nominals which have irregular forms (and list their irregular forms, too) where each of the nominals has a distinct way of getting across the meaning of this morpheme. (That is, give me five different types of irregularities— not five examples of the same type of irregularity. Do not be led astray. This question should take you only a few minutes to answer.)

Part 3

Consider the morpheme written as *'s* in:

the boy's book (as in: This is the boy's book.)
the boy who swam's book (as in: This is the boy who swam's book.)

(a) Does this morpheme attach at the end of an N or at the end of an NP? Justify your answer.

(b) What does this morpheme add to the semantics of a nominal? Consider nominals like:

Sally's brother
last night's party
the new kid's desk
Bill's lecture about health care
John's untimely death
Mary's photo of Bill that Jim owns

(Be careful. The answer to Part 2b above is short, but the answer to this question is much longer. Be sure to consider all these examples and any others that come to mind. Then, even if you have tons to say, limit your answer to Part 3b to one half of one page. Do not simply say that this morpheme always indicates possession. There is much more to it than that. In fact, possession often has nothing to do with the semantics here.)

Part 4

Given the answers to Parts 2 and 3 (if you did them the way I hoped), you now have a way to test whether the item you are looking at is an N or an NP. In the examples below underline the Ns with a wavy line and the NPs with two straight lines. (Be careful: one of the issues you are being faced with here is whether or not something can be both an N and an NP at the same time.)

(4)   Geese's beaks are powerful.

(5)   Did Sally's little brothers ever show up?

(At this point you might want to go back and reconsider your answer to Part 1 above.)

Part 5

Can an NP ever consist of simply an N? (That is, can a single word be both an N and an NP at the same time?) If so, give an example of such an NP in a sentence. Then explain why you think this word is both an N and an NP at the same time. (Hint: Look back at what you did in Part 4.)

Part 6

Consider the CONJOINED phrase (where "conjoined" means connected by *and*):

big cats and dogs

This phrase is ambiguous. State the two readings. Then explain why these two readings emerge. (That is, what leads to the ambiguity? Please use what you learned from Parts 3–5 above to answer this.)

Part 7

Consider NPs that contain a head N. Is there anything which must precede such a head N in every single NP? If so, what? If not, give an example of an NP that begins with its head N and use that NP in a sentence.

Part 8

Consider NPs that contain a head N. Is there anything which must follow such a head N in every single NP? If not, give an example of an NP that ends with its head N and use that NP in a sentence.

Part 9

Is it possible for an NP not to contain a phonetically audible head N? That is, does the definition of NP really have to include a phonetically audible N? If you think it does, explain why you came to this conclusion. If you think it doesn't, give an example of such an NP and use it in a sentence. Explain why you think there is no N in your example NP. In answering this, be sure to consider these examples:

(6)   The poor are always with us.

(7) *The poors are always with us.

(8) The poor's power is always marginal.

(Be careful here. If you claim that *poor* is a plural N in 6, you are claiming that it is irregular morphologically with regard to plural formation, since it does not use *s* (as in 7). But there are only a limited number of Ns in English that are irregular for their plural formation. (See your own answer to Part 2d above.) Ask yourself whether saying *poor* has an irregular plural is insightful or, in fact, misses a generalization. In thinking about this, you might consider examples like:

(9) Here are all the books the new dean sent. Let's arrange them in her office by color, okay? The *blue* go on the top shelf. The *red* go on the bottom shelf. And let's put the *purple* on the in-between shelves.

If *poor* has an irregular plural, are you going to have to say that *blue* and *red* and *purple* do, too? Is that insightful?)

*Problem Set 1.2: English Clefts

The diagnostic developed in this problem set will be used repeatedly in later chapters of this book.

Sentences like:

(1) It was Mary that my friend saw.

(2) Who my friend saw was Mary.

are called CLEFT SENTENCES. The cleft in 1 is an *it*-cleft, and the cleft in 2 is a *wh*-cleft (because the one in 1 begins with *it* and the one in 2 begins with a question word: most question words in English begin with *wh*).

It is possible to invert the *wh*-cleft around the form of the verb *be*:

(3) Mary was who my friend saw.

Let us take the liberty of calling the sentence in 3 a cleft sentence also. And let us call *Mary* the clefted item. This is the kind of cleft we will use in this exercise. So whenever I refer to cleft sentences below, I mean sentences with the form

(4) item + form of the verb *be* + *wh*-word + clause

In the clause at the end of the cleft sentence, we have a "hole" that corresponds to the clefted item:

(5) Mary is who my friend saw _____.

That is, we understand *saw* to have a Direct Object but the DO is missing. Furthermore, we understand the missing DO to be identical (in some sense that we have not defined yet) to Mary.

Do not make any assumptions about how we form cleft sentences, please. Just note that all cleft sentences have a corresponding noncleft sentence. The noncleft sentence corresponding to (3) is:

(6)   My friend saw Mary.

Cleft sentences always contain a form of the COPULA (the verb *be*) with material both preceding and following (although not all sentences that contain a copula are cleft sentences). So examples like those in 7, which have fronted items and are called TOPICALIZATION sentences, are not cleft sentences:

(7)   Mary my friend saw.
      Beans I like.
      That guy Sue just swears you're going to like.

Please do not consider topicalization sentences as you do this problem set. Instead, stick to clefts of the type seen in 3.

There may be a number of restrictions on the various parts of cleft sentences. But the clefted item in examples like 3 at first looks as if it has no restrictions on it with regard to category, although many people are not perfectly comfortable with clefted verbal items:

(8)   Quickly is how she went.
      Out is where Mary went.
      Intelligent is what she is.
      ?Run is what Mary did.

Quickly is an adverb. *Out* is a preposition. *Intelligent* is an adjective. *Run* is a verb. And in 3 above we found *Mary*, which is an N.

Actually, there is an important restriction on the type of category that the clefted item can be. Consider the following examples, where the "hole" is underlined for your benefit:

(9)   The girl is who my friend saw _____.

(10)   *Girl is who my friend saw the _____.

(11)   Those exact dogs over there are what I'd like to buy _____.

(12)   *Dogs are what I'd like to buy those exact _____ over there.

Part 1

If the clefted item is a nominal, is it an N or an NP? Support your answer with relevant data.

Part 2

In Problem Set 1.1, you learned that the genitive marker attaches to the end of an NP. Are the following sentences consistent with your answer to Part 1 of this problem set? Why or why not? (Do not worry about where the "hole" is in 13 and 14. That is not the point of this question.)

(13)   Jack's is whose book I saw on the table.

(14)   Your brother's is whose car needs washing.

(Not all speakers get 13 and 14 easily. If you do not, treat this question as though it were asking about a variety of English that you did not speak, and simply answer the question for the grammar of the variety in which 13 and 14 are good sentences.)

Part 3

Now consider prepositions and prepositional phrases. Ps are words like *in, out, after, with, to,* etc. PPs are made of a P plus its Object. Let us use the term PREPO- SITIONAL ITEM as a cover term for both P and PP (just like "nominal" is a cover term for both N and NP). If the clefted item is a prepositional item, is it a P or a PP?

(15)   Into the house is where she ran.

(16)   *Into is where she ran the house.

Part 4

Are the following sentences consistent with your answer to Part 3? Why or why not?

(17)   In is where she ran (not out).

(18)   Up is where Dukakis hoped to be headed.

(Hint: Recall from Problem Set 1.1 that an NP can consist of simply an N some- times, as in "*Dogs'* ears can be floppy." This fact will, I hope, open your mind to the possibilities with prepositional items.)

Part 5

A word like *pretty* is an adjective. A string like *very pretty* is an adjective phrase (or AdjP).

A word like *quickly* is an adverb. A string like *too quickly* is an adverb phrase (or AdvP).

A word like *eat* is a verb. A string like *eat the pizza* is a VP.

Give a cleft sentence in which the clefted item is adjectival. Is it Adj or AdjP that we find here? Support your answer. (Hint: Look at the contrast in 9 versus 10, 11 versus 12, and 15 versus 16. Use that as a model.)

Do the same for adverbials that have the category Adv or AdvP.

Do the same for VERBALS (where the term "verbals" covers V and VP).

Part 6

What is the general restriction on the category of the clefted item of a cleft sentence? (Do not talk about specific categories, like N, V, etc. Just state what type of category this initial item must be. Try to think in terms of heads versus phrases.)

Part 7

Looking back at 8, what category does the clefted item in each sentence belong to? Be sure to make use of the answer you just gave in Part 6 and to consider whether the clefted items are heads or phrases.

Part 8

Is the string of words *up the ladder* a PP in 19?

    (19)   She climbed up the ladder.

Give an argument using what you know about the clefted item of cleft-sentences to support your answer.

Part 9

Is the string of words *up the number* a PP in 20?

    (20)   She looked up the number.

Give an argument to support your answer.

Part 10

Some languages have postpositions (like Japanese). Here is an example, just for interest's sake:

    Toshio-ga   [Hitomi-to] [kuruma-de] [Kobe-ni] itta.
    Toshio-SUBJ Hitomi with car   by   Kobe to went
    'Toshio went to Kobe by car with Hitomi.'

(The *ga* following *Toshio* tells us that *Toshio* is the Subject of this sentence.)
    Some languages, including all the Romance languages, have only prepositions (and no postpositions). Here is an Italian example:

    Daria andrà [con Tonino] [al negozio] [dopo cena].
    'Daria will go with Tonino   to the store after dinner.'

And some have both. Included here are Dutch and German. The following examples are from Dutch.

    Prepositional Phrase:
    Joop heeft [aan haar] nog vaak gedacht.
    Joop has   of her   often   thought
    'Joop often thought about her.'

    Postpositional Phrase:
    Kom mee, [het bos   in].
    come with, the forest into
    'Come along, into the forest.'

Now the question for you is whether English has any postpositional phrases. A potential candidate is *the number up* in:

(21)   I can look the number up.

Is the string of words *the number up* a PP in 21 (where PP stands for postpositional phrase here)? Give an argument to support your answer.

Part 11

Compare 20 to 21. Please list three other combinations besides *look . . . up* that can have this same kind of varying word order. (This is not complicated. It should not take you more than a few minutes to find them.)

Part 12

Consider the word *right* with the sense of "directly," as in:

(22)   Mary went right into the house.
       Mary went right in.

We cannot say (with the sense of "directly"): ——————

(23)   *Mary right sat down.
       *Mary bought right a pizza.
       *Mary is right smart.
       *Mary ran right fast.

(Actually, some varieties of English can accept the final two sentences of 23. Please, if you can do this, answer the question for those varieties of English that mark all the sentences in 23 as ungrammatical. Then, as a separate exercise, you can discuss how your variety of English differs from the variety of English that rejects these sentences.)

Assume that *right* introduces only a phrasal level (that is, an XP, not just an X). (We have not justified this—that is why it is an assumption. At some later point in your syntactic studies you might try to prove this assumption.)

What (phrasal) category does *right* introduce?

Part 13

Is the single word *up* of 20 a PP? (Be careful to look at 20, not at 21!) Give two arguments to support your answer. (Please use what you learned in Parts 3 and 12 above. You use your clefting test and your *right*-test here.)

Part 14

What category do you think *up* is in 20? Why? Keep your discussion short. A couple of sentences should do. But the maximum limit is one half of one side of a page.

Problem Set 1.3: Italian Agreement

This problem set is on Italian and it is your first problem set on a language other than English, but it will not be your last. All the information you need to know in order to do this problem set is included. Relax and try it. None of the concepts presented are new to you.

Part 1

The color words in Italian typically show a morphological ending that indicates agreement with the item the color word modifies inside the noun phrase, as in:

(1) la   macchina nera   'the black car'
     the car (fs)   black (fs)

     le   macchine nere   'the black cars'
     the car (fp)   black (fp)

     il   piatto   nero   'the black plate'
     the plate (ms) black (ms)

     i   piatti   neri   'the black plates'
     the plate (mp) black (mp)

(Note that fs = feminine singular, fp = feminine plural, ms = masculine singular, mp = masculine plural.) In this way, the color word in 1 behaves like an ordinary adjective of Italian.

On the basis of 1, for what features do the color words agree with the noun they modify in Italian? What are the four morphological endings seen in the color word above and what are the features associated with these endings?

Part 2

A few color words, however, are invariable. One type is exemplified in:

(2) la macchina rosa 'the pink car'
     le macchine rosa 'the pink cars'

     il piatto   rosa 'the pink plate'
     i piatti   rosa 'the pink plates'

Rosa in Italian has more than one meaning. Just on the basis of your knowledge of English, suggest a second meaning for *rosa* beside 'pink.' Consider the semantic and pragmatic relationships between these two meanings for *rosa*. Why do you think *rosa* is invariable for agreement? Guess at another color word that might possibly be invariable, based solely on your knowledge of color words in English.

Part 3

A second type of color word that is invariable for agreement is exemplified in:

> (3) la macchina blù 'the blue car'
>   le macchine blù 'the blue cars'
>   il piatto blù 'the blue plate'
>   i piatti blù 'the blue plates'

The accent marks in 3 indicate stress on the final vowel. Consider the four mor-phological endings you came up with in Part 1. Now consider the root for the word which means 'black' to which these endings were attached in 1. If the color word here were to make use of these endings in agreement processes, what morphological questions would arise? (Hint: Consider what the root for the word that means 'blue' might be. How does it differ from the root for 'black' in Part 1? Could this difference be the source of the impossibility of adding the agreement suffix in 3? You don't have much to go on here, so just make a stab at it.)

Part 4

Tensed verbs agree with their Subjects in Italian. Consider:

> (4) Io canto.
>   'I sing.'

> (5) Tu canti.
>   'You sing.'

> (6) Il ragazzo canta.
>   'The boy sings.'

> (7) La ragazza canta.
>   'The girl sings.'

> (8) Noi cantiamo.
>   'We sing.'

> (9) Voi cantate.
>   'You (plural) sing.'

> (10) I ragazzi cantano.
>   'The boys sing.'

> (11) Le ragazze cantano.
>   'The girls sing.'

Whether the speaker is male or female, whether the person spoken to is male or female, 4, 5, 8, and 9 are all grammatical. While 5 and 9 have the same translation in English, the difference in Italian is that 5 is understood to say that a single person sings, whereas 9 is understood to say that more than one person sings.

On the basis of 4–11, for what features do verbs agree with their Subjects in Italian?

(Note: While 4, 5, 8, and 9 are grammatical, pronominal subjects in Italian are quite often omitted entirely. Thus 4, 5, 8, and 9 would also be grammatical if they consisted of the verb alone. In fact, 6, 7, 10, and 11, would also be grammatical if they consisted of the verb alone. But in that case they would be interpreted the same way as sentences with an expressed pronominal Subject. You will look more closely at this aspect of Italian grammar in Problem Set 2.5 of chapter 2.)

Part 5

As I said above in Part 1, the agreement phenomenon exemplified in 1 is typical of adjectives in Italian. Compare, then, the features for which adjectives agree in Italian (which you discovered in Part 1) with the features for which verbs agree (which you discovered in Part 4). What feature is reflected in both agreement processes? What feature is reflected in only adjective agreement? What feature is reflected in only verb agreement?

If you are doing this problem set as part of a course, you might want to discuss in class the differences you find in these two agreement processes. If not, be sure to read the Tangent 2.3 on agreement in chapter 2 when you get to it.

Problem Set 1.4: Japanese Word Order and Particles

This problem set is on Japanese. It has only one conceptual point. If you see that point, you will be able to answer the question here in a sentence or two.

Please read the caveats concerning the Japanese problem sets found in the introduction to this book before starting.

Consider these English sentences:

(1)   Jack gave Pete Sally.
       Jack gave Sally Pete.
       Pete gave Jack Sally.
       Pete gave Sally Jack.
       Sally gave Pete Jack.
       Sally gave Jack Pete.

In order to allow for a good context for these sentences, you may have to think of Sally, Pete, and Jack alternately as pets, perhaps. That is, in the first sentence Jack is giving Pete a pet named Sally; in the second sentence Jack is giving Sally a pet named Pete; and so on. These sentences do not mean the same thing.

Now consider the Japanese sentences:

(2)   Toshio-ga Hitomi-ni Hanako-o yatta.
       Toshio-ga Hanako-o Hitomi-ni yatta.
       Hitomi-ni Toshio-ga Hanako-o yatta.

Hitomi-ni Hanako-o Toshio-ga yatta.
Hanako-o Toshio-ga Hitomi-ni yatta.
Hanako-o Hitomi-ni Toshio-ga yatta.
'Toshio gave Hanako to Hitomi.'

All of these sentences can be used to describe the situation in which Toshio gave Hanako to Hitomi, as the translation at the end of 2 shows (although some of them are more peculiar than others and call for certain restrictions on the contexts in which they can be appropriately used). Again, in order to have a pragmatically suitable situation, we might allow *Hanako* to be the name of a pet in 2.

The important point for us in this problem set is that 2 contrasts sharply with 1. In 1, all the sentences were sharply distinct in meaning. They described different situations and they would be true in different situations. But the sentences in 2 are very similar in meaning. They describe the same situation and they are true in the same situations. (The differences in meaning are of a subtle sort, having to do with issues such as what is old and new information in the sentence, where our sympathies lie, and other factors of the discourse.)

In both 1 and 2 the verbs remained in a fixed position, but the noun phrases were arranged differently from sentence to sentence. Rearranging the order of the NPs in English resulted in drastic changes for the semantics. But rearranging the order of the NPs in Japanese did not.

Why?

(Hint: Reread Tangent 1.5 on Case. Then guess at the function of the PARTICLES *ga*, *o*, and *ni* in Japanese.]

(Note: You are led to a particular answer here that not all scholars of Japanese would agree with. As you go through this book, you will do many problem sets on Japanese. After you have finished the book, you may want to return to this question and see if you can recognize why the answer you gave now is controversial.)

Star Problem 1.1

Consider the pronoun *one*, as in:

(1)   You have a mean brother and I have a nice one.

Does *one* belong to the category N or to the category NP? Justify your answer. (You will need to make up other sentences with *one* to make your point. Be sure that in the sentences you make up you are using the pronoun *one* and not the numeral *one* in front of an N (as in *one dog*).)

Once you have your answer, then consider examples like:

(2)   You have a mean older brother and I have a nice one.

If an N consists of simply a head N and an NP consists of the entire phrase (that is, the head N plus *all* its paraphernalia), what problem does 2 present for the analysis of the category of the word *one*? How might we try to resolve this problem? (We return to issues involving *one* in Tangent 8.1.)

Star Problem 1.2

We have contrasted words like *Sally*, which are proper nouns, with words like *chair*, which are common nouns. Basically, a proper noun is used as a name; it has a referent. But a common noun has a sense only, and is related to a referent only by way of being the head of an NP.

Give a sentence in which *Sally* appears as a head N for an NP that contains at least one other word, as well.

Is a so-called proper noun like *Sally* in a sentence like:

(1) I invited Sally.

best analyzed as an N that happens to fill the NP, or best analyzed as an NP for which no internal analysis (that is, no breakdown into head N plus paraphernalia) makes sense? In thinking about this you may want to contrast examples like 2 to those like 3:

(2) The Sally in your class likes peanut butter.
     I've never met a Sally who liked her own name.

(3) Poor Sally left town in a huff.
     Have you met (my) darling Sally yet?

Star Problem 1.3

Given what you know about common and proper nouns from Star Problem 1.2, are the personal pronouns common or proper nouns in their ordinary uses? Give an example in which a personal pronoun is used in an extraordinary way. (Some people have claimed that the term "pronoun" is a misnomer. Now you know why.)

Star Problem 1.4

The morphological distinction between *my* and *mine* is not common to their counterparts in most languages. Discuss the distribution of *my* versus *mine*. Why do we call *my* an adjectival and *mine* a nominal?

Star Problem 1.5

In Part 9 of Problem Set 1.1 you were asked to consider NPs such as:

(1) Thank you for carrying in all my toy animals. Please put *the breakable* over here and the *unbreakable* on the floor.

Discuss the contrast between the sense of *breakable* above and the sense of *breakables* in:

(2) Do you have any breakables in this box?

The use of *breakable* in 1 is elliptical. In elliptical phrases we find that there is a syntactic "hole," so to speak: something is missing syntactically. In 1 the head N for the NP *the breakable* is missing. There are various possibilities for the analysis of an elliptical NP. We might say that there is no head N in this NP, either as a syntactic reality or as a semantic reality. This is the most concrete analysis.

We might, alternatively, say that there is a head N here, but that it is phonetically empty (that is, it is inaudible). In this analysis, we have at least two options. We could claim that syntactically there is no head N in this NP, but in the semantics we have a phonetically empty head N, or we could say that in both the syntax and the semantics we have a phonetically empty head N. Both of these approaches are abstract in calling for a semantic and/or syntactic entity that has no phonetic counterpart.

The crucial issue for us, as students of syntax, is whether there is a head N in the syntax or not (where if there is a head N, it is, of course, phonetically empty). We will not here go into the question of whether or not there is a head N in the semantics.

Now compare the use of *mine* in:

(3)   That book is mine.

(4)   Oh, you finally brought in the books. Please put mine over here and Bill's over there.

Number 3 does not contain any elliptical phrases; there is no syntactic hole in 3. But 4 contains the elliptical phrases *mine* and *Bill's*. Look back at your discussion in Star Problem 1.4 of the distribution of *my* and *mine*. Notice that *mine* but not *my* appears in elliptical phrases, as we see in 4 contrasted to:

(5)   *Please put my over there.

How does the fact that only *mine* but not *my* occurs in elliptical NPs bear on the issue of whether or not there is in the syntax a phonetically empty head N in elliptical NPs?

Overview

In chapter 1 we learned that anaphors (such as reflexives in English) must be bound. This fact will eventually be incorporated into Condition A of the *binding theory* (BT).

We also learned that pronouns need not be bound. This fact will eventually be incorporated into Condition B of BT.

We have recognized that words fall into categories and that strings of words group together into phrases. These facts will help us build the X-Bar Theory of chapter 4.

We learned that English has a Case system for its nominals. We will piece together Case Theory in chapter 5.

2

Subject

Anaphors

At the end of the last chapter we concluded that the reason *himself* and *Jack* had to have the same gender, number, and person in a sentence such as 1 was that *himself* and *Jack* must be understood as coreferential in this sentence:

(1)   Jack saved himself.

We labeled the word *himself* a reflexive and we said that reflexives are an example of anaphors, where anaphors are linguistic entities that must be bound within the same overall sentence. We labeled the something that anaphors are bound by their antecedents. Another example of an anaphor is the RECIPROCAL phrase *each other*, as in:

(2)   The boys saved each other.

Each other, unlike reflexives, is not (lexically or morphologically) distinguished for gender or person (girls can save each other; we can save each other; etc.). It is, however, used only with a plural antecedent, because of its distributive sense (that is, the *each* of *each other* picks out individuals distributed across a group):

(3)   *The boy saved each other.

As we go on in this book we will build up an inventory of properties that anaphors have by looking at the behavior of reflexives. You will have a chance to test whether reciprocals have these properties in Problem Set 7.10. For now let us assume they do.

Reflexives and reciprocals turn out to be anaphors in many languages, but not all. As we build up our inventory of anaphor properties, you might try to see if you can find anaphors in whatever other language(s) you know besides English.

The question now is whether we need to be more specific about our description of the distribution of anaphors. Is it enough to say that an anaphor and its antecedent must occur in the same overall sentence or do we need to say more in order to adequately describe all and only the possible locations of anaphors?

There are two kinds of sentences that, if they occurred, might help us answer this question. In one kind of sentence anaphors and their antecedents would appear, but the sentence would not be good. In another kind of sentence, anaphors would appear without (overt) antecedents, but the sentence would be good.

We, in fact, find both kinds of sentences. In 4 we have an anaphor and its antecedent (both italicized here), but the sentence is no good:

(4)   *We_i said that Sally shouldn't invite $ourselves_i$.

The INDICES in 4 on *we* and *ourselves* indicate that these two NPs are to be understood as entering into a binding relationship. In 4 the binding relationship would involve coreference.

In 5 we have an anaphor (again italicized) that has no OVERT antecedent, yet the sentence is good:

(5)   Working *oneself* to the bone is never a good idea.

(By overt I mean an element that is audible—in technical terms, one that has a PHONETIC MATRIX. We will discuss nonovert elements starting in chapter 6.) For the moment we will lay aside the questions that sentences like 5 pose and concentrate on the questions that sentences like 4 pose.

Given 4, we realize that we must tighten up our statement about the distribution of anaphors. It is not enough that an anaphor and its antecedent both appear in the same overall sentence. Instead, they obey certain additional restrictions. Those are the restrictions we are going to investigate now.

Just looking at 4 versus all the good sentences with reflexives in chapter 1, we might notice an important difference: 4 is a two-clause sentence, whereas every other sentence we have looked at with reflexives has had only one clause.

What do we mean when we say there are two clauses in 4? First notice that there are two VERB STRINGS in 4: *said* and *shouldn't invite*. We will explore the verb-string system of English in detail in Problem Set 2.4 and Tangent 2.1 of this chapter, and we will return to questions of its proper analysis in chapter 4 and Tangent 8.1 of chapter 8. For now assume that a verb string is a verb plus all its AUXILIARY (or helping) verbs. A helpful indicator (although it works only in most cases, but perhaps not all, as you will find in chapter 10) of the number of clauses we have in an overall sentence is the number of verb strings we find. In 4 we have two verb strings, and 4 has two clauses, where one clause is inside the other clause. The verb strings here are italicized:

(6)   [₁ We *said* [₂ that Sally *shouldn't invite* ourselves ₂] ₁.]

Can you think of a sentence with three verb strings? There are many, such as:

(7)   Bill *thought* that Jack *said* that Sally *shouldn't come*.

Can you think of a sentence with four verb strings? Easily, for all you need to do is add, "Jeffrey told everyone that . . ." to the beginning of 7 and you have a four-verb-string sentence. In fact, it is possible to have any number of verb strings in a single sentence, although your memory may tell you to quit at a certain point. (Sixteen verb strings in a single overall sentence is not conducive to easy discourse, for example.)

We will say that 7 has three clauses and, in general, that sentences with n number of verb strings have n number of clauses. All the clauses we have seen so far are tensed (also called FINITE) clauses. That is, the initial element of the verb string is morphologically marked for past or present tense (Tangent 2.1). This is not the only kind of clause we find in English, however. We have NONFINITE (that is, untensed) clauses, as well. One kind of nonfinite clause is called the INFINITIVAL clause (the *to* clause), as in:

(8) [Bill wanted [Sally to invite someone]].

Here *Sally to invite someone* is an infinitival clause inside the larger clause. That is, what Bill wanted was a PROPOSITION—he wanted something to happen. And that proposition is represented by way of the infinitival clause *Sally to invite someone*. The infinitival verb string is *to invite*, and you will be asked to explore exactly what this *to* is in Problem Set 2.4 of this chapter.

Sentences with more than one clause, where one or more is inside another, are called COMPLEX SENTENCES. We call the biggest clause of a complex sentence, inside of which all the others fall, the MATRIX (or ROOT, or MAIN) CLAUSE. We call all the other clauses EMBEDDED. When we have several clauses embedded one inside the other, we say that the most deeply embedded clause is the LOWEST CLAUSE and we go on up until we reach the HIGHEST, or matrix, CLAUSE. In 7, for example, the lowest clause is:

[that Sally shouldn't come]

The next-to-the-lowest clause is:

[that Jack said that Sally shouldn't come]

And the matrix clause is the full sentence:

[Bill thought that Jack said that Sally shouldn't come].

We have seen two types of embedded clauses, then: finite ones (as in 7) and nonfinite infinitivals (as in 8). There are other types of nonfinite clauses besides infinitivals. One of these has an *-ing* on the first verb of the verb string, as in:

(9) [We counted on [Bill inviting Sally]].
    [We counted on [Bill having invited Sally already]].

(A common remark in syntax classes is that the second sentence in 9 has a past tense in the embedded clause, as witnessed by the *having*. This remark is based on a mistaken idea of what tense is. After you have read Tangent 2.1, you will understand why infinitivals and the embedded clauses in 9 are to be classified as nonfinite.)

Actually, there are a number of different types of nonfinite verb strings with *-ing* on the main verb, as you will see in chapter 5 in Problem Sets 5.4 and 5.5. For now, if you come across an example in this book of a nonfinite clause with a V that ends in *-ing*, it will be of the type seen in 9.

The question before us is whether the fact that 4 has two clauses is in any way responsible for its ungrammaticality. Once more let us consider all the good sentences with reflexives in chapter 1. We find there that the antecedent of the reflexive is always in Subject position (and we will work at trying to understand the notion of Subject below). When we consider the ungrammaticality of 4 above, we notice that the antecedent of the reflexive is not in Subject position of the lowest clause that the antecedent is in. A proposal that might well come to mind is that an anaphor must find its antecedent in the Subject position of the lowest clause that the anaphor is in.

This proposal may well describe the distribution of anaphors and antecedents in some languages (for example, in Danish). However, for English the situation is more complex. But before we can see that complexity, it is important that we understand the proposal before us. And crucial to understanding that proposal is the notion of Subject.

Subject

What is a Subject? With this question we are embarking on a very long discussion of several hypotheses.

One common answer in introductory syntax classes is that the Subject of a sentence is what the sentence is about. Let us see if this is an adequate definition. Consider the following sentence, spoken three different ways, with the capital letters indicating where the audible STRESS PEAK of the sentence falls:

(10) a. BILL told Jenny.
      b. Bill TOLD Jenny.
      c. Bill told JENNY.

Certainly the situations in which we might use this sentence with these three different INTONATION CONTOURS (or patterns of PITCH and VOLUME) differ. For example, if the LISTENER (or hearer) knows that someone told Jenny but not who told Jenny, we might say 10a. If the listener knows that Bill did something with respect to Jenny but not what Bill did with respect to Jenny, we might say 10b. If the listener knows that Bill told someone, but not who Bill told, we might say 10c. Now if these different contexts mean that each of 10a through 10c is about something different, then we would be forced to say that the Subject of each of these sentences is different. But from a syntactic point of view, these sentences are identical. That is, the words in these sentences, the order in which they appear, and the ways they structurally relate to each other (you will learn about structural relations as you progress through this book) are the same. If we want a notion of Subject that has clear syntactic correlates, then talking about *aboutness* will not help us. So we have reached a dead end.

At this point you may feel convinced that a Subject of a sentence is not to be defined as what the sentence is about. But if you think that 10a, 10b, and 10c really are about the same thing, then you may be reluctant to drop this definition so quickly.

So let us try another tack in attempting to evaluate whether this elusive notion of aboutness is the key to the definition of Subject. What is the following sentence about?

(11)   Bertha gives blood after every phone call from her mother-in-law.

If you put this sentence in front of a hundred people and asked what it was about, you would undoubtedly not find uniformity in their answers. Instead, some people might say the sentence was about Bertha. Others might say it was about giving blood. Others might say it was about Bertha's mother-in-law. Others might even say it was about the possible effects mothers-in-law can have. And there might be stray answers in your sample that I cannot even guess at.

If you were to claim that all the answers you would get were equally valid, you would be led to saying that the Subject of the sentence varies according to the speaker. But then a sentence would not have a fixed Subject; it would have multiple potential Subjects, relative to each speaker. So talking about whether or not two sentences have the same Subject would be equivalent to talking about whether two sentences have the same set of potential Subjects and the same match between each potential Subject and each speaker. And the set is at least potentially limitless (so long as there is yet another speaker to ask, where that speaker might possibly give some new answer, and where speakers already asked might change their mind).

But if Subjects are entities that participate in grammatical processes, then with this variable (or relative or multiple) notion of Subject, we would expect different speakers to treat the same sentence differently with respect to these grammatical processes. While we have seen no grammatical processes that crucially look at the Subject of a clause yet, we will in this chapter. And we will find that different speakers do not, in fact, treat a given sentence differently with respect to the grammatical processes of Case assignment and SUBJECT-AUXILIARY INVERSION discussed below. Thus, this variable definition of Subject, based on the notion of aboutness, fails. Furthermore, we have set up an UNTESTABLE definition of Subject. *But if a definition is untestable, it is useless.*

This is an important point. Ask yourself what an untestable definition or hypothesis offers us. Do we learn anything about language from an untestable statement about language? Let me offer you another example of an untestable hypothesis: the Subject of a sentence is the thing the speaker pays the most attention to. In the absence of a way to test the degree of a speaker's attention to various parts of a sentence, this hypothesis is untestable. Did you learn anything about language from considering this hypothesis? I doubt it.

Because of issues like those above, linguists consider UNTESTABLE HYPOTHESES to be nonhypotheses, and untestable definitions to be nondefinitions.

Alternatively, if you are going to accept as valid only some of the answers you receive and not others as you do your survey of what people think 11 is about, you will need an independent standard by which to decide which ones are valid. That boils down to saying that you will need an independent standard by which to discern what a sentence is about. The burden is on you to come up with such a standard. And the very fact that the answers you gathered varied should make you doubtful of the promise of this approach. Keep in mind that this approach is theoretically possible. The point is that your independent standard is most likely going to have to be rather complex and sensitive to delicate distinctions of meaning. Until you come up with such a standard (and a testable standard, please), we must lay this line of inquiry aside.

We will therefore stop pursuing the notion that the Subject of a sentence is what the sentence is about.

Another common idea is that the Subject of a sentence is the noun phrase (NP) whose referent is understood to do the ACTION. By this definition, in 10 the Subject is *Bill*, since Bill is the one who performs the action of telling Jenny. In 1 *Jack* is the Subject, because Jack is the one who performs the action of saving himself. In 7, there are three Subjects, *Bill*, *Jack*, and *Sally*, each of which has an action that its referent performs. (By the way, we can now see that each of the three clauses in 7 has not only its own verb string, but also its own Subject.)

So what we need to do now in order to test our new hypothesis (that the Subject of a sentence is the NP whose referent is understood to do the action) is to look at more sentences. First of all, if we assume that every sentence has a Subject and if we can find a sentence whose meaning does not involve an action, we can conclude that this definition of Subject is wrong. And, definitely, there are sentences whose meanings do not involve actions, such as:

(12)   Mary is tall.

Tallness is not an action; it's a STATE. Yet 12 is a good sentence, and, in fact, most of us would say without hesitation that *Mary* is the Subject (where we would be basing that on some definition we seem to have picked up by osmosis, but which we are aiming to make explicit right now). So not all Subjects have referents that perform actions. In fact, even in sentences whose meanings involve actions, the referent of the Subject need not be the one who performs the action. Can you think of such a sentence? A common type is PASSIVE sentences (Tangent 2.2).

(13)   Everyone is frightened by that movie.

Again, we might call *everyone* the Subject, based on our so-far-amorphous definition. But the referent of *everyone* is not performing the action in this sentence. (Compare 13 to the active sentence *That movie frightens everyone.*)

Another way to attack the hypothesis that the Subject of a sentence is the NP whose referent performs the action is to find a sentence in which there seems to be more than one action involved but there is only one Subject. Consider 14:

(14)   John exchanged books with Mary.

Here two actions took place. Which NP is the Subject, then, *John* or *Mary*? Or, perhaps, both?

We are in trouble.

At this point I ask you to set aside all semantic notions of what a Subject might be. Instead, let us look at syntactically *simple* sentences (simple in the sense that they contain only one verb string), such as:

(15)   [Sally] [left].
       [The new postman] [arrived].

[The ship] [sank].
[Dogs] [bark].

In 15 each sentence has only two elements, an NP and a verb string that consists of a single verb. Assume one of them must be the Subject.

Why make such an assumption?

We started our investigation of Subjects because we wanted to try to make use of the notion of "Subject" in predicting the distribution of anaphors. If we were to look at a wide array of other phenomena (some of which you will examine in Problem Sets 2.1–2.3 at the end of this chapter), we would frequently find ourselves in this position—wanting a reliable definition of what Subjects are so we could use the notion "Subject" in a linguistic analysis. The notion of "Subject," then, turns out to be basic to issues of sentence analysis, regardless of any questions involving anaphors.

One of our goals in this book is to try to find a useful approach to the analysis of sentences. One way to go about this is to begin with general statements about all sentences. We can make a list of the properties we assume all sentences to have in common. Then we can go through that list and test to see if each property in fact holds of all sentences we can think of. In this way, we will winnow away the assumed properties on the list until we arrive at a (presumably) shorter list that contains properties we no longer assume but have verified.

In that spirit, let us assume that all sentences have a Subject. In fact, given that sentences can have multiple clauses (as in 7 above), we can be more precise and assume that all clauses have precisely one Subject. This second assumption is STRONGER than the first in that it rules out more possibilities. That is, the first assumption rules out the possibility of sentences that have no Subject. The second assumption rules out that possibility plus the possibility of a sentence with more Subjects than clauses or vice versa. If the second assumption is wrong, we will probably find out quickly once we check our data. If it is right, we will have made the strongest statement (and, thus, the biggest step forward in our knowledge of sentence structure) that we are capable of making at this point.

Turning back to 15 now, we assume one of the bracketed elements is the Subject. While we could arbitrarily call either one the Subject, traditionally it is the NP that has been called the Subject. This accords with the fact that many people offer the semantic definitions (which we have already set aside above) of "the element the sentence is about" or "the element whose referent performs the action" for the term *Subject*. They are stabbing at definitions that hold more easily of NPs than of verb strings.

Thus we will call the bracketed NPs in 15 the Subjects of these sentences.

At this point you might raise the objection that some sentences consist of only verb strings, so if every sentence must have a Subject, we should call the verb string the Subject. For example, in 16 we see what we will call IMPERATIVE sentences:

(16)   Leave!
       Stop!
       Move!

Imperatives are handled in Problem Set 2.3, where we will see that they do, in fact, contain nonovert Subjects. So this particular objection does not hold. In the discussion that follows we will not, then, consider imperatives problematic.

Let us return then to 15, calling the bracketed NPs the Subjects. How could we characterize these phrases so that in other sentences that consist of more than just an NP and a verb string we can pick out the Subject?

Let me bring up the ideas that have been raised in classes I have taught.

Phrases

One idea is that the Subject is the first phrase in the sentence.

In order to test this hypothesis, we need an understanding of what phrases are. In fact, in Problem Set 1.2 we found a test for picking out phrases from nonphrases, so we should already have that understanding. Basically, a phrase is an item of a particular CATEGORY that may be accompanied by paraphernalia such as modifiers and other types of items. We will be looking into phrase structure in depth in chapter 4.

What categories can a phrase be built around? There are different categories into which words fall. In Problem Set 1.1 we learned how to distinguish the category noun (or N) from all other categories. But we now need to distinguish among all non-nouns. We have already noted that we need the categories of verb (V), adjective, adverb, and preposition (P). But we have not given any tests for distinguishing these categories from one another.

Recall that our test for distinguishing N was morphological: Ns can take an -s affix to form the plural. (Actually, the picture is more complex than this, as we saw in Problem Set 1.1, but this statement will do here.)

Using that experience, let us try to find some morphological bases upon which to distinguish between the other categories. Consider adjectives and adverbs first. One thing they can do that the other categories cannot is form comparatives and superlatives by adding a suffix:

(17)   Adjective: taller, prettier
                tallest, prettiest

      Adverb: faster
            fastest

The comparative -er and superlative -est affixes attach only to monosyllabic words or disyllabic words where the second syllable is very light. For words with more syllables, we use *more* or *most* to form the comparative and superlative. Vs cannot do this; thus we find no forms like:

(18)   *elapser
      *elapsest

Forms like those in 19 are not counterexamples:

(19)   grower, organizer

These words are Ns, not comparative Vs. They are formed by adding the AGENTIVE suffix -er to a V. This process is called NOMINALIZATION, and this particular type of nominalization is typically taken to be a lexical process. That is, we take Vs from our lexicon and add -er to them to form agentive Ns. (In fact, the -er nominal is not always agentive, as you will see in Problem Set 3.4 of chapter 3.)

Ps also typically do not have comparative or superlative forms, although when a P is a PREDICATE (as in the first sentence of 20b—and you will learn about predicates in chapter 3) or when the PP MODIFIES a nominal (as in the second sentence of 20b), it can be preceded by more/less or most/least. Still, Ps never take the comparative or superlative affix:

(20) a. *arounder
     *aroundest

b. John's more into art than Mary is.
   John is the most into art person I know.

Forms like those in 21 are not counterexamples:

(21) upper, downer

Instead, we find again the Agentive -er which, besides being able to be added to many Vs, can also be added to some Ps to form an N.

Forms like those in 22 are also not counterexamples:

(22) inner, outer

These words are not comparative Ps. Rather, they are adjectives:

(23) the inner wall, the outer circle

And, finally, Ns do not take the comparative or superlative affix:

(24) *boyer
     *boyest

although we can certainly find more and most with Ns and we do have a distinct way of expressing the idea of a comparative for a predicative nominal:

(25) a. I have more milk than you do.

b. Bill's more of a scholar than I ever expected him to be.

And for a very few lexical items in the casual speech of at least some speakers one can hear superlatives of the following sort:

(26) He's the most man I could ever want.

(In 25b and 26 we are dealing with predicative nominals—compare to predicative prepositions, as in the first sentence of 20b above.) But, in general, Ns do not form comparatives or superlatives with -er or -est, in contrast to adjectives and adverbs.

We have at this point distinguished the categories of adjectives and adverbs from all others but not from each other. Many linguists lump adjectives and adverbs together into one larger category with the abbreviation A. Certainly, however, adjectives and adverbs are not morphologically identical. In fact, many adverbs can be derived from adjectives via the suffix -*ly*:

(27)   happy, happily
       quiet, quietly

But there is an important sense in which we can view adjectives and adverbs as being two sides of the same coin. This is because their distribution relative to each other is predictable: adjectives occur in positions where they modify or are predicated of nominals; adverbs occur in positions where they modify or are predicated of anything other than nominals. In chapter 3 we will discuss modification and predication at length. Thus the reader will have to hold off on the verification of this claim until that point.

Now we have to find a way to distinguish Vs and Ps from each other. Morphology can help again: the suffix -*ing* can be added productively to Vs only. It cannot be added to Ns, As, or Ps:

(28)   walking, sleeping

(29)   N: *contraptioning
       A: *talling, *quietlying
       P: *froming, *arounding

(Question: Why can we say *John's downing the last beer right now?* Hint: Consider what category *downing* belongs to in this sentence.)

We have, then, justified the existence of at least four categories: N, V, A, and P. The first three have been distinguished by morphological processes that only they can undergo. The last has been distinguished by its failure to undergo all the morphological processes that were used to distinguish the first three.

Phrases can be built up around any of these categories. They are called the MAJOR CATEGORIES, and they are said to head the phrase. Examples of phrases of each kind of category, where their heads are underlined, are:

(30)   NP: the ugly gray *dog* with big teeth that bit Billy

       AP: absurdly *fond* of Billy
            so exceedingly *sneakily*

       PP: right *through* the window

       VP: *jumped* wildly about on the bed

It is important to note even at this point that the head of a phrase need not come in initial position of that phrase. In 30 none of the phrases are head-initial.

If you have lots of questions about how we justify calling each of the examples in 30 a phrase, good. Establishing that a string of words forms a phrase is a complex matter. For now, use the cleft-test you developed as you did Problem Set 1.2 and have patience until you reach chapters 4 and 7.

Looking at 30 you can see that there are several words there that do not immediately look like N, A, P, or V. For example, what are *the, that, so,* and *right* in 30? Some of these are called MINOR-CATEGORY words, like the ARTICLE *the*. Minor-category words cannot head a phrase: they do not take any paraphernalia of their own. Rather, they are (part of) the paraphernalia of the heads of the phrases to which they belong. *So* is another minor-category word. The classification of others of the words here is controversial; for example, are auxiliaries like *may* major category or minor-category words? We will set all of these issues aside until chapter 4.

Back to Subjects

Now we can test the definition offered above that the Subject of a sentence is the first phrase in the sentence. Let us consider again the first example of 15, repeated here:

(31)   Sally left.

With our definition, *Sally* is the Subject. But now consider:

(32)   On the fourth night Sally left.

Here the first phrase is the P phrase (PP) *on the fourth night*. With our definition of Subject, we would be led to saying that the Subject of 31 is the NP, but the Subject of 32 is the PP. Even with very little knowledge of syntax, you are probably disturbed by this turn of events. That is, you have an intuition that the PP is semantically peripheral. It serves here to modify the EVENT denoted by the rest of the sentence. But the heart of the matter is that Sally left. Should we say that the Subject has changed as a result of this modification?

Consider also that the PP could appear at the end of the sentence as easily as at the beginning:

(33)   Sally left on the fourth night.

But *Sally* cannot appear at the end of the sentence, regardless of where the PP is:

(34)   *x Left x Sally x.

If we were to put *on the fourth night* into any one of the x slots in 34, we would still have a bad sentence. So, somehow the PP in 32 is syntactically freer than the NP *Sally* in either 31 or 33. This accords with the fact we noted earlier—that the PP is semantically peripheral.

While none of the comments above are proof, they are suggestive. And you probably did not even have to think about them to come to the conclusion that our definition of Subject is flawed. Most likely, you wanted to say that the Subjects of 31 and 32 had to be the same, right off the bat. But we have yet to discover what unstated reasons you have for wanting to say this. Still, we will follow our hunches and try for a better definition.

We might try altering our definition to say that the Subject is the first NP of the sentence. But notice that *the fourth night* is an NP, and it is the first NP in 32. So, still, we are going to have to ANALYZE 31 and 32 as having different Subjects—and all the problems we had with the previous definition of Subject lift their ugly heads again.

Alternatively, we might try saying that the Subject is the first NP of the sentence that is not CONTAINED inside a PP. That is, *Sally* in 31 would be the Subject because this is the first NP in the sentence and this NP is not part of a larger PP. Likewise, *Sally* in 32 would be the Subject, because the NP which precedes it (*the fourth night*) is inside a PP, so *Sally* is the first NP of the sentence that is not inside a PP. But now compare:

(35) I hate beans, not peas (, you idiot)!

(36) Beans I hate, not peas (, you idiot)!

In 35 we would be led to claim that *I* is the Subject. (Recall from the star problems of chapter 1, if you did them, that pronouns are NPs.) But in 36, *beans* would be the Subject. Again, a queasiness should enter your stomach; these sentences express the same event—the same person is doing the same action to the same entity. Without a doubt, 36 is a special sentence syntactically and semantically. It is called a topicalized sentence, and the problem, obviously, is that the word order in 36 is unusual. But is the difference between 35 and 36 one of different Subjects?

You may not feel sure that the answer to that last question is no, but you surely feel some dissatisfaction in our approach. Let us try again.

The definition of a Subject as the first NP in the clause not contained in a PP is a syntactic one. That is, this definition depends not on the sounds of the words (their phonology) or on their internal makeup (their morphology) or on their meanings (their semantics), but on their arrangement in the clause (which is part of the syntax of the clause). And since this is a book about syntax, this definition has been a welcome one. Regretfully, however, we must admit it is time to chuck even this syntactic definition of Subject.

The only assumption we are left with is that every sentence must have a Subject.

Let us take another look at all the sentences we have dealt with so far to see if we can find any other way to get a handle on this term. Actually, we have already talked about something in chapter 1 that can help us here: Case systems. We noted that English appears to have three Cases: Subjective (also and more frequently called "nominative," see Tangent 1.5 of chapter 1), Objective, and genitive. Subjective and Objective Cases are audible, however, only on non-neuter pronouns (as in *he* versus *him*). That means that if we want to test what Case a given NP has in a given sentence, we must substitute the appropriate pronoun for that NP and check its Case. If we now go back to our sentences in 15, in which we claimed that the NP must be the Subject, and if we substitute pronouns for every lexical NP, we come up with the following sentences:

(37) [Sally] [left]. → [She] [left].
[The new postman] [arrived]. → [He] [arrived].
[The ship] [sank]. → [It] [sank].
[Dogs] [bark]. → [They] [bark].

She, he, and *they* are Subjective Case (contrast to *her, him,* and *them* and *her*[*s*], *his,* and *their*[*s*]). *It* is not phonetically distinguishable for Case between the Subjective and the Objective (although it does have the possessive form *its*). Since we have no evidence to the contrary, the simplest proposal we can now make is that Subjects have Subjective Case.

Notice that while we cannot hear the Case of the NP *Sally* in the first sentence of 37, we are concluding that its Case is Subjective. This is because the substitution of a pronoun for *Sally* is grammatical only if the pronoun is Subjective. (Compare the first sentence of 37 to *Her left.*)

Since we are testing the assumption that there is precisely one Subject in every clause, we now predict that there will be at most one item in every clause that can have Subjective Case. Why do I say "at most one" instead of "precisely one"? There are two variables here. First, we will find in the text below that Subjects of some clauses have a Case other than Subjective. Second, while every clause must have a Subject, in English only NPs show audible evidence (as with the morphology of genitive NPs and with the lexical Case of pronouns) of having Case (although there are other ways of detecting whether a phrase has Case, as we will see in chapter 5, particularly in Problem Set 5.5). So if the Subject of a clause can be a phrase of some category other than NP, we will not have any audible Case on the Subject and we might question whether non-NP Subjects really do have Case.

Can you think of a clause that has some phrase other than NP as its Subject? If not, go back to Problem Set 1.2 and consider the cleft-sentences that we studied there again. (Actually, they were inverted *wh*-clefts, but we called them clefts for ease of presentation.) These sentences have two clauses. And the matrix clause takes a phrase of any category as its Subject:

(38)   NP: [Mary] is who I like.

   PP: [Into the house] is where she ran.

   AP: [Quickly] is how she did it.
   [Pretty] is how she looks.

   VP: [Run into trouble] is what you're gonna do.

In fact, it is quite unusual for clauses to have PP, AP, or VP as their Subjects. Other types of sentences besides clefts that allow this include ones in which the verb is a copula (or linking verb):

(39)   [From New York to Boston] isn't so far after all.

and ones in which the verb is special in another way, as the verbs *appear* and *seem* are (whose specialness we will learn about in chapter 7):

(40)   [From New York to Boston] seems farther every day.

Other than these types, we find such unusual Subjects only under pragmatically controlled interpretations of the sentences. For example, take the sentence:

(41)   [From New York to Boston] makes me absolutely sick.

This is a strange sentence out of context. However, as an answer to the question, "Which leg of the trip is the worst in your opinion?" 41 is fine.

Examples like 38–41 show that phrases of every major category can occur as Subjects. Furthermore, clauses can be the Subjects of other clauses. Can you think of any examples? Consider what type of verb would take a clause as its Subject. The verb would have to allow a proposition as a participant in whatever event the verb denoted. A verb like *eat*, then, is not a candidate: propositions do not eat. But a verb like *excite* or *amaze* or *mean* are candidates for taking a SENTENTIAL SUBJECT: propositions can excite and amaze and mean things. And we find that, just as we would expect, sentential Subjects are possible with such verbs:

(42)   [That Paul's doing metrics again] {excites/amazes} me.
       [That Paul's doing metrics again] means that a new theory will appear any day now.

But clauses, like all phrases other than NPs, do not show any audible evidence of having Case. So for now we must leave open the possibility that even in a tensed matrix clause the Subject might not be assigned Case. (In Problem Set 7.11 of chapter 7 we will take up this issue again.)

Returning now to our prediction that at most one item in a clause can have Subjective Case, we find, if we look carefully at all the good sentences presented thus far and at most other sentences that we come up with, that this is true.

However, there is one immediate type of counterexample found in formal or archaic speech, as in:

(43)   This is she.
       It is I.

It would appear that in 43 the elements on both sides of the copula are in the Subjective Case. We set these aside here and you will be asked to examine them in Problem Set 3.2 of chapter 3.

Even setting aside the type of sentence in 43, there is still another complication. Compare sentences 7, 8, and 9, with pronouns substituted for lexical NPs wherever possible:

(44)   Bill thought that Jack said that Sally shouldn't come.
       He thought that he said that she shouldn't come.

(45)   Bill wanted Sally to invite someone.
       He wanted her to invite someone.

(46)   We counted on Bill inviting Sally.
       We counted on him inviting her.

These are multiple-clause sentences; 44 has three clauses, and, in fact, three Subjective NPs. But 45 and 46 both have two clauses, with only one Subjective NP: the Subject of the matrix clause. In general all matrix clauses have Subjective Subjects if they have NP Subjects. But embedded clauses vary. Play around with several multiple-clause sentences, like:

(47)   That *I'm* discombobulated is no surprise to him.
       I expect (that) *she'll* leave before *he* does.
       After *we* had studied, there was total silence.

(48) For *me* to scare him would be a surprise.
      I expect *her* to leave before him.
      We all wonder about *him* truly understanding or not.

In 47 and 48 the sentences are arranged so that the first example has a sentential Subject, the second has a SENTENTIAL OBJECT, and the third has an embedded clause that is the Object of a P. In 47 all the embedded clauses have a Subjective NP. But in 48 none of them do. What is the crucial difference?

Many linguists have proposed that the difference is tense: tensed clauses have Subjective Case on their NP Subjects. Others have proposed that the difference is agreement: clauses in which the verb agrees with the Subject have Subjective Case on their NP Subjects (Tangent 2.3). But in English, all and only tensed clauses undergo Subject-Verb Agreement. So in English it is difficult to find evidence to support a choice between these two alternatives. In some languages, however, there is empirical evidence to make the choice. In Portuguese, for example, tenseless clauses can undergo Subject-Verb Agreement under certain conditions, and when they do, the Subject is in the Subjective (or nominative) Case. You will explore the Portuguese data in Problem Set 5.3 of chapter 5. Let us say that any clause in which the Subject and verb agree has the feature [+AGR] (and we will discuss the implications of this at greater length in chapter 5). We will, then, say that all NP Subjects of clauses in which we find Subject-Verb Agreement are Subjective Case.

We now have a diagnostic for NP Subjects of tensed clauses in English: the NP that receives Subjective Case is the Subject. We do not yet have any characteristics of Subjects, however, that will hold for all Subjects of all clauses. The present diagnostic holds for NPs only and for tensed clauses only.

There are at least two other diagnostics for the Subject of tensed clauses that we can develop at this point. Think for a moment about sentences that are used to ask questions (DIRECT QUESTIONS), as in:

(49) Are you coming?
      Where has Bill gone?

The first question here calls for affirmation or denial. For this reason it is called a YES/NO QUESTION. The second question, on the other hand, calls for more information than just simple affirmation or denial. Other questions that call for more information in their answer include:

(50) Who did Suzie say left?
      When will Jack be here?
      What have you done?
      Why was she ignored?
      How could they have done that?

Since most of the question words in the initial position of these examples start with the letters *wh*, these are called WH-QUESTIONS. Both kinds of questions, yes/no and wh-, exhibit a special word order. Look carefully at these examples. (And please do not consider other examples of wh-questions that may come to your mind and that do not have the characteristics described below. We will explore wh-questions thoroughly in chapter 8.)

If there is a question word (or phrase), it comes in initial position. Next comes the first auxiliary of the verb string. Then, instead of the rest of the verb string, in all the examples in 49 and 50 we find an NP, and not just any old NP. We find the precise NP which receives Subjective Case. We could posit, then, that the position after the first auxiliary in a direct question is filled by the Subject. To test this, we could see if any other element can appear there. And no other element can:

(51)   Has Ralph often given Paula a hard time?
       (cf. Ralph has often given Paula a hard time.)

       *Has often Ralph given Paula a hard time?
       (cf. Often Ralph has given Paula a hard time.)

Here we see that if *often* appears after the first auxiliary in a DECLARATIVE SEN-TENCE, in the corresponding direct question it will be separated from that auxiliary by the Subject. But if *often* is sentence-initial in a declarative sentence, there is no good corresponding direct question. You can now do a variety of permutations on the questions in 51 to prove to yourself that only the Subject can appear after the first auxiliary. The phenomenon of first auxiliary followed by the Subject has tra-ditionally been called Subject-Auxiliary Inversion. Do not make any assumptions at this point as to whether any real inversion has taken place here. Simply use this term as a label for the phenomenon. (We return to this issue in chapter 8.)

This diagnostic, unlike the Case diagnostic, is not by definition limited to NPs. Thus we can try applying it to (appropriate variations on) our cleft-sentences in 38 and our copular sentence in 39, repeated here for convenience:

(52)   Is [Mary] who you like?
       Is [into the house] where she ran?
       Is [quickly] how she really did it?
       Is [pretty] how she really looks?
       Is [get in trouble] what you really wanna do?

(53)   Is [from New York to Boston] too far for you?

Not everyone is perfectly comfortable with these questions. Still, with a little fid-dling with adverbs and tense and aspect and the appropriate context, most people will accept these questions or others that exhibit the same relevant structure. The position following the first auxiliary in a direct question, then, is a diagnostic for Subjects of all categories.

This diagnostic is of limited application, however. Consider:

(54)   I asked when she was coming.
       Ralph doesn't know what Sally saw.
       They wondered how Jill could get back up the hill.
       He's wondering {whether/if} we can come.

In these sentences we have INDIRECT QUESTIONS, that is, questions in embedded position. They are not direct in that they do not call for either a yes/no or an infor-mation answer. Embedded questions are introduced by the same *wh*-words that introduce direct questions, with the addition of *whether* and *if*. But the relevant point for us here is that we find no Subject-Auxiliary Inversion in indirect questions. Thus our diagnostic for Subjects will not identify Subjects of indirect questions. However, a similar diagnostic is available in these cases: in almost all indirect questions, the first element following the question word is the Subject. The few exceptions to this involve topicalization in embedded clauses—something that some, but not many, speakers find acceptable:

(55) I wonder if liberty he can live without.
      I doubt whether liberty anyone can live without.

The final diagnostic that we should be able to develop at this point is closely related to the diagnostic of Subjective Case, and that is the diagnostic of Subject-Verb Agreement. We have already noted that in English, verbs in tensed clauses show morphological agreement with some other element in the sentence. This element turns out to be the element that receives Subjective Case:

(56) I *am* here.
      She *is* here.
      We *are* here.

As with the other diagnostics, however, we are aided in the analysis of tensed clauses only, since tenseless verbs in English do not show agreement:

(57) They saw [{me/you/him/us/them} *leave*].

Back to Anaphors

We can now return to the issue we opened this chapter with: What is the proper way to describe the distribution of reflexives in English? The hypothesis that we wanted to test was: an anaphor must find its antecedent in the Subject position of the lowest clause it is in. We can test this hypothesis with our three diagnostics for the Subject position of tensed clauses.

There are at least two parts of this hypothesis that we are equipped to test. First, we can test whether the antecedent of the reflexive anaphor must be a Subject. Recall that in all the example sentences we looked at in the first section, the antecedent appeared to be a Subject. In fact, this was the very motivation for the hypothesis we are testing now. We now need to look for examples in which the antecedent of an anaphor is not a Subject.

While the examples are tricky to find because the contexts for using such sentences have so many conditions on them, it is possible to find sentences in which a reflexive has an antecedent in some position other than Subject:

(58) The surgeons carefully unwrapped the bandages. Then they showed John himself in the mirror.
      The psychiatrist introduced the patients to themselves at the final session.

In both of these examples, the antecedent for the reflexive is not a Subject.

How do we know that neither *John* nor *the patients* is a Subject in 58? We know because (1) if we replace these antecedents with appropriate pronouns, the pronouns are not Subjective Case, even though these are tensed clauses; (2) in the corresponding direct questions the antecedents do not immediately follow the first auxiliary of the verb string; and (3) the verbs do not undergo agreement with these NPs:

(59)   Then they showed {him/*he} himself in the mirror.
       The psychiatrist introduced {them/*they} to themselves at the final session.

(60)   When did they show John himself in the mirror?
       When did the psychiatrist introduce the patients to themselves?

(61)   Then the surgeons {show/*shows} John himself in the mirror.
       The psychiatrist {introduces/*introduce} the patients to themselves.

We must conclude that in English the antecedent of a reflexive need not be a Subject.

Second, we can test whether or not the antecedent of a reflexive must be in the lowest clause that the reflexive is contained in. Recall that earlier we saw an example in which the antecedent was in a higher clause than the reflexive and the result was ungrammatical (4, repeated here for convenience):

(62)   *We said that Sally shouldn't invite ourselves.

However, we did not at that time go searching for good examples of this sort. The crucial examples are, again, tricky to find. But this time the problem is not one of scarcity of appropriate contexts but of finding the few types of cases that arise. One is seen in:

(63)   John$_i$ knows that a picture of himself$_i$ hangs in the post office.

The index i here is a referential index. I have given the same index to *John* and *himself* in order to indicate that the sentence should be read with these two items being coreferential. In 63 *himself* is in the clause:

[that a picture of himself hangs in the post office]

but *John* is in the matrix clause. Another kind of example is:

(64)   I$_i$ never expected myself$_i$ to win.

Here *myself* is the Subject of the clause:

[myself to win]

but *I* is in the matrix clause.

Despite the above evidence, however, most reflexives in English appear in sentences in which the Subject of the lowest clause they are contained in is their antecedent. We know now that this fact does not follow directly from a grammatical rule that requires anaphors to take their Subject of their own clause as antecedent. Yet it is unlikely that their overwhelming tendency to do so is an accident. Notice that if we augment examples 63 and 64 by the addition of a medial clause (that is, a clause that comes between the matrix clause and the lowest clause), the sentences become unacceptable:

(65)   *John knows that we all think that a picture of himself hangs in the post office.

(66)   *I never expected you to want myself to win.

Contrasts like these show that there is some kind of LOCALITY RESTRICTION on the antecedent of the reflexive. That is, the antecedent must be local (as opposed to distant) in some sense. As we progress through this book, we will develop an explicit statement of that sense and we will also address problems with it of the type exemplified in 63 in chapters 9 and 10.

Before we leave this chapter, there is one more observation we are primed to make. In chapter 1 we realized that pronouns contrast with anaphors in that pronouns do not require a linguistic antecedent. Now we can get closer to the precise restriction on the binding of pronouns. Thus, in simple sentences, we do not find pronouns in Direct Object position that are bound by some other element in the clause:

(67)   John likes him.

Example 67 cannot mean that John likes himself; it can only mean that John likes some other person distinct from himself. Go back now through all the grammatical examples we gave above with reflexives, substituting in a coreferential pronoun instead. You will find that ungrammaticality results. On the other hand, if you substitute pronouns for reflexives in the ungrammatical examples above, grammaticality results. We are led, then, to the conclusion that while reflexives must be locally bound, pronouns cannot be locally bound. That is, pronouns must be locally free. But just as the restriction on anaphors is not absolute (witness examples like 63), the restriction on pronouns is also not absolute:

(68)   John brought his sister with him.
       All my socks have holes in them.

You will have a chance to explore this issue in Problem Set 4.6 of chapter 4.

Tangent 2.1: Tense

When I have asked students in introductory linguistics classes how many tenses English has, the most common answer I have heard is three: present, past, and future. The student with more experience in language studies might at that point want to add to the list conditional, perfect, pluperfect, and perhaps others. This sort of answer reflects a confusion between time frames and tenses. Certainly English has ways to express events that occur in a variety of time frames, including future time, at the present time, in a past time, and in a time before another time that is already past. And it has ways to express how we look at an event within a given time, including considering the event to be in a hypothetical world (conditioned in some way), to have happened habitually in the past, to happen continuously in the present, and many others. The question for the linguist studying the structure of English is how English goes about expressing various time frames and various ways ot looking at an event within a given time. We will begin talking about tense and then relate it to time frame later.

Compare:

> John parks in the lot across the street.
> John parked in the lot across the street.

The first sentence is in the present tense and the verbal suffix written as *-s* indicates that tense. The second sentence is in the past tense and the verbal suffix written as *-ed* indicates that tense. In English we have tense sequencing (or tense concordance) in some sentences whereby if a present tense is used in one clause, then a present tense must be used in another clause, and if a past tense is used in one clause, then a past tense must be used in another clause:

> After John parks in the lot across the street, he walks to the pharmacy.
> *After John parks in the lot across the street, he walked to the pharmacy.

> After John parked in the lot across the street, he walked to the pharmacy.
> *After John parked in the lot across the street, he walks to the pharmacy.

Certainly not all sentences involving multiple clauses call for the same tense in all clauses. Probably there are semantic and pragmatic reasons behind the tense sequencing seen above. Examples in which two clauses can have difference tenses are easy to find:

> John claims that Mary walks to work.
> John claims that Mary walked to work.

> John claimed that Mary walks to work.
> John claimed that Mary walked to work.

Now consider:

> I park in the lot across the street.
> I parked in the lot across the street.

Here there is no *-s* suffix on the verb in the first sentence. Yet we know that the first sentence is in the present tense and the second is in the past tense because of the sense of the sentences. But we can also show that the first sentence must be in the present tense by checking tense sequencing:

> After I park in the lot across the street, John walks to the pharmacy.
> *After I park in the lot across the street, John walked to the pharmacy.

In English the appearance of the present tense suffix *-s* depends on the Subject. Test a wide variety of Subjects with the verb *park*. You will find that only when the Subject is third-person singular does the present-tense suffix show up. However, as tense sequencing above proves, even verb forms that do not carry phonetically audible tense can bear tense. We will say, then, that the present tense in English is morphologically marked with the suffix $\emptyset$ in all persons except the third-person singular, which has an audible suffix. (And, as you have undoubtedly noticed, that audible suffix sometimes sounds like [s] (as in *walks*), sometimes like [z] (as in *swims*), and sometimes like [əz] (as in *clashes*). These three sounds are called the ALLOMORPHS of the present-tense morpheme. There is a phonological regularity here, but it does not concern us. We will proceed to call the present-tense suffix -*s* in this book, despite the fact that it has the allomorphs listed above.)

The past tense, however, is phonetically audible in all persons and numbers and is written as -*ed* for regular verbs: *park/parked, walk/walked* (although it, like the present tense, exhibits allomorphy—listen to yourself say *pecked, pegged, petted*). Of course there are plenty of irregular pasts, as well:

leave/left   go/went   buy/bought   put/put

But, for ease of presentation, we will call the past-tense morpheme -*ed* in this book.

And both the present and past tenses of the verb *be* are more highly inflected than all other verbs, both regular and irregular (a fact that has perhaps been nagging you throughout this discussion—consider *am, are, is, was, were*).

We know, then, that English has at least the two tenses of present and past. Do these two tenses correspond exactly to the time frames of present and past? And is there only one type of present and only one type of past? Consider:

I enjoy movies.

This sentence does not mean that I am at the present moment enjoying movies. Instead, it gives a characterization of a general tendency, which is not falsified if, in fact, I go to see *Look Who's Talking* and I don't enjoy it. Thus the following sentence is not a contradiction:

I enjoy movies but right now I'm not enjoying this one.

Still, the characterization of enjoying movies is understood to be asserted as true at the present moment. In that sense, there is a clear correlation here between present tense and a present habitual (or generic) event. The present tense, however, can also correspond to a nonhabitual event taking place in the present moment:

Bill feels sick.

Make a list of verbs that have a habitual sense when used in the present tense (like *enjoy*) and another of verbs that have a simple present sense when used in the present tense (like *feel* with an adjective phrase). You will find a semantic grouping here. Those verbs that DENOTE an ACTIVITY (the action verbs we taked of in chapter 1) exhibit the habitual sense in the present tense. Those verbs that denote a state (so-called STATIVE VERBS) exhibit the simple present sense in the present tense. ("??" below indicates extreme marginality of grammaticality.)

Activity:
I read. (cf. ??I read now./I am reading now.)
John works at McDonalds. (cf. ??John works at McDonald's at this very second./John is working at McDonald's at this very second.)

State:
I understand that. (cf. I understand that now./??I am understanding that now.)
John fears the dark. (cf. John fears the dark at this very second./??John is fearing the dark at this very second.)

Some verbs have both an activity and a state usage:

I {live/am living} in Pennsylvania.
John {hears/is hearing} all sorts of noises.

The sentences above that have the *-ing* ending on the verb are said to be in the PROGRESSIVE ASPECT, where *aspect* is a term that covers how we view an event within a given time frame. Here the relevant sentences are in the present tense, but the event is viewed as ongoing (in progress, hence the term *progressive*).

While progressive aspect is marked with the morpheme *-ing*, we have been talking about another aspect above, as well, that is not marked with any particular morpheme. Thus we can have the present tense with a present time frame that can be read as habitual or not (as in the contrast between *I enjoy movies* and *Bill feels sick*), where the distinction between a habitual action and one that is not is also an aspect distinction. In English this aspect distinction does not require any particular morphological marker, but in other languages it may.

There are further complications beyond aspect differences to the correlation between present tense and time frames. One is that under certain conditions we can use the present tense about a past time.

*Thomas Jefferson is a fine president.
Thomas Jefferson is one of the finest presidents that ever lived.

Another is that we can use the present tense to convey an event that will take place at some relatively near future time:

{Tomorrow/Next fall/??Five years from now} she leaves for London.

What about the past tense? We find that it can correspond to a simple past or a habitual past, thus giving the same aspect distinction we found for the present-tense usages:

Jill left the house at dawn.
In those days Jill left the house at dawn.

The first sentence tells us about some particular past point in time. The second one tells us about Jill's habitual behavior during an interval of time in the past. The PP *in those days* (which here functions as a time modifier) makes the crucial difference here, not the form of the verb. I will leave it to you to find other complications for making a one-to-one correspondence between past tense and a unique time/aspect frame.

A single tense, then, can correspond to a range of time frames. For that reason, it is important that we distinguish tense, as spelled out morphologically (by *-s* or *-ed*), from time frame. And within any time frame, it is important that we consider aspect.

We can now face the question of whether we have a future tense in English. Consider:

Mary will go to the pharmacy.

Surely we understand that the event here will happen at some future time. But the question is not what time frame this sentence is set in (particularly since we know that present tense, as well, can correlate to a future time), but what tense the verb holds. Actually, we have a verb string here: *will go*. And, clearly, it is the *will* that tells us that a future time is involved. But what tense is *will*? Our tense sequencing indicates that *will* is present tense:

After she drives to the market, she will get out of her car.
*After she drove to the market, she will get out of her car.

But if *will* is present tense, what is its past-tense form? Looking at the tense sequencing examples above, you have probably already answered that question for yourself—*would*:

After she drove to the market, she would get out of her car.
*After she drives to the market, she would get out of her car.

There is no affix that marks the future tense in English. Instead, *will* is a present-tense form, and we understand the future time frame from the combination of *will* plus another verb. Likewise, there is no affix that marks the conditional tense in English; *would* is a past-tense form. *Will/would* is called an auxiliary verb because it co-occurs in the verb string with a MAIN VERB.

There are a few types of auxiliary verbs in English. One type is called a MODAL VERB (*will* is a modal), because it tends to express modality (such as the modality of an unreal, or hypothetical, world). Another is called an ASPECTUAL auxiliary because it tends to express the way we view an event. You have already met the progressive aspect above. What auxiliary characterizes the progressive aspect in English? *Be* (as you can easily see from the examples with *-ing* on the main verb above). It can appear in both present and past tenses:

I'm studying now.
I was studying then.

There is a second aspectual auxiliary in English—the *have* that occurs with a PERFECT PARTICIPLE of a main verb:

John *has* left.
John *had* left.

And, of course, the perfect-aspect auxiliary can occur in the present tense or in the past tense:

After she has corrected her papers, the teacher always {smiles/*smiled}.
After she had corrected her papers, the teacher always {*smiles/smiled}.

Thus there is no affix for the perfect or pluperfect tense in English. Rather, we use the perfect-aspect auxiliary.

Another auxiliary expresses the PASSIVE VOICE (and see Tangent 2.2):

> They are shunned by the group.
> They were shunned by the group.

Problem set 2.-4 will help you understand both the active and passive verb strings of English better.

While English has only the two affixes -*s* and -*ed* indicating the two tenses of present and past, other languages can have multiple affixes to indicate complexities of tense, aspect, and modality. The analysis of other languages can get complicated fast, and any brief discussion risks raising more questions than it answers. Nevertheless, let me quickly mention two other systems.

Italian has five distinct such affixes:

> Mangio. 'I am eating.'—present tense
> Mangiavo. 'I was eating.'—imperfect tense
> Mangerò. 'I will eat.'—future tense
> Mangerei. 'I would eat.'—conditional tense
> Mangiai. 'I ate.'—past tense

It also has at least two types of aspectual auxiliaries, which I exemplify here in the present tense, but which can occur in the range of tenses seen above:

> Ho mangiato. 'I ate.'—perfect aspect
> Sto mangiando. 'I am eating.'—progressive aspect

And it expresses modality of necessity, probability, possibility, and ability not via auxiliaries but via main verbs.

While both English and Italian attach these time-oriented affixes to verbs only, this is not the only possible system. Japanese distinguishes what is called the imperfective (to denote an unfinished action or state) from the perfective (to denote a finished action or state) on both verbs and adjectives. Here the examples are in the AFFIRMATIVE forms (where NEGATIVE forms differ) and in the direct style (where more formal styles differ):

> Wakari*masu*. 'I understand.' (verb + imperfective)
> Wakari*masita*. 'I understood.' (verb + perfective)
> Omosiro*i*. 'It is interesting.' (adjective + perfective)
> Omosiro*katta*. 'It was interesting.' (adjective + perfective)

Tangent 2.2: Voice

When we speak of passive sentences, we are talking about voice. In English at least two voices are morphologically marked. One is called the active voice, and it is seen in:

> The entire class ignored Jack.
> A demented person assassinated Martin Luther King.

It is to be contrasted with the passive voice, seen in:

Jack was ignored by the entire class.
Martin Luther King was assassinated by a demented person.

The passive voice in English is always characterized morphologically by two things: (1) the presence of some form of the verb *be* (the copula or linking verb) immediately preceding the main verb (with at most negatives or adverbials such as *not* or *quickly* intervening between the two) and (2) the PASSIVE-PARTICIPLE form of the main verb. We also optionally allow a *by* phrase, as in the examples above. In the examples below, we have passive sentences with no *by* phrase:

Sally wasn't run over, thank heavens.
Pete won't be fired after all.

It is no accident that the passive voice is called "passive." One of the major uses of passive sentences is to describe an event without mentioning any agentive cause for that event—as in the passive sentences without *by* phrases. Furthermore, in passive sentences the item which is acted upon winds up in the Subject position—so the syntax has placed a relatively "passive" PARTICIPANT in the event in the most syntactically important position, that of Subject.

We will discuss events and participants in events at length in chapter 3.

Many languages, including most of the languages of Europe, have a passive that is similar in both form and meaning to ours. However, some languages have different characteristics to their passive voice. For example, some languages, such as German and Dutch, can have passives in which no participant in the event need be overtly mentioned. These are called IMPERSONAL PASSIVES. The following example is from German:

Es wurde gestern   (von uns) getanzt.
it was   yesterday (by us)   danced
'There was dancing (by us) yesterday.'

Here we have a form of a copula plus the passive participle of the main V, but the syntactic Subject, *es*, carries no sense of a participant (it is a dummy subject) and the *von*-phrase is optional.

Some languages require that their counterpart to the English *by*-phrase be present (as in the Austronesian languages Palauan and Indonesian). Other languages disallow the presence of a *by*-phrase. Polish, for example, disallows a *by*-phrase in its passive that makes use of a special verb form (which is also called "impersonal"):

Zapukano   w drzwi (*przez sasiada).
was-knocked at door (*by   neighbor)
'It was knocked at the door.'
(= 'Someone knocked at the door.')

If the material in parentheses in the Polish example is present, the sentence is ungrammatical: we simply cannot overtly state who did the knocking.

Some languages can express in the passive voice events that we do not treat in terms of an agentive and an acted-upon participant in English. For example, Japanese, besides having a passive that is quite similar to ours, also has what is called an ADVERSITY PASSIVE, illustrated in:

Taroo-ga ame-ni furareta.
SUBJ rain-by fallen
'Taroo got rained on.' = 'It rained on Taroo.'

The morpheme *-reta* on the sentence-final V here is an indicator of the passive voice. Here we understand Taroo to have been adversely affected by the fact that it rained. The active counterpart cannot express this adversity. So the active counterpart does not include *Taroo*:

Ame-ga futta.
rain- SUBJ fell.
'Rain fell.' = 'It rained.'

Tangent 2.3: Agreement

In Tangent 2.1 we saw that verbs agree with their Subjects for person and number in English. The morphological paradigm is, certainly, impoverished—we hear audible agreement on verbs other than *be* only in the third-person singular of the present tense—but it is there.

Generally, discussions of agreement in English stop at this point. For example, we have no morphological marker that we put on an adjective to indicate that it modifies or is predicated of a given phrase, as you saw in the discussion of gender, number, and person in Tangents 1.1–1.3 of chapter 1. Other languages (such as Italian), instead, morphologically mark both verbs and adjectives for features such as these, in agreement with the phrase they modify or are predicated of. Still other languages (such as Japanese) have no agreement at all in instances of either predication or modification.

Despite the fact that agreement appears to be an extremely limited phenomenon in English, I would like to challenge you to find other instances of it. For example, in:

I made a friend today.

we know that the speaker became friendly with one person. And in:

I made friends today.

we are told that the speaker became friendly with more than one person. However, in:

Jack and Bill made friends today.

we find the plural *friends*, and the singular is rejected, even though there are certainly readings in which Jack made only one friend and Bill made only one friend (where that friend could have been the other, or some third person that is the same or different for each of them). Agreement between *friends* and the conjoined NP that it is predicated of could be responsible for the plural marker here. This idea is supported by the facts below:

Jack made friends with Bill today.
*Jack made a friend with Bill today.

Jack made a friend of Bill today.
*Jack made friends of Bill today.

When *Bill* is introduced by *with*, we read the sentence as involving Bill's participation. Thus each boy winds up as a friend to the other. Therefore *friends* is predicated of both *Jack* and *Bill*, and agreement could account for the required plural marker. But when *Bill* is introduced by *of*, at least some speakers understand Jack to have turned Bill into his friend, without Jack necessarily becoming a friend of Bill's in return. So *friend* is predicated only of *Bill* for these speakers, and, accordingly, must be singular.

If the above discussion is on the right track, there may be a variety of other instances of agreement in English. I invite you to go hunting.

While verbs agree with their Subjects in English, it is arguable that this is not the only type of verbal agreement we find in languages. There are a variety of languages in which the verb indicates an "undergoer" (or patient). For example, in Fore, Marind, Yimas (all languages of New Guinea), and Navajo a prefix on the verb can indicate an undergoer. The question arises as to whether such a prefix is an agreement morpheme or a pronoun (which would be a CLITIC pronoun—and in Problem Set 5.6 of chapter 5 you can gain a working knowledge of clitic pronouns). We cannot go into this question here, but if it can be argued that the prefix is an agreement morpheme, then verbs can agree with multiple elements.

In Basque we definitely find agreement with other grammatical functions (GFs) than just Subject. The form of the auxiliary changes (by suffixation) when the agent (the initiator of the action), patient (the one the action is done to), and recipient (the one who benefits from or receives the product of the action) change. (You will learn about things like agents and patients in chapter 3, particularly in Problem Set 3.3. The agent, patient, recipient, and others are called the "arguments.") And these changes are affected both by whether or not and which arguments are present and by the number of the argument. And in many languages we find affixal agreement with both Subject and Object, including Quechua and several languages of native Canadians, such as Greenlandic and Labrador Inuttut.

*Problem Set 2.1: English Tag Questions

You will use the information learned in this problem set repeatedly in later work. So please be sure to do this one.

This problem set builds as it goes. So look at the first question, think about it, and then answer it. Then go on to the next question and answer it, etc. Do not read over the whole problem set before you begin, or you will not be able to see the progression that I want you to see. Please answer every question.

Consider the TAG QUESTION (the little question following the comma) in:

(1)   John's coming, isn't he?

A tag like 1 has a rising intonation (that is, the pitch of the voice goes up) at the end and means something like "Right?" That is, it is a CONDUCIVE TAG QUESTION—it is rhetorical in the sense that it presupposes the answer. For example, the speaker of 1 expects the answer to be "Yes."

There is another type of tag question. So, consider:

(2)   You're going to the party, are you?

Take the situation where the angry mother is talking to the adolescent daughter whose homework isn't yet complete. Here the intonation of the tag is falling at the end and it means something like, "I'm challenging you on this." It is called a BEL-LIGERENT TAG QUESTION, and rather than having the force of a question, it has the force of a challenge.

Then there are elliptical questions that are really independent questions and not tag questions at all. For example, the question in 3 is not a tag question.

(3)   John's going to the party. Are you?

The elliptical question is 3 means something like, "Are you going to the party?" and it neither presupposes the answer (unlike conducive tag questions) nor challenges (unlike belligerent tag questions). It is a true request for information, and its answer is independent of the preceding statement.

In the questions below consider only conducive tag questions.

Part 1

Think of lots of conducive tag questions, like:

> He can't read, can he?
> He should have spoken up, shouldn't he?
> They haven't left, have they?
> She wasn't christened, was she?
> She will be studying by the time I get there, won't she?
> We couldn't have been recognized, could we?

Do not limit yourself to just these—I give them only as a start.

In the tag there is always an auxiliary verb. What determines which auxiliary verb (*can, will, be*, etc.) appears in the tag?

Part 2

Will your answer to 1 account for the tag in:

> He left, didn't he?

If not, revise it to account for examples like this.

Part 3

Now consider lots more conducive tag questions, like:

> I said the truth to the man, didn't I?
> *I said the truth to the man, didn't it?
> *I said the truth to the man, didn't he?

> Bill should give the candies to Janet, shouldn't he?
> *Bill should give the candies to Janet, shouldn't they?
> *Bill should give the candies to Janet, shouldn't she?

(Note: The asterisks here indicate that these sentences are not good when spoken with the characteristic intonation of a conducive tag question. Surely, they can be good as elliptical questions—but they are not good as conducive tag questions.) Again, do not be limited by these—they are just a start.

A pronoun always occurs in the tag. What determines the choice of pronoun (*he*, *we*, etc.) in the tag?

Part 4

We say that a tag like that in 4 is negative and a tag like that in 5 is affirmative or POSITIVE. That is, the POLARITY of 4 is negative, and the polarity of 5 is positive.

(4)   Mary left, didn't she?

(5)   John couldn't have been studying, could he?

Look at the data list of tag questions that you have made up so far (your own list—not anything you are going to hand in to a teacher, if you are doing this as part of a course). What determines the polarity of the tag question? (That is, what determines whether the tag question will be negative or positive?)

Part 5

Consider sentences whose only verb is *be* or *have*, as in:

(6)   She's nice.

(7)   She has money.

Add the proper conducive tag questions to 6 and 7.

What determines which auxiliary will occur in these tags? Is your answer consistent with your answers in Parts 1 and 2 above? Now give a statement for the determination of the choice of auxiliary in these tags which will cover both the sentences you considered for Parts 1 and 2 and the sentences you considered here for Part 5. Your statement should begin:

> "The choice of auxiliary in a conducive tag question is determined by . . ."

Part 6

Now consider sentences with DUMMY SUBJECTS (also called INERT or EXPLETIVE SUBJECTS)—that is, Subjects that have no clear sense of reference about them (you will explore the semantic properties of some of these in chapter 7, Problem Set 7.3)—like:

   (8)   It's two o'clock.

   (9)   It can't be raining again.

Give 8 and 9 with the proper conducive tag questions added. What determines the choice of pronoun in the tags? Is your answer consistent with your answer in Part 3 above? Now give a statement for the choice of pronoun in the tags which will cover the sentences you considered for Part 3 as well as the sentences you considered here in Part 6. Your statement should begin:

   "The choice of pronoun in a conducive tag is determined by . . ."

Part 7

Consider these sentences:

   (10)   Bill hopes that Mary will come, doesn't he?
          *Bill hopes that Mary will come, won't she?

   (11)   Jack has decided that we can't come, hasn't he?
          *Jack has decided that we can't come, can we?

The tags here are at the end of complex sentences that consist of two clauses. For example, in 10 *hopes* is the verb string of the matrix clause and *will come* is the verb string of the embedded clause.
   Consider your answers to Parts 5 and 6. Will they uniquely pick out the correct auxiliary and pronoun for the grammatical tags in 10 and 11? Will your answer to Part 4 correctly pick out the polarity of the tag? If not, revise your answers to do so.

Part 8

Consider the sentences here:

   (12)   I suppose she isn't coming, is she?
          *I suppose she isn't coming, don't I?

   (13)   I figure he left already, didn't he?
          *I figure he left already, don't I?

Do your answers in Parts 4–7 cover these examples? I expect them not to. What determines the choice of auxiliary in the good tags in 12 and 13? What determines the choice of pronoun in the good tags in 12 and 13? What determines the polarity of the good tags in 12 and 13? Certainly, 12 and 13 are unusual (in that most sentences do not form tags in this way—the more typical pattern is seen in 10 and 11).

Yet they are entirely grammatical. Try to find another example like 12 and 13 which does not use the verbs *suppose* or *figure*. If you find one, give it. Discuss briefly why 12 and 13 form tags as they do instead of following the general rule that you came up with in your answers to the earlier parts of this problem set. (You may well have to consider semantic and pragmatic factors of a discourse here.)

*Problem Set 2.2: English *There*-Sentences

This problem set must be done.
   Part 1 of this problem set probably has its counterpart in most introductory syntax classes in the English-speaking world. I encountered a version of parts of it as a student at Harvard and then again later as a student at MIT. I hereby thank whatever persons are originally responsible for it.

Compare the sentences here:

   (1)   There's a problem on my mind.

   (2)   There they go.

In the first sentence the *there* is unstressed or receives very low stress. In the second sentence, the *there* receives normal word stress or can even be emphatically stressed. (Note, *there* in 1 cannot be emphatically stressed.) The second type of *there* is called "demonstrative" and we find it used as a locative:

   (3)   She put it down there.

   (4)   He went there.

   (5)   There is where I'd like to be.

   (6)   There goes John again, always mouthing off.

The first kind of *there* is called a dummy (just as the *it* of weather and time expressions that you looked at briefly in Problem Set 2.1, Part 6, is called dummy-*it*). Some sentences in written form are ambiguous between the two uses of *there* and we need intonation to disambiguate them out of context. For example, in 7 we can think of the sentence without stress on *there* meaning "another problem exists," or we can think of the sentence with stress on *there*, perhaps, in the context of a teacher leaning over a student's paper and pointing:

   (7)   I'm sorry. There's another problem.

Throughout this problem set consider dummy-*there* only, please. Thank-you.

Part 1

People have argued for years in a variety of theories over what dummy-*there* is. Is it best described as a word that fits a category (such as V, VP, N, NP, etc.) and, if so, which category does it fit? Or is it best described as a word that fills a grammatical function (that is, a GF, such as Subject, Direct Object, Indirect Object, or Object of a Preposition)? You have a working familiarity with only one GF at this point: Subject. Thus you need to limit yourself to asking whether dummy-*there* is best described as a word that fits a category or as a Subject. Consider the sentences below and any other relevant ones that you can think of that are good sentences of English and come up with arguments for what dummy-*there* is. If some data lead to one hypothesis and other data lead to another hypothesis, point that out. Wait until you have given every argument you can for the status of dummy-*there*, whether those arguments are contradictory to each other or not, before you try to resolve the conflict. (If you are doing this as part of a course, you are to write down all the arguments for the instructor.) But please do try to resolve the conflict at the end, even if you just make a wild stab at it.

The data are organized into groups of sentences so that a separate argument can be made based on the data in each group.

Data Set A

(8)   There hopped a little bunny out of the hole.

(9)   *I spoke there to Bill. (compare: I spoke Spanish to Bill.)

(10)   *Let's invite him to there.

(11)   *She hid under there.

(Remember to read these and all the sentences below with no stress on the *there*; that way the asterisked ones range from wildly unacceptable to quite strange.)

Data Set B

(12)   There's a tornado coming, isn't there?

(13)   *There's a tornado coming, isn't it?

(Here you should be applying what you learned in Problem Set 2.1.)

Data Set C

(14)   Will there be peaches for dessert?

(15)   Did the boys pick the peaches?

(If you do not see the issue here, go back to the text of chapter 2 and reread the parts about the inversion of auxiliaries.)

Data Set D

(16)   Frank knew that there would be a riot and indeed there was.

(17)   Joe said that the tall guy would show up and indeed he did.

(You are on your own here. This is new. But it is not so different from things you are already familiar with.)

(Overall hint: As you look at 8–17, think about whether the construction in a given sentence has any restrictions on it that involve categories [such as "only an X can go here" or "only an XP can go here"] or that involve GFs [where the only type of restriction you are expected to be familiar with at this point would be something like "only a Subject can go here"]. Then ask yourself whether *there* is satisfying the restriction. If it is, then it must have the requisite category or GF. For example, in 12 and 13 the interesting construction is the conducive tag question. Is there any restriction on categories or GFs inside the tag? Does *there* satisfy this restriction? In 14 and 15, the interesting construction is the inversion involved in a question. Again, is there any restriction on categories or GFs in questions with inversion? Does *there* satisfy this restriction? Etc.)

Part 2

Do the following sentences present a problem for your hypothesis? If so, how? Offer a suggestion for a solution to this problem. Be sure to consider what the appropriate tag questions to 18 and 19 would be and make your answer consistent with those findings.

(18)   There's a duck in the kitchen.

(19)   There are two ducks in the kitchen.

(20)   *There are a duck in the kitchen.

Part 3

Consider the following sentences and others that come to your mind:

(21)   There strode into town the ugliest gunslinger alive.

(22)   There went up a cry of protest.

(23)   There appeared a man in the doorway.

(24)   There lived a king in days gone by that I must tell you about.

(25)   There stood a little boy in the corner.

(26)   There suddenly burst in five policemen.

Sentences like 21–26 sound just fine (although some of them may be more or less dramatic). However, other sentences that begin with unstressed *there* sound very strange out of context:

(27)   ??There cried a little boy (in the corner).

(28)   *There telephoned a hysterical victim.

(29)   *There spoke an imposing woman in favor of ozone.

(30)   *There painted a woman on the bridge over the Seine.

And still others sound just terrible, no matter what the context:

(31)   *There ate a rotund gentleman pizza (at the next table).

(32)   *There wrote a friend of mine a letter.

(33)   *There put a student an amazing answer on the test.

The sentences in 31–33 are rejected for a syntactic reason. State the constraint that blocks these sentences. (Hint: Think about this in terms of the types of verbs in the good-versus-bad examples. What kinds of verbs can *there* simply not occur with regardless of context? This question is, strictly speaking, jumping the gun, since we have not yet discussed syntactic verb classes [although we will in chapter 3]. However, you probably have come across the crucial notion in English classes in high school.)

Part 4

The sentences in 27–30 most likely are rejected for a semantic reason. Compare the semantics of the acceptable sentences in 21–26 to those of 27–30. Briefly characterize the semantic class or semantic classes of the types of verbs that can occur with *there*. (Again, you are on your own here, since we have not discussed semantic classes of verbs and will not in any depth in this book. Think about the use of *there*-sentences in discourse and you may get a handle on this question.)

Part 5

Now consider the contrast between these sentences:

(34)   There is a salami in the refrigerator.

(35)   There is the salami in the refrigerator.

Both are grammatical sentences, but in different contexts. Describe the contexts for sentences that have an INDEFINITE NP following the copula as opposed to those that have a DEFINITE NP following the copula. (If you feel uncertain about the distinction between definite and indefinite NPs, look back at the discussion of old-versus-new information in chapter 1. If that does not help you enough, then wait until after you have read chapter 4 before returning to this question.) Please be sure to read these sentences with the dummy (the unstressed) use of *there*. (With the stressed use of *there*, the contexts for usage are quite different.)

*Problem Set 2.3: English Imperatives

The tests developed in this problem set will be assumed in later discussion.

In chapter 2 we noticed that one apparent exception to the statement that sentences have Subjects is imperatives, such as:

Go home!

Here we will explore this apparent exception.

Part 1

In 1 we have tag questions on an imperative:

(1)   Come home, won't you?
      *Come home, won't he?
      *Come home, won't we?

Test additional examples in your head and then state the restriction on the NP that shows up in the tag question with imperatives. (Do not try to account for this restriction yet, merely state it.)

Part 2

Now look back at Problem 2.1 and your statement of the restriction on the NP that shows up in tag questions in general. Use this statement plus your statement in Part 1 here to argue not only that imperatives have Subjects, but what that Subject must be.

Part 3

Consider the sentences here:

(2)   Jack$_i$ lost his$_i$ mind.
      *Jack lost our mind.
      *Jack lost their mind.
      *Jack lost Sam's mind.
      *Jack$_i$ lost his$_j$ mind.

(3)   *They lost Jack's mind.
      *They lost his mind.

(Note that when the referential indices match in the sentence *Jack lost his mind*, you are to read the sentence with *Jack* and *his* having the same referent, but when the referential indices do not match, you are to read the sentence with *Jack* and *his* having different referents.) Test additional examples in your head. There is a restriction on the phrase:

X lose Y's mind

State that restriction as simply as possible. (Be sure to use the notions we have been developing in the text, such as coreferentiality.) Do not try to account for the restriction. (That is, do not get into a discussion of why this restriction might exist. Just state what the restriction is, regardless of why we observe it.)

Give three other phrases that, like *X lose Y's mind*, exhibit this exact same restriction. (Be sure your phrases involve a restriction between a Subject and a genitive.)

Part 4

In the imperatives below, only one possessive pronoun is acceptable: *your*.

(4)   Don't lose your mind over it!
*Don't lose his mind over it!
*Don't lose our mind over it!

Use the restriction you arrived at in Part 3 to argue that imperatives have a Subject and to determine what that Subject is.

Part 5

Consider the sentences here with the idiomatic reading of "tease":

(5)   Jack pulled Jane's leg.
Jack pulled Sam's leg.
Jack pulled your aunt's best friend's leg.
*Jack$_i$ pulled his$_i$ leg.
Jack$_i$ pulled his$_j$ leg.

Test additional examples in your head. What is the restriction on the phrase:

X pulled Y's leg.

Give three other phrases that exhibit the same restriction. (Again, do not get into a discussion of why such a restriction might arise. Also, be sure your phrases involve a restriction between a Subject and a genitive.)

Part 6

Use the restriction you came up with in Part 5 to argue that imperatives have a Subject and to determine what that Subject is. (Hint: The relationship between Parts 5 and 6 is analogous to the relationship between Parts 3 and 4. Your argument should have a similar form. The difference is that in Part 4 you were given the relevant data about imperative sentences, but in the present question you must come up with those data on your own.)

Part 7

The imperatives here contain reflexives:

(6)   Clean yourself off.
Clean yourselves off.
*Clean {myself/ourselves/herself/himself/itself/themselves} off.

Use these data to build an argument that imperatives have a Subject and to determine what that Subject is.

Caveat Lector

Although you probably came to the conclusion that imperative sentences are best described as having a nonovert Subject, there is evidence that in some languages imperatives have a nonovert agent regardless of whether or not the agent is a Subject. Thus our conclusions here hold for English, but we must refrain from generalizing to other languages unless we actually examine those languages.

*Problem Set 2.4: English Verb Strings

Parts 1–7 of this problem set are taken (in altered form) from Joan Maling and Ray Jackendoff, whom I hereby thank.

Answer all parts of this problem set, even if the questions seem trivial to you. Each succeeding question depends on your having answered the ones before it. So please do not read through the whole problem set before beginning.

There are several words in English that function as auxiliary (helping) verbs, occurring between the Subject and the main verb in declarative sentences.

1. Modals: My frog *will* eat your lizard.
             can
             may

2. Perfect Aspect: My frog *has* eaten your lizard.

3. Progressive Aspect: My frog *is* eating your lizard.

Part 1

What effect does each kind of auxiliary verb have on the form (not the meaning) of the main verb? Answer separately for each of the three kinds of auxiliaries above. Consider sentences in which you have only a single auxiliary followed immediately by the main verb. Your answer should have the form:

    After a modal the form of the main verb is . . .
    After a perfect aspect the form of the main verb is . . .
    After a progressive aspect the form of the main verb is . . .

Please do not answer with a label like "participle." Instead, say what happens to the morphology of the main verb. That is, state whether a special morpheme appears on the main verb in each context and, if one does, give that morpheme. If no special morpheme appears in that context, say that the main verb is uninflected.

Part 2

Suppose we try to use more than one auxiliary in a single sentence. Think of all the combinations you can. Think of some ungrammatical combinations. Consider bad sentences such as:

> *The lizard has will eat my supper.
> *The sky is have fallen.
> *No one may will leave this room.

as well as good combinations like:

> That course of action may have proven unnecessary.

Give an example of a sentence with three auxiliaries.

Now state a general rule that describes which combinations are possible. (A really good general rule—that is, one that truly captures a generalization—will not just list the lexical items. Instead, you need to figure out if certain classes of auxiliaries behave in the same way with respect to how they can combine with other classes of auxiliaries.) Your answer should start out:

> When there are three auxiliaries before the main verb . . .

Part 3

Consider again Part 1. Does your answer generalize to sentences with more than one auxiliary? Why or why not? Which verb (whether auxiliary or main) does each auxiliary constrain the form of? State a general rule which will cover sentences with a string of auxiliaries.

Part 4

Consider the *be* we find in passive sentences, such as:

> Mary was ignored by her classmates.

This *be* is also an auxiliary. Specify precisely its linear order with respect to the other auxiliaries. (That is, where does it come in the auxiliary string?)

How does the passive *be* affect the form of the other verbs in the string? Is your answer consistent with your general rule from Part 3? It ought to be. Consider sentences like:

> The lizard has been eaten by the frog.
> *The lizard is have eaten by the frog.

> No one will be permitted to leave.
> *No one is will permitted to leave.

> The U.S. is being attacked by Fredonia.
> *The U.S. is been attacking by Fredonia.

as well as other sentences you think of to test your theory.

Now give a sentence with four auxiliaries.

Part 5

Which element in the auxiliary string carries the tense? (Please do not confuse time frame with tense here. See Tangent 2.1 of this chapter.)

Part 6

List all the modal verbs you can think of. (There should be at least nine of them, including present- and past-tense forms, and possibly more, depending on your own speech patterns. Remember that whatever you call a modal should have the same effect on the form of a following main verb that you claimed modals have in Part 1 above.)

Can you think of a syntactic test to show that *used to* (as in *John used to smile*) is not in the same syntactic class as *will*? State that test in simple terms and demonstrate that *used to* is different by this test from *will*.

(Hint: Possible syntactic tests might involve the placement of the sentential negative *not* [as in *Susie will not come*—think about what kinds of words *not* can follow], the order of words in direct questions [like *Will Susie come?* and *When will Susie come?*—see the discussion of Subject-Auxiliary Inversion in the text of this chapter], the formation of conducive tag questions [as in the end of the sentence *Susie will come, won't she?*—see Problem 2.1 above and consider what restrictions hold on the verbal form in the tag], etc.)

Your demonstrations should have the following form:

   I. Show that a certain syntactic test separates modals like *can* from main verbs like *eat*. (Of course, this test need not [and probably won't] distinguish modals from other auxiliaries. But it will, at least, distinguish modals from main verbs.)

  II. Show how the verb *used to* behaves with this syntactic test.

 III. Come to a conclusion based on I and II as to whether *used to* is a modal.

Each test you give will call for the same argument form.

If you can come up with three tests, that is perfectly adequate. If you come up with fewer, look harder at the hint above.

Now go back to your list of all the modals at the beginning of this question. Make sure that every item you called a modal behaves like *will* and not like *used to* with respect to the syntactic test(s) you have just offered. (If you had many more modals than nine to start with, you will now probably be able to eliminate some of them.)

Now take your syntactic test(s) and test whether *need to*, *have to*, and *might* fall with *used to* or with *will*. Use the argument form given above (in I–III) for each test.

Part 7

An auxiliary *do* turns up in negative statements (*Newts don't eat goldfish food*), in direct questions (*What do newts eat, then?*), in tag questions (*They eat brine shrimp, don't they?*), and in emphatic sentences (*Newts DO like bagels, though*).

How does this *do* affect the form of the main verb that follows it?

What are the rules governing its occurrence in the same sentence with other auxiliaries?

Why is the *do* in *Fred might have done the dishes* not the auxiliary *do*? Prove it. (By "prove it," I mean, use the tests and the argumentation form given in Part 6. Recall that the tests in Part 6 probably were for auxiliaries in general and not just for modals.)

Part 8

In chapter 2 we saw several examples of complex sentences (that is, sentences with more than one clause). We used the terminology of "main" (or matrix, or root) clause and "embedded" (or subordinate) clause. The main clause is the independent one—the one that the other clause is playing a GF (grammatical function) in or that the other clause plays a modifying role in. On the other hand, the embedded clause is the dependent one—the one that plays a GF in the main clause or that somehow modifies something in the main clause. For example, in:

John said that Susie left.

said is the verb of the main clause and *left* is the verb of the embedded clause. In this sentence the clause *that Susie left* is the Direct Object (DO) of the verb *said*.

Another example is:

Whenever Susie is cutting onions, John is crying.

Here *is crying* is the verb string of the main clause and *is cutting* is the verb string of the embedded clause. The embedded clause *Whenever Susie is cutting onions* is an adverbial modifier (telling time) of the main clause.

Now consider embedded clauses in which the verb string is not tensed, as in:

(1)   John wants *to leave*.

(2)   John expected *Bill to have left by noon*.

(3)   I arranged *for Bill to leave*.

(4)   John broke the dish *to upset his mother*.

In 1 *to leave* has the GF of a DO of the main verb *wants*. In 2 *Bill to have left by noon* has the GF of a DO of the main verb *expects*. In 4 *to upset his mother* is an adverbial modifier (telling purpose) of the main clause. In 3 it is debatable whether *Bill to leave* is the Object of the Preposition (OP) *for* or whether *for Bill to leave* is the DO of the main verb *arranged*. (But that debate does not concern us here, since we are not yet ready to enter it.)

State a general rule which describes the full range of possibilities of the verb string in an embedded tenseless clause like those in 1–4. (Be careful not to consider other types of tenseless clauses, such as those with a verb form ending in *-ing* where there is no progressive aspect *be* around to account for that *-ing*.) Your rule should tell the order of the auxiliaries and the effect each auxiliary has on the form of the following verb.

In doing this, ask yourself whether any of the modals you listed in Part 6 can occur in these infinitival verb strings, and if they can, where they occur. Then ask whether the perfective *have* can occur, and where. Then ask whether the progressive *be* can occur and where. Do not forget to cover the possibilities of a passive *be* and the *do* of Part 7, if these possibilities arise in these tenseless clauses.

Is *to* in these clauses an auxiliary? Give one argument for your answer. (Hint: Go back to the tests you developed in Part 6. Will *to* pass any of the tests for modals? Of course, the tag-question and direct-question tests are not applicable here, because those tests apply only to tensed clauses, but others may be applicable.) Why can this *to* and the *do* of Part 7 not appear in the same verb string? (If you can not get a handle on this, go back to Part 7 and look at your answers there. They should help.)

Problem Set 2.5: Japanese versus Italian—Zero-Pronoun versus Pro-Drop

This problem set has two parts. Part 1 may be done alone. However, Part 2 cannot be done unless you have first done Part 1.

Part 1

The following are some brief conversational exchanges in Japanese. No word-by-word gloss is given. Instead, following each exchange is a loose translation:

(1) —Wakarimasu-ka?
    —Ee, wakarimasu.
    —Do you understand?
    —Yes, I understand.

(2) —Tukurimasita-ne?
    —Hai. Kinoo tukurimasita.
    —You made it, right?
    —Yes. I made it yesterday.

In 2 *kinoo* means 'yesterday.' In 1 *ee* means 'yes,' and in 2 *hai* means 'yes.' These two words are not equivalent, however. They differ with regard to the level of politeness and with regard to style. We will not concern ourselves with these differences here.

Looking at these sentences, what category do you think the words *warakimasu* and *tukurimasita* belong to? (Think of the categories we discussed in this chapter of N, V, A, P.) Why? What function do you think these words play in these sentences? (Think of the functions we discussed briefly of referring, modifying, and being predicative.) (Note: You have a rudimentary knowledge of categories at this point, but no firm notion of the functions of modifying and being predicative. However, you should have a vague working knowledge of these notions just from reading this chapter. You will get a much clearer sense of these notions in chapters 3 and 4.)

Ka in the question in 1 and *ne* in the question in 2 are called sentence particles. Based solely on these examples, what functions do you think these two sentence particles play? What semantic difference is there between them?

Is there any single word or part of a word (that is, morpheme) in 1 and 2 that you can point to and say it means 'I' or 'you'?

Now consider one more exchange:

> (3) —Asita kimasen-ne?
>   —Iya, kimasu-yo.
>   —You're not coming tomorrow, right?
>   —No, I AM coming.

Asita in 3 means 'tomorrow.'

Based on 1–3, what category do you think *kimasen* and *kimasu* belong to?

Note that in 1 and 2, the words *wakarimasu* and *tukurimasita* are absolutely identical phonologically and morphologically in the question and the answer. But in 3, in the question we have the form *kimasen* and in the answer we have the form *kimasu*. To what do you attribute the difference in phonological and morphological forms in 3?

Based on 1–3, what function do you think the sentence particle *yo* in the answer in 3 plays?

Given all of 1–3, can you point to any word or morpheme and say it means 'I' or 'you'?

Part 2

Consider the following Italian conversational exchanges:

> (4) —Capisci?
>   —Sì, capisco.
>   —Do you understand?
>   —Yes, I understand.
>
> (5) —Lo leggi, no?
>   —Sì, lo leggo ora.
>   —You are reading it, right?
>   —Yes, I'm reading it now.

Ora in the answer in 5 means 'now.' The *lo* in both question and answer in 5 means 'it.'

Compare 4 and 5 in Italian to 1 and 2 in Japanese in Part 1. While in Japanese the questions and answers were identical but for the particles and the interjections meaning 'yes,' in Italian, the questions and answers differ in other ways. Can you point to any one word or morpheme in 4 and 5 that you think means 'I'? Can you point to any one word or morpheme in 4 and 5 that you think means 'you'? If so, give those words or morphemes.

Now consider:

(6) —Non canti domani, vero?
     —No. Canto di sicuro.
     —You're not singing tomorrow, right?
     —No. I'm singing for sure.

Domani in the question in 6 means 'tomorrow.' *Di sicuro* in the answer in 6 means 'for sure.'

Again, compare the Italian exchange in 6 to the Japanese exchange in 3 above. Are your ideas about the morphemes that mean 'I' and 'you' confirmed here?

Assume that both Japanese and Italian have phonetically null (that is, inaudible, or nonovert) pronouns in the Subject position in all these sentences. If your answers to whether the language has audible morphemes in these examples that indicate 'I' and 'you' differ for Japanese and Italian, how can you account for this difference?

Discuss whether there is any evidence in this problem set for claiming that one or the other or both of these languages has nonovert Object pronouns.

Japanese is called a ZERO-PRONOUN LANGUAGE. It is claimed that while pronouns can be overtly expressed in Japanese, they often are not. If you are going through this book as part of a class, discuss with the class interpretation strategies that you might expect, based on common sense alone, to come into play in a zero-pronoun language like Japanese.

Based only on 1–3 above, if a question is asked out of the blue (without previous context), and its Subject is not overtly expressed, how do you think that Subject is to be interpreted?

Guess at how a missing Subject is to be interpreted for a statement made out of the blue.

Guess at how a missing Subject is to be interpreted for a statement when there is previous context.

Guess at how a missing Subject is to be interpreted for a question when there is previous context.

Italian, in contrast to Japanese, is called a PRO-DROP LANGUAGE. That is, a pronominal Subject need not be overtly expressed (although it often can be, as you saw with the Subject pronouns in Problem Set 1.3 of chapter 1). It differs from a zero-pronoun language in that the features of person and number of the referent of the Subject are supplied in the sentence even in the absence of an overt Subject. (There is, however, variation in the literature in the use of these terms. Thus you may well find Japanese referred to as a pro-drop language—and then find the term applied to all languages that allow the Subject not to be overtly expressed.)

Problem Set 2.6: English Verb Phrase (VP) Ellipsis

This problem set is a continuation, in a sense, of Problem Set 2.4. Do not attempt it until you have completed Problem Set 2.4.

There is a construction in English which is called VP DELETION or VP ELLIPSIS. It is found in the clause introduced by *and* in these sentences:

(1)   John has left, and Sue has, too.

(2)   John may leave, and Sue may, too.

Part 1

Just on the basis of 1 and 2, what does the verb string in a VP ellipsis construction consist of? (Make a general statement. Do not simply say that it consists of *has* or *may*.)

Part 2

Now consider:

(3)   John may have left, and Sue may have, too.

(4)   John may have left, and Sue may, too.

Do not concern yourself with any possible meaning differences between 3 and 4.

Think of other examples of VP ellipsis constructions where the clause(s) preceding the VP ellipsis clause have more than one auxiliary in the verb string. Give a revised general statement of what the verb string in VP-ellipsis constructions consists of. (This should be a revision of the generalization you gave in Part 1. Do not worry about distinguishing between the meanings associated with the various forms (as in 3 versus 4). Instead, just state the possible verb strings in general terms.)

Part 3

Now consider:

(5)   John left, and Sue did, too.

Consider the *did* that shows up in 5. What other constructions have you seen it in? (Look back at Problem Set 2.4 for this.) Is the appearance of a form of *do* in this VP-ellipsis construction a problem for your generalization in Part 2? If so, revise that generalization to handle all the data thus far.

Part 4

Now consider:

(6)   John wanted to leave, and Sue wanted to, too.

(7)   John wanted to leave, and Sue did, too.

Again, please do not worry about whether there is a meaning difference between 7 and 8.

Account for the grammaticality of both 7 and 8. That is, why can we get both *wanted to* and *did* in the VP-ellipsis construction here? What is the VP-ellipsis construction "standing for" in 7? What is it "standing for" in 8?

Part 5

Look back at example 7 above. How does this example bear on the issue of what category the *to* that introduces infinitivals belongs to? (See Part 8 of Problem Set 2.4.) Be sure to make use of the generalization you arrived at in Parts 1–3 above as you answer this.

Star Problem 2.1

Lots of sentences can be used as orders, given an appropriate context. For example, if a mother says to her son:

Your bike is in the driveway.

this ordinary declarative sentence could be taken as an order to the son to get his bike out of the driveway (fast). Likewise an ordinary question like:

Where's your bike?

could be taken as an order under the same circumstances. However, when we talked about imperatives in this chapter, we limited ourselves to looking only at sentences that lacked an explicit Subject and that are typically taken as orders or requests regardless of context. It is only this latter sort of sentence that is called an imperative in linguistics.

The question for you here is whether imperatives must lack an explicit Subject. Consider examples such as:

You sit down!
Nobody move!
Everybody lie flat on the floor!

If these are imperatives, then imperatives need not lack an explicit Subject. Are these imperatives? If you can make use here of anything you learned doing Problem Set 2.3 above, do so.

Star Problem 2.2

The passive participle can appear inside a noun phrase, modifying the head noun:

(1)   an enlightened idea
      the abandoned shoes

It can also appear as the last element of a verb string, of course:

(2)   Mary was eventually enlightened.
      Those antiquated ideas must be abandoned.

Is the participle in its modifier use an adjective or a verb? (You might look back at the discussion of morphological bases upon which to distinguish between categories in the text of this chapter. But do not limit yourself to that. Consider other factors like the distribution of *very* versus *very much*.)

Star Problem 2.3

What is the category of the word *born* in:

    (1)   Mary was born at 8 A.M.

Star Problem 2.4

In Tangent 2.2 you were introduced to the adversity passive of Japanese. English just might have a parallel. Characterize sentences with the *on*-construction found in:

    (1)   My dog got lost on me.
          Jane's car stalled on her.

In doing this, you should notice that we do not say:

    (2)   ??My sister won an award on me.
          ??Pete's dog got found on him.

except in rather unusual circumstances. Think about the typical circumstances for 1 and 2 and consider the acceptable and unusual circumstances for 3 and 4 and come up with many other examples to support your discussion.

Overview

Binding Theory

We have advanced our binding theory considerably. We now know:

    (A) Anaphors must be locally bound.

    (B) Pronouns must be locally free.

We have not defined precisely what it means to be locally bound or free. One major issue to face is the definition of locality. Another is the hierarchical relationship that one item must have toward another in order to bind it. We have not yet entered into any explicit discussion of structural relationships that are hierarchical, so do not worry if you did not realize that this lies ahead.

X-Bar Theory

X-Bar Theory has not yet been fully explained, but we have, in fact, been working on it. X-Bar Theory is the theory of the structure of phrases. We know that there are major categories and minor categories: major categories can head phrases that consist of the head and its paraphernalia but minor categories consist of isolated words that do not group together with other words to form phrases. In chapter 4 we will go more deeply into these matters.

Case Theory

We have seen that in English, Subjects of tensed clauses have Subjective Case, whereas nominals in other positions have the Objective or genitive Case. In chapter 5 we will give a more complete discussion.

Theta Theory

You have not yet met the term "Theta Theory," but, as with X-Bar Theory, we have been working on it in this chapter. Theta Theory involves the thematic relations of the items in a sentence. We discussed and rejected in this chapter the hypothesis that the Subject of a clause is the entity whose referent performs the action of the clause. By doing this, we were recognizing that different elements in the sentence play different participant roles. You will explore this type of participant role in chapter 3. Other semantic roles include modification and predication, which you will also explore in chapter 3.

3

Grammatical Functions, Complete Functional Complex, Theta Theory, and Licensing

Locality

At the end of chapter 2 we concluded that reflexives require an antecedent that is somehow local to them. Our job now is to try to develop a useful notion of locality.

An item can be local to, or near, another item either in a syntactic sense or a semantic sense or both. Here we will try to get closer to a notion of both syntactic and semantic locality, using a clue from the last chapter. We noticed there that typically (although this is not a rule) a reflexive and its antecedent are members of the lowest clause that contains the reflexive. For example:

(1)   John said that Mary likes herself.

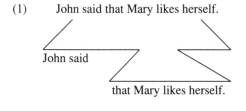

(2)   *John said that Mary likes himself.

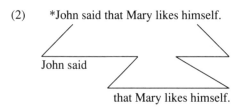

Here the triangles indicate clauses, and the lower triangle is contained in the larger triangle. In 1 (the grammatical sentence), *herself* and its antecedent *Mary* both appear in the lowest clause that contains the reflexive NP. But in 2 (the ungrammatical sentence), *himself* and its antecedent *John* do not both appear in the lowest clause that contains the reflexive.

What is there about the organization of a clause that might be responsible for the tendency of reflexives to find their antecedents within the lowest clause that contains the reflexive? Earlier we mentioned that a highly reliable method for determining how many clauses a sentence contained was to count the verb strings. So the question above could be rephrased as: What is there about verbs and the structures that revolve around verbs that might be responsible for this tendency?

We have already talked about the fact that all the words in a given utterance can be classified as belonging to a given category. The categories we have mentioned thus far include Verb (V), Noun, Adjective, Adverb, and Preposition. There are others, as well, and we will discuss them in chapter 4. At this point we want to concentrate on verbs. For now, consider the facts you already know about verbs in English: (1) only verbs take the *-ed* past tense affix; (2) only verbs agree with their Subject; and (3) only verbs co-occur with the aspectual auxiliaries *have + -ed* and *be + -ing*. (See Problem Set 2.4.) We can use these facts as diagnostics for the category V. I will expect you to apply these diagnostics yourself as you search for examples in your head to back up the discussion below.

What are the syntactic characteristics of verbs? One of them is that verbs can be SUBCATEGORIZED (that is, the category of Verb can be broken down into smaller subcategories) with respect to what other items cannot, may, or must co-occur with them, where typically the other items we are talking about play grammatical functions. You are already familiar with one of the major criteria for subcategorizing verbs: whether or not they take Direct Objects. Verbs that take a DO are called TRANSITIVES. Verbs that do not take a DO are called INTRANSITIVES. For example, the verb *elapse* can never take a DO; *eat* optionally takes one; and *arrange* requires one:

(3)   The requisite time period finally elapsed.

(4)   Jack ate (pizza) at five o'clock.

(5)   I'll arrange the flowers.

(6)   *I'll arrange.

We are, clearly, jumping ahead of ourselves in that we have not defined the term *Direct Object*. In fact, defining the term *Direct Object* presents many difficulties, just as defining the term *Subject* did in chapter 2. But let us make a stab at it.

Direct Objects—Diagnostics, Categories, Position, and Semantic Role

You probably noticed right off that within a single clause (as in examples 3–6) the DO is the noun phrase (NP) that follows the V. Does a DO have to be an NP? You saw in chapter 2 examples of clauses that function as the DO of a higher V, as in:

(7)   Jeff thinks [(that) Sue's left].

We are not ready yet to face the question of what category the embedded clause in a sentence like 7 belongs to. For now let us call it S (for "sentence"). So we can say the DO is the NP or S that follows the V.

But is every NP or S that follows a V within a single clause the DO of that V? Consider:

(8)   I was talking about Sue.

Here the NP *Sue* follows the V, yet we traditionally do not call this NP the DO. Instead, we say that *Sue* is the Object of the Preposition *about*. This may not strike you as terribly well motivated, and, in fact, there are many problems with this approach. Nevertheless, we can already show that the P and the NP in 8 form a syntactic unit, namely, a Prepositional Phrase (PP). Recall your cleft-test for phrases, developed in Problem Set 1.2, and exemplified here:

(9)   It was [about Sue] that I was talking.

So the NP here is inside a PP. For the moment, let us say that if a P intervenes between the V and the relevant NP and if the P and the NP form a PP, then the NP is the Object of the P and is not the DO (that is, is not the Object of the V).

We might, then, try to say that the DO is the NP or S that IMMEDIATELY FOLLOWS the V within a single clause (that is, nothing can intervene between the V and its DO). However, this definition still has problems. One problem is that it does not carry over to languages which are otherwise quite similar to English in terms of criteria for identifying GFs. For example, while in English an adverb may not intervene between a V and a following DO under most circumstances, in Italian an adverb may so intervene:

(10)   *She sang too rapidly that song.

(11)   Ha cantato troppo rapidamente quella canzone.

(If you feel uncertain that 10 is truly unacceptable in your speech, try to have faith in my claim for the moment. We will talk more about the possible intervention of adverbials between the V and its DO in chapter 5.) But even if we limit ourselves to considering only English data, problems arise. Are the bracketed phrases in 12–14 DOs?

(12)   She read [every day].

(13)   She spent [her whole life] on it.

(14)   She weighs [a ton].

There are good arguments for claiming that these bracketed phrases are NPs (and you will be able to come up with those arguments yourself after reading chapter 4). And certainly they immediately follow the V. Yet their function is quite different from that of the DOs we identified in 4, 5, and 7 above. The phrase *every day* functions to modify the time frame of the action. The phrases *her whole life* and *a ton* are measure phrases (one measuring time, one measuring weight) that give us information about the extent of the action. This contrasts with *pizza* in 4 and *the flowers* in 5, repeated here for convenience:

(15)   Jack ate (pizza) at five o'clock.

(16)   I'll arrange the flowers.

The DOs here do not modify the action in any sense. Rather, they tell us some of the entities that were involved (in a way to be more clearly specified below) in the action.

At this point we might modify our definition of DO to be the NP or S that immediately follows the V and that is an entity involved in the action of the V. To test this definition, we need to explore what this involvement might be. But even without doing that, we can see that this definition of DO has taken on a semantic flavor. In chapter 2 we found that any semantic definition of Subject failed for English, so we might be suspicious of a semantic definition of DO.

Can you think of any sentence in which an element that you might be tempted to call a DO is not "an entity involved in the action of the V" (whatever that means)? What about:

(17)   Wilt couldn't take care of his dog.

Here *care* is an NP which immediately follows the V, yet it is not an entity involved in the action of the V. Instead, the V here does not denote an action on its own. The action of this sentence is conveyed by the string of words *take care (of)*. (The *of* is in parentheses because it might well not be part of the action. We will return to a discussion of why *of* occurs in strings like this in chapter 4.) Is *care* the DO or not? A similar question comes up for idioms, like:

(18)   Old man Reese finally kicked the bucket.

In the idiomatic sense (in which the man died), the action is conveyed not by the V alone but by the string of words *kick the bucket*. Is *the bucket* the DO or not?

Semantically both *care* in 17 and *the bucket* in 18 fail this test for being a DO. Yet if they are not DOs, are we to say these sentences are intransitive? If so, then they would be structurally similar to the example in 3, repeated here for convenience:

(19)   The requisite time period finally elapsed.

Even with only the most rudimentary sense of English syntax, you probably suspect this is wrong. The semantic test has led us to a regrettable conclusion and we should at this point abandon it, just as we abandoned semantic tests for Subjecthood in chapter 2.

Direct Objects—Potential Diagnostics and Passive

So we need a diagnostic for the DO independent of semantics now. When we were looking for diagnostics for Subject in chapter 2, we settled upon three, involving Case, Subject-Auxiliary Inversion, and Subject-Verb Agreement. We might ask whether there are any parallels to these diagnostics for DOs. With respect to Case, we find that, while only Subjects have Subjective Case, Objects of Ps as well as DOs have Objective Case:

(20)   I saw [him].

(21)   I enjoyed the show with [him].

You can test this claim for yourself with the full range of pronouns. DOs and Objects of Ps are always homophonous. In fact, any NP that isn't Subjective or genitive appears in the Objective Case. Furthermore, the Objective Case appears in utterances that consist of solely an NP, whereas in a corresponding sentence these NPs might get Subjective Case:

(22)   —Who's in the closet?
       —Me.

(23)   —I'm in the closet.

We can conclude, then, that if an NP has some Case other than Objective, it is not the DO. However, if it has Objective Case, it is not necessarily the DO (as in 21 and the answer in 22).

With respect to Subject-Auxiliary Inversion, there is no parallel word-order peculiarity involving only the DO in questions or any other structure. The only word-order peculiarity we have noted is the strong tendency for the DO to immediately follow the V.

Finally, with respect to Subject-Verb Agreement, there is no parallel morphological phenomenon involving only the DO in English (although there are languages in which an affix on the V is determined in accordance with the DO, as you learned in Tangent 3 of chapter 2).

Some linguists have claimed that passive sentences can help us recognize DOs. They note that generally if you take a pair of sentences in which one is active and the other is passive, the DO of the active sentence will correspond to the Subject of the passive sentence:

(24)   Everybody ate the marshmallows.

(25)   The marshmallows were eaten by everybody.

We will return to a possible explanation for this observation in chapter 6.

Passive and Verb-Particle Combinations

For now we can note that while the observation holds true for most active/passive pairs, it is not obviously true for others. What is happening in:

(26)   Bill turned on the television.

(27)   The television was turned on by Bill.

In 26 the NP *the television* does not immediately follow the V, so it does not appear in the position we have said DOs generally appear in. Nonetheless, this NP appears as the Subject of the corresponding passive sentence in 27. Is passive, then, an inadequate test for DOs or is our generalization about where DOs appear at fault?

Compare 26 to example 7, which is repeated here.

(28)   I was talking about Sue.

We noted that *Sue* is the Object of the P in 28, and, accordingly, it can be clefted along with the P:

(29)   It was [about Sue] that I was talking.

Is *the television* the Object of *on* in 26? Our clefting test is negative here; 30 is not grammatical on a reading similar to the reading of 26 and 27:

(30)   *It was on the television that Bill turned.

So the *on* is not part of a larger PP. What is *on* doing here? You have most probably already answered this question for yourself: *on* together with *turn* tells us what the action is. That is, *turn on* in the sense of "start" is a multiple-word string that should be listed in the lexicon as a single lexical item. Its meaning is not compositionally derivable from the meanings of *turn* plus *on*. We can see this clearly if we look at a sentence which is more obviously AMBIGUOUS:

(31)   Bill turned on the merry-go-round.

Take the situation in which Bill is on the merry-go-round practicing his ballet turns. Here *on* forms a PP with the following NP:

(32)   It was on the merry-go-round that Bill turned.

Now take the situation in which Bill threw the switch that made the merry-go-round start turning. Example 31 can be used in this instance, but 32 certainly would not describe this situation.

Another syntactic property of *on* in its capacity as part of the lexical item *turn on* is that it need not appear immediately following *turn*, but can, instead, follow an NP:

(33)   Bill turned the television on.

In fact, if the NP is a pronoun, *on* must follow the pronoun:

(34)   Bill turned it on.

(35)   *Bill turned on it.

Number 35 is a grammatical sentence, but not with the reading in which Bill started the television—only with the bizarre reading in which Bill stood on the television and turned around.

Items like *on* in the lexical item *turn on* have been called PARTICLES. Another particle that you have already seen is the *up* of *look up* in Problem Set 1.2. Other examples of verb-particle combinations that show the syntactic behavior in 34 and 35 include those here:

(36)   Harold turned the radio down.
         Harold turned down the radio.
         Harold turned it down.
        *Harold turned down it.
         Bring your friend along.
         Bring along your friend.
         Bring him along.
        *Bring along him.

In Star Problem 3.1 of this chapter you are asked to show that particles are a special type of P. However, they are problematic, in a way pointed out there. We will, therefore, continue to recognize their specialness among Ps by calling them particles. We can still use the abbreviation P for them, however, without being inaccurate.

Certainly *turn on* is not a V. We know this because if we put it in the past tense, for example, the *-ed* affix goes on *turn* and not on *on* (*turned on*, **turn oned*). *Turn on*, then, is a MULTIPLE-WORD LEXICAL ITEM that consists of a V plus a P. That lexical item denotes the activity and has been called the predicate. So we can modify our generalization about the position of DOs to say that the DO typically is the NP or S that immediately follows the predicate. With this generalization, 26 and 27 present no problem for the claim that passive is a good test for picking out DOs.

Passive and Affectedness

Still, there are other problems with the passive test. Compare:

(37)   George Washington slept in that very bed.
         That very bed was slept in by George Washington.

Here we do not want to say that *sleep in* is a multiple-word lexical item since the sense of this string of words is certainly COMPOSITIONAL, based on the sense of *sleep* and the sense of *in* (compare to the sense of *sleep on*, *sleep under*). Furthermore, *in* here introduces a PP, as clefting shows:

(38)   It was in that very bed that George Washington slept.

A better stab at the restriction on the Subject of a passive sentence might be to say not that it should fill the DO function in the corresponding active sentence, but that the action should have such an effect on it that this NP (or S) can thereafter be characterized as having undergone that action. Accordingly, Vs whose actions do not have a great effect on their DO do not lend themselves easily to passive sentences:

(39)   John watched the movie.
         ?The movie was watched (by John).

(40)   John smelled the smoke.
         ?The smoke was smelled (by John).

Simply watching or smelling an inanimate object usually does not affect that object. However, touching an object can affect the object if the object feels the touch or is somehow changed (perhaps damaged) by the very touch.

(41)   John was touched by the monster's slimy finger.

(42)   *The Statue of Liberty was touched by the children.

(43)   Oil paintings should never be touched.

And in 37 above, the fact that George Washington slept in the bed made that bed famous. Thus the action did have an effect on the NP.

Now look back at 39 and 40 and find an appropriate context for a passive sentence with the verbs *watch* and *smell*.

With the approach above, the reason the passive test typically works to pick out the DO is that in active sentences the DO is generally AFFECTED by the action of the V (this is the involvement we mentioned above in our discussion of 12–16), so the passive counterpart is semantically appropriate. But DOs need not be affected by the action of the verb (as in 39 and 40), and the thing affected need not be the DO (as in the active sentence in 37). So we can see that with this analysis of passive sentences, the Subject of a passive sentence need not correspond to the DO of an active sentence, after all.

However, even an analysis of passive sentences based on the idea of affectedness has its limitations. The expression *take care (of)*, as in 17, can have a passive counterpart in which *care* is the Subject of the sentence:

(44)   (Decent) care was taken in this matter, I assure you.

Clearly the referent of *decent care* is not affected by any action here. Furthermore, certain measure phrases, as in 13 above, can appear as the Subject of passive sentences, but they cannot be taken to have been affected by the action:

(45)   The last mile of the race was run in five minutes flat.
         Five hours were spent on that problem set.

So perhaps if we had a more nearly adequate analysis of passive sentences, we might be able to come up with a reliable diagnostic for DOs.

More on Passive—Natural Predicates and Light Verbs

Let's try a third way of grappling with the analysis of passive sentences. We can come at them by analyzing the predicate rather than the Subject. Some have claimed that if an NP in an active sentence follows a string of words that can be called a NATURAL PREDICATE or a NATURAL WORD, that NP can show up in the Subject position of the corresponding passive sentence. That is, only strings that form natural predicates can appear in the passive voice. One would then look back at *turn on* and claim that since this string describes a single activity, it is a natural predicate, so the NP following this string in the active sentence (as in 26) could appear in the Subject position in the corresponding passive sentence (as in 27). It becomes a little more difficult to justify calling *sleep in* (as in 37 and 38) a natural predicate, but with the proper definition of natural predicate (which we have not attempted here), perhaps one could do that. However, examples like 44 are still problematic. The *take* here is SEMANTICALLY BLEACHED; it does not have the same denotation as the *take* in sentences like:

(46)   He took the reins in his hand.
       He took my money.

Instead, it plays the verbal role of carrying tense and showing agreement, but it leaves most of the job of carrying the sense of the predication up to the N *care* (compare to *take heed, take a shower, take a rest*, etc.). Certainly *take* does make a semantic contribution. For one thing, the Subject of sentences with such predicates are typically understood to have undertaken the activity of the predicate with conscious INTENTION, whereas the Subject of corresponding sentences without *take* need not be understood in this way:

(47)   a. She took care of them.
           She cared for them.

       b. She took a rest.
           She finally rested.

However, there are instances in which *take* fails to attribute intentionality to the Subject:

(48)   She took a chill.

So *take* alone is not the predicate in these expressions. The word(s) following *take* tells us the actual activity that occurred or state that existed. The entire string, then, is the predicate (*take care (of), take a chill*, etc.). For this reason verbs like *take*, when used as in 47 and 48 are often called LIGHT VERBS. They are semantically lightweight.

We might then try to say that a DO is that NP that follows a natural predicate in an active sentence, where we can use the passive as a test for identifying natural predicates. However, this definition fails, too. Looking back at 44 we can see that it is not true that only the NP following a natural predicate in an active sentence can appear as the Subject of the corresponding passive sentence: *take* is not a natural predicate here. (Notice that it is also not true that only natural predicates can show up in the passive voice, since the *take* in 44 is not a natural predicate, but only part of a predicate, yet it shows up in the passive voice.)

A Final Definition of DO

At this point we conclude that our understanding of the restrictions on passive Subjects is incomplete and, since this is not a book devoted to the study of only passive sentences, our understanding must remain incomplete for now. We have not developed any firm diagnostic for a DO, then. Let us just say, knowing full well that our statement is problematic, that the DO is the NP or S (clause) that immediately follows the V within a clause and that is not a modifier of the action. (I am including measure phrases as a type of modification at this point.) This definition will allow NPs that are parts of idioms (as in 17 and 18) to qualify as DOs; thus this definition does not require any particular semantic role for the DO. Yet we know that typically the DO is somehow involved in the action of the verb.

The Double-Object Construction

This definition has interesting consequences. For one, in sentences like the following, only *John,* and not *the present,* will be called the DO:

 (49) We shouldn't give John the present.

This result might upset you, since 49 is semantically close to:

 (50) We shouldn't give the present to John.

Yet for 50 our definition would have us select *the present,* not *John,* as the DO. Still, this turn of events shouldn't alarm you. In fact, English has many types of paired sentences that are semantically close and in which a given NP is the DO in one, but not in the other. Examples include:

 (51) We sprayed the wall with paint.
   We sprayed paint on the wall.

   We loaded the wagon with hay.
   We loaded hay onto the wagon.

   We wrapped the child in the blanket.
   We wrapped the blanket around the child.

   We stuffed feathers into the pillow.
   We stuffed the pillow with feathers.

Verbs that occur in pairs like those in 51 are called the SPRAY/ LOAD VERBS. Still, the pair in 49 and 50 is special in that it presents a perplexing question: if the first NP following the V in 49 is the DO, what grammatical function does the second NP have? Sentences like 49 are traditionally called DOUBLE-OBJECT SENTENCES. And in order to understand them better, we need to first discuss 50.

 Looking at 50 we find another way that verbs can be subcategorized: by whether they must, may, or cannot co-occur with an Indirect Object.

 (52) a. I handed the newspaper to Mary.

   b. I sent the letter (to Mary).

   c. I drank the milkshake (*to Mary).

Indirect Objects are typically introduced by *to,* as above, or *for:*

 (53) Let's bake a cake for your sister.

And one important characteristic of sentences that contain both an IO and a DO is that there is typically a corresponding sentence without *to/for* in which the NPs appear in the reverse order. That is, 52a and 53 form pairs with 54 parallel to 50 and 49:

(54)   I handed Mary the newspaper.
       Let's bake your sister a cake.

For this reason (and others), many people would say that in the Double-Object construction, the first Object is the IO and the second Object is the DO. Not everyone agrees with this conclusion, however, and it is not a logical necessity. In fact, we already saw in looking at the *spray/load* verbs (as in 51 above) that the alternation between DO and OP does not correlate with any immediately obvious difference in semantics. Given this, we might even expect different DOs in the two variants of sentences that have two objects of a single verb (a DO and an IO).

We will not discuss further the proper labels for the two Objects in the Double-Object construction because at no point in this book will their label be important. Instead, we will rely on linear order only, referring to the first Object and the second Object of the Double-Object construction.

Not every NP introduced by a *to* or *for* is an IO. We can use the availability of the Double-Object construction as a diagnostic for IOs. That is, if the Object of a *to* or *for* in a given sentence can appear without the *to* or *for* in the position immediately following the verb in a (close to) synonymous sentence, the Object of the *to* or *for* in the given sentence is an IO. With this diagnostic we see that *to* can also introduce locative expressions, for example, that often function as modifiers of the action. *For* can also introduce a variety of modifying expressions:

(55)   She carried her brother to Rome.
       *She carried Rome her brother.

(56)   She wrote letters for three hours.
       *She wrote three hours letters.

The contrast between 55 and 56 and 52 and 53 is an important one for understanding why the Objects of the prepositions in 52 and 53 are called IOs (that is, Indirect Objects of the V), but the Objects of the prepositions in 55 and 56 are simply called OPs (Objects of prepositions). The locative *to* in 55 can be replaced by other locatives that are semantically appropriate for the action denoted by *carried*, such as:

(57)   She carried her brother {in/from/around} Rome.

Likewise, *for* in its duration sense in 56 can be replaced by other Ps that deal with time relationships so long as they are semantically appropriate for the action denoted by *wrote*, such as:

(58)   She wrote (the) letters {in/after/within} three hours.

But if we replace the *to* or *for* of 52 and 53 with another P, we find that either the PP is rejected, or the PP now has a modifying sense:

(59)   *I handed the newspaper {around/for/with} Mary.

(60)   Let's bake a cake {around/with/*to} your sister.

The verb *hand* requires that there be an IO introduced by *to*. (That is, *hand* is subcategorized for the property of requiring such an IO.) The verb *bake* optionally takes an IO introduced by *for*, and any other PP that co-occurs with it is interpreted as a modifying PP. (That is, *bake* is subcategorized for the property of optionally taking such an IO.)

IOs, then, are narrowly selected by the verbs they co-occur with. In contrast, most verbs either do not require modifying phrases (that is, phrases with an ADVERBIAL function) at all, or, if they do require a modifying phrase, it can be of a range of types. In 60 the verb *bake* does not require a modifying phrase, but if one occurs, it can be of any syntactic type so long as it is semantically appropriate. In 61 the verb *place*, in the sense of "put" or "arrange," requires some type of phrase in addition to its DO, but that phrase can be of a wide range of syntactic types:

(61)   Let's place the flowers {in the vase/carefully/so that everyone can see the daffodils/there}.

DOs and IOs are called COMPLEMENTS of the V, so we say that Vs are subcategorized according to the types of complements they take. One could subcategorize verbs as to whether they require some phrase other than a DO or IO (like *place* in 61), in which case one might call the phrases in braces in 61 COMPLEMENTS of the V, as well.

Subcategorization and Subjects

Can verbs be subcategorized according to whether they take a Subject? Limit yourself to considering only single clause sentences. What can you say about all of them regarding Subjects? They all have Subjects. This is a fact of English syntax: we require an overt Subject for every tensed clause (and all our independent clauses are tensed). This is the reason English exhibits dummy Subjects (like the *there* you analyzed in Problem Set 2.2). Not all languages do that. Italian and Japanese, for example, do not. But French and German do. So in English it makes no sense to subcategorize verbs according to whether they take an overt Subject, since all of them will occur with an overt Subject in a tensed clause. Furthermore, it has been argued that even clauses that have no overt Subject have what is called an EMPTY SUBJECT in the syntax for English, Italian, Japanese, and many other languages. You will see much of the evidence for this claim for English in chapter 7 and some of the evidence for it regarding Romance languages in a variety of problem sets on Italian, Spanish, and Portuguese found throughout this book. As a result, linguists generally do not talk about subcategorization regarding Subjects.

However, while all tensed clauses have an overt Subject in English, it turns out that there are distinctions to be made among verb types regarding their Subjects, and some of these distinctions should be made in terms of subcategorization. We will discuss relevant data and analyses in Problem Set 6.4 of chapter 6.

Back to Locality, Better Equipped

All right: what have we learned so far? We set out in the first section to discover why clauses appear to be special with regard to the notion of locality. Since each clause typically has precisely one verb string, that led us to explore verbs. We learned that verbs require, allow, or disallow DOs and IOs, and some verbs require other types of phrases (although I know of no verbs that disallow items other than DOs or IOs—for example, I know of no verbs that disallow all modifying phrases). We have arrived at this conclusion by discussing primarily the syntax (the form) of English sentences. So now we can say that clauses are special in that the grammatical functions are defined internal to them. In this sense, the GFs within a clause are all syntactically local to one another.

Let us now return to our original question, this time with attention to semantic considerations. If we are going to approach the question of what locality is from a semantic point of view, we need to understand the semantic contribution of verbs to the utterances they occur in. Consider this sentence:

(62)   Jack's mother clapped her hands.

Clapped here tells us the activity that took place. Jack's mother is the one who initiated and carried out this activity. It did not just happen to her; she brought it about. For this reason, we say that the NP *Jack's mother* is an agent. So the Subject position of this clause is not filled with just any old phrase. Instead, it is filled with a phrase whose referent is a participant in the activity denoted by the verb. The common term used for a participant is ARGUMENT.

Jack's mother is not the only argument here. Her hands are the objects that felt the effects of the activity, so they, too, are participants in the activity. Notice that the sense of *participant* used here does not require that participation be willing or even conscious. There are various labels given to the type of argument that *her hands* is in 62. We will use the label THEME, although PATIENT and OBJECT(IVE) can also be found in the literature, for arguments that are acted upon but have not initiated the activity and do not play one of the other argument roles described below.

Another argument role is exemplified in sentences that have an IO, as we have seen above, and repeated here:

(63)   I handed Mary the newspaper.
       I handed the newspaper to Mary.

       Let's bake your sister a cake.
       Let's bake a cake for your sister.

The IO in these sentences is the one who receives something or benefits somehow from the activity. It is called the BENEFACTIVE, or the BENEFACTEE, or the BENEFICIARY, or the RECIPIENT, or the GOAL. (Distinctions can be made among all these terms, but we will not have cause to do so in this book.)

A fourth argument type is exemplified here:

(64)   That key opens this door.
       Kate opened the door with that key.

In both these sentences, that key is the INSTRUMENT by which some agent brought
about the activity. Unlike an agent, an instrument does not initiate the activity
under its own steam or by its own volition.

An additional argument role is exemplified in:

(65)   Sally heard the bell.

Here the activity is not one that can be controlled. That is, we hear those things that
we perceive aurally, but that perception is beyond our control under ordinary circumstances. Normally we command people to do only those things they have control over. Contrast *hear* in this regard to *listen*:

(66)   *Hear closely!
       Listen closely!

Sally, then, is not an agent of the activity in 65, nor is she the benefactive or the
instrument. Some people might say that she is the theme here, in that the action
happens to her. Others have claimed that she is the EXPERIENCER of the activity.
We will take the position that she is the experiencer, and you will be able to find at
least one argument for why she is not a theme as you do Problem Set 3.3 at the end
of this chapter.

Argument roles like agent, theme, benefactive, instrumental, and experiencer are
called THEMATIC ROLES or THETA-ROLES. Many other argument roles in addition
to these five have been discussed in the literature. *The question of how many theta-
roles there are and what their defining properties are has yet to be answered conclusively. The issue for us (given that this is a syntax book) is not what nuances a linguist may see and hence how many different types of participation one can distinguish on some semantic basis, but, rather, how many and which different theta-roles
we must recognize in order to account for syntactic facts, such as the distribution of
grammatical items.* For example, many have noted that phrases like *voluntarily* do
not occur freely:

(67)   *Sally heard the bell voluntarily.
       *John grew voluntarily.
       *Mary was arrested voluntarily.

(68)   Sally listened to the record voluntarily.
       John ate more nutritious food voluntarily.
       Mary's father turned her in voluntarily.

In 67 no overt participant is an agent. But in 68 every sentence has an overt agent.
In order to describe the distribution of *voluntarily*, many linguists have taken the
position that we need to admit the theta-role of agent into our grammar, as contrasted to all other theta-roles. In Problem Set 3.3 you will be given some criteria
by which to recognize other theta-roles, although you will find that simple criteria
are hard to come by. Fortunately, however, it is often the case that the important

question for syntax is not which theta-role an item bears, but whether it bears a theta-role at all.

Look back for a moment at 62–68. What determines which theta-role a given item will bear? Compare the following sentences with respect to the theta-role of *the little boy*:

(69)   The little boy ate the apple.
        I saw the little boy.
        Sam gave everything to the little boy.
        Jack picked up Jill's brother and threw him across the room and that's
        how the little boy broke the window.
        The little boy feels sick.

If you think *the little boy* has each of the five different theta-roles discussed above in these sentences, then I chose good examples with which to make my point. If you do not think so, then choose better examples for yourself. Certainly a given NP (or a given phrase of any other category) does not determine its own theta-role independently of the sentence it appears in.

So what determines the theta-role? If you think in terms of activities, you can say that a given activity calls for certain kinds of participation—thus the theta-roles (which reflect participation types) are determined by the activity. You already know that not all sentences involve an activity. Consider the final sentence of 69 above. Is feeling sick an activity? We said in chapter 2 that most people call this type of event a state. Other examples of state-events are easy to come by:

(70)   We're fat.
        We resemble our mothers.

Come up with several yourself now. So it is the event itself (keep in mind that the term *event* covers both activities and states) that determines the theta-roles.

Determining Theta-Roles—Contributions of Predicates and Context

But what item(s) tells us the event? Generally the verb or the PREDICATIVE ADJECTIVE (as in the first example of 70) tells us the event. But as we can see in the fourth example of 69, repeated here, sometimes the larger context contributes to our determination of theta-roles:

(71)   Jack picked up Jill's brother and threw him across the room and that's
        how Jill's brother broke the window.

Perhaps, if we heard 72 out of context:

(72)   Jill's brother broke the window.

we would understand this sentence to contain an agent. But in the context in 71, we understand it to contain an instrument. And once we've heard 71, we can recognize 72 as allowing an agentive or an instrumental reading. Does that mean that theta-roles cannot be discussed independently of context? It would at first appear so.

Yet it is quite true that the extrasentential context cannot change the theta-role of *John* in:

(73)   John assassinated the king.

The denotation of *assassinate* includes the notion of killing with forethought and purpose (usually political) and attributes some sort of importance (again usually political) to the object killed. No amount of fiddling with the context will change that.

Is *assassinate*, then, somehow different from *break* with respect to theta-role assignment? To answer this, consider the following sentences:

(74)   John assassinated the king.
       John murdered the king.
       John killed the king.

We have already seen that *assassinate* can be used only in very limited contexts. *Murder* can be used in all the contexts *assassinate* can be used in, but not vice versa. For example, if a gunman named John holds up the bank and his stray bullet kills the king, we can say he murdered the king (by statutory definition, since it is a death in the course of a felony) but we would not say he assassinated the king (since he did not intentionally, with forethought, kill a political figure for a political reason). Likewise, *kill* can be used in all the contexts *assassinate* and *murder* can, but not vice versa. We see here a cline, going from a verb of high information (a notion we have come across before), which puts severe limitations on the contexts in which it can be used appropriately, to a verb of low information, which puts only a few limitations on the contexts in which it can be used appropriately.

For high-information verbs it is easy to say that their arguments bear a particular theta-role. But for low-information verbs we know that the contexts they can appear in are quite varied, and therefore we must recognize that they set up a range of possible theta-roles (corresponding to the variety of appropriate contexts). *Break* is a relatively low-information word: therefore, to say that its Subject could be an agent or an instrument is not inconsistent with the claim that it is the verb or the predicate adjective that determines the theta-roles of the arguments.

Why do verbs and predicate adjectives typically do this? These are the words that are generally our event words. We call them predicates, and we've mentioned them on and off since the beginning of this book. We will develop a better understanding of the notion of "predicate" as we progress through this book. For now, let us say that every predicate has a set of arguments (that is, participants). And many have argued that each argument of a given predicate must have a unique theta-role (you will explore this carefully in Problem Set 3.3, particularly Part 3). We will call a predicate and all its arguments a COMPLETE FUNCTIONAL COMPLEX or CFC (and we will revise this definition in the last section of chapter 4). We now have a semantic notion of locality that corresponds to our syntactic notion of locality: a CFC is to semantics as a clause is to syntax. (This is not the only possible analogy that can be made between CFCs and semantics, on the one hand, and syntax, on the other. But it is the only analogy that we are able to see at this point.)

CFCs and Subcategorization, or Semantics and Syntax

In fact, we can make a relatively straightforward correlation between a CFC and a clause. Think about what allows a given clause to have a DO and/or an IO. The subcategorization of the verb (or, as you will see in chapter 4, of the lexical item of any category that heads a phrase) determines whether we may or must have any particular GF except Subject (since all tensed clauses—and we will later see, even untensed clauses—in English have Subjects, regardless of any facts of subcategorization). Is a lexical item's subcategorization truly independent of its argument structure or does the first follow from the second?

We have already seen evidence above that we need to treat subcategorization as an independent factor from argument structure. Consider once more pairs of the type seen in 51 above, repeated here:

(75)   We sprayed the wall with paint.
       We sprayed paint on the wall.

       We loaded the wagon with hay.
       We loaded hay onto the wagon.

       We wrapped the child in the blanket.
       We wrapped the blanket around the child.

       We stuffed feathers into the pillow.
       We stuffed the pillow with feathers.

Verbs that enter into such pairs are often called the SPRAY/ LOAD VERBS. We can see from them that the fact that a verb takes a theme does not tell us that this theme will automatically appear in any particular GF. In fact, in Problem Set 3.3 you will see conclusively that, with only one exception, there is no fixed theta-role for any given GF and, with no exceptions, there is no fixed GF for any given theta-role.

Furthermore, we can find verbs which are very similar in meaning, but which are subcategorized differently:

(76)   We tried.
       *We attempted.

Try need not have a syntactic complement; *attempt* requires one.

The subcategorization FRAME of a lexical item, then, is independent of its argument frame, and vice versa. But when we put words together to make a sentence, these two frames interact. For example, if we note that *eat* is subcategorized to optionally take a DO and if we note that *eat* can take both an agent and a theme, we cannot insert both arguments into a transitive structure freely and come out with the same semantic interpretation:

(77)   The mouse ate the cheese.

(78)   The cheese ate the mouse.

So 77 is not synonymous with 78, even though they involve the same words and the same GFs.

We must admit into our grammar a LINKING (or MAPPING) mechanism that links the subcategorization and argument frames. For *discuss* it might look something like:

(79)   *discuss*
      argument frame: agent   ⟨theme⟩

      subcategorization frame: Subject DO

This is to be read as saying that *discuss* has an argument frame that calls for an agent and a theme. (The angled brackets around the theme argument indicate that this argument is internal to the Verb Phrase. You will learn more about VPs in chapter 4.) Example 79 also tells us that *discuss* takes a Subject (which is not, as we have said above, a subcategorization fact) and a DO (which is a subcategorization fact) and that the agent argument gets mapped into the Subject position and the theme argument gets mapped into the DO position. Verbs in the *spray/load* class have two subcategorization frames that are linked to a single argument frame (or, at least, that is one possible way to handle them).

If you have read other works on syntax, you may be familiar with a different type of subcategorization frame from that given in 79—one given not in terms of grammatical functions, but in terms of categories. For *discuss* we might find:

(80)   *discuss:* _____ {NP, S}

Example 80 is to be read as telling us that *discuss* can fit into the slot before an NP or an S. That is, *discuss* is immediately followed by an NP or a clause (as in *Let's discuss whether he's coming*). There are several problems with a subcategorization frame given in terms of categories rather than GFs. One is obvious from 80: *discuss* in 80 looks like it has two possible contexts (before an NP and before a clause). But, in fact, the generalization is that *discuss* must take a theme argument in the DO position regardless of the category of the DO. If *discuss* is followed by an NP or S which is not an argument, but, instead, a modifier (such as the clause *because she left*), we will get a deviant result, even though we are conforming to 80; for example:

(81)   *We discussed because she left.

Thus the framework in 80 misses an important fact about *discuss*.

The difference between 79 and 80 is that 79 involves a linking between arguments and syntax (the GFs), while 80 is purely structure-based. They are not competing formalisms for conveying the same information. We will continue to state our subcategorization frameworks in terms of GFs, then, and to relate them to argument frames, as in 79.

Get yourself a piece of paper and write down several simple sentences now. Circle the arguments of the predicate. Now box in the GFs. What do you notice? Let me give you three more:

(82)   Mary sent a letter to Bill last Thursday.
       There came a train around the bend.
       The boys put the papers down.

If you have limited yourself to one-predicate clauses, the correlation we have been working toward will jump off the page at you: arguments get mapped into GFs (Subject, DO, IO, OP). (If you think this is not true for the example with *put* in 82, you will after you have done Part 2d of Problem Set 3.1.)

However, not every GF need be filled by an argument. Subjects can be filled by dummies, as you well know. And, as we have seen in this chapter, DOs can also be filled by elements that are not arguments, but, instead, parts of a multiple-word predicate (often an idiom), as in 17 (with *take care (of)*) and 18 (with the idiom *kick the bucket*). The same is true of OPs:

(83)   The teacher took the students to task.

Here the predicate is the discontinuous string *take . . . to task*, and the Object of the P *to* is not filled with an argument of the predicate. In fact, OPs are often not arguments of the predicates, since PPs function very often as modifiers:

(84)   She left [on Thursday].
       She dressed [with good taste].
       She laughed [out loud].

Can an IO ever be filled by a nonargument? (You will ponder this further as you do Problem Set 3.3.)

Conclusion

This chapter has focused on the syntactic and semantic components of simple sentences and the connection between the two. We say that all of the members of a grammatical unit need to be LICENSED. An item can be licensed because it is an argument, a modifier, or a predicate, or because it satisfies some structural requirement (such as the requirement that a clause have a Subject). As this book proceeds, you may decide to add to the list of functions that can license grammatical entities. In a structure such as:

(85)   *The elephant the cheese saw the idea the generator.

incomprehensibility follows from there being too many nominal items in the sentence. For example, if *the elephant* is the Subject, what is *the cheese* doing here? If *the idea* is the DO, what is *the generator* doing here? In other sentences we may allow a pileup of NPs before or after or on both sides of the verb:

(86)   [Last night] [the elephant] saw the idea.
       The elephant saw [the idea] [last night].
       [Next year] [I] will eat [meals] [anyplace I want].

But in 86 the extra NPs (*last night, next year,* and *anyplace I want*) can be interpreted as serving to modify the predicate. This type of NP is often called a BARE NP ADVERBIAL (and we will see some properties of them in Problem Set 5.2). In contrast, none of the NPs in 85 has a referent that is a time or a place or a reason, so they cannot be interpreted as bare NP adverbials. That is why the pileup of NPs in 85 leads to ungrammaticality: Not all of these nominals can be licensed. (*See* allows only two arguments, the syntax restricts us to one Subject and one DO, and none of the nominals in 85 is a modifier.)

We can now state a principle called the THETA CRITERION:

(87)   Every argument must be assigned a theta-role and every
       theta-role must be assigned to an argument.

The Theta Criterion assures that arguments will get theta-roles. In 85 the predicate cannot assign all these NPs a theta-role, so 85 is a violation of the Theta Criterion. Furthermore, the Theta Criterion assures that a predicate which takes a certain range of thematic arguments will, in fact, occur in structures in which there are constituents that can bear the appropriate theta-roles. You will see the effects of the Theta Criterion in Problem Set 3.3 and throughout the rest of this book.

We can now return to the question posed at the start of the chapter: what notion of locality is relevant to the distribution of anaphors and their antecedents? We need to test whether clauses (whose members are local to one another syntactically) or CFCs (whose members are local to one another semantically) are useful notions in getting at the type of locality that matters for anaphors. We will do that. But first we will need a more thorough understanding of phrase structure, which is the topic of the next chapter.

*Problem Set 3.1: English Subcategorization

This problem set is basic to your understanding of syntax. It must be done.

Read this problem set through to the end. Then go about your business and let it brew in the back of your mind. Come back to it every few hours and you'll find that examples will come to you.

Part 1

In this chapter we discussed Grammatical Functions, including Subject, Direct Object, Indirect Object, and Object of a preposition. Now think about the different verbs of English and answer the following questions. Please do not try to account for the data you give, merely give them.

(a) Give one verb in English that must occur without a Direct Object and also without an Indirect Object. Do not use *be* or a passive sentence.

(Be careful here and below. A verb like *run*, for example, can be used transitively in a sentence like *She runs marathons.* You must find a verb that can *never* occur with any Direct or Indirect Object, such as *elapse* in example 3 in the text. Note also that some intransitive verbs allow so-called "cognate" Objects:

(1)   She slept the sleep of the weary.

(2)   He lived {a life of leisure/a fantasy}.

Try to find a verb which disallows even cognate Objects.)

(b) Give one verb in English that can optionally occur with a Direct Object but must never take an Indirect Object. An example is *eat* in example 4 in the text.

(c) Give one verb in English that must occur with a Direct Object. (Again, be very careful. There are many verbs that are typically transitive but in common contexts can be used intransitively. For example, *buy* is typically transitive, but we can easily understand a sentence like *Are you buying again today?* said in the context of one person asking if the other will pay for lunch. Make sure the verb you give doesn't lend itself to easy comprehension when used intransitively. An example is *confuse*, as in, *Mary confuses the issues*, but not **Mary confuses on most days, so I'll do the confusing today.* Watch out for variations in tense and aspect that affect whether an object is required. You want examples where the DO is required in all tenses and aspects.)

(d) Give one verb that must occur with a Direct Object and also requires some other element (beyond the Subject) to be there—perhaps an Indirect Object, perhaps a prepositional phrase, perhaps something that is locative (that is, telling a place or position or direction), perhaps something that modifies the action of the verb. This verb must be different from the one you used in (c) above. (I am not giving you an example here, because if I do, I will give away the class of verbs for you, since they tend to be quite similar. Instead, let me give you an example of an intransitive verb that requires a locative: *lurk*, as in *She lurked in the bushes*, but not **She lurked all day.* Now you need to find a verb that requires both some other phrase plus a DO.)

Part 2

Prepositions, like verbs, can occur in different environments, and we can subcategorize them according to these environments. For example, like most verbs, most prepositions are only optionally transitive:

(3)   Susie went <u>in (the house)</u>.
          P   NP

Compare to an optionally transitive V:

(4)   Susie <u>drank (the beer)</u>.
             V   NP

Also, prepositions, like verbs, can introduce another prepositional phrase rather than only an NP Object:

(5)   Susie fell <u>down [through the hole]</u>.
                  P   PP

Compare to a V introducing a PP:

(6)   Susie <u>fell [down the stairs]</u>.
             V   PP

And prepositions, like verbs, can introduce clauses rather than just NPs or PPs:

(7) *In* [*that there's nothing left to say*], I'm leaving.
     P   clause

     I wouldn't cry just on account *of* [*his mother yelled*].
                                    P   clause

(You may not find the second sentence of 7 grammatical, but many people do and this is an ATTESTED—that is, actually heard—EXAMPLE.) Compare to a V introducing a clause:

(8) I *think* [*that there's nothing left to say*].
       V   clause

     I *noticed* [*his mother yelled*].
       V   clause

There are many prepositions in English, and they are easily recognized once it is seen that a preposition does not require an NP Object. As you learned in Problem Set 1.2, a typical diagnostic for a PP is whether it can be introduced by *right* or *directly*. Thus for most speakers of English, these specifiers do not introduce any category other than one headed by P:

(9) She went {right/directly} [into the house].
                                    P

     *She's {right/directly} [intelligent].
                                  A

     *She {right/directly} [cried].
                             V

     *It fell {right/directly} [quickly].
                                  A

The *right*-test for PP is sufficient, but not necessary. That is, if an item can be introduced by *right*, it is a PP. But not all PPs can be introduced by *right*:

(10) *She bought a basket [{right/directly} of peaches].

In 10, *of peaches* is surely a PP, but *right/directly* cannot introduce it.

Now try to answer the following.

(a) Give one preposition that can never take an NP Object. (It is okay if your example can introduce another PP.) Use it in a sentence.

(b) Give one preposition that must take an NP Object. Use it in a sentence.

(c) Give one preposition that must introduce only a clause. Use it in a sentence.
(Hint: Think about the kinds of words that can be used to introduce clauses of all sorts. Then compare which of these words seem to be semantically like Ps and ask if any of them pass the *right/directly* test.

PPs can be used in lots of ways. They can indicate location (as in: *in the bath*), or time (as in: *at 5 o'clock*), or reason (as in: *(I did it) for Bill's sake*), or purpose (as in: *(I need that brush) for cleaning the tub*), or many other things. So as you answer this one, try to think of words that introduce clauses in cases in which the clause functions to indicate location or time or reason or purpose or the other kinds of things that PPs do. You may not have previously considered the words I am looking for to be Ps. Discard your old ideas of what Ps are and trust your *right*-test.)

(d) What is the category of each of the bracketed phrases below? Give an argument to support each of your answers:

(11)   Mary ran [back].

(12)   Mary went [home].

(13)   Mary found it [there].

(I expect this to make you unhappy. Try to follow your tests and forget your preconceived notions about categories. If you know another language well, you might try to see if you can find similar examples in the languages you know.)

(e) Some verbs cannot take DOs, most can optionally take DOs, and a few must take DOs (as you found out in Part 1). No category other than V and P can take an Object. However, nouns and adjectives can take complements which are PPs. Usually, these PPs are optional:

(14)   destruction (of the city)/the rumor (about Pete)
       sick (of milk)/dependent (on Pete)

Find one adjective of English that requires a PP when it is used predicatively. There are only a handful, but if you bring this up at the dinner table, maybe your friends can help you find one. I will give you an example just so you believe there are some:

(15)   Joe is fond of Sue.
       *Joe is fond.

(Notice that the subcategorization frame of an adjective may vary between its use as a modifier and its use as a predicate:

    a fond look
??Her look was fond

    my fondest memory
*That memory is fondest.

For this reason, please demonstrate with a predicative use of an adjective.)

Problem Set 3.2: English Prescriptive Case

Part 1

Consider the sentence:

(1)   (*)It is I.

You might well say a sentence like 1 yourself, but most people do not in ordinary conversation. Instead, 1 is familiar to many of us who do not use it simply because we have been told by someone somewhere along the way that it is "correct" English. The asterisk in parentheses in 1 indicates that 1 belongs to normative or prescriptive speech for most of us (and see remarks on prescriptive-versus-descriptive linguistics in the introduction to this book). Rather than 1, most of us would say:

(2)   It's me.

Discuss which of these two alternatives, 1 or 2, is consistent with the way we have developed English syntax up to this point. In particular, think about our diagnostics for Subject (and you can look back to the text and the problem sets of chapter 2 for them). In your discussion, please be sure to consider examples like:

(3)   *It am me.

(4)   It's us.

(5)   (*)It's we.

(6)   *It are we.

(7)   Who is it?

(8)   I wonder who it is.

(9)   It's them.

(10) (*)It's they.

(11)   It's them, isn't it?

(12) *It's them, {isn't them/isn't they/ aren't them/aren't they}?

(13) *It's they, {isn't them/isn't they/ aren't them/aren't they}?

Your discussion should touch on matters of Case assignment, Subject-Verb Agreement, Subject-Auxiliary Inversion, tag questions, and anything else you would like to bring up.

Part 2

Just as 1 above is often called correct, so are:

(14) (*)Whom did you see?
       (*)Whom did you talk with?

as opposed to the sentences that most people actually say:

(15)   Who did you see?
       Who did you talk with?

Discuss here what determines the choice of *who* versus *whom* in the speech of those who use 14 rather than 15. In case you cannot say 14 yourself, note that those who say 14 would accept 16–18, but reject 19 and 20 (as all of us would):

(16) (*)Whom did you think Bill saw?
      (*)Whom did you think Bill talked with?

(17) Who did you think saw Bill?
      Who did you think talked with Bill?

(18) Who came?

(19) *Whom did you think saw Bill? (cf. 17)
      *Whom did you think talked with Bill? (cf. 17)

(20) *Whom came? (cf. 18)

Part 3

In ordinary speech, when we question the Object of a P, most of us leave the P
STRANDED. Thus in 21, *with*, *to*, and *for* are stranded in the sense that their Object
does not follow them:

(21) Who did you visit with?
      Who are you speaking to, young lady?
      Who did you bake the cake for?

However, if we are speaking prescriptively, we might place the P in sentence-initial
position. If we do, the following grammaticality judgments are common:

(22) With whom did you visit?
      To whom are you speaking, young lady?
      For whom did you bake the cake?

(23) *With who did you visit?
      *To who are you speaking, young lady?
      *For who did you bake the cake?

Describe the distribution of *who* versus *whom* in this speech pattern in general
terms (that is, do not phrase your statement in terms of the specific Ps *with*, *to*, and
for, but in terms of P in general, etc.).

Part 4

Despite the fact that most people have the pattern you described above in Part 3,
we can find many people saying both 24 and 25:

(24) You went with who?

(25) You went with whom?

Say 24 and 25 aloud. Describe the intonation contour that you would assign to
these sentences in order to accept them.
    Now think about the types of contexts you might use 24 or 25 in. Describe two
such different contexts.
    Finally, how does the fact that both 24 and 25 are heard, whereas 23 above is

ungrammatical, affect the generalization you came to in Part 3? Why do you think this problem arises?

Part 5

Finally, if you do not belong to any of the speech groups whose grammatical pattern is exemplified in Parts 2 and 3 of this problem set, show with examples how you differ from these groups and discuss what determines the choice of *who* versus *whom* in your own speech.

*Problem Set 3.3: English Theta-Roles

This problem set may seem very difficult at first. Read it through. Organize which example sentences seem relevant to which questions. Then dig in. And try to remember that in syntax there are rarely clean answers—so do not try to force any. State what you see.

In chapter 3 we isolated the grammatical functions (GFs) of Subject (S), Direct Object (DO), Indirect Object (IO), and Object of a Preposition (OP). For the purposes of this problem set, assume these are the only GFs.

We also discussed the thematic roles that arguments of a given verb may have. These are typically called theta-roles. They concern the semantics of a sentence. For example, in:

(1)   John threw Susie a ball.

John has the GF of S, and the theta-role of agent; *Susie* has the GF of IO, and the theta-role of benefactee (also called recipient, also called beneficiary, also called goal, but various linguists make various distinctions between these different labels—do not worry about it for now); *a ball* has the GF of DO and the theta-role of theme (also called patient).

Another theta-role is experiencer. So in:

(2)   John went crazy.

John has the GF of S and the theta-role of experiencer.

A fifth theta-role is instrument. So in:

(3)   This key opens that door.

This key has the GF of S and the theta-role of instrument.

There are no clean and clear definitions for the various theta-roles and there is no easy way to determine how many theta-roles a given language makes use of. For the sake of this homework, consider only the five theta-roles of AGENT, BENEFAC-TEE, THEME, EXPERIENCER, and INSTRUMENT exemplified above.

Diagnostics for Agent

There are several diagnostics for agent. First, an agent can license the occurrence of the adverbial *voluntarily*, as pointed out in the text. A theme, a benefactee, an experiencer, and an instrument cannot. Thus if a sentence has no agent, it cannot have the adverbial *voluntarily*. And if a sentence can have the adverbial *voluntarily*, it does have an agent. In other words, the ability of *voluntarily* to occur in a sentence is a necessary-and-sufficient test for whether the sentence has an agent. (This is generally taken to be true for most speakers. Some speakers have the same restriction on the occurrence of *on purpose*, but others don't. For the sake of this problem set, use only *voluntarily* as a test.)

There is another diagnostic for agent, but the use of this test requires some judgment calls. Consider:

(4)   I promise to come home on time.

(5)   *I promise to be five feet tall.

Certainly the first promise is just fine. But the second one is odd. Still, in spite of the fact that it is asterisked, it is a statement that might be made. For instance, let us assume it is fall tryouts for the basketball team. But the team will not actually start playing until late winter. Let's further assume that to be on the team one must be five feet tall. Now if a seventh grader is trying to convince the coach to allow her/him to be on the basketball team, but that seventh grader is presently too short, she/he might say, "I promise to be five feet tall by Christmas." No, it is not a real promise. It is more a declaration of hope or belief in the pediatrician's words to the effect that this seventh grader will keep growing. Whatever, the sentence might be said. If we can distinguish the nonpromise sentences with *promise* from the true promises, we can say that whenever you can truly promise with an infinitival (like "I promise to come home on time"), then you have an agent (the guy that is going to perform the event of the infinitive—that is, the one who is going to come home on time).

Another diagnostic for agent is progressive aspect. Consider:

(6)   I'm talking to you.

(7)   *I'm understanding French.

If the Subject is an agent, then it has potential control over the event, and so the progressive is possible. This test, while necessary (that is, every verb with an agentive Subject can be in the progressive so long as the extrasentential context of the particular sentence permits), is not sufficient. Thus, even experiencers can occur as the Subjects of verbs with the progressive aspect:

(8)   You've gone and left—and I'm so blue—*I'm hurting* over you.

And a fourth possible diagnostic for agent involves RATIONALE CLAUSES: they can occur only with an agent present:

(9)   She shouted in order to make everyone look.

(10)   *She had good reflexes in order to impress everyone.

(Note: Rationale clauses are distinct from PURPOSE CLAUSES, which do not require an agent: *I know a book [to read to the kids]*.) As far as I know, this test is both necessary and sufficient. However, it is tricky, too, because we have another use of *in order to* that means "if" (conditional), and that use is not a test for agent:

(11) We need money in order to impress his mother.
  (cf. *We are needing money.
      *We need money voluntarily.
      *I promise to need money.)

Diagnostics for Theme

There is at least one test for theme. A RESULTATIVE adjective can be predicated of a theme, but it cannot be predicated of an agent, a benefactee, an experiencer, or an instrument. For example, consider:

(12) John scrubbed the floor clean.

The reading in which John scrubbed the floor until it became clean is called resultative. With that reading, we understand only *the floor*, the theme, to wind up clean—not *John*, the agent. Of course there is the reading in which John scrubbed the floor while he was clean, parallel to,

(13) John came home clean.

Here the adjective *clean* is predicated of *John*, but *clean* is not a resultative. (We don't come home until we wind up clean.) The resultative test is only a sufficient test, however, not a necessary test. That is, if a resultative can be introduced into a sentence, then the sentence has a theme. But if a resultative cannot be introduced into a sentence, we cannot conclude that no theme is present. Instead, there may be extraneous interfering factors that prevent the resultative. For example, *the paper* is the theme in:

(14) John saw the paper.

but no resultative can be added here:

(15) *John saw the paper flat.

Why do you think that is? If you give it just a moment's thought, you will realize that just seeing some inanimate object does not typically result in some change happening to that inanimate object. So the problem with *John saw the paper flat* is that it could never happen, not that there is no theme here. (Compare *John pressed the paper flat.* By the way, if you think my explanation of the ungrammaticality of *John saw the paper flat* is wrong, write up why and give it to your professor or send it to me.)

Diagnostics for Instrument, Benefactee, and Experiencer

Some have proposed a diagnostic for instrument. If an NP is an instrument and it is not the Object of *with*, there is often another parallel sentence very close in meaning in which the relevant NP shows up as the Object of *with*:

(16) The key opened the door.

(17) Someone opened the door with the key.

However, this is not always the case:

    (18)   The medication made me sick.

    (19)   *I got sick with the medication.
            (cf. I got sick from the medication.
               I got sick with the flu.)

Furthermore, a subject that is not instrumental in one sentence might occur as the Object of *with* in a sentence with similar meaning:

    (20)   John and Mary left the party.

    (21)   John left the party with Mary.

Here we have a sense of accompaniment, rather than instrument. Because of problems like these, *with* is not considered a good diagnostic for instrument.

I know of no good test for benefactee or experiencer, either. If you can think of one that works for any of these, write it up and give it to your professor or send it to me.

Now answer the questions in Parts 1–4. Use the example sentences (1–47) that follow to support your answers.

Part 1

Is there any GF that always gets a fixed theta-role? If so, which? And which theta-role does it get?

Part 2

Is there any theta-role that always goes with a certain GF? If so, which?
(Note: the answers to Parts 1 and 2 are not dependent upon each other. That is, Part 1 asks if GF x can only have theta-role y in a case in which theta-role y might also be allowed with GF z. But Part 2 asks if theta-role x can only be allowed with GF y in a case in which GF y might also allow theta-role z.)

Your answers to Parts 1 and 2 should have the following form, please. Set up a matrix in which the columns are the GFs and the rows are the theta-roles, like so:

	Subject	*DO*	*IO*	*OP*
Agent				
Theme				
Benefactee				
Experiencer				
Instrument				

If one of the example sentences that follows has an agentive Subject, enter the number of that sentence in the proper grid space. If an example sentence has an agentive DO, put the number of that sentence in the proper grid. And so on. If you find that a certain column is empty except for one row, then that GF has only one theta-role associated with it. If you find that a certain row is empty except for one column, then that theta-role has only one GF it can fill.

Do not try to assign every sentence to a grid space (and see Star Problem 3.2, if you find a sentence with a phrase that does not fit). Just one example in each grid is enough to show that that grid space is not empty.

You can answer this by using only my sentences (I think). But if you think you have an example of your own that fills in a grid space that would otherwise remain empty, please write that sentence and show where it fits in the grid.

Part 3

Some people have proposed that each GF in a sentence can have at most one theta-role and that the theta-roles for all the various GFs in a given sentence must be different. Since you know that arguments are generally linked only to GFs, it follows that each argument of a given predicate has a unique theta-role. (That is, you cannot have two experiencers; you cannot have two instruments; etc. Be careful here: a conjoined DO, for example, is still a single DO with a theta-role that goes for the whole DO:

   I bought milk and spaghetti.

Here the conjoined NP *milk and spaghetti* is the theme.)

Do sentences like example 30 present problems for this claim?

Be sure that, if you say there are two GFs with the same theta-role in 30, you check to make sure that both pass whatever diagnostic tests you have for that theta-role.

Limit this discussion to one half of one side of a page.

Part 4

Discuss briefly (limit: half of one side of a page) the issues that pairs of sentences like the following raise for an approach to meaning in which we talk about predicates and theta-roles as distinct entities.

   John buttered the bread.
   John put butter on the bread.

Give another pair of sentences (from the examples) that demonstrate the same kind of problems.

And here, finally, are the example sentences (in no particular order). I think it is possible to answer the questions posed in Parts 1–4 by considering only these data. But so long as you consider all these sentences, if you want to consider others, you are welcome to. If you disagree with my grammaticality judgments, please nonetheless use my judgments to arrive at an answer to the questions. Then if you want to go through the questions a second time using different judgments, you can do that.

Some of the sentences here present questions that are, strictly speaking, not relevant to this homework because they do not speak to the particular questions asked here. I include them because they may get you to thinking about new issues that lie ahead.

Please do not spend countless hours trying to identify the theta-role of every word with a GF in these sentences. Remember, first of all, that not all words are participants in some event, so not all words will get theta-roles. And remember that linguists have argued for years about precisely which theta-role some GF in a given sentence may have. So do not force yourself to do the impossible. Simply identify the theta-roles of enough words to answer the questions. Then stop.

1. John broke the window with a hammer.

2. John caught the ball.

3. John understood the theorem.

4. We drew Mary a picture.

5. The martyr was shot down by the police in order to restore law and order.

6. We regaled Mary with jewels.

7. John broke the window when Mary knocked him against it.

8. Mary was knocked down by accident.

9. Mary was given a diamond ring.

10. We fed Mary fine foods.

11. We surprised Mary.

12. We sent a letter to Sue.

13. John caught a cold.

14. John battled Bill voluntarily. [Only John's will is expressed.]

15. John fought with Bill voluntarily. [Only John's will, again.]

16. We ate the peas after Bill.

17. We ate the peas after the steak.

18. We ate the peas after dark.

19. We ate the peas after our bath.

20. Bill rolled down the hill just for fun.

21. Bill rolled down the hill limp as a rag after he was hit by the tractor.

22. We gave Mary jewels.

23. We feted Mary with fine foods.

24. We feted Mary nude. [We or Mary or both can be nude.]

25. *We feted Mary fat. [There is no resultative reading here.]

26. The kettle was polished shiny by the brute. [Only the kettle winds up shiny.]

27. *John understood the theorem voluntarily.

28. Sue tickled Mary silly voluntarily. [Only Sue's will is expressed; Mary ends up silly.]

29. Mary was chosen by fiat.

30. Bill exchanged books with Mary.

31. John told Mary a lie voluntarily. [Only John's will is expressed.]

32. We paid John.

33. We paid John the money.

34. We paid John with money.

35. John used the hammer to open the door.

36. John died.

37. Mary hit Bill.

38. The flu hit Bill.

39. This piece was written by Mozart in order to please his wife.

40. Mary got arrested by the police voluntarily. [Only Mary's will is expressed.]

41. A piano concerto by Mozart is just what we need.

42. *A piano concerto by Mozart in order to please his mother is just what we need.

43. John helped his parents.

44. Who will take care of Bill?

45. I gave Mary the flu.

46. Let's hammer the door open.

47. I put the blanket around Mary to keep her warm.

*Problem Set 3.4: English Deverbal Nouns and Unaccusatives

Later parts of this book assume you have the acquired the knowledge that is to be gained by doing this problem set.

This is a time-consuming problem set, largely because you need to come up with examples. It is best done by a group of people working together.

In English we can add -*er* to a V to derive an N:

(1) drink, drinker
     swim, swimmer
     eat, eater

The referent of each of the particular nouns in 1 is the person or thing that does the action of the verb. The referent of the noun, then, is identical to the agent argument of the verb in these instances. Thus, a swimmer, for example, is a person or animate thing that swims. However, the referent of these deverbal nouns need not be identical to the agent argument of the verb only, as you will discover below.

Part 1

Think about as many DEVERBAL Ns with -*er* as you can (where a deverbal N is an N that is morphologically derived from a V root). Give an example of a verb-noun pair whose argument for the V and referent for the N is:

(a) an agent (as in 1 above)

(b) an experiencer

(c) a benefactee

(d) a theme (This is harder.)

(e) an instrument (Here, of course, you will also find an agentive reading—but find an example whose most immediate or common referent for the N is instrumental.)

(f) a locative (There are some—relax and try it—think about trains.)

Part 2

Sometimes an -*er* nominal inherits the argument structure of the V, so if the verb takes an Object, the noun can take an Object also (where that Object is most commonly introduced by *of*—a fact we will discuss in chapter 5).

(2)   a loader of hay

But sometimes the noun does not inherit the argument structure of the V:

(3)   Don't break the *toaster*, please.
      *Don't break the toaster of bagels, please.
      (cf. She passes her day as a toaster of bagels.)

Give five examples of -*er* nominals in a sentence where they inherit the argument structure of the V.

Give five examples of -*er* nominals in a sentence in which they do not inherit the argument structure of the V.

Now look at your examples here and in Part 1 above. What can you say about the semantics of -*er* nominals that have argument structure as compared to those that do not? Consider the types of things they refer to.

Part 3

Consider the *spray/load* verbs:

(4)   Jack squirted water on the plants.

(5)   Jack squirted the plants with water.

Notice that the *with*-phrase in 5 is not an instrument, as shown by the fact that we can add a true instrument:

(6)   Jack squirted the plants with water with his new squirt gun.

Let us call the role that the NP *water* plays in 4 and 5 theme and the role that the NP *the plants* plays in 4 and 5 the LOCATUM (a new theta-role that is perhaps the same one we require with verbs like *put*, as you might have discovered in Problem Set 3.1).

Think of several pairs of verbs that fall into this class (that have pairs like 4 and 5). Give five examples. Put those examples in sentences. What argument can the *-er* nominal formed from these verbs take as its referent: agent, instrument, theme, locatum, or possibly more than one?

Part 4

Consider verbs like *fill* that do not fall into the *spray/load* class:

(7)   *Jack filled water into the buckets.

(8)   Jack filled the buckets with water (with a hose).

Here the locatum argument is a DO and the theme is an OP. Give five verbs that appear in a structure like 8 but not like 7. Put those five verbs into sentences. What argument can the *-er* nominal formed from these verbs take as its referent?

Part 5

Are any of the *-er* nominals you have listed so far in this homework derived from strictly intransitive Vs? If so, list them. If not, make a list here of at least five *-er* nominals that derive from intransitive Vs.

Part 6

In Problem Set 6.4 of chapter 6 you will analyze the so-called UNACCUSATIVE verbs of English. For now, let me introduce them briefly. Many of them can appear in both a transitive and an intransitive sentence. But unlike optionally transitive verbs like *eat*, which have an agentive Subject in the active voice regardless of transitivity, the unaccusative verbs have an agent as their Subject in transitive sentences, but a theme as their Subject in intransitive sentences:

(9)   Sally opened the door.

(10) The door opened.

Give five sentence pairs with unaccusative verbs. Then give the -er nominals formed from these unaccusative Vs. What argument do they refer to?

Part 7

Consider all the -er nominals you have thought about while doing this homework. Given them, is there any generalization you can make about the argument that is their referent? For example, think of:

(11)   creeper: *The baby* creeps.
       stripper: *Hal* stripped the walls.

etc. Be sure to line up each nominal with a sentence that it corresponds to and underline the argument of the V that the nominal takes as its referent.
   Now can you see any generalization about the underlined arguments of the V?

Part 8

Consider the nominal *broiler*, meaning "a chicken bred to be broiled" (compare to *fryer*—"a chicken bred to be fried".) *Broil* is an unaccusative verb:

(12)   Jessie broiled the chicken.

(13)   The chicken broiled in a half-hour flat.

And it can be used in a MIDDLE sentence:

(14)   Chickens broil up delicious, believe me.

Again, in Problem Set 6.4 of chapter 6, you will meet the MIDDLE VOICE. For now all you need to keep in mind is that in a middle voice sentence, not only is the verb an unaccusative verb, but the sense of the voice is that the predication happens because of something inherent to the theme, not because of some unstated-agent argument.
   Now which argument in which sentence (the transitive, the unaccusative intransitive, or the middle intransitive) would the nominal *broiler* have to be related to in order to maintain whatever generalization you came to in Part 6 above?
   (Note: If you came to a different statement in Part 6 and a different generalization in Part 7 from what I am thinking of, Part 8 may not seem interesting to you. That does not mean you are wrong. You probably came up with a different range of data from mine—so different generalizations emerged. Do not worry about it.)

Part 9

Some people have claimed that in a nominal like:

(15)   Jack's admirer

the genitive is the theme argument of the nominal (parallel to *Someone admires Jack*).

Other people say that genitives never bear a theta-role. Instead, their semantics is UNDERDETERMINED (or UNDERSPECIFIED) with respect to the head N. So in:

(16)   Jack's photograph

we might have a photograph by Jack, of Jack, that Jack owns, that Jack talked about, that Jack likes, etc. The genitive then just characterizes the photograph as having some underdetermined relationship toward Jack, and the rest of the sentence or the discourse or pragmatics may help us to figure out what that relationship might be.

Still others find a middle ground and argue that with nominals which do not have events as referents (such as *wallet*, *table*, etc.), the genitive has an underdetermined relationship to the head N except when the N is relational, where the genitive's relationship to the head N is then rather tightly constrained (such as *father* in *John's father*, or *partner* in *my partner*). But with nominals that do have events as referents (such as *destruction*, *lecture*, *evaporation*, etc.), the genitive may bear a theta-role. Thus *Jack* would bear no theta role in 17 but would be an agent in 18:

(17)   Jack's chair

(18)   Jack's lecture on birth control

We will discuss these ideas further in chapter 4.

Now consider your answer to Part 2 above. To be consistent with it, how do you (specifically you—not the generic you) have to analyze 15? That is, in your analysis, can or must *Jack* be an argument, or must *Jack* not be an argument? How do the following examples bear on your answer?

(19)   the king's taster

(20)   Jack tastes all the food for the king.

(Please be sure to contrast 19 with 15.)

Part 10

Consider the following -*er* nominals and what they refer to. Do any of them bear on the issues already raised in this problem set? If so, how. If not, discuss the new issues that these raise:

(21)   hammer
        porker (as a derogative term for a fat person)
        whaler (as a ship)
        shutter
        sneakers
        wrecker (as a name for a tow truck)
        looker (as in: *Jeff's a real looker*)
        stickers (as in: *She walked through the overgrown field
        and her socks got full of stickers*)
        creamer (as in: *sugar bowl and creamer*)
        bummer
        jobber

Part 11

If you have studied morphology, you might want to consider the new issues these nominals present:

(22)   philosopher
       burglar
       traitor
       prayer versus *pray-er*
       insider
       outsider

Problem Set 3.5: English Measure Phrases

In the text we met both DOs and measure phrases. A given V might take either a DO or a measure phrase after it. So in 1 we see a DO, but in 2 we find a measure phrase with the same V:

(1)   Jack ate pizza.

(2)   Jack ate a lot.

On our first reading of 2 (that is, without prior context) *a lot* does not tell us what Jack ate, but the extent to which he ate. What about:

(3)   Jack ate a lot of pizza.

Here *a lot of pizza* is what Jack ate, so it is a DO. The words *a lot* tell us that the amount of pizza he ate was large, and so, indirectly, give us information about the extent to which he ate.

In Problem Set 1.1 you learned that it is possible for an NP not to contain a phonetically audible head N (as in [*The poor*] *are always with us*). Although the NPs discussed there did not contain a P (unlike 3, which has the P *of*), the possibility should be entertained that there could be NPs which do not contain a phonetically audible *of* + N. It would be conceivable, then, that 2 is ambiguous between a reading in which *a lot* is a measure phrase and that in which *a lot* is a regular referential NP which is lacking an audible *of* + N. That is, 2 and sentences like it should have not just the measure phrase reading, but also the DO reading. Do they?

In answering this, you should construct dialogues that 2 (or a sentence with a similar syntactic structure to 2) can be a part of. For example, consider the following dialogue:

(4)   —What happened to the cupcakes?
       —I'm sorry. The children ate a lot already.

Does the answer in 4 have two interpretations? If you do not think so, consider whether the answer here leads you to believe that the children did eat cupcakes or did not eat cupcakes or either. Give a paraphrase of the answer in 4 if the children did eat cupcakes. Give a paraphrase if they did not.

How is *a lot* used in 5: as a measure phrase or as a quantifying expression for an NP?

(5)   I like them a lot.

Is *many* in 6 a measure phrase or a quantifying expression for a (missing) NP?

(6)   The children ate many.

Problem Set 3.6: Italian NP Argument Structure

We learned in this chapter that predicates assign theta-roles and that a reflexive usually finds its antecedent within the lowest clause and within the lowest Complete Functional Complex that contains it, where the clauses we looked at had only one predicate and the CFCs we looked at were essentially identical to clauses. We used data from English to come to these conclusions.

Now consider the following Italian NPs:

(1)   l'ultima lezione di Carlo sulla   guerra
      the last lesson of Carlo on-the war
      'the last lesson of Carlo's (by Carlo) on the war'

(2)   la   reazione brutta di Gigina alle   notizie
      the reaction ugly   of Gigina to-the news
      'the bad reaction of Gigina at the news'

(3)   l'annuncio   alla   folla   della decizione finale
      the announcement to-the crowd of-the decision   final
      'the announcement to the crowd of the final decision'

Part 1

Underline the head N in the largest NP (that is, the most inclusive NP) in each of 1–3. Now circle every full NP contained inside the overall NP. Just from these three examples, do you think it makes sense to talk of nouns assigning theta-roles to other members of the NP they head in Italian? If you say yes, tell which theta-role each NP you circled might reasonably bear. If you say no, discuss why not. Notice that if you say yes, you are saying that NPs can be potential CFCs in Italian.

Part 2

Now consider this NP:

(4)   la   lettera di Carlo a se   stesso
      the letter of Carlo to self same

      'the letter by Carlo to himself'

Se stesso, like its English counterpart *himself,* is an anaphor.
What is the antecedent for the reflexive in 4?
(Note: If you know Italian, please do not substitute the stressed reflexive *sè* for *se stesso* in this problem set. The facts involving the stressed reflexive are much more complicated than those involving *se stesso* and can—and have—served as the focus of lengthy manuscripts.)

Part 3

Now let us place the NP in 4 in a sentence:

> (5) Ho trovato la lettera di Carlo a se   stesso.
>   have found the letter of Carlo to self same
>   '(I) have found the letter by Carlo to himself.'

What is the antecedent for the reflexive in 5?

Part 4

Consider now these sentences:

> (6) *Ho   trovato la   lettera di Carlo a me stessa.
>   have found   the letter of Carlo to me same
>   *'(I) found the letter by Carlo to myself.'

> (7) *Carlo ha trovato la   lettera di Maria a se   stresso.
>   Carlo has found   the letter of Maria to self same
>   *'Carlo has found the letter by Maria to himself.'

If 6 and 7 are ungrammatical because they are violations of Binding Theory, what condition of Binding Theory do you think they violate? In answering this, you will have to think more about locality. The real question you need to ask yourself is: can an NP be a CFC? Once you have come to grips with this question, then you will be able to tie the ungrammaticality of 6 and 7 into Binding Theory.

Part 5

The sentence in 8 is not ambiguous. What does it mean?

> (8) Giorgio ha trovato la lettera di Carlo a se stesso.

Be sure to point out the antecedent for the reflexive.

Part 6

Choose English examples to show that everything you have discovered about Italian NPs above is true of English, as well.

Part 7

Now consider the following English and Italian NPs ("Calvino" is the name of a novelist):

> (9)   her book of Calvino's
>   il suo libro di Calvino

> (10) *her book of Calvino's about herself
>   *il suo libro di Calvino su di se stessa

(cf. her; book of Calvino's about her;
il suo; libro di Calvino su di lei;)

(11)   her book of Calvino;'s about himself;
il suo libro di Calvino; su di se stesso;

What is the semantic function of *her/suo* in these examples? What is the semantic function of *Calvino* in these examples? (If you think an NP bears a theta-role, say that and specify which theta-role you think it bears.)

For now you have no explanation for the fact that the examples in 10 are ungrammatical, while the examples in parentheses under 10 are grammatical. The explanation for 10 is controversial. You will eventually find one possible explanation for these facts in this book in chapter 8, where we develop the idea of A-binder versus non-A-binder. For now, you should tuck this fact away along with all the other mysteries of binding that you have been and will be coming across in the material up to chapter 8.

Problem Set 3.7: Japanese Passives

Japanese has passive sentences in which transitive verbs are found (as in English):

(1)   Sensei-ga   seito-ni   kerareta.
teacher-SUBJ pupil-BY was kicked
'The teacher was kicked by the pupil.'

The *ga* and *ni* after the Ns in 1 are called particles (and they are quite different from particles as in verb-particle combinations like *look up*). They are often claimed to mark the GF of a NP (but we will see some problems for this claim in later problem sets). So the Subject is marked by *ga*, the DO by *o*, and the IO by *ni*. The agentive in a passive sentence is also marked by *ni*, as you can see in 1. Furthermore, Japanese distinguishes a TOPIC NP with the particle *wa*. A sentence with a topic NP can often be translated by "as for NP" followed by the rest of the sentence. That is, the topic is introduced and some statement that relates to the topic is then uttered. Do not worry too much about the particles in this problem set. Just use the brief information given here.

In addition to passives like that in 1, Japanese also has passive sentences in which intransitive verbs are found (unlike in English):

(2)   Sensei-ga   seito-ni   nakareta.
teacher-SUBJ pupil-BY was cried
literally: The teacher was cried by the pupil.
'The pupil cried, which affected the teacher.'

However, not all active sentences that lack a Direct Object have a good passive counterpart in Japanese. In 3–5 we find three good passives with active counterparts that lack a Direct Object. These passives are characterized as "funny" but grammatical by Washio (1986/87, listed in the bibliography). Other native speakers have told me that they are marginal or ungrammatical (especially examples 4 and

5). However, for the purposes of this problem set, please assume they are grammatical:

> (3) Boku-wa taiya-ni pankusareta.
>   I-TOP   tire-BY was gone flat
>   literally: I was *gone flat* by the tire.
>   'The tire went flat, which affected me.'

> (4) Boku-wa tokei-ni   tomarareta.
>   I-TOP   clock-BY was ceased
>   literally: I was *ceased* by the clock.
>   'My watch ceased, which affected me.'

> (5) Boku-wa inku-ni kawakareta.
>   I-TOP   ink-BY was grown dry
>   literally: I was *grown dry* by the ink.
>   'The ink grew dry, which affected me.'

In 6–8, on the other hand, we find three ungrammatical passives with active counterparts that lack a Direct Object. (The verb morphology here indicates a combination of passive and potential. The important point for us is the presence of the passive morpheme.)

> (6) *Boku-wa mado-ni   warerareta.
>   I-TOP   window-BY was broken
>   literally: I was *broken* by the window.
>   'The window broke, which affected me.'

> (7) *Boku-wa kutu-no himo-ni hodokerareta.
>   I-TOP   shoe-OF lace-BY was untied
>   literally: I was *untied* by the shoelace.
>   'My shoelace untied, which affected me.'

> (8) *Boku-wa zubon-ni nugerareta.
>   I-TOP   pants-BY was undressed
>   literally: I was *undressed* by the pants.
>   'My pants fell off, which affected me.'

Assume that the subcategorization frames for the Japanese predicates in 3–8 are identical to the English glosses that I have chosen for you above. (Note: The English word-by-word glosses—not the translations—that I have supplied in 3–8 may not be the ones that a bilingual Japanese/English speaker would choose. I have selected them so that you may safely make the assumption I am asking you to make in this paragraph. Look particularly at the italicized predicates in the English glosses. Even if you are a native speaker of Japanese, I ask you to focus on these glosses as you do this problem set.)

  Try to make a statement that will account for which types of verbs can appear in passive sentences in Japanese. Use your knowledge of subcategorization frames in doing this.

Star Problem 3.1

In this chapter we mentioned that some lexical items consist of a V plus a particle, such as *run over* and *look up*.

Give at least one argument to the effect that particles are Ps.

Give at least one argument supporting the idea that particles are not PPs.

If you have given these two arguments, you now find yourself in an uncomfortable situation. Why would a P be blocked from filling the whole phrase, and thus be blocked from being a PP? Is there some sort of semantic integrity that a phrase must have that particles don't have? If you try that tack, you will have to face the question of why *care* in *take care (of)* seems to be a phrase, given that it can be the Subject of a passive sentence:

(1) (Decent) care must be taken of those patients.

Star Problem 3.2

In Problem Set 3.3 a list of sentences is given from which you are to find examples to use in the matrix table (thus exploring the match between theta-roles and GFs). Some of these sentences may have presented questions for you about theta-roles in general (that is why I explicitly told you not to try to force every example into a grid space). These problematic sentences were placed there on purpose. Take one or more of those problems and explore them here. Present a problematic sentence. State clearly what question or problem it presents. Offer a hypothesis that will either answer the question or solve the problem. Find supporting or disconfirming evidence for your hypothesis. If a first hypothesis is disconfirmed, offer another. Find supporting or disconfirming evidence, and so on, until you find a hypothesis that seems to work.

Star Problem 3.3

In chapter 3 we noted that when you have a string like:

(1) NP V NP {to/for} NP

we can test to see if the second NP following the V is an IO by seeing if it can occur preceding the first NP following the V. By this test, *the new kid* is an IO in 2:

(2) Martin gave a book to the new kid.

(3) Martin gave the new kid a book.

An example with *for* is:

(4) Martin baked a cake for the new kid.

(5) Martin baked the new kid a cake.

This is a sufficient test for IO, but not a necessary one. Sometimes we have *to* or *for* introducing an NP, but there is no DO, as in:

(6)   I sang to Martin.

So the test can't apply directly to 6 and we do not know whether *Martin* is an IO or not. However, the fact that the test works when we do add a DO to 6 suggests that even in 6 *Martin* is an IO:

(7)   I sang a lullaby to Martin.

(8)   I sang Martin a lullaby.

Still, sometimes even NPs that certainly seem to be IOs by other criteria (such as the fact that they have the theta-role of benefactee or recipient) fail the test:

(9)   I spoke to Martin.

(10)   I spoke Latin to Martin.

(11)   *I spoke Martin Latin.

From here on, please consider IOs that involve *to* only, not *for*.

In this problem I would like you to try to figure out what factors make a *to* appropriate or inappropriate in introducing an IO. You will find yourself naturally discussing the participatory role of the NP that immediately follows the V in the action of the sentence. In doing this, you should uncover some subtle semantic differences between sentences with a *to* and sentences with the Double Object construction. Please expect exceptions to arise. The point is to come up with a generalization that holds of most of the sentences you can think of. Then list all the exceptions you have come across and perhaps you will find motivation for their exceptional behavior (but perhaps not). You might consider examples such as:

(12)   Jack gave Mary a book.
       Jack gave a book to Mary.

(13)   Jack gave Mary the creeps.
       *Jack gave the creeps to Mary.

(14)   Measle germs give you measles.
       *Measle germs give measles to you.

(15)   The judge spared John the ordeal.
       *The judge spared the ordeal to John.

(16)   *We left chance the outcome.
       We left the outcome to chance.

(17)   *Cast the wind your fate.
       Cast your fate to the wind.

(18)   *I donated charity money.
       I donated money to charity.

(19)   *Sock me it. (Compare: Hand me it.)
       Sock it to me.

Once you have an idea of what's going on, consider the contexts in which you might choose to say 20 and those in which you might choose to say 21:

(20)   I paid Stuart the rent.

(21)   I paid the rent to Stuart.

There is a difference here, though delicate. Will the generalization you came to above account for this difference?

Star Problem 3.4

Consider the sentence:

(1)   Fred paid the criminal.

Is *the criminal* a theme or a benefactee here? In answering this, consider the sentences below and use what you learned from doing Star Problem 3.3 above:

(2)   Fred paid the criminal the ransom.

(3)   Fred paid the ransom to the criminal.

(4)   *Fred paid to the criminal.

Other sentences that pattern like 1–4, where I give the example parallel to 2 in each case, are:

(5)   Patty served the fat man two desserts.

(6)   We telephoned Mamma the bad news.

(In discussions of tennis, *serve* can be used with a *to* phrase in the absence of a DO. But in the context of serving food as in a restaurant, *serve* patterns as claimed above.) On the other hand, I do not believe there are any sentences parallel to 1 with a verb that takes a *for* benefactee:

(7)   Please choose a coat for me.
      Please choose me a coat.
      *Please choose me.

(8)   Sally cooked a chicken for us.
      Sally cooked us a chicken.
      *Sally cooked us.

These sentences, however, can have a *for* benefactee in the absence of a theme argument, in contrast to 4 above:

(9)   Please choose for me.

(10) Sally cooked for us.

The contrast between verbs that take *to* and those that take *for* is not that clean, however, since most verbs that take *to* exhibit the pattern in 7–10 and not the pattern in 1–6:

(11)   I read a long poem to Sue.
        I read Sue a long poem.
        *I read Sue.
        I read to Sue.

Verbs like *pay* and *serve* and *telephone*, then, are exceptional and you will need to try to figure out why.

Once you have a handle on the two patterns above (that in 1–6 and that in 7–10), you might try to account for a third pattern exhibited with a handful of verbs:

(12)   She wrote a letter to Bill.
        She wrote Bill a letter.
        She wrote Bill.
        She wrote to Bill.

Star Problem 3.5

Compare pairs like:

(1)   John got hurt.

(2)   John hurt himself.

1 is called a "get-inchoative." "Inchoative" is the term generally given to verbs that involve a change of state which simply happens to the Subject, rather than being brought about by the Subject, as in:

(3)   The sky reddened.

(4)   The soup thickened.

(5)   The little children gradually sickened.

The question for you is: Is 2 an inchoative or a true reflexive sentence. (If 2 is an inchoative, it would mean that John wound up hurt, but he was not the agent in the hurting. If 2 is a true reflexive sentence, it would mean that John wound up hurt and he was the one who brought about the hurting.) Are there any inchoatives in English that use reflexive pronouns? (Inchoatives in the Romance languages, for example, typically use reflexive pronouns.)

Star Problem 3.6

Discuss the interpretation of the NP that follows *than* in sentences such as:

(1)   Mary is taller than Bill.
        Mary kissed Pete more than Bill.

Does this NP have a fixed theta-role? Does it have the same theta-role as some other NP in the clause preceding *than*? Does it lack a theta-role entirely?

Compare the interpretation of *than NP* phrases to *than* followed by a clause, as in:

(2)   Mary is taller than Bill is.
       Mary kissed Pete more than Bill did.
       Mary kissed Pete more than she did Bill.

Be sure to consider more fanciful comparatives such as:

(3)   Mary eats faster than a tornado.

If you come to the conclusion that the NP in a *than NP* phrase receives a theta-role, how does this affect our claim that each argument of a given predicate has a unique theta-role?

If you come to the conclusion that the NP in a *than NP* phrase does not receive a theta-role, how do you account for the licensing of this NP?

Star Problem 3.7

There are many types of compounds in English. Pick one of the types listed below and discuss any restrictions on it that involve Theta Theory, subcategorization, modification, or predication. Do not limit yourself to just these examples.

Noun Compounds

Compounds made up of two Ns, where the second is an -*er* nominalization:

(1)   record player, pipe smoker, wall paper hanger, hair dryer

Compounds made up of two Ns:

(2)   apron string, teakettle, sunshine, mill wheel, linguistics student, hubcap

Compounds made up of P plus N:

(3)   overdose, underdog, uprising, onlooker, uptown, inland

Compounds made up of A plus N:

(4)   high school, smallpox, sharpshooter, well-wisher

Compounds made up of V plus N:

(5)   swearword, whetstone, scrubwoman, rattlesnake

Adjective Compounds

Made up of N A:

(6)   headstrong, honey-sweet, skin-deep, nationwide

Made up of A A:

(7)   icy cold, white-hot, worldly-wise, widespread, highstrung

Made up of P A:

(8)   overwide, overripe, ingrown, underfed, above-mentioned

Made up of N V, where the V is a progressive participle:

(9)   pipe-smoking, tobacco-chewing, mind-boggling, beer-chugging

Made up of A V, where the V is a progressive participle:

(10)   sweet-smelling, loud-talking, bitter-tasting, easygoing

Made up of A with a small set of (usually) obscene words infixed into the A to form an emphatic A:

(11)   fanfreakingtastic, unfreakingbelievable, otherfreakingworldly

(There are some interesting constraints here: *fantastfreakingtic, *unbefreak-inglievable, etc. If you know something about phonology and morphology, this could be particularly fun to work on.)

Verb Compounds

Made up of P V:

(12)   outlive, overdo, offset, uproot, underfeed, overstep

Made up of N V:

(13)   globe-trot, stage-manage, air-condition, window-shop

(Perhaps these are formed via their noun-compound counterpart:

globe-trotter, stage-manager, air-conditioner, window-shopper.)

Made up of A V:

(14)   sharpshoot, dry-clean, whitewash, roughcast

(Again, these might be formed via their noun-compound or adjective-compound counterparts:

sharpshooter, dry-cleaning, whitewashed, roughcast.)

Multiple-Word Compounds

(15)   bathroom towel rack, law-school language requirement, term-paper proposal

Overview

Binding Theory

We have not learned anything new about BT in this chapter. Thus, we still have only two conditions to BT:

(A) Anaphors must be locally bound.

(B) Pronouns must be locally free.

We have set the stage for testing whether two items are to be called local to one another if they are members of the same clause or if they are members of the same CFC. And we have pointed out that these are not the only possible definitions of locality, but that they are reasonable ones to test first.

X-Bar Theory

We remain with the knowledge we had at the end of chapter 2. There are major and minor categories, and the first can head phrases.

Case Theory

We remain with the knowledge we had at the end of chapter 2. In English Subjects of tensed clauses have Subjective Case, whereas nominals in other positions have Objective or genitive Case.

Theta Theory

Our major advance in this chapter has been the development of a Theta Theory. We argued that predicates assign theta-roles to their arguments within their CFC. The roles we pointed out are agent, theme, benefactee, instrument, and experiencer. We pointed out that the ability of a predicate to assign a theta-role is part of the lexical information we know about words and that each argument is assigned a unique theta-role.

We also pointed out that there is a linking mechanism that maps between the predicate-argument structure of a lexical item and its subcategorization frame. We know that GFs other than IO (as you discovered in Problem Set 3.3) need not be filled with arguments, but all arguments (so far as we know at this point) must be linked to a GF.

We adopted the Theta Criterion:

> Every argument must be assigned a theta-role and every
> theta-role must be assigned to an argument.

After doing Problem Set 3.3, you know that the Theta Criterion is to be interpreted as limiting a given argument to receiving only one theta-role from a given predicate and as limiting a given theta-role to being assigned to only one argument of a given predicate.

Licensing

We also learned that every element in a sentence must be licensed: An argument, a modifier, a predicate, and a GF are the functional roles we have discussed thus far that license an element. (For that last point, consider the licensing of dummy Subjects in clauses that require an overt Subject.)

4

X-Bar Theory

Subcategorization of Heads

In chapter 3 we discussed the fact that verbs can be subcategorized according to whether or not they must, may, or cannot take DOs, IOs, and sometimes other types of items. In Problem Set 3.1 you found that prepositions, also, can be subcategorized as to whether they must take Objects:

(1)   Jack went [into the house].
       *Jack went [into].

or may take Objects:

(2)   Jack went [in the house].
       Jack went [in].

or, perhaps even cannot take Objects:

(3)   Jack went [there].

(Certainly *there* passes the *right*-test for PPs that you learned in Problem Set 1.2. But you may have concluded either that *there* itself is a P—in which case, it is a strictly intransitive P—or that *there* is the Object of a phonetically null P. At this point in our studies we have no way to choose between the two possibilities.) We can add here another parallel between Ps and Vs that you discovered in Problem Set 3.1: some Ps take only sentential Objects, just as some Vs do:

(4)   She left [while he was talking].
       *She left [while the lecture].

(5)   I suppose [that he's coming].
       *I suppose [{the result/ the fact}].

You were also exposed in that problem set to the idea that Adjectives can be subcategorized for whether they must take an Object (which is preceded by a P, a point to which we return in chapter 5):

(6)   Jack is [fond of Sue].
       *Jack is [fond].

or may take an Object:

(7)   Jack is [dependent on Sue].
       Jack is [dependent].

or cannot take an Object:

(8)   The cow is [domesticated].

In fact, even nouns can be subcategorized in this way. Thus some may take Objects (introduced by a P, again, just as adjectives' Objects are introduced by a P):

(9)   the destruction of the city
       the destruction

and others cannot take Objects:

(10)   the wallet

PPs can occur inside NPs like the one in 10, but only when they serve to modify the N (as in: *the wallet of pigskin*). So 10 gives an example of an obligatorily "intransitive" N. Unlike Vs, Ps, and As, however, there do not seem to be any Ns that must take an Object. Can you think of any?

What Is Subcategorization All About?
The Analysis of *While* Phrases

Before we pursue the structural questions raised by these facts, let us stop a moment and ask whether there possibly are semantic explanations for them. Consider 4 and 5 again:

(11)   a.   She left [while he was talking].
       b.   *She left [while the lecture].

(12)   I suppose [that he's coming].
       *I suppose [the result/the fact].

Certainly lectures (as in the asterisked sentence of 11) take place over a period of time, so there should be no semantic incoherence in *while the lecture*. That might lead us to the conclusion that the restriction seen in 11 is a syntactic one. On the other hand, it is not, in fact, strictly true that only clauses can appear as the Objects of *while*:

(13)   a.   She met him while on vacation.
       b.   While in the Bahamas, she decided to quit her job.

Here there is a PP complement of *while*. And, in fact, certain APs can be the complement of *while*:

(14)   a. She drew that, you're not gonna believe this, while asleep!
       b. While depressed and impoverished, she still managed to raise those
          children.

In fact, if we consider the "despite" sense of *while* that can arise in 14b, we find that
even though NPs that could easily evoke a sense of duration are rejected as possible
complements of *while*, as in 11 above and in:

(15)   a. *She left him while autumn.
       b. *She learned everything while the army. (cf. She learned everything
          while in the army.)

NPs that are predicational are accepted:

(16)   a. While a rather inexperienced person, she is still no fool.
       b. While a blithering idiot, he is still the chairman.

These facts offer strong evidence that the restriction on the range of complement
types of *while* is not syntactic in nature, after all, but semantic.

What do the clauses, PPs, APs, and predicational NPs in the acceptable sentences
above have in common that the NPs in the unacceptable sentences do not? Ask
yourself how you would expand the *while* phrases above if someone were to ask you
what they meant. Reasonable expansions include:

(17)   (cf. 13a) while on vacation → while she was on vacation
       (cf. 14a) while asleep → while she was asleep
       (cf. 16a) while a rather inexperienced person → while she is a rather
                  inexperienced person

So the complements of *while* in these phrases are all mapped onto PROPOSITIONS
in semantic structure. That is, their semantic status is the same as that of a clause
and differs from the ordinary semantic status of NPs. They semantically indicate
events with a predicate (a state or action) and arguments (role players), in contrast
to NPs, which typically indicate reference only. Accordingly, phrases that generally
modify only predicates can occur in these *while* phrases:

(18)   She must have written that while [still] off her rocker. While in trouble
       [often], she was still a pretty good kid.

(In chapter 3 we used the term *adverbial* to refer to modifiers of a verb, regardless
of their category. So, for example, the adverb *quietly*, the PP *without a sound*, the
embedded clause *after he came in*, and the NP *last Tuesday* can all be adverbials.
We will now extend that term to cover all modifiers (regardless of their category) of
anything other than a nominal. Thus the bracketed phrases in 18 are adverbials.)

But this cannot be the whole story. Looking back at the unacceptable complements to *while*, we find that these NPs also could just as reasonably be mapped onto
propositions:

(19)   a. (cf. 11b) while the lecture → while the lecture was in progress
       b. (cf. 15a) while autumn → while it was autumn
       c. (cf. 15b) while the army → while she was in the army

There is, however, an important difference between the propositions that we are led to construct in 19 and those that we are led to construct in 17. This difference is not immediately apparent, so we need to take a closer look. Let us start with 17.

Uses of the Copula

In 17 the only verb we need to add in our construction of the proposition is the copula, which is, in fact, among our least predicative verbs (that is, it is semantically quite uninformative). For example, in 20 the APs, NPs, and PPs tell us the state or action, not the copula:

(20) Mary is finally quiet.
      Jack is a doctor.
      Mavis is outside.

What function does the copula play in these examples? Ask yourself what information we would lose if English allowed sentences that did not have verb strings. Besides the usual information of state or action, a verb string can show the tense, aspect, and modality of the event, as we learned in chapter 2. If we allowed sentences without verb strings, we would have to find other strategies for figuring out the tense, aspect, and modality of the event. There are many languages, which, in fact, do exactly that. The Egyptian Arabic translations of 20, for example, would not include a form of the copula. But if these English sentences were in the past tense, their Egyptian Arabic translations would include the copula. Russian behaves exactly as Egyptian Arabic in this respect. That is, if the copula does not appear, the strategy is to read the event as having the same time frame we would assign to a present-tense verb. (You can explore the Egyptian Arabic constructions in Problem Set 8.8 of chapter 8.) The copula in 20, then, while the only verb in the sentence, behaves semantically like an auxiliary (and you will see more of this in Problem Set 4.1). (By the way, take a look at the use of *while* in the sentence you just read!)

This is not to say that the copula never contributes any information of a different sort from an auxiliary. It can contribute a sense of intention or probability that some linguists might argue is not to be identified with the typical auxiliary contribution of modality:

(21) Mary is to leave tomorrow.

And it can (archaically) indicate existence:

(22) I think therefore I am.
      God is.
      The government just is!

Returning to *While*

But in the expansions in 17 we see only the semantically auxiliary use of the copula. Furthermore, the tense of that copula matches the tense of the verb string in the main clause (for 13a and 14a, past tense; for 16a, present tense).

The only other element we find in the expansion of 17 is a pronoun that is understood as coreferential with an NP in the higher clause of 13a, 14a, and 16a.

That means that the complements of *while* in 17 before expansion already contained predicates and that the subjects of these predicates were already present in the overall sentence in 13a, 14a, and 16a before expansion. Thus all the semantically meaningful elements that appear in the expansion of 17 are uniquely determined by the elements in the main clause. The appearance of *be* in the expansion does nothing more than carry tense, and the tense matches the main clause's tense. The pronoun that appears in the expansion must be coreferential with some NP in the main clause.

On the other hand, the expansion in 19, repeated here for convenience, calls for additional elements that are not determined by elements already present in the main clause.

(23)   while the lecture → while the lecture was in progress
       while autumn → while it was autumn
       while the army → while she was in the army

Here the predicate *in progress* is added; the so-called dummy-*it* of weather and time expressions is added; the relational P *in* is added. These elements are not determined by anything in the main clause. Nothing in the main clause, for example, tells us that the lecture had to be in progress as opposed to ending ("while the lecture was ending") or just beginning ("while the lecture was beginning"). And expansions of these *while* phrases that are parallel to the expansions in 17 are inappropriate:

(24)   while the lecture ↛ while she was the lecture
       while autumn ↛ while she was autumn
       while the army ↛ while she was the army

I suggest, then, that *while* selects a complement of any category, but in semantic structure that complement must be mapped onto a proposition. If the complement is a clause, then ordinary rules for mapping clauses into propositions will apply. If the complement is some category other than a clause, then the mapping onto a proposition must be entirely determined by elements already syntactically present in the overall sentence.

This approach is adequate for the *while* examples we have studied here. In Star Problem 4.1 you can determine whether a similar approach adequately accounts for the behavior of sentences with *suppose*, as in 5 above, or whether some other syntactic, semantic, or combination restriction is at work.

The point of the above discussion is that very often there are relevant semantic factors that can serve to obfuscate what the syntactic subcategorization facts really are. You have now been alerted to this fact and you can seek those factors in the future.

X-Bar Syntax: Phrase Structure across Categories

We are now about to set out on a garden path that we will not abandon until the end of the next text section. Many have followed this path before us, and articles written before the mid-1980s may well have adopted some of the analyses we are about to discuss and reject. My hope is that by considering this path seriously before rejecting it, you will have a better appreciation of our final conclusion.

The discussion of examples 1–10 suggests that there are some similarities between VP, PP, AP, and NP with regard to internal structure. In fact, it has been proposed that all major categories have parallel internal structure, of the form in 25:

(25)

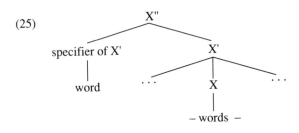

(In example 25 and throughout the rest of this book, we will speak of "specifier of X'." However, some works use the phrase "specifier of X"" to refer to the same item—the left sister of X' in 25.) For many years linguists took the position that structures like that in 25 were GENERATED by PHRASE STRUCTURE (PS) RULES (rewriting rules), as in 26:

(26) $X'' \rightarrow$ spec of X', X'
      $X' \rightarrow \ldots X \ldots$
      $X \rightarrow$ lexical items

Today, however, many linguists have dispensed with PS rules. They argue that (1) the recognition that lexical items have argument frames that are linked to syntactic positions (as we saw in chapter 3), plus (2) the recognition of subcategorization frames, and (3) certain facts about Case Theory (which we will discuss in chapter 5), allow us access to all the information that PS rules would give us. Thus PS rules are redundant. We will not be making use of PS rules in this book, so we will not enter into this debate. Once you have read chapter 5, you may want to return to this issue and ask yourself whether we need PS rules to determine which items can fill the dots on either side of X in 25 and to determine which order the elements under X' come in.

In the diagram in example 25, X ranges across all major categories (V, P, A, and N—the only major categories we know at this point). At the lowest level, called the lexical level and written as X (sometimes with a zero superscript, as in X^0), we have the nodes from which our lexical items hang. (So in a given diagram a V might have *run* under it, an N might have *dog* under it, and so on.) The lexical-level node X is the head of its phrase (a term we have been familiar with since Problem Set 1.1).

At the next level up, the head X is found with dots on either side. This head, of course, determines the category of the whole phrase. Thus if the head is an N, the whole phrase will be an NP; if the head is a V, the whole phrase will be a VP; and so on. The dots on either side of the head represent possible positions for items that either modify the head or are arguments of the head. Any item that is on the same level as X and hangs from the same node is called a SISTER to X. X plus all its sisters makes up the intermediary level that we call X' (read "X bar"). (While I will represent below all complements and modifiers of a head X as sisters to X, there are arguments that the X' level has a more complex internal structure. We will discuss some of these arguments in Tangent 8.1 of chapter 8.)

The sister to X' for now is written as *specifier of X'*, and we will replace that label with a category label once we demonstrate what "specifier of X'" means below. X' and the specifier of X' together make up the X" level (read "X double-bar level"). X" is the symbol used for the phrasal level, and it is entirely interchangeable with the symbol XP.

There are at least two reasons for you to feel discomfort with the schema in 25. First, we have not demonstrated what any of these symbols other than X" or X might be filled by in terms of lexical items, so the discussion of 25 is ungrounded for you. Second, we have not justified the breakdown of the intermediary level, X'. That is, we all recognize that X exists—an easy recognition to make since most Xs are single words of our vocabulary. And surely we all recognize that X" exists, since right from chapter 1 on we have dealt with the notion of phrases and used our cleft test to identify phrases. But unless you did Star Problem 1.1, you may not yet have considered any evidence that is pertinent to the internal breakdown of the phrase. Thus the idea that X' exists is new to us. We will now work to gain a greater understanding of the specifier of X' and of the X' level.

Let us begin our demonstration with NPs. We learned in Problem Set 1.1 that NPs can consist of just a simple N:

(27)   My brother likes [milk$_{NP}$].

Find at least ten other Ns that we could substitute for *milk* in 27 and still have a grammatical sentence. Not all Ns work:

(28)   #My brother likes [friend].

Example 28 is ungrammatical unless we understand *friend* to be the name of something (perhaps Jeff's nickname, for example). The symbol "#" indicates that this sentence is ungrammatical outside of the special context. Find at least ten other Ns that, like *friend*, yield an ungrammatical sentence if we substitute them into 27 for *milk*. Now look at your two lists of Ns. Do you notice anything about them that might account for why they pattern as they do? Try pluralizing the nouns. Suddenly we find that *milks* is odd in 27 unless we mean it as types of milk (cow milk, goat milk, pig milk, etc.) or discrete quantities of milk (pints of milk, quarts of milk, etc.).

(29)   #My brother likes milks.

But *friends* is fine with no special context called for:

(30)   My brother likes friends.

Why should this be? We call Ns like *milk* MASS NOUNS and Ns like *friend* COUNT NOUNS. The latter can be counted with ease (one friend, two friends, many friends);

the former can be counted only if it is taken to mean types or specific quantities (one milk, two milks, many milks). Thus it is a semantic property of the N which determines the ease with which we understand it when it occurs alone to fill an NP. For that reason we will say that from a syntactic point of view, N can fill NP—and we will leave any refinements on that claim to the semanticists.

But, of course, Ns need not fill NP. The most common accompaniment to an N within an NP is some sort of SPECIFIER, of which you have already been introduced to the type called the DETERMINER, including the DEFINITE ARTICLE (which is invariant for number) and the INDEFINITE ARTICLE (which appears only with singular Ns):

(31)   the dog, the dogs
        a dog, *a dogs
        an apple, *an apples

As we mentioned in chapter 1, the definite article typically appears with NPs that are old information to the discourse, whereas the indefinite article introduces new NPs into the discourse. Accordingly, we do not expect them to co-occur, and they in fact cannot.

Appearing in complementary distribution to articles are the DEMONSTRATIVE ADJECTIVES:

(32)   this dog, these dogs
        (cf. *a this dog, *this a dog)

        that dog, those dogs
        (cf. *the those dogs, *those the dogs)

Like the definite articles, these adjectives typically introduce NPs that are old information to the discourse. They are, additionally, DEICTIC (or INDEXICAL) in that they point out an item. For example, *this/these* points to close objects, while *that/those* points to (comparatively speaking) more distant objects. Once more, given the sense of demonstrative adjectives and the sense of articles, we may feel satisfied that their inability to co-occur within an NP follows from their sense.

Numerals and quantifiers can also introduce Ns:

(33)   five dogs . . .
        all dogs, many dogs, few dogs, most dogs . . .
        each dog, every dog

Again, since these words function to pick out the number or quantity of items with the sense of the head N that are playing a role in the utterance, they contribute to our ability to find the intended referent of the NP. However, numerals and quantifiers can co-occur with each other and with articles and demonstrative adjectives:

(34)   those five dogs
        all the dogs

Not all combinations are grammatical, of course. As we would expect, the singular indefinite article cannot co-occur with either numerals or quantifiers, since most of those involve the notion of plurality somehow (*a five dogs, *all a poodle). The only numeral that does not involve plurality is *one*. And, in fact, some linguists have proposed that *a/an* is a phonetically reduced form of *one*, accounting thereby for their inability to co-occur (*a one dog). (However, stressed *one* can co-occur with singular demonstrative adjectives (*that one dog*), unlike *a*.) Likewise, singular demonstrative adjectives cannot co-occur with numerals or quantifiers (*that five dogs, *all that poodles).

NPs like those in 33 and 34 are called QUANTIFIED NPs (QNPs) because they have a numeral or a quantifier introducing the N. You will be asked to examine one kind of QNP in Problem Set 4.2. However, even without giving much thought to any wider range of data, you should already be somewhat suspicious of any analysis of quantifiers that would label them specifiers. Why? Look closely at 25 and then consider 34. How could all the lexical items in 34 fit into the schema in 25? If specifier of X′ is a lexical node under which a minor-category word hangs, then we'd be led to claim that a string like *those five* or *all the* is a single lexical item. This is nonsense. We need a more adequate analysis of quantifiers, and, accordingly, a more adequate analysis of phrases that contain nominals. But we are getting ahead of ourselves. Hold onto this niggling problem and let us continue on the path we set out on.

In all the NPs we have examined thus far, the specifier of NP introduces it both in the sense that it relates the NP to the rest of the discourse semantically and in the sense that it is the first item within the NP linearly. The specifier usually relates the NP to the rest of the discourse by giving us information such as whether the NP is new, whether it is close, and how much of the type of N we are discussing is involved. Thus the specifier helps us to pick out the appropriate referent in the universe of the utterance for this NP.

Besides a specifier, an NP can contain arguments of the head N and modifiers of that N. You already have a good idea of what arguments are (we discussed them in the context of verbs in chapter 3) and an operative idea of what modifiers are, so for the moment, let us rely on those ideas as background and discuss specifiers of phrases other than NP and then return to a more complete discussion of arguments and modifiers of N.

Determiners (articles and demonstrative adjectives) have been called minor-category words because it would appear that, unlike N, for example, they do not take their own specifiers, modifiers, or arguments. In this sense, they are not EXPANDABLE. (They do not head their own phrase.)

Does an AP, like an NP, have a specifier? First note that most adjectives can occur alone, forming a single-word AP:

(35)   the [tired] boy
        The boy is [tired].

The few that cannot are the obligatorily transitive ones (like *fond* in 6 above). If AP had a specifier, and if its specifier were similar in function to the specifiers of NP that we have looked at thus far, we would expect specifiers of AP not to add information about the basic sense of the A, but either to relate the A to the context (as determiners do for NPs) or to indicate the degree or extent of the A (just as numerals and quantifiers indicate the quantity of the N). With that clue, it is easy to come up with words that seem to be AP specifiers:

(36)   {that/rather/quite/very/ . . . } intelligent

We will call these words INTENSIFIERS. As with determiners, they cannot co-occur, although some of them can be repeated for emphasis:

(37)   a.   *quite, very intelligent
            *that, more intelligent

       b.   very very intelligent
            quite quite intelligent

Like the numerals and quantifiers that appear in NPs, there are quantificational words that occur in APs:

(38)   {more/not/most/so . . . } intelligent

And just as the numerals and quantifiers can co-occur with each other and with determiners in NPs, so these quantificational words can co-ocur with each other and with intensifiers in APs:

(39)   not more intelligent
       not very intelligent
       rather more intelligent
       so very intelligent

Once more, we are struck by the fact that quantificational words create obvious problems for the schema in 25: 39 (with APs) is just as difficult to align with 25 as 34 (with NPs) was.

(If you were surprised at the inclusion of *so* in the list of quantificational words in 38, you are not alone. Many linguists would not include *so* in this list. However, the fact that *so* behaves like quantificational elements in 39 is evidence for its membership on the list. And there are a variety of other ways in which *so* shows characteristics that are common to quantificational elements. The syntactic and semantic behavior of *so* could certainly serve as a topic for research once you have completed this book.)

Does PP have any elements parallel to the determiners, numerals, and quantifiers of NPs or the intensifiers and quantificational elements of APs which function as specifiers for PP? You have already come across one: the *right* that we have used since Problem Set 1.2 as a diagnostic for PPs:

(40)   She went [right in (the house)].

Certainly, this *right* is homophonous with at least two adjectives *right*:

(41)   a.   You're wrong and she's right.
       b.   He put on the left shoe and she put on the right shoe.

But in its use in 40 it means neither "correct" (as in 41a) nor the directional opposite to *left* (as in 41b). Instead, it means something like "immediately" or "directly." And, in fact, both of these words appear to function well as specifiers to PP:

(42)   The example [immediately below this one] is wrong.
       She went [directly out the door].

Again, both of these words are homophonous with adverbs:

(43)   She left immediately.
       She spoke directly (instead of indirectly).

In this specifier function, *right*, *immediately*, and *directly* behave like minor category words in not allowing specifiers or modifiers of the word, whereas in the adjective or adverb function, these words behave like major-category words. (The "?*" below indicates that the judgment of ungrammaticality is not quite as strong for some people in regard to this example.)

(44)   *The example [very right below this one] is wrong.
        *The example [so immediately below this one] is wrong.
        ?*The example [absolutely directly below this one] is wrong.

(45)   In this instance, he's very wrong and you're [very right].
       She left [so immediately] that I didn't have time to say good-bye.
       She spoke [embarrassingly directly], and no one, but no one, could
       mistake her meaning.

Let us call these specifiers of P′ intensifiers (giving them the same label we gave to specifiers of A′).

What about VP? VPs present an extra complication in that quite often an adverb phrase that modifies the VP or the entire clause can appear between the Subject and the verb string:

(46)   She quickly ran out the door.
       She obviously ran out the door.

If we want to determine whether *quickly* or *obviously* is inside the VP the only test we have at this point is clefting. But clefting does not sound lovely, regardless of whether we cleft the AP with the VP or not:

(47)   *It was quickly run out the door that she did.
        *It was obviously run out the door that she did.
        ??It was run out the door that she did quickly.
        *It was run out the door that she did obviously.

And, in fact, clefting VP is not perfect for many speakers even if no AP is present:

(48)   ?It was run out the door that she did.

We therefore do not have a way right now to test the CONSTITUENCY, that is, the syntactic groupings, of these sentences. We cannot say, for example, whether the APs in 45 are part of the VP or not. In the following discussion, we will accordingly limit ourselves to examples in which no adverbial intervenes between the Subject and material that is recognizably part of the VP.

In fact, the positioning of all adverbials, not just ones that precede the verb string, is often left out of consideration in works that aim to develop a syntax for English.

The rationale might be that if we can develop some sense of how the VP works without looking at adverbials, perhaps we can then add in the adverbials and have a chance of making some sense out of the complex puzzle that presents itself. (You can investigate issues in the positioning of adverbs by doing Problem Set 8-16 in chapter 8 later.)

With the above limitation, we find that VPs by and large start with the verb string. As with the other major categories, a V may fill the VP:

(49) Mary ran.

But the V can also be preceded by auxiliaries, as you well know from Problem Set 2.4. These auxiliaries tell the modality and the aspect of the action or state. It is not, I do not believe, stretching the imagination too much to see an analogy here between the auxiliaries and the specifiers of other categories. Auxiliaries do not change the sense denoted by the verb. Rather, they place that sense (the action or state) in some possible, probable, or necessary light:

(50) Mary might run.
      Mary must run.

and tell us to view it as unfinished or finished:

(51) Mary has run (before).
      Mary is running.

and so forth. They give us the extra information that allows us to pick out among all the instances of running, for example, which particular instance the utterance is about. For this reason we will now call the auxiliary string the specifier of the VP and we will see where this analysis leads us.

The discussion thus far, then, has led us to the following realizations of 25 for the categories of NP, AP, PP, and VP, using examples above:

(52)

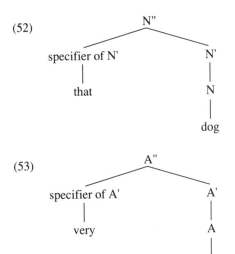

(53)

(54)

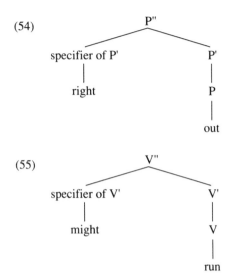

(55)

Take a careful look at the diagrams here, which are called syntactic TREES; each label on the tree is called a NODE or a PHRASE MARKER, and the words that hang off the bottom nodes are called the TERMINAL STRING (that is, the terminal string consists of the lexical items that make up the phrase or sentence). We see that the nodes for the heads (the N, A, P, or V) are all categories. Furthermore, all the other nodes are PROJECTIONS of categories (the two projections are the medial one, X′, and the MAXIMAL one, X″), except for the nodes with the label "specifier of X′." (If you feel overwhelmed with terminology, you might turn right now to Tangent 4.1 and read this tangent before continuing with the rest of the text of the narrative.)

Syntactic trees show us quickly the CONFIGURATIONAL HIERARCHIES that hold between the various nodes in a given syntactic structure. We will be focusing more and more on those hierarchical relationships as we progress through this book.

Many languages tend to be either HEAD-INITIAL or HEAD-FINAL in their phrase structure. That is, within a phrase all the modifiers and arguments of the head will either follow it (so that the head is initial) or precede it (so that the head is final). The Romance languages are fairly strongly head-initial. Japanese is head-final. English tends to be head-initial. (The arguments generally follow the head, for example), but displays some variation with respect to the ordering of modifiers of a head.

"Specifier" Structurally Defined

The term *specifier* in 52–54 could be interpreted as a functional term if we limited ourselves to considering only the examples discussed thus far in this chapter. That is, the specifiers we have discussed up to this point all serve to relate the phrase they introduce to the rest of the discourse or to indicate a quantity or degree. So they share a common function. If *specifier* were a functional term, it would then differ strongly from the category labels, since categories are defined morphologically (see Tangent 1.4 and Problem Set 1.1 of chapter 1 and, particularly, chapter 2), independently of their function.

For example, if we examine Ns, we can find Ns heading NPs that function as Subjects, Direct Objects, Indirect Objects, and Objects of a preposition, as you well know from earlier chapters. But we can also find NPs that function as adverbials (that is, as modifiers of non-nominals):

(56)   She left [yesterday].

We know that *yesterday* is an NP because only NPs can take the genitive marker:

(57)   She left after [yesterday's] lecture.

We can also find NPs that function as modifiers of nominals:

(58)   a [leather] wallet

(59)   a moment of [beauty]

One might argue that the N *leather* has undergone a derivational process in 58 to become an adjective, or, alternatively, that the string *leather wallet* is a compound N, like *goose bumps* or *teakettle*. And *leather* is not special in this way: one might try either of these approaches to account for any NP that is ADNOMINAL (that is, adjacent) to an N (*a [stone] column, a [candy] heart*). We cannot go into further discussion of either of these possibilities since they involve a reasonable knowledge of morphology (or word formation). The point of mentioning them is that in either of those cases, *leather* would not be an NP functioning as a modifier of another N. However, in 59 neither of those alternative analyses is even remotely available to us. Here an *of* introduces the NP (just as we saw an *of* in 6 and 9—and we will return to a discussion of this *of* in chapter 5), but there is no question that the NP is the element that gives the sense of the modification. A reasonable paraphrase of 59 is:

(60)   a beautiful moment

We can also find NPs that are predicated of other NPs:

(61)   John is an excellent student.

Here the NP *an excellent student* attributes a property to John (that of being an excellent student).

And many linguists argue that besides predicative NPs, as in 61, we have NPs that merely identify (or equate):

(62)   The coach is Mr. Randolph.

The name *Mr. Randolph*, which is an NP in 62, is said to serve only to give another label to the referent, not to assign the referent any additional property (and see Problem Set 4.3).

Thus the category N and all its projections are not associated with any fixed function.

The category Adjective, likewise, is morphologically defined and the phrasal projection of this category can correspond to at least two functions: predicate and modifier. We developed a rudimentary notion of predication in chapter 3, but up till now we have been operating with no explicit notion of modification. The contrast between the two functions is seen in:

(63)   Paint the red cows, please.

(64)   Paint the cows red, please.

If you gave a group of people some paints and a set of wooden cows and uttered 63, they might search for a cow that was red and then, hopefully, commence to paint it whatever color they pleased, as in:

(65)   Eva painted the red cow blue with orange polka dots.

But if you uttered 64 in the same situation, the people might pick up any old cow and paint it red (and not blue with orange polka dots). *Red* in 63 helps us to pick out the particular cows that the speaker intends us to pick out—those that already have the property of redness. *Red*, then, contributes to the determination of the referent of the NP *the red cows*. This use of the AP is modification. *Red* in 64, on the other hand, does not help us pick out the referent of the NP *the cows*. Instead, those cows are identified independently of whatever color they happen to be. *Red* tells us that those cows should wind up with the property of being red once they have been painted. The AP therefore assigns a property to the NP *the cows* whose referent is identified in independent ways, and the AP is thus a predicate.

We could formalize the difference between modification and predication by noting that a modifier assigns a property to a head X while a predicate assigns a property to a phrase X''.

The presence of the predicative AP in 64 is not necessary to the grammaticality of this sentence:

(66)   Paint the cows, please.

And *paint* is not subcategorized for whether it can take a SECONDARY PREDICATE like *red*. For this reason, the AP is called an ADJUNCT, rather than an argument, of the verb *paint*. Most modifiers, as well, are adjuncts, in the sense that typically a lexical item is not subcategorized to take a modifier. (All unsubcategorized for items besides the predicate and its Subject are adjuncts.) However, not all adjuncts are modifiers (that is, modifiers are a proper subset of adjuncts). In 64, while it is clear that *red* is predicated of *the cows*, it is debatable whether *red* modifies the verb or stands in some other semantic relationship to it. We will touch upon this issue later in this chapter.

Not all secondary predicates are adjuncts. There are other verbs that call for predicates as arguments, as in:

(67)   The medicine rendered Jill [ill].

Rendered requires both a theme argument and a predicate argument. But that predicate need not be an AP:

(68)   The medicine rendered Jill [a paraplegic].
       The medicine rendered Jill [totally out of her mind].

Adjectives can, in particular structures, serve other functions, as well. We have seen that adjectives can be the subjects of sentences, such as clefts:

(69)   —Hey, that photograph is charming.
       —Charming? Then I failed. Beautiful is what I want.

Here *beautiful* is being used referentially; the sense of the AP emerges as something to consider independently of its association with any particular entity.

However, except for in these more atypical situations, APs function as modifiers or predicates.

Ps are similar to As in their range of functions. Thus, they can head a PP that modifies,

(70)   the girls [in blue dresses]

or is predicated of an NP:

(71)   The girls are [in blue dresses].

And they can head a PP that occurs as the Subject of sentences under special circumstances:

(72)   From New York to Boston is a long way.

Here *from New York to Boston* is used referentially to indicate a distance.

Verbs, once again, are the most difficult category to discuss with respect to their functions. Clearly their most common function is as predicates, and one might at first say that is the only function. But verbal participles (progressive or passive) can head a phrase that modifies:

(73)   The girl [*sitting* on the bench] is my friend.
       The girl [*dressed* in blue] is my friend.

If one wanted to push the hypothesis that verbs could function only as predicates, one might look for evidence that the participle forms in 73 belong to the category A rather than V. (You can consider some of the types of evidence one might bring to bear on this issue by doing Star Problem 4.2.) The evidence is not clear-cut, however. We will learn more about V as we progress through this book. In the meantime, each time you think you have come across a new function for V or VP, you might note it and, if you are taking a syntax class, bring it up for class discussion.

The important point of the above discussion is that categories are defined independently of function. So when we look at the trees in 52–55 we can recognize that all the nodes on the tree have syntactic category labels that give no indication of function, with a single exception: the label "specifier, X'" (for any X') is the one label in our trees so far which is potentially functional in character. That alone makes it suspect: in general, linguists try to use node labels that are independent of function, since the relationship between form (which is represented clearly in a syntactic tree) and function is not in any obvious way a simple one. Thus instead of the label "specifier," we might put 74–77.

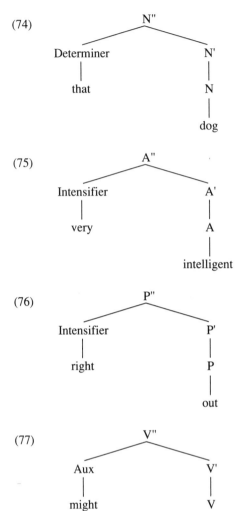

(74) N"
(75) A"
(76) P"
(77) V"

In 74–77 the labels for the LEFT BRANCH off of X" indicate a CLOSED SET OF
LEXICAL ITEMS. That is, there are only a handful of determiners and we are unlikely
to add any new ones. The same is true for the intensifiers and the auxiliaries. Minor-
category words in general form closed sets. Major categories, on the other hand, are
usually OPEN SETS. There are huge numbers of nouns, for example, and speakers
are free to add new ones. The one major category we have looked at for which this
is not true is the Preposition. There are several Ps, not just a handful—in contrast
to the number of determiners, intensifiers, and auxiliaries. But there are many fewer
Ps (probably in the range of fifty to 100) than Ns, As, and Vs (which number in the
thousands). Also, we are highly unlikely to add new Ps to our language.

Are the trees in 74–77 truly free of any functional labels? That is, if determiners form a small closed set whose members are not identifiable morphologically but simply have to be listed and whose members function only to specify N', isn't the label "determiner" equivalent to a functional label? Surely the answer is yes. (First, one would want to confirm that determiners are not morphologically identifiable and function only to specify N'. Only after that could one conclude that this label is functional. You can confirm both contentions yourself now.)

Is it possible to label our trees so that no functional labels appear? Why would we want to do that? If whenever X" branches, the left branch of X" serves the function of specifying X', why would we want to have a label that was function-free for this node?

One might answer that we want all the phrase markers in our tree to be categorial only so that the tree does not mix information types. To this, another might respond that the function of specifier could be read off the tree relationship anyway, so whether we label the node with a category symbol or with the term *specifier* amounts to a mere terminological difference.

Before getting more deeply into this debate, we need to ask whether, in fact, the left branch of X" always functions to semantically specify the phrase. In all the examples we have considered thus far, the answer seems to be yes, and that is why we have been led to think of the term "specifier" as a functional term. But we find that sometimes major-category phrases can appear as the left branch of X". For example, we find N" as the left branch of N", A", and P" (see examples 78–80, below).

(78)   [a bit of] ice

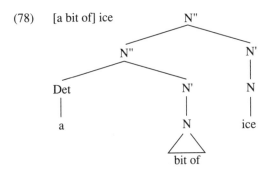

(79)   [a bit] dusty

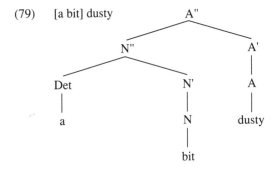

(80)   [a bit] off the wall (as in: That comment is . . .)

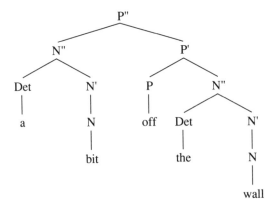

(Once more an *of* appears in 78. A discussion of this *of* appears in chapter 5. At that point, be sure to look at Star Problem 5.5.) In all of these instances, however, the N″ on the left branch is telling us an amount or degree—so the function is still what we have been calling a specifier function. However, we can find N″ as the left branch of N″ where no sense of degree or quantity, etc., is involved (see example 81).

(81)   the boy's book

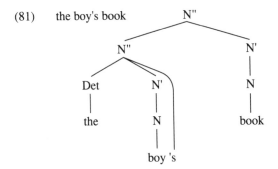

(For justification of the attachment of the genitive marker to N″ rather than N, see Problem Set 1.1.) Here the boy may own the book or have written the book or be the main character in the book or have a variety of other possible relationships to the book that the context may help to determine. As far as the grammar is concerned, the relationship between the boy and the book is underdetermined. But what is clear is that *the boy's* does not function as a specifier in the sense of that function as developed above. For this reason (and others that we will find in chapter 5), many people rewrite the general schema for major categories as in example 82.

(82)

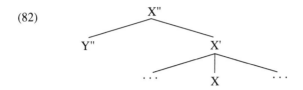

This schema allows a phrase of any category (here represented as Y″) to be the left branch of X″ and involves no particular function for the left branch of X″. In fact, in light of examples like 81, we can use the schema in 82 to give a definition of *specifier* that is in no way functional:

(83) A specifier is the maximal projection that is the immediate daughter of another maximal projection.

An immediate problem with this definition is that it does not cover the cases in which the left branch of the higher X″ in 82 is a minor category, since we have analyzed minor categories as not having the usual breakdown into projections. That is, 52-55 are all problematic. If nodes with the label "Determiner" and "Auxiliary," for example, are the lowest level (the X level), then how can they fill the Y″ slot (a phrasal slot) in the tree in 82?

Instead, nodes like determiner, intensifier, and auxiliary look like heads (that is, X^0s). In fact, that that is exactly what they are. Please turn now to Tangent 4.2 for a discussion of Determiner Phrases (DPs) and Quantifier Phrases (QPs). We will hold off on a discussion of the proper analysis of auxiliaries until chapter 8. And we will not seriously consider the proper analysis of intensifiers of A and P in this book, although given the structure in 82 we must analyze intensifiers as heads, just as we must analyze determiners and auxiliaries as heads.

Throughout the rest of this book we will adopt the DP and QP analyses that you just read about in Tangent 4.2. Thus the term "specifier" will refer to that maximal projection that is immediately dominated by another maximal projection. And a specifier node will have no set function. However, we will typically not represent phrases containing nominals as DPs or QPs, but continue to represent them as NPs. This is simply for expository convenience. The DP and QP analyses call for complexity that often is not of interest to our discussion, and an unnecessarily complicated tree may, in fact, take your attention way from the real issues at hand. Thus we will talk about NPs below, even though you know that what we are really talking about is DPs and QPs.

Modifiers and Arguments of the Head

Looking at 82, which is a revised version of 25, we can now return to the question of what fills the dots on either side of the head of the phrase and what evidence there is for the existence of an X′ level. You are already familiar with the notion of both modifiers and arguments as they pertain to verbs and you know that both modifiers and arguments can fill these dots in a VP. Thus in 84, *quickly* modifies the V and *the room* is an argument of the V:

(84)   Sally [swept the room quickly].

Furthermore, we already said for N that these dots can be filled by modifiers or arguments. You are very familiar with the notion of modifier for a N:

(85)   the happy girl

And if you did Problem Sets 3.4 and 3.6 of chapter 3, you know that Ns may take arguments. But, even if you did not do those problem sets, you have dealt implicitly with this idea in this chapter—when you noted in 9 that Ns can take Objects. Consider 9 again, repeated here for convenience. The sense of this N is an action and it assigns the theta-role of theme to *the city*:

(86)   the destruction [of the city]

(Our *of* appears again. You will find it discussed in chapter 5.) In fact, many linguists would argue that arguments of the N may occur not only as a sister to the N, but also as the left branch of N″:

(87)   [the Huns'] destruction of the city

Contrast 87 to 81 above, *the boy's book*. In 87 the relationship between the Huns and destruction is not underdetermined. Rather, we understand the Huns to be responsible for the destruction of the city. *The Huns'* is, then, the agentive argument of the head N *destruction*.

Do adjectives take modifiers and arguments? Modifiers are easy to find:

(88)   [childishly] happy
       [serenely] content

And we have also already seen instances of arguments of A, in which, again, we called them Objects above and in Problem Set 3.1 of chapter 3:

(89)   Jill is [fond [of Sue]].

Here *fond* is the predicate, taking two arguments—one INTERNAL to the AP (*Sue*) and one EXTERNAL to the AP (*Jill*). Many other adjectives can take arguments, and those arguments are always introduced by a P, a point to which we will return in chapter 5:

(90)   talented [at tennis]
       sick [of cats]
       annoyed [with her brother]
       equal [to nothing]

How about Ps? Can Ps be modified? We have seen that Ps can take intensifiers. But modification is another matter. Modification is not limited to notions of degree or of old-versus-new information. Modification can introduce entirely new and independent senses, as we see in 87, for example. Can Ps be modified? To answer this, we need to recognize three contexts for Ps.

Most Ps in most of their uses are relational words. They typically set up a spatial or temporal relationship between their Object and either the rest of the sentence or something in the rest of the sentence (and we will return to a discussion of this fact at the end of the chapter). So far as I know, Ps in their relational sense are not open to modification of the ordinary sort. Instead, the only types of elements that are potential candidates for modifiers and that co-occur with relational uses of P concern notions of degree or quantity:

(91)   *almost* in; *not* out; *halfway* through; *altogether* inside; *barely* outside; *all* around

However, when a PP as a whole has an idiomatic usage, modifiers are acceptable:

(92)   Her behavior was [*childishly* off the wall].
        I'm [*serenely* off my rocker]—don't bother me!

Also, when a P is used as a predicate which assigns properties to various arguments, it can take modifiers:

(93)   Mary is [*sinfully* into Greek art].
        Jim is [*unabashedly* after his neighbor's wife].

Here *into* and *after* do not set up spatial or temporal relationships between their Objects and something else. Instead, they are predicates which assign theta-roles to the Subject of the sentence and to their Objects. So with examples like these, we can see that the category P, like the categories of N, A, and V, allows both modifiers and arguments.

The X′ Level

The task for us now is to find evidence for the existence of an X′ level. Consider 87 again, repeated here:

(94)   the Huns' destruction of the city

If the schema in 82 were correct, *destruction of the city* would form an N′. How can we test for this constituency? Our cleft test will not help us here, since only the maximal projection (the X″ level) can be clefted. However, we do have another diagnostic: coordination. Back in Problem Set 1.1, you accounted for the ambiguity of the phrase:

(95)   big cats and dogs

Here *big* can be understood to modify only *cats* or to modify both *cats* and *dogs*. Give a tree analysis for each of those readings. The major difference, of course, will be in whether we have a conjunction of N″s or of Ns (see example 96).

(96)

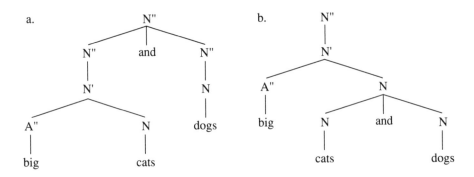

a.

b.

Conjunction appears to apply freely to both the X and the X″ levels. We might expect it, then, to apply freely to the X′ level, as well. So if there really is an N′ level inside N″, we should find conjunctions of N′s.

Look again at 94. Can you think of an example using conjunction to show that *the Huns'* is a sister to N′? Easily:

(97)   the Huns' destruction of the city and theft of the cows

One reading of this NP has the Huns as the agent argument not only of *destruction*, but of *theft*. On that reading we have a conjunction of N′s (see example 98).

(98)

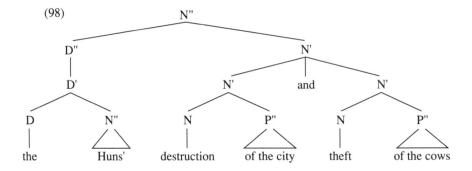

(In 98 I have represented the nominal *the Huns'* as a DP, just to remind you of the DP analysis. But no other nominal is represented as being a DP. Actually, it is logically possible that every nominal is introduced as a complement to a determiner or Q, where the D or Q node might be empty.)

It is more difficult for us to demonstrate the existence of V′. Consider this example with conjunction:

(99)   She might [win at tennis and lose at ping-pong].

In 99 the material in brackets forms a node made up of conjoined nodes. However, if auxiliaries (like *might*) are not specifiers inside V″ (as we will argue they are not in chapter 8), then the bracketed material in 99 might be conjoined V's or conjoined V"s.

Now consider the question for A' and P':

> (100) Mary is very [focussed at the piano and spacey about everything else].

> (101) They went straight [through the door and into the ballroom].

Certainly there is a reading for 100 and 101 in which the material in brackets forms a node that is a conjunction of two nodes. If intensifiers are the left branch of the phrasal node, as in 53 and 54, 100 and 101 would be evidence for the existence of A' and P'. However, if intensifiers, like determiners and auxiliaries, are better analyzed as heads that take A" and P" complements, then examples such as 100 and 101 are no more conclusive than examples such as 99.

Still, we have reason to accept the idea that V', A', and P' exist. We have seen many parallels between the lexical categories, and these parallels are the motivation for a general schema such as that in 82 in the first place. Lexical categories appear to have similar internal structure. On those general grounds, the fact that N' exists (as we saw with 97 and 98) leads us to conclude that X' exists for all the lexical categories.

One important remaining issue concerning phrase structure is the question of what determines the linear order of modifiers and arguments with respect to the head. We will consider evidence relevant to this issue in chapter 5 and again in Tangent 8.1 of chapter 8.

The Relationship between Phrase Structure and Semantic Structure

One final question for us to consider before we conclude this chapter is what the relationship is between the syntactic notion of phrase structure and the semantic notion of Complete Functional Complex.

For example, if a P is used as a predicate, are all its arguments contained inside the PP? Based on the sentences we have examined thus far, we must answer no. As we saw in chapter 3, with such predicates one argument is always external to the PP. *Mary* in 102 is external to the PP:

> (102) *Mary* is [$_{P''}$ *into* Greek art].

So a PP can never be a CFC.

If an A is used as a predicate, are all its arguments contained inside the AP? Again, the answer is negative:

> (103) *Mary* is [$_{A''}$ *talented* at the clarinet].

So an AP can never be a CFC.

What about VP? Can it be a CFC? Generally the Subject position of a clause is filled with an argument of the V:

> (104) *Mary* [$_{V''}$ *laughed* out loud].

So it would appear that a VP cannot be a CFC. However, the Subject position is sometimes filled with a dummy of some sort:

(105)   *It* [$_{V'}$ *seems* that John is happy].

It is not an argument of any predicate in 105. So if *seems* is a predicate (where it would take its sister clause as its only argument), then VP can be a CFC.

What about NP (that is, DP)? Can it be a CFC? If N is used as a predicate in a copular construction parallel to those in 102–103, the NP it heads is not a CFC because one of the N's' arguments is external to the NP:

(106)   *Mary* is [$_{N'}$ a *master* at chess].

But if an NP is used referentially and if its head N is a theta-assigner, the NP can contain all the arguments of the head N, as with our familiar example:

(107)   the Huns' destruction of the city

Is 107 a CFC or not?

In chapter 3 we defined a CFC as a predicate and all its arguments. But in chapter 3 we had not yet recognized theta-assigners that were not predicates. Now that we have seen examples like 107, we can revise our definition of CFC to be a theta-assigner and all its arguments, where an NP, then, can be a CFC so long as it contains a Subject argument of the head N (and, perhaps, other arguments, depending on the argument structure of the particular head N). We will see positive ramifications of this revision in chapters 9 and 10.

We conclude that NP, S, and, perhaps, VP are the only structures we know of yet that can be CFCs.

In this entire discussion, we have taken the approach that a predicate need not be a maximal projection. This is not a common approach. If one took the alternative (and more common) position that predicates must be maximal projections (so that there is no identity between predicates and theta-assigners), then the entire PP in 102, AP in 103, and VP in 104 are the predicates and they always take an external argument (their Subject argument). With this approach the matrix VP in 105 can be a predicate only if we allow predicates to take dummy arguments (since every predicate must have at least one argument—and the only potential argument outside the matrix VP in 105 is the dummy *it*). While the choice in definition of the term "predicate" matters to various parts of our grammar, in fact nothing crucial to our discussion above is affected by which definition we choose. And, of course, once we revise our definition of CFC to be a theta-assigner and all its arguments, the choice of definition of "predicate" is totally irrelevant to the discussion above.

Summary

What we have been developing in this chapter is known as X-Bar Theory (a term you are familiar with from the chapter overviews at the end of Chapters Two and Three). According to X-Bar Theory the major syntactic categories are internally similar in their structural analysis. They have the breakdown shown in 82. Furthermore, we have considered seriously and rejected any semantic or functional definition of the term "specifier."

We also learned in this chapter that the sisters of X typically function as modifiers or arguments of X. But we have seen that the sisters of X can also have other functions that are not so easily classifiable. For example, in its relational use, P takes an Object that is not an argument in the sense of the term as we developed it in chapter 3: the Object of a relational P is not its agent or theme or benefactee or instrument or experiencer. Relational Ps are not predicates. They set up a relationship (typically temporal or spatial) between their Object and some other entity. Perhaps we need to allow the notion of temporal or spatial RELATOR into our grammar. The Object of the P would, then, play no specific role in the event of the clause that contains the PP. Instead, it would be understood in a certain relationship (that of the sense of the P) to some other entity in that clause. In most uses, relational PPs function as modifiers of material outside the PP.

Likewise, adjunct predicates to V, as in 64, repeated here, raise questions.

(108)   Paint the cows red, please.

Red is not an argument of *paint*, it is an adjunct, as we discussed above. Certainly it has something in common with modifier adjuncts. For example, it tells something about the painting, just as the modifier does in:

(109)   Paint the cows carefully, please.

But *red* is doing more: it tells us also that the cows will wind up red as a result of the painting. The adjunct predicate *red*, then, MEDIATES the predication relationship between *paint* and its theme argument. We might then need to admit mediation as another function.

One side effect of our X-Bar Theory that we did not note earlier is that we can now attempt a new kind of definition for Direct Object. Draw a tree for the VP *ate pizza*. Can you pick out the DO in structural terms? The DO will always be an XP sister (an NP or S) to V. But certainly not all XPs that follow V are DOs, not even all NPs or Ss (as with the adverbial NP in the VP *left the other day*). If adverbials are also sisters to V, we have a structural characteristic that is necessary in order to pick out DOs, but not sufficient. We will return to this question in Tangent 8.2 of chapter 8.

The X-Bar Theory does not constrain or in any way direct our notions of the function of categories. Instead, it concerns only the syntactic breakdown of projections of the major categories. Furthermore, maximal projections are not to be automatically identified with CFCs (which we have now defined as theta-assigners and all their arguments, where an NP can be a CFC only if it contains a Subject argument). Rather, it would appear that only N″ (in certain uses), S, and perhaps V″ can be CFCs.

The picture of X-Bar Theory given in this chapter is highly constrained: there are only three projections of any major category (X, X′, and X″) and arguments and modifiers of a head are sisters to the head. Many less-restrictive versions of X-Bar Theory can be found in the literature. We will discuss some of the types of issues that arise in arguments about X-Bar Theory in Tangent 8.2 of chapter 8. In the meantime, we will work with the restrictive version developed here.

In this chapter we have completely sidestepped the original question of this book, which involves the distribution of anaphors and their binders. We will briefly touch upon that issue in Problem Set 4.6. It has been necessary to lay aside the question of anaphors in order to build up a picture of those components of the grammar that we will need as background when we return to this question. In the next three chapters we will continue assembling this background. Have patience. We will eventually return to the question of anaphors.

Tangent 4.1: Trees and Constituency

Diagrams have gradually and without any fanfare been insinuated into the discussion, starting with the large triangles in example 1 of chapter 3. With this chapter, however, it is necessary to face these diagrams and become comfortable talking about them.

Diagrams of the sort in 52–55 in the text, as we said, are called trees. We say that each category label on the tree is a node in the tree. For example, if we have the tree:

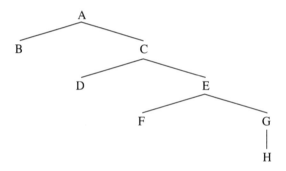

the nodes of this tree are A, B, C, D, E, F, G, and H.

But sentences do not consist merely of category labels. They consist of words. So the bottom line of any tree will consist of a terminal string of lexical items, as in:

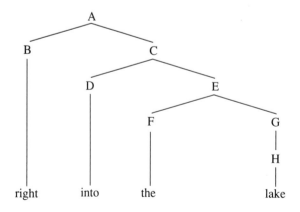

The words must occur in the terminal string in the same order as you say them in the phrase. The nodes immediately above the lexical items are called LEXICAL NODES. You are familiar with many types of lexical nodes: N, V, P, A, Det(erminer), Int(ensifier), Aux(iliary). We say that the lexical nodes DOMINATE the lexical items under them. In fact, any node dominates all the material below it. Nodes that immediately dominate other nodes (rather than lexical items) are generally PHRASAL NODES of the level of X′ (an intermediary projection) or X″ (the maximal projection). The one exception to this is when we have coordination (that is, connection with *and, or,* or *but*) at the lexical level, as in:

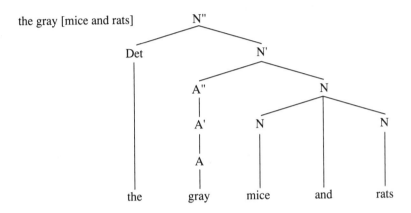

Here the coordinated Ns are immediately dominated by another node N, which is also of the lowest projection (the lexical projection).

In the first tree, repeated here for convenience, A dominates every node. We will ignore any unshown lexical material that must be under the terminal nodes and talk about domination relationships between nodes only.

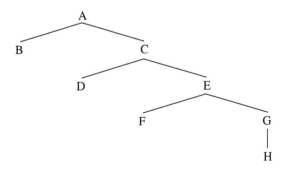

B dominates nothing (except the lexical item that is not shown here). C dominates D, E, F, G, and H. D dominates nothing (again, except unshown lexical material). E dominates F, G, and H. F dominates nothing (except unshown lexical material).

G dominates H. And H dominates nothing (except unshown lexical material). Some of the nodes on this tree are discretely related to one another: that is, they neither dominate nor are dominated by the other node. Thus A is not discretely related to any other nodes, since it dominates all of them. But B is discretely related to all the nodes in the above tree except A. G is discretely related to B, D, and F, but not to A, C, and E (all of which dominate it) nor to H (which it dominates).

A node that immediately dominates more than one item is said to BRANCH. Nodes A, C, and E above are branching nodes. G is an unbranching node. In general, all lexical nodes are unbranching except in unusual cases (such as coordination, as we saw above). *One of the most important conventions of syntactic theory that we will adopt in this book is that branches do not cross.* Hence, a tree like the one that follows is disallowed.

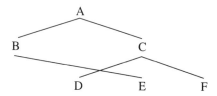

We can view a given tree has having multiple analyses. Any analysis of the tree must include a string of nodes such that (1) every terminal lexical node will either appear in the string or be dominated by a node that appears in the string, and (2) every node in the string will be discretely related to the other nodes in the string.

For example, the tree above can be analyzed as simply A, because A dominates all the nodes in the tree. It also has four other possible analyses. Can you find them? They are:

    B C
    B D E
    B D F G
    B D F H

We say that A is analyzable as BC or BDE or BDFG or BDFH. The flip side of this relationship is the *IS A* relationship. We say BC is an A; BDE is an A; BDFG is an A; and BDFH is an A.

Since any node of a tree defines a subpart that is also a tree, we can talk about the *IS ANALYZABLE AS* and the *IS A* relationships for all the nodes of the tree above. What are all the possible analyses of C, for example? (C is analyzable as DE, DFG, and DFH.) What is FG? (FG is an E.) What is H? (H is a G.)

We call any node that immediately dominates other nodes the MOTHER of those other nodes; those other nodes are the DAUGHTERS. (Note: motherhood involves IMMEDIATE DOMINATION only.) Thus A is the mother of B and C and B and C are the daughters of A. What is the mother of F and G? What are the daughters of C?

We call nodes that have the same mother sisters. D is the sister of E. What is the sister of B?

Most people do not talk about grandmothers, aunts, and cousins, but it would certainly be possible to talk about the nodes of a tree in that way.

Now we can define the notion of constituency. A string of nodes is said to form a constituent X if those nodes stand in the IS A relationship with respect to the node X. That is, FH above is the constituent E (that is, FH is an E). DE is the constituent C. And so on. Constituency is an important notion in syntax. Way back in Problem Set 1.2 you discovered that the cleft construction is a test for constituency at the maximal phrasal level. For example, consider the instantiation of our tree above, repeated here:

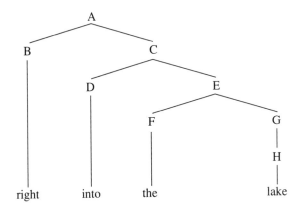

What is A in terms of actual category labels that you know? What are B, C, E, F, G, and H? Let us redo this tree with the actual labels:

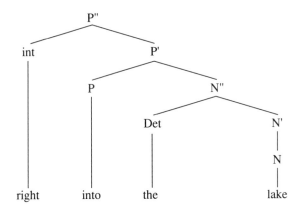

Now let us put this PP into the larger sentence:

The frog jumped right into the lake.

We find that if we form cleft sentences using elements from the analyzed part of this sentence shown in our tree here, we get:

> Right into the lake is where the frog jumped.
> The lake is what the frog jumped right into.

But we cannot cleft a string that does not form a constituent (such as the string P-Det):

> *Into the is where the frog jumped right lake.

And we cannot cleft a node that is not phrasal (such as Int or P'):

> *Right is how the frog jumped into the lake.
> *Into the lake is where the frog jumped right.

You can and will use these facts about constituency in future problem sets.

If you have some experience and background in syntax other than what you have gained by working in this book, you may well be wondering why I have thus far discussed only clefts as a test for constituency and not pro-forms (such as the *do so-*test). In this book we will not use pro-forms as a test for constituency. The reasons for this are stated in Tangent 8.2 of chapter 8.

An alternative to trees is LABELED BRACKETS, as in:

$$[_{P''} [_{Int} \text{right}] [_{P'} [_P \text{into}] [_{N''} [_{Det} \text{the}] [_{N'} [_N \text{lake}]]]]]$$

Labeled brackets give the same information trees give. However, when the brackets pile up (as they do at the right-hand side of this example), they can be difficult to interpret. Trees may be more immediately understood for such structures. We will use both trees and labeled brackets throughout the rest of this book.

There will be times when we do not care about particular details of a structure. We can employ triangles in trees to indicate that we could give a more detailed analysis, but we do not care to. For example, in the tree below the NP has a triangle below it, indicating that the internal structure of the NP is not shown:

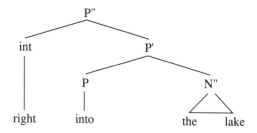

Likewise, with labeled brackets, we need not include all the brackets, skipping those that are not of particular interest at the moment. Thus the labeled bracketing corresponding to the tree above would be:

$$[_{P''} [_{Int} \text{right}] [_{P'} [_P \text{into}] [_{N''} \text{the lake}]]]$$

Before ending this tangent, let me make an aside for the sake of sexual politics. As you may have noticed, the terminology for relationships between nodes is feminine (mothers, sisters). Furthermore, the terminology for relationships between clauses is feminine. (The top clause is the matrix: *matrix* means "mother" in Latin.) This is a tradition in linguistics and you will find this terminology frequently in linguistics articles. It has no sexist roots, as far as I am aware. In addition, the actual lexical items in a string are often called by the masculine term "guys" (or sometimes by the more gender-neutral term "animals") in informal classroom discussions. So a professor might say, "This guy over here is the antecedent for this guy," when talking about two words or phrases. Or the professor might say, "This word over here is a whole nother kind of animal from that one." I do not recall seeing this terminology in linguistics articles, but do not be surprised if you hear it in class. (And linguists almost have to say things like "a whole nother"—it is close to obligatory.)

Tangent 4.2: Determiner Phrases and Quantifier Phrases

In recent years linguists have argued that instead of the two types of categories we have called minor categories and major categories, the real split is between functional categories and lexical categories. Lexical categories would be A, N, P, and V, the categories that dominate lexical items that are semantically "whole." But functional categories would be quite different in at least the following ways:

(a) They would not be semantically "whole" or rich, but instead would serve to functionally introduce their complement.

(b) In accordance with (a), they would not assign a theta-role to their complement.

(c) In accordance with (a), they would be limited to taking only a single complement, since they are not semantically rich or complex enough to introduce multiple elements.

(d) In accordance with (a), they would be stressless under most circumstances.

(e) In accordance with (a), they would be a closed set.

(f) In accordance with (a), their maximal projection would function to "close off" the phrase, giving it an integrity or wholeness.

Elements like determiners would be strong candidates for functional categories: they are not semantically rich; they do not assign a theta-role to the NP; they take only a single complement (the NP); they are stressless under most circumstances; they are a closed set; their maximal projection (which is the entire nominal phrase, called the Determiner Phrase [DP]) has a semantic integrity in that it is the referential level. Proponents of this approach might analyze a string like *the blue book* (what we have been analyzing as an NP) as a DP, with the structure shown at the top of the next page.

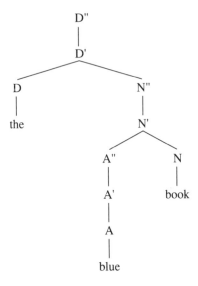

Some linguists have argued further that lexical categories do not have any max-imal projection, since they can always add some other element (a complement or modifier) and thus are never truly semantically complete or integral. Thus X-Bar Theory would have to allow two schemas: one for functional categories and another for lexical categories. They would look something like this:

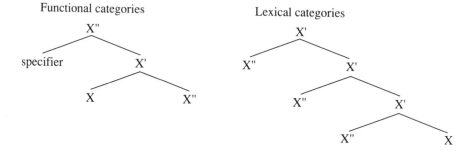

Functional categories would allow a single specifier and a single complement of the head. Lexical categories would be optionally iterative (X' can dominate X' over and over again—although in the above schema I have given a representation with only two iterations) and, depending on the particular linguist, X might be allowed to take only one sister (as I have represented in the above schema) or multiple sisters. (We will return to a discussion of BINARY BRANCHING versus multiple branching in Tangent 8.2 of chapter 8.) While I have placed the sisters to the various projections of X in the lexical-category schema on the left, their actual placement would be dependent upon the particular category that heads the phrase and the particular language we are talking about.

While we will adopt the determiner phrase analysis in the tree above for *the blue book*, we will not assume the position for English that lexical categories have no maximal projection. However, there is evidence that in some languages, such as Japanese, lexical categories may, in fact, have no maximal projection. You can consider some of this evidence in Problem Sets 8.2 of chapter 8 and 10.8 of chapter 10.

Before returning to the text, let us take a quick look at quantifiers. Is Q a functional or a lexical category? Regarding characteristic (a) in the list above, Qs have lexical sense (*all* is different from *no* or *six*), although their sense is typically in relation to the item they quantify. However, adjectives, also, have a sense that generally is related to the item they modify or are predicated of.

With regard to characteristic (b), Qs do not assign a theta-role to their complement. But it can be argued that many Ps, as well, do not assign theta-roles to their arguments (as you saw in Problem Set 3.3).

As for (c), Qs take only a single complement.

As for (d), Qs typically have ordinary word stress (in contrast to determiners).

As for (e), Qs form a closed set except for the numerals, but so do Ps.

And as for (f), any difference between functional and lexical categories in this regard would be vitiated in English if both types of categories have maximal projections.

Given (a)–(f), we are unable to say with any certainly what type of category Q is. However, unless this issue becomes important for some reason, it is not necessary for us to resolve it. The important point is that Q certainly heads its own phrase. Thus a nominal like *absolutely all the big animals* would have the structure:

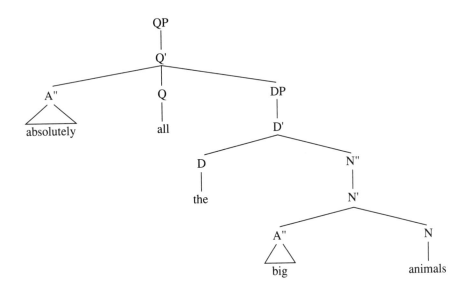

Problem Set 4.1: English Auxiliaries

Part 1

In the text we saw that the copula is semantically more like an auxiliary in many of its uses even when it is the main (that is, final) verb of the verb string:

    (1)   Sally is nice.

Is the so-called main verb *be* syntactically more like other main verbs or more like auxiliary verbs? Find at least three arguments for your position. You might consider Subject-Auxiliary Inversion, Conducive Tag-Question formation, the placement of *not* in copular sentences, the appearance or lack of appearance of *do* in negative sentences and questions, or anything else we have covered or perhaps new arguments.

Part 2

Now consider *have*, which, like *be*, can occur both inside the auxiliary string (as the perfect aspect marker) and as the main verb:

    (2)   a. She has left.
           b. She has five brothers.

Is *have* syntactically (please do not discuss semantics here) more like an auxiliary verb or more like a main verb when it occurs as the final verb of the verb string, as in 2b? Again, give at least three arguments for your position.

Part 3

What about *will* when it occurs as the final verb of the verb string?

    (3)   God willed the firmaments to come together.

Again, please present three arguments.

Part 4

Now address the question of whether the semantic contribution of *have* and *will* when they are the final verb of a verb string like that in 2b and 3 corresponds to the syntactic status (as an auxiliary or main verb, depending on what you decided above). Compare your findings to the correspondence between the semantic contribution of *be* (as discussed in the text) to the syntactic status of *be* (as you argued above).

    (This should be an informal discussion. Go with your intuitions and common sense.)

Problem Set 4.2: English Quantifiers

In the text we mentioned NPs that are introduced by a numeral or quantifier along with some other element, such as:

(1)   those five dogs
        all the dogs

There is an alternative structure that English can employ when numerals or quantifiers co-occur with other introducers of NPs:

(2)   five of those dogs
        some of the dogs

NPs like those in 1 and 2 are called quantified NPs (QNPs). Certainly the first QNP in 2 is not semantically equivalent to the first QNP in 1, and you can easily find contexts in which it would be appropriate to say *those five dogs* and others in which it would be appropriate to say *five of those dogs*.

There is one main question for you to answer in this problem set: what is the internal structure of QNPs like those in 2?

In answering this, consider sentences such as those below and answer all of the intermediary questions.

Data Set A

(3)   I'll buy five of the apples, please.
        I'll buy five, please.

        I'll take some of the apples, thank-you.
        I'll take some, thank-you.

        Each of the boys came in.
        Each came in.

        Few of the boys understand.
        Few understand.

(4)   *I'll buy every of the apples.
        *I'll buy every.

        *The of the boys came in.
        *The came in.

What regularity do 3 and 4 point out for you? (Please limit yourself to considering only the data in 3 and 4 for now.) What do they indicate with regard to the determination of the head of NPs like that in 2?

Data Set B

(5)   *I like those of the boys.
        I like those.

(6)   I like those of the boys that wear loafers.

How does 5 threaten the correlation you found in 3 and 4 above? How does 6 rescue the correlation? What semantic function does the relative clause *that wear loafers* play in 6 that allows the quantified NP to be grammatical?

Data Set C

(7)   *A(n) of the boy(s) came in.
      One of the boys came in.

How does 7 bear on the issue? Notice that 6 versus 5 above led you to a semantic understanding of the correlation seen in 3 and 4. Can semantics be called upon to account for the grammaticality difference in 7? If not, which of the two sentences in 7 is surprising and what might be an alternative explanation for the grammaticality judgment here?

Data Set D

(8)   All of the boys came in.
       ??All came in.

How does 8 bear on the issue? (Just state its relevance; do not try to account for it.)
Now consider:

(9)   all three of those boxes
       each one of the boys

but:

(10)   *some five of the boys
       *few three of the boys

(11)   *every five of the boys
       *the five of the boys

Does 9 present any new problems for your analysis of our QNPs thus far? If not, give the analysis for 9. If so, revise your analysis for our QNPs so that 9 is not problematic. If you cannot do that, explain what the problems are and why you cannot solve them.

Data Set E

(12)   two of those five boys

Discuss the semantics of 12. Is your discussion here consistent with or problematic for your discussions of the earlier data? If it is consistent, fine. If it is problematic, explain how your earlier discussion might be revised to make the two discussions consistent with one another.

Data Set F

(13)   the two lightest of the boxes

Discuss the position of *lightest* here. What is it modifying? What does its position suggest about the structure of this phrase? (Focus on the syntactic status of *two*.)

Data Set G

(14)   Of those five boxes, I can carry only the two lightest.

Discuss the fronting of *of those five boxes* here. What does this fronting tell us about the constituency of phrases like that in 13 above?

*Problem Set 4.3: English Prediction

This problem set deals with predication and related concepts. It will serve as a basis for later discussion in the book, so it should be done.

Adjectives

Part 1:   In the text you learned that APs can modify or predicate. Take the sentences below and argue whether the AP is inside the NP (whose head) it modifies or is predicated of.

(1)   I considered the [long] argument.

(2)   I considered the argument [long].

(Hint: You can consider clefting as a test for constituency, as pointed out in Tangent 4.1 of this chapter. You can also consider the makeup of ordinary NPs.) In which sentence is *long* a predicate?

Part 2:   Find one adjective of English that can never be used to head a predicative AP. Just to get you going, an example is *mere*, as in:

(3)   She's a mere child.

(4)   *That child is mere.

Part 3:   In the text you saw an example of an AP that was used as a predicate, but that was not the only predicate in its clause:

(5)   The medicine rendered Jill [ill].

Render is itself a predicate, which takes three arguments: the agent *the medicine*, the theme *Jill*, and the result [*ill*]. The usual terminology calls *rendered* the PRIMARY PREDICATE and, as you learned in the text, *ill* the secondary predicate.

In 5 the secondary predicate is an argument, and if we leave it out, the sentence is ungrammatical. But in 6 it is an adjunct and, accordingly, it is optional.

(6)   She ironed the shirt [flat].

We have not discussed what the theta-role of resultative predicates is, and you can see from 6 that since some resultatives are not arguments, at least some resultatives bear no theta-role. Probably the argument resultative in 5 would be assigned the theta-role of goal by many linguists, where these linguists would be making a distinction between the two theta-roles of benefactee and goal (and see Problem Set 3.3). Nothing in this book will rely on resultatives having any particular theta-role, so we need not go into this question further. Please just accept the label "result" or "resultative."

There are other types of secondary predicates besides resultatives. One kind is called DEPICTIVES:

    (7)   She sat at the desk [tired and depressed].
           He left [a babbling idiot].
           She fell on the floor [half out of her mind].

Find at least one more verb which, like *render*, takes an argument predicate, whether that argument is resultative or depictive. (Remember, if omission of the secondary predicate results in the sentence becoming ungrammatical, then the secondary predicate must be an argument of the primary predicate.)

Give a list of at least five sentences in which a secondary predicate is an adjunct.

We can see from 7 that depictive secondary predicates can be APs, NPs, or PPs. In 5 and 6 above the resultative secondary predicates are APs. Find an example of a resultative NP and of a resultative PP.

Part 4: APs that modify can be understood to be RESTRICTIVE or NONRESTRICTIVE. For example, in:

    (8)   The philosophical Greeks wrote plays.

we could read this restrictively to mean "Those Greeks who were philosophical wrote plays," or nonrestrictively to mean "All Greeks were philosophical and they wrote plays." This difference corresponds to a difference in relative clauses:

    (9)   The Greeks that were philosophical wrote plays.
           The Greeks who were philosophical wrote plays.

    (10)   The Greeks, who were philosophical, wrote plays.

That relative clauses have only a restrictive reading. *Who* relative clauses have a restrictive reading if they are not marked off by pauses (indicated by commas), and a nonrestrictive reading otherwise. *Which* relative clauses, on the other hand, for some speakers have only a nonrestrictive reading:

    (11)   Whales, which are large sea mammals, talk.

    (12)   *Whales which are large sea mammals talk.

Give an NP that contains an AP that can be read as restrictive or nonrestrictive and describe both readings of that NP.

Give an NP that contains an AP that can be read only as restrictive in that NP. Describe the reading.

Give an NP that contains an AP that can be read only as nonrestrictive in that NP. Describe the reading.

Nouns

Part 1: In the text you learned that NPs can be used predicatively and also equationally or identificationally.

(1)   John is an excellent student.

(2)   The coach is Mr. Randolph.

Some linguists have claimed that in most contexts the indefinite article on an NP in a copular sentence favors the predicational reading, whereas the definite article favors an identificational reading:

(3)   John is a doctor.

(4)   John is the doctor.

Describe a typical (that is, not unusual) context for 4. Discuss whether *the doctor* in that context gives merely another name for John or assigns a property to John.

Describe a context in which *the doctor* in 4 clearly has a predicational reading.

Offer a sentence with a definite NP after the copula in which that NP favors a predicational reading in most contexts. (It might take a while to find such an example. Hint: NPs with demonstrative adjectives as their specifiers are considered morphologically definite. However, they might introduce material that is new to the discourse.)

Offer a sentence with a definite NP after the copula in which that NP must be understood as identificational.

*Problem Set 4.4: English Argument Structure of Nonverbals

This problem set covers basic concepts. It should be done.

Part 1

In this chapter we have seen that not only V can take thematic arguments, but so can N, A, and P, as in:

(1)   a. [$_{VP}$ like [books]]
      b. [$_{NP}$ a master [at chess]]
      c. [$_{PP}$ into [Greek art]]

In example 1a *like* is the head V and *books* is its theme argument; in example 1b *master* is the head N and *chess* is its theme argument; in example 1c *into* is the head P and *Greek art* is its theme argument. Here I would like you to consider N only.

Give an NP in which the head N has a theme argument internal to the NP. Show that the theme argument is, in fact, internal to the NP. Discuss why you judge that argument to be a theme. (Look back to Problem Set 3.3 for relevant criteria.)

Give another NP (with a different head N) in which the N has an agent argument internal to the NP. Again, give supporting evidence that the argument is, in fact, internal and is, in fact, an agent.

Give another NP (with a different head N) in which the N has a benefactee argument internal to the NP. Give the relevant supporting evidence.

Give another NP (with a different head N) in which the N has an experiencer argument internal to the NP. Give the relevant supporting evidence.

Give another NP (with a different head N) in which the N has an instrument argument internal to the NP. Give the relevant supporting evidence.

As you find the required NPs above, avoid GERUNDS (that is, avoid Ns made up of a V plus -*ing*—like *Bill's reading of Shakespeare*). Instead, use Ns that have typical N morphology (like *book* or *lecture* or *demonstration*). Also, notice that if *voluntarily*, as a modifier of a V, is a test for an agent argument of a verb, then *voluntary*, as a modifier of an N, should be a test for an agent argument of N.

Part 2

You have seen examples of idioms that involve verbs in which one could say the verb somehow heads the idiom, as in:

(2)   John *kicked* the bucket.
      figuratively: 'John died.'

(3)   John *burned* the candle at both ends.
      figuratively: 'John worked hard.'

Try to find at least three idioms that involve nouns in which one could say the noun somehow heads the idiom. Let me give you two examples:

(4)   flight of fancy

(5)   rules of thumb

Now give the trees for the NPs you presented, being sure to give all projections of every major category in your phrase. For example, if an NP is contained inside one of your NPs, and if that contained NP consists of just a single word (an N, like *fancy* or *thumb* in 4 and 5), be sure to give the N″, N′, and N levels, even though N′ and N″ would have only one daughter in such an example.

Problem Set 4.5: English Adverbs

In the text we demonstrated the X-Bar Theory's validity for the category A by using only adjectives. However, as we discussed in chapter 2, A is the cover label used for adverbs, as well. And, in fact, it is reasonable to see A as a coherent category in that adjectives and adverbs occur in complementary distribution, where the form that is morphologically an adjective occurs if modification or predication of a nominal or a clause is involved, but the form that is morphologically an adverb occurs if modification (and, perhaps, predication) of a non-nominal occurs:

(1)   the beautiful idea
      She is beautiful.
      That she would give you that is beautiful.

(2)   She sings beautifully.
      She is beautifully warm and gentle.

Does the category Adverb have the internal analysis that we would expect with X-Bar Theory? Be sure to address the questions of whether Adverb Phrases can take specifiers, modifiers, and arguments.

*Problem Set 4.6: English Reflexives

What you learn from this problem set will be assumed repeatedly in later chapters, so this set should be done.

We know that anaphors must be bound by a local antecedent and we know that pronouns cannot be bound by a local antecedent. That means that within a local context, anaphors and pronouns should have complementary distribution. However, we pointed out in the very end of chapter 2 some instances in which an anaphor appeared to have a somewhat distant antecedent and in which a pronoun appeared to have a terribly local antecedent. An example of each type is repeated here:

(1)   John knew that there would be a picture of himself hanging in the post office.

(2)   My socks have holes in them.

In this problem set, we are going to explore the type of problem that 2 presents.

Part 1

Make a list of five sentences that, like 2, consist of a single clause with a single predicate, but have a pronoun in them that is coreferential with some other NP in the same sentence. Please be sure to avoid possessive adjectives (like *his*) here. To get you started, here are a few more examples:

(3)   The box has books in {it/*itself}.

(4)   Does that list have my name on {it/*itself}?

(5)   Bill brought a friend with {him/*himself}.

Part 2

Look at the list of five sentences that you have come up with and compare them to 2–5. Considering these examples and all the others you have thought of by now, make a generalization about the GF of the pronoun. If you are having any trouble doing this, compare your list and 2–5 to:

(6)   Jack$_i$ likes {*him$_i$/himself}.

(7)   Jack$_i$ talks to {*him$_i$/himself}.

Part 3

Now consider the argument structure of 2–5 and the sentences on your list of five examples. What can you say about the pronoun that can occur with a local antecedent with regard to its semantic function in the sentence? If you are having trouble seeing a generalization, contrast 2–5 with 6 and 7 and with the following examples:

(8) Jack$_i$ depends on {*him$_i$/himself}.

(9) [We have to encourage Jack to be more sociable.] Jack$_i$ is into {*him$_i$/himself} too much.

(Hint: Consider predicate-argument structure in all the relevant sentences.)

Part 4

Sometimes people vary on whether they prefer an anaphor or an antecedent in a given sentence. Take the sentence:

(10) John$_i$ pulled the blanket over {himself/him$_i$}.

(11) The woman$_i$ clasped the child to {herself/her$_i$}.

If you have a strong preference for one over the other in either of these sentences, state that and then try to account for why in a way that is consistent with your answers to Parts 2 and 3. If you have no preference, but could accept either the anaphor or the pronoun in both sentences, try to find a context in which you prefer the anaphor and a different context in which you prefer the pronoun. Give these contexts and discuss them in light of your answers to Parts 2 and 3.

If you feel completely unsure of your own judgments about 10 and 11 (and that happens often to syntacticians), do some data-gathering. Find at least five informants who are native speakers of English. Ask them when they would use 10 and 11 with an anaphor and when they would use them with a pronoun. Listen carefully to their answers and fiddle with the contexts they supply you with until you see some sort of generalization emerging. Relate that generalization to your answers to Parts 2 and 3.

Part 5

We have ignored thus far in this book the so-called EMPHATIC reflexive, as in:

(12) The President himself is coming.

(13) The President is coming himself.

Examples 12 and 13 mean (very close to) the same thing. In 13 we say that the emphatic reflexive is in FLOATED-position. You probably put a stress peak on *himself* as you say the sentence with a floated emphatic.

Does the emphatic reflexive receive a theta-role? If not, what function(s) does it have in the sentence?

Part 6

Now consider sentences like:

(14)   I can do that myself.

(15)   Pam can fix the bike herself.

Here there is nothing introducing the reflexive, yet the reflexive does not seem to be a floated emphatic reflexive. Discuss the difference in meaning between 14 and 15, and 16 and 17, with emphatic reflexives:

(16)   I myself can do that.

(17)   Pam herself can fix the bike.

Part 7

Consider the reflexives in:

(18)   I would never run home by myself.

(19)   She trimmed the tree by herself.

Does the reflexive here receive a theta-role? If not, what function(s) does the *by*-phrase have in the sentence?

Discuss the *by*-reflexive phrase uses in comparison to the bare final reflexive uses like those seen in 14 and 15.

Problem Set 4.7: French Adjective Order

In French, adjectives generally follow the N they modify within the NP. However, many adjectives can precede the head N, as well. Usually, however, there is a semantic distinction associated with the linear distinction. For example, compare the translation of the (a) NPs (in which the N precedes the modifier) to the translation of the (b) NPs (in which the N follows the modifier) in 1–7. Beneath each example I have given a single one-word translation of both the N and the A; these translations represent commonly used senses of these words.

(1)   a.   un menteur furieux 'an angry liar'
      b.   un furieux menteur 'a compulsive (that is, a terrible) liar'
         (menteur = 'liar'; furieux = 'angry')

(2)   a.   un poète heureux 'a happy poet'
      b.   un heureux poète 'a successful poet'
         (poète = 'poet'; heureux = 'happy')

(3)   a.   un homme pauvre 'an impecunious man'
      b.   un pauvre homme 'a wretched man'
         (homme = 'man'; pauvre = 'poor')

(4)   a.   un soldat simple 'a simple-minded (that is, uncomplicated) soldier'
      b.   un simple soldat 'a private'
         (soldat = 'soldier'; simple = 'simple')

(5)   a. une route mauvaise 'a bad(ly paved) road'
      b. une mauvaise route 'a wrong (that is, mistaken) road'
          (route = 'road'; mauvaise = 'bad')

(6)   a. un livre méchant 'a wicked (that is, evil) book'
      b. un méchant livre 'a third-rate book'
          (livre = 'book'; méchant = 'bad')

(7)   a. un roi ancien 'an ancient king'
      b. un ancien roi 'a former king'
          (roi = 'king'; ancien = 'ancient')

Part 1

Think about the specfic semantic difference that correlates to word order in each of
1–7 above. Now consider those specific differences and try to find a thread that will
tie together 1–7 so that you can make a generalization about the type of meanings
we associate with a modifier that follows the N as opposed to the type of meanings
we associate with a modifier that precedes the N. Do not yet write any of this down.
Based on your thoughts about 1–7, which order in 8 would mean 'a long-standing
friend' and which would mean 'an elderly friend'? (I have used the feminine noun
for friend here.)

(8)   une amie vieille (amie = 'friend'; vieille = 'old')
      une vieille amie

Part 2

Guess at the English translations for the French NPs below. Use the data in 1–7
above to aid you. There are several theoretically correct answers here. The point is
for you to see the *types* of meanings that are most probable.

(9)   un mangeur furieux (mangeur = 'eater')
       un furieux mangeur

(10)   un billet simple (billet = 'ticket')
       un simple billet

(11)   un cheval méchant (cheval = 'horse')
       un méchant cheval

(12)   une église pauvre (église = 'church')
       une pauvre église

Part 3

The French word for 'French' is *français*. How do you think one would say *'Old
French'* (as when referring to an earlier stage of the language)? Why?
    Fille means 'girl' and *vieille* is the form of the adjective for 'old' that would agree
with a feminine singular noun like *fille*. What do you think *une vieille fille* would
mean? Why?

Part 4

Look over all the data thus far and state a generalization about the correlation between word order and meaning with regard to modifiers and Ns within an NP in French.

Part 5

You may well have noticed that the single-word translations in 1–7 (the translations in parentheses after each pair of examples) were helpful for the N but quite unhelpful for the A. Why might that be? (Hint: This question is, frankly, difficult and carries you into the realm of semantics much further than we have yet treaded in this book. You need to consider the senses of Ns as compared to the senses of As. Please aim for a relatively simple answer and do not let yourself get sidetracked by details that do not conform to the general picture. Think here about the sense of Ns and the sense of As and how these relate to context.)

At this point you have completed the regular problem set. However, the next three parts are added for those who are interested in trying to find some comparisons between the French phenomenon above and English or Spanish.

Part 6

If you did Problem Set 4.3, explain why the difference in meaning associated with the differing word orders in the English sentences below is not an example of the same phenomenon seen in the French examples in Parts 1–3.

(13) a. A hungry lion is a danger to all.
      A lion hungry is a danger to all.

  b. An unhappy man is seldom in control of his emotions.
     A man unhappy is seldom in control of his emotions.

Part 7

Consider the differences in meaning associated with the differing word orders in the English sentences below:

(14) He rudely spoke to me.
      He spoke to me rudely.

(15) They courteously stepped aside.
      They stepped aside courteously.

(16) He once hit me.
      He hit me once.

(17) She simply told me.
      She told me simply.

(18) We often eat.
      We eat often.

Give a brief paraphrase of each pair of sentences in 14–18 which makes clear the difference in meaning between the members of each pair.

Next give at least two other pairs of sentences with adverbs (like *rudely, courteously, once, simply,* and *often* above) which display a similar meaning difference associated with different word orders.

Now give a general statement of the meaning difference associated with the word-order difference in these sentences with adverbs.

Finally, compare the phenomenon in this part of the problem set to that explored in Parts 1–5. Is this the same phenomenon or not? Defend your answer.

Part 8

If you know Spanish, discuss these examples in light of the French semantic distinction you came up with in Part 4.

(19)   cierta cosa
       una cosa cierta

(20)   varios libros
       libros varios

(21)   la pura verdad
       la verdad pura

Problem Set 4.8: Japanese Reduplication

Consider the following Japanese sentences (where "TOP" stands for "topic", as in Problem Set 3.7):

(1)   a. Kinoo-wa   susi-o   tabeta.
         yesterday-TOP sushi-OBJ ate.

         'Yesterday (I) ate sushi.'

      b. Kinoo-wa   susi-o   tabe-ni tabeta.
         'Yesterday (I) ate sushi to an extreme extent.'

(2)   a. Hanako-wa Yosio-o   nikunda.
         Hanako-TOP Yoshio-OBJ hated

         'Hanako hated Yoshio.'

      b. Hanako-wa Yosio-o   nikum-i-ni nikunda.
         'Hanako hated Yoshio to an extreme extent.'

(3)   a. Kinoo-wa   Yamada-to   akegata   -made nonda.
         yesterday-TOP Yamada-with dawn   -until drank

         'Yesterday (I) drank with Yamada until dawn.'

      b. Kinoo-wa   Yamada-to   akegata   -made nom-i-ni nonda.
         'Yesterday (I) drank to an extreme extent with Yamada until dawn.'

The final word in each of these examples is a verb, and the final syllable of that verb (the *ta* or *da*) is a past-tense affix. The rest of the verb is its root.

Assume that a regular phonological rule is responsible for the alternation between *m* and *n* in forms like "niku*m*-ini" and "niku*n*da" in 2b and "no*m*-ini" and "no*n*da" in 3b.

Assume further that the -(*i*)-*ni* of *tabe-ni, nikum-i-ni*, and *nom-i-ni* is either an affix or a particle.

State briefly the syntactic and morphological difference you see between the (a) and (b) examples above. (This is as simple a job as you think it is.)

What semantic correlation is there to these syntactic and morphological differences?

Is this type of phenomenon (which is often called REDUPLICATION) found as well in English? If so, give an example and discuss restrictions on reduplication in English.

Is this type of phenomenon found as well in any Romance language you know (if you know one)? If so, give an example and discuss restrictions on reduplication in that language.

Japanese allows a variety of word orders in its sentences (as you learned in Problem Set 1.4). However, no word may come between the reduplicated elements of examples like 1–3. Thus, for example, we find:

(4)   *Kinoo-wa Yamada-to nom-ini akegata-made nonda.
        *Kinoo-wa akegata-made nom-ini Yamada-to nonda.

How might you account for this fact? (Note: You are making a stab in the dark here. But certain kinds of stabs should seem reasonable to you at this point, whereas other kinds should not.)

Discuss briefly whatever questions for phrase structure that you see this phenomenon raising.

Star Problem 4.1

In the text we pointed out that some verbs require sentential Objects:

(1)   I suppose that he's coming.
        *I suppose {the result/the fact}.

However, as we saw with the preposition *while*, it is not immediately obvious whether this restriction is best handled by a syntactic account or a semantic account. Let us try to approach that question for *suppose* here.

Can *suppose* have a PP complement? Can it have an AP complement? Can it have an NP complement?

Consider the following dialogues:

(2)   —Where did he go?
        —I suppose [to the store].

(3)   —How does she feel?
        —I suppose [lousy].

(4) —Who is she with?
    —I suppose [Noam].

The answers in all these examples are called elliptical. How do we know how to interpret them? What conversational strategies are involved? In answering this, discuss how this PP, AP, and NP would be expanded in the semantics.

Notice that the strategies involved in interpreting 2–4 are quite different from those involved in interpreting the complements of *while* discussed in the text. In fact, if someone began a conversation with:

(5) While in Florida, . . .

you might encourage a continuation with:

(6) —Well, go on, what happened?

But if someone began a conversation with:

(7) —I suppose strawberry jam.

you might be completely confused. If you gave the person the benefit of the doubt, you might ask:

(8) —What do you suppose about strawberry jam?

Use the fact that 5 seems incomplete, whereas 7 seems at first blush inappropriate as you discuss the restriction on the complements of *suppose*.

Now consider the complements of *suppose* below:

(9) I suppose [so].
    I suppose [not].
    I supposed [that], too, before I met her.
    I supposed [the very same thing] before I met her.

What are the appropriate types of contexts for such sentences? Given those contexts, discuss the possibility that the words *so*, *not*, and *that* are PRO-CLAUSES (just like some words are pronouns) in 9. How does the NP *the very same thing* fit in? Is it semantically like an ordinary NP or is it semantically more like a pro-form (pro-clause or pro-NP)?

Now compare *suppose* with PP, AP, and NP complements (as in 2–4) with *ask*, which most commonly takes a clausal complement:

(10) She asked what he was doing.

but can take an NP complement that is not elliptical:

(11) She asked the time.

Discuss the expansion in semantic structure of the complement of *ask* in 11. When can we say things like the following?

(12) She asked {what/when/why/how/who/whether or not/where}.

Are the examples in 12 more like 11 or more like the answers in 2–4 with respect to the processes we go through in order to interpret them?

Find your own examples of other elliptical NP complements. Analyze them as we have done for *while* and *suppose* NP complements.

Star Problem 4.2

In the text I raised the possibility that participles, when used to modify, might be of the category A rather than V. We know at least two ways to investigate that possibility at this point. One is to ask whether participles as modifiers can have morphological properties that As take but Vs do not, or vice versa. The other is to ask whether participles as modifiers can co-occur with other items that As can occur with but Vs cannot, or vice versa, such as particular intensifiers.

You might begin, then, by considering examples such as:

(1)   The tireder boy of the two is John.
      (cf. We tired John out.
          *We tireder John out.
          She is {taller/ happier/ calmer/ gentler/ . . . }.)

(2)   The very tired boy is John.
      (cf. *We very tired John out.
          She is very {intelligent/ tall/ calm/ rational . . . }.

(3)   The very much appreciated gift is still in the drawer.
      (cf. We very much appreciate that gift.
          *She is very much {intelligent/ tall/ calm . . . }.)

Be sure to follow up on how these kinds of tests break participles, adjectives, and verbs down into subclasses.

Warning: Do not expect a clean answer. Just have fun exploring.

Overview

Binding Theory

In this chapter we put on hold our discussion of Binding Theory (BT) in order to get a firm grasp on phrasal analysis. Thus we still have only two conditions to BT:

(A)   Anaphors must be locally bound.
(B)   Pronouns must be locally free.

We still need to explore locality and we still need to explore the potential hierarchical relationships between one item and another that it binds.

However, there is one new fact relevant to BT that we uncovered in doing Problem Set 4.6. We found out that pronouns can be locally bound if they do not receive a theta-role. Locally bound pronouns in all the examples we have seen thus far are adjunct OPs, and never DOs or IOs.

On the other hand, anaphors generally receive a theta-role, unless they are used emphatically.

These facts suggest that BT is intricately related to Theta Theory in a way we must develop further later.

X-Bar Theory

We now have a good picture of X-Bar Theory. We have argued that every major category has the internal structure:

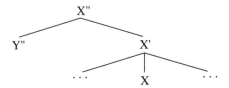

We have adoped the convention that branches of a tree cannot cross.

We have introduced labeled brackets as an alternative graphic representation of a structural analysis.

We have discussed the contrast between a minor/major-category distinction and a functional/lexical-category distinction. We have adopted the idea that both functional and lexical categories can have maximal projections. All nominal phrases will be analyzed as Quantifier Phrases or Determiner Phrases from now on, although we may represent them as NPs in trees if their internal structure is not relevant to the discussion at hand in a given passage of the text. We have put off the proper analysis of Auxiliaries until chapter 8.

Case Theory

We remain with our slim knowledge that in English Subjects of tensed clauses have Subjective Case, whereas nominals in other positions are Objective or genitive.

Theta Theory

We have a complete Theta Theory (TT). Each argument is assigned a unique theta-role. You can look back to the Overview of chapter 3 for details.

We also learned in this chapter that the only nodes that we know of thus far that can be Complete Functional Complexes are NPs, Ss, and perhaps VPs.

Licensing

We learned in earlier chapters that every element in a sentence must be licensed by serving some function. The functional roles we had prior to this chapter included being a predicate, a modifier, an argument, and filling a GF.

In this chapter we learned that Ps can license their Objects by serving to relate them to all or part of the material outside the PP, even if the Object of the P does not receive a theta-role. We suggested that the function of "relator" be added to our list of functions. However, since Object of P is a GF, Objects of P are licensed, so we need not claim that the relator function licenses any elements.

We also learned that secondary predicates can occur either as arguments or as adjuncts of primary predicates. We pointed out that sometimes the secondary predicate serves the function of "mediating" the relationship between its Subject and the primary predicate. However, we need not claim that the mediation function licenses any elements. Adjunct secondary predicates would be licensed by virtue of the fact that they are predicated of some other element that is, in turn, licensed independently of the adjunct. For example, the resultative adjunct predicate we discussed in this chapter is predicated of the theme argument of the primary predicate.

5

Case, Government, and C-Command

Introduction

In Chapter 4 we developed the X-Bar Theory, according to which every lexical category has the following internal structure:

(1)

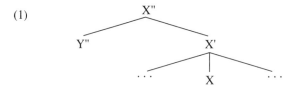

A phrase can be filled by a single lexical item, typically the head of the phrase, as in:

(2) I like [dogs] . She [runs] . We went [out] . He's [nice] .
      NP = N   VP = V   PP = P   AP = A

Heads can also be accompanied by modifiers. Modifiers can be of a range of categories. The modifier is underlined in example 3; this list is representative (but not exhaustive) of the range of categories that can modify the various heads:

(3) I like [*big* dogs].   (AP modifies N.)
     I like [birds *with claws*].   (PP modifies N.)
     She [runs *fast*].   (AP modifies V.)
     She [runs *a great deal*].   (NP modifies V.)
     Mary is [*sinfully* into Greek art]. (AP modifies P.)
     He's [*obviously* nice].   (AP modifies A.)
     He went [blue *in the face*].   (PP modifies A.)

And whole clauses, whose category we have simply written as S thus far, can modify a variety of head types:

(4) a. I like [dogs *that you train*].   (S modifies N.)
     b. He [spoke *how I told you he would*].   (S modifies V.)
     c. He's [as interesting *as I had hoped*].   (S modifies A.)

Heads can also be accompanied by arguments inside their phrase. Arguments are usually NPs or clauses, but they could be PPs or APs (as you saw in chapter 3). (And some have argued that VPs can be arguments. Each bracketed phrase below contains an italicized phrase that can be argued to be an argument of the element(s) in boldface.

(5) a. I like [**stories** about *Jim*].
     b. She [**runs** *marathons*].
     c. We **went** [**out** *the window*].
     d. He's [**nice** *to children*].

Notice that in an example like 5c I am taking the position that *the window* is an argument of the multiple-word theta-assigner *go out*. If this is correct, then theta-assigners not only can consist of more than one word—the words that make up a theta-assigner need not form a syntactic constituent (or unit). In my view Vs and Ps often act together to assign theta-roles. Thus a V like *go*, for example, would be part of many different theta-assigners (compare *go in, go through, go on*, etc.).

Certainly this analysis of 5c is not the only possible one. And, in fact, it is not a common one. Others might well take the position that the P *out* assigns a theta-role to its Object. We have already discussed the fact that some Ps in some uses seem to be true theta-assigners, like *after* in:

(6) She's after that prize.

Others seem to relate their Object to the rest of the sentence in a range of ways, like *after* in:

(7) I'll eat after my bath.

And, finally, others seem to work with another word or words to assign a theta-role to their Object, like *after* in:

(8) I'll look after the child for you.

Thus each use of a P in a given sentence demands scrutiny before one can say whether the P alone is a theta-assigner. (Compare to *look after* the following V-plus-P combinations: *take after, worry about, depend on*, and many others.)

While my analysis of 5c is highly debatable, the claim that it rests on, that strings of words which do not form a syntactic constituent can form a semantic constituent, is better accepted. There are many semantic units that do not appear to form syntactic constituents, such as the italicized words in:

(9) The teacher *took* the students *to task*.
     The cat's got Bill's *tongue*. (on the idomatic reading)
     Mary *made a face at* her sister.

Add some of your own examples to 9.

Nevertheless, a prevalent idea in linguistics is that semantic units correspond to syntactic constituents—as they often do. Thus a variety of somewhat abstract analyses might be offered for examples like those in 9 (analyses that you probably cannot begin to guess at yet—but which you may well consider after you have read through the end of chapter 8). Certainly, if there were a strict parallel between semantic structure and syntactic structure (some people even argue that these two components of the grammar are ISOMORPHIC, claiming that for each element in one, there is a corresponding element in the other, and for each principle or operation in one, there is a corresponding principle or operation in the other that acts on the corresponding elements), the mapping between the two might be relatively simple. A theory of grammar that included such a mapping would be desirable. Thus it is easy to understand why many linguists are loathe to give up the claim that semantic units form syntactic constituents. As you continue through this book, you may want to keep track of all those points at which I claim that a string which does not form a syntactic constituent is a semantic constituent and try to find evidence yourself for or against each particular analysis.

A good foundation in X-Bar Theory and the ability to draw trees will be assumed in the rest of this chapter. You can review your knowledge of trees by doing Problem Set 5, followed by Problem Set 5.7, which uses those skills and will, I hope, convince you of some of the explanatory power of X-Bar Theory.

Case Assignment

One thing we noted repeatedly in chapter 4 was that when we set up parallels between N, V, P, and A, often N and A would group together in needing a P (frequently *of*) to introduce their Object, whereas V and P did not generally call for any (additional) preposition:

(10) NP: the destruction [of] the city
      VP: destroy the city
      AP: destructive [of] her self-esteem
      PP: with the boy

(Of course, the NP in 10 is really a DP, as you know. But the point is that *the city* is the argument of the N *destruction*, not of the D.) In 10 the preposition *of* in the NP and AP examples does not contribute any easily identifiable semantic information to the phrase, although some might want to claim that *of* introduces theme arguments of Ns and As. Notice, however, that *of* is not needed to introduce theme arguments of V or P. Whether *of* is itself meaningless or marks a theme argument, the question remains: Why can V and P take a "Direct" Object, while N and A cannot?

In order to answer this, we need to look at a wide range of examples like those in 10. As you know, in addition to NPs, whole clauses can be Objects. But when whole clauses are Objects, no *of* or other P appears to introduce them regardless of the category of the head whose Object the clause is:

(11) NP: the knowledge [that Jim is here]
      VP: know [that Jim is here]
      AP: upset [that Jim is here]
      PP: in [that Jim is here]

If you test lots of examples for yourself, you will find that if the Object is an NP, both N and A heads require *of* or some other P to introduce the Object. If the Object is a clause, however, no P appears. So now the question asked above can be revised to: Why can V and P take Direct NP Objects, while N and A cannot?

A speaker of English faced with this question is often at a loss as to how to begin to answer it. But speakers of other languages that exhibit similar patterns to those in 10 and 11 above and also have a well-developed audible Case system for NPs (such as German and Russian) sometimes find the question less baffling. If you know a language that exhibits data like those in 10 and 11 and that DECLINES NPs with audible morphemes (that is, assigns NPs Case endings based on the structural position in the sentence, as discussed in Tangent 1.5 of chapter 1), you may find the question easier to attack, as well.

The answer many linguists have given is that V and P are CASE-ASSIGNERS, whereas N and A are not. That is, whether Case is audible or not, Vs and Ps assign a Case to their Object, but Ns and As in English cannot do this. Let us assume the tenet known as the CASE FILTER:

(12) Every NP with a phonetic matrix must receive Case.

(Note: An NP with a phonetic matrix is audible. The Case Filter restricts audible NPs only. We will discuss the possibility of silent, or phonetically empty, NPs in the next chapter and in following ones. There we will face the issue of the Case properties of empty NPs.) With the Case Filter we can account for the different behaviors of NP and clauses above, because NPs require Case (that is, they must be assigned Case) but clauses do not.

Notice that the fact that phrases other than NPs (such as clauses) do not require Case does not prevent them from receiving Case if they should appear in a position to which Case is normally assigned. We will explore data that bear on the issue of whether non-NPs can or must receive Case in Problem Set 7.11 of chapter 7.

We now need to formulate rules that assign Case. One simple possibility is that V and P assign Case to their NP sisters. Let us call this STRUCTURAL CASE ASSIGNMENT since this rule is sensitive to structural factors (here sisterhood of nodes). If N and A do not have this capability, then a sister to N or A would fail to receive Case, and the result would be a violation of the Case Filter. The *of* that appears in 10, then, can be viewed as a P whose function is to assign Case to the following NP. Thus Ns and As take "prepositional Objects" rather than Direct NP Objects because Ns and As are not Case-Assigners. Let us assume this formulation of Structural Case Assignment for the moment.

For every category we have looked at thus far, the head precedes its arguments within the phrase. This is the main reason some people have classified English as a head-initial language. These arguments are sisters to the head, so our Structural Case Assignment rule will account for their receiving Case. There is one exception that we have seen, however: the argument that can occur as the left branch of NP, as in 13.

(13)   [the professor's] discussion of war

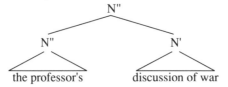

(You will see a different tree analysis for 13 in Tangent 8.2 of chapter 8. But the same issue arises in both analyses.) Immediately we are faced with a problem regarding Case: How does the bracketed NP in 13 receive Case? It is not the Object of a V or P, not even the P *of* which might have been expected to appear (since *the professor* is an argument of an N, and since this N introduces its other argument, the NP *war*, with *of*). Furthermore, it is not a sister of the head N, but instead a sister to the N' node. If we place the entire NP in 13 inside a complete utterance, we find that it is free to appear in any of the positions that NPs (or DPs or QPs, of course) ordinarily appear in:

(14)   [The professor's discussion of Vico] was extraordinary.
       I hated [the professor's discussion of Vico].
       I thought {of/about} [the professor's discussion of Vico].

The NP in 13 can be a Subject, a DO, and an OP, as we see in 14. We already know that the Case of an NP is determined by its syntactic properties (as we very informally said in Tangent 1.5 of chapter 1). Interestingly, however, the Case of *the professor* is invariable, regardless of the syntactic properties of the larger NP within which it is contained. That is, *the professor* is genitive (as the *-s* indicates), even when the NP that contains it is in the Subject position of a tensed clause, where Subjective Case (or Nominative Case) is expected. What might account for the fact that the NP *the professor* in 13 and 14 is always genitive regardless of the Case of the containing NP? If genitive Case is assigned internally, that is, if the genitive Case of the NP *the professor* is determined by factors present entirely inside the containing NP, then we can explain why the syntactic environment external to the containing NP does not affect the genitive Case here. So we are led to proposing a special rule, which we will call the GENITIVE RULE:

(15)   In:

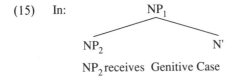

(In 15 NP$_2$ could, of course, be DP or QP. As we said in chapter 4, we will label all nominal phrases NP unless the recognition of DP or QP is of particular pertinence to the discussion at hand.) The Genitive Rule, then, accounts for Case on an NP which is the left branch of a containing NP. That is, an NP that is in specifier position of a larger NP typically receives genitive Case. (You will consider consequences of this claim in Star Problem 5.5.) There is no Case-Assigner involved here. Instead, any NP in that structural configuration can undergo this rule.

Now that we have handled the Case of genitive arguments, we can take a closer look at our Structural Case Assignment rule involving sisters to a head. Consider:

(16)   NP: the destruction *of an entire city* in six days
                the destruction in six days *of an entire city*

         VP: destroy *the city* brutally
                *destroy brutally *the city*

         AP: destructive *of her self-esteem* in unforeseeable ways
                destructive in unforeseeable ways *of her self-esteem*

         PP: in the box completely
                *in completely the box

In each example here, the head is followed by two constituents, one is an argument (italicized) and the other is a modifier. Arguments and modifiers of N and A that follow the head may appear in either order in these examples, but that is not true for V or P. With the V and P here, the Object must immediately follow the V or P. A modifier can follow the Object (as in 16) or precede the V or P (*brutally destroy the city, completely in the box*).

Is the restriction that the V/P be immediately followed by its Object peculiar to the V *destroy* and the P *in*, or is it general to the categories V and P? If we substitute *see, enjoy, explore*, or any other transitive V that is semantically suitable into 16, we find that this restriction holds. Likewise if we substitute any other transitive P that is semantically suitable into 16, the restriction still holds. So we can assume it is a restriction general to the categories V and P.

Is this an ad hoc restriction we find on V and P, or does it follow from some other fact? Notice that DOs are not the only type of argument that V takes. What happens to word order within VP if we consider an IO argument and a modifier?

(17)   talk *to Bill* quietly
          talk quietly *to Bill*

Suddenly we find that a modifier can intervene easily between the V and its argument. What makes the DO such a special argument of V? In all the instances in which the word order is flexible, we find that the arguments of N, A, or V are introduced by Ps (here *of* for arguments of N or A, and *to* for the IO argument of the V). Only DOs of Vs and Objects of Ps are not introduced by a separate P. So we can use this fact in accounting for 16. If Structural Case Assignment in English operates only on an immediately ADJACENT NP (that is, on a sister node with nothing intervening between the Case-Assigner and its sister), then DOs of Vs and Objects of Ps must immediately follow them, but arguments of N and A, which have an additional P to assign them Case, need not immediately follow the N or A (so long as they immediately follow the relevant Case-Assigning P). We can now restate Structural Case Assignment:

(18)   V and P assign structural Case to an immediately following sister NP.

(We will have occasion later to revise this formulation of Structural Case Assignment. Notice that 18 does not distinguish argument sisters from modifier sisters. You will have a chance to ask whether such a distinction should be made as you do Problem Set 5.2.)

Direct Objects That Do Not Immediately Follow Verbs

You might well be objecting at this point because you may have noticed that there are, in fact, instances in English in which a DO that is an NP does not immediately follow the V. One common type of example involves PARENTHETICALS or certain types of sentential adverbials that intervene between a V and its DO, set off by a pause (indicated by commas here) from the material surrounding them:

(19)   I ate, you're not gonna believe this, the very pizza . . .
       I ate, unfortunately, the very pizza you told me not to.

Parentheticals and sentential adverbials can appear in a variety of NICHES in a sentence, and if we were to construct a grammar taking their distribution into account from the start, we would have difficulty seeing otherwise-relatively-straightforward generalizations about English grammar. For that reason, we will build our grammar without considering their placement for now. We will return to a discussion of adverbials in chapter 8, and you can do some exploration of the factors that affect their placement in Problem Set 8.16.

A second type of sentence in which the DO need not immediately follow the V is one in which a particle (see discussion in chapter 3) appears:

(20)   Harry looked up the number.
       (cf. Harry looked the number up.)

If we admit *look up* as an item in our lexicon, then we could argue that here there is a complex V made up of a V plus a P, as in 21.

(21)

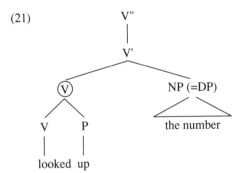

(Recall that the triangle in 21 indicates that we could give a more detailed breakdown of the phrase here, but we will not because those details are not relevant to the discussion.) With this analysis, the circled V in 21 is immediately followed by the NP and can be taken as its Case-Assigner.

The analysis in 21 is brought up simply to remove V plus particle combinations from the list of cases in which a DO is not immediately adjacent to the V. However, it creates a number of other problems. For example, this analysis requires that we allow a modification of our X-Bar Theory such that a lexical node like V can be expanded to V plus P instead of being restricted to dominating only a lexical item. Furthermore, the parallels between sentences in which a particle precedes a DO and sentences in which it follows a DO may now be more difficult to account for. We will leave these issues unresolved.

A third type of sentence in which the DO does not immediately follow the V is the Double Object construction, discussed in chapter 3:

(22)   Sally gave Bill the book.

Here two NPs follow the V in succession. Structural Case Assignment in 18 cannot account for 22. There are several alternatives here. One is that Case is assigned to both the NPs following the V in 22 by the V via a special rule of Case assignment that is structural in nature, similar to 18. In that instance, since we know that Structural Case Assignment is sensitive to linear adjacency, we might expect that if any modifier intervened between either of these NPs and the V, the sentence would fail. That is, in fact, what happens:

(23)   *Sally gave [surreptitiously] Bill the book.
       *Sally gave Bill [surreptitiously] the book.
       (cf. Sally gave Bill the book [surreptitiously].
       Sally gave the book [surreptitiously] to Bill.
       Sally gave the book to Bill [surreptitiously].)

Again, particles (as in 20) create complications. They can intervene between the two NP Objects for at least some speakers:

(24)   I'll give Jim [back] the book, if he'll just be patient.
       (cf. I'll give Jim the book [back], if he'll just be patient.)

But they cannot come between the V and the first NP in the Double-Object construction (although they can in the DO-IO alternative—see the discussion of 21 above):

(25)   *I'll give [back] Jim the book, if he'll just be patient.
       (cf. I'll give back the book to Jim, if he'll . . .)

A variety of explanations have been offered for these facts about particles. Once again, we will not go further into them in this book.

An alternative account of 22 would see the Double-Object construction as special with regard to Case assignment. You already know (from chapter 3 and Star Problem 3.3) that only some Vs, not all, can enter into the Double Object construction. It is possible that these Vs are marked in the lexicon as assigning Case—by some new method, let us call it INHERENT CASE ASSIGNMENT, to the second Object, whereas the first Object could easily be assigned structural Case. We will not choose between these alternatives because nothing we do in the rest of this book hinges on that choice. Instead, we will merely refer to the DOUBLE-OBJECT CASE RULE and not worry about exactly how this rule operates.

Before we leave the Double-Object construction, there is one more alternative analysis that we not only should bring up, but can also dismiss. Students I have had in classes over the years often suggest that in a sentence like 22, the first NP is introduced by a phonetically null *to* which gives it Case. Then the second NP gets Case by Structural Case Assignment. There are at least two serious problems with this proposal. First, Structural Case Assignment would have to overlook the intervening PP (the silent *to* plus the first NP) between the V and the second NP. But how is this Case rule to recognize that this PP is special, as opposed to other PPs, like that in 26?

(26)   *Jack ate [on Tuesday] pizza.

Second, sentences with the Double-Object construction do not always have a corresponding sentence in which an IO is introduced by *to*. Instead, they might have a corresponding sentence in which an IO is introduced by *for*, or they may lack any corresponding sentence in which the benefactive argument appears preceded by a P:

(27)   a.   We baked Mary a cake.
              We baked a cake for Mary.

        b.   We spared John the ordeal.
              *We spared the ordeal {to/for/from/of/ . . . } John.

Thus we would have to posit a silent *for* to handle the first sentence of 27a, and we would be at a loss as to what silent P to posit for 27b. We must conclude that positing a phonetically null P before the first Object in the Double Object construction gains us nothing.

There is another account of the Double-Object construction involving a null P that has been proposed in the literature. In this proposal the second Object is introduced by a null P. The motivation for such a proposal involves theoretical concerns that we will not address now (such as how many daughters a given node may have— see Tangent 8.2 of chapter 8). Therefore we will not discuss this analysis further. However, it is interesting to note that in Yoruba, a Kwa language of the Niger Congo family, we can have a theme argument preceding a benefactee argument or vice versa, but in either order the linearly second NP is preceded by a P.

A fourth type of apparent exception to 18 is presented by sentences like:

(28)   Jack bought with only two dollars [the most magnificent fox skin you'll ever set eyes on].

Here what is called a HEAVY NP is placed at the end of the sentence. Compare the awkwardness of the same constituent order when the DO is very short:

(29)   *Jack bought with only two dollars {it/diamonds}.

The phenomenon seen in 28 is typically called HEAVY NP SHIFT. The exact definition of heaviness is the topic of much literature and is a point of controversy. What is clear is that no simple definition in terms of phonological length or syntactic complexity suffices. We will return to a discussion of sentences with a heavy NP in final position in chapter 7. There we will offer an account of 28 that allows us to maintain ordinary Structural Case Assignment for these examples.

We will, therefore, go forth with 18 for now, repeated here for convenience:

(30)   V and P assign structural Case to an immediately following sister NP.

Example 30 has as a consequence the fact that NP Objects of V and P must immediately follow the V or P. The ordering of other constituents within a phrase, however, is not constrained in any way by Case Theory.

We have recognized and discussed the following four types of apparent exceptions to 30, all of which involve questions for Case assignment by V, not by P, since a constituent intervenes between the V and its Object:

(31)   a. parentheticals and sentential adverbials
          I ate [{you're not gonna believe this/unfortunately}] the very pizza
          you told me not to.

       b. particles
          Harry looked [up] the number

       c. Double Objects
          Sally gave [Bill] the book.

       d. heavy NPs
          Jack bought [with only two dollars] the most magnificent fox skin
          you'll ever set eyes on.

With the picture we have developed thus far of Case Theory, figure out how each NP in the sentences below gets Case.

(32)   *Sam* ate [a peach] with [that neighbor].
       The boy gave /Sally/ /a dollar/ for [{the teacher's} ruler].

Here the NPs in brackets receive Case by Structural Case Assignment from a V or P. The NP in braces receives Case by the Genitive Rule. The NPs between slants receive Case by the Double-Object Case Rule. But we still have two NPs to account for: the italicized NPs in Subject position of both sentences.

Assigning Case to Subjects

We know that the Subject position of the clauses in 32 is a position to which Case is assigned. We know this simply by virtue of the fact that NPs can occur in this position and we have adopted the Case Filter. But no rule of Case assignment we have yet discussed will give Case to the Subject NPs in 32.

How do Subject NPs get Case? Subject NPs are not inside any larger phrase headed by N, V, P, or A. Instead, the next larger syntactic phrase that contains them, so far as we know at this point, is the clause. So now we need to ask exactly what the structure of clauses is.

For a long period within modern linguistics people assumed that clauses, unlike NP, VP, PP, or AP, were EXOCENTRIC, or unheaded (as opposed to ENDOCENTRIC, or headed). Thus S had the structure shown in 33.

(33)

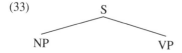

With this analysis, S was an unusual category and, while it was a phrasal level (immediately dominating other nonterminal nodes) and not a lexical level (immediately dominating lexical items), it was not a projection of any category. Even today it is not uncommon to find trees drawn as in 33, although they are usually just a shorthand for the trees we are going to develop below.

The very fact that S as analyzed in 33 was an exceptional category for X-Bar Theory made this analysis suspect. That is, unless we are forced away by weighty evidence to the contrary, we should pursue the position that all major categories have the same internal breakdown. Thus the search began for a way to align S with the other major categories. An immediate proposal was that S was really a projection of V, maybe a V with triple bars, something like:

(34)

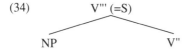

Still, S was unusual in that now V had a triple-bar level, but the other categories did not. The sorts of evidence one might have hoped to find that N and P and A could also have a triple-bar level were either elusive or were not as closely analogous to the situation encountered with V as one would have liked. (We discuss some in Tangent 8.2 of chapter 8.) Furthermore, seeing the Subject as internal to the phrase headed by V created other problems for the theory and made V stand apart from the other categories. That is, in all the examples that follow *Jim* is the Subject argument of the italicized item (the theta-assigner), but with the analysis of S in 34, only in 35a is *Jim* an argument internal to the phrase that its theta-assigner heads. That is, assuming 34, *Jim* is internal to the VP (which is a triple-bar level) in 35a, but *Jim* is external to the NP, PP, and AP of 35b–d.

(35) a. V: [Jim *swam* five laps every day].
      b. N: Jim was [a *champion* at tennis].
      c. P: Jim was [*out* yesterday].
      d. A: Jim was [*friendly* to newcomers].

Thus analyzing S as a projection of V still did not pull S into alignment with the other major categories. (In Tangent 8.1 of chapter 8 you will see a more recent analysis of verb phrases in which Subjects are internal arguments. We are not yet ready to discuss that analysis here, however.)

Furthermore, since the Subject would be internal to the VP in 35a, but external to the NP, PP, and AP in 35b–d, we might expect to find syntactic behavior differences between sentences like 35a and those like 35b–d with regard to either the Subject or the predicate or both. But we apparently do not. All likely phenomena that I have tested treat 35a–d equally. For example, the phenomenon known as VP Deletion or VP Ellipsis (which you studied in Problem Set 2.6) treats them all the same:

(36) a. Jim swam five laps every day and Bill did, too.
      b. Jim was a champion at tennis and Bill was, too.
      c. Jim was out yesterday, and Bill was, too.
      d. Jim was friendly to newcomers, and Bill was, too.

(The auxiliary *did* in the second conjunct in 36a shows up whenever the first conjunct has no auxiliary, a situation we are familiar with from Problem Sets 2.1 and 2.4.)

On the other hand, we have already noted that Ns can take a Subject argument internal to the NP (which is the specifier of the whole NP):

(37) [the Huns'] destruction of the city

One might suggest that this genitive NP is a sister to an N'' level, so that N, like V (as in 34), has a triple-bar level. However, we have already seen that the Subject argument in 37 is the left branch of NP, and does not call for any newly proposed triple-bar level. (See chapter 4.) Still, the parallel between Subjects of nominals and Subjects of verbals (and other types of predicates) is an important one and our X-Bar Theory should ideally account for it.

We have, then, in NP a model of an X'' that allows another maximal projection to be the left branch of X'' while functioning as an argument. This is precisely the sort of arrangement we would like to have to handle the internal structure of S.

There is no category among those we have discussed that could possibly head S without calling for significant adjustments in X-Bar Theory and without still probably meeting with serious problems (as we just saw in our criticisms of 34). We might therefore try a new tack.

The Category I (NFL) and Bringing S into the X-Bar Theory

Let us propose that there is some abstract head of S such that S is the maximal projection of that category. Let us call the head I, so that S = I''. Now if we consider 37 again, we find that this one example is representative of a wide range of examples in which an NP is parallel in thematic structure to an I'':

(38)   Sal's lecture on drug abuse
       Sal lectures on drug abuse.

       the boy's insistence that she leave
       The boy insists that she leave.

       the girls' reaction to the announcement
       The girls react to the announcement.

The tree for the last NP example in 38 would be as in 39.

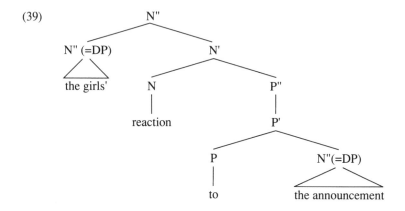

Since the Subject argument of the N in these instances appears in the left branch of
NP, let us propose that the Subject argument in the clauses appears in the left
branch of IP:

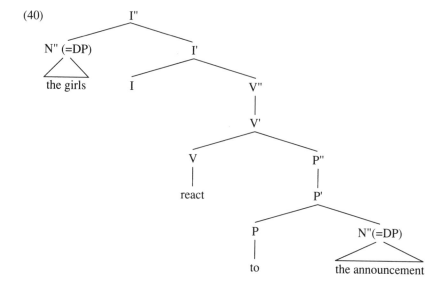

What we have done with this type of analysis of clauses is to pull S into the schema set up by X-Bar Theory. There is a major inconsistency here, however. With the NPs in 38, the left branch of NP is an argument of the head N, as we see in 39. But with the IPs in 38, as analyzed in 40, the left branch of IP is an argument not of the head I but of the head of the VP that is a sister to I. Thus even though the structure offered in 40 makes I″ parallel to other X″s syntactically, there is still a semantic difference to be addressed. We will hold off on addressing this issue until chapter 8.

Furthermore, we have not yet addressed the question of what I is. We will get at this important question by examining additional issues of Case assignment.

Let us return then to the question posed earlier: how do the Subjects of sentences receive Case? This can be rephrased as: how do the Subjects of clauses receive Case?

Two Types of Clauses and Their Subjects

There are at least two kinds of clauses that we have already used for demonstration of various concepts in earlier chapters. One is the tensed clause, as in 40 above and 41 here, in which both the matrix and the embedded clauses are tensed. The other is the tenseless clause, as in 42, where the embedded clause is tenseless.

(41)   Jim believes [(that) I *am* a fool].

(42)   Jim believes [me to *be* a fool].

Play around with the particular embedded clauses in 41 and 42. Put them in a variety of syntactic environments. Test their distribution with and without *that* introducing them. Ask if they can stand as INDEPENDENT CLAUSES. See what categories of heads they can be complements to. List your discoveries.

First, we see that the tensed clause here can be introduced by *that*, but the tenseless one cannot.

Second, you may have noticed that the tensed clause, minus the *that*, can occur as an independent clause, but the tenseless one cannot:

(43)   I am a fool.
        *Me to be a fool.

Third, the tensed clause (this time with the *that*) can be the Subject of an independent tensed clause, but the tenseless one cannot:

(44)   [That I am a fool] means nothing.
        *[Me to be a fool] means nothing.

Fourth, the tensed clause (again, with the *that*) can be the Object of an A, but the tenseless one cannot:

(45)   She is upset [that I am a fool].
        *She is upset [me to be a fool].

Fifth, the tensed clause (again, with the *that*) can be the Object of an N, but the tenseless one cannot:

(46)   the knowledge [that I am a fool]
        *the knowledge [me to be a fool]

Sixth, both can be the Object of a P, although there are different restrictions on which Ps are acceptable:

(47)   In [that I am a fool], you needn't answer me.
        Everyone arranged for [me to be a fool].

Seventh, both can be the Object of a V, as you saw in 41 and 42 above.

What can you make of these facts? Line up the fourth through seventh points above. What categories can tensed clauses be the Object of? What categories can tenseless clauses be the Object of? Tensed clauses can be Objects of all categories, but tenseless ones can be Objects of only V and P. Why? How do V and P differ from N and A? You have already seen a way in which V and P are special, in contrast to N and A: V and P are Case-assigners, but N and A are not. It appears, then, that *tenseless clauses can appear only in those positions to which Case can be assigned.*

Consider now the second point above, that tensed clauses may occur as independent (that is, matrix) clauses, but tenseless ones can be only embedded clauses. Does the generalization we have arrived at account for this point? Yes. An independent clause is not in a structural position to which Case is assigned. Thus a tenseless clause cannot stand as an independent clause.

What about the third point, that tensed clauses can be the Subject of a higher tensed clause but tenseless ones cannot? Here we have a puzzle. In 48 the Subject position of *means nothing* is certainly a position to which Case is assigned, otherwise NPs could not occur here, but they can:

(48)   [That idea] means nothing.

Let us set this particular point aside for the moment and return to it later.

Based on the other points, we can say that tenseless clauses have to appear in positions to which Case can be assigned, but tenseless ones are not limited in this way. Why should that be so? What is it about tenseless clauses that makes them sensitive to their environment in this way? The answer surely lies in issues of Case assignment.

And now we are back to our stubborn question: how do the Subjects of clauses receive Case? We want an answer that will account for the freedom of distribution of tensed clauses (as Subjects of I'', as Objects of any category, and as independent clauses) as opposed to the restricted distribution of tenseless clauses (as Objects of only the Case-Assigners V and P). If we make the single assumption that Subjects of tensed clauses are assigned Case from something internal to the tensed clause, but Subjects of tenseless clauses are assigned Case from something external to the tenseless clause, then all the facts we noted above will fall into an understandable pattern. Tensed clauses will not rely on anything external to them with regard to Case Theory—so their distribution is free. But tenseless clauses will rely on an external Case-assigner to give Case to their Subject, so they will appear only as the

Objects of Case-Assigning Vs or Ps. These Vs or Ps will give Case to the Subject of the tenseless clause.

Tensed Clauses and [+Agr]

What does all this mean? Looking to 40, repeated in 49 for convenience, we now must find something internal to this tensed clause structure that assigns Case to the Subject NP.

(49)

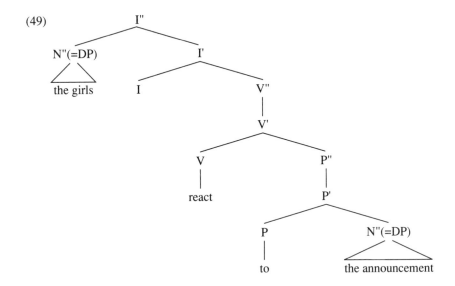

There are only three candidates here, since there are only three heads that could possibly assign Case to the Subject N″. Those are I, V, and P. Both V and P are Case-Assigners, we know. However, we also know that V and P assign Objective Case, but Subjects of tensed clauses receive Subjective Case. For this reason, we might propose that I is the Case-Assigner here, giving Subjective Case to the Subject.

There is at least one other compelling reason for preferring I as the Case-Assigner in 49. We can see this by looking for a moment at the tenseless counterpart:

(50)   the girls to react to the announcement

Example 50 is, of course, ungrammatical when it stands alone, but fine as an embedded clause:

(51)   We expected [the girls to react to the announcement].

Example 52 is structurally identical to 49 with regard to the V and the P that appear in it.

(52)

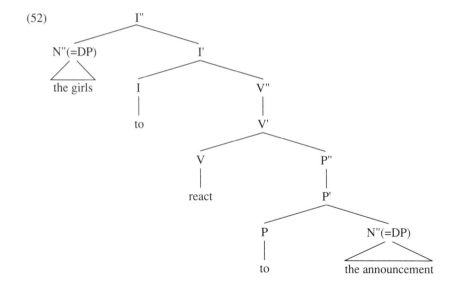

(A discussion of the *to* found in infinitival clauses appears in Tangent 8.1 of chapter 8. For now please just accept my having placed it under the I node.) We came to the conclusion that Subjects of tenseless clauses do not receive their Case from anything internal to the clause. That means that no node in 52 can assign Case to the Subject NP here.

Looking back at 49, then, we realize that if the V or the P in 49 were assigning Case to the Subject NP, we would have no way of blocking the V or the P in 52 from assigning Case to the Subject NP.

Instead, if we propose that the I in tensed clauses (like that in 49) is the Case-Assigner for the Subject and if we propose that the I in tenseless clauses (like that in 52) cannot be a Case-Assigner, then we can account for the fact that Subjects of tensed clauses receive their Case from something internal to the clause (the tensed I), while Subjects of tenseless clauses do not.

This argument involves an important leap as stated in the claim that the I nodes in tensed and tenseless clauses can be different. How could 49 and 52 have a different I as their head? What is this I? The immediate answer is that the I is the head that bears the feature of [+tense] or [−tense], where [+tense] allows the I to be a Case-Assigner (giving Subjective Case), but [−tense] does not.

Actually, as you learned in chapter 2, there is another major difference between tensed and tenseless clauses: the former witness Subject-Verb Agreement, but the latter do not. So in English an I that has the feature [+tense] automatically has the feature [+Agr] ([+Subject-Verb Agreement]); but an I that has the feature [−tense], automatically also has the feature [−Agr]. For this reason, it is impossible in English to determine whether it is the feature of [+tense] or the feature of [+Agr] that allows an I to be a Case-Assigner. In Problem Set 5.3 you will learn that in European (E.) Portuguese the features of tense and Agr are independent of one another. Therefore, it is possible in E. Portuguese to determine which of these two features allows I to be a Case-Assigner. Throughout the rest of this book we will use the feature [+Agr] in our trees as the indicator of an I that can assign Case. However, in our discussion we will typically talk of tensed-versus-tenseless clauses as an expository convenience. You will find both features used in trees and in discussions of Case in many works on English.

The fact that the category I is marked by the features of tense and Agr is responsible for its name; I is short for INFL, which is short for INFLECTION. You will find I and INFL alternating with each other in linguistics articles and books.

The Case-Assigners V, P, and I

We now have three Case-Assigners in English: I, V, and P. But I is a Case assigner only if it has the feature [+Agr]. What about V and P? Are they always Case-Assigners? You already learned in chapter 3 that some Vs and some Ps do not allow (in the sense of "do not subcategorize for") NP Objects, even though they may allow or require sentential Objects. Some examples include:

(53)   V: *We *hoped* [the candy].
            *John *thought* [the reason].
       P: *She sang right *while* [the movie].
            *She walked out right *when* [the catastrophe].

Hope can take sentential Objects (*We hoped it would rain*) and PPs with the head *for* (*We hoped for the candy*), but no NP Object. Likewise, *think* in most contexts (but see Star Problem 5.1) allows no NP Object, although it can take a sentential Object (*John thought it was raining*) and PPs with the head *of* or *about* (*John thought {of/about} the reason*). *While* and *when* are Ps (as the *right* test can verify) that disallow referential NP Objects but require sentential or otherwise propositional Objects (including predicational NPs—for some complexities of the issue, see chapter 4). In 53, then, we have Vs that allow a propositional member of their argument structure to be linked to DO position and a referential member of their argument structure to be linked to OP position. Furthermore, the P *while* has a semantically close P *during* that can take referential NP Objects. Therefore, the restriction exemplified in 53 probably does not have to do with argument structure. Rather, we can propose that these Vs and Ps lack the ability to assign Case. That is why they cannot take referential NP Objects (and you will get a chance to look more closely at this issue in Problem Sets 5.2 and 5.3).

Thus while the categories of I, V, and P are potential Case-Assigners, each particular I, V, or P may or may not have the feature which allows it to assign Case. (For I, the relevant feature is [+Agr].) All Case-Assigners are similar in this regard.

However, there are differences that set I apart from V and P as a Case-Assigner. Let us repeat 18, our first attempt at a statement of Structural Case Assignment, as a starting point for this discussion:

(54)   V and P assign structural Case to an immediately following sister NP.

If I in the tree in 49 assigns Case to the Subject NP, then I, unlike V and P, can assign Case leftward.

Furthermore, V and P require that their Case-Receiver not only follow them, but follow them immediately. Does the NP to the left of I have to be immediately adjacent to I in a linear sense? This is difficult to answer. Ask yourself what items can come between a Subject NP and I. Since I has no phonetic realization independent of verbal inflections (that is, tense and agreement markers), this task amounts to asking yourself what constituents can come between a Subject NP and the start of the V".

You will find that only parentheticals and sentential adverbials are potential intervenors (potential in that one might analyze at least some of these adverbials as being inside the V" rather than between the Subject and the V"). But we have already had more than one occasion to point out that the placement of parentheticals and sentential adverbials presents confounding data to the statement of otherwise relatively straightforward generalizations about syntax. We would prefer, then, not to build arguments on the basis of the placement of these constituents at this time. Still, the very fact that the two types of constituents that we have decided to ignore for the time being in our syntactic analyses are the only possible intervenors should lead us to conclude that in some sense (a sense that will become clear in chapter 8) nothing, in fact, can intervene between a Subject and the start of the V".

However, there may be slight evidence that what comes between the Subject and the V" is irrelevant to the Case assignment from I to the Subject NP. If you compare tensed clauses with tenseless clauses, you will find that the same range of items can intervene between the Subject NP and the V" in both. If linear adjacency were relevant to Case assignment by an I, we might expect to find that tensed clauses, where the I assigns Case to the Subject NP, had a more restised range of items that could intervene between the Subject and the V" than tenseless clauses, in which no Case assignment takes place between the I and the Subject NP. Since this is not what we find, it appears likely that linear adjacency is irrelevant to Case assignment from I to the Subject NP.

There is yet another difference between I and V and P, given the statement of Structural Case Assignment in 54: the Subject NP is not a sister to I. Why should this difference arise? Consider first what we know about V and P. Their Objects always follow them. But given our picture of X-Bar Theory, if the Objects follow the head, they must be sisters to the head. That is because the only X" node within a minimal Y" that is not a sister to the head Y is the specifier node—and in English the specifier node precedes the head. Thus the sisterhood requirement in 54 is a consequence of the fact that the Objects follow the heads. We can therefore do away with the sisterhood requirement in 54.

A caveat is in order here. Our conclusion that sisterhood is not a requirement for structural Case assignment is English specific. Languages vary in terms of whether the specifier position is initial or final to a phrase and whether arguments of a head precede it, follow it, or both. It is quite possible—and, perhaps, likely—that sisterhood may be the key relationship to Structural Case Assignment in some languages.

Returning to English, we can ask: is linear adjacency to the right for V and P the only structural requirement on Structural Case Assignment then? No. Consider the sentences here:

(55) I [bought [the little boy's book]].

(56) I went [with [the little boy's mother]].

The trees for the V″ and the P″ above are given in 57 and 58.

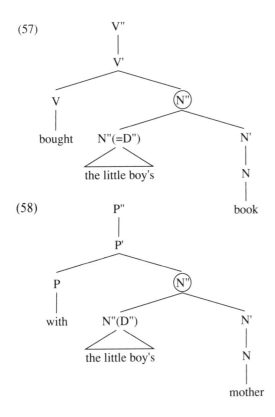

If we look at the lowest string of nodes, the terminal string, presented in 57 and 58, we find that the first N″ following the V and P in these examples is the N″ *the little boy's*. But the V and P do not assign Case to this N″ witness the fact that V and P assign Objective Case and not genitive Case in English. Instead, the V and P are assigning Case to the higher NP, the one that we recognized earlier as being their sister. This Case trickles down and is realized in English on the head of the NP (*book* in 57 and *mother* in 58).

How could we state the restriction on Structural Case Assignment in such a way as to allow V and P to assign Case to their sisters but not to the genitive NPs in 57 and 58 and at the same time allow I to assign Case to its nonsister Subject NP? If we think of X-Bar Theory here, we can find a rather simple answer. A Case-Assigner X can assign Case to all elements within the X″ that it heads, but it cannot assign Case to elements within another phrase (that is, within another X″). That is, any maximal projection will act as a BARRIER to Case assignment. So V and P in 57 and 58 can assign Case to the circled NP (and the Case gets realized on the head of that

NP), but not to any NP inside that NP (that is, not to the left branch of the circled NP in 57 and 58).

Adding the Notion of Government to Case Theory

Let us define the relationship between a head and all the other members of its maximal projection that are not separated from it by another maximal projection GOVERNMENT. That is, a head GOVERNS all the elements in its maximal projection that are not separated from it by another maximal projection. We can now state a generalization about Structural Case Assignment:

(59)   A Case-Assigner X can assign Case to any element that it governs.

With 59 we can see Case assignment from I to a Subject NP as an instance of Structural Case Assignment, since I governs the Subject NP.

An alternative now arises. In a tensed clause, I assigns Case to the Subject. In a tenseless clause, I does not. We said earlier that a.. I which is [+Agr] is a Case-Assigner, but an I which is [−Agr] is not. We now have another potential way of accounting for the Case of Subjects of clauses. We could say that [+Agr] is a governor, but [−Agr] is not. Since Case is assigned only by governors, it then follows that [−Agr] cannot assign Case.

Upon what distinction might we base our claim that [+Agr] can govern but [−Agr] cannot? Other governors are lexical heads—so they contain some sort of lexical information. Now [+Agr] has the features of person and number in English (while in other languages [+Agr] might have a different range of features), which are, in a sense, lexical features. We can now capture a generalization: only heads that contain lexical information can govern. That is why [+Agr] and all the lexical heads can govern, but [−Agr] cannot.

Let us stop for a moment and consider that last paragraph again. There are two possible ways to interpret it. In one way, we could be saying that any node which has the feature [+Agr] is a governor. In another way, we could be saying that [+Agr] is in some sense a lexical head. While the second interpretation might seem farfetched at first, it is really no different from admitting pro-forms of any category into the set of lexical items, for, as we have noted earlier, pro-forms are essentially feature bundles. You will find both interpretations in the linguistic literature. We will procede with the latter interpretation, although nothing we do below hinges on this choice.

Exceptional Case-Marking

Now let us return to the hypothesis we made above—that the Subjects of tenseless clauses receive their Case from a Case-Assigner external to their clause. For example, in 51 above, the NP *the girls* would receive Case from the matrix V *expected* (see example 60).

(60)

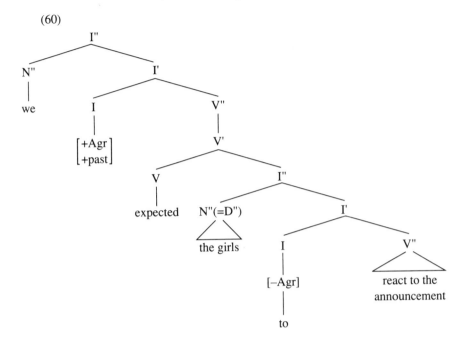

And, as we would predict if the V is giving Case, this Case is Objective, as we can see if we have a pronoun for the embedded Subject:

(61) We expected [*them* to react to the announcement].

(62) *We expected [*they* to react to the announcement].

Furthermore, as we would predict if the V is giving Case, linear adjacency is relevant. Here I demonstrate with a different matrix verb, but the same point is made:

(63) We [very much] *wanted them* to react to the announcement.
       *We *wanted* [very much] *them* to react to the announcement.
       We *wanted them* to react to the announcement [very much].

This analysis is immediately problematic for Structural Case Assignment, since a tenseless clause is an I″ (so far as we know), so the I″ should act as a barrier against Case assignment to any N″ contained inside I″ from a Case-Assigner external to the I″. One way around this is to claim that the V *expected* in 60 assigns Case to the embedded I″, and this Case trickles down to the head I, which then transmits the Case to the Subject NP. Whatever the merits of this approach, it cannot obfuscate the fact that we have exceptional behavior here. The fact is that if we have this same verb with a tensed clause as its complement, we cannot allow Case to be assigned to the I″ and trickle down to the head I and thence be transmitted to the Subject NP—because that embedded Subject NP receives Subjective and not Objective Case.

(64)   We expected they would react to the announcement.

(65)   *We expected them would react to the announcement.

An alternative is to claim that somehow the V or P that is external to the tenseless I″ governs the Subject position of that I″. This is, in fact, the alternative we will adopt, and we will see further evidence in chapter 7 that the V and P behave as though they are governing the specifier position (in these instances, the Subject position) of their complements with respect to Binding Theory, as well.

Now we can explain a fact that perhaps you already noted and that may have been bothering you: the addition of *for* to the middle sentence of 63 above rescues it:

(66)   We wanted [very much] *for them* to react to the announcement.

Here *wanted* is not immediately followed by *them*, but *for* is. So if *for* is the Case-Assigner for the embedded clause's Subject, the contrast between 66 and 63 is accounted for. In other words, *for* governs *them* in 66.

The idea that if a node X governs a node YP then X also governs the head and the specifier of YP is fairly well accepted today, but keep in mind that it has some problems. As we saw above in 57 and 58, the specifier of NP does not appear to be governed by anything outside the NP, at least so far as the data on Case show. Thus this extension of government helps make Case assignment to Subjects of infinitival clauses more nearly regular, but it has other costs.

For these reasons, we will say that the Case-marking of infinitival clause Subjects is exceptional in a number of ways and we will label it EXCEPTIONAL CASE-MARK-ING and say that it takes place via EXCEPTIONAL GOVERNMENT. It is exceptional in many ways.

First, it is exceptional in that we have to restrict exceptional government to the Subjects of tenseless clauses only.

Second, this exceptional government does not recognize the I″, which is a maximal projection, as a barrier, as we have just discussed above.

Third, only V and P can assign Case by Exceptional Case-Marking, but [+Agr] cannot. Thus, tenseless clauses can be the Object of V and P, but not the Subject of a higher clause (in contrast to tensed clauses), as we saw above in 41 and 42, 47, and 44, repeated here for convenience:

(67)   Jim believes [(that) I am a fool].
        Jim believes [me to be a fool].

(68)   In [that I am a fool], you needn't answer me.
        Everyone arranged for [me to be a fool].

(69)   [That I am a fool] means nothing.
        *[Me to be a fool] means nothing.

Since V and P typically have a sense content, but I does not, this fact suggests that Exceptional Case Marking (and exceptional government) is sensitive to the meaning of the exceptional governor. But the relationship cannot be a simple one because of the fourth point, immediately below.

Fourth, as we might expect, not all Vs and not all Ps can assign Case by Exceptional Case Marking, since not all Vs and not all Ps are Case-Assigners. The surprising fact, however, is that even some Vs and some Ps that are Case-Assigners still cannot assign Case by Exceptional Case Marking to the Subject of an infinitival clause that is governed by the V or the P:

(70)   Bill *said* [$_{NP}$nothing].
        *Bill *said* [$_{I'}$Jill to be nice].
        (cf. Bill *said* that Jill was nice.)

(71)   John left *after* [$_{N'}$Bill].
        *John left *after* [$_{I'}$Bill to leave].
        (cf. John left *after* Bill left.)

Fifth, Exceptional Case Marking does not have a counterpart in many other languages of the world, whereas Structural Case Assignment does. In this way it is more like both the Genitive Rule and the Double Object Rule, which are not common in other languages.

We will, therefore, not collapse Exceptional Case-Marking (ECM) with Structural Case Assignment. Instead, we state ECM as:

(72)   A V or P that is so marked can exceptionally assign Case to the Subject
        of a tenseless embedded clause that is its complement if that Subject
        immediately follows the V or P.

We recognize that ECM applies because the relevant V or P can exceptionally govern the specifier of its complement.

Exceptional Case Marking and exceptional government are ad hoc at this point and beg for grammar-internal motivation. As I said above, we will see other evidence for exceptional government based on facts about binding in chapter 7. Still, the exceptionality here must be considered one of the weakest points in Case Theory until such motivation can be found.

We have now reached the end of our discussion of Case Theory. Four different rules of Case assignment were presented in this chapter: the Genitive Rule, the Double-Object Rule, Structural Case Assignment, and ECM. The problem sets should help you to understand better some issues involved in Case Theory. But if you presently feel overwhelmed, rest assured that you will become comfortable with Case Theory as you use it throughout this book.

Implications of This Chapter for Theory in General:
The Role of Government

Our discussion of Case Theory has led us naturally into a discussion of government. We said above that a lexical head and [+Agr] govern all the material within their maximal projection that is not separated from them by another maximal projection. For example, in 73, I$_1$ (being [+Agr]) governs N″$_1$ and V″$_1$, but it does not govern N″$_2$ or anything dominated by V″$_1$. Likewise V$_2$ governs A″, but it does not

(73)

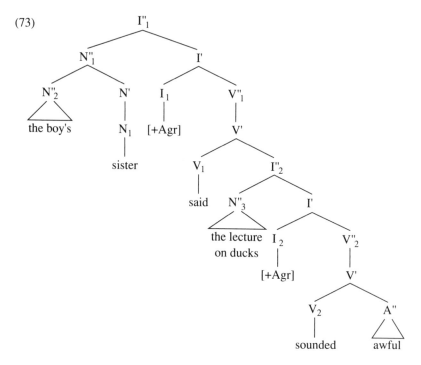

govern anything outside of V''_2. What does I_2 govern? It governs N''_3 (but not any-thing inside N''_3) and V''_2 (but not anything inside V''_2).

Structural Case Assignment makes use of the notion of government in that a Case-Assigner can give Case only to those items it governs. Exceptional Case-Mark-ing makes use of the notion of government in that the Exceptional Case-Marker exceptionally governs the specifier of its complement.

Notice that we now have a simple structural definition for the Subject of a clause (a welcome relief after chapter 2's discussion): the specifier of I' is the Subject of the clause.

We might well ask whether the other modules of our grammar that we have stud-ied thus far make use of the notion of government. An interesting module to con-sider is Theta Theory. Does a theta-assigner assign a theta-role only to those items that it governs? With regard to N, V, A, and P, this is generally true. But the big exception in theta-assignment for all categories is Subject position of a clause. The Subject position of a clause is governed only by INFL with our X-Bar Theory, and INFL is not a theta-assigner. Of course, Subjects can receive a theta-role—the point here is that INFL is not the theta-assigner for the Subject. So Theta Theory is (uncomfortably) complicated: theta-assignment is under government except for the Subject of a clause. (You will find in Tangent 8.1 of chapter 8 that there is a version of X-Bar Theory that can simplify Theta Theory to make all theta-assignment be under government.)

Is government relevant to Binding Theory? For right now the only proposal we can test is whether a binder of an anaphor must govern it. But, clearly, the whole question is a silly one. That is because binders are phrasal projections (such as NP), but governors are lexical projections (N, V, P, A, and [+Agr]). The answer is, trivially, no.

On the other hand, a notion hierarchically similar in some ways to government has been claimed to be relevant: the notion of C-COMMAND.

(74)   A node B of any category and of any level of projection is said to c-command all the nodes that are dominated by the first branching node above it, except for the nodes dominated by B itself.

So, for example, in 73, N''_1 c-commands everything in the clause, since the first branching node that contains N''_1 is the I''_1. Notice that N''_1 governs nothing, since only the lexical level can govern. On the other hand, I_1 c-commands V''_1 and everything contained inside V''_1, but it does not c-command N''_1, although it governs N''_1. And note that N''_1 does not c-command N''_2 or N', since it dominates these nodes.

Now let us try to see some reasons why linguists have claimed that the notion of c-command is relevant to Binding Theory. Consider the following pair of sentences:

(75)   John likes himself.

(76)   *Himself likes John.

There are at least two ways in which the structural relationships between the anaphor and the potential antecedent differ between 75 and 76: linear order and hierarchical relationships. In the good sentence, the antecedent both precedes and c-commands the anaphor. In the unacceptable sentence, it does neither.

You might want to argue that 76 is ungrammatical not for any syntactic reasons, but because *himself* simply cannot appear in Subject position of a tensed clause. One reason for this ban might be that *himself* is not in the Subjective Case. But such an answer is not only unverifiable (that is, how can we be sure that *himself* is not a homophonous form for Subjective and Objective Cases?), it also begs the question, which would then become: why does English lack a Subjective Case anaphor? Furthermore, *himself* can be the Subject of an infinitival clause:

(77)   Bill considers [himself to be rather nice to James].

In 77 the anaphor is accepted, so its Case is appropriate to its structural position. However, the only good reading for this sentence is that in which *himself* is co-indexed with *Bill*, not with *James*. Once more, the only good antecedent (here *Bill*) both precedes and c-commands the anaphor (*himself*).

Given the data in 75–77, we could as easily conclude that a binder must precede, or must c-command, or both, the bindee. Yet most linguists take the position that only c-command is relevant to binding, not linear precedence. A major reason for that position is the binding behavior of items other than anaphors. For example, in 78 the pronoun precedes its antecedent, but binding is possible because the antecedent c-commands the pronoun.

(78)   After [he$_i$] recognized the car, [John$_i$] got in.

Actually, I am less convinced that c-command is the sole structural factor in bind-ing than the majority of GB linguists. I suspect that in English local binding (as of anaphors) is syntactically restricted in different ways from nonlocal binding (as of pronouns). For now, however, let us adopt the mainstream position, and we can return to this issue in chapter 10.

It is easy to show, however, that c-command is the relevant structural relation-ship between binder and bindee in nonlocal binding instances other those in which the bindee is a reflexive or reciprocal, although we are not ready yet to consider any of these cases. We will certainly see some of these instances in later chapters (start-ing with chapter 7). If binding of reciprocals and reflexives is really an instance of the same kind of binding that we find in these other cases, then for reasons of con-sistency alone we would choose the definition of binding that requires the binder to c-command the bindee.

It is now time to continue exploring the notions of government and c-command with respect to the binding of elements other than reflexives and with respect to other modules of the grammar. That is the direction of our next chapter.

*Problem Set 5.1 English Syntactic Trees and Case

This problem set is directly related to the material of chapter 4 rather than chapter 5. I have put it here to give you more practice with drawing trees and to remind you of X-Bar Theory.

X-Bar Theory tells us that modifiers and arguments of a head are typically sisters to it. It also tells us that the sister to the X′ level is another phrasal level Y″ (which we have called the specifier of X′). The functional category of Determiner heads its own phrase and takes NP as its sister:

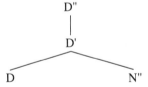

We will assume also that the functional category of Auxiliary heads its own phrase and takes VP as its sister, as in the following illustration (but we will see distinctions between types of auxiliaries and their placements in chapter 8):

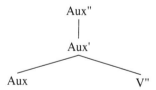

Finally, let us assume that intensifiers of A (such as *very*) and of P (such as *right*) head their own phrase and take A″ and P″ as their complements, respectively, as in the next illustration (facing page; although nowhere in this book will we consider evidence for or against this last assumption).

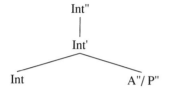

Thus we have the analyses in the two succeeding illustrations of these phrases:

NP$_1$: Sally's cherubic boy in a bulldozer very dirty with dust

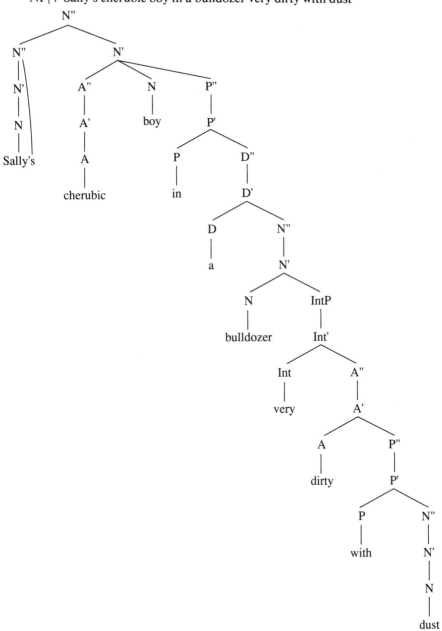

AuxP₁ : has absolutely ruined the fabulous dinner we prepared

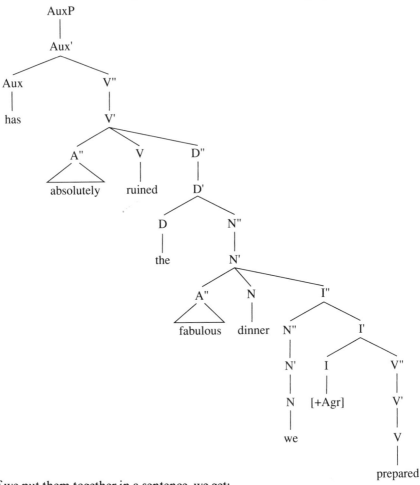

If we put them together in a sentence, we get:

Sally's cherubic boy in a bulldozer very dirty with dust has absolutely ruined the fabulous dinner we prepared.

The tree for this would be as follows:

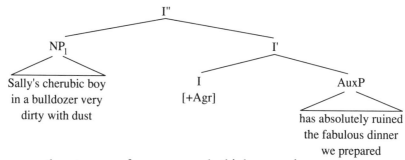

You can use these trees as reference as you do this homework.

Part 1

Match the trees in parts A–D of the next illustration to the sentences in 1–4. Write in the words in the terminal string of each tree. Mark each INFL as to whether it is [+Agr] or [−Agr]. Assume that infinitival *to* is located under a [−Agr] INFL node (as in example 52 in the text of this chapter).

(1) Bill's voice frightened me.

(2) Today's temperature gave me shivers.

(3) Jeff's brother expected Bill to leave.

(4) Ralph's mother thought they left.

(Note: When an I″ is a right sister to a V, we have a sentential Object. Most sentential Objects can be introduced by *that*. Just set aside for now any questions you have about how such a *that* fits into the tree. We will answer your questions in chapter 8.)

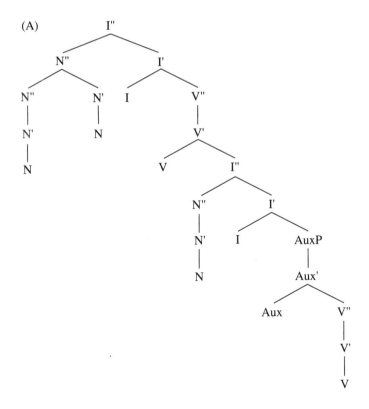

(A)

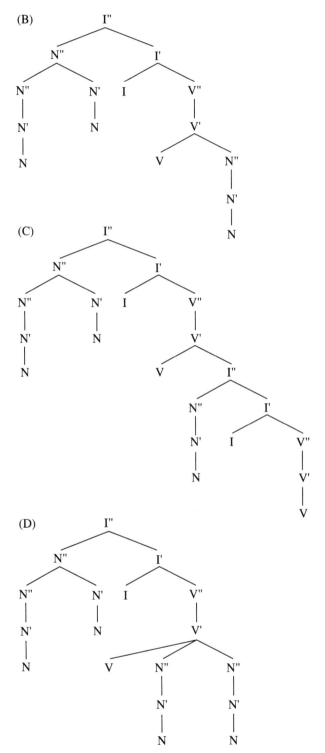

Part 2

Take the structures in the two preceding trees and list every NP in each structure. Tell whether each NP gets Case. If the NP gets Case, tell which rule gives this NP Case: Structural Case Assignment, the Genitive Rule, the Double-Object Rule, or Exceptional Case-Marking. If the rule is either Structural Case Assignment or Exceptional Case-Marking, say whether the Case-Assigner is V, P, or [+Agr].

Part 3

Give the trees for the following sentences:

   (5)   John has lied right to the teacher's face.

   (6)   The tall child is slightly crazy.

   (7)   Jack put the candle in the pumpkin.

Be careful with *slightly* in 6. Its morphology tells you that it is an adverb. And since it has no paraphernalia, you can see that in 6 it fills an AP. The question for you is whether this AP modifies the verb or the adjective *crazy*. If it modifies the V, you want it to be a sister to V under V'. If it modifies the A, you want it to be a sister to A under A'. Ask yourself what the sentence means before you draw the tree. This sentence is not ambiguous—so only one tree is correct.

   As for 7, the important question is whether the PP is a sister to both the V and the NP Direct Object, or whether the PP modifies the N *candle*, and so is inside the DO. You can use the cleft-test: *The candle in the pumpkin is what Jack put* versus *The candle is what Jack put in the pumpkin*. What does clefting tell you about where the PP is syntactically attached? (After you have done Problem Set 6.8 of chapter 6, you might want to return and give one more argument for the analysis of this PP.)

Part 4

Fill in a good sentence of English for the trees on page 222. Remember: An I″ sister to a V is a sentential Object.

(Note: We have not yet discussed any sentences that would fit into the final tree, but they are common. You need to find a matrix verb that can take both a nominal complement (here I have asked you to find a quantified NP) and a following clause as sisters. I will give you one example, but you should use a different one in your tree: *convince*—*We convinced [few boys] [(that) Mary was right]*.

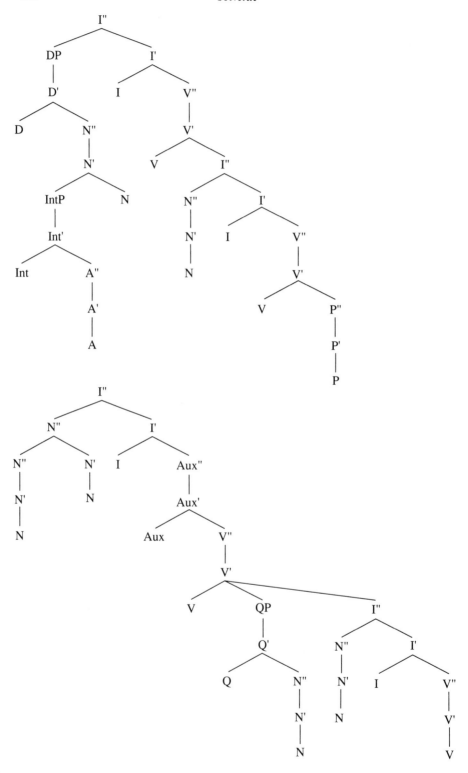

*Problem Set 5.2: English Non–Case-Assigning Verbs

You need to know the material covered in this problem set for later chapters.

Part 1

The Case Filter says that every audible NP (that is, every NP with a phonetic matrix) must receive Case. We have seen that clauses can appear in any GF that NPs can appear in. In the text we stated that clauses need not be assigned Case. How do the following examples bear on the issue of whether clauses must be assigned Case?

(1) *I'm afraid John.
I'm afraid of John.
I'm afraid (that) it will rain.

(2) *The expectation money made her happy.
The expectation of money made her happy.
The expectation that she'd get money made her happy.

Part 2

Not all Vs can occur with an NP Object immediately following them. You came up with such Vs as you did Problem Set 3.1. If such Vs also disallow sentential Objects, they are typically called intransitive. Another way to look at these Vs is to see them as Vs which lack the ability to assign Case, as we stated in the text. That is, while only members of the categories V, P, and I can assign Case, not all members of these categories can. Consider the data below (where every example is to be read as nonelliptical). Discuss whether they are consistent with your answer in Part 1 above.

(3) *Mary thought Bill.
Mary thought of Bill.
Mary thought (that) Bill would come.

(4) *Mary hoped rain.
Mary hoped for rain.
Mary hoped (that) it would rain.

(If you find "Mary thought Bill" grammatical with a nonelliptical reading, you are pretty odd. But you may be assigning this sentence the special interpretation discussed in Star Problem 5.1 later.)

Part 3

Consider the NP in brackets:

(5) Sally cooked marvelously [last night].

This NP cannot be receiving Case by Structural Case Assignment. Why not?
   Now consider the NPs in brackets below:

   (6)   I invited Sam [someplace new].

   (7)   She arranged the flowers [any old way].

The tree for 7, for example, would be as follows:

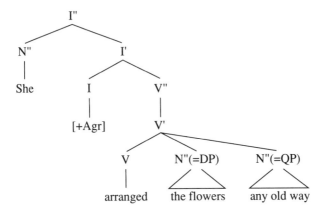

These NPs (which we identified as bare NP adverbials in chapter 2), likewise, cannot be receiving Case by Structural Case Assignment. Why not?
   Come up with at least three other sentences in which there is an NP which cannot be receiving Case by any of the four Case rules discussed in this chapter (Structural Case Assignment, the Genitive Rule, the Double-Object Rule, and Exceptional Case-Marking).
   How are the bracketed NPs in 5–7 functioning in these sentences? (Please be sure to consider the large classes of functions that we have developed in this book: the GFs of Subject, DO, IO, OP, as well as modifiers, and predicates.) Are the relevant NPs in the examples you came up with functioning in the same way?

Part 4

Consider the NPs in brackets:

   (8)   We waited [two hours].
         We waited [a lifetime].

   (9)   She jump-roped [a mile] at least.

The tree for the first sentence of 8, for example, would be as follows:

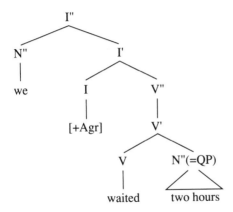

The bracketed NPs in 8 and 9 cannot be receiving Case by Structural Case Assignment. Why not? Be careful. The reason here has to do with properties of these Vs. Be sure to consider sentences like:

(10) *We waited John.

(11) *She jump-roped the house.

Is there any other rule of Case assignment that we discussed that will give these NPs Case? What is the function of these NPs? Compare their function to the function of the bracketed NPs in Part 3. Give three sentences with other NPs with a similar function which also occur in positions to which Case is not assigned by any of our rules thus far.

Part 5

Consider the NP in brackets:

(12) I consider Sally [a fine doctor].

This NP cannot be receiving Case by Structural Case Assignment. Why not? Is there any other rule of Case assignment that we discussed that will give this NP Case? What is the function of this NP? Give three sentences with other NPs with a similar function which also occur in positions to which Case is not assigned by any of our rules thus far.

Part 6

Parts 3–5 here point out problematic issues in Case Theory. Do you see anything they have in common? How could you revise Case Theory so as to account for the data here? (Note: There is a simple answer consistent with all the data in this problem set that makes use of our knowledge of theta-role assignment. Unfortunately, it is probably wrong. But the point is for you to see that simple answer. You could then go on to write a monograph about why it is wrong—but not as part of this homework.)

Part 7

Consider:

  (13)   Come [right this way].

  (14)   I'll leave [right now].

What category do the bracketed phrases here belong to? How do you know that? What does that suggest about the possible Case-Assigner for NPs like those inside the brackets here and in Part 3?

*Problem Set 5.3: Portuguese Infinitivals

This problem set addresses basic issues in Case Theory. It should be done. It is long, but only because you are asked to consider many data that are new to you, not because there is anything conceptually difficult here.

We have pointed out that not all verbs are Case-Assigners. In general, it looks like only verbs that can be followed by a DO that is an NP can assign Case. This accounts for some of the facts you encountered in Problem Set 5.2 above.

Furthermore, Exceptional Case Assignment operates with only some Vs and with only some Ps, as we saw in the text.

Assume our discussion of Case Theory in this chapter is correct. Now answer the following questions about European Portuguese (EP). EP will present a new idea to you, but once you see that idea, the rest of Case Theory will operate just as it does in English.

As you do this, keep in mind the Case Theory we have developed thus far for English.

  (A) Every NP with a phonetic matrix must get Case.

  (B) I in tensed clauses, V, and P are the Case-Assigners for English.

  (C) The rule of Structural Case Assignment is from a Case-Assigner onto an NP within its maximal projection that is not separated from it by any other maximal projection.

There are three other parts of Case Theory that we have developed, but which certainly do not hold for Portuguese (or many other languages):

  (D) Exceptional Case-Marking allows a Case-Assigner V or P to give Case to an adjacent Subject of an infinitival clause that is the Object of the V or P, even though a maximal projection intervenes. This is because the V or P exceptionally governs the specifier of its complement.

  (E) The Genitive Rule allows an NP in specifier position of NP to get genitive Case (*Bill's house*).

(F) The Double-Object Rule allows the second Object in a V-NP-NP string to get Objective Case (*gave Mary a ring*).

Finally, here are the problems.

Part 1

In Portuguese a finite verb agrees with its Subject in person and number (as in English), and its Subject is Subjective Case (as in English). In each example, the first gloss under a verb is V (for "verb") followed by person and number features, while pronouns and nouns have only person and number features on the first gloss. (Note: Only those items relevant to the question have a first gloss. Also, while pronouns vary for person, in Portuguese, as in English, nouns do not vary for person: all are third person. Still, I mark nouns for person here to help you focus on the issues.)

    (1)   Carolina tomou   óleo-de-rícino. (*tomaram, *tomamos, etc.)
          3s   V3s   V3p   V1p
                [+tense]
          Carolina took   oil-of-castor
          'Carolina took castor oil.'

("Ricino" is the name of the castor oil plant.) *Like English, EP Case is audible only on pronouns, not on full NPs.*

    In EP (but not in other varieties of Portuguese) an infinitive verb may agree with its Subject in person and number under certain conditions. We are not concerned in this problem set with what the conditions are for agreement. *Take the fact that agreement does or does not occur as a given. Do not try to account for agreement.* Instead, use the facts concerning agreement to help you answer the questions below.

    (2)   Julio   disse   para nós   não sairmos de casa.
          3s   V3s   1p   V1p
                [+tense]   SUBJ   [−tense]
          Julio   said   for   we   not leave   from home
          'Julio said we shouldn't leave home.'

    (3)   Vi-os   assaltar   a velha.
          V1s-3p   V-unmarked
          [+tense]-DO [−tense]
          saw-them   assault   the old lady
          '(I) saw them assault the old lady.'

The single Portuguese word *velha* is translated 'old lady' here. In 3 the Portuguese example does not have an overt Subject pronoun. Portuguese, like Italian (as you have seen in various problem sets), is known as a pro-drop language. Do not let that throw you off. It does not complicate anything in this part of the homework. The pronoun *os* in 3 above is also found in 4:

    (4)   Vi-os   regar   o jardim.
          V1s-3p   V-unmarked

[+tense]-DO [−tense]
saw-them   water   the garden
'(I) saw them water the garden.'

While the pronoun *nos* in 2 is a Subjective pronoun, the pronoun *os* in 3 and 4 is an Objective pronoun. (By the way, the pronoun in 3 and 4 is a "clitic" pronoun— it forms a phonological word with the verb it follows. Objective pronouns in Portuguese may or may not be clitics. Do not worry about this. It will not affect your answers. If you want to learn more about clitic pronouns, see Problem Set 5.6 and Star Problem 5.2 below.)

In 2 *sairmos* is an infinitive form (it is not tensed), yet it agrees for person and number with the pronoun *nos*. In 3 and 4 *assaltar* and *regar* are infinitive forms and they have no agreement markers on them. (They are in the unmarked form.)

Consider the data in 2–4 above and those in 5–7 below.

(5) *Julio disse   para os meninos não sair   de casa.
                              3p   V-unmarked
           [+tense]   [−tense]
     Julio said   for the boys   not leave   from home
     'Julio said the boys shouldn't leave home.'
     (cf. Julio disse para os meninos não sairem de casa.)
                              3p   V3p
            [+tense]   [−tense]

(The *os* in 4 above is an Objective clitic pronoun. But the *os* in 5 is the third-person plural masculine definite article that introduces the NP headed by *meninos* 'boys.')

(6) *Vi-os   assaltarem a velha.
           3p   V3p
     [+tense]-DO [−tense]
     saw-them   assault   the old lady
     '(I) saw them assault the old lady.'
     (cf. 3 above and:Vi   eles   assaltarem a velha.
                              3p   V3p
            [+tense] SUBJ [−tense]
                  saw   them   assault   the old lady
                  '(I) saw them assault the old lady.')

(7) *Vi-os   regarem o   jardim.
           3p   V3p
     [+tense]-DO [−tense]
     saw-them   water   the garden
     '(I) saw them water the garden.'
     (cf. 4 above and: Vi   eles   regarem o   jardim.
                              3p   V3p
            [+ tense] SUBJ [−tense]
                  saw   them   water   the garden
                  '(I) saw them water the garden.')

How does Case of a Subject correlate with agreement on a verb in EP judging from 1–5? The only verbs you have had above are the verbs for "take," "say," "leave," "see," "assault," and "water." But these verbs are entirely representative of how verbs in general behave in such structures.

Does your statement cover both finite (that is, [+tense]) and nonfinite (that is, [−tense]) verb forms? Try to make it do that.

Note: Even if you know EP, do not bring data beyond those given in this problem set to bear in your answers. You may well arrive at different answers if you consider more data (particularly if you consider the informal registers of the language). Make sure that the answer you give is justified by the data that are given to you here. At the very end if you speak EP and you think that the actual answers are different from those that these data lead you to, you should write up the problem set again, using the data you know.

Part 2

Portuguese, unlike English, allows sentences to have no expressed Subject. That is, it is a pro-drop language like Italian. But even when the Subject is not overt, we have agreement with it, as in 3 above (where the top clause has a missing "I" subject) and in 8 below.

(8) Tomaram óleo-de-rícino.
     V3p
     [+tense]
     took   oil- of- castor
     '(They) took castor oil.'

Again, unlike English, there are no dummy subjects in Portuguese. So parallel to the *it* of *It seems that things are hot in Belfast*, we find:

(9) Parece que as coisas estão   quentes em Belfast.
     V3s   3p   V3p
     [+tense]   [+tense]
     seems   that the things are   hot   in Belfast
     '(It) seems that things are hot in Belfast.'

In 9 both verbs are tensed (*parece* and *estão*).

Now keeping the facts that 8 and 9 demonstrate in mind, why is 10 good but 11 bad?

(10) Parece   estarem as coisas quentes em Belfast.
      V3s   V3p   3p
      [+tense] [−tense]
      seems   be   the things hot   in Belfast
      '(It) seems things to be hot in Belfast.'

(11) *Parece   estar   as   coisas quentes em Belfast.
          V3s   V-unmarked   3p
          [+tense] [−tense]
          seems   be   the things hot   in   Belfast
          '(It) seems things to be hot in Belfast.'

Your explanation for 10 versus 11 should present no new problems for the Case system you have developed thus far for EP. If it does, revise your system to account for 10 versus 11.

(Hint: In doing this, assume *parecer* is similar in its predicate argument structure and in its subcategorization to our *seem*. Notice that our *seem* is not a Case-Assigner:

(12) *It seems [$_N$ John].
       *It seems [John to be nice].

Furthermore, our *seem* takes a complement that is sentential and that is its only true argument.

(13) It seems (that) John is nice.

Do not consider the structure that *seem* occurs in here:

(14) John seems to be nice.

We will be discussing structures like this in chapter 7.)

Part 3

Now translate the following sentence into EP:

(15) It seems that the boys are assaulting the old lady.

There should be only two ways that you know of to grammatically translate 15 into EP. You can give one translation just from the data on this homework. However, you cannot give the other translation. Why not? (What information are you lacking that keeps you from being able to do the other translation?)
[NOTE: The progressive aspect in the embedded clause in example 15 should be translated into EP by a simple form of *assaltar* without any aspect marker. Your job is to figure out whether the form of *assaltar* should appear with agreement.]

Part 4

Try to come up with three statements that are part of Case Theory parallel to A, B, and C above that will cover both all the EP data given here and English, as well. You will have to revise one of A, B, or C. Actually, a quite small revision will do it. Pick out which of the parts of our Case Theory is affected by the EP data—and make the necessary revision.

*Problem Set 5.4: English *-ing*

We will use the results of this problem set repeatedly in later chapters. It should be done.

We have seen at least four kinds of constructions that have a word with the *-ing* ending.

A. One is the progressive participle, which can be used as an auxiliary in the verb string:

Jill is winning the race.

or can be used as a modifier of a noun:

Her winning smile always makes me glad.

You know this one well from Problem Set 2.4.

B. There's a construction that has a word ending in *-ing* plus an Objective Subject to that word. We have not discussed this construction at all; it has only been mentioned in passing.

I counted on Jill reading Shakespeare.

C. There's a construction that has a genitive Subject to the *-ing* word in which if you have an Object of the word, it can be a Direct Object.

I counted on Jill's reading Shakespeare.

Some people have argued that the *-ing* word here is a verb, thereby accounting for why it can take a Direct Object. However, the construction is an NP externally (because it has the distribution of an NP and because its Subject is genitive Case, which is the Case given to NPs which are the left branch of a containing NP). The structure is then as follows:

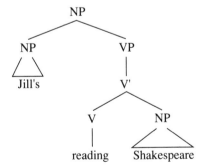

D. There is another construction that has a genitive Subject to the *-ing* word in which if you have an Object of that word, it can only be a prepositional object and not a Direct Object.

I enjoyed Jill's reading of Shakespeare.

This construction seems to be an NP both internally and externally. The structure is then as follows:

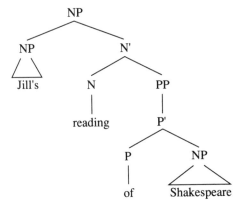

Now for the questions. I want you to concentrate on examples like those in C and D above and make sure you are not using examples of -*ing* words like those in A and B. We will study examples like those in B in Problem Set 5.5.

Account for the differences between the following sets of sentences by using the analyses in C and D. Each of the six sets of sentences below shows a distinction between verbals and nominals. Be sure to point out what the distinction is in each set and how the analyses in C and D can account for the data.

(1)   I enjoy no reading of Shakespeare.
       *I enjoy no reading Shakespeare.
       *I enjoy not reading of Shakespeare.
       I enjoy not reading Shakespeare (anymore).

(2)   I recall Bill's having read Shakespeare last year.
       *I recall Bill's having read of Shakespeare last year.

(3)   I can't stand Bill's reading Shakespeare pompously.
       *I can't stand Bill's reading of Shakespeare pompously.
       *I can't stand Bill's pompous reading Shakespeare.
       I can't stand Bill's pompous reading of Shakespeare.

(4)   I count on Bill's readings of Shakespeare. (They always stimulate us.)
       *I count on Bill's readings Shakespeare.

(5)   I enjoyed that reading of Shakespeare last night.
       *I enjoyed that reading Shakespeare last night.

(6)   I enjoy every reading of Shakespeare.
       *I enjoy every reading Shakespeare.

Now comment briefly on what problems an NP like *Bill's reading Shakespeare* presents for X-Bar Theory.

*Problem Set 5.5: English Accusative-*ing*

We will use the results of this problem set repeatedly in later chapters. It should be done.

At this point we'll turn our attention to the construction in B of Problem Set 5.4 above, the -*ing* word plus an Objective Subject.

(1)   I counted on Mary reading Shakespeare.

Part 1

Is the -*ing* word here a noun or a verb? Give three arguments for your answer. (Certainly, you can give more. But just give three, as cleanly as you can.) Be sure to give the relevant data to back up your arguments. [Hint: If you think you cannot give any arguments, look at what you said about examples 1–6 in Problem Set 5.4 above. Each set of example sentences there gives you a test for noun versus verb.]

Part 2

Is the -*ing* phrase in 1, *Mary reading Shakespeare*, an NP or an I″? Let us call this the Accusative-*ing* construction. (We could have called it the Objective-*ing* construction, since we know that *Mary* in 1 is Objective. But in the literature this construction goes by the name of Acc-*ing*—so we will follow tradition.)

Please take as a GIVEN that tensed clauses are I″ and infinitivals are I″. Also take as a given that a phrase like:

(2)   Bill's use of marijuana

is an N″ (in fact, a very ordinary N″), and a phrase like:

(3)   Bill's reading of Shakespeare

is an NP (both internally and externally—and see Problem Set 5.4 for arguments), and a phrase like:

(4)   Bill's reading Shakespeare

is an NP externally (although internally it is headed by a V, as you discovered in Problem Set 5.4).

Use the sets of data that follow to build arguments as to whether the Acc-ing construction is an I″ or an N″. Each set of data will give you an argument. Be sure to give every argument.

The data are organized so that the first example shows you what happens with tensed I″. The second example shows you what happens with infinitival I″. The third example shows you what happens with ordinary NPs (like that in 2 above). The fourth example shows you what happens with -*ing* NPs like that in 3 above. The fifth example shows you what happens with our complicated -*ing* NPs like that in 4 above. And, finally, the sixth example shows you what happens with our mystery Acc-*ing* form.

You are expected to use everything you have learned in this text and on the problem sets up to this point in doing this. For example, on Problem Set 2.2 of chapter 2 you learned that *there* in:

(5)   There's a fly in my soup.

is a dummy that appears only in the Subject position of a clause. The other good candidate for a dummy that appears in Subject position only is the *it* of weather and time expressions that you looked at briefly in Problem Set 2.1 of chapter 2 (but see also Problem Set 7.3 of chapter 7).

Data Set A

(6)   That John plays the piano and that Fred sings is terrifying.
       *That John plays the piano and that Fred sings are terrifying.

(7)   For John to play the piano and for Fred to sing is terrifying.
       *For John to play the piano and for Fred to sing are terrifying.

(8)   John and Fred are terrifying.
       *John and Fred is terrifying.
       John's use of marijuana and Fred's use of cocaine are terrifying.
       *John's use of marijuana and Fred's use of cocaine is terrifying.

(9)   John's reading of Shakespeare and Bill's reading of Thomas are terrifying.
       *John's reading of Shakespeare and Bill's reading of Thomas is terrifying.

(10) John's playing the piano and Fred's singing were terrifying.
       *John's playing the piano and Fred's singing was terrifying.

(11) John playing the piano and Fred singing was terrifying.
       *John playing the piano and Fred singing were terrifying.

Data Set B

(12) There is a problem in this homework.

(13) I expect there to be a problem in this homework.

(14) *I never heard of there's existence of a problem.
       (cf. I never heard of the existence of a problem.)
       *I never heard of there's existence of a devil.
       (cf. I never heard of the existence of a devil. and: There exists a devil.)

(15) *I never heard of there's existing of a problem.
       *I never heard of there's being of a problem.

(16) *I wouldn't count on there's being a problem.

(17) I wouldn't count on there being a problem.

Data Set C

(18)   It rains in Spain.

(19)   I found it to rain unbearably much in Spain.

(20)   *I never heard of its downpour in Spain.

(21)   *I never heard of its raining of cats and dogs in Spain.

(22)   *I wouldn't count on its raining.

(23)   I wouldn't count on it raining.

Data Set D

(24)   What do you imagine that Fred said?

(25)   What do you expect Fred to say?

(26)   *What did you hear Fred's lecture about?

(27)   *What did you hear Fred's reading of?

(28)   *What did you hear Fred's reading?

(29)   What did you hear Fred reading?

The data sets in A–C probably all made sense to you. The data set in D is new to you. You do not have to understand why the data fall as they do and at this point you probably have no idea why the data fall as they do in Data Set D. The point is that clauses go one way and NPs go the other. So you can use this to argue about whether the Acc-*ing* structure is I″ or N″.

Part 3

Presumably you have now discovered that the category of the -*ing* form is a V and you have argued that the Acc-*ing* construction is an I″. Since this is a tenseless clause, you have now discovered that not all tenseless clauses are infinitivals. In fact, not all tenseless clauses exhibit the same properties when it comes to Case assignment. In the text every example of a tenseless clause was an infinitival, so the statements made there about Case Theory are not really about tenseless clauses but about a specific type of tenseless clause: the infinitival. Here you will discover something new about the Acc-*ing* tenseless clause.

The important issue you must face is how to account for the Case assignment to *Mary* in:

(30)   I counted on Mary reading Shakespeare.

Begin by considering the distribution of these Acc-*ing* clauses:

(31)   [Mary reading Shakespeare this fall] means Bill has lost his touch.

(32) I enjoyed [Mary reading Shakespeare this fall].

(33) I was shocked by [Mary reading Shakespeare this fall].

Given this distribution and given our Case Theory, does the Subject NP *Mary* receive Case from something outside its clause via Exceptional Case-Marking, or from something inside its clause? Why? Be sure to note the contrast in pairs like:

(34) *Children to beg for food would be a shock.

(35) Children begging for food is always a shock.

If the Subject of the Acc-*ing* clause receives Case from something inside the clause, what might that thing be? (Here you are guessing, but there is really only one reasonable guess, since you can muster arguments against proposing any others.)

Look back at A through E of Problem Set 5.3. How could the statement in B be revised in order to account for Case assignment to Subjects of Acc-*ing* clauses?

Part 4

Consider the fact that 36 and 37 are grammatical but 38 is not:

(36) I heard, I must tell you, John reading his poetry.

(37) I heard, I must tell you, John's reading of his poetry.

(38) *I heard, I must tell you, John read his poetry.

In 38 we have a new nonfinite clause, one in which the verb appears without *to* or *-ing*. This kind of verb string is found after verbs of perception (such as *hear, see*) and verbs of causation (such as *make, let*). If we were to account for the ungrammaticality of 38 with Case Theory, how do you think Case is assigned to *John* in 39? Explain your answer.

(39) I heard John read his poetry.

Problem Set 5.6: French Clitics

This problem is not directly related to the text of this chapter. It is here for those people who became intrigued with the Portuguese clitic pronouns in Problem Set 5.3. Also, doing this problem set will allow you to at least attack Star Problem 5.2 below.

Object pronouns have two forms in French: strong (TONIC) and weak (ATONIC). (*Tonic* means the pronoun gets primary stress and *atonic* means it gets no stress or very weak stress.) The tonic form may appear in many places in the sentence. The atonic form appears only preverbally, except in positive imperatives, where it is postverbal. For example, *elles* (feminine plural—fp) is the tonic form and *les* (plural masculine or singular—p, m or f) is the atonic form in the examples below:

(1) Marie ne connaît qu' elles.
     Marie not knows   but them
     'Marie knows only them.'

(2) Marie ne les   connaît pas.
     Marie not them knows not
     'Marie doesn't know them.'

(3) Présentez-les   à Paul.
     introduce-them to Paul
     'Introduce them to Paul.'

Elles and *les* cannot be interchanged in the examples above. They have complementary distribution:

(1') *Marie ne connaît que les.

(2') *Marie ne elles connaît pas.

(3') *Présentez-elles à Paul.

(Note: For first and second persons in the singular, the atonic pronouns are *me* and *te* and the tonic ones are *moi* and *toi*. However, in positive imperatives in which atonic pronouns for all other persons and numbers appear, *me* and *te* do not appear; instead, only *moi* and *toi* are used:

(4) Regardez-moi.
     regard-   me
     'Look at me.'

(5) Amuse-toi.
     amuse-you
     'Amuse yourself/enjoy yourself.'

(6) Présentez-les- moi.
     introduce-them-me
     'Introduce them to me.'

This fact need not be considered when doing the next problem. You may ignore imperatives altogether, since no new insights for this problem will be gained by their examination.)

Note also that in a given sentence one does not generally have freedom to use either the atonic pronoun (in preverbal position) or the tonic pronoun (in regular NP position). Thus in a sentence like 7, we must use the atonic pronoun:

(7) Elle les   connaît.
     she them knows
     'She knows them.'

(8) *Elle connaît elles.

In general, if a pronoun is the Object of a preposition other than à *or* de, *or if it appears after* que *in the* ne ... que *construction (seen in 1), or if it appears in a position to receive contrastive stress, then the strong form is used and it appears in normal NP position.* Otherwise the weak form is used. (That is, preverbal position is required for ordinary direct and indirect Object pronouns, except in positive imperatives.) Do not get too concerned about this. Just stick to the data given below in 9–16 as you answer the questions below.

The weak forms are called "clitics." In the list of examples below many differences and similarities between clitics and the strong form are exemplified. (Most patterns below give examples with a clitic first, then a strong form pronoun, then a full NP.)

Please use this chart as you answer the questions that follow the data sets.

DIRECT-OBJECT PRONOUNS: atonic form/tonic form

	singular	*plural*
first person	me/moi	nous/nous
second person	te/toi	vous/vous
third-person m.	la/elle	les/elles
third-person f.	le/lui	les/eux

INDIRECT-OBJECT PRONOUNS: atonic form/tonic form

	singular	*plural*
first person	me/moi	nous/nous
second person	te/toi	vous/vous
third-person m.	lui/elle	leur/elles
third-person f.	lui/lui	leur/eux

Note that only in the third-person singular is a difference in gender heard.

Data Set A

(9) a. *Marie *lui* parlera.
         Marie him will speak
         'Marie will speak to him.'

     b. Marie l'a   acheté pour *lui*.
         Marie it has bought for him
         'Marie bought it for him.'

     c. Marie l'a acheté pour *Jean*.
         'Marie bought it for Jean.'

(Note: In 9 the italic means that a word receives contrastive stress; 9a is ungrammatical with contrastive stress—but good with ordinary weak stress on *lui*. Please use this fact when answering the questions below.)

Data Set B

(10) a. Jean, paraît-il, me préfère.
          Jean seems it me prefers
          'Jean, it seems, prefers me.'

      b. *Jean me, paraît-il, préfère.
          Jean,   it seems, prefers me.'

      c. Jean l'a   acheté, paraît-il, pour moi hier soir.
          Jean it has bought seems it for me last night.
          'Jean bought it, it seems, for me last night.'

      d. Jean l'a   acheté pour moi, paraît-il, hier soir.
          'Jean bought it   for me,   it seems, last night.'

Data Set C

(11) a. *Jean me et te   voit.
          Jean me and you sees
          'Jean sees me and you.'

      b. Jean l'a   acheté pour moi et toi.
          Jean it has bought for me and you
          'Jean bought it for me and you.'

      c. Jean l'a acheté pour Marie et Paul.
          'Jean bought it for Marie   and Paul.'

Data Set D

(12) a. Jean me le donnera.
          Jean me it will give
          'Jean will give it to me.'

      b. *Jean le me donnera.
          Jean it me will give
          'Jean will give it to me.'

      c. Jean l'a   acheté pour moi et toi.
          Jean it has bought for me and you
          'Jean bought it for me and you.'

      d. Jean l'a acheté pour toi et   moi.
          'Jean bought it for you and me.'

      e. Jean l'a acheté pour Marie et Paul.
          'Jean bought it for Marie and Paul.'

      f. Jean l'a acheté pour Paul et Marie.
          'Jean bought it for Paul   and Marie.'

(Note: The examples in 12a and b are not parallel in GFs to the examples in 12c and d and 12e and f. Please do not let that throw you off. Consider instead the linear order of the pronouns only. Then I think you will be able to make a generalization.)

Data Set E

(13) Question: Qui as- tu vu?
who have-you seen
'Who did you see?'

Answers: a. *Le.
'Him.'
b. Lui.
Him.'
c. Jean.

Data Set F

(14) Question: Vois-tu Marie?
see- you Marie
Do you see Marie?

Answers: a. Oui, je la vois.
yes I her see
'Yes, I see her.' (*la* = 3fs)
b. *Oui, je le vois. (*le* = 3ms)
c. *Oui, je te vois. (*te* = 2s, f or m)
d. *Oui, je les vois. (*les* = 3p, f or m)

(15) Question: L' as- tu acheté pour Paul?
it have-you bought for Paul
'Did you buy it for Paul?'

Answers: a. Oui. Je l'ai acheté pour lui.
yes I it have bought for him
'Yes. I bought it for him.' (*lui* = 3ms)
b. *Oui. Je l'ai acheté pour elle. (*elle* = 3fs)
c. *Oui. Je l'ai acheté pour toi. (*toi* = 2s, m or f)
d. *Oui. Je l'ai acheté pour eux. (*eux* = 3p, f or m)

Data Set G

(16) a. *Elle va les lire deux.
she goes them read two
'She's going to read two of them.'
b. *Elle va deux les lire.
c. *Elle va les deux lire.

d. Elle l'a   acheté pour eux   deux.
   she it has bought for   them two
   'She bought it for the two of them.'
e. Elle l'a acheté pour les deux garçons.
   'She bought it for the two boys.'

(There is no grammatical counterpart to 16a–c that uses the atonic form *les*. Instead, the partitive clitic *en* could appear in 16a in place of *les*. Again, do not concern yourself with this fact. The point is that 16a–c with the clitic form of the personal pronoun is ungrammatical, whereas 16d and 16e, with the tonic pronoun and the ordinary NP respectively, are grammatical.)

Finally, here are your questions. Answer all the questions, please. And follow directions word for word.

Part 1

Make a list of six properties of clitics that are not shared by strong pronouns. (From the brief data sets above, you might come up with many possible—but, in fact, incorrect—hypotheses. The factors I'd like you to consider are: the ability to bear contrastive stress; the ability to be quantified; the ability to stand alone, independent from the rest of a sentence; the ability to show person and number (and sometimes gender) marking; the ability to conjoin; the ability to be separated from the constituents on either side by a parenthetical; and freedom of linear order.)

Part 2

What is the one property illustrated above that is shared by all object pronouns?

Part 3

How do full NPs compare with clitics on the properties you just discussed in Parts 1 and 2? How do full NPs compare with strong pronouns on these properties?

Part 4

Using the list of properties you made in Part 1, determine whether the Subject pronouns (*je, tu, il, elle, nous, vous, ils,* and *elles*) are clitics by making up sentences that test each of these properties. For example, you could try putting the parenthetical *paraît-il* between *je* 'I' and its following verb to test whether *je* can be separated from the verb by a phrase. Or you could try a sentence with *je et tu* 'I and you' as the Subject to see if these pronouns can be conjoined (in either order), and so on. (You need not show each test. Just say "clitic" or "not clitic" after each pronoun or after the whole group, if you think they all behave the same way.)

Please use a native-speaker informant to complete this part of the problem set, even if you speak French very well (unless you are yourself a native). (Note: If

is a language you do not know at all and you do not want to do this part,
\ut if you are part of a syntax class, at least try to touch base with someone
.11e class who is doing this part, so that you can see how French works.)

Part 5

If you found any Subject clitics in doing Part 4, what are the corresponding strong
forms? (If you did not do Part 4, you cannot do Part 5.)

Part 6

Object clitics exist in Spanish, Portuguese, Italian, and Romanian. If you know any
of these languages, test whether Subject clitics exist in them. List any languages you
tested among these that have Subject clitics.

Part 7

I hope you came up with a contrast between French and one of the other Romance
languages in Part 6. Make a guess as to why such a contrast should exist. (This is a
guess—so guess. But do not be irrational about it—try to use anything you know
about language. One thing to do is listen to some French sentences and listen to
some Spanish [or Italian, etc.] sentences and compare what you hear.)

Problem Set 5.7: Italian Syntactic Doubling

*This problem set relates to the material learned in chapter 4. It is placed here so that
you can do it after you have had a reasonable amount of practice drawing trees. It
should be done after Problem Set 5.1.*

Italian has an EXTERNAL SANDHI RULE called raddoppiamento sintattico (RS).
External sandhi rules in general bring about a phonological change at the beginning
or end of a word. They differ from ordinary phonological rules that operate strictly
within word boundaries in that they are sensitive to the syntactic relationship of the
words involved in the rule. (Actually, there is considerable debate as to whether it
is the syntactic relationship between the relevant words or the phonological phrase
relationship between the relevant words that sandhi rules are sensitive to. We will
not get into that debate here, since the point I hope you'll get out of this exercise
could be arrived at regardless of which approach to sandhi one takes.)
    The principal phonological rule involved in RS is a rule that lengthens word-
initial consonants (for Tuscan, only when the preceding word ends in a stressed
vowel). Let us call the two words Word 1 and Word 2. This rule applies only if Word
1 and Word 2 stand in a certain syntactic relationship to one another that you will
discover in this exercise. A slash (/) between two words means that RS could not
apply here (that is, Word 2 is not pronounced with a lengthened initial consonant).
A double dash (--) between two words means that RS can apply here. The data are
from a sample collected by me and Marina Nespor in 1978. They represent the

Sicilian and Tuscan dialects we studied; all the examples marked as acceptable with RS are good in the Sicilian dialects and most are good in the Tuscan dialects, and all the examples marked ungrammatical with RS are rejected by all our informants.

As you do this problem set, please assume for Italian that quantifiers (including numerals and quantificational intensifiers like *più* 'more') and auxiliaries head their own phrases (called QPs and AuxPs). Thus a Q or an Aux would be a head that takes its own XP complement as a sister under the Q′ or Aux′ level.

RS can take place in the four contexts exemplified below. After each set of examples answer these questions:

(A) What category does the bracketed phrase belong to?

(B) What is the head of the bracketed phrase?

(C) What is the function of Word 1 within the minimal XP that contains it?

(D) What is the function of Word 2 within the bracketed phrase?

(E) Draw a tree for the minimal XP that contains both Word 1 and Word 2. Circle the nodes that immediately DOMINATE Word 1 and Word 2.

Context One

(1) Maria è più [--calda che mai].
'Maria is more [--hot (= hotter) than ever].'

(2) Ho visto tre [--cani].
'(I) have seen three [--dogs].'

(3) Mario ha [--fatto tutto].
'Mario has [--done everything].'

Context Two

(4) È più [--chiaramente bravo per i principianti].
'(He) is more [--clearly good for beginners].'

(5) Ho visto tre [--grandi cani].
'(I) have seen three [--big dogs].'

(6) Ha [--sempre parlato bene di te].
'(He) has [--always spoken well of you].'

Context Three

(7) È [blù--nella faccia].
'(He) is [blue--in the face].'

(8) Ho visto tre [gru--galleggianti].
'(I) have seen three [cranes--floating].'

(9)   Carlo [fa--tutto].
      'Carlo [does--everything].'

Context Four

(10)   Questa maestra è [chiaramente--contenta con i principianti].
       'This teacher is [clearly--content with the beginners].'

(11)   Ho visto tre [grandi--cani].
       '(I) have seen three [big--dogs].'

(12)   Ha [già--parlato].
       '(He) has [already--spoken].'

RS is impossible in the two contexts below. Answer questions A–E for these examples, as well.

Context Five

(13)   È [chiaramente brava / per i principianti].
       '(She) is [clearly good / for beginners].'

(14)   Ho visto tre [grandi gru / galleggianti].
       '(I) have seen three [big cranes / floating].'

(15)   Ha [già visto / Carla].
       '(He) has [already seen / Carla].'

Context Six

(16)   È [bagnato di pipì / sulle gambe].
       '(He) is [wet with piss / on his legs].'

(17)   Ho visto tre [cani blù / misteriosi].
       '(I) have seen three [dogs blue / mysterious].'

(18)   Ho [accompagnato Artù / nel bar].
       '(I) have [accompanied Artu / into the bar].'

Now look at all the trees you have drawn and all the nodes you have circled. Is the category of a word significant relative to the ability of RS to apply to it? Is the function of a word significant relative to the ability of RS to apply to it? Try to make a generalization about which two words RS can take place between with respect to their structural relationship to one another. Remember that the first word in any X'' or in any X' is the syntactic start of X'' or X', regardless of its category. Thus in 13 (reproduced here), for example, *chiaramente* is the first word of both the A'' and the A' that *brava* heads, as well as being the left branch of the A', as well as being a modifier:

(13)   È [chiaramente brava / per i principianti].
         (She) is [clearly good / for beginners].

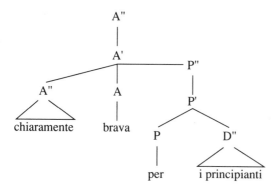

(Hint: Be sure to pay attention to the notion of left branch.)

Problem Set 5.8: Japanese *Sika* Scope

In this problem set you are to figure out (1) the syntactic category, (2) the syntactic distribution, and (3) the semantic contribution of the word *sika* in Japanese.

Syntactic Category

With respect to syntactic category, ask yourself whether *sika* behaves like some projection of N, V, P (here, postposition), A, or I, or like a particle.

With regard to postpositions, assume that Japanese postpositions are comparable to English prepositions for this problem set. (If you are particularly interested in Japanese, you might notice that Japanese postpositions are often written with a hyphen between them and the final word of their Object, which indicates a phonological weakness, similar to that of particles. The difference between postpositions and particles could serve as the topic for a research paper or even a dissertation.)

With regard to particles, there are at least three types in Japanese. One is the sentence particle (and you looked at some of these in Problem Set 2.5 of chapter 2). These particles attach to the verb or adjective that is the predicate of the clause.

Another is the GF particle. Recall from earlier problem sets that Japanese assigns particles to Subject (*ga*), DO (*o*), IO (*ni*), and genitive NP (*no*). We will not look at the genitive particle *no* in this problem set and I ask you now to set it aside completely and do not consider it as you do this problem set. (If you are particularly interested in Japanese, the analysis of *no* could serve as a topic for a research project.) GF particles can attach to both nominal phrases and clauses.

The third type of particle is often called the adverbial particle. The one we are familiar with so far is *wa*, which marks a topic. It can attach not only to phrases that play GFs, but also to phrases that have other roles, such as PPs. Another adverbial particle is *mo* 'also.'

In general, at most one particle can be attached to a given NP. No combination of GF particles would make sense, of course. Thus we never expect (and never find) combinations like *ga-o (Subject-DO). And while a combination of a GF particle and adverbial particle would make sense some of the time, we never find them for *ga* or *o*. Thus where we might expect to find a combination like *ga-wa* (Subject-Topic), for example, we find simply *wa*.

Postpositions, likewise, cannot co-occur with GF particles. This is because the GF particles attach only to N″ and I″, so we never find the combination of postposition followed by GF particle. And it is also because the Object of a P does not have any particle of its own in addition to the P, so we never get a postposition following a GF particle. However, nothing stops us from having a postposition plus an adverbial particle. Thus we can find combinations such as *de-wa* 'from-Topic.'

One tricky problem is the behavior of *ni*, the morpheme that attaches to the IO. Above I called it a GF particle. However, it has some unusual properties:

(a) Like the GF particles and like postpositions, it cannot co-occur with other GF particles.

(b) Unlike the GF particles *ga* and *o* but like postpositions, it can co-occur with the adverbial particles *wa* and *mo* (as in *ni-wa* and *ni-mo*).

(c) Unlike postpositions, it may optionally be omitted before an adverbial particle for some speakers (but not all, by any means). Thus some people would use simply NP-*wa* sometimes where others would have to use NP-*ni-wa*. (Note that this behavior is not precisely that of *ga* and *o*, since these two GF particles must be omitted before an adverbial particle.)

Again, the analysis of *ni* could serve as the topic for a research paper or even a dissertation. For now, just note its behavior with postpostions and with GF particles and adverbial particles, because this behavior can help you figure out the correct syntactic category of *sika*.

Syntactic Distribution

Figuring out the syntactic distribution of *sika* is perhaps less difficult. Ask yourself where *sika* can appear and whether anything else must co-occur with it. If something else must co-occur with *sika*, what is that something else? Let us call that something else X for now. What sort of structural relationship must X stand in with respect to *sika*? Be sure to consider the structural relationships that we talked about in this chapter, including government, c-command, and linear precedence. (That is, must *sika* linearly precede or follow X? Must *sika* c-command or be c-commanded by X? Must *sika* govern or be governed by X?)

Semantic Contribution

With respect to semantic contribution, *sika* is relatively straightforward, so a brief statement will suffice.

Please make the following crucial assumptions as you work:

A. The Japanese clause consists of a projection of V with all arguments and modifiers of the V as sisters to the V. Japanese also has sentential particles, negatives, and tense markers which occur cliticized or affixed to the verb. Let us represent these three types of items as being part of a single word with the V root.

B. GF and adverbial particles attach as sisters to the phrasal level, and are taken to c-command all that material that the phrase they are attached to c-commands.

With these assumptions, the structure of a Japanese sentence is something like this:

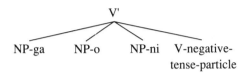

```
                    V'
       _____
      /      /         \        \
   NP-ga   NP-o       NP-ni    V-negative-
                               tense-particle
```

(This is an oversimplification of the phrase structure. I ask you to use this assumption because it will allow you to see the point of the problem and for our purposes no more complex structure is necessary. In fact, however, there is much evidence that the Subject argument is external to the VP in Japanese. So please keep this caveat in mind for your own future research.)

The data follow. Be sure to ask yourself what each set of examples shows you and include that restriction in your final statement.

(1) a. Taroo-sika Noriko-ni tegami-o   kakanakatta.
       Taroo-only Noriko-IO letter- DO write-neg-past
       'Only Taroo wrote a letter to Noriko.'

    b. Taroo-ga   Noriko-ni tegami-o   kakanakatta.
       Taroo-SUBJ Noriko-IO letter- DO write-neg-past
       'Taroo didn't write a letter to Noriko.'

    c. Taroo-ga Noriko-ni tegami-o kaita.
                                    write-past
       'Taroo wrote a letter to Noriko.'

(2) a. Taroo-sika Noriko-ni tegami-o kakanakatta. (= 1a)
       Taroo-only Noriko-IO letter-DO write-neg-past
       'Only Taroo wrote a letter to Noriko.'

    b. *Taroo-sika Noriko-ni tegami-o kaita.
                                        write-past

(3) a. Taroo-ga Noriko-(ni)-sika tegami-o kakanakatta.
       'Taroo wrote a letter only to Noriko.'

    b. Taroo-ga Noriko-ni tegami-sika kakanakatta.
       'Taroo wrote to Noriko only a letter.'(not a book, for example)

(Note that in 3a many speakers insist that *ni* be present, but some optionally allow it to be omitted.)

(4) a. *Taroo-ga-sika Noriko-ni tegami-o kakanakatta.
     b. *Taroo-sika-ga Noriko-ni tegami-o kakanakatta.
     c.   Taroo-ga Noriko-ni-sika tegami-o kakanakatta.
     d. *Taroo-ga Noriko-sika-ni tegami-o kakanakatta.
     e. *Taroo-ga Noriko-ni tegami-o-sika kakanakatta.
     f. *Taroo-ga Noriko-ni tegami-sika-o kakanakatta.

(5) a. Uma-ga   biiru-o   nomu koto-sika omosirokunai.
         horse-SUBJ beer-DO drink that- only uninteresting
         'Only (the fact) that horses drink beer is interesting.'

     b. Uma-ga biiru-o nomu koto-ga omosiroi.
                                      interesting
         '(The fact) that horses drink beer is interesting.'

In 5 and the examples below *koto* introduces an embedded clause, similar to *that* in English. As expected in a head-final language like Japanese, it follows the embedded clause that it introduces. *Koto* is typically followed by the GF particle that indicates whether the embedded clause is Subject (*ga*), or DO (*o*). (Not all speakers find 5a perfectly grammatical. I have taken it from Oishi [1986], who marks it grammatical. Many of my informants agree. Please assume it is grammatical for the purposes of this problem set.)

(6) a. *Uma-sika biiru-o nomu koto-ga omosirokunai.
     b. *Uma-ga biiru-sika nomu koto-ga omosirokunai.

(7) a. Uma-sika   biiru-o   nomanai koto-ga   omosiroi.
         horses-only beer-DO drink-neg that-SUBJ interesting
         'It's interesting that only horses drink beer.'

     b. Uma-sika biiru-o nomanai koto-ga omosiokunai.
         'It's uninteresting that only horses drink beer.'

Let me repeat: the job is to figure out the syntactic category, the syntactic distribution, and the semantic contribution of the word *sika*.

Now translate 8 and 10. (You will learn nothing new from doing this. The idea is just to make you see how much you know about Japanese already.)

(8) Uma-ga biiru-sika nomanai koto-ga omosiroi.

(9) Gakusei-ga   kodomo-ga   kono uti-ni   sundeinai koto-o   tasikameta
     students-SUBJ children-SUBJ this   house-in live-neg   that-DO made sure
     'The students made sure that children weren't living in this house.'

(10) Gakusei-ga kodomo-sika kono uti-ni sundeinai koto-o tasikameta.

Finally, there is one more complication with *sika*'s distribution that I would like to raise. Make a stab at it based on these sentences:

(11) a. Tokyo-made ikanakatta.
Tokyo-till   go-neg-past.
'I didn't go up to (as far as) Tokyo.'

   b. Tokyo-made-sika ikanakatta.
'I went only till Tokyo.'

   c. *Tokyo-sika-made ikanakatta.

Made is a postposition. In considering why 11c is ungrammatical, be sure to consider the structural relationship between *sika* and whatever other element it must co-occur with. You probably decided above that that other element must stand in a particular structural relationship with respect to *sika*. I am now asking you to propose what structural relationship *sika* must stand in with respect to that other element. Do not get frustrated. These are very few examples to go on, but your first stab at an answer will probably be correct.

Star Problem 5.1

Think is a non–Case-Assigner. However, it can occur with an NP immediately following it under certain conditions. An example is:

(1) She thinks computers night and day.

Gather many examples of this type with *think* and with any other verbs you can find that do this. Make a list of all the restrictions these sentences observe. Pay attention to features of the NP following the V as well as tense, aspect, and anything else you find relevant.

Star Problem 5.2

Consider the following information on English.

Data Set A

In English we can easily say either sentence 1 or 2; both have very similar (although you know they are not identical, if you did Star Problem 3.3 of chapter 3) meanings:

(1) Mary gave a watch to Tom.

(2) Mary gave Tom a watch.

When the Direct Object is a pronoun, however, we find that only 3 is good, and not 4:

(3) Mary gave it to Tom.

(4) ??Mary gave Tom it.

(Note: 4 is to be read with ordinary light stress, not contrastive stress, on *it*. It should sound like the *it* in *I know it, after all*.)

But when both Direct Object and Indirect Object are pronouns, both 5 and 6 are good (for many speakers):

(5)   Mary gave it to him.

(6)   Mary gave him it.

Data Set B

In English we can easily say both 7 and 8; where they have very similar (if not identical) meanings:

(7)   I messed up that problem but good.

(8)   I messed that problem up but good.

When the Direct Object is a pronoun, however, we find that only 9 is good, and not 10:

(9)   I messed it up but good.

(10)   *I messed up it but good.

Now answer the following questions.

Part 1:   Considering the information in Data Sets A and B above, and using the French tests for clitics in Problem Set 5.5 above, do we have Object clitics in English? Why or why not? Bring in any other data you think relevant.

Part 2:   Is *I* a Subject clitic or a strong pronoun? What properties of clitics does it have? What properties is it lacking? Is there a corresponding strong form? If so, what is it?

(Note: As you do Part 2, please try to use the way you really talk to your friends as the basis for your answers. The way you were taught to speak in school (when you were corrected—remember?) may reflect archaisms. It is interesting to compare how we speak now in informal contexts to how our grandparents spoke in informal contexts (or even our parents). The former is today's ordinary (and often scorned) talk; the latter is today's fancy (and often archaic) talk. Please do not let yourself confuse normative language with ordinary comfortable daily language as you do this question. And see Problem Set 3.2 if you want to compare the "logic" of normative speech to the "logic" of ordinary talk.

Star Problem 5.3

This is a problem for someone seriously interested in Romance languages who would like to investigate Case Theory further. You will need to work with a native speaker informant.

No other Romance language has inflected infinitives like European Portuguese in Problem Set V-3 above. However, at least some other Romance languages have instances in which a Subjective pronoun can occur as the Subject of an infinitival clause. For example, in Italian you can say:

(1) L'esser { io/*me}   disposto ad aiutarvi non significa niente.
          SUBJ DO
     the to-be I/me   ready   to help-you not means   nothing.
     'The I to be ready to help you does not mean anything' =
     'That I'm willing to help you doesn't mean anything.'

Look at some Romance language you know and find out whether the construction in 1 exists in that language. If it does, make a list of uses of Subjective NPs as Subjects of infinitives. See if you can come up with a list of syntactic and/or semantic characteristics of these sentences. If you have a hypothesis about how the Subjective pronoun gets its Case, give it and try to support it.

Besides infinitives, some Romance languages have nonfinite ABSOLUTIVES which take Subjective pronoun Subjects, too. Let me exemplify two types with Italian:

(2) Avendo lui   accettato di aiutarci, potremo   risolvere il problema.
          SUBJ
     having he   accepted to help-us, we-will-be-able to-solve the problem
     'He having agreed to help us, we'll be able to solve the problem.'
     *Avendolo accettato di aiutarci, potremo . . .
            DO
     'Having him accepted to help us, we'll be able . . .

In 2 we have the progressive participle of the verb *avere* 'have', which is here an auxiliary to the perfective participle of the verb *accettare* 'accept.' The verbal form *avendo accettato* is not marked for tense—it is a nonfinite verb form.

(3) Arrivata {io/* me}, Gianni se   ne   andò.
          SUBJ DO
     arrived I /   me Gianni self from-it went
     'Arrived I, Gianni went away' =
     'With me arrived, Gianni went away.'

In 3 we have the perfective participle of the verb *arrivare*. Again, this verbal form is not marked for tense.

In both 2 and 3 only a Subjective pronoun can be used as the Subject of the nonfinite verbal form.

Look at either the construction in 2 or the construction in 3 in some Romance language that you know (if it exists in that language). Make a list of various sentences in which this construction is used. Come up with a list of semantic and/or syntactic characteristics of such sentences. If you have a hypothesis about how the pronoun gets Subjective Case, give it and try to support it.

Star Problem 5.4

English has no counterpart to 1 in Star Problem 5.3 that uses a Subjective pronoun. But English does have a counterpart to 2 of Star Problem 5.3 above with a Subjective pronoun:

> (1) I having helped already, it's perfectly reasonable that I should be allowed to goof off now.

There is clearly something fancy and snooty about such talk, but it sounds grammatical to my ear. If it sounds good to your ear, study it. Make a list of sentences using this construction. Make a list of syntactic and/or semantic characteristics of the construction. Make a stab at how the pronoun gets Subjective Case and try to support it.

Star Problem 5.5

In chapter 4 we saw nominal phrases like:

> (1) a bit of ice

Very early in that chapter (before encountering the DP analysis of nominal phrases) we analyzed them as having the structure:

(2)

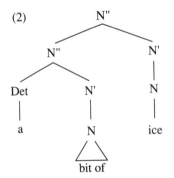

In this chapter we analyzed NPs like 3 as in 4.

> (3) the professor's discussion of war

(4)

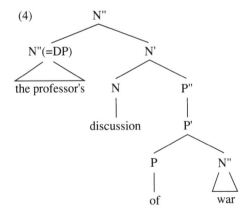

There is a problem here. If 1 has the structure in 2, what prevents the Genitive Rule from applying here, adding the suffix -*s* (as it does in 3)? Furthermore, why does *of* appear after the specifier of the overall NP in 1 but not in 3? From these data, one could conclude that the analysis we gave of 1 in chapter 4 is wrong. Instead, one might propose for 1 the structure in 5.

(5)

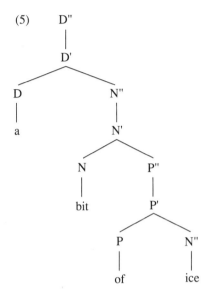

Discuss the arguments in favor of 2 over 5 or 5 over 2. You might want to consider semantic as well as syntactic ones. (That is, what is the referent of the overall nominal phrase?)

Overview

Binding Theory

Our BT has taken a step forward in this chapter. We still maintain Conditions A and B:

(A) Anaphors must be locally bound.

(B) Pronouns must be locally free.

We have just learned that a binder must c-command its bindee. We did not develop that idea on our own. Rather I stated it for you as a given. We will see the demonstration of this claim in later chapters (and a challenge to it in chapter 10).

Otherwise, BT remains as in the Overview of chapter 4.

X-Bar Theory

We have maintained the picture of X-Bar Theory that we had at the end of chapter 4 with the addition of the major (abstract) category I(NFL), which replaces S. The structure of a clause (so far as we know now) is as follows:

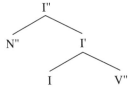

Here N″ is the Subject and V″ contains the predicate. I is marked as [+Agr] or [−Agr], and it is the site for the tense feature.

Case Theory

We have developed a complete Case Theory in this chapter. We have the Case Filter:

Every NP with a phonetic matrix must get Case.

We know that the Case-Assigners for English are [+Agr], V, and P. We also have four rules of Case assignment:

1. The rule of Structural Case Assignment is from a Case-assigner onto an NP that it governs.

2. Exceptional Case-Marking allows a Case-Assigner V or P to give Case to an adjacent Subject of an infinitival that is the Object of the V or P, even though a maximal projection intervenes. This is because in these instances the V or P exceptionally governs the specifier of its complement. Such infinitival clauses are called "ECMs."

3. The Genitive Rule allows an NP in specifier position of NP to get genitive Case (*Bill's house*).

4. The Double-Object Rule allows the second Object in a V-NP-NP string to get Objective Case (*gave Mary a ring*).

Theta Theory

We have the same (and complete) picture of Theta Theory (TT) that we had at the end of chapter 4. We pointed out in this chapter that theta-assignment is under government except for the assignment of a theta-role to the Subject of a clause.

Licensing

We have the same picture of licensing that we had at the end of chapter 4.

Government Theory

In this chapter the structural relationship of government was introduced. A lexical projection (N, V, P, A) as well as I that is marked [+Agr] governs all the elements within its maximal projection unless those elements are separated from it by another maximal projection. In this way, maximal projections can be viewed as barriers to government.

The notion of government is relevant to Case Theory: Structural Case Assignment takes place under government.

The notion of government is relevant to Theta Theory: theta-assignment takes place under government, with the exception of theta-assignment to a Subject of a clause.

6

Empty Categories and Movement

Introduction

In chapter 5 we noted that tensed clauses and tenseless clauses have different distributions. We attributed this fact to Case Theory: the Subject of tensed clauses receives Case from the I internal to the I″ (which is [+ Agr])—hence tensed clauses have a relatively free distribution; the Subject of tenseless clauses receives Case from a preceding adjacent V or P by Exceptional Case-Marking—hence tenseless clauses can appear only as the Objects of Case-assigning Vs or Ps which have the property of being able to exceptionally govern. Actually, while we talked in the text of chapter 5 about tensed-versus-tenseless clauses, we illustrated all our points with tensed-versus-infinitival clauses. In Problem Set 5.5 we looked briefly at another kind of tenseless clause, the Accusative-*ing* clause (as contrasted to NPs with a genitival Subject argument in which the head has an -*ing* ending). You discovered there that the Subjects of these tenseless clauses are assigned Case by something internal to the I″. As expected, the Accusative-*ing* clause need not be the Object of a V or P:

(1)   [Children dying of starvation] is a ghastly thought.

So we must revise our notion of the whole discussion in chapter 5 and consider it to be about tensed-versus-infinitival clauses. You should make this revision in your head, since we will not go through the steps again together.

Infinitivals without Overt Subjects

The infinitival clauses we looked at in chapter 5 all had phonetically realized Subjects, as in:

(2)   We expected [*Bill* to win].

These are not the only kinds of structures in which we find infinitival verb strings, however:

(3)   We expected [to win].

Our Case Theory incorporated the Case Filter, repeated here:

(4)   Every NP with a phonetic matrix must receive Case.

But since there is no audible Subject in the infinitival structure in brackets in 3, we might expect that this structure would have a different distribution from infinitivals with an expressed Subject NP. In fact, if these infinitival structures are full clauses with an EMPTY NODE or EMPTY CATEGORY (phonetically empty) in Subject position, then we might expect them to have the same distribution as tensed clauses.

Can you see why? Reread the second sentence of this chapter. Now look again at 3. If the structure in brackets in 3 is a clause, its Subject need not receive Case from any source, so this clause need not be limited to positions to which Case can be assigned by a V or P that exceptionally governs.

Our expectation is by-and-large met. Infinitivals of the type seen in 3 can be in the Subject position of tensed clauses; infinitivals with an expressed Subject are rejected but tensed clauses are accepted:

(5)   [To leave now] would be a mistake.
       (cf. *[Bill to leave now] would be a mistake.
       [That Bill should leave now] would be a mistake.]

And they can be in Object position, as in 3 above, where both infinitivals and tensed clauses can appear. In Problem Set 6.1 you will find another environment which accepts infinitivals without overt Subjects as well as tensed clauses, but rejects infinitivals with overt Subjects.

However, for most varieties of modern English infinitivals without overt Subjects cannot appear as the Object of a P:

(6)   *For to leave would be a mistake.

The fact that some varieties of English accept sentences like 6, however, would suggest that, rather than attributing the ungrammaticality of 6 to a basic principle of grammar, we should attribute it to some relatively minor grammatical mechanism that most varieties of English have but which is lacking in the varieties that accept 6. That is, we would not expect varieties of English that are similar to each other in most respects regarding Case Theory to differ on a basic principle of Case Theory. In fact, it has been proposed that there is a filter in most varieties of English that blocks the string *for to*:

(7)   *for to

(7 is to be read as: mark ungrammatical any structure containing the string *for to*.) If this filter is correct, the failure of 6 has nothing to do with Case Theory. (And notice that you are probably familiar with the sequence *for to*, as in the song "Oh! Susanna!" in the line "I'm goin' to Louisiana, my true love for to see.")

In support of the filter in 7, we can note that in instances in which we expect the string *for to* to appear, it does not:

(8)   We hoped (*for) to leave on time.

As you know from Problem Set 5.2, *hope* generally takes *for* to introduce its theme arguments:

(9)   We hoped for [rain].

(10)   We hoped for [Bill to win].

However, *for* cannot introduce our empty-Subject infinitivals, as we see in 8. Instead, the sentence is good if we omit *for*. We might propose, then, that there is a rule which deletes *for* before *to* (generating 8 without *for*, for example):

(11)   for → ∅/ —————— to

(11 is to be read: *for* becomes nothing before *to*.) In fact, we would expect *for* to show up before tensed sentential Objects with *hope*, but it does not:

(12)   We hoped (*for) (that) it would rain.

So perhaps 11 should be generalized to delete *for* before tensed I″, as well.

Alternatively, 12 was historically offered as evidence that there is a filter in English which marks as ungrammatical any structure in which two COMPLEMEN-TIZERS (that is, introducers of clauses) occur in the same clause. If both *for* and *that* in 12 are complementizers, this filter, known as the DOUBLY FILLED COMP FILTER, would rule out 12. This account of 12, however, works only for the version of 12 that includes *that*. Furthermore, this account of 12 depends on *for* being a comple-mentizer, but there is good evidence that *for* is a regular P. We will get a sense of what complementizers are semantically and syntactically as we work our way through chapters 8 and 9, (and you can do Star Problem 6.1 at the end of this chapter to whet your appetite). At that point you might want to return to the issue of what mechanism best handles these data (a filter like 7, or a Doubly Filled Comp Filter, or something else, such as perhaps the claim that *for* in 12 must assign [or DISCHARGE] a Case, but it has no appropriate phrase it can assign that Case to).

For now let us assume that the proper account of these data, whatever it might be, is compatible with our Case Theory as developed thus far. This is a reasonable assumption since none of these data threatens our four rules of Case assignment.

Returning to 3, repeated here:

(13)   We expected [to win].

we need to delve further into the analysis of the string in brackets. We noted that if this string is a clause whose Subject is an empty node, symbolized by "e" in 14, the distribution of these clauses as noted above is accounted for. In 14 we find the tree of the relevant section of 13 with the analysis:

(14)

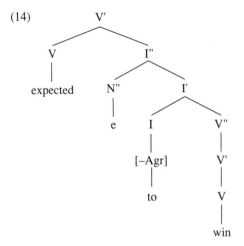

An alternative would be to analyze the bracketed material in 13 as a V″ (what has been called an ORPHAN VP), as in 15.

(15)

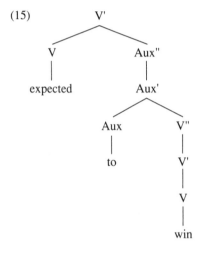

(In 15 I have arbitrarily labeled as Aux″ the node that *to* heads. Since we will reject the orphan VP analysis below, this choice will be of no consequence.) The fact that orphan VPs have a similar distribution to tensed I″, then, would follow from the fact that no Case need be assigned to any element of either orphan VPs or tensed I″s from any Case-Assigner external to the VP or tensed I.

The analysis in 14 has consequences for both the syntax and the semantics of our grammar in that it requires that we admit a new element: the empty category, which plays a syntactic role and must be semantically interpreted. The analysis in 15 has consequences for both the syntax and the semantics, as well. It requires that we increase the possible complements of V to include V″ as well as the maximal projection of all other categories. Likewise, N and A would allow orphan VP sisters (although additional complications arise in these constructions: [_NP_a girl [to talk with]], [_AP_interesting [to talk with]].) The analysis in 15 also requires that we admit into our semantics a rule that allows us to read an orphan VP as corresponding to a full proposition.

Most of the arguments that pertain to the choice between the analyses in 14 and 15 and to the larger question of whether the grammar should include empty nodes in general depend on analyses of other structures that we have not yet addressed. We will now look at one of those other structures, passive sentences, in a long aside which will eventually bring us back to the issue of the choice between 14 and 15.

Selectional Restrictions

With this section we begin a long discussion that may seem to stray far from the types of concerns we are accustomed to considering in syntax. In fact, we are delving into a realm best handled in a semantics class. Nevertheless, the relevance of this discussion will eventually become apparent. So let us apply whatever rudimentary knowledge of semantics we have put together thus far and forge ahead.

Consider the following sentences:

    (16)   Bill fainted.

    (17) #The tub fainted.

Example 16 is an ordinary sentence, but 17 is not. It may strike you not so much as ungrammatical as inappropriate (which is why the symbol # is there). That is, tubs are not the sort of thing we generally think of as participants in the act of fainting. If we play around with 17 and put it in a special context, we might accept it as a silly extension of language, but we would probably always admit that there is something special about such sentences:

    (18)   Jack took off his robe and the poor tub fainted.

All right, we agree that tubs cannot faint. But what sorts of things can faint? Some of you might argue that only animate things can faint—hence rocks and trees and tubs cannot. But can all animate things faint? Consider:

    (19)   The boy fainted.
             The German shepherd fainted.
             The lizard fainted.
             The earthworm fainted.
             The amoeba fainted.

Everyone agrees that boys can faint. But some people in classes I have taught do not feel comfortable saying that dogs faint. A dog certainly can lose consciousness. But some people claim that fainting requires that consciousness be lost in a way that requires a certain amount of intelligence. That is, if someone comes along and hits a boy over the head with a bat and the boy loses consciousness, you might not say the boy fainted. But if someone comes along and shocks the boy with bad news and he loses consciousness, then you might say he fainted. What about sentences like:

(20)   It was so hot, the boy fainted.

Here something purely physical, the heat, caused the boy to lose consciousness. Yet many people who can say 20 still reject 19 with dogs as subjects. There are even fewer people who accept 19 with lizards or other reptiles as subjects. I have been told by no adults (although some children) that earthworms can faint. And no one yet has told me amoebas can faint.

You may well not agree entirely with the comments above, but you undoubtedly recognize some tendency within your own speech to select more intelligent beings as the Subject of the verb *faint*. But can all intelligent beings faint?

(21)   The baby fainted.

Some people find 21 odd unless we explicitly say that the cause was purely physical, such as by adding at the outset, "It was so hot. . . ." Other people accept 21 but balk at:

(22)   The newborn fainted.

If you are sensitive to 21 and 22 in this way, perhaps you have some sort of experience requirement on possible fainters. That is, someone cannot faint unless they have had a certain amount of experience with life so that they can have expectations and be shocked by the failure of those expectations, or some such thing.

What about:

(23)   The sleeping man fainted.

Can you faint if you are asleep? Fainting requires a passage into unconsciousness, but from what state must it begin?

We could go on like this, but the point I want to make should be clear: it is difficult to describe exactly what characteristics the Subject of *faint* must have. Yet you, as a native speaker of your language, have a strong sense of whether any given Subject is appropriate in a given sentence. We can say that *faint* SELECTS its Subject, and that what we have been discussing above are SELECTIONAL RESTRICTIONS. We could have used any number of other sentences to make the same point.

(24)   Bill sawed the board in half.

(25)   #Bill sawed the air in half.

What sorts of things can be sawed in half? Raise that question at a dinner table and you may find that the discussion has no natural end within the span of a single evening.

While many people state selectional restrictions in terms of the verb's selection of the other elements in the sentence, others say simply that all the elements of a sentence select each other as to appropriateness. Nothing we do with selectional restrictions below will hinge on which approach you take to them.

Are selectional restrictions something that we learn as we learn a language or are they something that we learn as we gain experience in the world? Consider 24 versus 25 above. Probably most speakers will say that 24 is an ordinary sentence and 25 is extraordinary. But what about:

(26)   Bill sawed the diamond in half.

Is this sentence fine or deviant (in the sense of straying from our sense of appropriateness)? If you know that diamonds are crystals, you might conclude that they are impossible to saw in half. If you know, on the other hand, that diamonds can be cut, you might conclude that it would be possible to saw them in half. But in any case, the person without specialized knowledge of diamonds probably is uncertain as to whether this sentence is odd or not—because the person is uncertain as to whether this sentence has the potential to be true in the world as we know it.

Are selectional restrictions always sensitive to our understanding of the world—and hence, in strict terms, not specifically linguistic matters—or can they be part of our understanding of the limitations of a given lexical item? Consider the English sentences:

(27)   The postman is short.

(28)   The film was short.

(29)   The string is short.

In Italian each instance of the word *short* above would be translated by a separate lexical item:

(30)   Il postino è [basso].

(31)   Il film era [breve].

(32)   La stringa è [corta].

Basso relates to physical spans of height or depth—vertical measurement. *Breve* relates to temporal spans. *Corto* relates to physical length. To the *basso/corto* difference we can compare the analogous difference in English *tall/long* (Italian *alto/lungo*). But *short* is indifferent to this difference in English. Is the choice of lexical item in Italian made on a linguistic or a pragmatic basis?

Whether you decide that selectional restrictions are at least partially grammatical entities or are strictly pragmatic entities, keep in mind that *selectional restrictions exist and they are extremely difficult to state*. This is the first fact that we will use in our argument below.

Idiom Chunks

Now let us turn to a different sort of data. Consider the following sentence:

(33)   The team made headway.

This sentence is very special in one respect. Fiddle around with it. Change the Subject. Lots of different Subjects work:

(34)   The {coach/women/mathematician/ . . . } made headway.

All right, now keep the Subject fixed and change the DO. Again, a variety of DOs work:

(35)   The team made {progress/money/ noise/ . . . }.

But if you hold the DO constant and try to fiddle around with the V, you find that the result is unnatural at best and absurd at worst. This is so even if you fiddle with both the V and the Subject:

(36)   The team {?gained/?lost/*wanted/*bought/ . . . } headway.
       The {coach/women/mathematician . . . } {?gained/?lost/*wanted . . . }
       headway.

What you have discovered is that the word *headway* when it is a DO in English is extremely limited in its distribution: it can be the Object of *make* only. Furthermore, in active sentences, *headway* can occur only as a DO:

(37)   *Headway is super.

Make headway is called an IDIOM CHUNK. Idiom chunks are combinations of words in which one word cannot appear without the other(s). In this idiom chunk, *headway* cannot appear without a form of *make*. If *headway* has an article and/or modifier with it, the restriction is less strongly felt:

(38)   The team lost all that hard-earned headway in the last five minutes of
       the game.

There are a handful of idiom chunks in English (such as *give vent to, make amends, take umbrage, keep tabs on*) and all of them involve nouns that appear without an article or modifier.

The term "idiom chunk" is an unfortunate one in that it can easily be confused with the term IDIOM. But the two are distinct. Idiom chunks involve lexical items that are FROZEN in a given construction (above the frozen items are *vent, amends, umbrage,* and *tabs*). Idioms, on the other hand, are strings which have both a literal and a figurative (or idiomatic) reading, like the VP idiom *kick the bucket* or the whole sentence idiom *The earth moved*). Besides having two readings, idioms involve words which are not frozen. Thus *the bucket* need not co-occur with a form of *kick; the earth* need not co-occur with a form of *move*. Be very careful to distinguish idiom chunks from idioms.

Looking back at 33–38, is *headway* restricted in this way because of its meaning? Probably not. With enough appreciation for diversity (and, sometimes, perversity), we can call just about anything super—so 37 is not rejected for semantic reasons. And notice that the near synonym *progress* is not restricted to only the Object position of *make*, supporting our contention that the restriction on *headway* is not semantically motivated:

(39)   We all want progress.

(40)   Progress is our most important product.

Is *headway* restricted in this way because of our knowledge about the way the world works? Again, probably not, and for the same reason: the near synonym *progress* is not so restricted. Idiom chunks, then, are something a person must memorize when learning the language, whether as a first language or not. They are not predictable. That is, no one from another language background learning English will say when they learn the word *headway*, "Hey, I bet that word is part of an idiom chunk." Idiom chunks are accidents in the history of the language. And, in fact, the older an idiom chunk is, the more syntactically frozen it is (that is, the more limited in its distribution and in its ability to participate in rules of grammar it is). *The fact that idiom chunks exist and that they are not predictable* is the second fact that we will use in our argument below.

Passive and Selectional Restrictions

Now let us turn to a structure we discussed in chapter 3: the passive sentence. Consider this pair:

(41)   Bill sawed the board in half.

(42)   The board was sawed in half by Bill.

Example 42 is called the passive counterpart to 41. What other NPs could be substituted into 42 for the Subject? Instead of making a list, try to characterize that list. This characterization should begin to sound familiar. You already faced it above when you thought about 24 versus 25. What can you say about the selectional restrictions on the Subject of the sentence in 42 as compared to anything you know about the selectional restrictions operative in 41? In fact, the selectional restrictions on the Subject of the passive sentence are identical to the selectional restrictions on the DO of the corresponding active sentence.

Is this correspondence accidental to 41 and 42 or common to all active/passive pairs? While it is not always the DO that is involved in the correspondence:

(43)   Mary was given the ring by Bill.
       (cf. Bill gave Mary the ring.)

(44)   Mary was taken care of by Jill.
       (cf. Jill took care of Mary.)

there is always a correspondence: The selectional restrictions on some NP inside the VP of the active sentence are identical to the selectional restrictions on the Subject of the passive sentence.

How could we account for such a correspondence? It could just be accident, but that is an absurd hypothesis. That is, if it is accident, why should the selectional restrictions on the DO of *eat*, for example, not correspond to the selectional restrictions on the Subject of *be enjoyed* or *be listened to* or any other randomly chosen passive string instead of the particular string *be eaten*?

It could be that people learn these selectional restrictions independently. That is, we learn the selectional restrictions on *eat*, for example, and we learn the selectional restrictions on *be eaten*, and they happen to be the same because both involve the same matching between words and the world—and call for the same judgments of appropriateness. But then we are saying that the child who learns this correlation between *eat* and *be eaten* will have to independently learn that the same correlation occurs between *see* and *be seen* and *enjoy* and *be enjoyed*. Each time the child will have to learn the correlation for each pair.

Instead, linguists have taken the position that there is only one set of selectional restrictions to learn and that the correlation observed above follows because there are rules in the language that account for this correlation. One possible rule is a syntactic rule of MOVEMENT. We could say that in a passive sentence, the Subject of the sentence is generated (that is, starts out) not in Subject position but in some position within the VP. Then it is moved into Subject position. The DERIVATIONS of 42–44 would then be as in:

(45) [e] was sawed [the board] in half by Bill. →
[The board] was sawed [e] in half by Bill.

(46) [e] was given [Mary] the ring by Bill. →
[Mary] was given [e] the ring by Bill.

(47) [e] was taken care of [Mary] by Jill. →
[Mary] was taken care of [e] by Jill.

(The "e" in the second sentence of each pair (the SS level—as defined in Tangent 6.1) marks the site from which movement took place. We discuss it in the section after next.) As long as selectional restrictions are met on the UNDERLYING LEVEL, it will follow that only those things that can be the DO (or the IO or the OP, depending on which sentence you look at above) of the V (whether the V is in an active or passive V string) can appear as the Subject in these passive sentences. (Tangent 6.1. Please read this tangent before continuing with the main text narrative.) This is because the DERIVED Subjects are underlyingly members of the VP. The difference between active and passive sentences with this analysis is that the passive ones are generated with some form of the verb *be* and with the V in the passive participle form and the passive ones must have an empty node in Subject position at the DS. (The term DS was introduced in Tangent 6.1.)

You may well have ideas right now about some correlation between the Subject of active sentences and the NP that shows up as the Object of *by* in the corresponding passive sentences. We will address those ideas below, so please set them aside for the moment.

Another point about the derivations in 45–47 that might be bothering you is that our grammar now generates underlying levels which do not sound like acceptable sentences to our ears. That is, no one says, "Was sawed the board in half by Bill," for example. These derivations, then, involve ABSTRACTION. With them, we are positing a syntactic level which will always have to undergo some changes before it is acceptable as a surface structure. Evidence for the existence of the abstract DS level will have to be based on theoretical concerns. The two things that make the underlying levels in 45–47 abstract are (1) the empty node in Subject position, and (2) the presense of the NP (the one that moves) inside the VP despite the fact that the V is in its passive participle form and the passive auxiliary *be* is present. (Recall that from Problem Set 2.4 on we have used the term "passive participle" to refer to that form of the verb that follows the passive *be*.) We will address the issue of the empty Subject node below. But the issue of the correct placement at the underlying level of the relevant NP (the NP that moves) is exactly what our selectional restriction argument is addressing. So let us get on with that argument.

An alternative to accounting for the similarities between active and passive sentences with a movement rule in the syntax is to say that in the lexicon we have a rule which relates lexical pairs like *eat* and *be eaten*. This lexical rule tells us that the range of participants for both verbs is the same, but that the participant which is linked to the DO with *eat* is linked to the Subject with *be eaten*. That is, active and passive sentences are generated as is at DS, and the lexicon, via LEXICAL REDUNDANCY or LEXICAL CORRESPONDENCE RULES, tells us what is in common between the active and passive verbal forms (that is, their predicate-argument structure) and what is different (that is, the linking of predicate-argument structure to GF positions). Again, this analysis has the advantage of having the child learn the selectional restrictions only once. The fact that active and passive pairs have the correlation noted above will follow from the lexical rule which relates active and passive lexical items. With this analysis we need not posit any empty nodes because no movement is involved.

Are these alternatives equivalent empirically? Let us assume that our grammar is cleanly organized so that we first do operations in the lexicon, and then we locate our lexical items in syntactic structures, and finally we do operations in the syntax, as in:

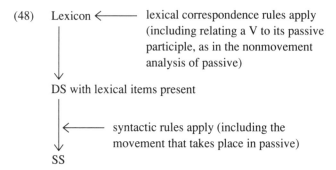

(48)   Lexicon ⟵——— lexical correspondence rules apply
                        (including relating a V to its passive
                        participle, as in the nonmovement
                        analysis of passive)

       DS with lexical items present

                   ⟵——— syntactic rules apply (including the
                        movement that takes place in passive)
       SS

The organization of the grammar shown in 48 assumes that each COMPONENT OF THE GRAMMAR is DISCRETE. Also, we cannot reverse direction. We cannot, for example, go from DS to the lexicon. One result is that no syntactic rules will be sandwiched between lexical rules and no lexical rules will be sandwiched between syntactic rules. If we could show that some process in the syntax took place before the Passive Rule applied, then, with this model of the grammar, we would have to conclude that the Passive Rule belongs to the syntax. If, on the other hand, we could show that some process in the lexicon took place after the Passive Rule applied, then we would have to conclude that the Passive Rule belongs to the lexicon. Do you see this? If not, reread this paragraph until you do. This is an extremely important point.

Unfortunately, to demonstrate either one of these situations, we would already have to have in place the analysis of some other syntactic or lexical process. We are not yet in that position. In chapter 7 you will meet a syntactic rule (which we will call the Raising Rule) that can precede the Passive Rule. At that point you will be able to justify treating the Passive Rule as a syntactic movement rule. Thus for now I ask you to adopt the movement analysis and go forward.

Passive and Idiom Chunks

A second argument for the existence of the Passive Rule is easily found by looking at sentences with idiom chunks.

(49) a. Our team finally made headway.
       b. Headway was finally made by our team.

Without the Passive Rule we must claim that people learn as two separate facts that *headway* can occur only as the Object of *make* or the Subject of *be made*, and we have no explanation for why it should be precisely this pair and not the pair *make* and *be listened to* (or any other passive V string). On the other hand, with the Passive Rule we need to learn only that *headway* can occur as the Object of *make*, whether *make* is in an active or passive V string. The fact that it can occur as the Subject of *be made* is a consequence of the movement rule. The derivation of 49b, then, would be:

(50) DS: [e] was finally made [headway] by our team. →
       SS: [Headway] was finally made [e] by our team.

Justification for Empty Nodes

Looking at the derivations in 45–47 and 50, we see that both in DS and in SS we have posited an empty node. The empty node at DS is in the Subject position. The empty node at SS marks the site from which movement has taken place. What is the advantage gained by positing these empty nodes? First, the underlying Subject SLOT must be empty, for if it were not, the NP inside the VP that moves could not move into Subject position.

(51) DS: Bill was sawed the board in half. →

       SS: *Bill [the board] was sawed in half [e].
           *[The board] Bill was sawed in half [e].

So the empty node in the underlying structure in 50 is a necessity imposed by our movement analysis.

What about the empty node posited in SS? Intuitively, it is the DO slot that these Vs subcategorize for. In our analysis it is the slot that was vacated by the NP that moved to Subject position: since the contents of that slot moved, it is now empty.

But why not assume it just disappears (that is, deletes) after movement? What advantages does positing this empty node give us? Here I present three.

First, consider any active sentence that has a passive counterpart:

(52)   Mary ate the potatoes.

If the verb *eat* appears in a passive sentence, such as:

(53)   The potatoes were eaten by Mary.

what mechanism allows us to interpret *the potatoes* as the theme argument of *eat*? In the lexicon we know that *eat* can take an agent and a theme argument and that the agent is linked to the Subject position while the theme is linked to the DO position. In 53 the linking is not as we expect it at all, yet we have no trouble interpreting this sentence. If the SS of 53 is enriched with an empty node that marks the position from which *the potatoes* moved, then we need not change any of our ideas about theta-assignment and about the linking between argument structure and GF. That is, the theta-role of theme is assigned by *eat* to its closest sister to the right (the canonical DO position), whether or not the sentence is passive. But in the passive instance, this sister is the empty node e (the hole left by *the potatoes*). If we did not have an e in this sister slot, the nearest sister to the right of *eat* would be the PP *by Mary*. We would end up either having *eat* assign the theme role to *(by) Mary* (a wrong thematic assignment) or being forced to complicate our otherwise straightforward theta-assignment process. Positing an e here, then, is very beneficial.

This argument assumes that we are reading semantic information from our SS. If, instead, one assumed that theta-assignment took place exclusively at DS, certain objections to this argument (and to the following two arguments, which are also based on theta-assignment) could be raised. Please lay your objections aside temporarily. We will return to this issue in the next section.

Let us call the particular type of empty node that is left behind by movement a TRACE, or simply t, and let us CO-INDEX it with the item it is a trace of:

(54)   [The potatoes]$_i$ were eaten [t]$_i$ by Mary.

Here *eat* assigns the theta-role of theme to that argument that appears in DO position. The trace is co-indexed with the NP in Subject position. Via this co-indexation, we can interpret the NP in Subject position as the theme argument of *eat*.

At this point you might balk: we have seen indices earlier, but only in binding relationships. Are the indices in 54 binding indices or something new? We will answer this question in chapter 7 (where we will argue that the relationship indicated by the indices in 54 is, indeed, a binding relationship).

Returning to the matter of the existence of traces, we can now recognize a second advantage of traces in SS that is quite similar to the first. Consider sentences with a verb that obligatorily calls for some element inside its VP:

(55)   Mary put the potatoes there.

Put requires a DO (as well as a locative). Yet we have no trouble accepting the passive sentence in 56, where *put* appears without any overt DO, but with only a locative and a PP (the *by*-phrase).

(56)   The potatoes were put there by Mary.

If the SS is enriched by traces, then we can see the trace in 57 as fulfilling the requirement that *put* be transitive, and we can correctly accept 56 and 57, but reject 58, with no DO at all (whether a trace or a full lexical item).

(57)   [The potatoes]$_i$ were put [t]$_i$ there by Mary.

(58)   *Mary put there.

Third, we know from Problem Set 3.3 that resultative secondary predicates can be predicated of a theme argument only. Thus we accept 59a but reject 59b with a resultative reading:

(59)   a.   Jack ironed the shirt flat.
       b.   *Jack ironed the shirt exhausted.

That is, 59a cannot mean that Jack ironed the shirt with the result that he became exhausted. Thus a resultative predicate (here *flat* or *exhausted*) can be predicated only of the DO of *iron*, not of the Subject. Yet 60a is fine with a resultative reading:

(60)   a.   The shirt was ironed flat.
       b.   [The shirt]$_i$ was ironed [t]$_i$ flat.

If we allow a trace (as represented in 60b), then *flat* can be predicated of the trace and we will understand *flat* to be predicated of the SS Subject via the mechanism of co-indexation.

As you continue with this book, your knowledge of grammatical analysis will grow and you will find additional benefits that traces in SS give us. Consider one more argument for traces—one that does not rely on theta-assignment. It involves sentences which have undergone more than one movement rule. For example, in 61 the Passive Rule has applied (witness the string *was introduced*):

(61)   I recognized the woman the man was introduced to.

Another movement rule that we will study in chapter 8 (see Problem Set 8.7) has also applied: the rule that forms relative clauses. The issue for us is why 61 is not ambiguous. That is, why do we understand 61 to include the proposition that the man was introduced to the woman but not to include the proposition that the woman was introduced to the man? While we cannot answer that question yet, traces turn out to be crucial. (After you have read chapter 8, please come back and go through the derivation of 61 so that you can verify this claim for yourself.)

We will take as an axiom, then, that movement always leaves behind a trace which is co-indexed with the moved item. This axiom constitutes a base for what is known as TRACE THEORY.

Global-versus-Discrete Models of Grammar

You might have objected to each of the three supposed advantages above by claiming that if we allow all our rules access to DS, we need not have traces in SS. So, for example, in order to interpret 53 correctly, all our interpretive rules need see is its structure at DS:

(62)   [e] were eaten [the potatoes] by Mary.

Let us see how.

First, given 62, we will know that *the potatoes* in 53 is a theme because it started out in the DO position of the verb *eat*, which assigns theme role to its DO. No trace is needed. Second, if all rules have access to DS, then we have no problem accounting for the grammaticality of 56 because we can say that *the potatoes* started out in DO position of *put*. Again, no trace is needed. And, finally, 60 is not problematic because we can see that *flat* is predicated of *the shirt*, where *the shirt* was in the DO position, and thus receives theme role. No trace is appealed to.

So if we can see the structure *that used to be present*, we have no need of traces. Traces are needed only if each rule of the grammar has access only to the structure it operates on and not to structures which occurred earlier in the DERIVATIONAL HISTORY (that is, the development from DS to SS) of the sentence. That is, if in interpreting 53, 56, and 60, we cannot see earlier syntactic levels, then we need traces in order to maintain our simplest statements concerning how theta-assignment works, what subcategorization is, and what the restrictions are on certain rules of interpretation (such as those that involve predication—like the rule discussed above in relation to 59 and 60 that assigns a Subject argument to a resultative predicate).

Traces allow us to carry along certain information from one level of syntactic derivation to the next. This information is quite restricted in nature: only syntactic position is encoded in traces. But because we have an explicit relationship between syntactic position and thematic relations (encoded in the lexical linking rules between predicate-argument structure and GF positions), the use of traces allows us to see all lexical properties of the predicate at every syntactic level of the derivation. In fact, linguists have claimed that this property of traces follows from a formal principle of grammar: the PROJECTION PRINCIPLE.

(63)   All lexical features of a predicate that appear in DS must appear at every other syntactic level, as well.

By comparing these two alternatives, the one that allows rules of grammar to see all levels of the syntactic derivation at once and the one that uses traces and allows a particular rule to see only the level that serves as input to that particular rule, we have entered a debate that was hot in linguistics two to three decades ago. In those days people often argued over whether rules of grammar could be GLOBAL (seeing the entire derivational history of a sentence) or were restricted to being LOCAL (seeing only the structure to which the particular rule applied). Today the term "local" is used more often in discussions of distance with regard to the behavior of anaphors and other items. You are very familiar with this more recent use of the term. Thus in this book we will not talk about global-versus-local rules in the old sense, but, instead, about a global model of the grammar versus a discrete model of the grammar; we already introduced the term "discrete" in the discussion following 48 above.

Which type of model, a global or a discrete one, is better? To answer this question we need to consider both theoretical standards and empirical adequacy. Certainly, a global model is more powerful in that it allows a wider variety of types of rules than a discrete model. For example, with a global model we could posit a rule which moved an NP only if that NP was the first element in the sentence at the second derivational level. (That is, if we call DS the first derivational level, the second would be the level to which one rule has applied; the third would be the level to which two rules have applied; and so on.) Such a rule could not be stated in a discrete model.

The global model could generate more different sorts of structures in the syntax, in the semantics, and in the phonology than a discrete approach would allow. For this reason, the discrete approach makes more easily testable predictions about what sort of syntactic, phonological, and interpretive rules there are in language. We will, as always, opt for the more-easily-testable theory and the less-powerful theory, on the grounds that if we are wrong, the evidence is likely to be forthcoming and we can then revise accordingly. If, instead, we opted for a theory that allowed many more sorts of rules, contradictory evidence would be hard to come by. Furthermore, if we opt for the more restrictive theory and it turns out to be empirically adequate (that is, it generates all and only the good sentences of language), then we have come a long way toward understanding how language works. But if we opt for the less-restrictive theory and it turns out to be empirically adequate, we still need to test the more-restrictive theory to see if it is equally empirically adequate.

You might object to the previous sentence. If a global account is empirically adequate, why do we need to search for and test a more restrictive account? The idea here is that we want the most elegant theory which accounts for all and only the data that arise. A simple account in linguistics, all other factors being equal, is to be preferred to a complex account. This standard is shared with many other fields, such as mathematics.

It would take us far astray of our present goal to enter into discussion of particular phenomena and analyses that have been offered in the literature in support of a global model. Suffice it to say that none of these cases is considered unassailable. Today the issue seems pretty much dead and the major grammatical theories adopt a discrete model of the grammar.

Let me outline the particular discrete model we have been implicitly adopting in this chapter. We assume that each rule of grammar belongs to a particular component of the grammar. Thus we know we have a lexicon and we know that certain information regarding theta-roles and linking to GFs is part of lexical information. We also know we have a syntax and we have relegated the Rule of Passive, for example, to the syntactic component of the grammar. We know we have rules of interpretation (involving predication relationships and binding relationships and others we will discover) and we call that component of the grammar LF (for LOGICAL FORM). And we know we have phonological rules and we call that component of the grammar PF (for PHONOLOGICAL FORM). The organization of the grammar that we have been assuming is as shown in 64.

(64)   Lexicon ──────→ DS

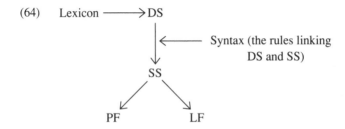

Here the lexicon FEEDS and, along with X-Bar Theory, creates DS by generating trees with nodes that have category labels and with a terminal string of lexical items. The DS is TRANSFORMED (hence, our grammar is TRANSFORMATIONAL) into the SS via rules which make up the syntax. SS is the input level to both the phonological component (PF) and the interpretive component (LF) of the grammar.

Before discussing this model of the grammar further, let us take a moment to consider an alternative account of theta-assignment. One might argue that theta-assignment takes place exclusively at DS (in contrast to the assumption we have been making—that theta-assignment takes place at both DS and SS) and that once a theta-role is assigned to a node, it is glued there. Wherever the node moves, then, it carries its theta-role along with it. This account of theta-assignment is not global in the sense of globality outlined above in this section. And with this account, we no longer need to have theta-assignment apply at SS. Therefore, three out of the four arguments in the previous section for the existence of traces are vitiated.

The arguments against this approach include at least the following two. First, this approach is inconsistent with the Projection Principle given in 63. The Projection Principle insists that theta-assignment take place at both DS and SS in identical ways. Insofar as the Projection Principle is motivated independently of theta-assignment questions, this is a valid objection.

Second, if theta-assignment applies to SS (as well as DS), then theta-assignment can be viewed as belonging to the interpretive component of the grammar (the LF in 64). Semantics, then, can be viewed as a coherent whole. If, instead, theta-assignment applies exclusively at DS, then one rule of interpretation—the rule of theta-assignment—is isolated from the others.

For these reasons we will assume that theta-assignment applies at SS as well as DS. However, even if you should feel unswayed by these arguments and decide to apply theta-assignment exclusively at DS, please note that there are still many arguments for the existence of traces. The final argument of the previous section (based on sentences in which two movement rules have applied) is a strong example of the type of evidence that one can bring to bear on the issue. We will now leave this issue and proceed with our discussion of the schema of the grammar given in 64.

There are many possible alternatives to the schema of the grammar in 64. One might argue that the components of the grammar are arranged in a different FEEDING PATTERN. Certainly no one is likely to object to having the phonological component operate off the output of the syntax, since phonological rules must follow the selection of inflectional endings such as Case-markers, and that selection cannot take place until after all syntactic movement rules have applied. (That is, the Subject of a passive sentence receives Subjective Case, just as the Subject of an active sentence does. So it is an SS configuration that feeds the Case rules.) Equally certainly, no one is likely to object to the lexicon being the input to the syntactic component. But the main issue of controversy has been whether the interpretive component operates off the DS (before any syntactic rules have applied), or the SS, or both. So long as a single rule of interpretation is shown to operate off of SS, then, with the principle of discreteness, all rules of interpretation must operate after the syntactic rules have applied.

We have already seen a single rule of interpretation that must operate after the syntactic rules have applied, and that is the RULE OF PREDICATION. Back in chapter 3 we discussed the interpretation of passive sentences. There we noted that generally the Subject of a passive sentence is interpreted as being characterizable by the predicate's action having taken place on it. For example,

(65)   The table was scratched.

(66)   His back was scratched.

Out of context, 65 is a somewhat ordinary sentence. We interpret it to mean that the table had a scratch in it as a result of being scratched (by some sharp object, for example). That is, we assign this sentence a vague context when we hear it, and that vague context is the same sort of context we expect if we have *scratch* in an active sentence with *the table* as its Object. Thus people do not generally scratch tables to relieve the table's itchiness. Example 66, also, is ordinary. We interpret it to mean that his back had scratch marks on it as a result of being scratched. It is significant, however, that this is not the first context we generally expect if we have *scratch* in an active sentence with *his back* as its Object. Thus in:

(67)   Bill scratched his back.

we might read this as "Bill simply relieved his itchiness without leaving any scratch marks," or as "Bill wound up with scratch marks on his back." (And notice that in the second instance we do not need to attribute agency to Bill; he might be a non-agentive experiencer here.) Both of these readings are ordinary. Yet for the passive sentence in 66, only the second reading is ordinary. That is, when we hear 66, we are more likely to think that the speaker can see scratch marks on his back than that the speaker is merely reporting that Bill relieved his itchiness. You can look back to chapter 3 to find other examples that make the same point. (For example, compare the uses of *I was touched* in two situations: one where a friend put a hand on my shoulder and the other where a slimy green monster put a hand on my shoulder. Which one do you think you would be more likely to use *I was touched (by so and so)* in?)

The operation of the Rule of Passive, then, affects our interpretation of the predication here. For this reason, we posit that the Rule of Predication follows the syntactic component of the grammar. Hence the LF component of the grammar follows the syntactic component of the grammar.

The Analysis of Passive Participles

Before leaving the analysis of passive sentences, let us reconsider one more aspect of their derivation, as in:

(68) a. That very arrangement was suggested earlier.
      b. [e] was suggested [that very arrangement] earlier

If 68b is the DS for 68a, are we then saying that the Rule of Passive is obligatory? Notice that 68b is not a good surface sentence:

(69) *Was suggested that very arrangement earlier.

How do we block 69? There are at least two things wrong with 69. As we have pointed out many times, tensed sentences in English require an overt Subject. Example 69 does not satisfy this requirement. However, while a dummy-*it* can rescue other types of Subjectless sentences, it cannot rescue 69:

(70) *It was suggested that very arrangement earlier.

So there must be something else wrong with 69, as well. Notice that passive participles (we have been using the term "passive participle" for the verbal form that follows the passive *be* auxiliary in the V string ever since Problem Set 2.4) can be used as modifiers of Ns:

(71) the [suggested] arrangement

We might propose then that passive participles have some of the properties of adjectives.

In support of this proposal, note that they can appear in the comparative and superlative constructions, just as adjectives can:

(72) the [*most* maligned] idea

(73) the [*more* valued] idea

And when they are in a verb string, the comparative *more* can precede them, just as it does adjectives, although it must follow other verb forms:

(74) She is more appreciated than Bill.
      She is appreciated more than Bill.

(75) *She is more talking than Bill.
      She is talking more than Bill.

(Note that examples like *She is more screaming than talking right now* are called the ABSOLUTE NEGATIVE or METALINGUISTIC COMPARATIVES, and they have different properties which are not pertinent to the discussion here.)

Furthermore, in Italian (and, also, French), there is a pro-adjective clitic, the *lo* (which I have glossed as 'that') in the example below, that appears in sentences where otherwise we might expect a full AP:

(76) —È contento Gianni?
        is content   Gianni
        'Is Gianni content?'
      —Sì, lo   è.
        yes that is
        'Yes, (he) is that.'

This clitic can also appear in sentences in which otherwise we might expect a passive participle (as in 77), but it cannot appear in sentences in which we might expect some other verbal form (as in 78, in which we expect a perfect participle):

(77) —È apprezzata Maria?
        is appreciated Maria
        'Is Maria appreciated?'
      — Sì, lo è.
        yes that is
        'Yes, (she) is that.'

(78) —È partita Maria?
        is left Maria
        'Has Maria left?'
      *Sì, lo è.
        yes that is
        'Yes, (she) has that.'

Again, we see that the passive participle shares a property that otherwise only adjectives have.

Now look back at 68b, repeated here:

(79)   DS: [e] was suggested [that very arrangement] earlier

If passive participles have some properties of adjectives, what property of adjectives might they have that makes them unable to be followed by an argument sister? Think back to Case Theory. Recall that adjectives are not Case-Assigners. If passive participles are, likewise, not Case-Assigners, we can say that 79 fails because the NP *Mary* cannot receive Case in the DO position. Example 79, then, is a violation of our Case Filter. Thus we need not state that the Rule of Passive is obligatory. Instead, it can optionally apply in 79. If it does apply, we will get a good passive sentence. If it does not apply, 79 will be marked ungrammatical because it violates the Case Filter (whether or not a dummy-*it* is inserted in Subject position—as in 70).

If this is a correct account, we would predict that when the DO is a tensed clause rather than an NP, the sentence will not fail even if movement does not take place, so long as some dummy Subject is inserted. That is so:

(80)   It was suggested [that we all leave town].

(81)   [That we all leave town] was suggested, and rather indelicately, I might add.

(Actually, there is an alternative account of 80 that involves a movement rule. You will learn about this rule in Problem Set 6.5 of this chapter. The movement analysis, however, will be challenged in Problem Set 8.1 of chapter 8.)

By-Phrases

A final question concerning passive sentences like 68a is whether these sentences contain an agentive argument at any point in their derivation. Consider:

(82)   Mary was arrested.

It has been argued that the passive-voice affix on the verb fills the role of an agentive argument. We will look at some of the evidence for this claim in Problem Set 7.1 of chapter 7. If this claim is correct, then the object of the *by*-phrase in passive sentences like 83 cannot be the agentive argument:

(83)   Mary was arrested by the police.

This idea is probably quite unsettling to you. You may very well have wanted right from the start of our discussion of passives to point out a correlation between the Subjects of active sentences and the Object of *by* in the corresponding passive sentences. For example, it at first appears that the same selectional restrictions hold on both slots. And in earlier models of generative grammars, many linguists represented passive sentences as coming from a DS that was, in fact, the corresponding active sentence. So the DS for 83 would have been the active sentence: *The police arrested Mary.*

There are important theory differences between the old analysis and the one presented in this chapter. Notice that in order to generate 83 from the active source, our grammar would have to allow us to add a form of *be*, to change the verbal form to the passive participle, and to not only add the preposition *by*, but attach the NP *the police* as its Object. This analysis is STRUCTURE-BUILDING (in that it adds *be* and *by* and whatever structure is needed to accommodate them). Certainly, we would want such structure-building rules to be highly constrained, or we would have a grammar that OVERGENERATED (that is, that allowed the generation of structures that never, in fact, appeared). The task of constraining structure-building rules turned out to be formidable. And there were several other problems with this analysis that concerned problems internal to the older theories.

But one of the major problems with the older approach is that the initial observation of a one-to-one correlation between the Subject slot of active sentences and the Object of the *by*-slot in passive sentences was flawed. One of those flaws is already apparent in 82 (which lacks a *by*-phrase altogether). And you will discover differences between these two slots as you do Problem Set 6.1 of this chapter. Thus the fact that our analysis of passive draws no correlation between these two slots is not to be taken as a fault of this analysis. It is quite likely that the *by*-phrase of passive sentences is functioning as an adverbial.

Back to Subjectless Infinitivals

We can now return to a question posed early in this chapter: Is it best to posit an empty node as the Subject of infinitival strings like those in brackets in 3, repeated here, in 85?

(84)   We expected [to win].

(85)

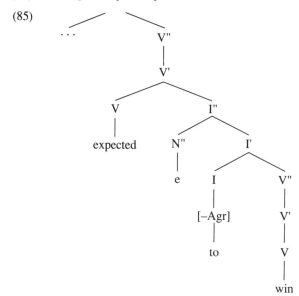

Or is it best to treat this string as an orphan VP, as in 86?

(86)

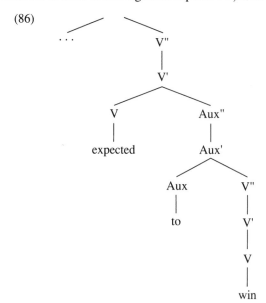

Let us see how our understanding of passive sentences can help us out. Can you think of any passive infinitivals that do not have an expressed Subject? There are many:

(87)   We expected [to be {ignored/appreciate/arrested/ . . . }].

We have argued that passives occur with an Object in DS. And, if you are a native speaker of English, you may feel that this analysis is intuitively appealing, since only transitive verbs occur in passive sentences in English (but see Tangent 2.2 of chapter 2 for discussion of intransitive passives in some languages). That is, we never find passivized verb strings like *be elapsed (as in *The due date was elapsed) or *be gone (as in *Home was gone by John). With that analysis of passive sentences, the DS of the examples in 87 have an Object inside the infinitival string. But this Object is not audible, so it must be an empty category.

(88)   DS: We expected [to be ignored [e]].

Now, since our Case Filter tells us only that audible NPs must be assigned Case, there is nothing to prevent 88 from being a good SS. So we still do not have evidence that we need to posit a Subject position in these infinitival strings.

However, 87 is not the only type of infinitival that can appear with a passive verb string:

(89)   We expected [Bill to be ignored].

Here the Rule of Passive has applied to move *Bill* from inside the VP into Subject position of the infinitival, and Case is subsequently assigned to *Bill* from the matrix V via Exceptional Case-Marking:

(90)   DS: We expected [[e] to be ignored [Bill]].

Since 90, then, is a good DS, we must be able to generate infinitivals with empty Subjects, given our movement analysis of passive. Rather than having two sources for infinitivals that lack a Subject, then, we will opt for a single type of generation for all infinitivals: all infinitivals are I″ at DS. With this analysis we are saying that every clause contains a Subject position, regardless of whether the Subject position is phonetically filled. This claim is known as the EXTENDED PROJECTION PRINCIPLE.

Inventory of Empty Categories

We have encountered three different types of empty categories thus far in this chapter. One is the empty node that is generated by way of movement. We called it trace:

(91)   Mary$_i$ was arrested [t$_i$].

Another is the empty node in a sentence like 3 (repeated here) that is present in both DS and SS and that we will call PRO (we will examine PRO in chapter 7):

(92)   We expected [PRO] to win.

The third is the empty node we posited in the generation of some sentences which appeared in DS but which was later filled during the derivation, as in:

(93) [e] was arrested John →
      John was arrested [t].

When we characterize empty categories later on, we will distinguish those that are present at SS. Thus the empty category represented by "e" in 93 will not be part of our discussion. Trace and PRO, however, will continue to be handled.

Actually, there is a fourth empty node that we must posit now, in light of the Extended Projection Principle. We have seen repeatedly in problem sets that some Romance languages allow nonovert Subjects (for Italian, Problem Sets 2.5, 3.6, 5.7; for Portuguese, Problem Set 5.3), and we will see this fact in later problem sets, as well (when Spanish can be added to our language list). If every clause has a Subject slot, as the Extended Projection Principle claims, then these Romance languages allow an empty category in Subject position of tensed clauses. But it cannot be trace, since it is not the result of movement. And it cannot be PRO, since it is not the Subject of infinitivals only. And it cannot be the empty category of 93, for example, since it is not just a placeholder at DS, but, rather, receives a theta-role from the predicate. We call this empty category "pro" (read as "little pro," to distinguish it from PRO). You will study pro in Problem Set 7.6 of chapter 7 and in Problem Set 8.6 of chapter 8.

Chains

At this point we need to take a step back and assess the import of our findings in this chapter. One of the major ideas of this chapter is that movement leaves behind a trace which is co-indexed with the moved element. The effect of a trace is to allow us to recover the thematic relations between the various items in a string. So if we find a trace in the DO position which is co-indexed with an NP in the Subject position (as happens in passive structures), we know that the theta-role which normally is assigned to the DO will be carried by the Subject at SS. Traces, then, ensure that predicate-argument structure is represented not just at DS, but at all intermediary syntactic levels, and at SS. Traces also let us know the syntactic history of a given item (that is, what structural position it was in at DS, at all intermediary levels, and at SS). We stated the motivation for traces in our basic principle of grammar known as the Projection Principle, repeated here for convenience:

(94) All lexical features of a predicate that appear in DS must appear at every
      syntactic level, as well.

This tells us that the predicate-argument structure as well as the subcategorization of a predicate will be represented at all syntactic levels.

Other principles of grammar now follow. First, with the Projection Principle, we are accepting the (absolutely sensible) idea that the semantic participant roles are assigned at DS and do not change during a derivation. We will find in later chapters that an item may move more than one time in the derivation of a single sentence.

Let us define a group of co-indexed items with trace as one of the members of the group a CHAIN. Trace would be the FOOT OF THE CHAIN. So in 93, for example, *John* and trace form a chain; trace is the foot of the chain and *John* is the HEAD OF THE CHAIN. The concept of the chain is one that we will have cause to appeal to repeatedly in later chapters. We can now state a generalization about chains:

(95)   There can be at most one theta-role assigned to a given chain.

Since predicate-argument structure is represented in DS, we could add to 95 that the theta-role of any chain will be assigned to the foot of the chain and then be associated with the rest of the items in the chain via co-indexation. So in 93, trace is assigned the theta-role of theme and then *John* is associated with this theta-role because *John* is a member of the chain which has this trace as its foot.

A consequence of 95 is that an item that is in a position to which a theta-role is assigned cannot move to another position to which a theta-role is assigned. Why not? Because the result would be semantic anomaly: a given item would be assigned two theta-roles. For example, if a predicate took arguments in both the DO and IO position and if a constituent could move from IO to DO position, then at SS the constituent in the DO position would bear two theta-roles. One would be linked to the DO position in the lexicon because of the argument structure of the predicate. The other would be associated with the DO via co-indexation with the IO slot:

(96)   predicate [$_{DO}$ XP$_i$]   [$_{IO}$ t$_i$]

This result is in conflict with the Theta Criterion that we first stated in chapter 3 and that we repeat here:

(97)   Every argument must be assigned a theta-role and every theta-role must be assigned to an argument.

The Theta Criterion is to be interpreted as limiting a given argument to receiving a unique theta-role from a given predicate (and as limiting a given theta-role to being assigned to a unique argument of a given predicate). Accordingly, 95 follows from other general principles (specifically, the Theta Criterion and the fact that movement leaves a trace co-indexed with the moved constituent), and we will not name it as a separate principle of our grammar.

The generalization in 95 together with the Projection Principle leads us to the conclusion that *movement can be only to a nonargument position.* That is, a moved node should not pick up theta-roles or other semantic roles during the derivation. Movement can be into the Subject position because GF Subject position need not be assigned a theta-role in DS (as you have already seen, since the dummies we have discussed up to this point have all been Subjects, and as you will argue for yourself in Problem Set 7.3 of chapter 7). Movement cannot be into DO or IO positions because they almost unfailingly are assigned theta-roles (exceptions being DOs or other GFs that are part of multiple-word predicates or part of unanalyzable idioms). Nor can movement be into the OP position, since OPs either are assigned a theta-role or bear some other semantic role (as we have pointed out repeatedly). The result is that the only GF position open as a LANDING SITE FOR MOVEMENT is Subject. We will discover other nonargument (and non-GF) positions to which movement can take place in chapter 8.

Now consider chains from the viewpoint of Case Theory. We argued in this chapter that passive participles have much in common with APs and cannot, in fact, assign Case. This fact motivates movement (as we argued in the discussion following 79 above), for if an NP moves into the Subject position, it will receive Case. *Movement, then, is from a non-Case position to a Case position. We might then suggest that at most one Case, just like at most one theta-role, may be assigned to a given chain.* Recall that our different Case assignment rules in chapter 5 applied in different contexts. So no NP will be assigned Case by more than one rule of Case assignment. If, then, no NP can have more than one Case associated with it via chain membership (as proposed here), we can see that the membership of an NP in a chain does not fundamentally change its Case potential: All NPs receive at most one Case.

Move Alpha

Given all of the above, we are now in a position to formulate the Rule of Passive. First consider the DS of a passive sentence, as in:

(98)   [e] was enjoyed the movie by the fifth-grade class.

There are several phrases in this sentence and so far as we know, all of them are free to move. But only one of them absolutely must move. Why must the NP *the movie* move? Recall that if it stays put, it will fail to receive Case, so we will have a violation of the Case Filter. Therefore, we will move this NP. We do not have to specify in our rule, then, which node is going to move.

Now, where can this node (here, an NP) move to? Note that this NP receives a theta-role from the V whose DO it is. Therefore, since every chain can have at most one theta-role associated with it, this NP can move only to a non-theta-receiving position. Looking at this tree, we see only one such position that is not filled: Subject position. (While we will discover other such positions in chapter 8, our discovery there will not impinge negatively on our reasoning here.) Therefore, the NP will move into the Subject position. We do not have to specify in our rule, then, where the NP is going to move.

But what moves and where it moves is all there is to the rule. Therefore, so far as we know at this point in our studies, all we need to say is: move anything anywhere. This is typically stated as 99, where "Alpha" stands for any node:

(99)   Move Alpha.

It has been claimed that 99 is the only rule of syntax. This is an amazing claim, and we will spend much time exploring it.

There are two stipulations on 99 that are very important. One is that Alpha be a node and never a string that does not form a node (that is, a nonconstituent string).

Thus in a DS like 98 above, the string *was enjoyed the* could never be moved as a unit, since this string does not form a constituent. But the string *was enjoyed the movie by the fifth-grade class* could potentially be moved, since this string forms the constituent Aux Phrase.

The second stipulation is that Alpha be a lexical node (an X) or a maximal node (an X″), but never a single-bar-level node (an X′). Passive movement involves the XP level. We will discuss an instance of movement of the X level in chapter 8 when we talk about the rule often called Subject-Auxiliary Inversion.

Caveat Lector

As usual, you should do or attempt all the problem sets of this chapter before you go on to the next chapter. *But you simply must do Problem Set 6.3 before you attempt to go on to later chapters.*

Tangent 6.1: Terminology

In early works in grammars that generated one structure from another, that is, GEN-ERATIVE GRAMMARS, people often spoke of the first input level as the DEEP STRUC-TURE. Many (though not all) people argued that the semantics of a sentence could be read off of deep structure.

To this structure a variety of syntactic (and, for some people, semantic) rules might apply. The output would be an INTERMEDIARY STRUCTURE, to which other rules might apply, giving the next intermediary structure, and so on. The final structure to which no further syntactic rules were applied was called the SURFACE STRUCTURE. At that point phonological rules would take over, yielding the sentence as we hear it.

In today's literature the first input level has been redubbed the D-STRUCTURE, or simply DS. While this new terminology may seem like a mere shorthand, it is meant as a new concept, free from the semantic associations that the term "deep structure" had for many linguists. DS is an abstract level (as discussed below in the text) which does not have a complete semantic interpretation associated with it. Rather, predicate-argument structure is apparent at DS (although even this claim can be argued to need qualifications), but binding relationships and various other types of semantic relationships (such as those involving the interpretation of quantifiers) are not determined from the DS. You will learn about this issue in chapter 9.

The final output of the syntactic rules has been redubbed the S-STRUCTURE, or simply SS. The term "surface structure" if used today is more likely to refer to the structure after all phonological rules have taken place. The SS, on the other hand, is the first input level to the phonological rules and to the rules of interpretation. It has been said to be ENRICHED by the presence of empty categories, whereas there is debate as to whether all or any empty categories are present in surface structure (that is, in phonological form).

Schematically, then, our grammar has the form shown as:

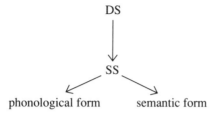

We have discussed this type of schema in more detail in the section Global-versus-Discrete Models of Grammar earlier in this chapter.

*Problem Set 6.1: English Infinitival Relatives, Raising, and *By*

This problem set is partially a review of certain points in the chapter and partially new applications of those points. It should be done.

Part 1

This NP contains a relative clause and our X-Bar Theory tells us it has the analysis shown in 1:

(1) the boy Gillian saw

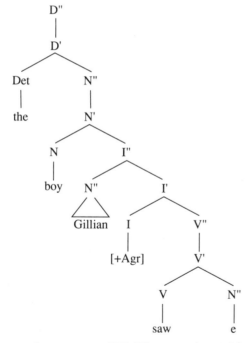

In this tree *saw* has an empty DO. We are not here taking a stance on which empty category this is (trace, PRO, pro, or an empty node that is present in the DS). You will not need to do anything with this e, so do not let it worry you. (In Problem Set 8.7 of chapter 8 you will analyze relative clauses.)

Now account for the differences in grammaticality of the sentences with relative clauses below:

(2)   The right kid [to study with] is the one who takes notes.

(3)   *The right kid [Bill to study with] is the one who takes notes.

(4)   The kind of kid [(that) everyone should study with] is one who takes notes.

(Hint: 2 and 3 contain infinitival clauses that are relative clauses; 4 contains a tensed clause that is a relative clause. Be sure to make use of Case Theory.)

Part 2

Give an account of the grammaticality or ungrammaticality of the following sentences (again, using Case Theory):

(5)   It was rumored that John likes tomato juice.

(6)   *It was rumored John to like tomato juice.

(7)   John was rumored to like tomato juice.

The NP *John* has moved in one of these sentences. Which one? (Please do not worry about whether or not this is an instance of the Passive Rule. You will study movement further in chapter 7. The job for you here is to figure out in which sentence of 5–7 *John* is located at SS at a different position from that in which he started in DS. If you do not understand the cause of the grammaticality contrast between 5 and 6, reread The Analysis of Passive Participles section of this chapter.)

Part 3

In the text we used the fact that the selectional restrictions on the Subject of a passive sentence are identical to the selectional restrictions on some element inside the VP of the corresponding active sentence as the basis for an argument that the Subject of passive sentences originates inside the VP in DS and moves into the Subject position by a syntactic movement rule. You probably noticed then that generally the selectional restrictions on the Object of the *by*-phrase in a passive sentence are identical to the selectional restrictions on the Subject of the corresponding active sentence. That observation led linguists in the early years of generative work (the 1950s through the 1970s) to propose that active sentences were the source of passive sentences (as discussed in the *By*-Phrases section of the text). We did not take this approach in the text. Instead, the sentence in 8 is argued to have the DS in 9 and not that in 10:

(8)   Mary was arrested by the police.

(9)   [e] was arrested [Mary] by the police.

(10)   The police arrested Mary.

Below you are asked to use Data Sets A–C and the material after them to point out five arguments for why 9 is a better source for 8 than 10.

Data Set A

(11)   Mary was arrested.

(12)   John was ignored.

(13)   The child's wagon was painted.

Examples 11–13 give passive sentences with no *by*-phrase. You can easily come up with many others. How do such sentences bear on the issue?

Data Set B

(14)   Margaret was appointed by executive fiat of the king.
       The new president was chosen by general acclamation of the common folk.

(15)   The package came by courier.

(16)   Mary is pregnant by John.

(Example 15 was offered to me by Emily McHugh. Example 16 was offered to me by Kristin Denham.) Discuss the semantic interpretation of these *by*-phrases. Then point out their relevance to the alternative sources for passive sentences in 9 and 10 above. Note that sentences like 15 and 16 present an additional problem to that presented by the sentence type exemplified in 14.

Data Set C

(17)   John was rumored to like tomato juice.
       *Everybody rumored John to like tomato juice.

(18)   Ken was born on the Fourth of July.
       does not equal: Someone bore Ken on the Fourth of July.

(The second example sentence of 18 does have a similar meaning to the first archaically. But in casual, modern speech, it does not.) How do the facts that the second sentence in 17 is ungrammatical and that the second sentence in 18 is not semantically equivalent to the first sentence in 18 bear on the issue of whether 9 or 10 is the correct source for 8?

The fourth argument you are to come up with does not call for a new data set. Consider the tree analyses of 8–10 in 19.

(19)　(=8)

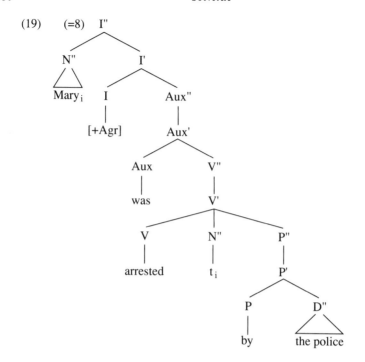

(20)　(=9)

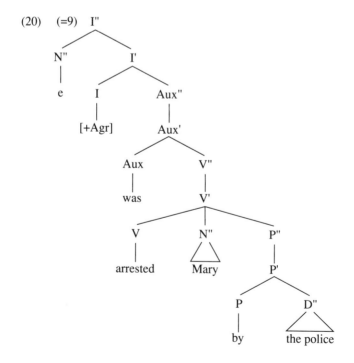

(21)   (=10)   I''

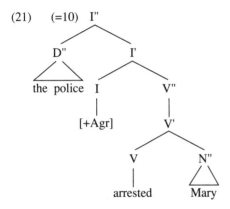

If 21 (= 10) were the source for 19 (= 8), both the passive auxiliary *be* and the *by* would have to be added, with concomitant changes in structure. Discuss what these structural changes would be and why this structure-building approach is undesirable.

The fifth argument you are to come up with likewise does not depend on any new data set. If 10 were the source for 8, a problem for Theta Theory arises. Discuss theta-assignment in 8 given 10 as its source and point out this problem. (Hint: Remember to assume that movement leaves behind a trace that is co-indexed with the moved item. It is via this co-indexation that we can figure out the theta-role of the moved items. Make use of the Theta Criterion here.)

Problem Set 6.2: Japanese Postposing

Many people have claimed that Japanese is a verb-final language. What they mean by that is that within a clause, the V or the predicative adjective must be the final element. In fact, some people claim the V is like a brick wall and nothing from the clause can appear after it except sentence particles. (You are familiar with some sentence particles from Problem Sets 2.5 and 5.8. They can indicate whether the sentence is a question, whether the sentence is tentative, whether the sentence is surprising, etc.) This claim is false, however: a variety of elements may follow the V or the predicative adjective.

Part 1

The matrix verb is in boldface in the following examples, as are any particles attached to it, and there is material following this verb in each example. For each sentence tell what category appears to the right of the V. For now just give the type of category without worrying about what projection of the category it is. So, for example, say that the category is A, N, V, P, or I, regardless of which projection (X, X', or X'') we find depending on the category of the head of the string. Recall (from Problem Set 2.5, in particular) that Japanese has a wide range of empty categories. Thus none of the sentences in 1–5 below have explicitly expressed Subjects.

(1) **Mita**, ano eiga?
     see   that movie
     'Did (you) see that movie?'

(You are aware from Problem Sets 1.4, 3.7, and 5.8 of the range of particles that occur on nominals in Japanese. The nominal in 1, however, has no particle on it. Do not let that throw you off. We return to this point in Part 3 below.)

(2) Tonikaku **syabette-hosii-no-ne**, ano, kotoba-de.
     anyway   talk-want   -Q   dialect-in
     'Anyway, (I) wanted (them) to talk, um, in dialect, you see?'

(In 2 "Q" = question particle. *No* is a particle that marks assertions (and is used primarily by women). The *ano* in 2 is a filler word, like the English "uh" or "um." It can be prolonged: *anooo* (like the English "uhhhh"). It is not the same *ano* that you see in 1.)

(3) Nani-ka   **site-ru**, itu-mo?
     something do   usually
     'Do (you) usually do something?'

(4) Kuruma-o **katta-yo**, sugoku hurui.
     car-DO   bought very   old
     'I bought a very old car.'

(5) **Samisii-wa-yo**, tomodati i-nakat-tara.
     lonely   friend   exist-not-if
     'It's lonely [if (there) aren't friends].'

(In 5 I have included *na(i)*, the negative morpheme, as part of the V, as I will do below again. In 4 and 5 *yo* is a particle marking emphasis. In 5 the use of *wa* suggests a female speaker.)

Part 2

Assume that the material that follows the V above was moved there by a movement rule. Now using 1–5 and the data that follow, tell what projection (X, X', or X") is moved by this postposing rule. Instead of using the symbol "S" for clause, switch over to use the correct projection of I(NFL).

(6) *Ano **mita**, eiga? (cf. 1)
     that see   movie
     'Did (you) see that movie?'

(7) *Kotoba tonikaku **syabette-hosii-no** ne, ano, de. (cf. 2)
     dialect anyway   talk-want   Q   um   in
     'Anyway, (I) wanted (them) to talk, um, in dialect, you see?'

(8) *Sugoku hurui- o   **katta-yo**, kuruma. (cf. 4)
     very   old-   DO bought   car
     'I bought a very old car.'

Make a general statement about what level (X, X′, or X″) gets postposed.

Part 3

Now tell what GFs can be postposed. Consider all the data thus far plus 9–12. (In 9–12 I have placed a particle on every nominal in order to aid you in answering this question. But, in fact, this postposing rule is prevalent in casual speech between friends, in which sometimes particles are omitted (as in 1 above). So if you are a Japanese speaker, you may prefer to omit some particles below.)

(9) Kondo **yar-oo-yo**, scrabble-o
sometime let's-play scrabble-DO
'Let's play Scrabble sometime.'

(10) Ima demo, soo, soo-yuu gakkoo-ga **an-no-yo**, syuukyoo-no
now even, uh, like-that school- SUBJ exist religion- GEN
gakkoo-wa.
school- TOP
{As for/With regard to/Talking about} religious schools, (there) are schools like that even now.'

(The *no* particle in 10 is glossed as a genitive marker. A close-to-literal translation of the NP that contains this genitive would be 'schools of religion.' The first *soo* in 10 is another filler, like the *ano* of 2 above. Fillers are typical of casual speech.)

(11) Watasi sugu **it-tyau-wake**, Hitomi nanka-ni.
I right away say Hitomi for example-IO
'I say (it) right away to, for example, Hitomi.'

(12) Soo **ossyatta-yo**, ano kata-ga.
so said (HON) that person (HON)-SUBJ
'That (honored) person said so.'

(The "HON" in 12 glosses an honorific form. There are a variety of honorific forms in Japanese which, generally, reflect social status of the various nominals in the sentence as well as of the speaker and the listener. The honorifics often work to humble or honor the people spoken about with respect to the person addressed.)

Part 4

Now give the landing site for the movement. (That is, tell where the postposed element can move to.) Consider all the data thus far, plus:

(13) [Naoki-ga kuru tte] **itte-ta-yo**, asita.
Naoki-SUBJ come that said tomorrow
'(He/She) said [that Naoki will come tomorrow].'

(14) [Asita kuru tte] **itte-ta-yo**, Naoki-ga.
tomorrow come that said Naoki-SUBJ
'(He/She) said [that Naoki will come tomorrow].'

(In 13 and 14 only the matrix V is in boldface, but there are two clauses here—thus two Vs.) Your answer should be purely in linear terms, since we have not discussed yet how a postposed string might be attached to the preceding material. The issue here is which verb the postposed material follows.

Part 5

Consider 15, in which we have two clauses and the V of each is in boldface:

(15)   Boku-wa [Toshio-ga   Chopin-o   **hiita**   tte] **kiita-yo.**
         I-TOP   [Toshio-SUBJ Chopin-DO played that] heard
         'I heard [that Toshio played Chopin].'

Postposing can yield 16 but not 17:

(16)   Boku-wa Toshio-ga   **hiita**   tte **kiita-yo**, Chopin-o.
         I-TOP   Toshio-SUBJ played that heard   Chopin-DO
         'I heard that Toshio played Chopin.'

(17)   *Boku-wa Toshio-ga   **hiita**   Chopin-o   tte **kiita-yo.**
         I-TOP   Toshio-SUBJ played Chopin-DO that heard
         'I heard that Toshio played Chopin.'

(Example 17 is ungrammatical even if there are pauses preceding and/or following *Chopin-o.*) What moved where in 16? What moved where in 17? Will your answer to Part 4 account for 16 versus 17? If not, adjust your statement of where a postposed item can move to in order to account for all the data thus far.

Part 6

Now consider:

(18)   Hasami **totte-kure-nai**, ano?
         scissors hand-won't   those
         'Won't (you) hand (me) those scissors?'

This example should surprise you. Based on its English gloss, what category do you think *ano* belongs to? What projection of that category seems to have postposed here?

(You will learn in Tangent 8.1 of chapter 8 and Problem Set 8.2 that Japanese does not have determiners. Thus *ano*, unlike English demonstratives, behaves syntactically like a true adjective. Therefore an A″ has moved in 18, and, accordingly, 18 is not a surprise, after all.)

*Problem Set 6.3: English *Wh*-Traces

This problem set cannot be skipped. It is assumed repeatedly in later chapters.

In this problem set, come up with as many arguments as you can for the very existence of empty categories by using *wh*-questions and sentences with relative clauses in them as your data base. A list of sentences of English that should help in building arguments follows. You are not limited to these sentences only. You are to assume that the *wh*-question or relative word has moved from the position marked with a trace in these examples. The point is for you to find reasons why positing a trace in the position indicated is desirable. In some examples PRO is also present. Just assume for the sake of the argument that PRO's existence is to be taken as a given. Concentrate on proving that t exists. For each sentence, come up with a distinct argument for the existence of t.

Be sure to bring to bear everything you have learned so far in this book. Let me remind you of a few things.

First, you have a Theta Theory which tells you that predicates assign theta-roles to their arguments and that those arguments are in GF positions. Furthermore, an argument may receive precisely one theta-role per complete functional complex that it belongs to, and each argument must have a different theta-role from the other arguments of the same predicate. This is part of the lexical structure or frame of a word. For example, *give* can take an agent and a theme and a benefactee. Remember that the GF positions are only Subject, DO, IO, and OP. They are never extra positions added to the end or beginning of a clause (as in the Japanese examples in Problem Set 6.2 above).

Remember also that you know certain facts about theta-roles. For one, only agents can license the presence of certain items that have to do with will—such as *voluntarily* and rationale clauses starting with *in order to* (as you learned in Problem Set 3.3). For another, only themes can be the Subject of resultative predicates (as in *I ironed THE DRESS FLAT*).

Second, you know that there is also another part of the lexical structure called subcategorization. The subcategorization frame for a word tells you which other GFs or modifiers it can or must take as complements. For example, the subcategorization frame of *prevail* will tell you that no DO is possible, whereas the subcategorization frame of *discuss* will tell you that a DO is necessary. Remember that there is a difference between argument frames and subcategorization frames. Argument frames give the theta-roles a theta-assigner has to assign; theta-roles are semantic in nature. Subcategorization tells you what GFs or modifiers must be syntactically realized with a given lexical item, regardless of semantics.

Third, you know that a reflexive must have a local antecedent, though we have only a vague idea yet of what locality means. You can assume for the sake of this problem set that a reflexive must have an antecedent within its complete functional complex.

(1)   I saw myself.
       *Jack saw myself.

(2)   Bill said Mary saw herself.
       *Bill said Mary saw himself.

That is the only fact about reflexives that you are expected to use on this problem set.

The traces are marked in the SSs, given in brackets after the examples that follow.

Please read through all these examples as well as the sample argument that follows before you begin.

(3) Where did Jack say Mary put the potatoes?
     [Where did Jack say [Mary put the potatoes t]?]

(4) This is the girl who Ralph insisted I ask to marry me.
     [This is the girl [who Ralph insisted I ask t [PRO to marry me]]

(5) Who did you insist perjure himself?
     [Who did you insist [t perjure himself]?]

(6) What did you think Jack painted red?
     [What did you think [Jack painted t red]?]

(7) Who did you think painted the barn red voluntarily?
     [Who did you think [t painted the barn red voluntarily]?]

(8) Jack I suppose did it again, didn't he?
     [[Jack I suppose [t did it again]], [didn't he]?]

(9) Which people did Jack say were yucky?
     [Which people did Jack say [t were yucky]?]
     but not: *Which people did Jack say was yucky?

(Hint: If you do not see the point of 8, look back to Problem Set 2.1 of chapter 2.)
Please try to make your arguments as concise as possible.

Let me give you a sample. I am going to build an argument for empty categories using so-called FLOATED QUANTIFIERS. You may not use this argument among yours.

First note the relevant data:

(10) Which boys did Jack say have all left?
      [Which boys did Jack say t have all left]

I. Quantifiers may float only off of plural Subjects and must remain in the same clause as the Subject they float off of. (I am stating this as a given. We have not discussed this and it might very well not be correct. I give it just so that I can offer you a sample argument. But in all your arguments you will be making statements that we have already justified in the text or in earlier problem sets. Please say where we justified your statement. If you come up with some generalization that we have not justified in the text or in problem sets, then you must take the time to justify that generalization here.)

II. In 10 the quantifier *all* is in floated position, since it is not inside an NP.

III. Therefore, from I and II, I conclude that *all* has floated off the Subject of the embedded clause.

IV. There is no overt Subject of the embedded clause.

V. Therefore, from III and IV, I conclude that there must be an empty Subject in the embedded clause (and furthermore, that that Subject is plural).

*Problem Set 6.4: English Unaccusative Movement

We will refer to unaccusative verbs repeatedly in later chapters, so it is a good idea for you to do this problem set just so you are very familiar with the properties of these verbs.

This problem set is messier than most. Do not let that bother you. (Syntax is messy.) Just do the best you can. If you see inconsistencies, state them.

Passive constructions have been argued to be underlyingly transitive (that is, underlyingly taking a DO) but on the surface intransitive, as we have seen in this chapter. But passive sentences are not the only types of sentences for which an underlying-transitive-but-surface-intransitive analysis is worth contemplating. There are at least two other candidates. One is what is called the ergative or unaccusative construction (which you first worked on in Problem Set 3.4).

(1)　The ice melted.

Another is what is called the middle contruction (and the sentence in 2 is said to be in the middle voice):

(2)　Ice melts quickly when you put it over fire.

Unaccusative verbs often appear in two kinds of sentences—ones that appear at SS to be intransitive (like 1), and corresponding ones that appear at SS to be transitive:

(3)　The fire melted the ice.

In fact, 1 and 3 together are called an UNACCUSATIVE PAIR or an UNACCUSATIVE/ INCHOATIVE pair.

Middle verbs also often appear in both intransitive (like 2) and transitive sentences. In fact, many verbs fall in both classes, like *melt.*

There are many differences between unaccusatives and middles. One is the semantics. Unaccusative sentences can be about specific situations—they need not have anything generic in them at all. But middles are most often generic in some way:

(4)　unaccusative: The bottle broke when she knocked it over.

(5)　middle: Glass bottles break easily if you knock them over.

Some people characterize this difference by saying that unaccusative sentences report an event, but middle sentences do not report an event, but, instead, a characteristic.

Unaccusative sentences in no way call to mind an agent or instrument, but middles do:

(6)　unaccusative: The clothes are hanging on the line.

(7)　middle: Clothes don't hang easily when the wind's blowing.

In 6 people say we have no indication of an agent at all. But in 7 people say that the presence of something like *easily* brings to mind an agent (whose ease or lack of it is reported here).

Not all transitive verbs have an unaccusative counterpart:

(8) unaccusative: *The chicken killed last night. (*in the sense of the chicken being the theme)

And a verb may have a middle even though it lacks an unaccusative, as in 9 (which a chicken farmer might say):

(9) middle: Chickens kill best in late summer.

And not all transitive verbs easily lend themselves to a middle usage:

(10) middle: *French acquires easily if you study hard.

Those that do not have a middle usage lack an unaccusative usage, as well:

(11) unaccusative: *French acquired yesterday.

Be sure to distinguish between unaccusatives and middles versus optionally transitive uses:

(12) John eats (dinner) at five.

Here *eat* optionally takes an object. But, either way, *John* is an agent. So 12 without *dinner* is neither unaccusative nor middle—it is just plain intransitive. (We will touch on the analysis of optional intransitives like 12 in Problem Set 7.6 of chapter 7.)

Part 1

Discuss the advantages of deriving unaccusatives and middles from underlying transitives with respect to the linking between the argument frame of a lexical item and the GF frame (that is, the linking between theta-roles and GFs). How will this linking be handled if 13 comes from 14, as opposed to being generated in the DS with *the ball/rubber balls* in Subject position? (In your discussion please be sure not to assume any meaning associated with DS other than lexical information, such as predicate-argument structure. In particular, note that an "e" at DS has no meaning associated with it whatsoever.)

(13) The ball bounced./Rubber balls bounce high.

(14) [e] bounced the ball./[e] bounce rubber balls high.

Part 2

Notice that neither unaccusatives nor middles have any particular suffix on the verb, nor can they appear with a *by*-phrase, nor do they co-occur with the passive auxiliary *be*. In these three ways they are unlike passives. What problem does this raise regarding the predicate-argument structure of the verb if 13 derives from 14 above?

Part 3

If 13 derives from 14, what problems for Case Theory will arise? (The issue is, once more, that unaccusatives and middles, unlike passives, have no special suffix; the verb is simply a verb and cannot be argued to belong to some other category such as adjective (in contrast to the predicate in passive constructions). So how is the Case-assigning property of the verb to be inhibited?)

Part 4

Some linguists have claimed that present participles of intransitive verbs occur freely in adnominal position (as modifiers of the N):

(15)   the prevailing idea
the dying flowers

But present participles of transitive verbs are generally excluded,

(16)   *the killing boy
*the persuading ideas

with the exception of those transitive verb participles which have become lexicalized as adjectives:

(17)   the exasperating class
the stunning idea

One piece of evidence that *exasperating* is an adjectival form while *prevailing* is a verbal form comes from superlatives:

(18)   *the most prevailing idea

(19)   the most exasperating class

If the above statement of the facts is correct, then the possibility of a present participle appearing as an adnominal modifier is a test for syntactic intransitivity.
Now consider the unaccusative verbs: *roll*, as in:

(20)   The log rolled down the hill.

bounce, as in:

(21)   The ball bounced out the window.

roast, as in

(22)   The turkey roasted in less than five hours.

all of which verbs can be used as middles, too.
And consider the middle verbs: *bribe*, as in:

(23)   Those bureaucrats bribe easily.

kill, as in 8 above; *paint*, as in:

(24)   Woodwork always paints with more difficulty than walls.

none of which verbs can be used as unaccusatives.

Test whether these unaccusatives behave as transitives or intransitives with respect to the present-participle test (that is, 15 versus 16).

Now test whether these middles behave as transitives or intransitives with respect to the present-participle test.

If you found that either unaccusatives or middles or both behave like transitives with respect to this test, what might account for this fact? (That is, will an analysis which derives 13 from 14 help account for this fact?)

Nota Bene: The above questions may have led you to contradictory arguments. If so, do not be upset. There is much controversy about the correct analysis of unaccusatives and middles.

Part 5

Notice that *away* can be used in a directional sense:

(25)   He ran away.
        We turned the boy away.
        The ball was hit away.

or in a durative sense:

(26)   He was eating away the whole time we were talking.

Some linguists have claimed that only verbs used without a DO can appear with the durative sense of *away*:

(27)   *He was eating away the pizza. (only elimination of pizza here—not duration of eating)
        (cf. He was eating away at the pizza.)
            *He was discussing away the project.

If this is correct, then the possibility of *away* appearing with a durative sense in a sentence is evidence that the verb of that sentence has no DO with it.

Consider the unaccusatives *sink*, *fracture*, and *flush*:

(28)   The ship sank fast.

(29)   Her hip bone fractured when she fell.

(30)   The toilet won't flush.

all of which can be used as middles also.

And consider the middles *wax*, *tint*, and *polish*:

(31)   Linoleum floors wax easily.

(32)   Blond hair tints more easily than brown hair.

(33)   Silver polishes up beautifully, don't you agree?

none of which can be used as unaccusatives.

Now test these unaccusatives for transitivity with the *away* test. Then test these middles. If either or both behave as transitive according to this diagnostic, how might we account for that?

What about passives? Can durative *away* occur in passives? What questions does your answer raise about the test?

Part 6

Out can be prefixed to obligatorily intransitive verbs to form transitives:

 (34)   John waited.

 (35)   John outwaited Bill.

It can also be prefixed to optionally transitive verbs in their intransitive use, to form a new transitive:

 (36)   John kills.

 (37)   John outkilled Fred.

But we do not find this -*out* prefixed to verbs when a DO is present:

 (38)   *John outkilled Bill chickens.

And we do not find this -*out* prefixed to obligatorily transitive verbs even in the absence of a DO:

 (39)   *John outdiscusses Bill.

Can *out* be prefixed to unaccusatives? Can it be prefixed to middles? How might we account for the answers you get?

I gave this warning before, but in light of the frustration you may now feel, I will give it again: The above questions may have led you to contradictory arguments. If so, do not be upset. There is much controversy about the correct analysis of unaccusatives and middles.

Problem Set 6.5: English Extraposition

Consider sentences like:

 (1)   [That Mary lied] shocked Frank.

 (2)   It shocked Frank [that Mary lied].

Many people have argued that there is a movement rule which derives 2 from 1. That rule would take a sentential Subject and extrapose it (the rule is called EXTRA-POSITION) to the end of the sentence, leaving behind a trace (since all movement leaves behind a trace). Then the trace would be "covered" by a so-called dummy-*it*, so the matrix clause would have a phonetically realized Subject at SS (as all tensed clauses in English must have). The derivation is as in examples 3 and 5 (next page), in which the tree analyses are given.

(3)   [That Mary lied] shocked Frank.

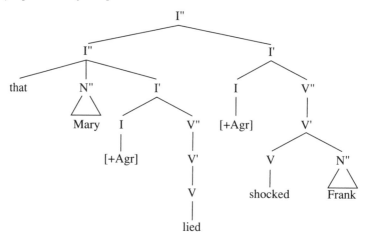

(4)   [t]ᵢ shocked Frank [that Mary lied]ᵢ

(5)   Itᵢ shocked Frank [that Mary lied]ᵢ

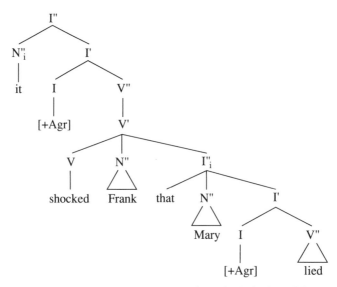

Notice that the *it* that covers the trace would inherit the index of the trace (accounting for the co-indexing of the NP *it* with the extraposed clause at SS).

   In these trees there are two details that might disturb you. One is that the complementizer *that* introducing the embedded clause appears not to fit within our X-Bar schema. If you noted that, you are quite right. The problem is that we have not yet developed a complete picture of X-Bar Theory. We will do so in chapter 8, and at that point you will find out where the complementizer *that* should go in the tree. For now, please adopt my strategy above and just attach it under the embedded I″.

The second point that might disturb you involves the tree for 5 only: the extraposed I″ is attached as a sister to V and N″ under the matrix V′. Logically, if an I″ moves to final position, it could as well be attached under the matrix V″, or I′, or even I″. You will be able to justify its attachment under V′ after you have done Problem Set 8.4 of chapter 8.

The goal of this problem set is to make sure you understand and feel comfortable with this movement analysis of Extraposition sentences.

Part 1

Give a simplified tree (you can draw in triangles for nodes whose internal analyses are not relevant to the issue) for the DS and all intermediate syntactic levels and then the SS of the following sentences:

(6) It amazed Pete that Sally left.

(7) It amazed Pete that it annoyed Mike that Sally left.

Be careful: in 6 you will have just two trees (the DS and SS); but in 7 Extraposition has applied twice, so you will have three trees (the DS, the intermediate tree in which one instance of Extraposition has taken place, and the SS in which both instances of Extraposition have taken place).

If you are having trouble drawing the trees for 7, think in terms of which predicates are higher in the tree. Let us go through the SS of 7 together. The matrix V is *amazed*. How do you know this? You know it because the only clause in 7 that is not introduced by the subordinating complementizer *that* is the one with *amazed* as its verb. So the structure is:

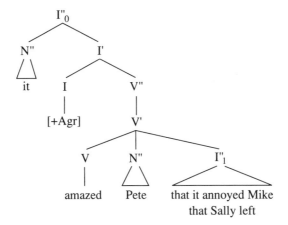

We need to analyze I″₁ further. So the next job is to figure out which is the next higher V: *annoyed* or *left*. Ask yourself whether the proposition involving annoying left, or whether the proposition involving leaving annoyed. The second, right? The first does not even make sense. So *annoyed* is the next higher V. Therefore the SS tree is as shown on the next page.

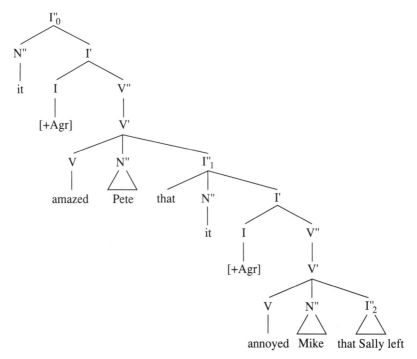

The SS terminal string must match the sentence as you say it, and this terminal string does match 7. So we are correct.

You can employ the same kind of strategy to figure out the DS of 7. You already know that the highest verb is *amazed*, the intermediary clause's verb is *annoyed*, and the lowest verb is *left*. Ask yourself, what amazed what? A proposition amazed Pete, right? So I''_1 is the Subject of *amazed* at DS. But what does I''_1 look like? We know its verb is *annoyed*. But what annoyed what? A proposition annoyed Mike. So I''_2 is the Subject of *annoyed*. The DS, therefore, is:

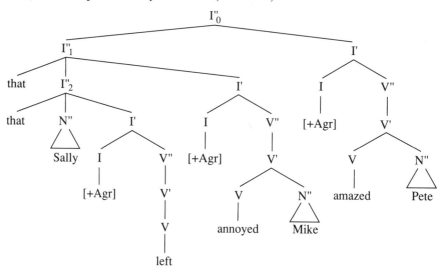

The terminal string for this DS reads, "That that Sally left annoyed Mike amazed Pete." It sounds awful. Remember that DS is an abstract level. DS need not sound good to the ear. Instead, DS must conform to X-Bar Theory and DS must reflect predicate-argument structure (that is, it should tell us who did what to whom). In Part 4 you will address the question of why structures like this DS immediately above sound so bad. For now, do not worry about it. Just use the strategy above and give the trees I ask for.

You still have one tree left to draw for 7, the intermediary tree in which I_2'' has extraposed, but I_1'' has not. (In the SS, both I_2'' and I_1'' have extraposed. In the DS, neither has extraposed.)

Part 2

Now draw the DS, all intermediate trees, and the SS for:

(8)   It was announced that Sally left.

(9)   It amazed Pete that it was announced that Sally had left.

In 8 assume that two rules have applied: Passive and Extraposition. Must they apply in a certain order? If so, in what order? Briefly describe an alternative analysis of example 8 in which Passive has not applied.

Part 3

Consider the following sentence:

(10)   The fact that Pete left upset Mark.

The clause *that Pete left* does not function here to modify *the fact*, unlike with the relative clause in:

(11)   The fact [which I'm about to tell you] will upset Mark.

Instead, in 10 the embedded clause tells us what the fact is. Thus 12 would be a non sequitur to 10, but not to 11:

(12)   And that fact is that Jenny married Paul.

Embedded clauses like that in 10 are typically called APPOSITIVE CLAUSES since the clause stands in a semantic relationship to the nominal preceding it that is similar to apposition. (Examples of ordinary nonclausal appositives include the italicized strings in:

(13)   Maybelle, *my best friend*, is coming to dinner.

(14)   She left on the Fourth of July, *Independence Day*.)

For the sake of this problem set assume that the structure for a sentence like 10 is that shown in 15.

(15)

```
                              I''_0
              _____/  _____
            N''                                    I'
        ___/  \___                            ___/  \___
      D''         I''_1                       I          V''
       |      ___/ | \___                     |          |
      D'    that  N''     I'                [+Agr]       V'
    __/\__        |    __/  \__                       __/  \__
  Det    N''      N'  I       V''                    V        N''
   |      |       |   |       |                      |         |
  the    N'       N  [+Agr]   V'                    upset      N'
         |      Pete          |                               |
        fact                  V'                              N
                              |                               |
                             left                           Mark
```

There is at least one troubling point in 15: the Subject of our matrix clause is an N'' that branches to D'' and I''_1, which is not consistent with the X-Bar Theory we have developed. Do you see why? According to our X-Bar Theory, the double-bar level should branch to a specifier and a single-bar level. But I''_1 is neither a specifier or a single-bar level. And we have the double-bar level of N immediately dominating another double-bar level of a nominal (the D''). Instead, given X-Bar Theory, we would have expected I''_1 to be a sister to the N level only.

As you might expect (given the X-Bar Theory problems with example 15), appositive clauses present complex issues that have led to disagreements in their analysis. Some have argued that appositive clauses must be sisters to a phrasal nominal (N'' or D''), as I have represented in 15 above. Others have proposed that appositive clauses must be sisters to N'; and still others say that they must be sisters to N. In fact, there is another proposal: that appositive clauses do not form a constituent with the nominal preceding them, but, instead, simply linearly follow that nominal and are attached as daughters to the mother of the nominal. In 15 that would mean that I''_1 would be a daughter of I''_0. This is the proposal I have argued for elsewhere. I have given the tree in 15, however, since the analysis in 15 is frequently found in the literature and since we are not prepared at this point to argue about the structure of appositive clauses. However, nothing we do with Extraposition sentences will depend upon this analysis. In fact, for our purposes, I''_1 could be attached as a sister to any projection of N or as a daughter to I''_0.

Give five sentences that contain an appositive clause with different nominals from *fact*.

Now give the DS, all intermediate trees, and the SS for:

(16)   The notion is absurd that Paul loves Mary.

Notice that you will be claiming that Extraposition can apply to move not just a sentential Subject, but an appositive clause that relates to the Subject (relates in a way explored in Problem Set 7.9).

Now find the DS for:

(17) It's obvious that the notion that the fact that bears are mammals is incorrect is absurd.

Part 4

The following example is a well-formed DS, but it is ungrammatical as an SS and it is considered fairly incomprehensible by most native speakers of English:

(18) No one doubts that that the fact that Marge likes Valentino bugs Pete surprised everyone.

Bracket the clauses in this sentence. Now give a tree for 18. Label the clause with the verb *like* as I″-4. Label the clause with the verb *bugs* as I″-3. Label the clause with the verb *surprised* as I″-2. And label the matrix clause I″-1.

Tell what clause (that is, which I″) or clauses extraposed to the end of what other clause (that is, to the end of which I″) or clauses to get:

(19) No one doubts that it surprised everyone that the fact that Marge likes Valentino bugs Pete.

(20) No one doubts that that the fact bugs Pete that Marge likes Valentino surprised everyone.

(21) No one doubts that it surprised everyone that the fact bugs Pete that Marge likes Valentino

Now if we let Passive apply on the matrix clause, we have additional possibilities, since I″-2 (which will be the derived Subject of I″-1 after Passive) can now extrapose to the end of I″-1. Tell which clauses have extraposed to the end of which clauses to get:

(22) It is doubted by no one that that the fact that Marge likes Valentino bugs Pete surprised everyone.

(23) It is doubted by no one that it surprised everyone that the fact that Marge likes Valentino bugs Pete.

(24) It is doubted by no one that it surprised everyone that the fact bugs Pete that Marge likes Valentino.

Now look over 18–24. Which one(s) of them sounds best to you? Which one(s) sounds terrible? Try to make a generalization about the terrible sentences based on (1) the linear string of words involved and (2) the shape of the SS tree. Try to make a generalization about the good sentences based on the shape of the SS tree. These generalization should be relatively gross. That is, I am not looking for any very detailed or refined generalization. Instead, I want you to study the trees and talk about general branching characteristics, and ignore details.

Part 5

Consider the sentence:

    (25)   It amazes me that it disturbs Paul that Mary left.

Draw a DS for this tree. Here Extraposition has applied twice.
  Now consider the sentence:

    (26)   *That it disturbs Paul amazes me that Mary left.

Which I″ moved to the end of which I″ to yield 26? Does 26 have any of the problems you found above for the unacceptable sentences among 18–25? I do not expect it to. Instead, 26 is utter garbage and the movement that took place here should be disallowed. Based on 26 in contrast to any of the good sentences you found in 18–25, what can you say in general about where Extraposition moves an embedded I″?

  That is all we will do on Extraposition at this time. We will return to Extraposition and challenge this movement analysis in Problem Set 8.1.

Problem Set 6.6: Japanese Center-Embedding

In Problem Set 6.5 you looked at a variety of sentences to which Extraposition did or could have applied. If Extraposition does not apply, sometimes we find that the embedded clause is both preceded and followed by material from a higher clause. You undoubtedly thought about this fact as you were working on Part 4 of that problem set.

  There are many instances in which we find embedded clauses that are both preceded and followed by material from a higher clause. Such clauses are said to be CENTER-EMBEDDED. Compare, for example, 1, in which we have multiple center-embedding, with 2, in which we do not.

    (1)   The rat [the cat [the boy [the girl knew] kept] chased] escaped.

    (2)   This is the cat that chased the rat that ate the malt that lay in the house that Jack built.

Native speakers find 1 very difficult to process, whereas they experience no difficulty with 2. If we remove the most deeply embedded clause of 1, it does not seem to improve in terms of ease of processing:

    (3)   The rat [the cat [the boy kept] chased] escaped.

But if we remove the most deeply embedded clause of 3, suddenly processing is easy:

    (4)   The rat [the cat chased] escaped.

Now consider the following Japanese sentences.

    (5)   Hirosi-ga   Masao-ga   katta   pan-o   tabeta.
         Hirosi-SUBJ Masao-SUBJ bought bread-DO ate
         'Hirosi ate the bread Masao bought.'

(6) Yoko-ga   Hiromi-ga   Asako-ga   kaita genkoo-o
      Yoko-SUBJ Hiromi-SUBJ Asako-SUBJ wrote draft-   DO
      kakinaosita syorui- o   yonda.
      rewrote   papers-DO read
      'Yoko read the papers that Hiromi rewrote based on the draft Asako
      wrote.'

(You might well be baffled by the fact that *genkoo* in 6 gets the particle *o*. If you are,
great; you are getting a feel for Japanese. If you do not see why *genkoo-o* is so baffling, ask yourself what GF you think the head of the relative clause that contains
genkoo-o is. We will not address this issue here. But if you should study the structure
of Japanese, you might want to attack the analysis of sentences like 6 at some later
point.)

Part 1

Put brackets around all the clauses in both 5 and 6. Doubly underline the head of
each relative clause. Which of these clauses are center-embedded?
   Now consider:

(7) Asako-ga   kaita genkoo-o kakinaosita syorui- o   yonda.
      Asako-SUBJ wrote draft-DO rewrote   papers-DO read
      'Somebody read the papers that somebody rewrote based on the draft
      that Asako wrote.'

Use the translation of 7 as a guide as you do the following parts of this problem set.
Please note that example 7 has other possible readings—but the reading of interest
to us here has *Asako* as the Subject of the most deeply embedded clause. Also in
this example you may be confused by the fact that *genkoo* takes the particle *o*, which
shows it is a DO. Assume that the gap in the clause whose verb is *kakinaosita* is a
genitive gap. Thus a more literal translation would be: 'Somebody read the papers
that somebody rewrote the draft of, (the draft) that Asako wrote.'

Part 2

Add in an "e" (for empty category) for all the missing NPs in 7. Now put brackets
around every clause. Doubly underline the head of each relative clause. Which of
these clauses are center-embedded?

Part 3

Japanese native speakers find 5 easy to process. But 6 is very difficult to process.
How do these facts compare to the facts on ease of processing in English sentences
with center-embedded clauses?

Part 4

Japanese native speakers find 7 significantly easier to process than 6. Discuss possible reasons why. (You are speculating here. However, you know enough about

ntax and Japanese—if you have been doing the problem sets on Japanese
ιok—to make intelligent speculations.)

Problem Set 6.7: Italian and English Lexical Passives

In the text of this chapter, we talked about two alternative analyses for passive sentences. In one, movement takes place. In the other, passive sentences are generated without movement, so their DS looks the same as their SS, and there are lexical correspondence rules that relate the forms and properties of active verbs to the forms and properties of passive participles. We argued for the movement analysis.

However, there is evidence that not all sentences that have the superficial form of a passive sentence (with a form of *be* and participial form for the main verb) are derived by movement. Instead, we have some sentences which "look like" passives, but are, instead, active forms. They have been called LEXICAL PASSIVES (as opposed to SYNTACTIC PASSIVES, which involve movement). Consider:

(1) John was {taught/educated}.

(2) John was {untaught/uneducated}.

These sentences are remarkably similar. Yet 1 involves movement and has a corresponding active sentence, whereas 2 does not:

(3) Someone {taught/educated} John.

(4) *Someone {untaught/uneducated} John.

Many lexical passives have a form that begins with the prefix *-un*.

In this problem set we will consider some evidence that points out the different properties of lexical and syntactic passives in both English and Italian. Take each data set below, state what property is at issue, and make a brief generalization as to the difference between lexical and syntactic passives regarding that property.

Data Set A

(5) Much was made of John.

(6) *Much was unmade of John.

(Hint: *Make much of* is idiomatic. Assume that *much* is a QP. Now consider whether *much* in 3 receives a theta-role. Given this, are there restrictions on the theta-assigning ability of the verbs in each kind of "passive" sentence?)

Data Set B

(7) John was taught French.

(8) *John was untaught French.

(9)   French was taught to John.

(10)   *French was untaught (to John).

(11)   John was known to be a fool.

(12)   *John was unknown to be a fool.

(Hint: Consider whether there are restrictions on the theta role of the surface Subject of each kind of "passive" sentence.)

In Italian *communicat-* behaves like a syntactic passive participle but *sconosciut-* behaves like a lexical passive participle with regard to the properties you discovered in considering Data Sets A and B above. We see examples of a syntactic and a lexical passive using these words below:

(13)   Non mi piace la verità che è stata communicata a Maria.
        not me please the truth that is been communicated to Maria
        'I don't like the truth that has been communicated to Maria.'

(14)   Non mi piace la verità che è sconosciuta a Maria.
                                      unknown
        'I don't like the truth that is unknown to Maria.'

In 15 and 16, which correspond to 13 and 14, respectively, we find that *a Maria* has been replaced with the clitic pronoun (CP) *le.* (You learned about clitics in Problem Set 5.6.) Clitic pronouns in Italian may attach only to verbal forms.

(15)   Non mi piace la verità che le è stata communicata.
                                   CP
        'I don't like the truth that was communicated to her.'

(16)   Non mi piace la verità che le è stata sconosciuta.
                                   CP
        'I don't like the truth that was unknown to her.'

Now you are ready to consider the next data set.

Data Set C

(17)   Non mi piace la verità communicatale
                                CP
        'I don't like the truth communicated to her.'

(18)   *Non mi piace la verità sconosciutale.
                                 CP
        'I don't like the truth unknown to her.'

At this point, you should be relatively convinced that there are a number of syntactic characteristics that distinguish syntactic from lexical passives. Let us consider one more data set. This time instead of finding a characteristic that differs between the two types of passives, use the data to build an argument in favor of claiming that the syntactic passive example involves movement while the lexical passive example does not.

Before you can do this, you need to know one fact of Italian that I will simply tell you: the clitic *ne* must be co-indexed with a quantifier in the DO position. (You will study this construction in depth in Problem set 9.4 of chapter 9.) This construction is illustrated here:

(19)   Ne$_i$ ho   visto [tanti$_i$].
       CP have seen [so many]
       '(I) have seen so many of them.' (*ne* = 'of them')

Data Set D:

(20)   Ne$_i$ furono riconosciuti molti$_i$.
       CP were   recognized   many
       'Many of them were recognized.'

(21)   *Ne$_i$ furono sconosciuti molti$_i$.
       CP were   unknown   many
       'Many of them were unknown.'

Now consider:

(22)   This island is inhabited by rodents.

(23)   This island is uninhabited by humans.

How does the fact that a *by*-phrase can occur in a lexical passive bear on the issue of the thematic role of the Object of the *by*? (If you do not see the point of this question, turn back to Problem Set 6.1.)

Finally, if lexical passives are not really passives in the sense developed in this chapter, what category do you think lexical items like *untaught, uneducated, unmade, unknown, uninhabited,* and the Italian *sconosciut-* belong to? Be sure to consider Data Set C in your discussion.

*Problem Set 6.8: English Trees

This problem set gives more practice with trees and labeled brackets. Trees are among the most commonly used graphic representations of syntactic analyses. And labeled brackets are convenient when you do not have the space for a tree, so journal articles are full of them. You should do this problem set.

Part 1

Fill in the trees in the following examples with good phrases of English.

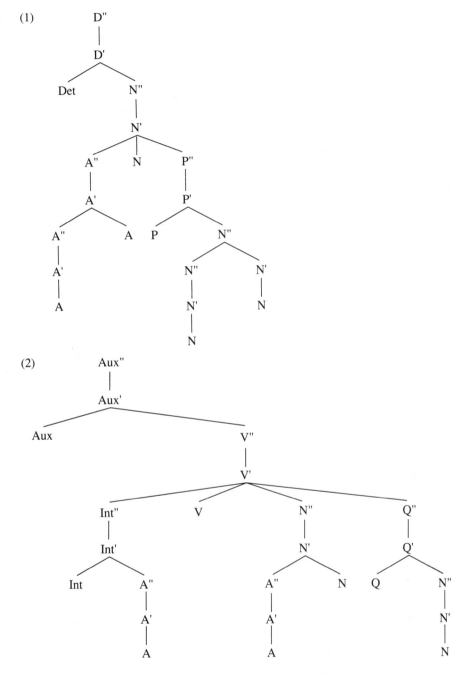

The "Q" in the expansion of V″ is to be filled in with a quantifier or a numeral. It heads a quantified nominal phrase (a QP) and takes a nominal phrase (here N″) as its sister.

Part 2

Give the trees for:

(3)   The young mare ran fast through the valley.

(4)   The cook laughed hysterically after Sally had eaten.

(For 4, you will have at least two questions on your mind. One is what to do with *after*. Let this be a P that heads an ordinary PP, where the Object of the P is senten-tial. The other question is where to attach the *after*-phrase. For now, attach it as a sister to the V and the AP under the V′. You will be able to argue for its proper position after you have done Problem Set 8.4 of chapter 8.)

Part 3

Consider the following sentences:

(5)   Mary ate the candy in the pumpkin.

(6)   The candy in the pumpkin was eaten by Mary.

(7)   The candy was eaten in the pumpkin by Mary.

Example 6 is the ordinary passive sentence corresponding to 5. But 7 is also a gram-matical sentence. The point is that 7 describes a bizarre situation. What is that sit-uation?

Once you see the good (though bizarre) reading for 7, can you now see that 5 is ambiguous? Give the two bracketings for 5—the one in which the candy (but not Mary) was in the pumpkin, and the other in which Mary was in the pumpkin when she ate the candy.

Now give the DS for 6 and 7 with labeled brackets.

Part 4

Consider these sentences:

(8)   Mary put the candy in the pumpkin.

(9)   *The candy in the pumpkin was put by Mary.

(10)   The candy was put in the pumpkin by Mary.

Example 9 is ungrammatical (in contrast with 6 above, which is an ordinary sen-tence). But 10 is ordinary (in contrast with 7 above, which describes a bizarre sit-uation). Give the labeled bracketing for 8.

Now give the DS for 10, with labeled bracketing.

Why is 9 ungrammatical? (Hint: Look back at our discussion in the text of the stipulations on the rule of Move Alpha; 9 has violated one of those stipulations. Which one?)

Star Problem 6.1

In the text we accounted for the ungrammaticality of 6, repeated here, with the filter below:

(1) *For to leave would be a mistake.

(2) *for to

There is at least one alternative explanation. We might claim that obligatorily transitive Ps must assign Case to some NP. Since *for* is obligatorily transitive, 1 is ungrammatical because *for* is not followed by an NP to which it can assign Case. The same explanation would account for the failure of *for* in the obligatorily transitive string of *hope for* before a tensed clause:

(3) We hoped (*for) (that) it would rain.

We would still, however, need a rule to delete *for* before *to* and tensed I″ in order to derive 1 and 3 without *for*. If this explanation were correct, we would expect that in the varieties of English that accept 1, *for* could be used intransitively—that is, *for* would not obligatorily have to assign Case to a following NP. I do not know the relevant data in this regard.

However, there are other facts that bear on the choice between this new account and the filter in 2 as an explanation for 1. Consider the data below and discuss how they pertain to this choice.

(4) *I've got faith; I certainly will count on.
     (cf. I've got faith; I certainly will count on you.)
     I certainly will count on Bill to be there.
     *I certainly will count on to be there.

(5) Mary knew (the truth), but she wouldn't tell.
     Mary knew Bill to act right in those situations.
     Mary knew to act right in those situations.

(6) Mary attempted chess.
     *Mary attempted.
     Mary attempted to leave.

Try to find contexts in which Ps are obligatorily transitive and others in which they are optionally transitive, where an infinitival clause with an expressed Subject can follow the P. Then test whether an infinitival with an empty Subject can follow the P.

Then do the same for V.

Overview: Complete Theory Overview

By this time you have realized that we are piecing together a THEORY OF GRAMMAR that has several interacting components or MODULES. The theory is a version of

GOVERNMENT AND BINDING THEORY, and the founder of this theory is Noam Chomsky. The modules we have been developing are:

1. Binding Theory
2. X-Bar Theory
3. Case Theory
4. Theta Theory
5. Government Theory
6. Trace Theory
7. Control Theory

The major principles of GB that we have worked to understand thus far are:

1. The Case Filter (under Case Theory)
2. The Theta Criterion (under Theta Theory)
3. The Principle of Full Interpretation (under Theta Theory)
4. The Projection Principle (under Theta Theory)
5. The Extended Projection Principle (under X-Bar Theory)

Let us see how far we have come.

In this chapter's overview I will give a full statement of the theory as we have developed it thus far, rather than referring the reader to the overviews of earlier chapters for various points. This overview, then, is a good review of all the positions we now hold.

Binding Theory

We have two conditions to Binding Theory (BT):

(A) Anaphors must be locally bound.

(B) Pronouns must be locally free.

A binder must c-command its bindee. In fact, we can now offer the following definition for binding:

(1)   A node B binds a node C if they are coindexed and B c-commands C.

We did not develop this notion of binding on our own, and we will challenge it in chapter 10.

We still need to explore locality.

Pronouns can be locally bound (contrary to Condition B) if they do not receive a theta-role. Locally bound pronouns in all the examples we have seen thus far are OPs, and never DOs or IOs.

On the other hand, anaphors generally receive a theta-role, unless they are used emphatically.

These facts suggest that BT is intricately related to Theta Theory in a way we must develop further later.

X-Bar Theory

All lexical-category phrases (NP, AP, PP, VP) as well as the nonlexical-category phrase IP have the same internal breakdown as:

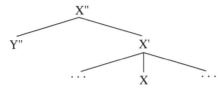

(Note that IP is exceptional throughout this discussion in that it falls with the lexical categories rather than the functional categories. We touched on this issue briefly in chapter 5 when we discussed whether [+Agr] is really a lexical head. We will address this issue in depth in chapter 8.)

We have adopted the convention that branches of a tree cannot cross.

We have introduced labeled brackets as an alternative graphic representation of a structural analysis.

We call X the head of the phrase. It immediately dominates a lexical item or, in the case of INFL, a feature bundle. The category INFLECTION (or INFL or I) is marked [+Agr] or [−Agr] and it is the place that the tense marker is located.

We call X' the X-bar level. It is a phrasal level (but not the maximal phrasal level) and it can take a Y″, which is called its specifier, as its sister.

We call X″ the X-double-bar level. It is the maximal projection of the category. (X is the lexical projection. X' is a medial phrasal projection.)

We call the sisters to X the complements. There is much variation on the use of this term in the linguistic literature. Some linguists use the term "complements" to cover both argument and nonargument sisters to X. We will do that. Furthermore, we have decided to call all nonargument sisters to X "adjuncts."

There are other uses of these terms. Many linguists today take the position that any node can have at most two branches under it. (See Tangent 8.2 of chapter 8.) Some of them argue that a sister to X is always an argument, so all complements of X are arguments. Others allow nonargument complements. If XP contains adjuncts to X as well as an argument(s) to X, the adjuncts would be attached not as sisters to X, but as sisters to a higher projection of X. (We discuss this in Tangent 8.2 of chapter 8.) For now, use the terminology as we have defined it, but be aware that many linguists use different definitions. (Note: Some linguists reserve the term "complement" only for arguments. So modifiers of a head would not be called complements. We have not made this distinction.)

Lexical categories and INFL can have a head, sisters, and a specifier. Lexical categories are to be contrasted with functional categories, which in English are limited to taking only one complement and do not have a specifier. (But, of course, for those linguists who admit at most binary branching, lexical categories also have only one complement.) We have discussed the functional categories Det(erminer), Int(ensifier), Aux(iliary), and Q(uantifier). You learned in Tangent 4.2 of chapter 4 that the claimed structural differences between lexical and functional categories are a controversial point and that the analysis of functional-category phrases might well vary in different languages.

Phrases headed by nodes of the same category as the phrasal node are called endocentric. There are some exocentric phrases, such as an NP that branches to specifier and AuxP as:

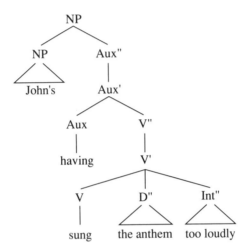

Exocentric phrases fall outside X-Bar Theory.

We have adopted the Extended Projection Principle, which ensures that every clause will have a Subject slot. Accordingly, we have recognized the empty node pro, which can be the Subject of clauses in a variety of languages (of which we have seen Italian, Portuguese, and Japanese).

Case Theory

We came up with the Case Filter:

(1)   Every NP with a phonetic matrix gets Case.

We also came up with some principles for Structural Case Assignment:

(2)   The Case-Assigners for English are [+AGR], V, and P.

(3)   The Case-Assigner must govern the phrase it gives Case to.

(4)   The Case-Assigners V and P must be adjacent (linearly) to the phrase they give Case to.

In addition to Structural Case Assignment, there are three other rules of Case assignment in English:

(5) Genitive rule: An NP in the specifier position of NP gets genitive Case.

(6) Double-Object Rule: The second NP in the Double-Object construction gets Objective Case.

(7) Exceptional Case-Marking: Certain verbs and prepositions (which are Case-Assigners in other contexts) can assign Case to the Subject of an infinitival clause that is adjacent to them if that infinitival clause is the complement of the V or P.

ECM occurs because in these instances the V or P exceptionally governs the specifier of its complement. Such infinitival clauses are called ECMs.

Theta Theory

We said that predicates may be of a range of categories (V, N, P, A, plus phrases that are indivisible semantically, such as the PP "off his rocker"). Actually, people debate a lot about this. Some people argue that all predicates are phrasal (so VP and not V would be a predicate, for example). But with that notion of predicate, each predicate takes only one role player: its Subject. If we want to allow a way to account for the thematic similarities of the different GFs, we need to allow heads to be predicates (so V is the predicate—and it can have internal arguments as well as the external argument in GF Subject position). This is not a matter we can settle in this book. It is just something to be aware of.

We also said that theta-assigners (including predicates) can be made of more than one word where the words do not form a syntactic constituent (such as *take care of* or *look after*) and might even form a discontinuous string (such as *take . . . to task*).

Theta-assigners set up a range of possible situations in which they can be used and in each situation they assign theta-roles (player roles, thematic roles) to their arguments (players, participants). The theta-roles we discussed are: agent, theme, benefactee, instrument, and experiencer. It is an open debate as to how to distinguish between different theta-roles and how many theta-roles any given language makes use of in its grammar.

We pointed out that the ability of a lexical item to assign a theta-role is part of the lexical information we have about words. There is a linking mechanism in the lexicon that maps between the predicate-argument structure of a lexical item and its subcategorization frame.

We came up with the following generalization (based on our work in Problem Set 3.3):

(1) Only GFs can have theta-roles, but not all GFs need to.

In particular, Subject position is often a nonargument slot, whereas IO is always (at least so far as we have seen) an argument slot. Since Subject position can be a non-argument slot, it can be filled at DS with an empty category. We have not given any particular name to this empty category. And in English it turns out that this empty category will never appear in SS. Instead, English demands a filled Subject slot at SS (audibly filled for tensed clauses; audibly or inaudibly filled for tenseless clauses).

The empty category in Subject position at DS, then, will either be filled by a movement rule (as in the case of passive sentences) or by a dummy Subject. (This empty category will never appear as the Subject of an infinitival clause for reasons that you will see in chapter 7.)

Looking again at 1 above, we note that DOs that are parts of idioms are not arguments (such as *the bucket* in the idiom *kick the bucket*). And, importantly, OPs are often not arguments. Instead, the P relates its Object to the rest of the material in the sentence, often via a spatial or temporal relationship. We suggested that the function of "relator" might be needed in our grammar to describe the function of many Ps. However, since OP is a GF, OPs are licensed, so we need not claim that the relator function licenses any elements.

We learned that the only nodes that we know of thus far that can be Complete Functional Complexes are NP, I″, and perhaps V″.

We also learned that secondary predicates can occur either as arguments or as adjuncts of primary predicates. We pointed out that sometimes the secondary predicate serves the function of "mediating" the relationship between its Subject and the primary predicate. However, we need not claim that the mediation function licenses any elements. Adjunct secondary predicates would be licensed by virtue of the fact that they are predicated of some other element that is, in turn, licensed independently of the adjunct. For example, resultative adjunct predicates are predicated of the theme argument of the primary predicate.

We noted that theta assignment from a primary predicate takes place under government except for the assignment of a theta-role to the Subject of a clause. We have not discussed any configurational restrictions on theta-assigment from a secondary predicate to its Subject, but you can easily go back now to the instances we looked at of secondary predication and see that theta assignment of a secondary predicate to its Subject is, likewise, not under government (for example: [*Jack*] *ate the pancakes* [*nude*]).

We also came up with the Theta Criterion, which was stated in a different way earlier, but which we will now amend:

> (2)   Only arguments of a theta-assigner get a theta-role and every argument of a given theta-assigner gets precisely one and a unique theta-role from that theta-assigner.

The reader is encouraged to compare this version of the Theta Criterion to that in the Overview of chapter 3. With this new statement, we have formalized our understanding that an argument must receive precisely one theta-role from a given theta-assigner and that a given theta-role can be assigned to only one argument of a given theta-assigner.

We also adopted the Projection Principle:

> (3)   All lexical features of a lexical item that appear in DS must appear at every other syntactic level, as well.

From this principle, Trace Theory follows.

In talking about theta-roles, we realized that subcategorization is a different thing from theta-roles. Lexical items can be subcategorized for whether they must, may, or cannot co-occur with certain GFs. Subcategorization frames give structural information, although they clearly have their roots in semantics. Still, there is no obvious mapping from semantics into syntactic subcategorization in all cases.

In all of this discussion we have been assuming a notion of licensing that is termed the Principle of Full Interpretation:

(4)   All nodes in a tree must play a role in the sentence.

Every node must be licensed; many different functions license a node, including being a predicate, an argument, a modifier, and filling a GF.

Government Theory

The notion of government is a configurational one and it is the topic of debate in much literature. We have thus far used the following formulation:

A node A governs another node B if:

(1)   A is a lexical category or [+Agr] and

(2)   B is contained within the maximal projection of A (that is, B is contained within A″), and

(3)   Every maximal projection that contains B also contains A.

So 1 allows any head (including I that is marked [+Agr]) to be a governor; 2 says that a governor governs everything within its maximal projection; 3 says that government cannot go across another maximal projection (that is, a maximal projection is a barrier to government). In ordinary words this says that a head governs everything inside its maximal projection up to another maximal projection.

Government Theory is relevant to other modules of the grammar. Thus far we have seen that:

1. In Case Theory, a Case-Assigner must govern a phrase in order to give it Case. (But keep exceptional government in mind.)

2. In X-Bar Theory, a head governs everything in its maximal projection.

3. Most instances of theta assignment are from a governor to the phrases it governs. The exceptions to this are theta assignment from a primary predicate to the Subject of a clause or from a secondary predicate to its Subject argument.

Trace Theory

Every movement leaves behind a trace. This fact must be so, in order to fulfill the requirements of the Projection Principle. (See Theta Theory.) We have, then, another empty category, trace, which is never present at DS, but is introduced as a result of movement.

We developed the Rule of Move Alpha and put two stipulations on it. First, only constituents (never strings of nodes that do not form constituents) move. Second, only the X and X″ levels (never the X′ level) move.

SYNTAX

We defined a chain as a group of co-indexed items with trace at the foot of the chain.

Now, since a trace and the item it is co-indexed with cannot have different functions, we can see that they cannot have different semantic functions, including theta-roles. We therefore came up naturally with the idea that only one theta-role can be associated with a given chain. That means that movement can only be to a position which is not automatically a theta-receiving slot. There is one such GF: Subject position. We know that Subject position can be filled by dummies, so it is not automatically a theta-receiving slot.

We have not offered any account of why Subject position is the only GF position that need not be assigned a theta-role. This issue connects to the fact that we have not yet fully accounted for the fact that IP acts like a lexical-category phrase. We will account for both in a unified way in chapter 8.

There are other non–theta-receiving slots (which are also non-GF slots) which we will meet in chapter 8. We will find there that movement can take place into these slots, as expected. (You may have already become aware of the need for one such slot as you did Problem Set 6.3 above.)

Control Theory

We have not yet faced Control Theory. It is the theory that tells us what can control the interpretation of a PRO, as in:

I promised Bill [PRO to leave].

We will deal with Control Theory in chapter 7.

In sum, we have recognized four empty categories (ec): pro, trace, PRO, and the ec that fills a nonargument Subject slot in DS.

A Map through GB

At this point it is helpful to have a map through Government and Binding Theory:

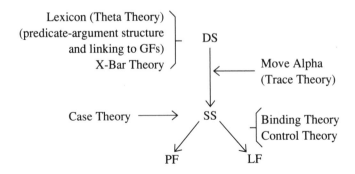

DS = the most underlying level, the first tree in the syntactic derivation. It is also called D-Structure.

SS = the last syntactic tree. It is also called S-Structure. It is enriched with the empty node trace, if movement has applied.

PF = Phonetic Form = the sentence as we actually hear it (with all the intonation contour in and all the contractions, etc.). It is SS with the phonology having applied. (Take a phonology course and be enlightened.) It is also known as the surface structure of the sentence.

LF = Logical Form = some formal representation of the sentence in which we have every instance of binding marked, and in which we can properly interpret quantifiers, adverbs, negatives, and other items. (We will learn more about LF in chapter 9.) It is an explicit representation of precisely how we understand the sentence. It is SS with the rules of semantic interpretation having applied. (Take a semantics course and be confounded.)

7

Control Theory, NP-Trace, and Governing Categories

In the last chapter we established that there are at least three types of empty categories in SS: trace, pro, and PRO.

The trace we discussed in the text of chapter 6 was the empty node that marks the position from which movement has taken place in the passive construction, as in:

(1) We were cheated by the government.
     at SS: We$_i$ were cheated t$_i$ by the government.

In Problem Set 6.3 you came up with a number of arguments for claiming that there are empty nodes in *wh*-questions and in *wh*–relative clauses, and we marked those empty nodes as trace there. We will not consider those empty nodes in this chapter, but, instead, return to them in chapter 8.

Next, "pro" is the label we have given to the empty Subject of many sentences in certain Romance languages.

(2) Italian: Vengo.   '(I) am coming.'
              come-1 sg.
     Portuguese: Tomarem óleo-de-rícino. '(They) took castor oil.'
                 take-3 pl   oil-of-castor

In the problem sets we have seen several Italian and Portuguese examples like those in 2. You will get a chance to explore questions related to pro in Problem Set 8.6 of chapter 8.

Finally, PRO is the empty category seen in 3, whose properties we have not yet discussed.

(3) We expected to win.
     at SS: We expected [PRO to win].

A major question in analyzing an empty category is how it receives its interpretation. This question is easily answered for trace: trace is interpreted via its co-indexation with the moved element. This question is at least partially answered for pro when it is in the Subject position of a tensed clause, because agreement inflection on the V gives us access to some features of pro. But what helps us interpret PRO? In 3, PRO's interpretation is CONTROLLED by the Subject of *expected*. For this reason, the phenomenon of the interpretation of PRO is called CONTROL. (It has also been called EQUI, for historical reasons, and verbs that allow one of their arguments to control PRO are called EQUI VERBS. We will not use that terminology, but you should know it.)

In this chapter we will look closely at PRO and continue to develop our understanding of trace. But we will not discuss pro further here.

Trace and all the elements it is co-indexed with are interdependent in important ways, and PRO is different in this respect. For one, trace forms a chain with all the elements it is co-indexed with, and every chain has associated with it at most one theta-role and at most one Case. The limitation of one theta-role per chain follows from the Theta Criterion, as discussed in chapter 6. The limitation of one Case per chain is at least partially a result of the fact that in all instances of movement in chapter 6, the NP that moved was in a position at DS to which no Case could be assigned. Had the NP not moved, by SS it would have failed to receive Case in the PF component of the grammar, and the resulting sentence would have violated the Case Filter (which requires every NP with a phonetic matrix to receive Case).

PRO, on the other hand, does not form a chain with its controller. Instead, PRO and its controller each play an independent role in their own clause. In 3, PRO and its controller each receive a theta-role from the predicate of their own clause. Do PRO and its controller always have to receive a separate theta-role within their respective Complete Functional Complex?

To answer this question, we need to look at all the positions that PRO can occur in and all the positions that its controller can occur in. But in order to do that, we need to be able to recognize PRO and its controller. So we will begin by gaining some familiarity with PRO sentences in general.

Obligatory and Nonobligatory Control

One important fact about PRO is that sometimes its interpretation is strictly delimited and sometimes it is not:

(4) John wants to leave.
     [John wants [PRO to leave]]

(5) To paint like Leonardo is the common fantasy.
     [[PRO to paint like Leonardo] is the common fantasy.

PRO in sentences like 4 is said to be controlled. We understand PRO to have the same referent as *John*, so *John* is the controller. PRO in sentences like 5, on the other hand, is not controlled. We understand PRO to mean some underdetermined person, in this instance perhaps anybody or perhaps anybody relevant to the context (such as if 5 were said by someone running an art school). This is called ARBI-

TRARY PRO (although its interpretation is not necessarily arbitrary), and it is often written as "PRO$_{arb}$" in the literature.

PRO occurs not only in infinitivals, but in other tenseless clause types, as well.

(6)   John stopped [PRO crying].

(7)   [PRO eating] is fun.

Example 6 is a controlled PRO. Example 7 is a PRO$_{arb}$. In our discussion we will talk primarily of PRO in infinitivals. In Problem Set 7.1 you will be asked to check whether certain of the conclusions we reach below about PRO in infinitivals hold for PRO in verbal *-ing* structures, as well.

There are two kinds of control of PRO. One is called OBLIGATORY CONTROL and the other is NONOBLIGATORY CONTROL. Obligatory control is control of a PRO that occurs in a position in which a lexical NP (phonetically realized) would be ungrammatical. For example, in 8 we must have a PRO as the Subject of the embedded clause:

(8)   John tried [PRO to understand].

      *John tried [Bill to understand].

Nonobligatory control is control of a PRO that appears in a position that could as easily be filled with a lexical NP:

(9)   John wanted [PRO to understand].
      John wanted [Bill to understand].

Obligatory and nonobligatory control have been claimed to differ on at least three other properties, as well. In order to see these three properties, we need to note first that infinitivals introduced by *for* often alternate with infinitivals without *for* precisely when there is a lexical NP Subject of the infinitival. For example, consider:

(10)   [PRO to leave without John] would be hard on me, not on you!

(11)   [For me to leave without John] would be hard on me, not on you!

(12)   *[Me to leave without John] would be hard on me, not on you!

These data are no surprise. The NP *me* in 12 fails to receive Case, so this sentence is a violation of the Case Filter. However, the presence of the *for* in 11 allows the infinitival to take a lexical Subject (here *me*), since the *for* will assign Case (by Exceptional Case-Marking) to the Subject of the following infinitival.

Example 10 might well be open to a PRO$_{arb}$ interpretation in your speech. But consider its control interpretation. On that interpretation, PRO is controlled by *me*. And on that interpretation, 10 is as close to synonymous with 11 as we can get. So if you are testing whether you have obligatory or nonobligatory control in an infinitival below, be sure to try PRO versus a lexical NP, and if the lexical NP is rejected, then try adding a *for* in front of the lexical NP. Obligatory control will never be saved by *for*:

(13)   *I tried [for Bill to leave]. (cf. 8)

but nonobligatory control may (as in 11 versus 12).

Restrictions on the Controller

Now that we have the above test to distinguish obligatory from nonobligatory control cases, we are ready to try to discover the three other properties that obligatory and nonobligatory control have been claimed to differ on. We already saw above that both obligatory and nonobligatory control can have a Subject control the PRO. Can a DO be the controller in an obligatory control sentence? What about in a non-obligatory control sentence?

(14)   I persuaded Bill [PRO to leave].

Here the DO is the controller. Is this obligatory or nonobligatory control? Your test of whether a lexical item can alternate with PRO here tells you that this is an instance of obligatory control:

(15)   *I persuaded Bill (for) [Mary to leave].

What about in:

(16)   [PRO to have been accused of cheating] humiliated Bill.

Here you might well allow a PRO$_{arb}$ reading. But on the controlled reading (where *Bill* is the controller), do we have obligatory or nonobligatory control? Again, your test of alternation with a lexical item tells you that 16 is an instance of nonobligatory control:

(17)   [For Sally to have been accused of cheating] humiliated Bill.

So both kinds of control allow a DO controller (obligatory in 14 and nonobligatory in 16).

What about a controller that is the Object of a preposition? Try to make up the relevant sentences to test. You will find right away that it it rare for an infinitival to follow a PP. The most everyday type is a rationale clause (with *in order*) or a purpose clause (without *in order*), as in:

(18)   I went [$_{PP}$with Bill] (in order) [PRO to upset his mother].

But as you already know from Problem Set 3.3 of chapter 3, rationale clauses are a diagnostic for whether the next higher clause contains an agent. You can now see why: the agent controls the PRO of a rationale clause. And since the canonical GF for an agent is Subject position, most rationale clauses have a PRO that is controlled by a Subject. However, you also know that there is debate over whether the Object of a *by*-phrase in a passive sentence is an agent (as you discovered in Problem Set 6.1 of chapter 6—see also the *By*-Phrase section of chapter 6). In particular, some have argued that the passive affix on the verb rather than the Object of the *by*-phrase is the true agent argument. We might, then, try to test whether the Object of a *by* can control PRO and, additionally, whether the passive affix can control PRO in both rationale clauses and purpose clauses. We will deal with this issue briefly in Problem Set 7.1. But ask yourself: if you came to the conclusion that the passive affix could control PRO, what would that mean about the possible GF positions for the controller of PRO? Is an affix in a GF position? Certainly not. Now is control into a rationale or a purpose clause obligatory or nonobligatorycontrol? The fact that you can have a lexical Subject (with a *for*) in these rationale and purpose clauses shows us that this is nonobligatory control:

(19)   I would do anything I could (in order) for you to be able to go.

So if an affix can control a rationale or purpose clause, we would expect that in nonobligatory control constructions there are no purely structural restrictions on the controller at all. We will not go further with the discussion of rationale or purpose clauses, but at least you can recognize the questions they present for Control Theory.

Besides rationale and purpose clauses, can you think of other infinitivals that can follow a PP? There are some. Consider:

(20)   I depended [_PP_on Bill] [PRO to be there].

Is this obligatory or nonobligatory control? Obligatory; witness:

(21)   *I depended on Bill (for) [Mary to be there].

And we already saw above in 10, repeated here, that nonobligatory control can have an OP controller:

(22)   [PRO to leave without John] would be hard on me, not on you!

So both types of control can have Subject (8 and 9), DO (14 and 16), and OP (22 and 10) as controllers. And it is possible (depending on how you do Problem Set 7.1) that you will conclude that nonobligatory control can have an affix as a controller.

Looking back over the examples we have had thus far, we begin to see a pattern that will help us to find a major difference between the two types of control. Is the order of controller and PRO fixed above for either type of control? Yes; for obligatory control the controller always precedes PRO, but for nonobligatory control, the controller may precede PRO (as in 9) or follow PRO (as in 16). Is this just an accident of the examples we have looked at thus far? Try to devise a sentence in which the infinitival clause is in the Subject position of the matrix clause. Can the PRO here ever enter into obligatory control? Compare, for example:

(23)   John tried {[PRO to leave]/ [PRO leaving]}.

(24)   a.   That's been tried before.

       b.   *[PRO to leave] was tried by John.
            *[PRO leaving] was tried by John.

Try is an obligatory control verb (as we saw in 8 and 13). We know from 24a here that *try* is a verb which can occur in passive structures. Yet the passive sentences in 24b are ungrammatical. If obligatory control requires the controller to linearly precede PRO, we can account for the ungrammaticality of 24b.

This then is our first of the three additional differences between the two types of control: *obligatory control requires that the controller linearly precede PRO.*

There is another difference between obligatory and nonobligatory control that will come out upon examination of the sentences in 23 and 24. In every case of control, go back and delete the controller. What happens to the grammaticality of the sentence? Obviously, if the controller is in Subject position, the resulting sentence is ungrammatical because tensed clauses require overt Subjects in English. But if we line up all the examples with a DO controller or an OP controller, and if we delete the DO or the entire PP (note, we must delete the entire PP, not just the Object of the P, since we do not want to strand the P), we find the following results:

(25)   [PRO to leave without John] would be hard. (cf. 10)

(26)   *I persuaded [PRO to leave]. (cf. 14)

(27)   *[PRO to have been accused of cheating] humiliated. (cf. 16)

(28)   *I depended [PRO to be there]. (cf. 19)

In 10, with nonobligatory control, the deletion of the controller results in the grammatical sentence 25 (with a PRO$_{arb}$ interpretation, of course). But in the other sentences, the deletion of the controller leads to an ungrammatical sentence. In 26–28 that is because the deleted element was required, regardless of the presence of the infinitival:

(29)   *I persuaded.
        *That humiliated.
        *I depended.

However, for at least some speakers, if we fiddle with the tense of the verb *humiliate*, we can allow the omission of the DO with a generic-time-frame interpretation:

(30)   That sort of yelling simply humiliates. Please don't do it.

The head of a nursery school might say a sentence like 30 to someone who had yelled at the children, for example. (Not all verbs that require a DO in specific-time-frame-interpretation sentences will allow the omission of the DO in generic-time-frame-interpretation sentences. Thus, for all speakers I have asked, *repair*, for example, requires a DO regardless of the tense/aspect interpretation. As you discovered in doing Problem Set 3.1 of chapter 3, the issue of how tense/aspect and subcategorization interact is complex. The point is that the interaction somehow allows 30, so for us this interaction is useful here, regardless of why.) Now if we use the simple present tense in 27 above (without the perfective aspect in the embedded clause), we find that 31 is grammatical for the same people who accept 30:

(31)   [PRO to be accused of cheating] humiliates. That is the overwhelming
        result: pure humiliation.

Can a bit of fiddling with the tense and/or aspect improve the other sentences of 29? Perhaps for some speakers. If we use the present progressive with a supporting adverbial, we get results such as:

> (32) I'm persuading all the time. It's the result of being in politics for so long. Please excuse me.
>   I'm depending all the time, in every way. I wish I was a stronger person.

Can you imagine a context for these sentences? No speakers I have asked are delighted with the sentences in 32, but there may well be other speakers who accept them. Yet using the present progressive in 26 and 28 cannot improve them, even with a supporting adverbial:

> (33) *I'm persuading [PRO to leave] (all the time).
>   *I'm (always) persuading [PRO to leave].

> (34) *I'm depending [PRO to be there] (all the time, in every way).
>   *I'm (always) depending [PRO to be there].

If you go through other examples in your head, you will find that *in general, if you omit the controller in an obligatory control situation, the resulting sentence is ungrammatical.* But if you omit the controller in a nonobligatory control situation, the resulting sentence may or may not be ungrammatical (depending on other factors, such as the subcategorization frame of the matrix verb and its interaction with varying time frames). That is the second additional difference between obligatory and nonobligatory control. And this difference accounts for the fact that obligatory control sentences are never ambiguous between a controlled reading and a PRO_{arb} reading, whereas nonobligatory control sentences often are.

Control and Reanalysis

A final claimed difference between obligatory and nonobligatory control is not one that I would expect you to arrive at by looking at the data above. That claim is that the controller in obligatory control sentences always c-commands PRO, and this hierarchical relationship is not necessary in nonobligatory control sentences. Recall that a node B c-commands another node D if and only if every branching node that contains B also contains D. (In other words, the first branching node above B dominates D.) You could not arrive at this conclusion by looking at the data we have discussed in this chapter because there is one example of obligatory control above in which the controller does not c-command PRO. Which one is that? It is example 20, repeated here for convenience:

> (35) I depended on Bill [PRO to be there].

Here *Bill* is the Object of the P *on* and the infinitival is not contained inside the PP, so *Bill* does not c-command PRO. In order to maintain the claim that the controller must c-command PRO in obligatory control sentences, one would have to analyze 35 in such a way as to allow *Bill* to c-command PRO. Such an analysis has, in fact, been proposed. Some have argued that there is a rule which allows a P following a V to be REANALYZED as part of the V, so that the NP that was underlyingly the Object of the P is no longer the OP, but is a daughter of V'. If Reanalysis were to apply to 35, we would have 36a and b.

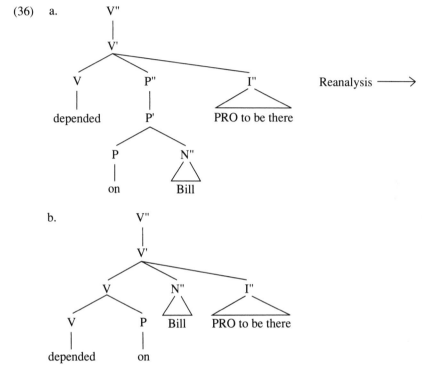

In 36a, before Reanalysis, *Bill* does not c-command PRO. (*Bill* c-commands only the material dominated by P'.) But in 36b, after Reanalysis, *Bill* c-commands PRO since the first branching node that contains *Bill* is V', and PRO is dominated by V'.

In Problem Set 7.8 you will be led to arguments that should make you reject Reanalysis as the correct analysis of 35. We will also discuss Reanalysis in chapter 10.

For now, what you need to know is that in general, the putative rule of Reanalysis is appealed to in order to account for OPs that behave not as though they are OPs, but as though they are DOs (as *Bill* does in 35). If Reanalysis is wrong, then the explanation for the behavior of the OPs in such instances is not syntactic. Instead, I would suggest that if an OP is an argument of the V (the lexical entry for the verb will tell us its argument structure), then that OP shares a range of semantic characteristics with other arguments of the V, including the ability to control PRO in both control constructions.

Let me point out to you, however, that the Reanalysis proposal is the generally accepted proposal in the literature today. So in bucking this proposal, I am going against the mainstream. If after doing Problem Set 7.8 you accept the conclusion that Reanalysis is not the correct analysis of 35, then unless you can defend an alternative analysis of sentences like 35 in which the relevant NP (here *Bill*) c-commands PRO, you will have to admit that the controller need not c-command PRO in obligatory control constructions.

Is there an alternative restriction on obligatory control that we should posit in its place? In all our examples of obligatory control thus far, the controller is an argument of the higher predicate. But in our nonobligatory control sentences, one could argue that the controller is not an argument in at least one example above: 10, repeated here for convenience:

(37)   [PRO to leave without John] would be hard on me, not on you!

Is *me* an argument of the matrix predicate here? Without a clear test for argumenthood, we cannot answer this question. Surely, if *me* is an argument, it is an experiencer, and we have no reliable test for experiencers. We will, therefore, leave this issue unresolved; that is, in obligatory control structures the controller must be an argument of a higher predicate, but in nonobligatory control structures we have been unable to determine if the controller must bear a theta-role. We will therefore go forward with only three diagnostics for distinguishing obligatory control from nonobligatory control (although in Problem Set 7.1 below I remind you of the c-command condition that so many others have accepted).

The three diagnostics we will work with, then, are: (A) obligatory control structures do not alternate with structures that have lexical Subjects, but nonobligatory control structures do; (B) obligatory control requires that the controller precede PRO, but nonobligatory control does not; and (C) obligatory control structures become ungrammatical if the controller is omitted, but nonobligatory ones might or might not, depending on other factors.

Now we can return to a question we posed very early in this chapter: Do the controller and PRO both have to bear theta-roles in their respective CFCs? We have seen above that the controller always bears a theta-role in instances of obligatory control, and we have not been able to determine if it does so in nonobligatory control. But in all the examples we have seen thus far, PRO not only bears a theta-role in its CFC, it is the Subject of its clause. Thus the answer is a definite yes for obligatory control and is as yet undetermined for nonobligatory control.

PRO's Position at SS

Can PRO ever appear in non-Subject position? Certainly, at DS it can. Try to devise a sentence with PRO in which you know that the PRO started out at DS in some position other than Subject. You will, undoubtedly, be searching for passive infinitivals—since we have argued at length for movement from a position inside the

VP of passive sentences to Subject position. Can PRO ever be the Subject of a passive infinitival? Consider:

(38)   I wanted [PRO to be recognized].

All right, now can PRO ever be a non-Subject at SS? What you are looking for at this point is an infinitival with a missing element inside the VP that is interpreted as being coreferential with some element in the next higher clause. If you search around long enough, you may come across what is known as the TOUGH-CONSTRUCTION, as in:

(39)   Jack is tough to follow.
       Jack is good to give things to.
       Jack is easy to count on.
       Jack is difficult to go anywhere with.

This is called the *tough*-construction because the adjective *tough* occurs in it frequently. But many other adjectives occur in this construction, as well, as you can see. The *tough*-construction, however, does not involve PRO inside the infinitival VP, but, instead, involves trace. We cannot yet argue for this analysis, but you can return to it and convince yourself after we have discussed *wh*-movement in depth in chapter 8. (By the way, what is the Subject of the infinitivals in 39? These are instances of PRO_{arb}.)

Unless you come up with other types of examples, we must admit that PRO occurs at SS only in Subject position, although at DS, of course, it can occur inside the VP. This is a fact we need to account for in our Control Theory. That is, this is not the sort of fact that should be accidental. It is not specific to any particular lexical item. It is not idiosyncratic in any way. That PRO can occur only in the Subject position at SS is a general statement about the distribution of a particular grammatical element. Such a general statement should be motivated on theoretical grounds.

Since the restriction on PRO's distribution is to be met at SS rather than DS, we might suspect that the issue of Case is somehow involved. That is, Case is assigned during PF, based on the SS position of an element. Is the Subject position of infinitivals special in any way regarding Case? Yes, certainly. We know that the I of infinitivals is [−Agr]; therefore this I is not a governor and cannot assign Case. So the Subject of an infinitival can receive Case only from outside the I″, by way of Exceptional Case-Marking. Since PRO has no phonetic matrix, it does not fall under the Case Filter and it need not receive Case. And in the examples above in which the infinitival control clause is in the Subject position (as in 5, 10, and 16), the PRO cannot receive Case. Furthermore, in the examples in which the infinitival control clause does not immediately follow a P or a V, the PRO cannot receive Case (as in 14, 18, and 19). We might then take a leap and hypothesize that PRO must not receive Case.

Will this create a problem for the analysis of any of our control sentences? Look back through them carefully. Notice that some of the verbs that can take infinitival control clauses can also exceptionally Case mark an overt Subject of an infinitival:

(40)   a. We expected [PRO to win]. (= 3)
       b. We expected [Mary to win].

(41)   a. John wants [PRO to leave]. (= 4)
       b. John wants [Mary to leave].

What we need to say, then, is that the ability of *expect* and *want* and other verbs to exceptionally Case mark is optional. So in 40a the verb does not exceptionally Case mark, but in 40b, it does. Likewise, in 41a it does not, but in 41b it does.

We might conclude that PRO cannot receive Case. However, this conclusion alone does not explain PRO's distribution, since the Subject position of infinitivals is not the only position to which Case need not be assigned, yet it is the only position that PRO can appear in at SS. Look back at 38, repeated here for convenience:

(42)   I wanted [PRO$_i$ to be recognized t$_i$].

At DS PRO is in the Object position of *recognized*, which is a position to which Case cannot be assigned, since a passive participle is not a Case-assigner. Why could we not as well analyze 42 as in:

(43)   I wanted [e to be recognized PRO].

That is, how do we know that PRO cannot occur as the DO of a passive verb at SS? We know, because in a simple sentence, we cannot have PRO as the DO of a passive verb at SS:

(44)   *It was recognized [PRO].

The only way to account for the failure of 44 with a PRO$_{arb}$ reading is to say that PRO cannot appear as a DO at SS.

Thus there must be something beside its apparent required Caselessness that motivates the fact that PRO occurs only in the Subject position at SS. Recall that [+ Agr] and every lexical head are governors and that every governor governs all the material within its maximal projection up to another maximal projection. That means that every node in every phrase is governed, except the Subject position of an I that is marked [− Agr] (we set aside all -*ing* constructions here—and see Problem Set 5.4 and, especially, Problem Set 5.5 of chapter 5.) But it is precisely the Subject position of an I that is marked [− Agr] that is the only position that PRO can occur in (so far as we know). That is, PRO occurs only in ungoverned positions. (And we therefore need not make any separate stipulation concerning whether PRO can receive Case. PRO's Case properties will follow from the positions it can appear in.)

Why should PRO occur only in ungoverned positions? This is an interesting question and it brings us to a central issue that we have not faced explicitly thus far. Let us turn our attention now to the place of PRO in the typology of NPs.

Typology of NPs

Right from the very first chapter of this book, we have recognized that among NPs that have a phonetic matrix, we must distinguish between anaphors (such as reflexives) and pronominals. We learned that anaphors must be locally bound (generally), and pronominals must be locally free (generally). In fact, while some pronouns are understood as coreferential with some other (nonlocal) item in the sentence (PROXIMATE PRONOUNS), as in:

(45)   Jack$_i$ asked Sally to accompany him$_i$.

other pronouns are not coreferential with anything else in the sentence (OBVIATE PRONOUNS), as in:

(46)   He left.

But not all NPs that have a phonetic matrix are anaphors or pronouns. What about *the sweet drink, an ounce or two, Bill,* and any number of other NPs you can think of? These NPs are called R-EXPRESSIONS, because they are fully referring expressions. That is, they contain a sense of their own that helps us to pick out their referent.

What happens to an R-expression when it enters into a binding relationship? We have seen many instances in earlier chapters in which an R-expression binds an anaphor or a pronoun, as in:

(47)   John$_i$ likes himself$_i$.

(48)   John$_i$ said that Bill was going with him$_i$.

But we have seen none in which an anaphor, a pronominal, or an R-expression binds an R-expression. Remember that in order for an element B to bind another element D, B must c-command D, not dominate D, and be co-indexed with D. Let us test whether an R-expression can be locally bound by substituting an R-expression for the anaphor in 47 above:

(49)   *John$_i$ likes John$_i$.

Example 49 is decidedly odd if we interpret the two instances of *John* as coreferential (hence the asterisk). If someone said 49 intending the coreferential interpretation, we would probably have what is called CONTRASTIVE STRESS on one or the other instance of *John*. That is, the intonation contour of the sentence would go up sharply on the second *John* and stay high with a slight drop at the very end of the sentence. Contrastive stress on an item can often allow it to pattern differently from how it would with the ordinary stress pattern (the so-called NUCLEAR STRESS RULE stress pattern). In fact, with contrastive stress on *me*, one might be able to say:

(50)   I like ME—that's all, no one else, just ME.

instead of the expected:

(51)   I like myself.

(The capitals in 50 represent contrastive stress.) So let us take 49 and 50 as ungrammatical without contrastive stress. If you try a range of examples, you will get similar results. R-expressions cannot be locally bound.

Can R-expressions be bound at a distance? Let us test by substituting an R-expression for the pronoun in 48 above:

(52)   *John$_i$ said that Bill was going with John$_i$.

Again, without contrastive stress on the second *John*, 52 is decidedly odd on the coreferential interpretation. If you consider a wide range of examples, you will get similar results. In general, R-expressions cannot be bound at a distance.

In conclusion, R-expressions are always free. This is called Condition C of the Binding Theory.

We have, then, three types of NPs with a phonetic matrix: anaphors, pronominals, and R-expressions, and all have different binding properties.

Now what about NPs with no phonetic matrix? Thus far we know only two such NPs intimately: PRO and the trace left by movement in a passive sentence. Since movement in a passive sentence is movement into Subject position, and since typically Subject position is filled with an NP, let us call this movement NP-MOVEMENT. (You know this is a misnomer, since whole clauses can move in passive sentences and since Subject position can be filled by a phrase of any category. Yet the term "NP-movement" is prevalent in the literature, so you need to know how it is used.) Let us call the trace left by NP-movement NP-TRACE. Now can PRO and NP-trace be classified as anaphors, pronominals, or R-expressions? That is, does our three-way classification of types for nominals with a phonetic matrix extend to nominals that lack a phonetic matrix?

An anaphor must be locally bound. Is NP-trace always locally bound? At the end of chapter 6 we argued that the correct formulation of the rule of passive was Move Alpha. That is, anything could move anywhere. But, in fact, because of independently motivated restrictions in the grammar, what happens in passive sentences is that an element inside the VP moves into the Subject position. Since the Subject position c-commands everything in the VP (given that the first branching node above it is I''), the moved element will always bind its trace. Is that binding relationship always local? If we look at sentences in which passive involves movement within a clause, of course the binding relationship is local, as in:

(53)   [e] was elected John. →
       [John]$_i$ was elected [t]$_i$.

But there are times when passive involves movement of an item from one clause into the next higher clause:

(54)   [e] was rumored [John to have failed]. →
       [John]$_i$ was rumored [t$_i$ to have failed].

Here is the binding relationship local? If we use the ability of an antecedent in Subject position of one clause to bind an overt anaphor in Subject position of an embedded infinitival clause as our guide, our answer must be yes:

(55)   Bill expected [himself to win].

Can passive involve movement from one clause to a position two clauses higher?

(56)   [e] was expected [that Sue wanted [Bill to win]] →
        *Bill$_i$ was expected [that Sue wanted [t$_i$ to win]].

No, it cannot. And, in fact, an antecedent two clauses up cannot generally bind an overt anaphor:

(57)   *Bill$_i$ expected [that Sue wanted [himself$_i$ to win]].

If you look through more sentences, you will find that *NP-trace must be locally bound. We can conclude that NP-trace is an anaphor.*

What about PRO? First of all, PRO$_{arb}$ has no controller, so it is not bound at all. In this way it is like an obviate pronoun. But PRO can have a controller in other constructions. As we saw for nonobligatory control structures, the controller of PRO need not precede it or stand in any particular hierarchical relationship to it. So the controller of PRO in nonobligatory control structures need not c-command it—that is, need not bind it. If we had accepted the Reanalysis proposal for 35, we would have concluded that the controller of PRO in obligatory control structures must c-command it. In that case, PRO would have been bound, and the question would have been whether that binding is local. Notice that we have, up to this point, always been talking about examples with PRO in which PRO was in the Subject position of an embedded infinitival and the controller, if there was one, was in the next higher clause. We know (from 54 and 55 above, in which an NP-trace and an overt anaphor are both accepted in the Subject position of an embedded infinitival, and thus are locally bound by an element in the next higher clause), that such a relationship is local. But can PRO ever have a controller that is two clauses higher?

(58)   *Jack$_i$ expected [Sue to want [PRO$_i$ to leave]].

Example 58 allows an interpretation with Sue wanting herself to leave, but not with Sue wanting Jack to leave. This is generally the case (and we will not see any evidence to the contrary until Star Problem 10.3): *PRO, if it is controlled, must be controlled by an element in the next higher clause.* That is, the controller must be local.

Because most linguists accept the Reanalysis proposal for 35, they also accept the proposal that obligatory control involves local binding. Thus they would conclude that PRO in obligatory control structures is an anaphor. We have not accepted the Reanalysis proposal for 35. However, as we will see in chapter 10, there may be evidence that c-command is not the proper restriction on binding of overt anaphors, anyway. In fact, in chapter 10 we will discuss the possibility that linear precedence is the only factor that matters for local binding of an overt anaphor in English. And since we have seen that in obligatory control structures the controller must precede PRO and that the binding must be local, we could also conclude that PRO in obligatory control structures is an anaphor.

On the other hand, PRO need not even be controlled (that is, we have PRO$_{arb}$). Furthermore, for controlled PRO in nonobligatory control structures, the controller need not c-command or precede it. In that way, it has properties of a pronominal.

Locality Revisited: Binding Theory in Terms of
Governing Categories

Could it be that PRO is both an anaphor (in its obligatory control uses) and a pronominal (in its nonobligatory control and arbitrary uses)? If it were, PRO would have to conform to both Condition A and Condition B of Binding Theory (BT). That is, according to Condition A it would have to be locally bound and according to Condition B it would have to be locally free. This situation seems at first a paradox. But, in fact, it is possible for an item to conform to both Condition A and Condition B of BT if we develop BT in a particular way.

How could we develop BT so as to prevent PRO, if it is both an anaphor and a pronominal, from violating either Condition A or Condition B or both of BT? Look back over our discussion of the properties of PRO. What is special about PRO, as opposed to the other anaphors and pronominals we have examined thus far in this book? Well, clearly, the answer is exactly the fact that we just uncovered above: PRO must be ungoverned at SS.

Think about this fact for a moment. Every nominal that we have examined so far in this book appears at SS in a governed position except Subjects of infinitivals and *wh*-nominals in questions and in relative clauses (as in Problem Set 6.3). We will put off all discussion of *wh*-nominals until chapter 8. For now, then, let us focus on Subjects of infinitivals. We know that the Subjects of infinitivals, if they are audible nominals, must receive Case. So we recognized in chapter 5 the mechanism of Exceptional Case-Marking, which takes place via exceptional government. That is, even these audible nominals are governed (though across a maximal projection— hence, the label "exceptional government").

Furthermore, PRO is distinct from NP-trace. In every example we have seen of NP-trace thus far, the nominal to be moved has originated inside the VP, governed either by the V or by a P. (We will see additional positions for NP-trace later, but none will be problematic for our discussion here.) Thus NP-trace is governed at SS.

That means that the fact that PRO is ungoverned makes it distinct from every other nominal we have examined thus far. Since Binding Theory concerns the interpretation of nominals, we might suspect that if PRO is a problem for BT and if PRO differs from all other nominals we know thus far by virtue of the fact that it is ungoverned, the concept of government is somehow crucial to BT.

Exactly how could the concept of government be crucial to BT? Our BT now has three conditions:

(59)   A. An anaphor must be locally bound.
        B. A pronominal must be locally free.
        C. An R-expression must be free everywhere.

The issue we have been vague about up to this point is exactly what locality is. So we should be led to propose that the notion of government is crucial to the proper definition of locality. And we must use the fact that PRO is ungoverned to allow PRO to violate neither Condition A nor Condition B of BT.

We have seen that items within a Complete Functional Complex (CFC) are local to one another, and CFCs are typically made of clause members or members of an NP that has a Subject:

(60)   Jack$_i$ likes himself$_i$.

(61)   [$_{NP}$Jack's$_i$ picture of himself$_{i/*j}$] surprised Bill$_j$.

In 61 *himself* can be read as coreferential with *Jack* (indicated by the index i), but not with *Bill* (indicated by the index j).

We have also seen that an item in the Subject position of an infinitival is local to material in the next higher clause, but not in more distant clauses, while an item in the Subject position of a tensed clause is not local to material in the next higher clause:

(62)   Jack$_i$ expects [himself$_i$ to win].

(63)   *Jack$_i$ expects [that himself$_i$ will win].

(64)   *Jack$_i$ expects [Sue to want [himself$_i$ to win]].

We will now make our notion of locality precise. First, let us review the notion of government: a head governs all the constituents within its maximal projection that are not separated from it by another maximal projection. We will use this notion of government as well as the familiar fact that local domains conform closely to clauses and to NPs (a fact that we have recognized from chapter 3 on), where the clauses and the NPs have Subjects. And, among constructions which typically form CFCs, we will be careful to single out tensed clauses (which can be distinguished by the fact that their heads are marked [+Agr]).

Let us define the notion of GOVERNING CATEGORY in the following way.

(65)   B is the governing category for E iff B is the minimal N″ or I″ that contains:
        (a) E,
        (b) the governor of E,
        and (c) a SUBJECT accessible to E.

("Iff" means "if and only if.") The governor of any node is the minimal node that governs it. For now let us define *SUBJECT* (read as "capital subject") as (1) the specifier of N′ or of an I′ that is [−Agr] or (2) [+Agr] in tensed clauses. That is, SUBJECT of N″ and of tenseless clauses is identical to Subject. But SUBJECT of tensed clauses is the node marked [+Agr].

This definition may seem reasonable to you with regard to N″ and to tenseless clauses, but arbitrary with respect to tensed clauses. What has [+Agr] got in common with Subjects? One of the motivations for calling [+Agr] the SUBJECT of tensed clauses is that in this way we can allow Subjects of tensed clauses to have their own I″ be their governing category. That is, if no constituent can serve as an ACCESSIBLE SUBJECT to itself (a point which we will face in chapter 9), Subjects of tensed clauses could not find an accessible SUBJECT within their own I″ if they were the SUBJECTs of their own clauses. But the minimal I″ that contains the Subject of a tensed clause must be the governing category for that Subject if we are going to account for why anaphors cannot occur in Subject position of tensed clauses (as we will see in the analysis below of the ungrammatical 63 above). Thus our definition of SUBJECT is motivated by the notion of ACCESSIBILITY.

The issue of what makes a SUBJECT accessible to a given node is something which, again, we will face in chapter 9. For now, in every example you will be given below in which we discuss governing category, the SUBJECT involved will be accessible to the relevant node we are discussing. So you need not worry about accessibility right now.

The claim is that locality is defined with respect to governing categories in such a way that Conditions A and B of BT can be rewritten as:

(66)   A. An anaphor must be bound within its governing category.
       B. A pronominal must be free within its governing category.

Let us go back through 60–64 above now. In 60 the governor for the anaphor is the verb *likes* (in boldface in 67).

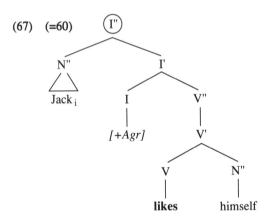

(67)   (=60)

The governing category is, therefore, the I″ (circled), and the accessible SUBJECT is [+Agr] (italic). Since *Jack* occurs inside this I″, the anaphor is bound within its governing category.

In 61 the governor of the anaphor is the noun *picture* (or, alternatively, the P *of*— the choice has no relevance to the discussion here—example 68).

(68) (=61)

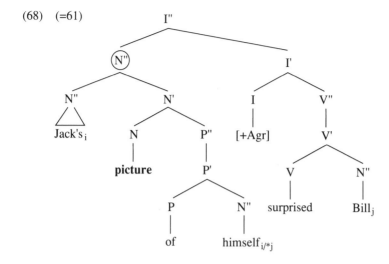

The governing category of the anaphor is the NP that contains *Jack's* (again circled), which is the accessible SUBJECT to the anaphor. Once more the anaphor is
bound within its governing category if we co-index it with *Jack's*. However, *Bill* is
outside the governing category and fails to c-command the anaphor; hence co-
indexation with *Bill* is not possible.

In 62 *himself* is exceptionally governed by *expects*. We know this because without exceptional government here, we could not get Case assigned to this anaphor:

(69) (=62)

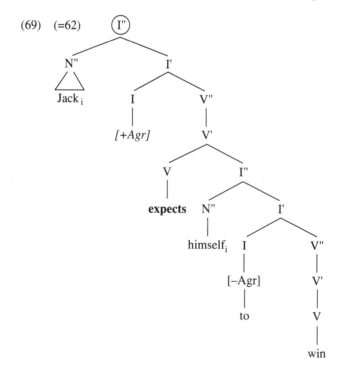

The governing category for this anaphor is the matrix clause I″, which contains the (exceptional) governor *expects* and the accessible SUBJECT [+Agr]. Since *Jack* is within the matrix I″, the anaphor is once more bound within its governing category. The behavior of overt anaphors in examples like 62, in fact, is the reason we opted in chapter 5 to say that exceptional government is responsible for Exceptional Case-Marking. If *expects* did not exceptionally govern *himself* in 62, the anaphor would be ungoverned and thus it would bypass Condition A of BT. But then we might expect that such an anaphor could be interpreted as coreferential with any other nominal anywhere in the sentence. Yet it cannot, as 63 clearly shows. Thus this anaphor is, after all, governed by exceptional government, and it does conform to Condition A of BT.

In 63, *himself* is governed by the [+Agr] of the embedded clause, which is an accessible SUBJECT.

(70)   (=63)

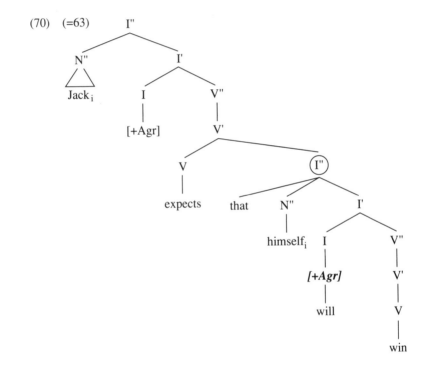

(The justification for placing the modals (like the *will* in 70) under the I node is found in Tangent 8.1 of chapter 8.) Thus the embedded clause is the governing category for this anaphor. But since the anaphor is not bound within its governing category, the sentence fails. (Note that we cannot claim that the matrix I″ is the governing category, because the definition of "governing category" in 65 specifies that the governing category must be the minimal N″ or I″ meeting the requirements.)

In 64 *himself* is exceptionally governed by the verb of the next higher clause *want*:

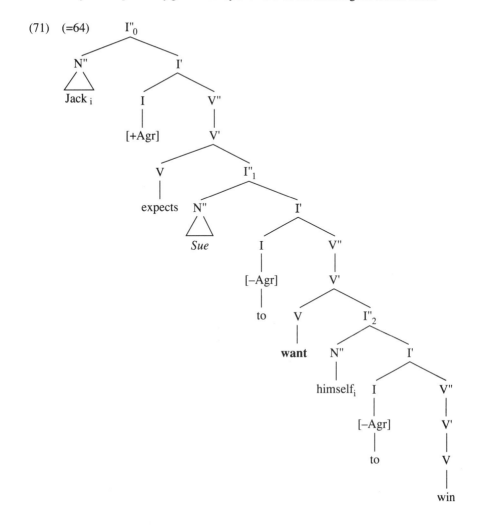

The Subject of the medial clause I″₁, *Sue*, is an accessible SUBJECT. Thus the governing category for the anaphor is I″₁. But since the anaphor is not bound within its governing category, the sentence fails.

We can see that infinitival clauses, while they are CFCs, are not governing categories for their own Subjects. This is because the governor of the Subject of an infinitival clause (if it has one) is not contained within the infinitival clause. (In fact, the Subject of an infinitival clause and the I″ of that clause will have the same governor, if, in fact, the Subject even has a governor.) It is also because no NP can be an accessible SUBJECT to itself (and, again, you must wait until chapter 9 for evidence). Thus the notions of "CFC" and "governing category" are distinct from one another.

The PRO Theorem

Now let us turn back to PRO. We said that PRO occurs only in ungoverned positions, and we are searching for motivation for this fact. We also said that PRO in obligatory control constructions shares properties with anaphors, but PRO in other constructions is more like pronominals. That suggests that PRO should conform to both Conditions A and B of BT. But PRO cannot possibly conform to Conditions A and B of BT. However, PRO can bypass both Conditions A and B of BT as rewritten in 66, since PRO has no governing category. That is, there is no possibility that PRO can ever violate either Condition A or B of BT, because PRO is ungoverned. In fact, the very fact that PRO must not be allowed to violate Conditions A and B of BT can be seen as the motivation for why PRO can occur only in ungoverned positions. The fact that PRO's distribution follows from the claim that it is both an anaphor and a pronominal is called the PRO THEOREM.

In all our examples PRO has no governor, so it cannot have a governing category. In a strict sense, however, the PRO Theorem does not require that PRO be ungoverned. Instead it requires only that PRO have no governing category. Look again at the definition of governing category, given in 65 and repeated here:

(72) B is the governing category for E iff B is the minimal N'' or I'' that contains:
      (a) E,
      (b) the governor of E,
      and (c) a SUBJECT accessible to E.

A node fails to have a governing category if it fails to have a governor, or if it fails to find an accessible SUBJECT, or both. PRO could fail to have a governing category, then, even if it were governed, so long as it had no SUBJECT accessible to it. This point is a technicality for us right now. But should you go on to study control structures more extensively, it might turn out to be important.

The PRO Theorem is disturbing, perhaps, in that we could well have expected that if an anaphor or a pronominal had no governing category in a given sentence, then, rather than that anaphor/pronominal being allowed to bypass Conditions A and B of BT, instead, the sentence would have simply been ungrammatical. The fact that sentences containing PRO are not all uniformly ungrammatical could be seen as a surprise. Why should PRO be allowed to disregard requirements that other anaphors/pronominals must meet? How can any sentence that contains an anaphor/pronominal that is ungoverned be grammatical? The PRO Theorem, in my view, begs the question. If you are disturbed by the PRO Theorem, as I am, then you might take upon yourself the challenge of finding a better account of PRO's properties. In the meantime, we will accept the PRO Theorem and work with it.

We have now developed as much of Control Theory as we are going to in this book. But before we leave PRO behind, there is one other issue we need to face together.

Semantic Rationale for Constituency

You have been introduced to sentences consisting of terminal strings of nodes that look very similar, such as in the second sentence of 9 and the example in 14, repeated here for convenience:

(73)   John wanted Bill to understand.

(74)   John persuaded Bill to leave.

Both consist of NP V NP VP. Yet we analyzed 73 in 9 as having *Bill* in Subject position of the infinitival clause, but we analyzed 74 in 14 as having *Bill* in Object position of the higher clause and PRO in Subject position of the infinitival clause, as in:

(75)   John wanted [Bill to understand].

(76)   John persuaded Bill [PRO to leave].

If you noticed this fact and were disturbed by it, good. Up to this point you have been asked to accept these different analyses on faith. Take a moment now to try to justify the different analyses to yourself on semantic grounds. It is not that hard to do. In 75 the sense of the sentence is that John wants a proposition to take place, not that he wants Bill. But in 76 the sense of the sentence is that John persuaded a person (in fact, it makes no sense to talk of persuading a proposition) of a proposition. Thus you can see why these two analyses make sense. And you will argue for these two analyses on a variety of semantic and syntactic grounds in Problem Set 7.4.

Empty Nodes and NP-Trace

It is now time to return to our general discussion of empty nodes, which will be the heart of chapter 8. But before we get there, let us take another look at NP-trace.

NP-trace occurs any time we have movement into Subject position. The only instance we have seen thus far of NP-trace is in passive sentences. However, many have argued that a sentence like 77 derives from a source like 78, via NP-movement:

(77)   John seems to understand math.

(78)   [e] seems [John to understand math].

The rule Move Alpha would take *John* from Subject position in the lower clause and move it to Subject position of the higher clause. Since the movement is going from a lower clause to a higher clause, this movement is often dubbed "Raising," and the types of matrix predicates that Raising takes place with are often called "Raising verbs" or "Raising predicates." You will argue for a Raising analysis of 77 in Problem Set 7.2 below, and you will identify other Raising predicates in Problem Set 7.7. Notice that while 77 consists of a similar string of nodes to that of 79, 77 does not involve PRO, but 79 does:

(79)   John wants [PRO to understand math].

Once you do Problem Set 7.2, you will be able to convince yourself quickly of the structural difference between 77 and 79, and you will be asked to explicitly argue for this difference in Problem Set 7.7 below.

Right now, what you should do is ask yourself whether the NP-trace in 77 behaves as an anaphor. We claimed above that the NP-trace of passive is an anaphor. If the NP-trace of Raising is the same animal, then it is an anaphor, as well; 77 at SS has the analysis here:

(80)   John$_i$ seems [t$_i$ to understand math].

What is the governor for this trace? This is not an easily answered question. Trace in 80 is in Subject position of an infinitival clause (whose I is, therefore, [−Agr]). So Trace is not governed within its clause. If it is going to be governed, then, it must be exceptionally governed by the higher verb *seem*. But if *seem* can exceptionally govern the Subject position of the embedded clause, why is 81 ungrammatical?

(81)   *It seems [John to understand math].

We have offered an explanation for the failure of 81 before—look back to Problem Set 5.3 of chapter 5. We noted there that not only are sentences like 81 ungrammatical, but also, sentences like 82:

(82)   *It seems John.

On the other hand, we can say,

(83)   It seems right.

(84)   It seems [that John understands math].

So AP and I″ that is marked [+Agr] can be complements of *seem*, but NP cannot (as in 82) and infinitival clauses (in which I″ is marked [−Agr]) that have an overt Subject at SS cannot (as in 81). This is the type of pattern we might expect if *seem* is not a Case-Assigner. That is, *seem* has the ability to exceptionally govern (as in 80), but since it is not a Case-Assigner, 81 is ungrammatical.

Let us analyze 80 with *seem* governing trace, then. Now, what is the governing category for trace here? That would be the matrix I″, because it contains trace, the governor of trace (which is *seem*), and a SUBJECT accessible to trace (which is [+Agr] of the matrix clause). So this trace is bound locally, as an anaphor should be.

Since all Raising structures are exactly like that in 80, all traces left by Raising are anaphors.

We can, then, maintain our claim that NP-trace in general (whether left behind by Passive or Raising) is an anaphor.

NP-trace is not the only kind of trace there is, however. And we will turn our attention in chapter 8 to a second kind of trace.

Problem Set 7.1: English Control in -*ing* Clauses, and *By*

This problem set is a good review of many points in the chapter. The ideas in Part 2, however, are somewhat elusive, and this part should be done with collaborators, if possible.

Part 1

Review the properties that distinguish obligatory from nonobligatory control.

(A) Obligatory-control PRO does not alternate with a lexical NP; nonobligatory-control PRO does.

(B) With obligatory control, the controller cannot be omitted regardless of the subcategorization frame of the verb; with nonobligatory control the controller may be omitted, depending on the subcategorization frame of the verb and its interaction with varying time frames.

(C) With obligatory control, the controller must linearly precede PRO; with nonobligatory control the controller may precede or follow PRO.

(D) In obligatory control the controller must c-command PRO, but this is not so with nonobligatory control. (Note: We did not adopt this property in the text, but it is one that is often adopted in the literature.)

Now consider Acc-*ing* complements (which you studied in Problem Set 5.5 of chapter 5) with control, such as:

(1)   John depended on [PRO winning].

(2)   John tried [PRO leaving].

Is control into Accusative-*ing* complements divided into obligatory and non-obligatory control? If you answer yes, then give examples to show the relevant properties. And if you make use of property D in your discussion, please give the relevant trees to make clear the c-command relationship.

(Please remember that INFL of the Acc-*ing* construction is [−Agr], so it is not a governor, even though it is possibly a Case-Assigner. Notice that if this INFL is a Case-Assigner (assigning Objective Case), then PRO can, in fact, receive Case, even though it cannot be governed.)

Part 2

Some have argued that in a passive sentence the passive morpheme (that is, the passive affix on the verb) carries the theta-role of agent, rather than the Object of the *by*. Discuss this proposal in light of the following sentences.

(3)   The price was decreased by the government [in order PRO to help the poor].

(4)   The price was decreased [in order PRO to help the poor].

Now consider the fact that many linguists have claimed that the specifier of N′ is the Subject position for NPs. So if an N takes an agent argument, we might expect that N to place the agent in specifier position. Just as an agent may not be realized by an overt NP in the passive sentence 4 above (but, instead, be realized by an affix on the verb), so one might posit that there is an agent in an NP like 5, even though there is no overt NP that functions as an agent here:

(5)   the destruction of the city

The point is that the N *destruction* surely allows an agent argument, as in:

(6)   the Huns' destruction of the city

so there is the possibility that a nonovert agent (what has been called an IMPLICIT agent argument) is present also in 5. If there were a nonovert agent in 5, what syntactic position would you associate that agent with? Argue for your answer using the following data:

(7)   the destruction of the city [in order PRO to make a point]

(8)   *the city's destruction [in order PRO to make a point]

(Assume that the NP *the city's* is moved from Object position of the head N (with a Case-marker *of*) to specifier position of N′ by Move Alpha, leaving behind a trace. Be sure to remember that no chain may have more than one theta-role associated with it.)

Can you account for 9 and 10 in a way consistent with your discussion of 7 and 8, with reference to both (1) whether the Object of a *by*-phrase is an agent, and (2) whether there is an implicit agent in nominals like 7? Try to.

(9)   the destruction of the city by the army [in order PRO to make a point]

(10)   *the city's destruction by the army [in order PRO to make a point]

Part 3

This sentence is ambiguous:

(11)   John was told [PRO to clean the house] [in order PRO to impress the guests].

First state the two readings by giving two different paraphrases of 11. Now account for the ambiguity.

*Problem Set 7.2: English and Portuguese Raising

The results of this problem set will be assumed in later chapters. You should do it.

As we noted in the text, people have argued that the sentence in 1 comes from the source in 2:

(1)   John seems to understand math.

(2)   [   ]$_{NP}$ seems [$_{I'}$ John to understand math]

The rule of Move Alpha would take *John* from Subject position in the lower clause and move (that is, raise) it to Subject position of the higher clause. For this reason, this particular instantiation of the rule Move Alpha is called Raising.

Now answer the following questions.

Part 1

Use the data in 3–6 to make an argument in favor of deriving 1 from 2.

(3)   {John/The children/Everyone/ . . . } understands math.

(4)   {John/The children/Everyone/ . . . } seems to understand math.

(5)   *{The wall/John's seductive wink/Aerobics/ . . . } understands math.

(6)   *{The wall/John's seductive wink/Aerobics/ . . . } seems to understand math.

(If you do not see the point here, turn back to the discussion of selectional restrictions in the arguments involving passive constructions in chapter 6.)

Part 2

Give the syntactic derivation of 7, including the DS, all intermediary structures, and the SS. You are free to use trees or labeled brackets here, but if you do use brackets, be sure to label them clearly. Be careful: Two applications of Move Alpha have applied here. Make sure you see them both.

(7)   Jack seems to have been invited by Susie.

(Refresh yourself on our analysis of passive sentences before attempting the analysis of 7.)

Part 3

Use the data in 8–11 to make an argument in favor of deriving 1 from 2. (Hint: the sentence in 10 has a derivation similar to that you gave above for 7.)

(8)   A friend {kept/*ignored/*enjoyed/*held/ . . . } tabs on my wife.

(9)   Tabs were {kept/*ignored/*enjoyed/*held/ . . . } on my wife.

(10)   Tabs seem to have been kept on my wife.

(11)   *Tabs seem interesting.

(If you do not see the point here, turn back to the discussion of idiom chunks in chapter 6.)

Part 4

Why is it impossible to derive 12 from 2? (That is, what makes 12 bad?)

(12)   *It seems John to understand math.

Part 5

Why is it impossible to derive 13 from 2? (Give at least one reason why 13 is bad. If you can give a second reason, terrific.)

(13)   *Math seems John to understand.

Part 6

Considering the derivation of 1 from 2, does this derivation force us into saying that *seem* gives a theta-role to its Subject or that *seem* does not give a theta-role to its Subject? (Hint: recall that in our Theta Theory we said that at most one theta-role can be associated with a given chain.) Use the sentences in 14–16 to argue whether this analysis of 1 makes correct predictions about sentences with *seem*.

(14)   There seems to be another hitch in GB.

(15)   It seems to be raining.

(16)   It seems that Jack left.

Part 7

Does *John* get a theta role in 1? If so, from which predicate? (Make sure your answer is consistent with your answer to Part 6.

Part 8

On Problem Set 5.3 of chapter 5 you were given data about European Portuguese (EP). You are expected to use the data from that problem set as well as the data given below in answering the following questions. (Again, as in Problem Set 5.3, I have glossed every verbal form with V (for "verb") plus person and number. Nominals are also glossed for person and number.)
    Consider the following data:

(17)   Parece   que as coisas estão   quentes em Belfast. (=9 in 5.3)
       V3s   3p   V3p
       [+tense]   [+tense]
       seems   that the things are   hot   in Belfast
       'It seems that things are hot in Belfast.'

(18)   As coisas parecem estar   quentes em Belfast.
             3p   V3p   V-unmarked
                    [+tense] [−tense]
       the things seem   be   hot   in Belfast
       'Things seem to be hot in Belfast.'

Give a string analysis of 18 with labeled brackets and mark whether the Subject of the embedded clause is t, or PRO, or *as coisas*. As you do this, assume that *parecer* here is like its English counterpart *seem* with respect to its predicate-argument structure, its Case-assigning properties, and its subcategorization frame.

Part 9

Now consider the additional data below:

(19)   As coisas parece   que estão   quentes em Belfast.
             3p   V3s   V3p
                   [+tense]   [+tense]
       things   seems   that are   hot   in Belfast
       'Things seem to be hot in Belfast.'

The translation of 19 is not literal. (Compare the word-by-word gloss to the translation and take a good look at the Portuguese.) What do you think is the string analysis of 19? Why? (EP is doing something here that English simply does not do. Shake the English out of your head and follow the EP. By the way, all the other Romance languages do the same thing that EP does in 19 regarding word order. [And sometimes in the written languages a comma is inserted after the initial NP, although in the spoken languages a pause is not found there.] But none of them can do what EP does in 20 below [not even other varieties of Portuguese]. This is because EP is the only one of the Romance languages that has an inflected infinitive.)

(Hint: The most important question here in determining the string analysis is: what is the Subject of the embedded clause? Is the Subject of the embedded clause t, or PRO, or *as coisas*, or a silent pro Subject of the type seen in Problem Set 5.3 in example 8 and in the matrix clauses of 3 and 4? Be careful here: clauses in Portuguese do not "overlap." That is, you do not find material from a higher clause completely surrounded by material from a lower clause.)

If you do not think *as coisas* is the Subject of the embedded clause in 19, does *as coisas* play a GF in the matrix clause? Why or why not? If not, what function do you think it has in this sentence?

Part 10

Now consider more data:

(20)   As coisas parece   estarem quentes em Belfast.
       3p   V3s   V3p
                [+tense] [−tense]
       the things seems   be   hot   in Belfast
       'Things seem to be hot in Belfast.'

(21)   Parece   estarem quentes em Belfast.
       V3s   V3p
       [+tense] [−tense]
       seems   be   hot   in Belfast
       'It seems (they) are hot in Belfast.'

Again the translations of 20 and 21 are not literal. Be sure to look back at 10 in Problem Set 5.3. Will the analysis you gave for 19 also work for 20? If not, explain why not. (I am not suggesting that it should not work; it all depends on what analysis you gave for 19. There is certainly at least one way to analyze 19 that will also work for 20.)

Part 11

Now more data:

(22)   *As coisas parecem estarem quentes em Belfast.
        3p   V3p   V3p
                 [+tense] [−tense]

Why is 22 bad? Argue for your answer.

Problem Set 7.3: English Ambient-*It*

In chapter 6 we argued that the Subject of passive sentences is moved there from some position inside VP. In Problem Set 7.2 you argued that the Subject of Raising predicates can be moved there from some position inside the embedded clause. Both of these analyses take as a given that English allows empty Subject slots in DS.

It would be important corroboration of those analyses if we could show that there are other constructions in English, besides movement constructions, in which there is an empty Subject slot at DS. That is the issue we will explore in this problem set, via the examination of sentences with so-called dummy Subjects.

You have been introduced to several items that have been called dummy Subjects. *There* of sentences like:

(1)   There's a fly in my soup.

is one example. We consider two alternative analyses of *there*-sentences in Problem Set 7.5 below, where one takes *there* to be a dummy that is inserted at SS, and the other takes *there* to be a somewhat mild locative that is present at DS. Neither analysis, however, requires that the relevant sentences have empty Subject slots at DS, so neither can shed light on the issue here.

Another putative dummy you have seen is the so-called AMBIENT-*it* (having to do with ambience in the most general sense) of weather and time expressions:

(2)   It's raining.

(3)   It's two o'clock.

And a third is the *it* with Raising predicates in which no Raising takes place:

(4)   It {seems/appears} that Jack isn't here.

Since there is no motivation whatsoever to posit dummies in DS, if either of these *it*s is truly a dummy, we must posit that it is not present at DS, but gets inserted (without any effect on the interpretation of the sentence—that is what it means to be a dummy) along the way. If the dummy fails to get inserted at SS, the sentence will be ruled ungrammatical because the INFL node will be unable to assign its Case. (But see the note at the end of this problem set.)

It is therefore our job now to examine whether both or one or neither of these two *it*s is a dummy. If we can show that either is, then we will have shown motivation for the positing of empty Subject slots at DS, independently of all considerations of movement, thereby lending credibility to our movement analyses of passive and Raising constructions.

There are several ways one might go about devising tests for dummyhood: (1) One possible test is to see whether the item to be tested can participate in a grammatical rule that otherwise only meaningful items participate in. (2) Another is to see whether the item to be tested can appear in a position where it must receive a theta-role. Since a dummy item could never, by definition, be assigned a theta-role, if the item tested can occur there, it cannot be a dummy.

*Consider the data below and give three arguments about the dummy status of ambient-*it *and of the* it *that occurs with Raising Verbs.*

(Caveat: If you decide to go off on your own and find examples, please be sure to keep straight the difference between the *it* of Raising Verbs, which we have in 4 above [with the verbs *seem* and *appear*] and the *it* of Extraposition, which can occur both with predicates that allow Raising—like [*be*] *likely*—and with predicates that do not—like [*be*] *clear*—as in:

(5)   a. It's likely that John has left.
      b. Raising: John is likely to have left.

(6)   a. It's clear that John has left.
      b. Raising: *John is clear to have left.

This problem set is not about the *it* of Extraposition, so do not consider examples like those in 5a and 6a. For more understanding of the *it* of Extraposition, see Problem Set 6.5 of chapter 6 and Problem Set 8.1 of chapter 8.)

Data Set A

    (7)   It got cold enough to snow.
            (cf.*The weather got cold enough to snow.)

            It got humid enough to finally rain.
            (cf.*The air got humid enough to finally rain.)

    (8)   *It seems (enough) that John died to upset me.

Data Set B

    (9)   I like it in California.

Data Set C

    (10)   It rained and ruined the picnic.
             It snowed but didn't stick.

    (11)   *It seemed that there were ants and upset me.
             *It only seems that he left but is obviously false.

Just by the way, it is interesting to note that in some languages that do not employ dummy Subjects, what we have called ambient-*it* sentences can be rendered either with a Subjectless sentence or with a lexical NP in Subject position. For example, in Mandarin Chinese we have both of the following sentences, which are considered largely equivalent (I have omitted the tone marks):

Xiayu-le.
raining
'(It's) raining.'

Tian xiayu-le.
sky   raining
Literally: 'The sky is raining.'

Perhaps you would like to comment on the relevance (if any) this sort of fact has for this problem set.

    Note: If you are really on your toes, you may have noticed that both ambient-*it* and the *it* of Raising predicates can occur in a tenseless clause:

    (12)   I want [it to rain].

    (13)   I want [it to seem that he's telling the truth].

This fact means that if one or both of them is truly a dummy, the assignment of Case by INFL cannot be the only motivating factor for the insertion of the dummy (since the INFL in 12 and 13 has no Case to assign.) It seems that English requires the Subject position in infinitivals to be filled at SS, although it can be filled by something that has no phonetic matrix. Thus PRO or trace can fill the Subject slot of infinitivals at SS. But a totally empty node from DS on cannot fill the Subject slot of infinitivals, accounting for the fact that we cannot say:

(14)   *I want [e to seem [that he's telling the truth]].

Tensed clauses, on the other hand, require that the Subject position be filled with something that has a phonetic matrix. These facts are independent of the issue addressed in this problem set and they should not affect your answers.

The fact that infinitivals require filled Subject positions at SS does not follow directly from our Extended Projection Principle (whereby every VP must have a Subject slot) because the Extended Projection Principle allows totally empty nodes to fill Subject position.

*Problem Set 7.4: English *Want* versus *Persuade*

This is a basic problem set that works on your argumentation skills. You should do it. Please read the entire problem set before beginning to answer the questions.

Part 1

You have seen that infinitival clauses can serve as Direct Objects, as in:

(1)   I wanted [Bill to leave].
      I expected [Bill to leave].
      I considered [Bill to be pretty smart].
      I found [Bill to be pretty smart].
      I like [children to act smart].
      I hate [children to act dumb].

There is another class of verbs, however, which do not take sentential DOs. Instead, they take NP Objects that are optionally followed by a second sentential complement, as in:

(2)   I persuaded Bill [PRO to leave].
      I forced Bill [PRO to leave].
      I encouraged Bill [PRO to leave].
      I ordered Bill [PRO to leave].
      I told Bill [PRO to leave].
      I convinced Bill [PRO to leave].

No evidence was presented to you in the text of this chapter that there really are two classes of verbs here beyond the fact that the semantics of the sentences in 1 are such that these verbs take propositional Objects, but the semantics of the sentences in 2 are such that these verbs take nominal Objects with an optional additional propositional Object. That is, in 1 we want, expect, consider, etc., propositions, not people. But in 2 we persuade, force, encourage, etc., people of propositions. Now you will be presented with relevant evidence of a variety of sorts that there really are structural differences between the two sets represented in 1 and 2. It is your job to come up with the arguments.

If there really are two classes of verbs, the structure for sentences with verbs like *want* and the other verbs in 1 would be as follows:

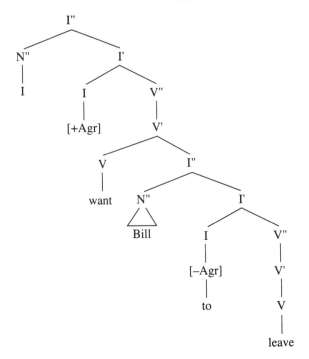

And the structure for sentences with verbs like *persuade* and the other verbs in 2 would be as in:

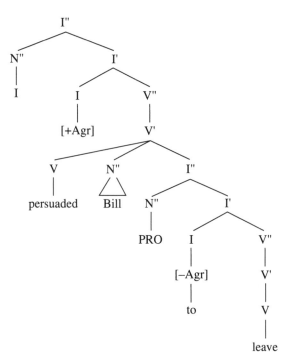

Take the data that follow and build arguments in favor of the preceding two structures. Describe in ordinary words what the data are showing in each set of examples below. Then build an argument supporting the claim that the structure of sentences with *want* is different from the structure of sentences with *persuade*.

Data Set A

(1) It's raining.
     (cf. *It's shouting. (No good unless the *it* is referential.)
          *I saw it. (No good unless the *it* is referential.))

(2) I wanted it to rain.
     *I persuaded it to rain.

Data Set B

(3) There's a party on November 21.
     *I saw there a party.

(4) Jeff wanted there to be a party.
     *Jeff persuaded there to be a party.

Data Set C

(5) Sally wanted to leave.
     *Sally persuaded to leave.

(Hint: your argument here is going to make use of the claim that *want* is subcategorized as taking either an NP Object or a sentential Object but not both, whereas *persuade* is subcategorized to take an NP Object and may optionally have a sentential complement, as well.)

Data Set D

(6) The doctor examined Mary.
     Mary was examined by the doctor.

(7) a. Sam wanted the doctor to examine Mary.
        Sam wanted Mary to be examined by the doctor.

     b. Sam persuaded the doctor to examine Mary.
        Sam persuaded Mary to be examined by the doctor.

(Hint: Your argument based on the data in 6 and 7 will deal with the explanation for the semantics. Be careful to compare the semantics of the pair in 7a to the semantics of the pair in 7b.)

From A–D you should be able to come up with two arguments easily, and a third argument with a little extra thought. The fourth argument may be a bit harder to come by, but you should be able to get it.

Please make your arguments based on the data in A, B, and D have the following general form (note, the argument based on the data in C will be slightly different in form):

(a) Give a generalization about something that will turn out to be relevant to the ungrammaticality or semantic differences in the pair of sentences with *want* and *persuade*. This statement will not mention *want* or *persuade* at all. Instead, it will talk about the data minus the sentences with *want* and *persuade*. That is, for the argument for Data A, the generalization will be based on the data in 1. For the argument for Data B, the generalization will be based on the data in 3. For the argument for Data D, the generalization will be based on the data in 6.

(b) State the facts about the particular sentences with *want* and *persuade*. That is, describe the relevant facts shown in 2 and 4 and 7.

(c) Give analyses for the particular sentences with *want* and *persuade* that are consistent with the generalization you came up with.

(d) Conclude that the structures given here for *want* and *persuade* are right.

Let me give you a sample argument.

Data Set E

(8)   The boys all left. (cf. All the boys left.)
        *I saw the boys all. (cf. I saw all the boys.)

(9)   Jeff wanted the boys all to leave.
        *Jeff persuaded the boys all to leave.

Argument
Generalization based on the data in 8: The quantifier *all* can have scope over an immediately preceding NP in Subject position, but not in Object position. (By the way, you are familiar with arguments built on the behavior of floating quantifiers, like the *all* in 8 and 9. Look back at Problem Set 6.3.)
Fact about our data in (9): *All* can have scope over an NP following *want* with an infinitival, but not over an NP following *persuade* with an infinitival.
Analysis: The NP following *want* with an infinitival is in Subject position, whereas the NP following *persuade* with an infinitival is in object position.
Conclusion: The structures given above are correct.

Part 2

Consider this sentence:

(10)   I begged Mother to go to the party.

For some people 10 is ambiguous between the reading on which I want to be allowed to go to the party and that on which I want Mother to go to the party. Give the two structures (with labeled brackets and all empty categories present) that correspond to the two readings.

Can you think of any other verbs that enter into this kind of ambiguity?

Problem Set 7.5: English *There*-Sentences

Part 1

Consider two analyses of *there*-sentences in English. One is a movement analysis, in which 3 derives from 2, which derives from 1.

(1) A bird is singing in the tree.

(2) t_i is [a bird]$_i$ singing in the tree.

(3) There$_i$ is [a bird]$_i$ singing in the tree.

The idea is that the Subject NP moves to the position immediately following the verb that triggers *there*-insertion. (Here *be* is the relevant verb—and see Problem Set 2.2 for an understanding of the semantics of this class of verbs.) The Subject leaves a trace when it moves. This trace is then covered by the insertion of *there* into Subject position.

The other is called the NP-Analysis. It derives 3 as a structure present at DS, with no movement.

A major difference between the two is that with movement, the derived structure of 3 is:

(4) [There] [$_{V''}$ is [a bird] [$_{V'}$ singing in the tree]].

That is, the NP *a bird* is plopped down in the middle of the verb string. (I put it in 4 inside the V″, but outside the V′. Actually, it is controversial whether or not it might be inside both the V″ and the V′.)

But with the NP-Analysis, the structure of 3 is:

(5) [There] is [a bird singing in the tree]$_{NP}$.

That is, the entire string, *a bird singing in the tree*, is an NP. The structure of 3, then, is similar to the structure of any other sentence with *be* followed by an NP, such as:

(6) There is a book.

Use the data below to argue for either the movement or the NP-Analysis. Each set of data will supply one argument.

Data Set A
In this data set the issue to consider is the semantics of the sentences.

(7) Someone is sick in the next room.

(8) Someone sick is in the next room.

(9) There is someone sick in the next room.

Data Set B

    (10)   A friend of mine is an impostor.

    (11)   *A friend of mine an impostor is in the next room.

    (12)   *There is a friend of mine an imposter.

Data Set C

    (13)   *A man is with a green coat (in the next room).

    (14)   A man with a green coat is in the next room.

    (15)   There is a man with a green coat in the next room.

Data Set D

    (16)   *A problem I must talk to you about is.

    (17)   There's a problem I must talk to you about.

Part 2

With the movement analysis, we must insert *there* and no other dummy and no other lexical item:

    (18)   There are flies in my soup.
           *It are flies in my soup. ≠
           They are flies in my soup.

With the NP-Analysis *there* is present in the DS. Discuss the issues that arise for the movement analysis regarding *there* insertion.

Part 3

Give the derivation of the following sentence first with a movement analysis and then with the NP-Analysis:

    (19)   There seem to be tons of problems here.

Part 4

With the movement analysis, *there* and the moved NP are co-indexed automatically since *there* inherits the index of the trace that it covers and the trace is co-indexed with the moved NP as a consequence of movement. Co-indexed items share many of their features, including person, number, and gender. This co-indexation, then, can account for the fact that *there* occurs with a singular verb in:

    (20)   [There]$_i$ is [a problem]$_i$ on my mind.

but a plural verb in:

(21)   [There]$_i$ are [many problems]$_i$ on my mind.

With an NP-Analysis, there is no automatic co-indexing between *there* and the NP that follows the verb:

(22)   There are [many problems on my mind].

The NP-Analysis, then, calls for some juggling in order to handle Subject-Verb Agreement in *there*-sentences.

There are at least two possible and simple ways the NP-Analysis could handle Subject-Verb Agreement in *there*-sentences. First, it could say that there is a special rule of agreement in *there*-sentences that makes the V agree not with the Subject (and *there* is the Subject, as you learned in Problem Set 2.2), but with the first NP to the right of the verb. Second, the NP-Analysis could call for co-indexation of *there* and the first NP to the right of the verb. Then agreement would proceed just as it does in the movement analysis.

Use the derivation of 19 above and 23 below to argue whether a special rule of Subject-Verb Agreement or co-indexation is a better solution for the agreement facts in *there*-sentence.

(23)   There seems to be an itty bitty problem here.

Problem Set 7.6: English and Chamorro Missing DOs

In chapter 6 we mentioned the proposal that the agentive argument in a passive sentence is realized by the passive-voice affix on the verb, and you briefly explored some evidence for this in Problem Set 7.1. So you have seen two proposals regarding missing arguments thus far: one is that they can be realized by affixes; the other is that they can be phonetically empty positions which are syntactically present and semantically interpretable, and these empty positions are not controlled (so they are not PRO), nor do they have an arbitrary or generic interpretation (so they are not PRO$_{arb}$), nor are they positions from which movement has applied (so they are not t).

Recall from the problem sets you have done on Portuguese, Italian, and Japanese that there are languages in which the Subject need not be phonetically realized.

Let us now look more closely into the idea of phonetically null arguments.

Part 1

Consider optionally transitive verbs of English (not unaccusatives, not middles— look for ones in which the same thematic role is played by the transitive and intransitive Subject), such as:

(1)   Jack eats (dinner) at 6.

(2)   She sings (arias) very well.

(3)   They clean (their house) all day long.

Give evidence for or against the hypothesis that the intransitive versions have a phonetically null but syntactically and semantically present Object.

You are on your own on this. Go in whatever directions you want. If you come up with arguments that contradict each other, fine. Just list all the arguments in favor and all the arguments against. If you do not know where to begin, you might try looking back at Problem Set 6.4 of chapter 6, where tests for transitivity are offered.

If you feel unchallenged by this question (in light of Problem Set 6.4 of chapter 6), you might ask it for sentences with verbs that take an optional IO (such as *serve* in *She served only cake* [*to the tourists*]).

You do not have to do this for English. If you know another language well, you could do this problem set for that language, instead. (French, for example, has exact translations of 1–3.) Please be sure to use native informants.

Part 2

Let us look at the Western Austronesian language Chamorro.

In Chamorro a verb agrees with the Subject for person or for number and sometimes for both.

(4) number only:
     T-um-angis i   neni.
     SUBJ(s)-cry the baby
     'The baby cried.'

(5) person and number:
     Ha-yuti'   si   Rebecca si Juan.
     SUBJ(3s)-drop Unm   Unm
     'Rebecca abandoned Juan.'

(Unm = unmarked—*si*, if used, marks the Case of both Subjects and DOs.) I am sorry, but I have no example of a sentence in which the verb agrees only for person. But it does happen.

The Subjects in 4 and 5 may also not be phonetically realized:

(6) T-um-angis.
     '(She) cried.'

(7) Ha-yuti' si Juan.
     '(She) abandoned Juan.'

Chamorro also allows an overt (phonetically audible) Subject pronoun. But only some of the time. Consider the examples below:

(8) Man-ma'udai (ham).
     SUBJ(p)-ride (we)
     '(We) rode.'

(9) Ha-fahan   (*gui') i   lepblu.
     SUBJ(3s)-buy (he)   the book
     '(He) bought the book.'

(10) Para bai infan-mattu (*ham) agupa'.
     will SUBJ(1p)-arrive (we)   tomorrow
     '(We) will arrive tomorrow.'

(11) Mattu   (gui') gi   petta.
     SUBJ(s)-arrive (he)   LOC door
     '(He) appeared in the doorway.'

(In 11 LOC = locative marker.)
   A Subject pronoun is possible in 8 and 11, but not in 9 and 10. Also, in 6 above
it is possible to have a pronoun, but in 7 it is not.

Question 1
When is an overt Subject pronoun disallowed?
   Now consider passive sentences. The verb agrees with the agent of a passive sen-
tence for number only:

(12) Kao ch-in-iku   si Maria as Juan?
     Q   SUBJ(s)-AGT(s)-kiss Unm   OBL
     'Was Maria kissed by Juan?'

(In 12 OBL = oblique marker. Here the OBL marks the Case of the Object of a
preposition.)
   All agents of passive sentences are third person—first and second person are simply ungrammatical:

(13) * Kao ch-in-iku   si Maria nu   hagu?
       Q   SUBJ(s)-AGT(s)-kiss Unm   OBL you
       'Was Maria kissed by you?'

(14) *Ma-bisita   i bihu   nu   hami.
      SUBJ(s)-AGT(p)-visit the old-man OBL us
      'The old man was visited by us.'

Passive sentences reject overt agentive pronouns:

(15) Kao ch-in-iku   si Maria (??nu guiya)?
     Q   SUBJ(s)-AGT(s)-kiss Unm   (OBL him)
     'Was Maria kissed (by him)?'

Note, of course, that the agentive pronoun may be omitted in 15 (just as the Subject
pronoun may always be omitted).

Question 2
Discuss how the data in 12–15 relate to the answer you gave to Question One.

Question 3

In the sentences of Chamorro in which no overt Subject appears (neither pronominal nor lexical), is there a phonetically null Subject pronoun? That is, is pro the Subject? Argue for your answer. (Use common sense and arguments involving theory here. There are no relevant additional data to give you beyond the fact that every sentence with a "missing" Subject behaves exactly like sentences with overt Subjects with regard to syntactic and semantic behavior.)

In Chamorro the verb does not agree with the DO, and the DO may be filled with a lexical NP, or with an overt pronoun, or it may be phonetically empty.

(16) In-bisita   (gui') gi   espitat.
      SUBJ(1p)-visit (him) LOC hospital.
      '(We) visited (him) at the hospital.'

(17) Ha-konni'   si Dolores   i   famagu'un gi   paingi. Kao
      SUBJ(3s)-take   Unm   the children last night Q
      ha-lalatdi   (i famagu'un)?
      SUBJ(3s)-scold (the children)
      'Dolores took the children last night. Did (Dolores) scold(the children)?'

(18) Ha-hahassu   ha' si   Maria$_i$ [na in-bisita   gi
      SUBJ(3s)-remember EMP Unm   that SUBJ(1p)-visit LOC
      espitat].
      hospital
      'Maria$_i$ remembers that (we) visited (her$_i$) at the hospital.'

For 16, of course, an appropriate extrasentential context (linguistic or pragmatic) is necessary in order for us to figure out that the DO is "him." In 17 I have given the appropriate extrasentential (linguistic) context. In 18, the empty DO slot is interpreted as coreferential with an antecedent in the higher clause: *Maria.*

We find that not every sentence with a transitive verb and only one unmarked argument (where both Subjects and DOs are unmarked arguments in Chamorro, as you learned above) can be interpreted as having an empty DO slot, however.

(19) *Para u-patmada   i   lahi.
       will SUBJ(3s)-slap the boy
       'The boy will slap her.'

(20) *Yanggin t-um-angis ta'lu i   patgun$_i$, para u-kastiga
        if   SUBJ(s)-cry again the child   will SUBJ(3s)-punish
       si Maria.
       Unm
       'If the child$_i$ cries again, Maria will punish (him$_i$).'

Contrast 19 and 20 to 16–18. An important fact is that both 19 and 20 are grammatical sentences, but not with the reading given above. Instead, 19 is good if it means:

(21) (She) will slap the boy.

And 20 is good if it means:

(22)   If the child$_i$ cries again, (he$_i$) will punish Maria.

Question 4

Come up with a strategy for interpreting sentences which do not have all their argument positions overtly filled.

Not all sentences like 19 and 20 have grammatical counterparts with a different reading. Consider:

(23)   *Ha-chalapun   si Maria.
       SUBJ(3s)-scatter Unm
       'Maria dispersed (them).'

Example 23 has no grammatical reading.

Question 5

The data in 23 may make you alter your answer to Question 4. If so, alter it now.

Question 6

What is the reading you would have expected for 23, given the interpretation strategy you came up with in questions 4/5, and why is this reading bad?

Question 7

I have no further data available to me on sentences that lack overt DOs. But just on the basis of what you have seen here, do you think Chamorro has phonetically null DO pronouns? Why?

*Problem Set 7.7: English Raising versus Control

This problem set is a good review of theory thus far. It should be done.

Part 1

In the text we noted that the SS of sentences with Raising and sentences with control can often look very similar, as in:

(1)   I seem [t to understand].

(2)   I want [PRO to understand].

Give at least three arguments for the claim that 1 involves movement, with a trace as the Subject of the embedded clause, but 2 involves control, with PRO as the Subject of the embedded clause. If you do not know where to begin, look back at both Problem Sets 7.2 and 7.4. You should be able to build arguments using:

(a) idiom chunks
(b) ambient-*it* (of weather and time expressions)
(c) the *there* of so-called *there*-sentences

Part 2

Now consider the following sentence:

(3) John is certain to win.

This sentence is ambiguous for many speakers of English (although not all). One reading expresses the speaker's attitude and could be paraphrased as, "It is certain that John will win." (Every speaker gets this reading.) The other reading expresses John's attitude and could be paraphrased as, "John is certain that he is going to win." (Not all speakers get this reading.)

Account for this ambiguity by offering two different structures for 3, one for each reading. Say which reading is associated with which structure and why.

Part 3

List at least five other predicates besides *seem* and *be certain* that allow Raising. One of these will probably be a verb. A few of these may consist of the copula plus an adjective. And still others may consist of the copula plus an NP, as in:

(4) John is a cinch to win.
   (cf. It's a cinch that John will win.
   That John will win is a cinch.)

Be careful here. Remember that Raising is from Subject position of an infinitival to Subject position of the next higher clause. Do not confuse yourself with examples of the *tough*-construction, as in:

(5) John is easy to understand.

This construction has quite different properties (and you can work on it in Star Problem 8.5 of chapter 8). You can recognize the difference between sentences like 4 and sentences like 5 by simply noting that *John* bears the theta-role assigned to the Subject of the infinitival in 4, but not in 5.

Problem Set 7.8: English Reanalysis

We pointed out in the text that examples like 35, repeated here, cause problems for the claim that the controller must c-command PRO in obligatory control structures:

(1) I depended on Bill [PRO to be there].

That 1 is an obligatory control structure is easily verified. The PRO does not alternate with a lexical item:

(2) *I depended on Bill [(for) Mary to be there].

The PRO must follow the controller:

(3) *[PRO$_i$ to be there] I depended on Bill$_i$.
   (cf. [PRO$_i$ to get there], I$_i$ depended on Bill.)

And the omission of the controller results in an ungrammatical sentence:

(4)   *I'm always depending [PRO to be there].

Yet the controller in 1 does not c-command PRO.

In order to maintain the c-command restriction on obligatory control, one might appeal to Reanalysis. Reanalysis is the rule brought up in the main text narrative that has been posited to apply to a string of a verb immediately followed by a preposition, reanalyzing them as a single constituent under a V node. (You might want to reread the discussion following 35 in the text right now.) If Reanalysis applied to 1, the structure would be:

(5)

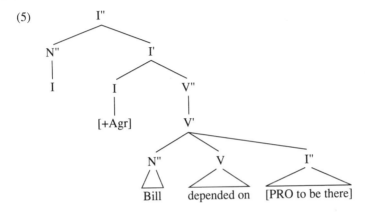

In 5, the N″ *Bill* is immediately dominated by V′, which dominates PRO, so the controller does, in fact, c-command PRO.

How do the following sentences bear on the issue of whether or not Reanalysis is the proper explanation for 1?

(6)   I depended, unaccountably I might add, on Bill$_i$ [PRO$_i$ to be there].

(7)   I depended entirely on Bill$_i$ [PRO$_i$ to make the arrangements].

(8)   On whom$_i$ did you depend t$_i$ [PRO$_i$ to make the arrangements]?

Problem Set 7.9: English Epithets, Appositives, and BT

Part 1

In the text we claimed that R-expressions must be free everywhere. Consider the epithet in boldface here:

(1)   Your sister left in a huff after someone caught **that witch** screaming at her kids again.

It is certainly possible to interpret *your sister* and *that witch* as coreferential in 1. Assume that the NP *your sister* c-commands the NP *that witch* (we will argue for this position in Problem Set 8.4 of chapter 8), so, if they are interpreted as coreferential, the NP *that witch* is then bound. What does that mean about the binding status of the NP *that witch*? Is it an anaphor, a pronominal, or an R-expression? Test other sentences with epithets and show whether *that witch* in 1 is doing something unusual or whether this is the pattern of epithets in general.

Very briefly discuss the naturalness or unnaturalness of your findings. (Certainly the concept of naturalness is a subjective one. Still, there are certain things you know about pronominals versus R-expressions, for example, that will allow you to see the grouping of epithets with one or the other as somehow natural or not.)

Part 2

Consider the appositive NP italicized here:

(2)   Maybelle, *the best Chinese writer I know*, is leaving.

Many questions about the correct tree structure of 2 arise. In fact, the analysis of appositives is problematic in numerous ways. We will not address them here. The important point for us is that the appositive NP is contained inside the matrix I″.

If the appositive NP were a referential NP, what problem for Binding Theory would 2 present?

Is the appositive NP in 2 a referential NP? Why or why not? If not, what else could it be? (Hint: You should be able to argue against appositives being referential items. Consider the predicate-argument structure of *leave* in analyzing 2.)

Part 3

Consider parentheticals, such as:

(3)   Jack, *I believe*, isn't so nice.

(4)   I saw the girls, *and you're not gonna believe this*, in the cemetery again.

(5)   I'm going with, *hold your breath*, the class president!

Make a list of as many different types of parentheticals as you can. Put them into sublists by syntactic and/or semantic characteristics.

What is the semantic function of parentheticals? (If you think there are many, give examples to make your point.)

Are there any grammatical characteristics that parentheticals and appositives (as in Part 2 above) have in common?

*Problem Set 7.10: English Reciprocals

This problem set is a good review of BT. It should be done.

In this problem set concentrate on Condition A of BT: an anaphor must be bound in its governing category. That means that an anaphor must find a linguistic antecedent, accounting for:

(1)   *Jeff likes ourselves.
      but: We₁ like ourselves₁.

It also means that if the anaphor finds itself in a tensed clause, its antecedent must be in the same tensed clause, accounting for:

(2)   *Jeff$_i$ said [that himself$_i$ would win].
      *Jeff$_i$ knew [we'd invite himself$_i$].
      *Jeff$_i$ knew [we'd give a book to himself$_i$].

This is because the [+Agr] of a tensed clause will be the accessible SUBJECT to all elements of the clause that are not members of some smaller CFC, and all elements inside a tensed clause will be governed. So the tensed I″ will be the governing category for all the elements within it that are not members of a smaller CFC.

But if the anaphor finds itself in a tenseless clause, its antecedent must be in the same clause only if the anaphor is not the GF Subject of the tenseless clause, accounting for:

(3)   *Jeff$_i$ expected [Sue to kiss himself$_i$].
      *Jeff$_i$ depended on [Sue talking with himself$_i$].

(4)   Jeff$_i$ knew [himself$_i$ to be a fool].
      Jeff$_i$ sensed [himself$_i$ losing the argument before it even began].

This is because the governing category of a non-Subject anaphor (as in 3) is the embedded I″, but the governing category of a Subject anaphor (as in 4) is the next higher I″. (Witness the fact that for the Subject of an infinitival, its [exceptional] governor is the Case-assigning V of the higher clause.)

And, finally, if the anaphor finds itself inside an NP and if the NP has a Subject (that is, a genitive specifier), the anaphor must find its antecedent inside the NP, accounting for:

(5)   *Jeff$_i$ threw out [Sally's pictures of himself$_i$].
      but: Jeff$_i$ threw out [an old picture of himself$_i$].

This is because an NP with a Subject forms a CFC and is, therefore, a governing category for the elements inside it (all of which are governed by the head N and all of which can find an accessible SUBJECT [so far as we yet know] within the NP). But an NP without a Subject does not form a CFC and does not have the potential to be a governing category for the elements inside it because it contains no potential accessible SUBJECT for those elements.

We also learned in Problem Set 4.6 of chapter 4 that Objects of prepositions can sometimes be reflexives and sometimes be pronouns when the antecedent is present in the governing category of the OP. You tied this variation in to thematic structure, I hope. That is, when the OP receives a theta-role, if it is coreferential with some other NP in its governing category, it must be a reflexive. Otherwise we find the pronoun only. As an illustration of that variable behavior, I give the following sentences.

(6)   must have reflexive:

      Jeff$_i$ talked to {himself$_i$/*him$_i$}.
      Jeff$_i$ baked a big chocolate cake for {himself$_i$/*him$_i$}.
      Jeff$_i$ depended on {himself$_i$/*him$_i$} alone.

(7) perhaps variable (multiple factors may enter here, such as how you view the event (that is, your detemination of arguments) and your regional variety of English):

Jeff$_i$ pulled the child to {himself$_i$/him$_i$}.
Jeff$_i$ put the pillow under {himself$_i$/him$_i$}.

(8) cannot have reflexive (at least in my speech):

Near {*himself$_i$/him$_i$} Jeff saw a snake.
Jeff walked down the street pulling the wagon behind {*himself$_i$/him$_i$}.

Assume the properties illustrated in 1–8 are common to all and only anaphors (which is, of course, the assumption we have held throughout this book thus far). That is, assume these properties define anaphors.

Here are your questions.

Part 1

Is the phrase *each other* an anaphor? Argue for your answer. (You must give sentences to illustrate whether *each other* has the properties that anaphors have, as shown in 1–8 above.)

Part 2

Explain why the following sentences are bad. Be sure to consider each sentence separately.

(9) *Sally expected the neighbors to invite herself.

(10) *Jeff knew himself had failed.

(11) *Rachel couldn't bear the class's rumors about herself.

(12) *Tullio insisted I carry himself.

(13) *Carmine thought I had bought your photo of himself.

Part 3

What is the antecedent of the anaphor in the following sentences? Where is that antecedent located linearly in relation to its anaphor? What GF does that antecedent play? (Remember that a GF is always with respect to a clause. So if you say "Subject," for example, you must say which clause the antecedent is the Subject of if there is more than one clause.) Be sure to consider each sentence below and to check that your analysis of the sentence is consistent with the way we have defined anaphors above.

(14) Jill wanted to enjoy herself.

(15) We all encouraged Lassie to perjure herself.

(16) Being true to oneself is important.

(Note: Look back at Problem Set 7.4 before doing this problem. There is a major syntactic difference between sentences with verbs like *want* and those with verbs like *encourage* when an infinitival complement is present. You must have that clear as you do this question.)

Part 4

The following sentence is a true exception to Condition A of BT. Which properties of anaphors are violated here?

(17)   Jeff$_i$ thought [that there was something wrong with himself$_i$].

In light of the fact that 18 is bad, which property of anaphors is respected in 17?

(18)   *There's something wrong with myself.

Finally, consider the way in which 17 violates Condition A of BT and give your own conjectures about why this violation results in an acceptable sentence. That is, is there anything about 17 that makes the violations not disturbing, as compared to the very disturbing violations in 1 and 2 above? In doing this, try to think of other sentences that illustrate violations like that in 17. You might list some of these as you give your discussion. Do not spend a great deal of time on this issue. We will address it at length in chapter 10. This question is asked more to make you aware of the issue than to get you to resolve it.

Problem Set 7.11: English *Seem*

This problem set presents some particularly thorny questions which could easily serve as the starting point for a research project.

Consider the sentence:

(1)   It seems to be happy.

The sentence in 1 has a good interpretation: that in which *it* is referential and there is a trace in Subject position of the lower clause:

(2)   It$_i$ seems [t$_i$ to be happy].

However, it does not have an interpretation that corresponds to the analysis in 3:

(3)   *It seems [PRO to be happy].

That is, we can neither interpret 3 with a referential *it* that controls PRO nor with a dummy-*it* and PRO$_{arb}$.

Part 1

Why is 3 out? That is, why is PRO blocked from being the Subject of the infinitive here? (You do not need to come up with any new constraint on PRO's distribution. A constraint you know already from chapter 5 will account for the blocking of PRO from 3.)

Part 2

Is *seem* a Case-Assigner? (If you did Problem Set 5.3, you can just look back there for your answer. If not, you can look back there to find data that will help you reach an answer.)

Part 3

In chapter 5 you learned that some verbs and prepositions that are Case-Assigners cannot exceptionally govern. (Look back at the discussion of examples 61 and 62 of chapter 5.) Now let us consider the flip side of the coin: Can a verb that is not a Case-Assigner exceptionally govern? Defend your answer. Is there any correlation, then, between the ability to Case-assign and the ability to exceptionally govern?

Part 4

In chapter 2 we raised the question of whether non-NP Subjects of tensed clauses received Case. That is, we know that [+Agr] can assign Case, but what we have not determined is whether a phrase that is not nominal can receive Case. With that question in mind, consider the following sentences, which compare to examples in 38 of chapter 2:

    (4)   *It seems [[into the house] to be where she ran].
          (cf. Into the house is where she ran.)

    (5)   *It seems [[quickly] to be how she did it].
          (cf. Quickly is how she did it.)

    (6)   *It seems [[run into trouble] to be what you're gonna do].
          (cf. Run into trouble is what you're gonna do.)

If Case Theory were responsible for the ungrammaticality of 4–6, what would that suggest about the relevant PP, AP, and VP in 4–6? Is the fact that 7–9 are grammatical consistent with your account of 4–6?

    (7)   Into the house seems to be where she ran.

    (8)   Quickly seems to be how she did it.

    (9)   Run into trouble seems to be what you're gonna do.

Now consider 10, which compares to 42 in chapter 2:

    (10) *It seems [that Paul's doing metrics again to mean that a new theory
          will appear any day now].
          (cf. That Paul's doing metrics again means that a new theory will
             appear any day now.)

What does 10 suggest about the ability of tensed clauses to receive Case? Is 11 consistent with that?

(11)   That Paul's doing metrics again seems to mean that a new theory will appear any day now.

Part 5

Consider the fact that 10 is ungrammatical but 12 is perfectly fine.

(12)   It seems [that Paul's doing metrics again].

Discuss what issues arise for Case Theory now. Reconsider the conclusions you arrived at in Part 4. How are they threatened by the contrast between 10 and 12? How could you resolve this problem? (Note: This is an open question, so far as I know. I am not trying to lead you toward any particular answer.)

One possibility you might consider is the claim that all Subjects are dominated by N″ (that is, the specifier of I′ is always N″), and this N″ can immediately dominate an X″ of any category. But Objects are not all N″. How would this proposal account for 12 versus 10?

Problem Set 7.12: Japanese Raising

We have seen that Raising takes place only out of tenseless clauses in English. We will now turn our attention to Japanese.

Part 1

Consider the sentences:

(1)   Ame-ga   huru.
      rain-SUBJ fall-PRES
      'Rain falls.' (= It's raining.)

(2)   Ame-ga   huru   hazu   da.
      rain-SUBJ fall-PRES expectation be-PRES
      'Rain is expected to fall.'

(PRES indicates that the predicate here is a tensed one, with present tense.) Our first job will be to analyze 2. The two possible analyses I want you to consider are that in which *ame-ga* is the Subject of the embedded clause at SS, so that a better gloss of 2 might be 'It is the expectation that rain will fall,' and that in which *ame-ga* is the Subject of the matrix clause at SS:

(3)   [$_{I''}$Ame-ga huru] hazu da.

(4)   [Ame-ga$_i$ [$_{I''}$ t$_i$ huru] hazu da].

The analysis in 4, of course, is a Raising analysis: *ame-ga* would have originated in Subject position of the embedded clause at DS and been moved into Subject position of the matrix clause by SS.

Form one argument that chooses between 3 and 4 as an analysis for constructions like 2 based on Data Set A.

Data Set A

In Japanese a predicate can show Subject honorification for the Subject of its own clause, not for the Subject of any other clause. (Actually, my informants do not all agree with this claim. I take it from Sells (1991—listed in the bibliography). For the sake of this problem set, please assume it.) In 5 we see Subject honorification in a simple sentence:

(5)   Sensee- ga   o-mie-ni-naru.
      teacher-SUBJ come-HON-PRES
      'The teacher comes.'

In 6 we see that Subject honorification is possible on the embedded predicate:

(6)   Sensee- ga   o-mie-ni-naru   hazu   da.
      teacher-SUBJ come-HON-PRES expectation be-PRES
      'The teacher is expected to come.'

In 7 we see that Subject honorification is possible on both predicates:

(7)   Sensee- ga   o-mie-ni-naru   hazu   de-irassyaimasu.
      teacher-SUBJ come-HON-PRES expectation be-HON-PRES
      'The teacher is expected to come.'

Do not get sidetracked by any questions of how the rule of honorification actually applies in 6 and 7. Merely use the generalization that Subject honorification can occur only with a Subject of a predicate's own clause in forming your argument.

Part 2

If you argued that 4 is the proper analysis of 2 in Part 1, we now have a problem on our hands. The embedded verb in 2 is tensed. Therefore the trace in Subject position of the embedded clause is assigned Case. Explain why this fact presents a problem for our theory. (Think of proper chain formation and the restrictions you know on chains.)

Part 3

One way around the problem you came up with in Part 2 would be to say that 4 is not the correct analysis of 2, after all. Instead, we could posit that 2 is a simple single-clause sentence, in which the discontinuous string *huru . . . da* somehow forms a single verb string. Use Data Sets B and C to argue whether constructions like 2 are complex (having two clauses) or simple.

Data Set B

(8)   Taroo-wa   Tokyo-e iku   hazu   da.
      Taroo-TOP Tokyo-to go-PRES expectation be-PRES
      'Taroo is expected to go to Tokyo.'

(9) Taroo-wa   Tokyo-e   itta   hazu   da.
     Taroo-TOP Tokyo-to go-PAST expectation be-PRES
     'Taroo is expected to have been to Tokyo.'

Data Set C

(10) Taroo-wa   soko-e   ikanai   hazu   da.
      Taroo-TOP there-to go-NEG-PRES expectation be-PRES
      'Taroo is expected not to go there.'

(11) Taroo-wa   soko-e   ikanai   hazu   de wa nai.
      Taroo-TOP there-to go-NEG-PRES expectation be-NEG-PRES
      'Taroo is not expected not to go there.'

Part 4

If you came to the conclusion that constructions like 2 involve two clauses, we are once more troubled because of the consideration you discovered in Part 2. We might then want to consider a third alternative analysis for 2:

(12) [Ame-ga$_i$ [$_{I''}$ pro$_i$ huru] hazu da.]

Here instead of the embedded Subject being a trace, we have a pro which is understood to be coreferential with the matrix Subject (indicated by the co-indexing). Movement would not, then, be involved in the derivation of 2 and 2 would involve no chains.

Choosing between 4 and 12 is not simple, and to do a decent job of arguing, we would need to know much more about other constructions in Japanese. However, let me give you one more data set and you can discuss what assumptions one would have to make in order to form an argument that helps us choose between 4 and 12.

Data Set D
Example 13 is an idiom:

(13) Musi-ga   siraseru.
      bug-SUBJ report-PRES
      Lit: 'A bug reports (to me).'
      Fig: 'I have a hunch.'

Example 14 has both the idiomatic and the literal reading:

(14) Musi-ga   siraseru   hazu   da.
      bug-SUBJ report-PRES expectation be-PRES
      Lit: 'A bug is expected to report (to me).'
      Fig: 'I expect to have a hunch.'

Problem Set 7.13: French Impersonal *II*

The so-called IMPERSONAL construction of French is illustrated in 1:

(1) Il est arrivé   trois femmes.
        3s
     it is   arrived three women
     'There arrived three women.'

Some have argued that a sentence like 1 is derived via a movement rule from 2, and
that the dummy-*il* is then inserted into Subject position to cover the trace (similar
to the movement analysis of extraposed sentential Subjects in Problem Set 6.5 of
chapter 6). The *il* in 1 would then be co-indexed with the moved NP (here *trois
femmes*).

(2) Trois femmes sont arrivées.
                      3p
     three women are   arrived
     'Three women have arrived.'

Let us call the proposed movement rule that would derive 1 from 2 Impersonal
Movement. Assume Impersonal Movement has applied in the impersonal construction in this problem set.

Part 1

State all properties you know of movement chains.

Part 2

Example 2 differs from 1 in other ways besides just word order. Describe the morphological differences you see.
    If we assume that ordinary Subject-Verb Agreement has applied in 1 and 2, what
do we know about the feature bundle of the *il* of 1?

Part 3

Now consider:

(3) Il a   été   arreté   plusieurs terroristes à la   frontière.
     it has been arrested several   terrorists at the border
     'There were arrested several terrorists at the border.'

Two movement rules have applied in 3. What are they and what order did they
apply in? Please give the DS, intermediate structure, and SS of 3. You may use
labeled brackets or trees. Please co-index all phrases in a chain.

Part 4

Give the structure of 1 with all indices added in. Now account for how the NP *trois
femmes* receives Case. (Note that the verb in 1 can never take a DO in other constructions.)

Part 5

If Impersonal Movement applies to either of the following sentences, the result is ungrammatical.

(4) Trois femmes ont embrassé Marie.
     three women have kissed   Marie
     'Three women kissed Marie.'

     *Il a embrassé trois femmes Marie.
     *Il a embrassé Marie trois femmes.

(5) Plusieurs policiers vendent les voitures.
     several   police sell   the cars
     'Several policemen sell the cars.'

     *Il vend plusieurs policiers les voitures.
     *Il vend les voitures plusieurs policiers.

In fact, Impersonal Movement does not apply when a DO is present. Give an account of why results of Impersonal Movement are ungrammatical in sentences like 4 and 5. (If you do not see the point here, look back at Part 3 and think about Case Theory.)

Part 6

Impersonal Movement is common with verbs of existence and motion, impossible with transitive verbs, and rare with intransitives of other semantic classes. However, it does occasionally occur with these other intransitives. Here are some examples:

(6) Il mange beaucoup de linguistes dans ce   restaurant.
     eat   a lot   of linguists in   this restaurant
     'There eat many linguists in this restaurant.'

(7) Il travaille des   milliers   d'ouvriers dans cette usine.
        work   some thousands of workers in   this factory
     'There work thousands of workers in this factory.'

(8) Il lui telephonait de   nombreuses personnes à cette époque.
        IO telephoned some numerous   people   at that time
     'There used to call him many people in those days.'

(9) Il a   violemment reagi   beaucoup de personnes à
        has violently   reacted many   of people   to
     l'annonce   de cette nomination.
     the announcement of this nomination.
     'There reacted many people violently at the announcement of this nom-
     ination.'

Discuss the semantics of the French impersonal construction in comparison with the semantics of the English *there*-construction. Be sure to consider the effects of using a dummy Subject in both constructions.

Star Problem 7.1

This problem is a natural continuation of Problem Sets 7.5 and 7.13.

Part 1

In English we have a variety of other ways of expressing presentation or existence, parallel to the *there*-sentences. Consider:

(1) New York has millions of people.
     There are millions of people in New York.

(2) New York has a new skyscraper.
     There's a new skyscraper in New York.

Play around with the *have*-construction here. Come up with a list of similarities and differences between the *have*-construction and the *there*-construction. This list can contain both syntactic and semantic characteristics. Offer a syntactic analysis.

Part 2

Instead of the *have*-construction, you could do Part 1 for the *get*-construction:

(3) This paper's got a lot of problems.
     There are a lot of problems in this paper.

or for the use of perception verbs exemplified here:

(4) I see a lot of problems in this paper.
     I heard some off notes in that Beethoven piece.

Part 3

If you know a language other than English, describe at least one way that that language has of expressing presentation or existence.

If you know French, you might compare the *il y a*-construction to the *voici/voilà*-constructions.

If you know Spanish, consider the *haber*-construction below. (Here all verbs are glossed with V (for "verb") plus number, while nominals are glossed for number.)

(5) Hubo una naranja.   *Hubieron dos naranjas.
     Vs   s   Vp   p
     has an orange   have   two oranges
     'There was an orange.'

(6) Hubo protestas.   *Hubieron protestas.
       Vs   p   Vp   p
     has   protests   have   protests
     'There were protests.'

Note that in this construction the verb is invariably singular.

If you know Italian, you might consider either the use of the copula with the clitic *ci*, or the *ecco*-construction:

(7) Ci   sono problemi qui.   C'è   un problema qui.
       Vp   p   Vs   s
     there are   problems here   there is a   problem here
     'There are problems here.'   'There's a problem here.'

(8) Ecco il libro che cercavo.
     'Here's the book that I was looking for.'

     Eccolo.
     'Here it is.'

Alternatively, you might compare the *ecco*-construction to the French *voici/voilà*-constructions.

Whatever construction you pick, come up with a list of syntactic and semantic characteristics of the construction(s) and give examples of every characteristic you describe.

Star Problem 7.2

Some have argued that PRO can occur in the Subject position of NPs (that is, in specifier position of NPs):

(1) I avoid [PRO discussions of Theta Theory].

(2) [PRO going trick-or-treating] is fun.

Find evidence for or against this position. If you decide that PRO can occur in the Subject position of NPs, test whether control into an NP divides into PRO$_{arb}$ versus controlled PRO and whether controlled PRO divides into obligatory and non-obligatory control. Would PRO be governed in 1? Discuss the problems that arise regarding government of PRO and how they might be resolved.

Overview

In this chapter we have worked on Binding Theory, Government Theory, Trace Theory, and, especially, Control Theory. The new principle we have added to our grammar is the PRO Theorem.

The reader should refer to the extensive overview at the end of chapter 6 for a discussion of those modules of the grammar not discussed here. Here we will state only changes or additions to the theory developed in this chapter.

Binding Theory

We now have three Conditions to BT.

 (A) An anaphor must be bound within its governing category.

 (B) A pronominal must be free within its governing category.

 (C) An R-expression must be free everywhere.

The definition for *governing category* is given under Government Theory in the next section. One gap in this definition still remains: we have yet to discuss what it means for a SUBJECT to be accessible.

The rest of BT remains the same as at the end of chapter 6.

Government Theory

We had already developed the hierarchical relationship of government.

Besides the structural notion of government, GT involves four other notions:

 (a) governor: The governor of a node B is the minimal node A that governs it.

 (b) governing category:
      B is the governing category for E if B is the minimal N'' or I'' that contains:
      (1) E,
      (2) the governor of E, and
      (3) a SUBJECT accessible to E.

 (c) SUBJECT: A SUBJECT is a Subject for N'' and for I'' that is $[-\text{Agr}]$. But in tensed clauses a SUBJECT is $[+\text{Agr}]$.

 (d) accessibility

We have not yet begun any discussion of the notion of accessibility.

We have seen in this chapter one new place where Government Theory is relevant to another module of the grammar: in BT the notion of locality is based on the notion of governing category.

The rest of GT remains the same as at the end of chapter 6.

Trace Theory

We argued in this chapter that NP-trace is an anaphor.

The rest of TT remains the same as at the end of chapter 6.

Control Theory

PRO can be uncontrolled (in which case we have PRO_{arb}) or controlled. If it is controlled, it can be an instance of obligatory control or nonobligatory control. The features that distinguish these two types of control are:

1. PRO does not alternate with a lexical item in obligatory control structures, but it can in nonobligatory control structures.

2. The controller always precedes PRO in obligatory control structures, but not in nonobligatory control structures.

3. If the controller is omitted from an obligatory control structure, the result is an ungrammatical sentence. But in nonobligatory control structures, omission may result in a grammatical sentence, depending on the subcategorization frame of the matrix verb and its interaction with varying time frames.

We also pointed out that many people take the position that the controller must c-command PRO in obligatory control structures, but not in nonobligatory control structures. We, however, found that c-command was not required in either type of control structure.

And, finally, the controller in obligatory control structures always bears a theta-role, but we were unable to determine if this is so in nonobligatory control structures.

PRO is ungoverned in every instance we have seen thus far. It therefore has no governing category. We noted, however, that PRO would also fail to have a governing category if it failed to have an accessible SUBJECT. The crucial property of PRO is that it never has a governing category. PRO has both the properties of an anaphor and the properties of a pronominal. It manages not to violate Condition A or B of BT by virtue of the fact that it has no governing category. The fact that PRO's status as both an anaphor and a pronominal makes it necessary that PRO be ungoverned (that is, the fact that the distribution of PRO follows from its status as both an anaphor and a pronominal) is known as the PRO Theorem.

8

Wh-Movement, Subjacency, and Barriers

Warning: This chapter is a killer. It pulls together the various modules of the grammar and plows through some of the most complex issues in linguistic theory. Allow yourself double the amount of time you ordinarily spend on a chapter. And do yourself the favor of trying as many problem sets as possible.

Wh-Movement

In chapter 7 we studied the behavior of PRO and of NP-trace. There is another kind of trace besides NP-trace: the trace that is left behind by a movement rule like *Wh*-Movement. Let us call that WH-TRACE and let us begin our discussion of it by looking closely at *Wh*-Movement.

In Problem Set 6.3 you came up with a number of arguments that claimed that there are empty nodes in *wh*-questions and in *wh*-relatives, such as:

(1) [Who$_i$] did Paul say [he saw t$_i$]?

(2) The girl [who$_i$] you know [t$_i$ came late] is Marie.

We will concentrate in the text of this chapter on *wh*-questions and leave the analysis of *wh*-relatives for Problem Set 8.7.

We have marked the empty nodes in 1 and 2 as traces (just as we did in Problem Set 6.3), but we have not justified labeling them traces as opposed to any other kind of empty node. Certainly, we know they cannot be PRO, since they are governed. (And, by the way, what is the governor of each trace shown in 1 and 2? In 1, the governor is the embedded verb *saw*. In 2, the governor is the embedded clause's I, which is [+Agr].) And certainly we do not want to generate these empty nodes at DS, since we have adopted the Projection Principle, which requires us to represent not just the subcategorization of all predicates at DS, but the predicate-argument

378

structure, as well. Thus, since these empty nodes receive a theta-role in 1 and 2, they must be filled at DS. It then follows that these empty nodes are, in fact, traces of the movement left by the question or relative words. So we are dealing with *wh*-traces.

Where does the *wh*-word move to in a question? Example 1 is a direct question (that is, it calls for an answer). Let us make a list of other direct *wh*-questions and study them:

(3) [What$_i$] did you see [t$_i$] in the park?

(4) [Why$_i$] did you leave [t$_i$]?

(5) [How$_i$] did he sound [t$_i$] yesterday?

(6) [Where$_i$] did she put the potatoes [t$_i$] when she came in?

(7) [When$_i$] is she leaving [t] for New York?

(Notice that not all the so-called *wh*-words begin with the letters *wh*. We will follow tradition here and let the term "*wh*-word" cover all the question words.) We find that the *wh*-word always occurs in sentence-initial position. So there is some slot at the beginning of the question that these *wh*-words are moving into.

Is it only single *wh*-words that can move in questions? That is, is the slot that these *wh*-words move into a lexical-node slot (an X-level slot)? Certainly not. Whole phrases can move:

(8) [Which book$_i$] did she buy [t$_i$] for him?

(9) [Into which house$_i$] did she flee [t$_i$]?

(10) [Whose brother$_i$] are you expecting [t$_i$] tonight?

(11) [With whom$_i$] did she leave [t$_i$]?

(12) [For what reason$_i$] did she leave [t$_i$]?

And the phrases above are both NPs (as in 8 and 10) and PPs (as in 9, 11, and 12). (The issue of what allows the P″ rather than just the OP to move in 9 is handled in Problem Set 8.13.)

The fact that the single words in 3–7 and the phrases in 8–12 all move to the front of the entire question suggests that the instances of single words are instances in which a single word simply happens to fill a phrase (a situation we have been familiar with since Problem Set 1.1). That is, in each case we are dealing with movement of a *wh*-phrase into an empty phrasal slot (that is, an X″ slot) at the front of the entire question.

Where does the *wh*-phrase move to in indirect (or embedded) questions? Consider:

(13) I wonder [[what$_i$] he saw [t$_i$] yesterday].

(14) I wonder [[who$_i$] he knows [t$_i$]].

(15)   I asked [[why$_i$] she left [t$_i$]].

(16)   I asked [[whose brother$_i$] she met [t$_i$] at the party].

(17)   I don't know [[with whom$_i$] she left the party [t$_i$]].

(You probably find 17 stilted or archaic-sounding. For analysis of its more collo-quial counterpart—in which *with* appears in sentence-final position—see Problem Set 8.13.) Again, the movement is to a slot at the front of the entire question, but this time the question is only the embedded clause, so the *wh*-phrase moves to the front of the embedded clause. We therefore must posit a phrasal slot in initial position of both direct and indirect questions into which the *wh*-phrase moves.

Subject-Auxiliary Inversion and the Status of Auxiliaries

But before we do that, notice that in the direct questions in 3–12 the order of the Subject and the first auxiliary are reversed, suggesting that a second movement rule has applied. We noticed this fact in earlier chapters and called this phenomenon Subject-Auxiliary Inversion. We assigned no particular analysis to the phenome-non and we will learn now that its name is a misnomer (although it is widely used in the literature). The movement rule involved in Subject-Auxiliary Inversion, unlike *Wh*-Movement, is restricted to applying only on matrix clauses, as we can see from the fact that it does not occur in the indirect questions in 13–17. (It is, then, a ROOT or MATRIX rule. You can examine other root phenomena in Problem Set 8.3.) We must, then, decide what is moving, the Subject or the auxiliary, and where it is moving to.

Were the Subject to move, it would be moving downward, right smack into the middle of the verb string. In 3–12 above, because these sentences have only one auxiliary, we find the Subject immediately preceding the main verb. But, in fact, if we consider sentences with more than one auxiliary, we find a different restriction:

(18)   a.   Why might [she] have been studying?
        b.   *Why might have [she] been studying?
        c.   *Why might have been [she] studying?

As we can see from 18, the Subject always ends up immediately following the first auxiliary, regardless of how many auxiliaries there might be in the verb string. As we might expect, given our familiarity with other phenomena that involve the first auxiliary (such as tag questions, as in Problem Set 2.1), when no auxiliary is present in the corresponding statement, a form of *do* shows up in the direct question:

(19)   —She left for some reason.
        —Why *did* she leave?

Let us now try to figure out what analysis of the verb string best accommodates these data. Back in chapter 4 we rejected the analysis of auxiliaries as being in the specifier node of V'. At that point we gave no arguments for our position. It is time to fill in the arguments.

Consider the VP of 18a if auxiliaries were to be located in specifier of V' and if the Subject were to have moved down inside the Aux string as in 20.

(20)

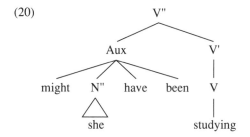

The result is a regrettable structure. First, no structure at SS we have seen thus far has a verb string interrupted by a Subject (not even *there*-sentences—as you saw in Problem Set 7.5). Second, actual Subject position would be left phonetically empty, which contradicts the fact that English requires an overt Subject in tensed clauses. One might try to claim that the *wh*-phrase fills the Subject position. However, if the same *Wh*-Movement applies in both direct and indirect questions, we cannot say that the *wh*-phrase is standing in Subject position in the direct questions in 3–12, since Subject position would not be available for the *wh*-phrase in the indirect questions in 13–17. Finally, downward movement of this type should be precluded from syntactic rules because of a principle (the ECP) which we will study in chapter 9. In sum, this analysis meets intractable problems.

If, instead, the auxiliary were to move in direct questions (such as 3–12), we could say that it moves to some position at the front of the clause (but after the slot that *wh*-phrases move into). Is this movement of an X (a lexical node) or is it movement of an XP (a phrasal node)? Given the analysis of the auxiliary system in 20, where we have put all auxiliaries under a single lexical-node Aux, this movement would be of "part" of an X node. That is, it would be movement of an actual lexical item, not of a node at all. We would then need to have separate rules for movement of the different lexical items that can be first auxiliaries, including *be, have*, and all the modals (there being at least nine and, depending on your speech, perhaps more, as you learned in Problem Set 2.4). This is clearly an uninsightful approach. *We want a rule that moves a node, not a rule that moves particular lexical items. The rule should be general enough to cover all the specific instantiations of it.*

Certainly Subject-Auxiliary Inversion shows that the simple picture of the auxiliary system in 20 is inadequate to account for the relevant data, as we have assumed without argument from the outset. (See our discussions in chapters 2 and 4.) We must recognize, then, that each auxiliary in the auxiliary string is dominated by its own X^0 node. There are at least two logically possible analyses that we should consider. One is that each auxiliary heads its own phrase (we leave open for now what category each auxiliary belongs to), as in 21.

(21)

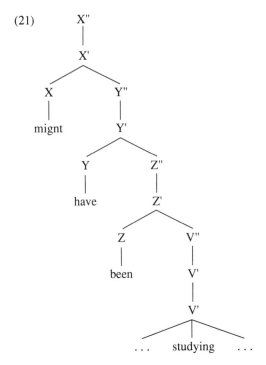

Another logical alternative is the structure in 22.

(22)

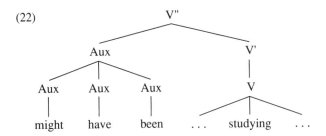

There are two major structural differences between 21 and 22. One is the category labels on each node in these trees. We address that issue in Tangent 8.1, which should not be read until you have completed reading the discussion about the second structural difference, which is constituency. In 21 each verbal word (auxiliary or main verb) forms a node (a phrasal node) with all the material following it, but the auxiliary string minus the main verb does not form a node. In 22 the constituency is exactly the opposite: the auxiliary string forms a node but no auxiliary other than the first one forms a node with all the material following it, and no string other than the entire one forms a phrase.

You are very familiar with at least one way to test the constituency of verb strings: the cleft-test. This test is not totally satisfactory since, as we have noted before, not all speakers feel comfortable with clefting verbal strings of any sort. However, many speakers do accept the cleft in 23:

(23)   Run down the street is what she did.

The fact that *run down the street* clefts, leaving behind the auxiliary *did,* is evidence that this string is a phrase (that is, an X''), since only phrases can be clefted. (See Problem Set 1.2.) Thus 23 is evidence in favor of 21, in which the verb and its arguments and adjuncts form a V'', over 22, in which the verb and its arguments and adjuncts form only a V'.

We would predict further with 21 that if an Auxiliary Phrase (the X'', Y'', or Z'' of 21) can cleft, we could get cleft-sentences in which one or more auxiliary is clefted along with the V''. (That is, X'', Y'', or Z'' might cleft, rather than merely V''.) With 22, however, we would predict that clefting should have to take all auxiliaries along with the V', since there is only one phrasal node in the whole structure (the V''). Unfortunately, these differing predictions cannot be tested since we never find any auxiliaries at all in a clefted phrase. (With the analysis in 21 we would say that only V'' can be clefted, never Auxiliary Phrases.)

Another way we could test the constituency of verb strings is to use the fronting rule called VP-FRONTING that is discussed in Tangent 8.2. In light of our presumption that movement is only of a single node (and, furthermore, only of the X or X'' level—see chapter 7), let us consider:

(24)   Mary said that she would run down the street, and run down the street she {did/may have}.

Again, the evidence supports the analysis in 21, according to which a V'' follows the final auxiliary, over that in 22, according to which a V' follows the final auxiliary.

Once more 21 and 22 would make different predictions if this fronting rule were to apply to strings that contain auxiliaries. Example 21 would predict that there is a choice of moving one or more auxiliaries along with the V'' (that is, the choice of moving X'', Y'', or Z'' in 21). Example 22 would predict that if any auxiliary is fronted, all must be. Once more, these predictions cannot be tested since we never find auxiliaries at all in these fronted verbal strings. (With the analysis in 21 we would say that the rule is well named: VP-Fronting fronts only V'', never auxiliary phrases.)

Other tests for the constituency of verbal strings could be and have been proposed. These tests are typically based on the assumption that pro-forms correspond to syntactic constituents. We have not adopted that assumption in this book; thus we will not discuss those tests here. However, you can read about this issue further in Tangent 8.2. (You should now read Tangents 8.1 and 8.2 before continuing with the text.)

Now that we have adopted 21 and rejected 22, we can see that the movement of an auxiliary in Subject-Auxiliary Inversion is movement of a node. But is it movement of a lexical node (an X) or of a phrasal node (an X")?

We already know that only the first auxiliary can move, not a string of auxiliaries, as in 18b and c. Furthermore, the whole verbal string (including all auxiliaries, adjuncts, and arguments, with the verb) cannot move:

(25)   *Why [$_{V'}$might have been studying] she?

The movement involved in Subject-Auxiliary Inversion, then, is of the first auxiliary only, not of any larger unit. And the first auxiliary is a single lexical node, not a phrase.

From Tangent 8.1 we know that the first auxiliary, regardless of whether it is a modal, *have*, or *be*, is located under the Tense (T) node at SS. If Subject-Auxiliary Inversion is, in fact, head movement of T into some higher head slot (whose category we do not yet know—indicated by X in 26), we have accounted for why only and precisely the first auxiliary moves in questions. (In 26 I have omitted Agr and all its projections since they are not of interest here.)

(26)

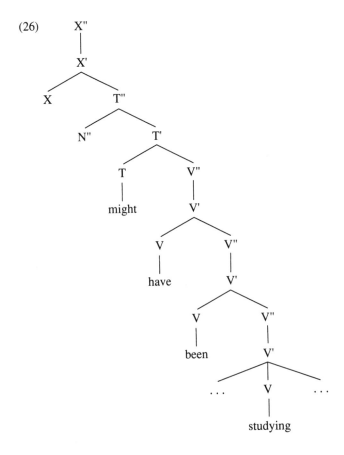

The Category C

We have come to the conclusion that at the outset of all questions there are two slots—the first a phrasal slot (into which *wh*-phrases move) and the second a lexical slot (into which, for direct (that is, matrix) questions only, the first auxiliary moves). But this sounds very much like the outset of any category phrase, given the X-Bar Theory. That is, all categories begin with a phrasal node Y″ (the specifier) followed by a lexical node (the head X), and perhaps modifiers or complements of X can intervene between the specifier and the head. If we posit that all questions are really phrases whose head node we will call C (for "Complementizer"), the structure of 3, for example, before and after *Wh*-Movement, Verb Movement, and Subject-Auxiliary Inversion (that is, head movement from T to C) is as shown in 27 and 28.

(27)

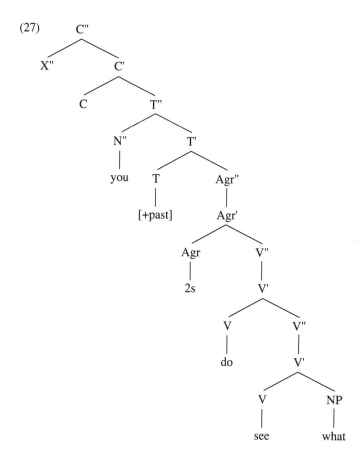

(28)

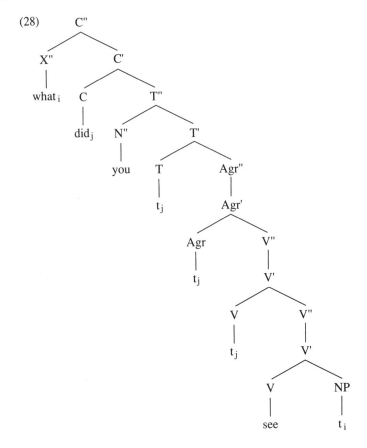

C″ would branch to its specifier, which is a phrasal node of any category, and C′. C′ would branch to C and T″ (or to C and I″, if the distinctions between T and Agr are not important to you). And the rest of the tree is familiar to you.

Wh-Movement, then, would be movement of the *wh*-phrase into the specifier of C′. (In 28 the trace of *Wh*-Movement (t_i) is co-indexed with the moved *wh*-phrase.) And Subject-Auxiliary Inversion would be movement of the first auxiliary (the T node) into C. (In 28 the traces of movement of the auxiliary (t_j) are co-indexed with the moved auxiliary.)

Are only questions dominated by C″, or are all sentences really C″ and not T″ (or I″)? Here, relative clauses help us. In 29 we see that *Wh*-Movement in relative clauses is to the front of the relative clause, immediately following the head of the relative (and you can turn back to Problem Set 6.3 for more examples):

(29)   The girl [[who$_i$] you like t_i] came in.

A relative clause like that in 29 is a statement (not a question), yet we clearly need to posit that it is a C″ in order to allow movement of the *wh*-phrase into the specifier of C′ position. Without the C″ structure for this relative clause, we have no slot that the *wh*-phrase can move into.

Is there any evidence for the C″ structure in sentences that do not involve *wh*-phrases? Back in Problem Set 6.5 you noted that at that point we had no satisfying and consistent (with respect to the rest of X-Bar Theory) way to deal with a *that* that introduces an embedded statement, as in:

(30)   [*That* she's here] is obvious.
       I know [*that* she's here].

We called the clause introducer *that* a complementizer. In fact, *that* could be considered the typical complementizer of embedded statements. We could consider *wh*-phrases, then, the complementizers of questions (both direct and embedded), since they introduce these questions. Thus we can posit that all clauses are really C″.

You probably immediately noticed that matrix statements seem not to be introduced by a complementizer. Yet we know that the C″ structure must be present for matrix clauses as well as embedded clauses, because direct questions (just like embedded or indirect questions) place the *wh*-phrase in clause-initial position.

We will find reason (and see the section The Position of *That* in chapter 9) to say that *that* is located in C, although *wh*-phrases are located in the specifier of C′. Still, both are typically called complementizers and both make use of the structure that the introduction of the category C and its projections adds to our trees.

That is often called the complementizer that has the feature [+th], and this feature is usually associated with definiteness. The complementizers of questions, on the other hand, have the feature [+wh], and this feature is usually associated with lack of information. So compare *that* to *what* and *there* to *where* (and in older stages of English *thence* to *whence*, *thither* to *whither*, and so on). (Star Problem 8.6 explores some ramifications of this idea.) These two features ([+th] and [+wh]) appear to be incompatible (most probably for semantic reasons), since we never find in modern English a clause that begins with a *wh*-phrase followed by *that* in C position of the same clause.

At this point we can say that in a question the questioned phrase, which we are calling the *wh*-phrase, moves from its DS position into the specifier of the C′ of the entire question (whether a matrix (direct) or embedded (indirect) question) at SS. (Notice that this movement is into the only available phrasal slot.) For any question, then, we know the important facts about its DS and about its SS. What we do not yet know is whether there are any intermediary steps in the transformation from DS into SS.

Bounded-versus-Unbounded Movement

In the two instances we have studied of NP-movement, the movement was limited (or BOUNDED) to happening either within a clause or between ADJACENT CLAUSES. (A clause is adjacent to the next lower clause it contains and to the next higher clause that contains it.) This boundedness allows Passive to occur in:

(31)   *movement within a clause:*
John$_i$ was sent [t$_i$] home.

movement between adjacent clauses:
John$_i$ was said [[t$_i$] to be a fine fellow].

But when Passive Movement is over a greater distance, the result is ungrammatical:

(32)   *John$_i$ was known [that Jane expected [[t$_i$] to win]].
(from: [e] was known [that Jane expected [John to win]])
(compare to the at least marginally acceptable:
It was known that John was expected to win by Jane.)

Likewise, Raising occurs from one clause to an adjacent one:

(33)   John$_i$ appears [[t$_i$] to like beans].

But when Raising is over a greater distance, the result is ungrammatical:

(34)   *John$_i$ appears [that Mary wants [[t$_i$] to eat the beans]].
(from: [e] appears [that Mary wants [John to eat the beans]])

*John$_i$ appears [that it seems [[t$_i$] to have eaten the beans]]
(from: [e] appears [that [e] seems [John to have eaten the beans]])

The locality of movement in both Passive and Raising structures follows from the fact that NP-trace is an anaphor, so it must be bound within its governing category. The NP-traces in 32 and 34 are not bound within their governing categories (the governing category in each case here is the intermediary embedded I″, not the lowest I″); thus 32 and 34 are violations of condition A of Binding Theory. (From here out I will be talking about I″ as a shorthand for the highest functional phrase in the verbal hierarchy, so this discussion is easily transferrable to languages in which Agr″ is higher than T″ as well as languages like English in which T″ is higher than Agr″.)

The fact that NP-trace is an anaphor accounts for the failure of a range of movements. For example, consider the DS:

(35)   [e] appears [that Mary likes Bill]

Here neither *Mary* nor *Bill* can move into the empty node:

(36)   *Mary$_i$ appears [that t$_i$ likes Bill].
*Bill$_i$ appears [that Mary likes t$_i$].

Example 36 is out because in both sentences the trace's governing category is the embedded I″; thus the trace fails to be bound within its governing category.

Is *Wh*-Movement also local?

(37)   [Who] did Mary hear t?

(38)   [Who] did Mary hear [Jim ask t]?

(39)   [Who] did Mary hear [Jim ask Paul [PRO to encourage t]]?

(40)   [Who] did Mary hear [Jim ask Paul [PRO to encourage Sally [PRO to invite t]]?

In 37 the trace is in the same clause as the final resting place of the *wh*-phrase. In 38 they are in adjacent clauses. In 39 they are two clauses apart. In 40 they are three clauses apart. Try to come up with an example in which they are four clauses apart. Five. You will find that the grammar does not limit the distance, although your memory may.

Does this mean that *Wh*-Movement, unlike NP-Movement, is UNBOUNDED? Can you find instances of *Wh*-Movement that sound ungrammatical to your ear? Consider the sentence:

(41)   Bill met [$_{N''}$friends of *someone you know*] yesterday.

Question the OP in 41. The result is:

(42)   ??Who$_i$ did Bill meet [$_{N''}$ friends of t$_i$] yesterday?

Example 42 is strange for most speakers of English. Now consider the sentence:

(43)   Bill met [$_{N''}$those old friends of *someone you know*] yesterday.

Again question the OP in 43. The result is:

(44)   *Who$_i$ did Bill meet [$_{N''}$those old friends of t$_i$] yesterday?

Many people find 44 absolutely ungrammatical. It appears, then, that movement out of NP is blocked, either somewhat weakly (as in 42), or strongly (as in 44). So *Wh*-Movement is bounded, after all. (If you can think of acceptable examples with *Wh*-Movement out of NP, please have patience. We will return to a discussion of such examples toward the end of this chapter.)

That *Wh*-Movement should be blocked out of NP is not perhaps unexpected, given that NPs are potential governing categories. In fact, if we try to question from within an NP that has its own Subject, almost all speakers find the result ungrammatical:

(45)   Bill heard [Sally's lecture on the war].
        *What did Bill hear [Sally's lecture on t]?

        Bill admired [Sally's talent at tennis].
        *What did Bill admire [Sally's talent at t]?

        Bill was disgusted at [Sally's dependency on drugs].
        *What was Bill disgusted at [Sally's dependency on t]?

The truly puzzling question, instead, is why *Wh*-Movement should show its bounded nature when we are moving out of an NP (as in 44 and 45), but not when we are moving out of a clause (as in 38–40). Consider the structure of an NP and the structure of a clause as:

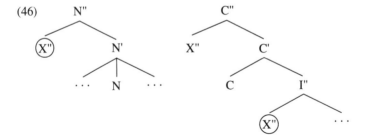

(46)

What is there about a clause as opposed to an N″ that gives it an ESCAPE HATCH for movement, so to speak? Compare the structures in 46. Both have a slot for the Subject (of the NP or of the clause), which I have circled. But C″ has the extra structure above I″, structure that is there for purely grammatical purposes, since neither predicates nor arguments (nor any of their modifiers) are generated at DS in C or in specifier of C′).

Look back now at what we just learned about *Wh*-Movement: the moved phrase winds up in the specifier of C′ position at the front of the entire question (or relative clause, as you will learn in Problem Set 8.7). If the specifier of C′ position were the escape hatch for movement, and if all *wh*-phrases that are moved out of N″ or C″ had to pass through an escape hatch, then we could account for the difference in bounding behavior for movement out of NPs and movement out of clauses. That is, NPs have no escape hatch, but clauses do. So movement out of NPs is blocked, but movement out of clauses is allowed.

We have identified the specifier of C′ position as the escape hatch for movement, but we have not explained why that precise position should be an escape hatch. That is, given the bounded property of *Wh*-Movement as exemplified in movement out of NPs, we expect *Wh*-Movement to be bounded out of I″ (which is also a potential governing category for a trace), as well. But our expectation is not met. It seems that the presence of C″ takes away the governing-category-ness of I″, so to speak. This effect needs to be accounted for (and we will account for it below).

Comp-to-Comp Movement and Chains

What we are proposing, then, is that all movement is bounded—that is, restricted to applying locally. We will get to a precise statement of that restriction later in this chapter. But first we need to discuss several new concepts. Keep in mind that we are trying to reach an understanding of the limitations on movement.

A *wh*-phrase moves into the specifier of the lowest C' that contains it. From there it hops from the specifier of C' to the specifier of the next higher C', to the specifier of the next higher C', and so on, until it reaches the front of the question (or relative). This hopping has been dubbed COMP-TO-COMP MOVEMENT (which is a SUCCESSIVE CYCLIC MOVEMENT, and we will return to a discussion of cycles below). Each time movement takes place (whether from the DS position into the first available specifier of C' or from the specifier of C' to the specifier of C' (that is, Comp-to-Comp), the movement is bounded. The derivation of 40, then, would be as shown in the following examples. In 47–50 the empty specifiers of the various C's are represented as gaps between brackets. The *wh*-phrase is represented as *who* all along.

(47) [[   ] Mary did hear [[   ] Jim ask Paul [[   ] PRO to encourage Sally [[   ] PRO to invite who]]].]

(48) [[   ] Mary did hear [[   ] Jim ask Paul [[   ] PRO to encourage Sally [[who$_i$] PRO to invite t$_i$]]].]

(49) [[   ] Mary did hear [[   ] Jim ask Paul [[who$_i$] PRO to encourage Sally [[t$_2$] PRO to invite t$_i$]]].]

(50) [[   ] Mary did hear [[who$_i$] Jim ask Paul [[t$_3$] PRO to encourage Sally [[t$_2$] PRO to invite t$_i$]]].]

(51) [[who$_5$] Mary did hear [[t$_4$] Jim ask Paul [[t$_3$] PRO to encourage Sally [[t$_2$] PRO to invite t$_i$]]].]

(52) [[Who$_5$] did Mary hear [[t$_4$] Jim ask Paul [[t$_3$] PRO to encourage Sally [[t$_2$] PRO to invite t$_i$]]]?]

There are, then, four instances of *Wh*-Movement in this derivation. The first is movement from DO position of the lowest clause into the specifier of the lowest C' (shown in 48). The next three are Comp-to-Comp movements (shown in 49–51). All the numbered traces marked in 49–52 are co-indexed with each other and with *who*—although I have numbered them for ease of exposition later, rather than simply putting the index "i" on all of them. (In 47–50, *who* has the index "i." But once the *wh*-phrase reaches its final destination, we can give it a numerical index that is one greater than the number of the closest trace—as in 51 and 52. You will see why we do that when you read about chain links.)

Of course, we also have movement of the auxiliary through T (indicated by I in the tree on page 392) and through Agr (all of whose projections have been omitted in this tree—that is, T and Agr have been conflated into I), into the highest C node from 51 to 52. Those head movements, as well, leave behind traces that are co-indexed with the auxiliary. I have left those traces out of the bracketed analysis in 52, since our focus right now is on the *Wh*-Movement, but they are shown in the

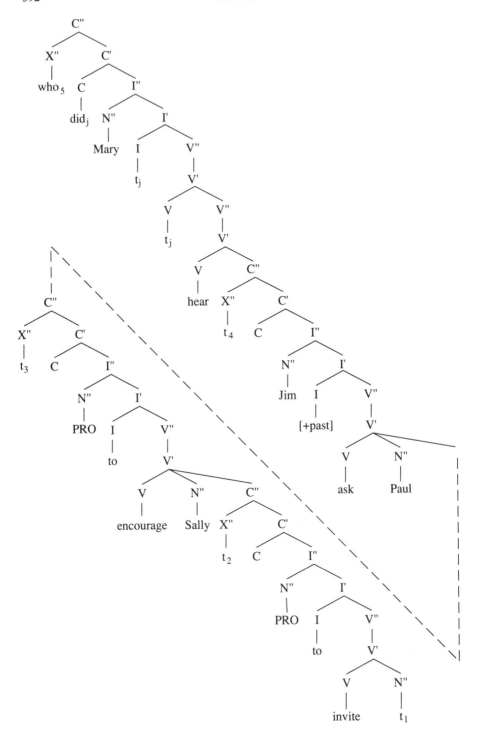

tree—with the simplification that T and Agr have been conflated into I. (In the tree of 52 I have marked INFLs that are not filled with trace or a lexical item as to whether they bear tense, as we discussed in Tangent 8.1.)

Consider the chain formed by *Wh*-Movement. If at most one Case and at most one theta-role can be associated with a given chain, do *Wh*-Movement chains create any problems for our understanding of chains? No. Specifier of C′ is not a position to which Case can be assigned, since C is not a Case-Assigner. Furthermore, specifier of C′ is not a position to which a theta-role can be assigned, since C is not a theta-assigner (given that complementizers have no argument structure). Therefore, if a Case or a theta-role is associated with a given *Wh*-Movement chain, it is because Case and/or a theta-role is assigned to the foot of the chain only. And, in fact, the *Wh*-Movement chain in 52 has both a Case and a theta-role associated with it: the Case and theta-role that *invite* assigns to its DO. In this way *Wh*-Movement chains differ from NP-Movement chains, where NP-trace can never receive Case, since NP-Movement is into a Subject position to which Case is assigned. Notice also that for every LINK IN THE CHAIN in 52 (a link is formed by any two co-indexed nodes in which at least one is a trace and the nodes have consecutive numbers, such as who_5-t_4 or t_2-t_3 in 52) the two members of that link are local to each other. (So t_n is local to both t_{n-1} and T_{n+1}.) This is just another way of saying that every movement is bounded.

Once a phrase is in specifier of C′, if it moves, the only place it can move to is another specifier of C′. Does this observation follow from a stipulation on movement or does it follow from other general principles? Think about chain formation. An item cannot move into a position where it will pick up a theta-role because of the Projection Principle. Thus movement into any position inside I″ is barred, except movement into a Subject position that is empty at DS. It is difficult to see how any principles thus far absolutely preclude movement of a *wh*-phrase into a Subject position that is empty at DS.

There is, however, at least one way we could handle our observation that *Wh*-Movement is only into specifier of C′ without an arbitrary stipulation on movement. If every clause is marked as having the feature [+wh] or [−wh] on its specifier of C′, we could say that *wh*-phrases can move only into empty phrase nodes that are marked [+wh]. Since empty Subjects at DS cannot have the feature [+wh], *wh*-phrases will be able to move only into specifier of C′ position. Thus it follows that once a phrase is in specifier of C′ position, the only place it can move to is another specifier of C′ position.

Given the proposal that *Wh*-Movement happens in short steps (as shown in 47–52) rather than in an unbounded fashion, we can make at least three predictions, the confirmation of which in turn confirms the proposal. First, we learned from 44 that movement from inside an NP to the specifier of C′ of the same clause is illicit (and results in ungrammaticality). From this we can predict that if we move from a specifier of C′ of a clause that is embedded inside an NP up to the specifier of the next higher C′, the result will be ungrammatical. Why? Because such a movement would be from inside an NP (the NP that contains the lower clause) to the specifier of C′ of the clause that contains that NP (the same illicit movement we have in 44). We say that the movement here would cross an NP node. Consider 53:

(53)   a. John heard [$_{NP}$ the rumor [that Sue met someone]].

       b. *Who did John hear [$_{NP}$ the rumor [[t] that Sue met t]]?

The movement from DO position of *met* into specifier of C′ of the lower clause is presumably grammatical. But Comp-to-Comp movement is blocked. Our first prediction is confirmed.

Strict Cyclicity

Second, part of our assumption above is that *Wh*-Movement must be into the specifier of the lowest C′ that contains the *wh*-phrase. We can then predict that if an embedded clause has an already-filled specifier of C′, *Wh*-Movement from inside the embedded clause to a position outside the embedded clause will be blocked. Consider:

(54)   Jack wonders [when [Mary saw someone]].

Here the embedded clause is an indirect question, so after *Wh*-Movement, the specifier of the embedded clause is filled with the *wh*-phrase *when*. If we wanted to question a second element of this embedded clause in a direct question, we would meet with an ungrammatical result:

(55)   *Who$_i$ does Jack wonder [when Mary saw t$_i$]?

(56)   *Who$_i$ does Jack wonder [when t$_i$ saw someone]?

Again, our prediction is confirmed.

    There is a serious problem with this account of 55 and 56, however. Notice that in 55 and 56, each specifier of a C′ is filled with only one *wh*-phrase at SS. So if we could find a way to arrive at the SSs in 55 and 56 without ever having a doubly filled specifier of C′ (often called a "doubly filled Comp" for short; you first met this concept in chapter 6), we might expect 55 and 56 to be grammatical. And there is a way to do this. First, let the *who* of 55 and 56 move, so that we have the intermediary structures:

(57)   Jack did wonder [[who$_i$] Mary saw t$_i$ when].

(58)   Jack did wonder [[who$_i$] t$_i$ saw someone when].

Now apply Comp-to-Comp movement:

(59)   Who$_i$ did Jack wonder [[t$_i$] Mary saw t$_i$ when].

(60)   Who$_i$ did Jack wonder [[t$_i$] t$_i$ saw someone when].

At this point the specifier of the C′ in the embedded clause is filled only with a trace. So if a lexical item can cover a trace (as in the classical analysis of *there*-sentences, outlined in Problem Set 7.5 of chapter 7), what is to prevent us from now applying *Wh*-Movement to the embedded *when* and moving it into the specifier position of the lower C'? If we did that, we would arrive at 55 and 56. So why are 55 and 56 ungrammatical?

Up to this point in this book we have never had the need to stipulate the ORDERING OF any RULES. For example, in a sentence such as:

(61) Jack seems to have been appreciated.

two rules have applied: Passive and Raising. In what order did they apply? It is easy to see that Passive applied on the lower clause before Raising applied to move *Jack* from Subject position of the lower clause to Subject position of the higher clause, because the NP *Jack* had to become the Subject of the lower clause before it could be raised. No other ordering of these two rules would result in 61. We did not have to stipulate that Passive preceded Raising here because there was no alternative.

But in order to account for the ungrammaticality of 55 and 56, we need to block the derivations outlined in 57–60. One way to do this is to make a stipulation about rule ordering.

(62) STRICT CYCLICITY: No rule may affect only the members of a given cycle once that cycle has already been passed.

The term CYCLE is new to you, although you encountered it above when I mentioned parenthetically that Comp-to-Comp Movement is a Successive Cyclic Movement. A cycle is a DOMAIN upon which rules operate. The Principle of Strict Cyclicity insures that all rules that affect only elements within a given rule-domain apply before rules that affect elements of a more inclusive rule-domain.

For example, if we were to say that the domain for *Wh*-Movement were C", then Strict Cyclicity would insure that all applications of *Wh*-Movement that operated within an embedded C" would take place before any applications of *Wh*-Movement that operated within a more inclusive (that is, a higher, containing) C". If we invoke Strict Cyclicity, we can rule out the derivations in 57–60. That is, the first *Wh*-Movement is grammatical. But Comp-to-Comp Movement cannot apply until after all applications of *Wh*-Movement have taken place on the lower C". Therefore *Wh*-Movement cannot apply to the intermediary structures in 59 and 60, and 55 and 56 cannot be generated, after all.

We will adopt the Principle of Strict Cyclicity. So we can maintain our original account of the ungrammaticality of 55 and 56 and conclude that our second prediction holds.

Notice that the presence of *that* in C in 63 does not block the movement of a *wh*-phrase. So contrast 63 to 55:

(63) Who$_i$ did Jack think [that Mary saw t$_i$]?

Why not? Contrasts such as 63 versus 55 give part of our motivation for analyzing *that* as being in C rather than in specifier of C' (as mentioned above, and as we will discuss further in chapter 9). Thus we never have the problem of a doubly filled specifier of C' in the derivation of 63.

You might notice, however, that the presence of *that* in C in 64 does result in ungrammaticality. Thus 64 seems to be like 56.

(64)   *Who$_i$ did Jack say [that t$_i$ did it]?
       (cf. Who$_i$ did Jack say [t$_i$ did it]?

However, the reason for the ungrammaticality of 64 is different from that respon-sible for the ungrammaticality of 56—a reason we will explore at length in chap-ter 9.

   We can therefore go ahead with the analysis of 55 and 56, adopting Strict Cyclic-ity and a restriction against a doubly filled specifier of C′ (the so-called Doubly Filled Comp Filter).

Movement from Within a Subject

Turning back now to our claim that *Wh*-Movement happens in short steps rather than in an unbounded fashion, we can see another prediction if we consider for a moment the nature of Subject positions in general. Be careful here. We will be led to conclude that certain nodes (N″ and I′) are intrinsically bounding nodes. But we will find reason to abandon this conclusion by the end of the section called Another Look at Subjacency.

   We argued in chapter 2 that Subject positions could be filled with phrases of any major category. However, in general, unless the verb is a copular verb or a Raising verb, its Subject position at SS is filled with an NP or a clause. Now consider the fact that [+tense] is a Case-Assigner. (Recall that we have identified the node I with [+ or − tense] in Tangent 8.1, where Agreement Phrase would be a sister to the I node. So everywhere we spoke of the feature of [+ or − Agr] in earlier chapters, we will now speak of the feature of [+ or − tense].) Whether all Vs, Ps, and Is are marked as being Case-Assigners or not (some Vs and Ps are optionally Case-Assign-ers), a reasonable assumption is that a Case-Assigner must assign its Case during PF. If this were so, a sentence like:

(65)   *Jack rescued.

would be ungrammatical not just because the subcategorization frame of the V requires a DO and the predicate-argument structure requires a theme argument, but also because in PF this verb needs to assign Objective Case but there is nothing to receive that Case.

   If this assumption were correct, we would expect that the Subject position of a clause whose I is [+tense] would have to be filled at PF with an element that can receive Case, but the Subject position of a clause whose I is [−tense] would not. In fact, that is so, as we already know:

(66)   You hoped [[Jack] had left].
       Who did you hope [[t] had left]?
       *You hoped [[PRO] had left].

(67)   You hoped for [[Jack] to leave].

(68)   You hoped [[PRO] to leave].

Looking at the Subject position of the embedded clauses only, we find that when I is [+tense], as in 66, a lexical NP and a *wh*-trace can fill Subject position, but PRO cannot. Both lexical NPs and *wh*-traces can receive Case, but PRO cannot. On the other hand, lexical NPs can fill the Subject position of a clause whose I is [−tense] if Exceptional Case-Marking is possible (as in 67, where *for* exceptionally governs and Case marks the Subject of the infinitival). But PRO can fill the Subject position of [−tense] clauses as well, because Exceptional Case-Marking need not apply (as in 68).

Let us follow where this assumption leads. Now if [+tense] must assign a Case and if NP is the only category that can receive Case, this means that the Subject position of clauses is an NP after all, in spite of the evidence to the contrary in chapter 2 and as you probably believed at the outset of chapter 2 before I led you away from that belief. In particular, this means that clauses that appear in the Subject position are dominated by NPs in some way that certainly looks at first glance to be problematic for X-Bar Theory. (But do not get involved in this issue, since we will eventually below abandon the claim that all Subjects must be NP.)

(69)

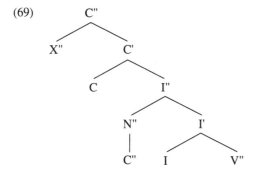

In 69 we have the tree for a sentence whose Subject is itself a clause. For example, 69 could be the tree for *That John met someone strikes you as odd.*

Since we know that movement into specifier of C′ from some position inside an NP is barred, as in 53 above, we now predict that *Wh*-Movement will be blocked out of Subjects. Again, the prediction holds. In 70 and 71 we see that movement is blocked out of sentential Subjects. In 72 and 73 we see that movement is blocked out of other NP Subjects.

(70)   [That John met someone] strikes you as odd.

(71)   *Who$_i$ does [that John met t$_i$] strike you as odd?
        (also:*Who$_i$ [that John met t$_i$] strikes you as odd?)

(72)   [Pictures of someone] strike you as odd.

(73)   *Who$_i$ do [pictures of t$_i$] strike you as odd?

We also predict, of course, that movement will be blocked out of what look like PP Subjects, and what look like AP Subjects. (Both the PP and the AP would be dominated by an NP if all Subjects are NPs.) However, we cannot test that prediction cleanly, since movement out of the sorts of PP and AP Subjects that arise is blocked even when these PPs and APs occur in non-Subject position:

(74)   [From Boston to someplace else] is quite far.
         *Where is [from Boston to t] quite far?

(75)   He went [from Boston to someplace else].
         ?*Where did he go [from Boston to t]?

We have strong evidence, then, that not just NP-movement (as in 31–34), but all movement is bounded. The question now is exactly how is movement bounded.

Bounding Nodes and Subjacency

We have noted that movement is allowed within clauses (as in passive and in simple—that is, single clause—questions). And we know further that movement is not limited to within a clause, because Passive can move a phrase from one clause to another (see 76) and Comp-to-Comp Movement is from one clause to another. But movement cannot move a phrase from one clause to two clauses higher in one fell swoop. Thus a clause is somehow a boundary for movement.

Furthermore, movement from one clause to an adjacent clause is not free. Passive can take a Subject and move it into Subject position of the next higher clause, as in the second example of 31, repeated here for convenience:

(76)   John$_i$ was said [[t$_i$] to be a fine fellow].

But *Wh*-Movement cannot take a Subject and move it into specifier of C′ of the next higher clause, witness the ungrammaticality of 56, repeated here:

(77)   *Who$_i$ does Jack wonder [when [t$_i$] saw someone]?

Notice that the difference in grammaticality between 76 and 77 cannot be attributed to any simple claim to the effect that traces cannot appear in Subject position of tensed clauses, since we get fine questions like:

(78)   Who$_i$ did Jack say [[t$_i$] left]?

So the problem is that movement is somehow not observing the proper bounding restrictions in 77, but it is in 76. Why? What are the proper bounding restrictions?

Certainly if a clause is somehow a BOUNDING NODE for movement, we must admit that movement can cross a bounding node. But why does movement across the embedded clause's bounding node result in grammaticality in 76 but not in 77?

We need to look at where the moved phrase ends up. In 76 the moved phrase ends up inside the thematic part of the clause, that is, inside I″, in Subject position. By "the thematic part of the clause" I mean that part within which all theta-roles and all functions of modification and predication take place. (That we could talk about Complete Functional Complexes way back in chapter 3, long before we recognized the existence of a C node and its projections, is suggestive that the thematic part of the clause is all within the I″ [the minimal node that contains Subject position as well as the V″—what we originally called S and what you will often find referred to in the literature as S].) But in 77 the moved phrase ends up outside the thematic part of the clause—that is, outside I″—in the specifier of C′.

Movement in 76, then, is from inside one I″ to inside the next I″ up the tree, as follows.

(79) $[_{C''}[_{I'}John_i$ was said $[_{C''}[_{I'}$ t_i to be a fine fellow]]]].

But movement in 77 is from inside I″ to outside the next I″ up the tree. So in 77 movement crosses two I″ nodes, as follows:

(80) $[_{C''}[who_i]$ does $[_{I'}$Jack wonder $[_{C''}$ when $[_{I'}[t_i]$ saw someone]]]]?
                                        —X—

In 78, on the other hand, there are two *Wh*-Movements. The first is from Subject position of the embedded clause into specifier of C′ of the embedded clause. The second is from Comp to Comp, as follows:

(81) $[_{C''}[who_i]$ did $[_{I'}$Jack say $[_{C''}[t_i]$ $[_{I'}t_i$ left]]]]?

The first movement is across the embedded I″. The second movement is across the matrix I″. But each movement is across only one I″.

Let us propose that the bounding node for clauses is I″ for English (which means, of course, T″). We have also recognized that N″ is a bounding node. We can now state a first approximation of a principle restricting movement:

(82)   THE SUBJACENCY PRINCIPLE: Movement can be across at most one bounding node, where the bounding nodes for English are I″ and N″.

We have appealed to the Subjacency Principle to account for the impossibility of *Wh*-Movement in sentences like 53b, 55, 71, and 73, repeated here for convenience:

(83)   *Who$_i$ did $[_{N''}$John hear $[_{N''}$the rumor that $[_{I'}$Sue met t$_i$]]]?

(84)   *Who$_i$ does $[_{I'}$Jack wonder when $[_{I'}$Mary saw t$_i$]]?

(85)   *Who$_i$ does $[_{I'}$ $[_{C''}$ that $[_{I'}$John met t$_i$]]$ strike you as odd]?

(86)   *Who$_i$ do $[_{I'}$ $[_{N''}$ pictures of t$_i$]$ strike you as odd]?

Island Constraints

We are going to settle on a version of the Subjacency Principle (though not the version in 82) as our final account of how movement is bounded, but it is important for us to step back for a moment and take a look at the history of some of the issues we have been addressing.

There are, historically, alternative explanations for all the examples in 83–86.

For 83, the most-well-known explanation is called the COMPLEX-NOUN-PHRASE CONSTRAINT (CNPC). According to the CNPC, movement is blocked from a complex NP where a complex NP is any NP with the structure:

(87)

In 83 the CNP is headed by the N *rumor*. (Actually, 87 is not a well-formed DS with our restictive notion of X-Bar Theory, since the NP immediately dominates NP. Thus a complex NP in our theory would have to be defined as an NP that contains a clause, where no phrasal node intervenes between the clause and the NP. That leaves unspecified whether the clause is attached as a sister to N, N', or N". The two types of clauses that are potential candidates for appearing inside NP like this are relative clauses [and you might look back at Problem Set 6.1 of chapter 6 to see where we attached them] and appositive clauses. [See Problem Set 6.5 of chapter 6.] [You will see an additional problem with 87 as an analysis of heads and relative clauses in Problem Set 9.2 of chapter 9.])

Besides this constraint, there was the SENTENTIAL SUBJECT CONSTRAINT (SSC), which blocked movement from a sentential Subject and would therefore account for the ungrammaticality of 85.

And among the original constraints to be proposed was the COORDINATE STRUC-TURE CONSTRAINT (CSC), which blocked movement from a coordinate structure, as in:

(88)   Mary likes [Paul and someone].
        *Who does Mary like [Paul and t]?

        Mary likes [someone and Paul].
        *Who does Mary like [t and Paul]?

        Mary [writes poems and sings madrigals].
        *What does Mary write and sing madrigals?
        *What does Mary write poems and sing?

This constraint was not demonstrated in any of our earlier examples.

Complex NPs, sentential Subjects, and coordinate structures were dubbed ISLANDS, since movement off them was disallowed. And these constraints came to be known as the ISLAND CONSTRAINTS.

Three additional structures were identified as being islands: the WH-ISLAND, which would be exemplified in 84 (the *when*-clause is a *wh*-island), all Subjects (people spoke of a SUBJECT CONDITION that blocked movement out of all Subjects), which would be exemplified in 86 (as well as in 85), and the ADVERBIAL-CLAUSE ISLAND, exemplified in:

(89)   Mary left [after Bill saw someone].
        *Who did Mary leave [after Bill saw t]?

(Recall that by "adverbial" we mean a phrase of any category that modifies a non-nominal. So the bracketed phrases in 89 are adverbials. If you are having no trouble following the text, you may want to turn now to Tangent 8.3 before continuing with the main text narrative. However, if you still feel a bit overwhelmed, you can hold off on reading this tangent until you have completed the entire text narrative.)

Today island contraints are still talked about, but usually as a shorthand for identifying a specific type or instance of some other principle or interaction of principles in the grammar. Thus, even though you might read a reference to *wh*-islands, for example, 84 would be accounted for in GB with the Subjacency Principle (or, as more typically stated, with Subjacency).

Notice that while Subjacency accounts for the CNPC, the SSC, the Subject Condition, and the *wh*-islands, it cannot account for the ungrammaticality of movement out of coordinate structures and out of adverbial clauses. Thus Subjacency is an improvement over the earlier approach of individual constraints and conditions because it captures a generalization that the earlier approach missed. But we still would like to see a motivated account for the islandhood of coordinate structures and of adverbial clauses (and of phrases like those in 74 and 75; see Star Problem 8.8).

Another Look at Subjacency

Consider once again the nature of Subjacency. We are dealing here with the notion that certain types of phrasal nodes make movement of material inside them to a position outside them difficult. That is, they act as barriers to movement somehow. Look back over the examples of acceptable *Wh*-Movement in this chapter and contrast them to the examples of unacceptable *Wh*-Movement.

Consider first movement from (or EXTRACTION from) clauses. There are essentially only four types of embedded clauses: those that are sentential Subjects of the next higher clause (***That John left*** *doesn't surprise me*); those that are sentential Objects of the next higher clause (*I thought* ***that John would leave***); those that are adverbial (modifying a non-nominal) (*John left* ***while his father was still asleep***); and those that are inside a complex NP (which turn out to be either relative clauses or, possibly, appositive clauses [but see Problem Set 6.5]) (*The remarks* ***that John made*** *didn't please anyone*).

You might object to this claim, since you have seen clauses which are Objects of Ps. Many of those clauses are adverbial in function, as with the *after* clause in 89 above. The only other ones are Objects of *for* or of some other P that is chosen by the V to introduce an argument of the V. Let us consider *for* first.

The *for* that introduces infinitivals seems to be present to allow Case marking of the Subject of the infinitival. These constructions occur both when the nonfinite clause is filling the thematic role that is assigned typically to the Subject of a V and when it is filling the thematic role that is typically assigned to the Object of a V. Extraction is possible in the latter case.

(90)   a.   For [Bill to leave Susan] would upset you.
            (cf. *[Bill to leave Susan] would upset you.)
            *Who would [for Bill to leave t] upset you?

b.   You wanted very much for [Bill to leave Susan].
     (cf. *You wanted very much [Bill to leave Susan].
     and *You wanted for [Bill to leave Susan].
     You wanted [Bill to leave Susan].)
     Who did you want very much for Bill to leave?

In 90a *Bill* could not get Case if *for* were missing, since the matrix I(NFL) does not have the ability to exceptionally govern. In 90b *Bill* could not get Case if *for* were missing, since Structural Case Assignment requires the NP to be immediately adjacent to the Case-Assigner (here, the V).

The remaining cases are clauses that are Objects of Ps that are selected by Vs to introduce arguments of the V, such as the Acc-*ing* clause that follows *on* in a sentence like 91. Again, extraction is possible in these instances:

(91)   I depend on [Susan finishing the job].
       What do you depend on [Susan finishing t]?

The generalization that emerges, then, is that we can extract from DOs (and certain OPs), but not from sentential Subjects, adverbial clauses, or clauses inside complex NPs.

Now consider extraction from NPs. We know that we cannot extract from a Subject NP (as we saw with 73 above, in which this sort of example was the original motivation for the so-called Subject Condition). And we saw earlier with 41–44 that extraction from Object NPs ranged from being slightly marginal to being quite unacceptable. Let me repeat those examples here:

(92)   Bill met [friends of someone you know] yesterday.
       ??Who did Bill meet [friends of t] yesterday?

       Bill met [those old friends of someone you know] yesterday.
       *Who did Bill meet [those old friends of t] yesterday?

However, there are other examples in which extraction from Object NPs is, in fact, perfectly acceptable. In fact, we can even get extraction from inside an OP if the OP is an argument of the predicate (such as the Object of *at* in a sentence with the predicate *look at*—but see Star Problem 8.9):

(93)   Bill bought [photos of someone].
       Who did Bill buy [photos of t]?

       You were looking at [pictures of someone].
       Who were you looking at [pictures of t]?

       You bought [a carton of something expensive].
       What did you buy [a carton of t]?

       Bill read [a news report about something].
       What did Bill read [a news report about t]?

       Bill gave [a lecture on something].
       What did Bill give [a lecture on t]?

We need to find an account of the difference in acceptability between 92 on the one hand, and 93 on the other, and you are asked to do just that in Star Problem 8.4 below. For now let us make the assumption that 93 illustrates the ordinary case, whereas 92 illustrates a complication. (This assumption will allow us to reach a generalization below, as you will see.) So extraction from Object NPs (and from certain OPs) is allowed.

What about extraction from NPs in positions other than Subject or DO? Can we extract from an NP that is an OP where the PP is a modifier (so that the OP is not an argument of the predicate)?

(94)   You went [p''with [N''a friend of someone]].
        *Who did you go [with [a friend of t]]?

        You left [p''after [N''the debate about someone]].
        *Who did you leave [after [the debate about t]]?

Extraction is blocked in these instances.

We now find that we must revise our initial conclusions. NP is not, after all, intrinsically a bounding node. Instead, in the examples given, an NP that is in any position other than DO (or sometimes OP) is a bounding node and only sometimes is an NP in DO position a bounding node. Likewise, I″ is not, after all, intrinsically a bounding node. Instead, an I″ that is in any position other than DO (or sometimes OP) is a bounding node.

L-Marking, Blocking Categories, Barriers, and a New Idea of Subjacency

In sum, extraction from inside a phrase that plays any role other than DO (and sometimes OP) is generally unacceptable. Why? What is special about DOs (and about certain OPs)? Of all the GFs in a sentence, the one that is almost assuredly going to carry a theta-role is DO. And now we can see the tie-in of the little addendum we have been putting on all our generalizations to the effect that certain OPs behave like DOs: The certain OPs are precisely those that are arguments of the predicate. So extraction is allowed out of arguments of the predicate that are located inside the VP.

Let us now formalize the restrictions we have discovered on extraction in this chapter.

First, we define the notion of L-MARKING (for "lexical-marking") as follows:

(95)   A predicate L-Marks its arguments that fall within the minimal phrase that contains the predicate.

(Please note: the definition in 95 is consistent with our notion that predicates need not be single nodes. Thus we allow a string like *look at* or *depend on* to be a predicate. And by 95, they would L-mark all their arguments within the VP. However, the more conventional notion of predicate takes it to be a single node and the more

conventional definition of L-marking says that a predicate L-marks its sister arguments. With that definition, the special OPs we noted repeatedly above are problematic for the account of extraction presented below (and call for a Reanalysis
Rule of the type we argued against in chapter 7 and will argue against further in
chapter 10). But with our definition, these OPs are not problematic.)

We can now define the notion of BLOCKING CATEGORY (BC) as in:

(96)   A is a BC for B iff A is not L-marked by a primary predicate and A dom-
       inates B, where A is phrasal.

(You will find in Star Problem 8.5 some of the issues that led to my defining BC in
terms of L-marking by a primary predicate instead of by any predicate.) So any
phrasal node that is not both an argument of a primary predicate and located inside
the VP is a BC to all the nodes it dominates. We can now formally define the notion
of barrier as in:

(97)   A is a barrier for B iff A is phrasal and:
           (a) A immediately dominates C, where C is a BC for B,
       or (b) A is a BC for B and A does not equal I″.

By (a) we see that a phrasal node A immediately dominating a BC for a node B
becomes a barrier for B. By (b) we see that all BCs are themselves barriers except
I″. In other words, I″ can be a barrier for a node B only if it immediately dominates
a BC of B (that is, only via [a] of 97). The two structures for barriers then are shown
in 98. (A is the barrier for B in both structures.)

(98)   a.   A   b.   A   (=BC for B and ≠ I″)

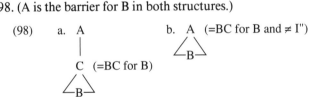

(The triangles in 98 are to be interpreted as showing that B is dominated by the node
above it, but not necessarily immediately dominated by that node.) We say that
barriers defined by (a) in 97 (schematized in 98a) INHERIT BARRIERHOOD (since the
BC below them allows them to become barriers).

A phrase of any category that has the GF of Subject, then, is a BC to all the elements contained in that Subject. That is because a Subject is never L-marked (since
it does not fall inside the VP). Since a Subject is also never I″ (and recall that sentential Subjects will be C″, not bare I″), every Subject node will be a barrier to all
the elements contained inside it.

(99)   C″

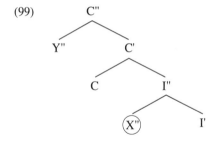

In 99, X'' is a Subject, and it is a BC and a barrier to all the elements it dominates.

A phrase of any category that functions as a modifier (adverbial modifier or relative-clause modifier) or as an appositive is, likewise, a BC to all the elements contained in that phrase. This is because modifiers and appositives are not arguments, so they cannot be L-marked. Again, modifiers and appositives will never be bare I'' (although they can be C''), so every modifier and appositive will be a barrier to everything contained within it.

Finally, only phrases that function as DOs or as OPs where the OP is an argument of the V (that is, L-Marked phrases) are not going to be BCs to the elements contained within them. These phrases will also not be barriers to the elements contained within them.

We can now think about Subjacency in a more intuitive way. The basic idea is:

(100)   Subjacency Principle: Movement that crosses at most one barrier is allowed. But movement becomes more difficult as more barriers are crossed.

This is similar to our original idea but different in important ways.

Our original notion of Subjacency (in 82 above) relied on the specialness of the categories N'' and I''. But the new notion that depends on barriers (in 100) sees nothing special about N'' and I'' (other than the unrelated fact that I'' cannot be a barrier except by inheritance). So all phrasal nodes are potential barriers.

Furthermore, the original notion of Subjacency saw N'' and I'' as being intrinsically special. But the barriers notion of Subjacency recognizes that no category and no particular node are intrinsically a barrier. Instead, different nodes will have different barriers. Thus an N'' in Subject position will be a barrier only with respect to the elements within it, and the I'' that immediately dominates that N'' will be a barrier only with respect to the elements within the Subject N''. That same I'' will not be a barrier to elements within the V'' of its clause. So our new notion of Subjacency is relative. That makes it conceptually more difficult, perhaps, but, as we will see below, better able to handle the complex data that arise.

There is an important qualification to Subjacency that we must make before we continue. So far our discussion has been in line with general GB literature. However, if you try to apply the Subjacency Principle in 100, you will meet one big, recurring question: how do the various levels of the verbal phrase fit into this schema. Are Tense Phrase, Agreement Phrase, Auxiliary Phrase, and Verb Phrase blocking categories and, hence, barriers? If they were, then no movement of any phrase out of VP should be acceptable, since that movement would cross at least two barriers (in fact, three: TP, AgrP, and at least one of AuxP or VP) in every clause. Yet movement out of VP is often possible.

If we want to preserve the concept of Subjacency given in 100, not all these verbal phrases can count as barriers for movement of a phrase from within a VP. But are these verbal phrases L-marked? Certainly it would be odd to think of any of these as receiving a theta-role from some head that takes them as arguments. Yet there is another sense in which each of them is chosen by the head of the next higher phrase. For example, an auxiliary chooses either another auxiliary phrase or a VP as its complement—and that is part of the lexical information we have about each auxiliary. We could claim, then, that this lexical selection keeps at least some of these verbal phrases from being BCs and, hence, from being barriers.

Alternatively, we could accept all these verbal phrases as BCs (and barriers) and then look for another way around the problem. We might try to say that instead of a single long movement taking place from within VP to the specifier of C′ position (as in an instance of *wh*-movement), a series of shorter movements takes place, where each short movement crosses only one barrier. For example, a phrase might move out of VP and adjoin to the left of VP as its sister. Then it might move from that position upward, and adjoin to the left of AuxP as its sister. And so on. This is a trivial way out of the problem. It is also a dangerous way, in that we now need to explain why this sort of small-jump adjunction process cannot take place to allow movement of any phrase out of any set of barriers. This kind of approach threatens to rob Subjacency of any predictive value.

Another alternative, and the one that we will opt for here, is to break down the verbal phrases into two types. The nonlexical verbal phrases, TP and AgrP, we will admit as BCs, but we will not allow them to become barriers except by inheritance. This is entirely in line with the definition of *barrier* in 97, since there we noted that I″ cannot become a barrier except by inheritance—and I″ is the conflation of TP and AgrP. The lexical verbal phrases, AuxP and VP, on the other hand, we will admit both as potential BCs and as potential barriers. However, if a clause has an AuxP, we will assume that the Aux L-marks its verbal phrase sister, so that only the AuxP but not the complement of the Aux will be a BC. Accordingly, in any given clause only the highest lexical verbal phrase will be a barrier to the phrases within it.

If you are not satisfied with this conclusion, that is fine. The more extraction sentences you analyze, the more problems you will find for this concept of Subjacency. Please consider 100 as a working definition and keep your mind open to revisions (which are constantly being offered in the linguistic literature). For now, however, let us adopt this approach and continue our discussion.

Let us look back at 83–86 above—the examples that we accounted for with our original formulation of Subjacency:

(101)   *$[_{C''}$Who$_i$ did $[_{I'}$John hear $[_{N''}$the rumor $[_{C''}$ that $[_{I'}$Sue met t$_i$]]]]]?

(102)   *$[_{C''}$Who$_i$ does $[_{I'}$Jack wonder $[_{C''}$when $[_{I'}$Mary saw t$_i$]]]]?

(103)   *$[_{C''}$Who$_i$ does $[_{I'}$ $[_{C''}$ that $[_{I'}$John met t$_i$]]$ strike you as odd]]?

(104)   *$[_{C''}$Who$_i$ do $[_{I'}$ $[_{N''}$ pictures of t$_i$]$ strike you as odd]]?

In all of these examples at least two barriers are crossed.

In 101 the offending movement is from specifier of C′ of the embedded clause to specifier of C′ of the matrix clause. (Note that the initial movement of the DO into the specifier of C′ of the embedded clause crosses only one barrier, the V″.) The barriers crossed are the C″ of the embedded clause (which is not L-Marked since it is not an argument of the head N *rumor*), and the matrix V″. In 105 we see this, where both movements are indicated and all barriers are labeled. The movement that crosses two barriers is indicated with an X and those barriers are circled.

(105) *Who did John [$_{V''}$ hear the rumor [$_{C''}$ t that Sue [$_{V''}$ met t]]]?

In 102 the offending movement is from DO position of *saw* to specifier of C′ of the matrix clause. The barriers crossed are the embedded V″ and the matrix V″. In 106 we see this.

(106) *Who does Jack [$_{V''}$ wonder [$_{C''}$ when Mary [$_{V''}$ saw t]]]?

Here the embedded C″ (which begins with the word *when*) is not a barrier since it is L-Marked. But the embedded V″ is a barrier since it is not L-Marked, it dominates the trace, and it is not I″. (Please note that Subjacency is not the only way to account for *wh*-islands. We will not consider other accounts in this book, but in the references for this chapter you can find other accounts.)

In 103 the offending movement is from specifier of C′ of the sentential Subject to specifier of C′ of the matrix clause. (Note that once more the initial movement from DO position to specifier of C′ of the sentential Subject is across only one barrier, the embedded clause's V″.) The barriers crossed are the C″ of the embedded clause (which is an argument of the primary predicate, but is not located inside the VP, so it is not L-Marked) and the I″ of the matrix clause (which becomes a barrier via inheritance, since it immediately dominates the embedded C″.

(107) *Who does [$_{I''}$ [$_{C''}$ t that John [$_{V''}$ met t] strike you as odd]]?

In 104 the offending movement is from OP to specifier of C′. The barriers crossed are the Subject NP and the I″ (which, again, is a barrier by inheritance since it immediately dominates the Subject N″, which is a BC—as well as a barrier—for anything within it).

(108) *Who do [$_{I''}$ [$_{N''}$ pictures of t] strike you as odd]?

So our new notion of Subjacency handles all the data that our original notion handled. It also has the advantage that we do not have to assume that all Subjects are dominated by NP, after all—a welcome result given our discussion in chapter 2. Furthermore, Subjacency can now account for adverbial islands, as in 89 above, repeated here.

(109) Mary left after Bill saw someone.

    *Who did Mary [$_{V''}$ leave after [$_{C''}$ t Bill [$_{V''}$ saw t]]]?

(For evidence that the adverbial clause is inside the V″ in sentences like 109, see Problem Set 8.4.) The offending movement is from specifier of C′ of the adverbial clause to specifier of C′ of the matrix clause. (Note that the initial movement from DO position to specifier of C′ of the adverbial clause is across only one barrier, the embedded V″.) The barriers crossed are the C″ of the adverbial clause (since this clause is not an argument of its sister predicate *left*) and the V″ of the matrix clause.

Our new notion of Subjacency can also help to account for the behavior of *Wh*-Movement out of nonargument PPs (as in 94 above), although we still have some unanswered questions here. Compare:

(110)   You [$_{V''}$went [$_{P''}$with someone]].
        Who did you [$_{V''}$go [$_{P''}$ with t]]?

(111)   You [$_{V''}$went [$_{P''}$with [$_{N''}$a friend [$_{P''}$of someone]]]].
        *Who did you [$_{V''}$go [$_{P''}$with [$_{N''}$a friend [$_{P''}$of t]]]]?

In 110 the movement is from Object of *with* to specifier of C′. The PP node is a barrier (since this PP is not L-Marked by *went*), dominates trace, and is not I″. Likewise the V″ is a barrier. However, for some reason, movement across these two barriers is acceptable. But in 111 the offending movement is from Object of the P *of* to specifier of C′. Neither P″ is L-Marked, nor is the N″ headed by *a friend* L-Marked (since *with* does not assign a theta-role, as you learned in Problem Set 3.4). Thus four barriers are crossed, and the result is ungrammatical. While we would not have expected full acceptability in 110, at least the fact that 111 is worse than 110 is expected.

And, actually, there is an analysis of 110 that will allow the movement to be across only one barrier: the P″. It has been proposed that nonargument PPs, like the *with*-phrase in 110 and 111, can be extracted out of V″ so that they are attached directly under I″. If we accepted this analysis, then the tree for 110 before movement would be as:

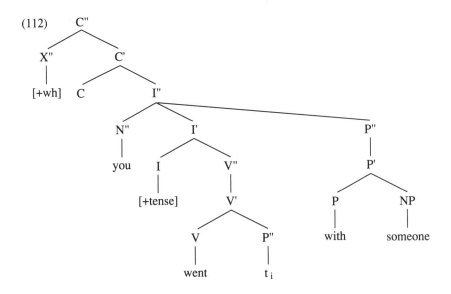

Now the P″ that is immediately under I″ (which is co-indexed with the trace) is a barrier for the OP, but it is the only barrier for the OP. Thus *Wh*-Movement of this OP into specifier of C′ results in grammaticality. In contrast, if we were to extract the *with*-phrase in 111 from the V″ and attach it immediately under I″, movement would still be across multiple barriers (the P″ headed by *of*, the N″ headed by *friend*, and the P″ headed by *with*), so it would still result in ungrammaticality.

We will not try to find independent motivation for the analysis in 112. The point is that with the proper analysis, it may be quite possible to account for the difference between 110 and 111 with Subjacency.

We cannot, however, use Subjacency to account for examples that motivated the Coordinate Structure Constraint (as in 88). That is because CSs are islands regardless of what GF or other function they may play. It is quite probable that a parallelism requirement on coordination is responsible for the unacceptability of extraction from CSs. That is, movement from only one conjunct of a conjunction, for example, would result in conjuncts that were not parallel: one would contain a trace and the other would not. In support of the idea that a parallelism requirement holds on conjunction (and other types of coordination) we can notice that if both conjuncts contain a trace, the result is grammatical:

(113)   What does Jack write and edit?

Example 113 is an instance of an ACROSS-THE-BOARD PHENOMENON (that is, the same effect is exhibited in all members of the coordinate structure). You can explore ways to account for 113 in Star Problem 8.2.

Wh-Trace and a Typology of NPs

We now have an excellent idea of how *Wh*-Movement proceeds. But we have yet to take a serious look at *wh*-trace. Does *wh*-trace have all the properties that NP-trace has? First, is *wh*-trace always bound within its governing category? No. Consider:

(114)   [c″ Who did [ı″ Mary see [t]]]?

The *wh*-phrase that binds the trace in 114 is outside the I″ which is the governing category of the trace.

Will a *wh*-trace ever be bound within its governing category? No. *Wh*-Movement is always to specifier of C′ position. So it is never within an I″ or N″. Therefore no *wh*-trace will ever be bound within its governing category.

In sum, *wh*-trace is not an anaphor.

Is *wh*-trace a pronominal or an R-expression? Given what we have said about Binding Theory thus far, you will undoubtedly say that *wh*-trace cannot be an R-expression, since R-expressions must be free everywhere, and *wh*-trace is always bound. You would be led, then, to conclude that *wh*-trace must be pronominal. However, it is troubling to think of *wh*-trace as being pronominal since in all the other instances we have examined thus far, pronominals were either free or bound (but not within their governing category) by some phrase that had an independent theta-role. *Wh*-trace is never free and the binder never has an independent theta-role.

So it is time for us to refine Binding Theory in order to accommodate *wh*-traces.

If we exclude all structures that involve *Wh*-Movement and look back at every other instance in this book in which we discussed binding, we will find that the binder was in a position that arguments can be generated in at DS. But for *wh*-trace, the binder is always in specifier of C', and no arguments can be generated in specifier of C' at DS. If we think then in terms of binding from an A-POSITION (a potential argument position at DS) versus binding from an A'-POSITION (A' means nonargument), we can say that our Binding Theory up to this point has really been limited to A-BINDING. In other words, anaphors must be A-BOUND within their governing categories; pronominals must be A-free within their governing categories; and R-expressions must be A-free everywhere. But now we can see that *wh*-trace could well be classified as an R-expression because it is always A-free.

Certainly, however, if *wh*-traces are R-expressions, they are special among R-expressions in that they are always A'-BOUND (that is, bound by something in a non-A position). *Wh*-traces have been called VARIABLES, where the very definition of a variable is something bound by a non-A-position. Variables must be bound; otherwise they would fail to receive an interpretation. That is, only through binding by some sort of OPERATOR can we assign an interpretation to a variable. The claim, then, is that *wh*-phrases are, in essence, operators. This whole discussion may be elusive to you, since you may not have even a vague sense of what an operator in language is. Do not worry about it right now. We will talk more about variables and operators in chapter 9.

We can now organize referring categories in the following way. Let us assume there is a feature of [+anaphor] or [−anaphor] and another feature of [+pronominal] or [−pronominal] and that all referring categories can be classified by using only these features.

There are, then, four logically possible types of referring categories. One has the feature bundle [+anaphor, −pronominal]. In this group fall all the anaphors, including those with a phonetic matrix (such as reflexives and reciprocals [as you argued in Problem Set 7.10]), as well as NP-trace.

Another group has the feature bundle [−anaphor, +pronominal]. In this group fall all the pronouns with a phonetic matrix, as well as pro of many languages other than English (including several Romance languages, and you can explore questions regarding pro in Problem Set 8.6).

A third group has the feature bundle [+anaphor, +pronominal]. This group consists of only those elements that have no governing category. There are two ways in which an element could fail to have a governing category: it could lack a governor, or it could lack an accessible SUBJECT (or both). If it lacked a governor, it could never get Case. Therefore, it could never have a phonetic matrix (since an N″ with a phonetic matrix must receive Case). We have not yet discussed in detail what it means to have or lack an accessible Subject. (That discussion awaits us in chapter 9.) So for now we must leave aside discussion of items which do have a governor but do not have an accessible SUBJECT. Given our knowledge thus far, then, we expect that only elements that lack a phonetic matrix could fall into this group. And, in fact, PRO is the only element we have placed in this group.

The final group has the feature bundle [−anaphor, −pronominal]. These are the

R-expressions. Those that have a phonetic matrix are known as referring expressions. Those that lack a phonetic matrix are variables, including *wh*-trace.

Chapter Results

In this chapter we learned that *Wh*-Movement is of an X″ into specifier of C′ position. That movement, and all movement, is bounded, and the barriers for movement are defined relative to the constituent being moved.

This conclusion has many consequences for your understanding of the grammar. For example, you discovered in Problem Set 6.5 that Extraposition, if it is indeed the product of a movement rule, moves a clause to the end of the next higher clause, but no higher. You can now account for the bounded nature of this movement rule with Subjacency. I invite you to go through the account for yourself.

Our focus in this chapter has been on *Wh*-Movement, specifically, questions. It has been claimed that *Wh*-Movement applies also in relative clauses; Topicalization structures (although this has certainly been challenged); comparatives; infinitival complements of *enough*; infinitival complements of *good, hard, difficult*, etc. (the so-called *tough*-construction that we saw in chapter 7), and other structures. If this were so, the term "*Wh*-Movement" would be a misnomer, in that not just *wh*-phrases, but all sorts of phrases, would undergo this movement rule. An investigation of all the structures for which *Wh*-Movement has been proposed is beyond the scope of this book. However, you should keep this claim in mind as you finish reading this book, and a good exercise would be to pick just one of these constructions and test whether it has the characteristics of *Wh*-Movement structures.

You are already quite familiar with one structure that has been claimed to involve *Wh*-Movement: clefts. Assuming that claim is correct, you can now see why clefting can be used as a test for phrasal nodes (that is, for X″, as opposed to X or X″): *Wh*-Movement is of phrasal nodes only.

In the introduction to this book I promised that we would not follow dogma, but instead question our approach at each step. At this point you may feel like we have strayed from that original goal quite a bit. Indeed, raising many alternatives at the outset of the study of syntax is easy because we have no background that is affected by these alternatives. However, the more constructions and theoretical issues we have studied, the more raising a new alternative means going back over a larger and larger background to test the consequences of each alternative for our entire picture of the grammar at that point. To truly follow all the ramifications of alternatives this book would have to grow in length dramatically. This may be a poor excuse for not following alternatives, but it is a genuine one.

However, there are some alternatives that we simply must consider. One is a nonmovement analysis of *wh*-structures. You will be asked to perform such an analysis in Problem Set 8.13.

There is certainly much more that could be said about all the issues raised in this chapter. In fact, many of the issues touched on here are at the forefront of linguistic inquiry and are, not surprisingly, points of heated debate. Since you are now prepared to enter that debate on your own, we will spend our time together on the new issues raised in the final two chapters.

Tangent 8.1: Verb Movement and Auxiliaries

In English, only tensed verbs exhibit agreement, and all verbs that exhibit agreement are tensed. This is not true in all languages, however, as we know from our study of European Portuguese (as in Problem Set 5.3). Thus the features of tense and agreement, which are often easily distinguished from one another in the verbal morphology of different languages, though not in English, are, in fact, two independent sets of features. Agr and T(ense), then, are functional categories which should each head their own phrases.

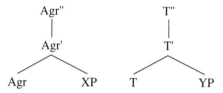

The question of whether T″ is embedded inside Agr″ or Agr″ is embedded inside T″ is to be answered by empirical considerations.

In Italian and related languages, there is evidence that the structure of a verbal phrase is as shown in the following example, which uses the verbal phrase *mangiava la pizza* 'was eating the pizza.'

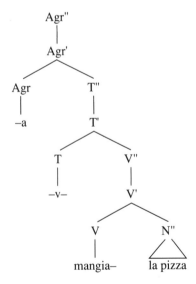

(In this tree the Agr morpheme *-a* indicates third-person singular and the T morpheme *-v-* indicates the imperfective.) The verb needs to pick up the tense and agreement morphemes above it in the tree. Let us assume here that this process takes place in the syntax. We will discuss in chapter 9 a principle that has the effect of blocking syntactic (and semantic) movement downward in trees. On the basis of that principle, we can take the position that the tense and agreement morphemes cannot move downward onto the verb in Italian. The only alternative, then, is that the V moves upward, from a head position to the next available head position, twice; first, as in the left side of the following tree and then as shown on the right side of the tree.

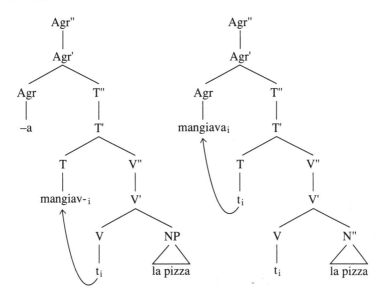

The movement of the V into T and then into Agr is called VERB MOVEMENT. It is a particular kind of HEAD MOVEMENT (since a head is moving). It has been proposed that all head movement is restricted in the following way:

> HEAD MOVEMENT CONSTRAINT: A head X can move into a head slot Y only if Y governs X″. (If Y is not Comp, then Y must also theta-mark or L-Mark X″.)

The part of the constraint that is in parentheses is largely uninterpretable to you at this point. We will learn about Comp and L-Marking later in this chapter. You can come back to this constraint at the end of reading the whole chapter. At that point you will realize that if the Head Movement Constraint is correct, then we must assume that both Agr and T L-Mark their complements. This is not intuitively obvious and I find this assumption one of the more questionable points in this constraint.

We can see from this analysis of the Italian verbal string above that the order of the morphemes in the final verb form (*mangia-v-a*) reflects the syntactic derivation; the morpheme that was lower in the tree is closer to the verb stem and the morpheme that was higher in the tree follows the morpheme that was lower. The principle at work here, what you might think of informally as the first-in-last-out principle, is called the MIRROR PRINCIPLE.

In English the T and Agr morphemes are not distinguishable from one another. Thus we cannot use a transparent morphology to figure out syntactic derivation. However, it has been argued on the basis of the placement of negatives and adverbs that in English, T″ is higher in the tree than Agr″. (You will have a chance in Problem Set 8.16 to consider questions of adverb placement in Italian. You can ask yourself at that time about the comparable issues in English.) So let us analyze a verbal phrase in a sentence such as *Mike [ate the pizza]*, as in:

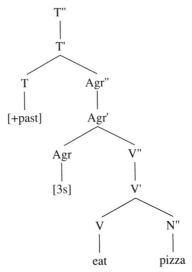

In both tree and labeled-bracket analyses we often find the node I rather than the nodes T and Agr when the details of the functional part of the verbal hierarchy of the tree are not of particular interest. We can think of I(NFL) as being a shorthand for T and Agr together.

Recall that in chapter 5 we noted that with respect to English, we could have flipped a coin to decide whether to indicate I as to tense or as to agreement features. It was the consideration of Portuguese that led us to choose agreement features. But now it appears that if we are going to conflate T and Agr together under the node I, for English it might be a better choice to indicate tense features (that is, the features of the higher funtional node) rather than agreement features of I. Notice that Portuguese is like Italian in having a transparent verb morphology. And this verb morphology indicates that in Portuguese Agr″ is higher in the tree than T. So for Portuguese (and Italian and Romance in general), it may make more sense to indicate agreement rather than tense features on I. From here on, I will feel free to indicate the features of I as agreement features or as tense features, making the choice on a variety of grounds, some of which are not always linguistic. In particular, in chapter 9 we will repeatedly use agreement features when talking about I because this will bring the discussion in line with the past literature on the topics discussed there.

Regardless of whether T or Agr is the higher node, we can identify Subject as the specifier of the higher node. So when we conflate the two, our already developed idea of Subject as the specifier of I′ can remain unchanged.

In English, unlike in Italian, lexical verbs cannot undergo Verb Movement. Why this is so is a complex matter and the topic of recent inquiry. For us right now, what matters is that lexical verbs in English never behave as though they have undergone Verb Movement into the T (or I) slot. (For example, they cannot undergo so-called Subject-Auxiliary Inversion:

*Sings Mary?

After you have read the analysis of Subject-Auxiliary Inversion in the text that follows in this chapter, you should come back and reread this paragraph.) That means that the tense and agreement morphemes must move downward onto the verb stem in English. We already said above that we will consider a principle in chapter 9 that should block downward syntactic movement. Accordingly, either English affix movement is an exception to this principle, or the principle is wrong, or affix movement is not part of the syntax proper (and, so, is not subject to principles of the syntax). We will not try to determine which of these three possibilities is correct because the chore is beyond the scope of this book. The sources listed in the bibliography can give you a head start on attacking the question if you decide to pursue it. And, as usual, the bibliography can give you sources that argue against the breakdown of IP into TP and AgrP.

Now let us consider the structure of auxiliaries. We learned in Problem Set 2.4 that within the verbal string we find the order modal-perfective-progressive-passive–main verb. *Have* (the perfective form) and *be* (the progressive and passive form) can occur without another V present in a nonelliptical use:

I have a book.
She is a nice person.

In other words, *have* and *be* have main V uses. What sets *have* and *be* apart from most other main verbs is that they can take a V″ as their complement. Thus the verbal phrase in the sentence *I [have eaten pizza]* would have the following analysis:

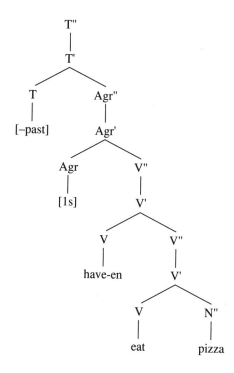

Auxiliaries in English do exhibit syntactic behavior that indicates that they undergo Verb Movement into I, witness Subject-Auxiliary Inversion:

Have I eaten pizza?

So English auxiliaries are like Italian lexical verbs in that they can undergo head movement. The structure of the English verbal phrase in the tree above, after all movement, would be:

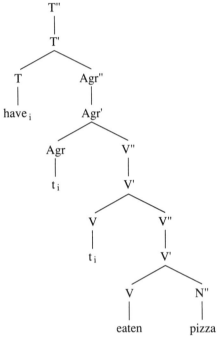

The modal auxiliaries, in contrast, have no main-verb usage. Furthermore, while modals can exhibit tense, they never exhibit agreement.

{I/you/she/we/you all/they} may eat pizza.

We could account for these two facts by generating modals under the T node:

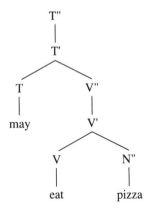

With this analysis, modals never pass through Agr, so they never pick up an agreement morpheme. However, since they are generated under T, they do undergo Subject-Auxiliary Inversion:

May I eat pizza?

The fact that auxiliaries in English undergo Verb Movement but lexical verbs do not is one of the more difficult facts of English to account for. If you are disturbed and intrigued by this (as well as by the possible consequences this has for affix movement in English), I urge you to research the issue. Perhaps you can come up with a more satisfactory account of the verbal string.

There is at least one more point we must make about auxiliaries in English. While we have generated *have* and *be* under a V node above, this V node must be distinguishable from main V nodes, since both the formation of clefts and Verb Fronting distinguish between the two types of Vs (as we just saw in the chapter text). For that reason, you may be inclined to talk about Auxiliary Phrases, and to say that *have* and *be* can head Auxiliary Phrases. I will feel free in the rest of this book to talk about *have* and *be* as heading Aux″ or V″, since this distinction will not be of relevance to us again in this book.

Finally, you can now figure out for yourself where the *be* of the passive verb string is generated. (The question is whether it heads an Aux″, like the progressive *be* and perfective *have*, or whether it is generated under T, like the modals.)

Tangent 8.2: X-Bar Theory and Constituency

There are several points of X-Bar Theory that we have not fully addressed. In this tangent we will address some of them.

One of the advantages that has been claimed for an X-Bar Theory that makes a distinction between functional and lexical categories (as we have done, with our distinction between Determiner Phrases and noun phrases, for example) is that it allows us to simplify Theta Theory. We have not yet seen this advantage because of the way we have treated Subjects of clauses.

Thus far, we have said that a head can assign a theta-role not just to arguments within its maximal projection, but to the specifier of I′ (the Subject of the sentence) and to the specifier of Det′ (the Subject of a nominal phrase when the head N is a theta-assigner). But if we make a distinction between functional categories and lexical categories, and if we agree further that functional categories have empty specifiers at DS and that the only truly meaningful element that the functional category governs is its complement, we are led to a simple Theta Theory. That is, the Subjects of not just N, but also of V and any other theta-assigner X, will arise inside the phrasal categories of N″, V″, and X″ at DS and then be moved up into their SS positions by Move Alpha. (There is an alternative approach to X-Bar Theory that claims that lexical categories, unlike functional categories, have no double-bar level. With this approach we could say Subjects will arise inside N′, V′, and X′. You can explore some of the benefits of this approach for understanding Japanese syntax in Problem Set 8.2.) Theta Theory, then, can restrict theta assignment from a head X to all its arguments within X″ (or, depending on your X-Bar Theory, within X′). So theta assignment can be within a government domain, a welcome result.

To see this, consider for a moment what the structure of I″ would be at DS and at SS for the simple sentence *Mary left*:

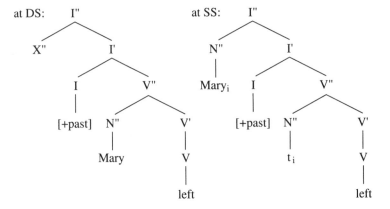

Here the Subject is generated in the specifier position of V′. Similarly, the structure at DS and at SS for the nominal phrase *Bill's lecture* would be:

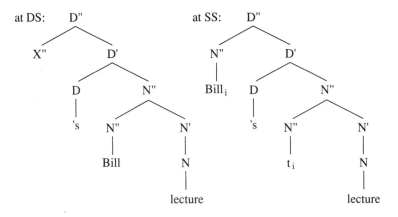

The Subject of the nominal above is generated in the specifier position of N′.

We will adopt the above analysis. However, throughout this book we will continue to draw trees with the Subject of a clause in the specifier of I′ position and the Subject of a nominal phrase in the specifier of Det′ position in our most underlying trees. We do that simply for ease of exposition (given that in almost every derivation we would otherwise have to talk about movement of a Subject up into the specifier of I′), since our interest from here on out will never focus on any distinction that would follow from generating these Subjects within the government domain of their theta-assigners. You should, however, keep the discussion here in mind and recognize that our way of drawing trees from here on is an expedient.

Let us note that Subjects are uniquely identifiable at SS as the specifier of I' or D'. We can now add that at DS Subjects are identifiable as the specifier of V' or N'. Furthermore, given that A and P can be theta-assigners and that either can serve as the primary predicate in a clause, we would want to generate their Subjects in specifier position of A' or P'. So Subjects are uniquely identifiable at DS as the specifier of X', where X is a theta-assigner. (Certainly in other languages it has been argued that other categories than nominals and verbals can take Subjects at SS. For those languages, Subjects would be uniquely identifiable at SS as the specifiers of various types of X'—perhaps even any X' (that is, perhaps they would have the same range of possibilities that Subjects do at DS in English). You can explore some of the issues related to this approach for Egyptian Arabic in Problem Set 8.8.)

Another issue in X-Bar Theory involves constituency. We have taken a very restrictive approach to X-Bar Theory, an approach in which all modifiers are generated at DS as sisters to a head. Many linguists do not accept this approach. Instead, while the idea that arguments are generated in DS only in sister position to a theta-assigning head (or in specifier of N' or specifier of V') is well accepted, the idea that all modifiers are at the sister level to a head is not.

For example, some have argued that restrictive AP modifiers are attached as sisters to N, but nonrestrictive AP modifiers are attached as sisters to N' (see the diagram below). (For a discussion of restrictive-versus-nonrestrictive modifiers, see Problem Set 4.3 of chapter 4):

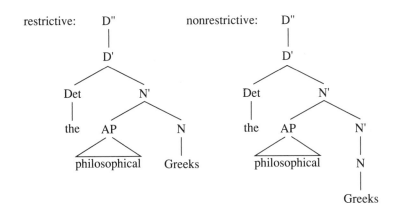

And other attachments have been proposed, also.

Another example is appositives; we briefly discussed the (very complicated) debate over their attachment in Problem Set 6.5.

Likewise, there are varying proposals for the attachment of adverbials. Some have argued that they can be generated as sisters to V, to V' (under another V'), to V" (under another V"), and even to projections of I and of C (and if we break down I into Agr and T, then under projections of Agr and T—as you will see in Problem Set 8.16 for Italian). Thus adverbials that modify a verb only might be generated somewhere inside the V", but adverbials that modify the entire proposition might be generated outside the V", as a sister to some projection of I or C.

Consistent with the above multiprojection approach to X-Bar Theory is another proposal, the Binary Branching Hypothesis (which we mentioned in Tangent 4.2 of chapter 4). Some have claimed that any given node either does not branch or branches only in a binary fashion. If this were so, we might have the following breakdown for a V″ such as *gave the books to Mary secretly last Sunday* (where the actual labels on each branching node that is a projection of V might vary in different linguists' analyses from being V′, as I have represented all but the maximal one, to being V with as many as four bars:

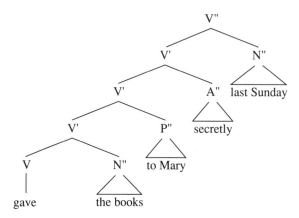

An alternative analysis, also consistent with the Binary Branching Hypothesis that has been proposed, follows:

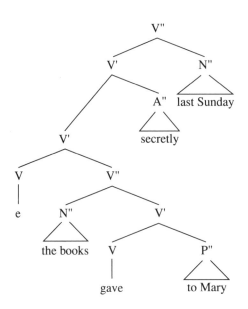

Here the lowest V, *gave*, will undergo head movement and wind up in the next higher V slot (which at DS is empty), yielding the correct word order at SS:

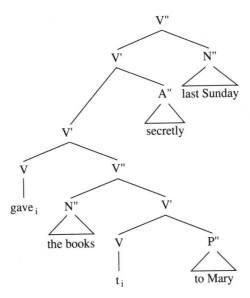

You might well wonder what sorts of considerations would make one choose one of these analyses of the verb phrase over the other. In particular, you might wonder what would justify the complexity of the second approach. The major motivation has been with regard to the analysis of the Double-Object construction. With the first approach, the VP *gave Mary the books* might have the structure at SS shown in:

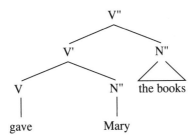

With the second approach this VP would have the analysis at SS shown in:

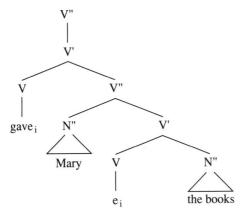

With the first approach the second object of the Double-Object construction asymmetrically c-commands the first; with the second approach the first object asymmetrically c-commands the second. We will discuss the second analysis of the Double-Object construction in chapter 10, where we will find that the original motivation for it is weak.

There are several advantages to recognizing various projections within any phrase. Notice that with this approach, so long as we generate all adverbials (no matter what category they are) as sisters to some higher projection of V, we would have a straightforward definition of DO: an NP sister to V is a DO. Also, we would have an explanation for why we generally do not have free word order within phrases. For example, arguments typically precede adjuncts within V″ in English, and neither arguments nor adjuncts are typically free to appear in varying order (except in instances of Heavy NP Shift, as discussed in chapter 5):

> gave the books to Mary secretly last Sunday
> *gave secretly the books to Mary last Sunday
> *gave to Mary the books secretly last Sunday

This relative rigidity of word order is observed even when none of the phrases involved is receiving Case from the V:

> spoke to Mary on Bill's behalf yesterday
> ??spoke yesterday to Mary on Bill's behalf
> ??spoke on Bill's behalf to Mary yesterday

Another claimed advantage of recognizing various projections within a phrase is based on arguments for constituency. The only tests we have accepted for constituency are based on the claim that movement is of a node only (and, furthermore, of X or X″ only). Thus if an AP or an appositive or an adverbial or any other XP can move alone with other material, we would conclude that it forms a node with that other material. For example, take the rule we called VP-Fronting (exemplified in 24 in the chapter text), leaving behind the first auxiliary, as in:

> Bill said he'd leave and *leave* he {did/may/will . . . }.
> Bill said he'd buy lunch and *buy lunch* he {did/may . . . }.

With this VP-Fronting test we can see that at least the adverbials in boldface below are inside the VP:

> Bill said he'd leave then, and *leave **then*** he did.
> Bill said he'd buy lunch without a second thought, and *buy lunch **without a second thought*** he {did/may . . . }.

This rule cannot front only the V:

> *Bill said he'd buy lunch and *buy* he did lunch.

Accordingly, the adverbials must move:

*Bill said he'd leave then and *leave* he did **then**.

*Bill said he'd buy lunch without a second thought, and *buy lunch* he {did/may
    ... } **without a second thought**.

While VP-Fronting shows us that the adverbials above are inside the VP, it also
shows us that the adverbials below are outside the VP:

*Bill said he'd leave, fortunately—and *leave, **fortunately*** he did.

Bill said he'd leave, fortunately—and *leave* he did, **fortunately**.

However, VP-Fronting does not give us any evidence as to what projection of V (or
of I or C) adverbials are sisters to. Thus VP-Fronting gives us no evidence relevant
to the issue of whether there are multiple projections within phrases.

    While we have limited ourselves to movement as a test for constituency, others
have claimed that certain pro-forms can be interpreted as corresponding only to a
syntactic constituent. Thus others would claim that the pro-string *do so* must be
interpreted as corresponding to some projection of V, as in:

Bill bought lunch and John *did so*, too.

With the *do so*-test one could argue that a variety of adverbials fall outside whatever
projection of V the *do so*-test identifies:

Bill bought lunch Tuesday and John *did so* **Wednesday**.

The fact that *Wednesday* can co-occur with *do so* in the second conjunct above
would be taken as evidence that such a time-adverbial is outside the relevant projection of V. However, our VP-Fronting test gives contradictory results:

Jim said he'd buy lunch Wednesday and *buy lunch **Wednesday*** he did.

Another pro-form that has been used to argue for constituency is *one* (which you
explored in Star Problem 1.1), as in:

You have *a brother* and I have *one*, too.

Here the *one* corresponds to an NP. Examples such as:

You have a mean *brother* and I have a nice *one*.

show that *one* can be interpreted as corresponding to the N level as well as the N″
level.

    From examples like:

You have a mean *older brother* and I have a nice *one*.

people could argue that each AP modifer of an N is attached at a different level,
like so:

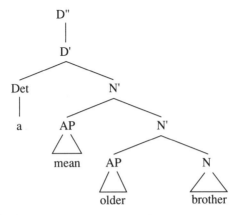

Thus the *one* in the last example above would correspond to the lowest N′ in the tree here. However, no movement rules operate on just N′ (since all movement applies to the X or X″ level, and never to the X′ level), so we cannot test whether movement corroborates the structure implied by the *one*-test.

Another very common pro-form that has been used as a test for constituency is the first auxiliary in the VP-Ellipsis construction (which you looked at in Problem Set 2.6 of chapter 2). Again, we find conflicts with evidence given to us by VP-Movement:

> Bill washed the car **on Tuesday** and I *did* **on Wednesday**.
> Bill said he'd wash the car on Tuesday and *wash the car* **on Tuesday** he did.

Tests for syntactic constituency based on the interpretation of pro-forms, then, cannot be corroborated by movement tests, since movement is restricted to only lexical levels (Xs) and phrasal levels (X″s).

We, therefore, might go look for other corroborating evidence. The nonpermutability of constituents with V″, as demonstrated above, for example, might be taken as corroborating evidence. However, this relatively fixed word order could also be taken as evidence for linear restrictions rather than hierarchical complexity. That is, one could as easily say that whatever is a sister to V in the hierarchical approach is linearly restricted to being generated as the immediate sister to V in a linear-restriction approach, and so on.

Furthermore, there is a serious theoretical problem involved here: Tests for syntactic constituency based on the interpretation of pro-forms rely on the assumption that these semantic units (these pro-forms) necessarily correspond to syntactic units. But we know in general that, while semantic units often correspond to syntactic units, this is not a necessary correspondence. We have repeatedly brought out the fact that semantic units can consist of syntactic strings that do not form constituents and may not even be continuous strings, as in the italicized parts of:

> *The cat has* John's *tongue*.
> We *brought* the students *to task*.

Why should pro-forms be restricted to corresponding only to syntactic constituents when other semantic units are not so restricted? And, in fact, there is evidence that pro-forms are not so restricted. Consider:

John brought his students to task and I *did so* to my students.

Here we have a strange *to* appearing in the second conjunct. But regardless of how this *to* is to be accounted for, the pro-form *did so* here corresponds to the nonconstituent discontinuous string *brought . . . to task*.

Similar complications arise for *one*. Consider:

John bought a new car and it has mag wheels. So I went out and bought one, too.

People judge this sentence as ambiguous between whether I bought a new car or I bought a new car with mag wheels. With enough information added to the sentence, they can favor the second reading:

John bought a new car and it has those mag wheels I've been dying to get. So I went out and finally bought one, too.

Here if *one* is interpreted as a new car with mag wheels, then it does not correspond to any syntactic constituent in the first sentence.

All the pro-forms are open to this sort of criticism. Thus *do so, one,* and the Aux in a VP-Ellipsis construction might all correspond to strings (continuous or discontinuous) that do not form syntactic constituents.

You might well decide that the advantages to having multiple projections within a phrase merit their proposal, regardless of what I have just said here. (And you might find flaws in my criticisms of the pro-form tests for constituency.) However, in this book we will not have reason to delve further into this issue. The important point is that you should be aware of the issue, and you should recognize some of the potential weaknesses of tests based on pro-forms. With that said, we will continue with our very simple X-Bar Theory, in which there is only one X' and it has only one sister (specifier of X').

Tangent 8.3: Terminology and Derivational Constraints versus Principles of Interpretation

You might have noticed that some of the older accounts of restrictions on movement constructions offered "constraints" (such as the CNPC). Later ones offered "conditions" (such as the Subject Condition). And today we talk about "principles" (such as the Subjacency Principle). This difference, however, is not purely terminological.

Early generative grammars focused on working out the particulars of different transformations, with all their restrictions. A major breakthrough of the 1960s was the discovery that what were then seen as different movement rules (such as Passive, Raising, *Wh*-Movement—which today are seen as different instantiations of the single rule of Move Alpha) all seemed to observe similar restrictions. These were stated as DERIVATIONAL CONSTRAINTS on movement in general. They represented a giant step forward in our understanding of linguistic theory. You were introduced to several of these constraints in the chapter narrative (the CNPC, the CSC, the SSC).

Another very important constraint, which was sometimes called a principle, sometimes a condition, and sometimes a constraint, is known today as the A-OVER-A PRINCIPLE. This principle says that if you have a structure in which a node of category A (A stands for any category) immediately dominates another node of category A, any rule of grammar applying to an A has to apply to the higher A and not to the lower A. For example, take the sentence:

You found some person's book.

The N″ *some person* is immediately dominated by another N″. Thus *Wh*-Movement, for example, should not be able to move the lower N″, but only the higher one. And that is, in fact, the case:

*Which person's did you find [t book]?
Which person's book did you find [t]?

*Whose did you find [t book]?
Whose book did you find [t]?

The A-Over-A Principle was proposed to handle a wide range of phenomena that are today handled by other principles. However, it is still invoked to handle data like those above (although, as you will see in the discussion below, it could well be interpreted as a principle of interpretation today rather than a constraint on rule application).

During the 1970s the focus of attention turned to trying to offer a description of the grammar that called for fewer abstractions. People asked what problems for our grammar would arise if the DS and the SS of a given construction (any given construction) were identical. Of course, this question had always been asked in generative grammar—and the answer had often been quick: a mess would arise, so transformations (such as movement, but also DELETION, INSERTION, and SUBSTITUTION) were adopted. But what was different about the 1970s was that, instead of throwing up one's hands at the mess, people took a close and serious look at the mess. It turned out that a grammar with fewer transformations would need to have some rather complex methods of interpretation.

The job then came to be the discovery and clear statement of principles of interpretation. That is, the point was to discover how we interpret structures at SS, regardless of their derivation. So derivational constraints took a back seat and interpretation took the front seat. The field of semantics moved forward in leaps and bounds.

While the grammar we are developing in this textbook no longer makes use of syntactic rules of deletion or substitution, it does incorporate movement (although not all modern theories of grammar do), in the single rule of Move Alpha (which has a variety of instantiations, including different types of NP-movement, *Wh*-Movement, and Head Movement—such as Verb Movement). Our theory also allows for rules of insertion, although you might well yourself be opting for a grammar without insertion rules, depending on your own analysis of *there*-sentences (see Problem Set 7.5), ambient-*it* (see Problem Set 7.3), Extraposition (compare Problem Set 6.5 to Problem Set 8.1), and other constructions.

When we talk of restrictions on movement today, then, we could be talking about restrictions on actual derivations or about restrictions on interpretations of sentences involving dependencies of two or more positions (such as structures to which movement has applied). Thus the Subjacency Principle, which we stated as a restriction on movement in 82, could as easily be stated as a principle that restricts how we can interpret sentences with traces:

> A trace and another constituent separated by more than one bounding node cannot be co-indexed.

This principle would disallow us from seeing such a trace and such a constituent as part of a single chain. It would result in some traces being left in the lurch, so to speak—not co-indexed with anything else. Such abandoned traces would lead to a breakdown in interpretation.

A theory of grammar that did not incorporate movement could make use of this new version of Subjacency so long as that theory of grammar could recognize positions that in our theory we fill with *wh*-trace. But any theory of grammar is probably going to have to be able to do that, since variables (which are defined toward the very end of this chapter's text) need to be recognized for a number of reasons (as you will see in chapter 9).

Thus Subjacency could easily be viewed as a principle of interpretation, and not a derivational constraint. However, there is evidence that Subjacency really should be viewed as a principle that restrains syntactic movement. This evidence comes from analyses that call for a different kind of movement in the semantic component of the grammar (we will look at the semantic component briefly in chapter 9). It appears that movement in the semantic component of the grammar does not obey Subjacency.

Problem Set 8.1: English Extraposition

We looked at Extraposition in Problem Set 6.5 of chapter 6. There we discussed the proposal that a sentential Subject or an appositive clause inside a Subject is moved to the end of the containing clause, as in:

(1) [That Mary lied] shocked Frank.

(2) [t]$_i$ shocked Frank [that Mary lied]$_i$.

(3) It$_i$ shocked Frank [that Mary lied$_i$].

We are now going to challenge this analysis.

Part 1

In 4 and 5 it is possible to have a proximate interpretation of the pronoun.

(4) That Frank couldn't stop crying upset him.

(5) That he couldn't stop crying upset Frank.

But out of 6 and 7, only in 7 is a proximate interpretation allowed.

(6)   *It upset him; that Frank; couldn't stop crying.

(7)   It upset Frank; that he; couldn't stop crying.

Assume that 6 is out because it is a violation of Binding Theory (BT). What condition of BT does it violate?

Where must the extraposed clause in 6 be attached (as a daughter to V′, V″, I′, I″, or some higher level) in order for 6 to be accounted for as a BT violation?

Part 2

Now give a tree for 3. Make sure you use the information you discovered in answering Part 1 to do this.

Part 3

Assume that a clause is an R-expression. (After all, what else could it be?) What problem does the co-indexing of the subject *it* and the extraposed clause cause for BT?

Part 4

Now that we can see that the analysis in 1–3 causes problems for BT, let us abandon it. Instead, let us assume that 1 and 3 are both base generated. That is, let us assume that these structures are generated as is at DS and no movement has applied. Let us further assume that *it* and the final clause are not co-indexed, but that they have some other semantic relationship (which we will not argue for, but which has been argued to be a predication relationship).

It has often been noted that a sentence like 8 has no parallel sentence like 9.

(8)   That Mary lied means that Jeff'll go to jail.

(9)   *It means that Jeff'll go to jail that Mary lied.

With the old movement analysis, people used to just claim there was an arbitrary restriction on not extraposing when you had an Object clause.

What would be the explanation for 9 with the no-movement analysis? That is, give the tree structure for 9 and argue why this is not a well-formed structure at DS. (Hint: Consider the expansion of V″ in English in general. What complements do we allow for V in our base? What complements will we have to allow for the verb *mean* in 9?)

Part 5

With our no-movement analysis, the *it* could be either a dummy (that is, we could base generate a sentence like 3 with an empty subject that then gets filled with a dummy-*it*) or it could be a normal pronominal. One thing you know about normal pronominals is that they can control PRO. Is the grammaticality of the sentence in

10 relevant to the question of whether our *it* is a dummy or a pronominal? If yes, how?

(10) It's likely enough that John did it [PRO to convince me we ought to question him].

Problem Set 8.2: Japanese Categories and Phrase Structure

We have taken the position that both functional and lexical categories can head phrases. Consider the structure shown below, if X is a functional category (such as a Determiner).

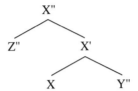

A functional category does not assign a theta-role to its complement, although it might assign Case. (Actually, we have a problem here, since, as we noted in Tangent 8.1, if the Head Movement Constraint is correct, the functional categories T and Agr L-Mark their sisters. Please set this issue aside for the sake of getting through the major points of this problem set.) There is only one specifier position and there is only one complement allowed. Note that whether the specifier is the left or right sister of X′ and whether the complement of X (the YP in the tree above) is the left or right sister of X are language specific. I have given the tree as it would be proposed for English (which is generally a head-initial language).

Some linguists have argued that lexical categories have a different projection, as in:

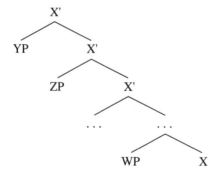

Here there is no X″. That is, lexical categories in this theory have no maximal projection. (We have not adopted this position, but please consider it for this problem set.) If X is lexical, X can assign a theta-role not just to its sister, but to any of the phrases that are sisters to the X′s (YP, ZP, WP). Furthermore, there can be any number of iterations of X′ with a sister phrase. And notice that whether the phrase is the left or right sister of X' (or X) is language specific. I have given the tree above as it would be proposed for Japanese (which is a head-final language).

Some of the strongest arguments for this approach to X-Bar Theory come from the analysis of Japanese. So let us take a brief look at some Japanese data.

Japanese differs from English in a number of ways. Below is a list of some of those differences with exemplification.

1. Japanese has no *Wh*-Movement.

   (1) Naoki-ga   nani-o   kaimasita-ka?
        Naoki-SUBJ what-DO bought - Q
        'What did Naoki buy?'

   (*Ka* is a sentence particle in 1, indicating that the clause is a question.)

2. Japanese has no overt dummy elements (that is, it has nothing comparable to dummy-*it* in English). There are no examples to give here. In cases in which we might expect a dummy element, Japanese uses a full NP (as in 2) or an empty category.

   (2) Ame-ga   futta.
        rain-SUBJ fell
        'It rained.'

3. Japanese has so-called multiple-Subject constructions.

   (3) Bunmeikoku-ga   dansei-ga   heikinzyumyoo-ga   mizikai.
        civilized   SUBJ male- SUBJ average lifespan-SUBJ is short
        'It is civilized countries that men, their average lifespan is short.'

   (Not all speakers of Japanese accept example 3, which is taken from Kuno [1973]. Please assume for the sake of doing this problem set that sentences with this structure are grammatical in Japanese.)

4. Japanese can "scramble" the arguments of the predicate within the confines of a clause. Thus all the examples in 4 are grammatical and all are very similar (if not identical) in meaning.

   (4) a. Mariko-ga   Naoki-ni sono hon- o   watasita.
           Mariko-SUBJ Naoki-IO that book-DO handed
           'Mariko handed Naoki that book.'

        b. Naoki-ni Mariko-ga sono hon-o watasita.
        c. Naoki-ni sono hon-o Mariko-ga watasita.
        d. Sono hon-o Mariko-ga Naoki-ni watasita.
        e. Sono hon-o Naoki-ni Mariko-ga watasita.

5. Japanese has no specifier of nominal position. That is, all complements and modifiers of the nominal are on an equal footing syntactically, and the presence of one does not preclude the presence of another on any syntactic basis. Thus, for example, we can find both demonstrative adjectives and genitives inside an NP:

(5) kireina   Mariko-no   sono hon
     beautiful Mariko-GEN that book
     'Mariko's that beautiful book'

Importantly, we find nothing that is equivalent to our articles in English.

6. Japanese exhibits no Subject-Verb Agreement. Thus a sentence like 6, with no overt Subject, can be understood in any of the ways indicated there, and context is the determining factor. If there were overt Subjects, the verb form would stay the same, regardless of the features of the Subjects.

(6) Hon-o   katta.
     book-DO bought
     '{I/We/You/He/She/They} bought the book.'

7. Pro-forms in Japanese can be modified.

(7) un, demo [kinoo-no   kare-wa] sukosi   yoosu-ga
     yes but   yesterday's he-TOP somewhat state- SUBJ
     hend   dat-ta.
     strange be-past
     'Yes, but, as for yesterday's him, the state was somewhat strange.' (That is, the person he was yesterday was pretty unusual.)

It has been proposed that Japanese has no functional categories (for example, no INFL, no Comp, no Determiner), and is limited to lexical categories alone. Discuss how this proposal can account for the data in 1–7 above.

Problem Set 8.3: English Root Phenomena

Part 1

We pointed out in this chapter that Subject-Auxiliary Inversion is limited to matrix clauses. It is a so-called root phenomenon. Other phenomena that have been put in this class are exemplified here:

(1) Never before have prices been so high.
     ?*Nixon regrets that never before have prices been so high.

(2) Squatting in the corner was a spotted tree frog.
     *I never enter the room when squatting in the corner is a spotted tree frog.

(3) John says he'll win it, and win it he will.
     *John wants to win it, but the claim that win it he will is absurd.

(4) In came the milkman.
     *John thinks that in came the milkman.

(5) Boy, are we in for it.
     *He discovered that boy, are we in for it.

(6) Not a bite did he eat.
     *Mary says that not a bite did he eat.

(7)   Lo and behold, there was a unicorn among the roses.
     *I realized that lo and behold, there was a unicorn among the roses.

(8)   Gotta go now.
     *I guess (that) gotta go now.

And there are many others. Actually, several root phenomena do occur in embedded clauses under certain conditions. Your job in this homework is to explore any single root phenomenon. You could pick one out of 1–8 above, or you might pick a different one that you demonstrate to be a root phenomenon.

Questions you might try to answer are:

(a) What moves?

(b) Where does it move to?

(c) Does this movement obey Subjacency?

(d) What characteristics does the trace left behind have?

(e) Are there any particular characteristics that the clause must have in order for this root phenomenon to occur?

(f) Are there any particular characteristics that the discourse must have in order for this root phenomenon to occur appropriately?

(g) If you pick a phenomenon that can, with certain limitations, occur in embedded clauses, what are those certain limitations?

(h) Is there any connection between your answer to (g) and your answers to (e) and (f)?

Part 2

Consider the following:

(9)   I {am/*is} the cause of the revolution.

(10)   The cause of the revolution is me.

(11)   The cause of the revolution am I.

(12)   You {are/*is} out in the cold again.

(13)   Out in the cold is you.

(14)   Out in the cold are you.

Examples 9 and 12 in most varieties of English require the verbal agreement indicated above. But in the other sentences, either *is* or a verb that agrees with the NP following it is allowed. If you have trouble finding 11 and 14 grammatical, say them aloud. With the right intonation (often the intonation of an exclamation) or the right stylistic setting (perhaps poetry), they might be good for you, and, if so, they contrast in meaning to 10, and 13, respectively. Describe that contrast in meaning.

(If you simply cannot find 11 and 14 grammatical, then this agreement pattern is archaic for you. You might then do the rest of this problem set as though this variety of English is a language you are not a speaker of. So just use my data and answer the questions.)

Now try to embed 9–11. You find the pattern:

(15)   I know that I am the cause of the revolution.

(16)   I know that the cause of the revolution is me.

(17)   *I know that the cause of the revolution am I.

Offer an analysis of sentences like 10 as opposed to sentences like 11 that will account for the fact that sentences like 10 can be embedded while sentences like 11 cannot and that will account for the agreement facts.

*Problem Set 8.4: English Adverbial Clauses

This problem set explores where adverbial clauses are attached. Be sure to review Binding Theory (by looking back at the overviews at the ends of chapters 6–8) before doing it. This problem set shows you how Binding Theory can give us information about tree structure, so it should be done.

Part 1

Consider the three logically possible attachment spots for initial adverbial clauses: in the XP slot (the specifier slot) immediately dominated by C″, as a left sister to C immediately dominated by C′, or as a left sister to N″ immediately dominated by I″. (Note: I am assuming that an *after* clause like that in example 1 is a PP, and the P introduces a whole clause. So the P″ in A–C below indicates an adverbial clause.)

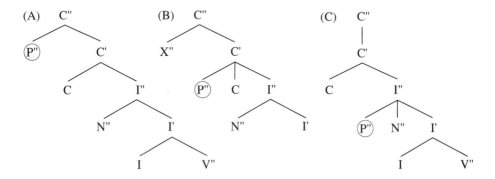

Use 1 to eliminate one of the trees A, B, or C, above. Explain how 1 supports your answer.

(1)   After John$_i$ realized the mistake, he$_i$ cried.

(The indices tell you that a proximate reading of the pronoun *he* is acceptable here.)

Between the remaining two trees, which one would our X-Bar Theory choose for us and why?

Part 2

Consider these six logically possible attachment spots for final adverbial clauses: as a daughter of C″, of C′, of I″, of I′, of V″, and of V′. As in A–C on the previous page, the P″ below indicates the adverbial clause.

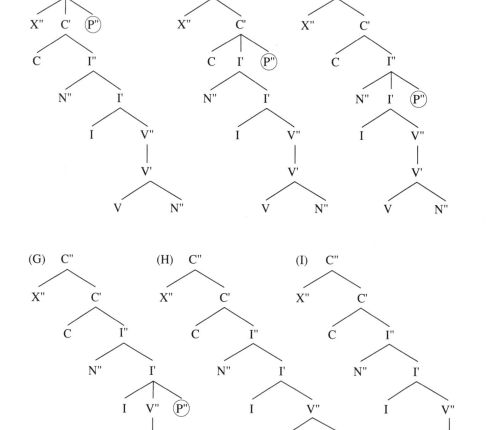

Assume that 2 and 3 are bad because they are violations of Binding Theory. Use 2 and 3 to determine where final adverbial clauses are attached. Explain how 2 and 3 support your answer.

(2) *He$_i$ cried after John$_i$ realized the mistake.

(3) *Bill slapped her$_i$ after Mary$_i$ lied.

(Note: 2 can help you eliminate two of the six trees; 3 can help you eliminate five of them.)

Part 3

Consider the analyses in D–I above once more. Use the VP-Fronting test discussed in Tangent 8.2 of this chapter to explore which of these analyses is a more adequate structure for adverbial clauses. You might test on sentences like:

(4) Bill said he'd leave when Mary came and . . .

Remember that if the adverbial clause can front along with the rest of the VP, then it must be generated inside the VP. (If you find that the adverbial clause appears to have a choice of fronting or not with the VP, then you must still conclude that the adverbial clause is generated inside the VP in order to account for its ability to front with the rest of the VP. Then a separate rule would be responsible for extraposing the adverbial clause outside the VP—either before or after VP-Fronting.)

This test should help you eliminate four of the possible analyses in D–I.

Do your findings corroborate those you reached in Part 2 above? (They should.)

Problem Set 8.5: English Gapping

Part 1

Sentences 1 and 2 are similar, if not identical, in meaning:

(1) Max wrote a novel, and Alex wrote a play.

(2) Max wrote a novel, and Alex a play.

Example 2 is called a GAPPED sentence.

Describe the form of gapped sentences in general. As you do this be sure to consider (1) what is missing (what is the gap?) and (2) where the gap is (on the right, left, or middle of any other specific structures).

If the gap is to be considered an empty node at SS, is it properly governed?

Argue either that gapped sentences are base generated (so that at DS 2 has the same form that it has at SS) or that they are derived from ungapped sentences via a deletion rule called GAPPING, which you must state precisely in ordinary words. With the first analysis, 1 and 2 come from different DSs. With the deletion analysis, 1 and 2 come from the same DS.

Sentences 3–16 are all gapped sentences. Consider these examples as you develop your arguments. Be sure that whatever analysis you opt for, you account for most of these sentences. If you cannot account for all of them with your analysis, point out which ones you cannot account for and explain why.

(3)   Max is careless, and Albert irresponsible.

(4)   Max spoke fluently, and Albert haltingly.

(5)   Susan eats with chopsticks, and Max with a spoon.

(6)   Max wants Sue to win, and Bill, Paula.

(7)   Max was ignored by his wife, and Geoff, by his lover.

(8)   Max seems to understand Julia, and Ted, Alice.

(9)   Max wants to understand Julia, and Ted, Alice.

(10) Max wants to try to begin to write a novel, and Alex a play.

(11) Paul Schachter has informed me that the basic word order in Tagalog is
      VOS; Ives Goddard that the unmarked word order in Algonkian is
      OVS; and Guy Carden that the basic order in Aleut is OSV.

(12) Bill discovered you, and Sally, me.
      (cf. *Bill discovered you, and Sally, I.)

(13) Bill killed himself, and Sally, herself.
      (cf. *Bill killed himself, and Sally_i, her_i.)

(14) Bill depends on Alice, and Alice, on Kate.
      (cf. *Bill depends on Alice, and Alice {with/in/for/to/of/after/ . . .}
      Kate.)

(15) Sam spoke slowly and Mary in great haste.
      (cf. *Sam spoke slowly and Mary in Italian.)

(16) On the table there's a book and on the desk a pencil.
      (cf. *On the table there's a book and a pencil on the desk.)

Part 2

According to your analysis, are the following sentences gapped sentences or not? If
not, explain why not. If so, account for them with your analysis.

(17) Susan spoke before Jack, and Mary after.
      (cf. Susan spoke before Jack and Mary after him.)

(18) The priest christened my baby Robert and my friend's baby, Antonio.

(19) Ralph is coming at three, and I am, too.

(20) Ralph shelled the peas and ate them.

(21) Ralph shelled, and Mary ate, the peas.

(22) Ralph invited Sue and Mary.

(23) How come he gets everything and me nothing?

(24) Today you'll get the first question and tomorrow, the second.

Part 3

Do gapped sentences always get mapped into a specific meaning or can their meaning be underdetermined? Give examples to make your point. What determines the meaning of gapped sentences with your analysis?

Part 4

When do you use gapped sentences?

Part 5

The following is from *The Franchise Affair* by Josephine Tey. Discuss the gaps in it.

> They were in and out of his place all day. He for his paper in the morning, and then *her* for her cigarettes shortly after, and then back for his evening paper and her back for the third time probably for cigarettes again. . . .

Problem Set 8.6: Italian Indefinite Subject and Object

We have seen a variety of problem sets in this book in which it is clear that Italian (and Spanish and Portuguese) allows an empty pronominal to fill the Subject position of tensed clauses. We called this empty pronominal pro (read "little pro") and we said it has the features [−anaphor, +pronominal]. The question of this problem set is: can pro occur in other positions, as well?

Part 1

Below are data that pertain to the question of whether Italian and English allow pro to fill DO position. Please restrict yourself to considering only these data when coming to your conclusion. Assume that the subcategorization frames for the Italian verbs below are identical to those of their English glosses. (Note: Under certain Italian verbs, we find V—for verb—plus the person and number marking on the V. Under certain nouns and adjectives we find the gender and number. You will not use that information in this part of the problem set. But you will use it in Part 2.)

(1) a. This sign cautions against avalanches.

b. Questo cartello mette in guardia contro le   valanghe.
    this   sign   puts on guard   against the avalanches
    'This sign puts (one) on guard against avalanches.'

(2) a. *This leads [PRO to conclude that avalanches are dangerous].

b. Questo conduce a [PRO concludere che le   valanghe   sono
    this   leads   to   conclude   that the avalanches are
    pericolose].
    dangerous.
    'This leads (one) to conclude that avalanches are dangerous.'

(3) a. *Good music reconciles with oneself.

    b. La buona musica riconcilia con se stessi.
              fs   V3s   mp
        the good   music   reconciles with selves
        'Good music reconciles (one) with oneself.'

(4) a. *A serious doctor visits nude. (with the reading: 'A serious doctor vis-
        its nude people.')

    b. Un medico serio   visita nudi .
              ms   V3s mp
        a   doctor serious visits nude
        'A serious doctor visits (one) nude.' (with the reading 'A serious doc-
        tor visits nude people.')

(5) a. *This music renders happy.

    b. Questa musica rende   allegri.
              fs   V3s   mp
        this   music renders happy
        'This music renders (one) happy.'

Part 2

You probably came up with at least three reasons for positing a pro in DO position
in the Italian sentences in Part 1. However, actually, the data do not support the
conclusion that the empty node in DO position is necessarily pro, but only that
there is an empty node in DO position. Pro is special in that it can be interpreted
as having any person (1, 2, or 3), number (s or p), or gender (m or f):

(6) Sembro {contento/contenta}.
     V1s   ms   fs
     '(I) seem content.'

     Sembri {contento/contenta}.
     V2s   ms   fs
     '(You) seem content.'

     Sembra {contento/contenta}.
     V3s   ms   fs
     '({He, She, It}) seems content.'

     Sembriamo {contenti/contente}.
     V1p   mp   fp
     '(We) seem content.'

     Sembrate {contenti/contente}.
     V2p   mp   fp
     '(You) seem content.'

Sembrano {contenti/contente}.
   V3p   mp   fp
'(They) seem content.'

But there is another element in Italian, called the INDEFINITE SUBJECT and usually realized by the clitic *si*, which is interpreted as being [+human] (as the examples in 7 show), always has the feature [+plural] (as seen in 8), and is typically [+masculine] unless the context makes a masculine referent impossible (as seen in 9).

(7)   Si lavora. 'One works.'
     *Si nevica. 'One snows.'
     *Si ulula. 'One howls.' (where *ululare* is restricted to taking as a Subject uvulating animals, so it is [−human])

(8)   Si arriva {*stanco/*stanchi*}.
                 s   p
     'One arrives tired.'

(9)   Si arriva *stanche.* (good only if the group referred to is exclusively
                        fp   female)
     'One arrives tired.'

     Quando si è *incinte,* non ci si sente bene.
                  fp
     'When one is pregnant, one doesn't feel well.'

One of the most perplexing facts about the Indefinite Subject *si* is that if there is a tensed verb with it, the verb is marked singular, although all participles (such as *arrivati* in 10 and *chiamati* in 11), adjectives (such as *stanchi* in 8 and *stanche* and *incinte* in 9), and predicative nominals (such as *cafoni* in 11) that normally agree with the Subject are plural.

(10)   Si è   *arrivati* in ritardo.
      V3s   mp
      'One arrived late.'

(11)   Se si lavora troppo, si è   *chiamati cafoni.*
                     V3s   mp   mp
      'If one works too much, one is called {bumpkins/ rednecks}.'

The interpretation of a sentence with the Indefinite Subject *si* has the predication be of an underspecified set of humans (often the generic interpretation), as indicated in the examples. In this way it is similar to sentences with *on* in French or *Man* in German.

Now the question for you is: Is the missing Object in the Italian sentences of 1–5 pro or a silent Object counterpart of Indefinite Subject *si*—let us call it "INDEFINITE OBJECT e"? You may use the data in 1–5 above, as well as:

(12)   *La buona musica riconcilia con se stesso. (cf. 3.)
          fs   V3s   ms

(13)   *Un medico serio visita nudo. (cf. 4, with the
              ms   V3s   ms   reading there)

(14)   *Questa musica rende allegro. (cf. 5.)
              fs   V3s   ms

Part 3

Mark all empty categories in the (b) examples of these Italian sentences:

(15)   a. Quando Carla è contenta, le   viene la   voglia di cantare.
                                        IO
          when   Carla is happy (to) her comes the desire to sing
          'When Carla is happy, she wants to sing.'

(Note: The *le* of the embedded verb is a dative clitic. It fills the GF of IO. It could
be translated "to her.")

       b. Quando si   è contenti, viene la   voglia di cantare.
          when   one is content, comes the desire to sing
          'When one is happy, one wants to sing.'

(16)   a. Maria tende a dimagrire   quando viaggia in Inghilterra.
          Maria tends to lose weight when   travels in England
          'Maria tends to lose weight when (she) travels in England.'

       b. Si tende a dimagrire quando si viaggia in Inghilterra.
          'One tends to lose weight when one travels in England.'

Be careful to look closely at the Italian and to use the word-by-word gloss, rather
than the loose translation, as your guide. (Note: The [a] examples are given purely
to acquaint you with the relevant facts of the Italian sentences.)

Now identify all the empty categories you found. Be sure to distinguish between
pro and Indefinite Object e (the silent Object counterpart to Indefinite Subject *si*).
If you claim that any of these empty categories are Indefinite Object e, give your
reasons.

(Hint: With regard to 16, ask yourself whether *tendere* 'tend' is a Raising verb.
The question is whether we have an instance of controlled PRO or an instance of
NP-movement with a trace left behind in 16.)

Based on this entire problem set, what GFs can the various counterparts of Indefinite *si* (that is, Indefinite Subject *si* and Indefinite Object e) fill at DS? (Be sure to
look carefully at 16 for this.)

Based on this entire problem set, what GFs can the various counterparts of Indefinite *si* fill at SS?

*Problem Set 8.7: English Relatives and Topicalization

This problem set ensures that you understand Wh-*Movement. You should do it.*

In the text of this chapter we looked at *Wh*-Movement in questions. Here we look
at two other structures which have been analyzed as involving movement. One is

the relative clause, which you are already familiar with (look back to Problem Set 6.1 for a quick review right now—you will be glad you did), as in 1:

(1)   I finally met the man [**who** you told me about].

The other is called the Topicalization structure:

(2)   [These baked beans] I just know you're gonna love!

Please note that there are relative clauses that do not use *wh*-words as well as relative clauses that do. One that does is given in 1. Two that do not are given in 3:

(3)   I finally met the man [that you told me about].
      I finally met the man [you told me about].

Also note that there are topicalization structures that begin with NPs (as in 2 above) and other structures that begin with various other phrases that introduce a topic, as in 4:

(4)   [As for John,] he's a fool.
      [Talking about baked beans,] I hate them.

Answer the following questions considering only the structures in 1 and 2 and not the structures in 3 and 4 until you reach Part 10, in which you will explore the structure in 3. (We will not address the structure in 4 in this problem set.)

Part 1

What moves in a relative clause? Be sure your answer covers all the sentences below as well as any others you can think of. The relative clauses are in brackets here. The head of the relative clause (that is, the N node that the relative clause modifies) is italicized. The moved string is in boldface.

(5)   I remember the *time* [**when** Mary lost her first tooth], don't you?
      I've never understood the *reason* [**why** Jeffrey wrote that scandalous novel], even though I pretended to.
      I love the *kid* [**who** just walked in] more than you'll ever realize.
      I love the *pasta* [**which** you prepared] and I sincerely hope you'll make it again sometime.
      I love *anyone* [**who** I can talk to without feeling bored].
      Isn't that the *house* [**where** Giorgio was born]?

You should also consider more formal relative clauses, as in:

I visited the town [**from which** my ancestors came].

Your answer should consider whether the moving string is limited to being of any particular category, of any particular projection (X or X″), or of any particular GF.

Part 2

Where does the moved item land at SS? Again, be sure to consider all the sentences above and below as well as others you can think of.

(6)   I met the *teacher* [**who** came to the party].
        I met the *teacher* [**who** you invited].
        I met the *teacher* [**who** Jeff said that you invited].
        I met the *teacher* [**who** Jeff said he persuaded you to invite].
        I met the *teacher* [**who** Jeff said he persuaded you to convince your sister
            to invite].
        *I met the *teacher* [Jeff said **who** he persuaded you to invite].
        *I met the *teacher* [Jeff said he persuaded you **who** to invite].

Part 3

Does this movement obey Subjacency? Defend your answer. In doing this, consider sentences like those in 7 and 8 as well as any others you can think of. Be sure to put in the trace that is the foot of the chain before you begin answering.

(7)   Whatever can Jeff want with the *cat* [**which** I took pictures of]?
        *Whatever can Jeff want with the *cat* [**which** I found Sarah's pictures
            of].

(8)   I enjoyed meeting the *director* [**who** Jeff said that Bill would hire].
        *I enjoyed meeting the *director* [**who** Jeff spread the rumor that no one
            would hire].

Part 4

There are two relative *wh*-words that are [+human]: *who* and *whom*. When do we use *who* and when do we use *whom* in casual speech? (Note: this is different from how we use them in writing and in formal speech. Do not be prescriptive. Remember that this book is a descriptive grammar, not a prescriptive one. You might want to look back at Problem Set 3.2 before you do this.) Below are pairs of sentences for you to say and listen to. Make a judgment as to which you prefer. If you feel yourself losing the ability to judge (and that happens in syntax a lot), ask a native speaker of English who is not a linguist. But make sure that person understands that what you want is a reaction of "normalcy"—not of "correctness." Then use your judgments to help answer this question.

(9)   I don't like the *man* [**who** left].
        I don't like the *man* [**whom** left].

(10)   I don't like the *man* [**who** you invited].
        I don't like the *man* [**whom** you invited].

(11)   I don't like the *man* [**who** you talked about].
        I don't like the *man* [**whom** you talked about].

Why do both sentences in 12 sound at best odd and at worst terrible in casual speech?

(12)   I don't like the *man* [**about who** you talked].
          I don't like the *man* [**about whom** you talked].

One of the sentences in 12 sounds much worse than the other. Which one and why?

Part 5

What moves in topicalization? (Please reread the initial directions to this problem set before you answer this question.) Consider here whether the movement is best stated with some restriction on GFs or on theta-roles or on other functions or simply on categories. If only a certain projection of a category moves (X or X″), say that. Below are some relevant sentences to consider as you answer.

(13)   **Jeffrey** I'm absolutely sure did it.
          Jeffrey I'm absolutely crazy about, I swear.
          Jeffrey I gotta talk to right now!
          Jeffrey I'm absolutely sure Sally married her first time around.
          *****Tuesday morning** I'm absolutely sure she left.
          *****The worst fool in the world** I'm absolutely sure he was.
          The worst fool in the world she's going to marry!
          *****Ridiculous** I know she considers him.

Be careful here. If you are not someone who uses these topicalizations a lot, you may have trouble feeling secure about what is acceptable and what is not. If you find yourself in that situation, please just stick to the examples in 13 with the judgments given there and do not confuse the issue with unsure judgments of your own that may lead to unreliable results.

Part 6

Where does the moved item move to in topicalization structures? Again, be sure your answer can account for the sentences in 14 as well as those in 13.

(14)   *****I never dreamed **Jeffrey** Sue'd marry.
          Jeffrey I never dreamed Sue'd marry.
          *****I never dreamed Sue'd say **Jeffrey** Margaret should marry.
          *****I never dreamed **Jeffrey** Sue'd say Margaret should marry.
          Jeffrey I never dreamed Sue'd say Margaret should marry.

Part 7

Does topicalization obey Subjacency? Please consider the sentences below as you answer. Again, be sure to mark in the trace that is the foot of the chain before you begin.

(15)   **Jeffrey** I heard Bill say that Margaret married.
        *__Jeffrey__ I heard Bill repeat the rumor that Margaret married.
        Jeffrey I'll buy photographs of.
        *__Jeffrey__ I'll buy Sue's photographs of.

Part 8

16 is probably an exception to one of the answers you have given above. Which one? Make a stab at an explanation for this exception. (Just make an educated guess. This is not an easy question. It is intended to whet your curiosity.)

(16)   He's a man who *liberty* we could never deny.

Part 9

Example 17 is probably an exception to one of the answers you have given above. Which one?

(17)   **Beans** I don't think I'd ever date a man who eats.

Do not even try to account for 17 here. Tuck it away in your bag of riddles and maybe someday you can write a monograph on it.

Part 10

Given your answers to Parts 1–3, is the movement in relative clauses NP-movement or *Wh*-Movement? Given your answers to Parts 5–7 is the movement in topicalization, NP-movement, or *Wh*-Movement? Argue briefly for your answers.

(Hint: List all the things you know about the two types of movement. The foot of an NP-movement chain is always in a position where it will not receive Case and where it is locally A-bound. [It is an anaphor.] It can be in a position where it will receive a theta-role. Remember that NP-movement is not limited to moving NPs only (it can move sentential Objects, for example), and movement is always into Subject position. Do not let the name "NP-movement" throw you off: it is a type of movement, not movement of only NPs.

On the other hand, the foot of a *Wh*-Movement chain, if it is a referring nominal, will be in a position to receive Case. [But, of course, it need not be a referring nominal—it could be a predicative nominal or it could be a non-nominal, such as a P″.] The foot of a *Wh*-Movement chain will always be locally non-A-bound. [It is a variable.] The foot of a *Wh*-Movement chain might or might not be in a position to receive a theta-role. And remember that *Wh*-Movement is not limited to moving only *wh*-phrases, and movement is always into the closest specifier of C′ position. Again, do not let the name "*Wh*-Movement" throw you off: it is a type of movement, not movement of only *wh*-phrases.

Ask yourself what properties the movements above display, regardless of whether the element moved is an NP or a *wh*-phrase.)

Part 11

Consider the formation of relative clauses without a *wh*-phrase. They can be introduced by nothing or by *that*:

    (18)   The *boy* [(that) I saw is nice].

Argue that these relative clauses involve *Wh*-Movement by showing that they obey Subjacency and could not involve NP-movement. (Hint: Look at Part 3 for the issue of Subjacency. And look at the hint for Part 10.)

Part 12

Is the *that* that can introduce relative clauses (such as in 18) a pronoun? To answer this, consider what you know about pronouns. You should be able to come up with two arguments by looking at the following sentences.

    (19)   He is nice.
            *Him is nice.
            The boy who sang is nice.
            *The boy whom sang is nice.
            The boy that sang is nice.
            The boy that I heard is nice.

    (20)   I went with him.
            The boy with whom I went is nice.
            *The boy with that I went is nice.

(Hint: What do 19 and 20 tell you about the Case of pronouns in comparison to *that*? What do 19 and 20 tell you about the possible GFs of pronouns in comparison to *that*?)

Part 13

What position in the tree are *if* and *whether* located in? Use the sentences below to support your answer.

    (21)   You asked {if/whether} Mary saw someone.
            *Who did you ask {if/whether} Mary saw?

    (22)   *She is the girl who I don't know {if/whether} Mary met.

    (23)   I don't know {if/whether} Mary met that girl.
            *That girl I don't know {if/ whether} Mary met.

(Hint: Ask yourself why the asterisked sentences here are out. What could they possibly be violating? Than ask yourself where *if/whether* must be located in order for that account of the ungrammaticality to hold.)

Problem Set 8.8: Egyptian Arabic Phrase Structure

This problem set is on X-Bar Theory.

Part 1

Let us turn to Egyptian Arabic (EA). Sentences that take a copular verb in English often do not have any verb phonetically expressed in EA, as in:

(1) ʔil-bent zakeyya
     the-girl intelligent
     'The girl is intelligent.'

(2) ʔil-mudi:r   hina
     the-director here
     'The director is here.'

(3) wald-i   mudarris
     father-my teacher
     'My father is a teacher.'

(4) ha:ni fi l-be:t
     Hani in the-house
     'Hani is in the house.'

(The question marks at the front of 1 and 2 are meant to symbolize a type of consonant called the glottal stop. Also, there is no word for *a* in EA. Do not let that confuse you. Assume that *mudarris* is an NP in 2.)

What is the string analysis of 1–4 at SS in terms of categories?

Part 2

There are also normal sentences of EA that have verbs in them:

(5) nadya ra:Hit   is-sinema
     Nadia she-went the-movies
     'Nadia went to the movies.'

The *ra* on the verb in 5 is a resumptive pronoun. (See Problem Set 8.9.) Ignore it for the sake of this problem set. Write a single string analysis for surface structures of simple sentences in EA that will cover 1–5.

Part 3

One question you should consider is whether equational sentences like those in 1–4 have no Inflection and no V, or whether they do, in fact, have Inflection and a V, where the V is phonetically empty and, therefore, the Inflection is also not heard.

If there is no Inflection node, do sentences like 1–4 present any problem for Case Theory?

Part 4

If there is no Inflection node, is the GF Subject position in 1–4 governed?

Part 5

Given your answer to Part 4, did you expect the sentences in 6–9 to be grammatical? Why?

    (6)   *PRO zakeyya
               intelligent (feminine)
               'Some girl is intelligent.'

    (7)   *PRO hina
               here
               'Someone is here.'

    (8)   *PRO mudarris
               teacher (masculine)
               'Some man is a teacher.'

    (9)   *PRO fi l-be:t
               in the-house
               'Someone is in the house.'

(Note: The PRO in 6–9 is the PRO we discussed in chapter 7 for English, which is [+anaphor, +pronominal]. It would have had the arbitrary interpretation here [since it is not controlled] if these sentences had been good. It is not the little pro that we know occurs in Subject position of tensed clauses in Italian, Spanish, and Portuguese and that we studied in Problem Set 8.6.)

Part 6

Now look at other equational sentences in EA:

    (10) ?il-bent ka:nit zakeyya
           the-girl was   clever
           'The girl was clever.'

    (11) ?il-mudi:r   ha-yku:n hina.
           the-director will be   here
           'The director will be here.'

    (12) wald-i   ka:n mudarris
           father-my was teacher
           'My father was a teacher.'

    (13) ha:ni ha-yku:n fi l-be:t
           Hani will be   in the house
           'Hani will be at home.'

And consider the contrast in meaning between 14, with the copular verb phonetically expressed and 15, without it:

(14) ?ana ca:yez ?ibn-i   yeku:n muhandis
      I   want son-my he-be engineer
      'I want my son to be an engineer' (when he grows up . . .)

      (compare to: ?ibn-i muhandis
                  son-my engineer
                  'My son is an engineer.')

(15) ?ana ca:yez ?il-ba:b madhu:n
      I   want   the-door painted
      'I want the door painted.' (now—this is an order of sorts)

      (compare to: ?il-ba:b madhu:n
                  the-door painted
                  'The door is painted.')

When does a form of the copular verb show up?

Part 7

Now in EA there are two ways to negate. One is with *ma* attached to a verb:

(16) ka:nu   il-ciya:l   naymi:n
      they-were the-children asleep
      'The children were asleep.'

(17) ma-kanu:-s   il-ciya:l   naymi:n
      not-they-were the-children asleep
      'The children were not asleep.'

The other way is with *mis* attached to a nominal:

(18) ?abilt il-kuba:r   mis il-ciya:l
      (I) met the-grown-ups not the-children
      'I met the adults, not the children.'

But *mis* cannot attach to a form of the copular verb:

(19) *il-ciya:l   mis ka:nu naymi:n
      the-children not were asleep
      'The children were not asleep.'

Neither *ma* nor *mis* can occur in an equational sentence that has no phonetically audible verb:

(20) *ma il-ciya:l   naymi:n
      not the-children asleep
      'The children are not asleep.'

(21)   *mis il-ciya:l   naymi:n
       not the-children asleep
       'The children are not asleep.'

Do the facts on negation help us to determine whether equational sentences in EA that lack a phonetically audible V really have an (empty) I and V? If yes, how?

Part 8

In English we have a single schema for all expandable categories, shown in:

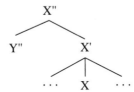

The dots on either side of X may be filled with other phrases.
     In particular, the schema for a sentence is shown in:

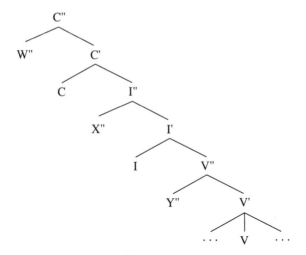

From all you have done on EA here, what do you think the schema for EA sentences is? In other words, take a stance on the issue of whether all equational sentences have an I and a V. (Please conflate the Agr Phrase with IP here, as I have done for English above, since there are no data given to you in this problem set that would allow you to distinguish between the two.)

*Problem Set 8.9: English Resumptive Pronoun Relatives

This problem set continues to work on your understanding of Subjacency. It should be done.

In Problem Set 8.7 you studied relative clauses introduced by a *wh*-phrase or by *that* in which the relative clause had a trace (realized at PF as a phonetic gap or hole). There is a third kind of relative clause found in English, but it is found in speech only and most speakers will probably consider it substandard. However, if you listen carefully at the dining hall table, or to the television, or just eavesdrop on conversations, you will find that people do use these relatives sometimes. Some examples are in 1 and 2; the relative clause is in brackets and the head of the relative is italicized.

(1) Let me tell you about this *problem* [that my chemistry professor wondered whether or not anyone could do it].

(2) I met this fabulous *kid* [that my mother had been trying to get me to babysit for him and another neighbor's child for weeks, but I didn't want to hear about it].

Here we get relative clauses introduced by *that*, but instead of a gap inside the relative clause, we find an ordinary pronoun (*it* in 1 and *him* in 2). This kind of pronoun is called a RESUMPTIVE PRONOUN. It is a typical way to form standard relative clauses in many languages (including Hebrew, Chinese, Romanian, and the Zurich variety of German).

Part 1

Do you think that the resumptive pronoun relative clause involves movement? Give one reason why or why not, based on 1 versus 3 (where 3 gives ordinary relatives with a trace indicated).

(3) *I met the *boy* [who Bill wondered what Jeff said to t].
     *I met the *boy* [that Bill wondered what Jeff said to t].

Give a second reason why or why not, based on 2 versus 4:

(4) *I met the *boy* [who Bill invited me and t to the party].
     *I met the *boy* [who Bill invited t and me to the party].
     *I met the *boy* [that Bill invited me and t to the party].
     *I met the *boy* [that Bill invited t and me to the party].

Part 2

Collect other examples of relative clauses in English with resumptive pronouns. Is the ordinary *wh*-counterpart to these relatives grammatical? Is the ordinary *that*-counterpart to these relatives grammatical? Can you make a general statement about the types of structures we are most likely to use the resumptive-pronoun-relative-clause strategy in?

Part 3

Consider 5, which is from Garrison Keillor's *We Are Still Married*:

(5)   I was once a tall dark *heartbreaker* [who, when I slouched into a room, women jumped up and asked if they could get me something]. . . .

(The brackets are mine.) There is a resumptive pronoun here—where? This relative differs from those in 1 and 2 in an important way. What is it? This relative, however, is similar to those in 1 and 2 in an important way. What is it? (Hint: look back to the general statement you arrived at in doing Part 2.)

Problem Set 8.10: Fieldwork on the Accessibility Hierarchy

This problem set is not conceptually difficult. But it takes some informant time. Please use only native speakers when you gather your data. Someone who moved to a country after the onset of adolescence, even if that person speaks the language of the new country beautifully, is not a reliable informant for that language.

There are many relative-clause strategies in the languages of the world. *Wh*-relatives of English have their parallels in many languages. *That*-relatives are even more common. And resumptive pronoun relatives (as in Problem Set 8.9) are not uncommon. If you know another language besides English, do some fieldwork. Determine whether these three relative-clause–forming strategies occur in the language you examine. If there is some fourth strategy present in the language you examine, describe it, with examples.

For every relative-clause–forming strategy, be sure to test whether the strategy works with the position inside the relative clause (the position from which you are relativizing) being a Subject, DO, IO, OP, and then genitive, as in:

(1)   The boy whose sister I like is Ralph.

And then test with Object of a Comparative, as in:

(2)   The boy that Mary is taller than isn't my brother.
      The boy who Mary is taller than isn't my brother.

Give examples of each type of relative that you find, with all the GFs tested.

Not all languages can relativize from all these GFs. Many languages have no way of relativizing from Object of a Comparative (Basque, Dutch, etc.). Many have no way of relativizing from either Object of a Comparative or genitive position (Catalan, North Frisian, Iban, etc.). Some cannot relativize from either of these two positions nor from an OP (Javanese, etc.). Some cannot relativize from any of these three positions nor from an IO (Malagasy, etc.). Some cannot even relativize from a DO (Tagalog, Maori, Minang-Kabau, etc.). But every language (so far as we know) has at least one strategy for relativizing from Subject position. Linguists have claimed that each of the GFs stated here is relatively more inaccessible to relativization than the next position. For this reason, people talk about the ACCESSIBILITY HIERARCHY (AH), which is

Subj > DO > IO > Obl > Gen > Object of Comparative

In this hierarchy you find the term "Obl" (for "oblique") instead of "OP." In English, our oblique objects are introduced by a P. But in many languages, oblique objects may be introduced by a P or by a special Case-marking (such as Latin ablative). "Oblique" is the cover term for both possibilities. Thus the claim of this hierarchy is that if a language cannot relativize from a given position in the hierarchy (such as Obl, for example), it cannot relativize from any position to the right of that one on the hierarchy, either (such as Gen and Object of Comparative).

Tell whether the language you look at can go all the way down the AH. If it cannot, does it have discontinuous gaps in the hierarchy (say IO and Gen, for example) or does it merely stop at a certain point so that every GF after that point is impossible to relativize from? Of course, the prediction of the AH is that you will not find discontinuous gaps. Instead, relativization will simply be impossible after a certain point on the hierarchy. But you should test all the way down the hierarchy so that you can either corroborate or refute the claims of the AH.

Problem Set 8.11: English *Though*-Preposing

Consider the phenomenon that has been called *though*-preposing, as in:

(1) [Though I may love her], that won't affect the grade.
     [Love her though I may], that won't affect the grade.

(2) [Though he may seem intelligent], he does not seem deep.
     [Intelligent though he may seem], he does not seem deep.

Is this movement of a lexical node or movement of a phrase? (You may have to make some assumptions about the structure of verbal strings here. State your assumptions explicitly.)

What categories can move?
Where does the category move to?
Is this a root phenomenon?
Does this movement obey Subjacency?
Give examples to support all of your answers.

Problem Set 8.12: English Asymmetric *And*

We noted in the text that movement out of coordinate structures is blocked. Yet the *Wh*-Movement structures in 2 and 3 are grammatical:

(1) You went to the store and bought something.

(2) What did you go to the store and buy?

(3) This is the whiskey that I went to the store and bought.

Study VPs like those in 1–3 that are connected by the conjunction *and* but allow extraction. Make a list of the characteristics of these VPs. Use the following data in making this list.

(4) I went to the store and bought whiskey. Here's the whiskey I went to the store and bought.

I earned \$5 at Mr. Jones' house and bought whiskey. *Here's the whiskey I earned \$5 at Mr. Jones's house and bought.

(5) You ran to Broadstreet and picked up the shirts. Which are the shirts you ran to Broadstreet and picked up?
     You ran to Broadstreet and didn't pick up the shirts. *Which are the shirts you ran to Broadstreet and didn't pick up?

(6) She's gone and ruined her dress! That's the dress she went and ruined.
     She's gone and will ruin her dress! *That's the dress she went and will ruin.

(7) She went and jumped in the lake. That's the lake she went and jumped in.
     She jumped in the lake and went. *That's the lake she jumped in and went.

Discuss why extraction might be allowed in the good examples. In doing this consider the semantic contribution of the first CONJUNCT to the second conjunct. Conjuncts are the strings coordinated by *and*.)

In many of these instances, a counterpart without *and* exists in the imperative, the future modality, and the infinitival form for many speakers:

(8) Run buy me some whiskey, please.

(9) She'll run buy you some whiskey if you ask nice.

(10) She wants to run buy some whiskey now.

In all these instances the verbal form has no inflectional ending. Can you tie this fact in to your discussion of why extraction is allowed in the good examples of 1–7?

By the way, the *and* in this problem set has been called the ASYMMETRIC *and* for reasons that now should be obvious to you.

*Problem Set 8.13: English Questions without Movement

This problem set challenges the text by asking you to consider seriously a nonmovement analysis of one phenomenon we have been attributing to Wh-*Movement. You should do it.*

Consider questions only (not relatives or any other structure you found Wh-*Movement to apply to).*

Part 1

If we were to generate in the DS all questions with the *wh*-phrase in specifier of C′ to start with, what rules would we need to interpret these questions properly? For example, if 1 is a good DS:

(1) Who did Mary say John insisted Paul invite?

what mechanisms must we propose in order to interpret the *wh*-phrase as being the theme argument of the verb *invite*? Can this interpretation be based on an UNBOUNDED DEPENDENCY between the *wh*-phrase and the DO position of *invite,* or must we form some sort of "dependency chains" (parallel to movement chains) that go from specifier of C' to specifier of C' for all the clauses in 1?

Part 2

How can island constraints (or violations of Subjacency in a movement approach) be handled with a nonmovement analysis of questions?

Part 3

It has been claimed that a nonmovement analysis of questions turns out to need all the mechanisms that a movement analysis needs, so the two analyses, according to some linguists, are terminological variants on each other. Does your preceding discussion offer any evidence with respect to this claim? How?

Part 4

Notice that we can question OPs either by having the OP in specifier of C' position or having the entire P'' in specifier of C' position:

    (2)   You talked to someone.

    (3)   **Who** did you talk to?

    (4)   **To whom** did you talk?

Chomsky has claimed this is because the feature of being [+wh] on the OP can optionally PERCOLATE up to the P'' that contains it. If percolation of this feature takes place, then the P'' (which now has the feature [+wh]) will move. If percolation does not take place, then the OP alone will move.

    In fact, not only a whole P'' can appear in specifier of C' position, but sometimes a whole N'' that contains the *wh*-phrase can appear in specifier of C' position:

    (5)   These are the *reports* [**which** I drew the lettering on the covers of].

    (6)   These are the *reports* [**on the covers of which** I drew the lettering].

    (7)   These are the *reports* [**the lettering on the covers of which** I drew].

The phenomenon exemplified in 4, 6, and 7 is called PIED-PIPING.

    Proponents of a nonmovement analysis of *wh*-structures have raised the issue of why, if Pied-Piping is optional, we cannot have a pied-piped P or part of an N'' stranded in specifier of C' position as we move from Comp to Comp. That is, why do we not find:

    (8)   Mary said Paul talked to someone.

    (9)   *Who did Mary say [$_{C''}$ [to] [$_{C'}$Paul talked]]?

Example 9 would be generated with a movement analysis by first moving the P″ that contains the *wh*-phrase into the specifier of C′ of the embedded clause:

(10)   Mary said [$_{C'}$[to whom] [$_C$Paul talked t]]

Then Comp-to-Comp movement would apply, but since Pied-Piping is optional, this time only the *wh*-phrase would move, and the *to* would be stranded in the specifier of C′ of the embedded clause, yielding 9.

The nonmovement analysis, however, would never generate 9 in the first place.

Is this an insuperable criticism for a movement analysis? Can you think of a reason why 9 should not be generated with a movement analysis?

*Problem Set 8.14: English Empty Categories

This problem set could easily serve as part of a final exam for a course based on this book. It pulls together several points of theory and it should be done.

We have argued that there are five possible types of phonetically empty categories (here called "ec"s):

(a) A slot can be completely empty, not having any sort of features at all. (This is what we find at DS in the GF Subject position of passive verbs and of verbs like *seem*, which assign no theta-role to the GF Subject slot. We argued that GF Subject position is the only GF position that can be completely empty at DS, since GF Subject position is the only GF position required by X-Bar Theory [in the form of the Extended Projection Principle] even when the lexical features of a predicate do not require it. That is, whether we have a DO is determined by the choice of lexical items in the V slot. Whether we have an IO is determined by the choice of lexical items in the V slot. Whether we have an OP is determined by the choice of lexical items in the P slot. But we always have a GF Subject.)

(b) An ec can be [−anaphor, +pronominal]. (This is what we argued that pro of languages like Portuguese can be. Little pro is like other pronominals in that it receives a theta-role.)

(c) An ec can be [+anaphor, +pronominal]. (This is what we argued PRO to be. In order for PRO not to violate Conditions A and B of the Binding Theory, we concluded that at SS [which is what BT operates off of] PRO cannot have a governing category. Like other pronominals [and anaphors], PRO receives a theta-role.)

(d) An ec can be [+anaphor, −pronominal]. (This is what we argued trace of NP-movement to be. So trace of NP-movement is always A-bound within its governing category.)

(e) An ec can be [−anaphor, −pronominal]. (This is what we said trace of *Wh*-Movement is. Remember that *wh*-trace is always locally non-A-bound.)

Assume that we were right, and there are only these five kinds of phonetically empty slots. (If you did Problem Set 8.6, on Italian Indefinite *si* sentences, you might have come to the conclusion that we need a sixth ec, the Indefinite Object e. Please ignore that finding here.)

Assume also that completely empty slots—as described in (a)—occur at DS but not at SS.

Use these assumptions as you answer the following questions.

In Problem Set 7.2 of chapter 7 we looked at sentences like:

(1)   John seems to have been invited by Susie.

You were led there to argue for a derivation in which *John* originates at DS as the DO of *invited* and two movements are involved. First *John* moves into GF Subject position of the lower clause (an instance of Passive); then it moves into GF Subject position of the higher clause (an instance of Raising). The DS of 1 would then be:

(2) $[_{I''} \ldots [_{V''}\text{seems} [_{I''} \ldots [_{V'}\text{to have been invited John by Susie}]]]]$

(The dots in 2 represent totally empty slots at DS. Only those brackets that we need in order to understand the structure are given.) And the SS of 1 with traces added would then be:

(3) $[_{I''}\text{John}_i \text{ [seems } [_{I'}t_i \text{ [to have been invited } t_i \text{ by Susie}]]]]$

Now consider an alternative derivation. Assume that 2 is the DS for 1, but that instead of two movements, we have only one movement, from Object position of the lower clause to Subject position of the higher clause. Then there would be only one trace: in Object position of the lower clause. And what is in Subject position of the lower clause is a mystery. Let me label this mystery node ??? for now:

(4)   [John [seems [???[to have been invited t by Susie]]]]

Part 1

Does the movement in 4 violate Subjacency? If not, just say no. If so, how? That is, name the nodes that are barriers for the trace. You should draw a tree that includes all projections of every C and every I so that you can be sure of your answer.

Part 2

Does the SS in 4 violate any principles of Case Theory? If not, just say no. If so, how?

Part 3

Now consider separately the remaining four of the five potential phonetically empty slots outlined in (a)–(e). (That is, skip trace of NP-movement.) For each one tell whether it could appear in the slot marked ??? in 4. If it cannot appear there, explain why not. (Remember that 4 is a representation at SS, not at DS.)

Part 4

Why are the constructions in 5 and 6 ill-formed?

> (5)   *John seems that Jack loves Susie.
>
> (6)   *John arrived Alf.

Part 5

Why is 4 not a well-formed derivation of 1? (Use all you learned in answering Parts 1–4 in your conclusion here.)

Problem Set 8.15: English Contraction

Consider the contrast between 1 and 2.

> (1)   Who do you wanna introduce to Sally?
>   (cf. Who do you want to introduce to Sally?)
>
> (2)   *Who do you wanna introduce me to Sally?
>   (cf. Who do you want to introduce me to Sally?)

Some linguists have claimed that the fact that *want to* can contract to *wanna* in 1 but not in 2 gives evidence not only of these sentences having syntactic structures that differ in some important way, but of the claim that the phonology recognizes some empty categories and not others.

First, give the SS for 1 and 2 with all empty categories filled in, with all necessary co-indexing, and with arrows to indicate the locus of any movements.

Second, explain why phonology is involved here. What distinction does phonology appear to be making?

Problem Set 8.16: Italian Verb-String Structure

As you learned in Tangent 8.1, Italian has been analyzed as having an Agreement Phrase which contains a Tense Phrase:

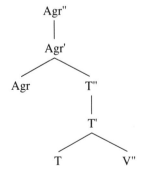

It has also been proposed that there is a Negative or Positive Phrase (Neg″ or Pos″) that comes between the two, in which the head would be *non* 'not' or a silent affirmative morpheme, as in:

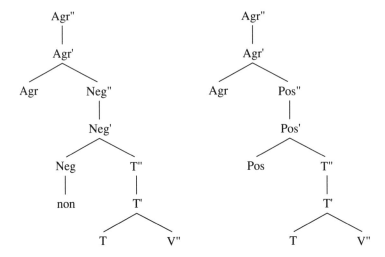

This proposal goes along with the further proposal that *non* (and the silent affirmative morpheme) is a clitic that must cliticize to Agr by ADJOINING to Agr, forming a new Agr node, as in:

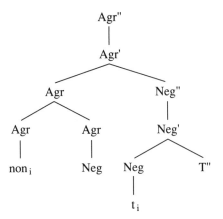

The type of adjunction seen here is called CHOMSKY-ADJUNCTION. Chomsky-adjunction is adjunction to a node in which a new mother node of the same category as the one adjoined to is formed, dominating the old node plus the moved node.

Italian has a handful of words that can accompany a negative which have been analyzed as adverbs that modify the whole Neg″, so they are generated as sisters to Neg′:

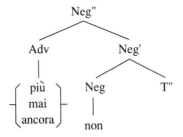

(For those of you who speak French, you might note that French has similar adverbs: *plus, jamais*, etc.) We can see these adverbs in:

(1) Gianni non parla più.
    'Gianni doesn't speak any more.'

(2) Gianni non parla mai.
    'Gianni does not speak ever.' = 'Gianni never speaks.'

(3) Gianni non parla ancora.
    'Gianni doesn't speak yet.'

In all of these sentences at least two rules have applied: the negative *non* has cliticized and the verb has moved through the head of Tense and on up into the head of Agr:

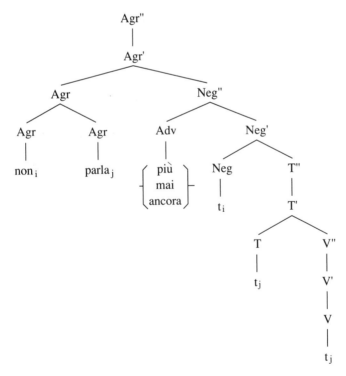

Now, when there is an auxiliary present, it takes its own tense and agreement morphemes in Italian, and the main verb shows up in a participle form. We will label
the morpheme of this participle as an Agr (but you might well, instead, want to label
it as Asp (for Aspectual)):

(4)   Gianni non ha parlato.

The derivation of 4 would be as shown in 5 and 6 below, where Subject will be in
specifier of Agr' position (analogous to specifier of I' position). In 5 we see the DS
of 4. In 6 we see the SS after *non* cliticization, head movement of the auxiliary up
through the T node and into the higher Agr node, and head movement of the main
verb up into the lower Agr node:

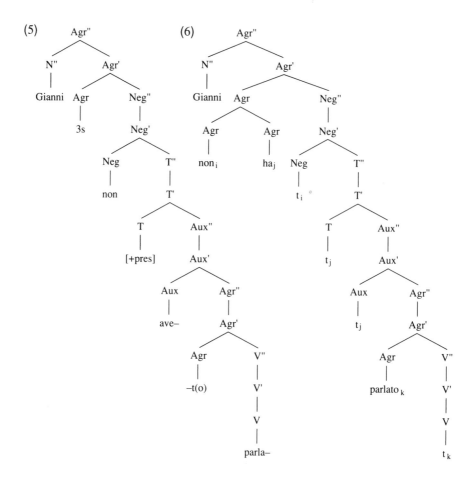

Part 1

Give a DS and SS tree for:

(7)   Gianni non ha mai parlato.
      'Gianni has never spoken.'

Part 2

Besides 7, we can also find:

(8)   Gianni non ha parlato mai.
      'Gianni has never spoken.'

Why is 8 surprising? If we assume that there is no rule allowing syntactic movement downward in a tree (and see the discussion in Tangent 8.1 of this point), then where might you propose that *mai* is generated in 8 at DS, as opposed to where *mai* is generated in 7 at DS?

Besides the movement rules of NP-movement, *Wh*-Movement, and head movements, Italian also has at least two other potential movement rules. One is called DISLOCATION. This rule can move a phrase (of any category) to the right or left periphery of a clause (RIGHT DISLOCATION [RD] or LEFT DISLOCATION [LD]), resulting in Chomsky-adjunction. The dislocated material is characterized by a pause between it and the rest of the phrase, indicated here by a comma. (As usual, the inflected verb is marked by V plus person and number.)

(9)   RD: L'ha fatto, Gianni.
            V3s
            '(He) did it, Gianni.' (= Gianni did it.)

      LD: Gianni, l'ha fatto.
            V3s
            'Gianni, (he) did it.'

At SS the structure of 9 is:

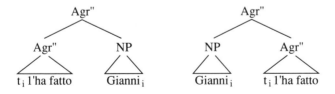

The other potential movement rule is called Topicalization; people have argued that Topicalization in Italian is not an instance of *Wh*-Movement, but, instead, a movement of a phrase (of any category) into a Topic Node that is somehow adjoined to a whole clause at DS (rather than being created by Chomsky-adjunction, in contrast to dislocation structures). (You are familiar with the idea of a topic node from Japanese, as in Problem Set 3.7.) Topicalization is only to the left and it is characterized by an intonation peak on the topicalized phrase, indicated by capitals below:

(10)   GIANNI ho visto.
            V1s
        'Gianni I have seen.'

The structure of 10 at SS is (something like—and please do not let the details of how the various projections of Topic are to be handled worry you—those details need not be worked out in this problem set) as seen in:

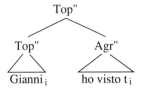

In a given sentence, if we believe that a phrase has been moved to initial position, we can identify whether that movement is LD or topicalization by the presence or lack of a pause and by the presence or lack of an initial intonation peak. There is another difference, however. Indefinite quantifiers cannot be Left Dislocated, but they can be topicalized.

(11)   *Nessuno, (l')ho visto.
        *Qualcuno, (l')ho visto.
        '{Nobody/Somebody}, I saw (him).'

(12)   NESSUNO ho visto.
        QUALCUNO ho visto.

Now, let us assume that adverbs that modify the entire proposition, that is, SENTENTIAL ADVERBS, are generated as sisters to the Agr″, perhaps as in 13.

(13)   Probabilmente Gianni telefonerà.
        "Probably Gianni will telephone."

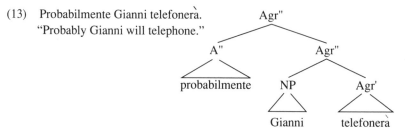

Part 3

Discuss two potential derivations of 14 (I have left out all potential pauses and given no indication of intonation peaks) and give both the SSs. With each derivation discuss whether and where there would be pauses and/or intonation peaks. (You can simplify by using triangles for details that do not interest us here, as I have in the trees above.)

    (14)   Gianni probabilmente telefonerà.
             'Gianni probably will telephone.'

There is only one analysis available for 15, in contrast to 14. Why?

    (15)   Nessuno probabilmente telefonerà.
             'Nobody probably will telephone.'

Mark where any pauses or intonation peaks should go in 15.

Part 4

Discuss the derivation of 16 and give a simplified SS for it.

    (16)   Gianni telefonerà, probabilmente.
             'Gianni will telephone, probably.'

There must be a pause preceding the adverb. Why?

Part 5

Now we find that while we do not get 17 without a pause, we do find sentences like 18, with no pause on either side of the adverb:

    (17)   *Gianni sbaglia probabilmente.
             'Gianni makes a mistake probably.'

    (18)   Gianni ha probabilmente sbagliato.
             'Gianni has probably made a mistake.'

Go back to our tree that shows the structure of sentences with auxiliaries in Italian. Now reread the description of where sentential adverbs are attached. Where could the sentential adverb in 18 be generated at DS in order to account for the word order of that sentence at SS? Give a DS and a SS for 18, using a complete tree with all the details you know how to put in.

    Adverbs that modify only the verb phrase are more difficult to talk about because they display a variety of syntactic behaviors. Here we will look at the single adverb *spesso* 'often,' but if you were to do the same exercise with a different adverb, you might well encounter quite different acceptability judgments and be led to different analyses.

    Let us propose that *spesso* is generated at DS adjoined either to the left or the right of V″:

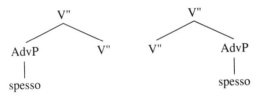

Part 6

Discuss the derivations of 19 and 20.

(19) Quel medico risolverà spesso i tuoi problemi.
'That doctor will solve often your problems.'

(20) Quel medico risolverà i tuoi problemi spesso.
'That doctor will solve your problems often.'

In particular, account for why *spesso* follows the verb in 19.

Part 7

In 21 we find we must get an initial intonation peak and we cannot have a pause after the adverb:

(21) SPESSO Gianni sbaglia.
'Often Gianni makes mistakes.'

Account for the position of *spesso* in 21 and for the intonation and pause facts.

Part 8

Now consider 22:

(22) Gianni SPESSO sbaglia.
'Gianni often makes mistakes.'

Give a derivation for 22 that will account for the word order here. You might want to use 23 in support of your analysis:

(23) *Qualcuno spesso sbaglia.
*Nessuno spesso sbaglia.
'{Somebody/Nobody} often makes mistakes.'

No amount of playing with the intonation or with pauses can salvage 23; these sentences are simply ungrammatical.

Star Problem 8.1

In most complex sentences it is easy to distinguish embedded clauses from the matrix clause. For one, *that* introduces only embedded clauses. For another, all tenseless clauses are embedded (with the one possible exception being imperatives, depending on your analysis for imperatives). And, of course, you can use Binding Theory to test whether one clause is contained in another, since BT makes predictions about the binding possibilities of elements in different clauses. (Look back at Problem Set 8.4.)

Consider sentences like the following, in which on the surface there is no complementizer to tell which clause is the embedded one:

(1)   You couldn't see five feet ahead, the snow was coming so fast.

(2)   The snow was coming so fast, you couldn't see five feet ahead.

(The concatenation of clauses with no obvious marker of subordination has been called ASYNDETON by some.) Argue for the structure of 1 and 2.

Star Problem 8.2

In the text of this chapter and in Tangent 8.3 you saw a variety of explanations for why *Wh*-Movement is ungrammatical in many structures (including various island constraints, the A-Over-A Principle, and Subjacency). *Wh*-Movement has applied in the sentences below. Identify why the application of *Wh*-Movement in each example below is problematic. Then discuss what additional factor might be responsible for the grammaticality here:

(1)   Who did Sue marry after Jill divorced?

(2)   What did Jack buy but Sally make?

(3)   He's a boy who if you meet, you'll like.
      (cf. *He's {a/the} boy who if you like, I'll pay you $50. but: He's the boy
      that if you like him, I'll pay you $50.)

You should reread the discussion at the end of the last section in the text. Structures with multiple gaps, like those in 1–3, are called across-the-board phenomena. So your job here is to discuss the mechanics of across-the-board movement.
      Hint: Many people can say not only 1–3, but also sentences like:

(4)   Sue actually married after Jill divorced [that crummy Tom].

(5)   Jack may have bought but Sally made [a perfect cake].

(6)   I swear. If you meet, you will definitely like, [this kid].

And if you find 4–6 ungrammatical or marginal, you might want to compare them to the fully grammatical examples:

(7)   He both reads and writes [poetry].

(8)   I'll have to buy or bake [a cake].

(9)   I ate, but didn't enjoy, [those doughnuts].

If you find 4–6 acceptable, the issue may not be one of *Wh*-Movement, but of some other movement that precedes *Wh*-Movement. This other movement rule (the one that has applied in 7–9) has been called RIGHT NODE RAISING (RNR). Your job here, if you decide to opt for RNR before *Wh*-Movement in 1–3, is to figure out what kind of structures RNR applies to. You might want to look at the description of Chomsky adjunction in Problem Set 8.16.

Star Problem 8.3

On November 30, 1990, Johnny Carson, on his television program, held a closed envelope up to his ear and, pretending to be a seer, said, "On top of old Smokey." This was supposed to be the answer to the question on a card inside the envelope— a question he supposedly had not yet seen. Then he opened the envelope and read, "Where Yogi Bear came home to find his wife." Let us convert this into an ordinary direct question by adding Subject-Auxiliary Inversion here:

(1)   *Where did Yogi Bear come home to find his wife?

This is not an acceptable sentence. How is the *Wh*-Movement in Johnny Carson's question a problem for GB Theory?

Why can quiz shows get away with questions like this, particularly if they do what Carson did, and not employ Subject-Auxiliary Inversion?

Star Problem 8.4

In the text we noted that extraction from an Object NP is often possible, but not always:

(1)   Jack took [pictures of someone].
      Who did Jack take pictures of?
      Jack opened [a bottle of wine].
      What did Jack open a bottle of?

(2)   Bill introduced [a friend of mine] to Sue.
    ??Who did Bill introduce [a friend of] to Sue?
      Bill bought [a wallet of fine leather].
    *What did Bill buy [a wallet of]?

Come up with many more examples in each list. State whatever generalizations you might see in terms of characterizing the factors that are relevant to a sentence's being in one list or the other. Now discuss those generalizations in light of the barriers notion of Subjacency.

Star Problem 8.5

When we gave a formal definition of blocking category in the text, we paid attention to whether or not a node was L-Marked by the primary predicate of the clause. At that point you might have wondered what other possibilities arise.

The possibilities that arise depend on a variety of other assumptions you might be making about the grammar. What I would like you to address here is the issue of whether a secondary predicate plays any role in the determination of blocking categories and barriers.

Consider:

(1)   I proved [the theory] [false].

In chapter 10 we will face the question of whether the two constituents following *proved* form a larger constituent. For now, do not make any assumptions one way or another. The only thing you need to assume is that the NP *the theory* is a sister to the predicative AP *false*.

In 1 many would argue that *proved* does not assign a theta-role to its DO. That is, this NP is not an argument of the V. Instead, the secondary predicate is the argument of the V. On the other hand, the NP is the argument of the secondary predicate. Thus it receives a theta-role from that secondary predicate. And this predicate is its sister. So it is L-Marked by the secondary predicate. Now does this L-Marking of the DO prevent the DO from being a blocking category, and therefore, from being a barrier to elements inside it? Consider:

(2)   You proved the theory about something false.

(3)   *What did you prove the theory about false?
       (cf. What did you prove a theory about?)

Find other examples to back up your conclusions. You might consider:

(4)   You found [pictures of someone] [amusing].

(5)   *Who did you find pictures of amusing?
       (cf. Who did you find pictures of?)

If you come to the conclusion that secondary predicates should not count in the determination of barriers (consistent with my approach in the text), why do you think that is? What makes secondary predicates not relevant to movement?

And does all movement behave the same way with respect to secondary predicates? Above we see examples involving only *Wh*-Movement. Is it possible to construct examples that involve NP-movement to test whether secondary predicates play a role in determining barriers? If so, do it. If not, explain why not.

Star Problem 8.6

Part 1

Compare:

(1)   It's odd that a man is chairing the Women's Concerns Committee.

(2)   It's odd for a man to chair the Women's Concerns Committee.

There is a semantic difference between these two sentences, and it must be attributed to the fact that one sentence has a tensed embedded clause introduced by *that* and the other has an infinitival embedded clause introduced by *for*.

Another pair is:

(3)   She asked whether Jack should come.

(4)   She asked that Jack should come.

Try to find other minimal pairs like these, in which a semantic difference is involved but the only syntactic difference is one of the type of embedded clause we have. These sorts of data have been used to support the claim that every clause is marked as to whether it has the features of [+th] or [−th] and [+wh] or [−wh]. Do we need to add any other possible features for clause types?

Part 2

Questions that involve more than one *wh*-phrase do not allow multiple *Wh*-Movement in the syntax (since the specifier of C' can be filled by only one phrase), but instead exhibit *wh*-phrases *in situ*:

(1)   Who gave [what] to [whom]?

Both the *wh*-phrases *in situ* in 1 are NPs. It's been noted that not all *wh*-phrases are grammatical *in situ* in multiple *wh*-phrase questions. Thus locative and temporal *wh*-phrases are grammatical, but manner and reason *wh*-phrases are not:

(2)   What did you find {when/where}?

(3)   *What did you find {how/why}?

It has been proposed that *when/where* are NPs while *how/why* are PPs. Can you find any evidence using your knowledge of the features [+wh] and [+th] for this categorial distinction?

    Right now you have no idea of how the claim of a categorial difference between *when/where*, on the one hand and *why/how* on the other can help account for the grammatical difference between 2 and 3. The claim is that after syntactic rules have applied, semantic rules may apply that can be parallel in many respects to syntactic rules. A semantic rule could front all the *wh*-phrases in a multiple *wh*-phrase question like 1–3. But the traces left behind would have to be properly governed. If *when* and *where* are NPs introduced by phonetically empty Ps (and notice that both can be introduced by *right*: *He left her {right when she most needed him/right where she wanted to be}*), then those Ps could govern their traces in 2 after the semantic *Wh*-Movement had fronted only the *wh*-NPs. But if *how* and *why* are PPs, then nothing will govern their traces in 3. After you have read chapter 9, this discussion will make sense to you. At that time you might want to approach these data again and evaluate this analysis for yourself.

Star Problem 8.7

Sometimes a *with* phrase is optional and the sentence, at least at first glance, seems to mean pretty much the same thing with or without it:

(1)   She picked up a knife and cut the steak (with it).

Actually, 1 without the *with* phrase is different in meaning from 1 with the *with* phrase. Thus 2 is not a contradiction, but 3 is:

(2)   She picked up a knife$_i$ and cut the steak, but not with the knife$_i$, with the laser beam!

(3)   *She picked up a knife$_i$ and cut the steak with it$_i$, but not with the knife$_i$, with the laser beam!

Now the object of a *with* phrase sometimes must be lexically realized:

(4)   *She picked up a knife and cut the steak with.

and other times cannot be lexically realized:

    (5)   Here's a fork to eat your supper with.
           *Here's a fork to eat your supper with it.

    (6)   Mary is ready to go out with.
           *Mary$_i$ is ready to go out with her$_i$.

Why?

Star Problem 8.8

In the text we noted that movement out of bracketed phrases like these results in ungrammaticality:

    (1)   [From Boston to someplace else] is quite far.
           *Where is [from Boston to t] quite far?

    (2)   He went [from Boston to someplace else].
           ?*Where did he go [from Boston to t]?

Will any of the principles we have yet discussed account for 1 or 2 or both? If not, explore the unaccounted-for restriction and try to offer your own account.

Star Problem 8.9

In the text we concluded that extraction out of an NP that is an OP is blocked unless the OP is an argument of the primary predicate (in which case it is L-Marked, and therefore not a barrier to the elements within it). But we find some interesting quirks here. The Object of *in* in 1 is L-Marked, yet extraction results in ungrammaticality:

    (1)   You got involved [$_{P'}$in [$_{N'}$the debate about something]].
           *What did you get involved in the debate about t?

However, for some speakers, if we have *who* instead of *what* in 1, the extraction results in a grammatical question:

    (2)   You got involved [$_{P'}$in [$_{N'}$the debate about someone]].
           Who did you get involved in the debate about t?

Will any of the principles we have yet discussed account for the difference between 1 and 2?

    Actually, 1 seems to be more the rule than 2 (even though our notion of Subjacency would lead us to see 2 as the rule and 1 as an aberration). Thus many OPs seem to resist extraction of any of their subparts, even though the OPs are L-Marked.

    (3)   You talked [about [the lecture on something]].
           *What did you talk about the lecture on t?

What is going on? (You might want to compare your study here to the results you came up with for Star Problem 8.4.)

Star Problem 8.10

Where is *unless* located in the tree in examples such as:

(1) I'll cry *unless* you come.

Is *unless* in C or in specifier of C', or is it a P whose complement is a clause, or what? Argue for your analysis.

Overview

In this chapter we have worked primarily on Trace Theory and Binding Theory in the text and we have looked at many issues of X-Bar Theory in the tangents. The new principles we have added to our grammar are Subjacency, Strict Cyclicity, the Mirror Principle, and the Head Movement Constraint. We have also discussed a new type of movement, head movement, and one instantiation of it, Verb Movement.

The reader should refer to the overviews at the ends of chapters 6 and 7. Here we will state only changes or additions to the theory developed in this chapter.

Binding Theory

We now have a typology of referring expressions, using the features [+anaphor]/[−anaphor] and [+pronominal]/[−pronominal], as in this chart. Here the items listed under 1 have a phonetic matrix, while those under 2 are empty categories.

	[+*anaphor*]	[−*anaphor*]
[+pronominal]	1. 0 2. PRO	1. pronouns 2. pro
[−pronominal]	1. reflexives, reciprocals 2. NP-trace	1. lexical NPs 2. *wh*-trace

The rest of BT remains as in chapter 7.

X-Bar Theory

We took a closer look at X-Bar Theory (in Tangents 8.1 and 8.2) and explored some issues further in the problems (Problem Sets 8.2 and 8.16, in particular). We discussed how there is considerable debate over whether modifiers must all be attached as sisters to an X at DS or whether some are attached as sisters to X' or to a variety of other potential projections of X.

We reiterated our claim that movement is a valid test for constituency, and we pointed out problems with using the interpretation of pro-forms as a test for syntactic constituency.

We finally made explicit our analysis of the verbal string. We argued that Tense and Agreement are independent features and that each head their own phrase. We analyzed the auxiliary system, arguing that modals are generated under T (which we have identified as I for English) and never pass through Agr, which is why they show inflection for tense only and never for person/number. *Have* and *be*, however, are generated lower in the tree. They each head phrases and take VP as their complement. Verb Movement moves the highest auxiliary in the tree and moves it upward if there are available nodes above it to move into (which will be the case unless the highest auxiliary is a modal). The moved auxiliary will pass first through Agr, picking up that morpheme, and then into T, picking up that morpheme.

This analysis of the auxiliary system accounts for the facts on Subject-Auxiliary Inversion, so long as we take that rule to be an instantiation of Head Movement from I into C.

We discussed the fact that it has been proposed that all head movement is restricted in the following way:

> Head Movement Constraint: A head X can move into a head slot Y only if Y governs X″. (If Y is not Comp, then Y must also theta-mark or L-mark X″.)

If the Head Movement Constraint is correct, both Agr and T L-Mark their complements. This is not intuitively obvious and I find this assumption one of the more questionable points in this constraint.

We also pointed out that with an analysis of verbal phrases in which every feature heads its own phrase (that is, T heads its own phrase, and Agr heads its own phrase) if the language has a relatively transparent morphology, the order of the morphemes in the final verb form reflects the syntactic derivation. That is, morphemes that are lower in the tree are closer to the verb stem than morphemes that are higher in the tree. The principle at work here, what you might think of informally as the first-in-last-out principle, is called the Mirror Principle.

We also learned that while Romance languages have Agr″ higher than T″, English has T″ higher than Agr″. It seems that the feature of the higher node in each language (in Romance [+Agr] or [−Agr], in English [+tense] or [−tense]) is the important one when it comes to characterizing binding domains.

The rest of X-Bar Theory remains the same as at the end of chapter 6.

Trace Theory

In this chapter we looked at *Wh*-Movement and compared it to NP-movement.

NP-movement leaves behind an NP-trace, which is an anaphor. The foot of an NP-movement chain is in a position to which Case cannot be assigned and to which a theta-role may be assigned.

NP-movement is always into Subject position. *It is important to realize that if we generate Subjects within the government domain of their theta-assigner (as discussed in Tangent 8.2), the specifier position which is the sister to I′ is a non-theta-receiving position automatically. Thus the fact that the only GF that can have movement into it is Subject position is nicely motivated.*

NP-movement is not limited to moving NPs only (it can move sentential

Objects, for example). Do not let the name "NP-movement" throw you off: it is a type of movement, not movement of NPs only.

Wh-Movement leaves behind a *wh*-trace, which is a variable and shares binding properties with R-expressions. All variables are locally non-A-bound (by definition). If the foot of a *Wh*-Movement chain is a referring nominal, it is in a position to receive Case and to which a theta-role might or might not be assigned.

We noted that *Wh*-Movement is always into an empty phrasal position that has the feature [+wh]. Since this feature is limited to specifier of C', *Wh*-Movement will always be into specifier of C'. A *wh*-phrase can move from one specifier of C' to the next adjacent specifier of C' in what is called Comp-to-Comp movement.

Wh-Movement is not limited to moving only *wh*-phrases. Again, do not let the name "*Wh*-Movement" throw you off: it is a type of movement, not movement of only *wh*-phrases.

We have maintained the claim that every chain (whether the result of NP-movement or of *Wh*-Movement) can have at most one theta-role and at most one Case associated with it.

All movement is bounded by the Principle of Subjacency:

> Subjacency Principle: Movement that crosses at most one barrier is allowed. But movement becomes more difficult as more barriers are crossed.

We said that every primary predicate L-Marks its arguments that fall within the minimal phrase that contains the predicate. We then defined the notion of blocking category as in:

1. A is a BC for B iff A is not L-Marked by a primary predicate and A dominates B, where A is phrasal.

We then defined the notion of barrier, as in:

2. A is a barrier for B iff A is phrasal and:
   (a) A immediately dominates C, where C is a BC for B,
   or (b) A is a BC for B and A does not equal I".

By (a) we see that a phrasal node immediately dominating a BC for a node B becomes a barrier for B. By (b) we see that all BCs are themselves barriers except I". In other words, I" can be a barrier for a node B only if it immediately dominates a BC for B—that is, only via (a). We said that barriers defined by (a) inherit barrierhood (since the BC below them allows them to become barriers).

A phrase of any category that has the GF of Subject, then, is a BC as well as a barrier (assuming Subjects will never be bare I") to all the elements contained in that Subject. A phrase of any category that functions as a modifier (adverbial modifier or relative clause modifier) or as an appositive is, likewise, a BC to all the elements contained in that phrase. Only phrases that function as DOs or as OPs where the OP is an argument of the primary predicate are not going to be BCs to the elements contained within them.

Finally, we adopted the Principle of Strict Cyclicity:

3. Strict Cyclicity: No rule may affect only the members of a given cycle once that cycle has already been passed.

Since the only rules we have concerned ourselves with in detail thus far are movement rules, I have placed this principle here under Trace Theory. However, it should apply generally to the entire grammar.

The rest of Trace Theory remains as it was at the end of chapter 6.

9

Accessibility, the Empty-Category Principle, and Crossover

A Typology of Referring Items

In chapter 8 we studied *Wh*-Movement and in the process we came up with the following typology of referring items.

(1) [+anaphor, −pronominal]
    with a phonetic matrix: reflexives, reciprocals
    without a phonetic matrix: NP-trace

(2) [−anaphor, +pronominal]
    with a phonetic matrix: pronouns
    without a phonetic matrix: pro

(3) [−anaphor, −pronominal]
    with a phonetic matrix: R-expressions
    without a phonetic matrix: *wh*-trace

(4) [+anaphor, +pronominal]
    with a phonetic matrix: none
    without a phonetic matrix: PRO

The one gap in this typology is the slot for [+anaphor, +pronominal] that has a phonetic matrix. We would like either to fill that slot or to find the reason it is empty. So let us now go on a hunt to fill that slot.

We know that if an item is [+anaphor], it must conform to Condition A of BT. We know that if an item is [+pronominal], it must conform to Condition B of BT. The one way we know of for an item to conform simultaneously to both Conditions A and B of BT is for that item to lack a governing category. An item can lack a governing category either because it lacks a governor (as is the case with PRO) or because it lacks an Accessible SUBJECT, or both.

If a referring expression were to be [+anaphor, +pronominal] and have a phonetic matrix, it would have to receive Case, which means that it would have to be governed (by its Case-Marker) or else be in the specifier of N′ (where it would receive genitive Case). But we have already noted instances in earlier chapters in which the possibility has been raised that the governor of a given X″ also governs the specifier of the X′ of that given X″. If that were generally true, then the specifier of any N′ would be governed by whatever node governed the relevant N″. Rather than pursue this question here (since it would lead us into a very extensive discussion of government), let us turn in a different direction to seek the item we are after.

The alternative, then, in looking for our NP that lacks a governing category, is to seek a [+anaphor, +pronominal] with a phonetic matrix that has no Accessible SUBJECT (although it is most probably governed). We now need to define the notion of "Accessible SUBJECT" and explore its ramifications for our picture of the theory.

Accessibility and i/i

Previously in this book we have taken the tack of developing concepts for ourselves. But we will not do that here. Instead, I will present to you a common definition of the notion of accessibility. And we will then see that this notion is founded on an incoherent assumption. Thus we could not have come up with it ourselves (I hope). We will then opt for a grammar that does not include the notion of accessibility.

The first thing for us to consider is the assumption upon which the notion of accessibility is dependent. This assumption is given in:

(5)   The I-WITHIN-I CONDITION:
        *$[_A \ldots B \ldots]$, where A and B bear the same index.

Example 5 is typically called "the i-within-i condition," and we will write it here as "i/i" for shorthand. i/i tells us that no node can be co-indexed with another node that properly contains it.

In this book so far indices have indicated only coreference or binding relationships; many binding relationships are based on coreference. Thus when we have seen two nodes with the same index, either they both had the same referent or one was an operator and the other was the variable that fell within the scope of that operator. If we consider only referential indices for a moment, i/i tells us that no node can bear the same referential index as another node that properly contains it. i/i as pertaining to referential indices surely exists as a condition independently from the notion of accessibility. Consider:

(6)   *[a picture of [itself]$_i$]$_i$
        *[the owner of [his]$_i$ boat]$_i$
        *[the conclusion of the text that precedes [it]$_i$]$_i$

These NPs are nonsensical (hence the asterisks in 6) with the assigned referential indices, and this ungrammaticality has been attributed to violations of i/i.

The particular applications of i/i in 6 are intuitively appealing. In these examples the reference of the entire NP is dependent upon the reference of all the parts of the NP. However, the reference of *itself, his,* and *it* in 6 are, in turn, dependent upon the reference of the entire NP. We have a circularity here that results in semantic anomaly. In Problem Set 9.1 we will study the type of referential circularity that i/i rules out. For now, we can see that when i/i applies to a structure involving referential indices only, i/i seems coherent as a principle of grammar. (And if you have already thought of examples that seem problematic for i/i even with respect to referential indices, please be patient until Problem Set 9.1. You will have a chance there to analyze them fully.)

Now let us turn to the definition of accessibility:

(7)   Accessibility:
       A is accessible to B iff B is in the c-command domain of A and assignment
       to B of the index of A would not violate i/i.

(Recall that if B is in the c-command domain of A, the first branching node that dominates A also dominates B, but A does not dominate B.) With regard to governing categories and the issue of Accessible SUBJECTs, 7 tells us that a node A can be an Accessible SUBJECT to another node B only if A c-commands B, A is a SUBJECT, and the co-indexation of B and A would not result in a violation of i/i. It is important to recognize that 7 concerns the hypothetical state of what would result if A and B were assigned the same index, but it does not require that A and B have the same index in order for A to be accessible to B.

You may well be asking yourself how on earth co-indexation of A and B could ever result in a violation of i/i. After all, if A c-commands B, then A does not contain B. So co-indexation of A and B will never result in A and B together constituting a violation of i/i. However, the co-indexation of A and B could result in some other violation of i/i. That is, co-indexing A and B might mean that some other node already co-indexed with A or B, let us call it C, would now constitute an i/i violation with A or with B or even with another node D, where D is already co-indexed with A or B.

Your imagination should be severely taxed at this point, for the only indices we have talked about up to this point in this book are referential indices, and binding indices (including those on traces and their antecedents or operators). However, many other types of indices have been proposed in the linguistic literature (and you will see one type, predication indices, and test i/i's relevance to it in Star Problem 9.2).

Before turning to an example that uses one of these other types of indices, let us look at an example to illustrate the notion of accessibility with indices that are already familiar to us. Consider:

(8)   *They expected [me to hear [stories about [each other]]].

Each other is an anaphor and must be bound in its governing category. What is the governor for this anaphor? It is the P *about.* Now where is the lowest SUBJECT? The NP headed by *stories* has no SUBJECT. But the infinitival clause does have a

SUBJECT (the NP *me*). Is that SUBJECT accessible to the anaphor? That is, if we were to co-index *me* and *each other*, would any violation of i/i result? No. So *me* is an accessible SUBJECT for the anaphor. Therefore, the governing category for the anaphor is the I″ of the infinitival clause. The problem with 8 is that the anaphor is not, in fact, bound within its governing category because the anaphor is co-indexed with *they*, not with *me*. So the anaphor is free in its governing category and 8 is ungrammatical because it violates condition A of BT. (If, by some chance, you find 8 or a minor variation on 8 grammatical, hold on. There is much variation in speakers' grammaticality judgments on sentences in which anaphors are not bound within their governing category. We will discuss this issue in chapter 10.)

Extensions of i/i

Now let us turn to an example which makes use of the notion of accessibility and of a new type of index. Consider:

(9)   They expected that [[pictures of each other] would be on sale].

Again we have an anaphor (the reciprocal). Its governor is the P *of* that is its sister. The NP headed by *pictures* does not have a SUBJECT. The embedded clause, however, does have a SUBJECT. What is that SUBJECT? Recall that the SUBJECT of a tensed clause is the INFL that is marked [+Agr] (or, in light of what we learned in Tangent 8.1 of chapter 8, [+ tense]). Now we must ask ourselves if [+Agr] is accessible to *each other*. If we were to co-index them, with our present knowledge of indices, we would come to the conclusion that no violation of i/i results, so [+Agr] is an accessible SUBJECT. However, it has been proposed that the following co-indexation rule exists:

(10)   Co-index Agr with the NP it governs.

Notice that this co-indexation is not based on coreference or on any notion of binding familiar to you. There is no sense in which Agr is an operator with Subject as the variable it binds. The indices proposed here are, then, a new kind of animal. In the linguistic literature, however, we find that many people treat these new indices as though they are indistinguishable by the grammar from binding and referential indices. Given 10, we will have co-indexation between [+Agr] and the Subject NP *pictures of each other*. But if the anaphor *each other* were to be co-indexed with [+Agr] (as we must test when checking out accessibility), the anaphor would also be co-indexed with the Subject NP that contains it:

(11)   They expected that [[pictures of [each other]$_i$]$_i$ would be on sale].

The co-indexation in 11 would be a violation of i/i. Therefore, we must conclude that [+Agr] is not, after all, an Accessible SUBJECT for the anaphor. That means that the governing category for the anaphor is the only other potential governing category in the sentence: the matrix I″. But, then, the anaphor, even though it is in a separate tensed clause from its antecedent, is, in fact, bound within its governing category. Thus 9 presents no problems for BT—hence its grammaticality.

What has happened here? By adopting 10, we have insured that for any item within the Subject of a given I″, the governing category cannot be that I″. That is, from 10 we can predict that anaphors embedded within a Subject of a clause can find their antecedents outside the clause (as in 9). We have thereby accounted for one type of nonlocal anaphor binding.

What about an anaphor that is itself the Subject of its clause? Is it always free to find an antecedent outside the clause? Think of examples. You can easily come up with the contrast we have noted repeatedly in earlier chapters between the Subjects of tenseless clauses and the Subjects of tensed clauses.

(12)   a.   They expected [each other to leave].
       b.   *They expected [that each other would leave].

We know that [+Agr] is a governor, but [−Agr] is not. So in 12a we know that the reciprocal is not governed within the embedded clause. Therefore the governing category for the reciprocal must be the matrix clause. Hence the reciprocal is bound within its governing category and 12a is grammatical. But in 12b [+Agr] of the embedded clause governs the reciprocal. Is this [+Agr] an Accessible SUBJECT for the reciprocal? If we were to co-index the reciprocal with [+Agr], no violation of i/i would result, since the reciprocal completely fills the Subject of the embedded clause instead of being properly contained in that Subject (in contrast to 9 above). So we must conclude that [+Agr] is, indeed, an Accessible SUBJECT here. Therefore, the governing category of the reciprocal is the embedded I″ and the reciprocal in 12b is not bound within its governing category. Example 12b, then, is a violation of Condition A of BT.

In sum, the adoption of 10 allows anaphors that are properly contained within Subjects to find antecedents outside their clause, while still blocking the binding of an anaphor that is the Subject of a tensed clause by some element outside the clause. In fact, many examples of anaphors that are properly contained within Subjects and that find antecedents outside their clause are cited in the literature, such as:

(13)   They think [[some letters for each other] are waiting at the post office].
       The models insisted that [[descriptions of themselves] be given to all the magazines].

       John and Mary said [[each other's photos] were on sale].

This behavior demands explanation. So the adoption of 10 does a lot of work for us. (We will discuss this behavior in chapter 10.)

However, the adoption of 10 in our account of 11 also calls for us to interpret i/i as applying to the new kind of indices created by the application of 10. While the invocation of i/i to rule out 6 above has intuitive appeal, since referential circularity is involved, the invocation of i/i in the analysis of 11 is completely without intuitive appeal. That is, we know that certain kinds of referential circularity lead to semantic anomaly (and see Problem Set 9.1), but there is nothing about the indices created by the application of 10 that would suggest that i/i should apply to such indices. In particular, we have no semantic sense of what the indices created by 10 represent, so we have nothing to guide us as to why i/i should apply to them. It would appear that 10's only motivation is to allow i/i to account for the behavior of binding in examples like 11. The ad hoc nature of 10 makes it suspect. Add to that the fact that once we extend i/i to handle indices other than referential and binding indices, its coherence is lost, and we should certainly begin to lose faith in our notion of accessibility as a useful notion in grammar.

Empirical Inadequacy of This Notion of Accessibility

Another point against the account of 11 based on this notion of accessibility is empirical: There is evidence that anaphors properly contained within Subjects can find their antecedents outside their clause even when an account parallel to that offered for 11 above cannot serve us. For example, consider:

(14)   They said [that nothing could {stop/prevent/interfere with/stand in the way of} [each other's pictures being put on sale]].

Here we have three clauses. The anaphor *each other* is properly contained in the NP *each other's pictures*, which is the Subject of the lowest clause (the Acc-*ing* clause we have been familiar with since Problem Set 5.5). The INFL of the lowest clause is co-indexed with the NP *each other's pictures* via 10. Now either the INFL of the lowest clause is a proper governor (since it assigns Case to its Subject, even though it is [−Agr]), in which case the lowest clause cannot be the governing category for the anaphor because the INFL is not an Accessible SUBJECT to this anaphor because of an i/i violation, or the INFL of the lowest clause is not a proper governor and, again, the lowest clause cannot be a governing category for the anaphor. However, the intermediary clause does contain both an Accessible SUBJECT for the anaphor (the NP *nothing*) and the governor for the anaphor (the head N *pictures*); thus the intermediary I″ is the governing category for this anaphor. The antecedent for the anaphor, however, is the Subject of the matrix clause, which is outside the governing category of the anaphor. Example 14, then, stands in violation of condition A of BT. Its grammaticality begs for an account, but the account offered for 11 does not serve here.

If we could find an account for 14 that also served for 11, we would not need to posit the rule in 10, nor would we need to interpret i/i as applying to indices other than referential and binding ones. Let us call binding of anaphors by an antecedent outside their governing category LONG-DISTANCE ANAPHORA. We will discuss L-D Anaphora in chapter 10 and offer there an account of 14 and 11 that makes use of neither 10 nor i/i.

For now, we see that our notion of accessibility incorrectly rules out the grammatical example 14. There are other grammatical examples of L-D Anaphora that our notion cannot handle adequately. One type is exemplified in:

(15)   Mary complained [that the teacher gave extra help to everyone but herself].

Here the anaphor *herself* is governed by the P *to* (which has as its Object the coordinate structure *everyone but herself*) and finds an accessible SUBJECT in the [+Agr] of the embedded clause. Thus the governing category for the anaphor is the lower clause. The antecedent, however, is in the matrix clause. Example 15 stands in violation of condition A of BT, yet it is grammatical for many speakers. We will return to such examples in chapter 10.

For the above reasons, we will not appeal to accessibility in order to account for L-D Anaphora. But, then, the whole raison d'être for the notion of accessibility has been vitiated and we will find no use for this notion at all in our grammar.

Please note that many linguistics articles today still make use of the notion of accessibility when determining the governing category for a given node. Thus the position we have arrived at in this chapter is not (yet) the mainstream position.

Back to a Typology of Referring Items

Returning to our typology of referential items, we were searching for an NP with the features [+anaphor, +pronominal] that had no governing category. We can conclude now that such an NP must lack a governor, since we have rendered meaningless the alternative possibility that such an NP lacks an accessible Subject (given that we have debunked the whole notion of accessibility). But, as we said at the end of the first section of this chapter, that means the NP must lack a phonetic matrix. Thus PRO is the only such item. The gap in the typology in 1–4 (found in the slot under 4 for an item with a phonetic matrix) is now accounted for.

The *That*-Trace Effect and the Empty-Category Principle

There remain a series of other major questions that arise from looking at the *Wh*-Movement phenomena of chapter 8 that we did not address there. I will now take the opportunity to discuss two briefly—one in this section and one in the next.

The first question regards a contrast in grammaticality that is well noted in the literature and that is exemplified here:

    (16)   Who did Jack say left?

    (17)   *Who did Jack say that left?

We find that while *Wh*-Movement in 16 is fine, in 17 it results in ungrammaticality. The only apparent difference between 16 and 17 is the presence of *that* in 17. But certainly we can apply *Wh*-Movement out of *that*-clauses in other sentences:

    (18)   Who did Jack say Bill saw?
            Who did Jack say that Bill saw?

Find additional grammatical examples of *Wh*-Movement out of *that*-clauses, like that in 18. Now find additional ungrammatical examples of *Wh*-Movement out of *that*-clauses, like that in 17. Do you notice a pattern? The ungrammatical examples involve movement of a Subject that is adjacent to the *that*. For this reason, the phenomenon exemplified in 17 has been referred to as the *That*-TRACE EFFECT.

Let us take a closer look at the SS of 16 and 17. For 16, the analysis is straightforward:

(19) $[_{C''}[\text{Who}_i]\,[_{C'}[_C\text{did}]\,[_{I''}\text{Jack say}\,[_{C''}[t_i]\,[_{C'}\,[_{I'}[t_i]\,\text{left}]]]]]]$?

There is a trace in Subject position of the embedded clause that is co-indexed with a trace in specifier of C' position in the lower clause, that is co-indexed with the *who* in specifier of C' position of the matrix clause. This arrangement of traces and their binders is grammatical, witness the acceptability of 16.

Now what about the SS of 17? Suddenly new questions present themselves. We argued in chapter 8 that *Wh*-Movement is always into the specifier of C' of the lowest clause that contains the *wh*-item. So in 17 we will have a trace in Subject position of the lower clause, and we know that movement will have taken place into the specifier of C' of the lower clause. Then Comp-to-Comp movement will have applied, leaving a trace in specifier of C' of the lower clause that is bound by the *who*. The problem is that the lower clause is introduced by *that*. Where is *that* located and how does the presence of the *that* affect the position of the trace that we know is somehow present in the specifier of C' of the embedded clause?

We talked in chapter 8 of how clauses seem to be marked by the specifier of C' as being [+wh] or [+th]. If this general approach is correct, we might expect that *that* would appear in specifier of C' position, just as *wh*-items appear in specifier of C' position. (But we will address an alternative analysis of *that* later.) With this assumption, we now have a problem for the analysis of 17: does *that* cover the intermediary trace, or does the specifier of C' branch, containing both *that* and trace?

(20) $[_{C''}\text{Who}_i\,[_{C'}\,[_C\text{did}]\,[_{I''}\text{Jack say}\,[_{C''}[\text{that}]\,[_{C'}\,[_{I'}\,t_i\,\text{left}]]]]]]$?

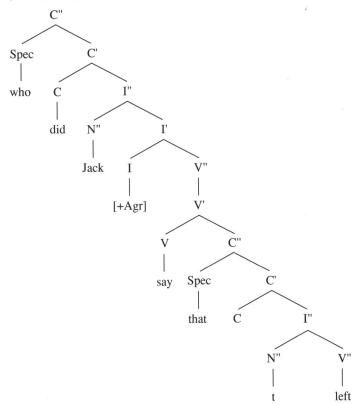

(21)   [$_{C''}$ Who$_i$ [$_{C'}$ [$_C$ did] [$_{I''}$ Jack say [$_{C''}$ [that–t$_i$] [$_{C'}$ [$_{I''}$ t$_i$ left]]]]]]?

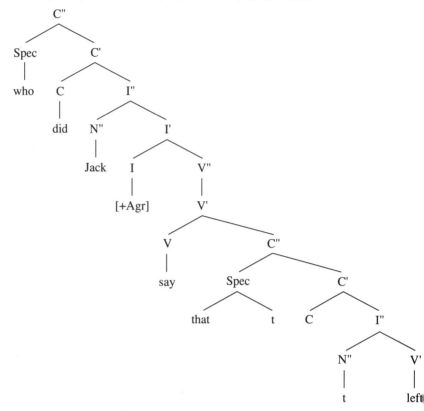

(In 20 and 21 I have used the label "Spec" for specifier of C′ slot. I have also omitted the trace of the Subject-Aux Inversion—which we know is really head movement of the Auxiliary from I into C—and all details of the tree related to the auxiliary system. These simplifications are made for ease of presentation.) Whichever one of these structures is correct (if either, as discussed later), the resulting binding arrangement is not grammatical, witness the unacceptability of 17.

Somehow the chains in 20 and 21 are ungrammatical. Why? Let us begin approaching this question by first looking at the chains we would have for 18.

(22)   [$_{C'}$Who$_i$ [$_C$did [$_{I''}$Jack say [$_{C'}$t$_i$ [[Bill saw t$_i$]]]]]]?

(23)   [$_{C'}$Who$_i$ [$_C$did [$_{I''}$Jack say [$_{C'}$that [[Bill saw t$_i$]]]]]]?

(24)   [$_{C'}$Who$_i$ [$_C$did [$_{I''}$Jack say [$_{C'}$[that-t$_i$] [[Bill saw t$_i$]]]]]]?

Example 22 is the structure for 18 without *that*, and it is parallel to 19. Examples 23 and 24 give possible structures for 18 with *that*, and they are parallel to those in 20 and 21. Yet while 20 and 21 are ungrammatical structures, 23 and 24 are grammatical. Whatever account we offer for the ungrammaticality of 17, 20, and 21 must be consistent with the fact that 18, 23, and 24 are grammatical.

The asymmetry between Subjects (as in 16 and 17) and Objects (as in 18) that we see here is not new to us. We have already discussed other areas of the grammar in which asymmetry between Subjects and Objects can be observed. For example, Objects are always Case-Marked by something internal to their clause, but Subjects need not be. Object positions at DS generally are theta-marked (except when they are parts of idiomatic phrases), but Subject positions at DS can freely be non-theta-marked (as in passive sentences and in sentences that wind up with an expletive Subject at SS). (Recall, by the way, that theta-assignment is to a position, not to a particular lexical item.) Both of these facts follow from the more general fact that Objects are lexically governed and their lexical governor gives them Case and, for Direct Objects, at least, theta-marks them. But Subjects are not lexically governed unless Exceptional Government into a tenseless clause takes place. When a clause is introduced by *that* (as in 16–18 above), the clause is tensed. So Subjects of *that* clauses are never lexically governed.

If we could make the difference in grammaticality between 17 and 18 follow from the fact that Subjects of *that* clauses are not lexically governed, whereas Objects are, we would be seeing a connection between the asymmetry above and other Subject-Object asymmetries. Such an approach is theoretically desirable, of course.

Our account needs to incorporate the fact that *empty categories that are lexically governed are not problematic, but empty categories that are not lexically governed are problematic,* as we just discovered. In particular, the empty categories that are not lexically governed in examples like 16 and 17 must be co-indexed with an antecedent in a particular way in order to be grammatical. We might even think of this co-indexing as another type of government, a type of ANTECEDENT GOVERNMENT.

In figuring out how to state the requirement on co-indexation with an antecedent, we must take another look at 20 and 21. If we take 20, in which *that* covers the intermediary trace, the antecedent of the foot of our chain is *who*, and we may say that this relationship is too distant. (We will leave the notion of distance undefined here.) If we take 21, in which the specifier of C′ branches to *that* and *wh*-trace, we can notice that the intermediary *wh*-trace does not c-command the foot of the chain (by virtue of the branching of the specifier of C′). That means that the intermediary *wh*-trace does not bind the foot of the chain. So regardless of whether we choose 20 or 21 as the correct SS for 17, *who* is the binder of the foot of the chain. And somehow the co-indexation between the foot of the chain and *who* is too distant to be grammatical. So antecedent government requires binding at not too great a distance.

These remarks can be formalized in the EMPTY-CATEGORY PRINCIPLE (ECP):

(25)   Every empty category must be properly governed.

(26)   An item is properly governed if,
        (a) it is lexically governed, or
        (b) it is antecedent governed.

Antecedent government is defined as in:

(27)   A node A antecedent governs a node B iff A binds B and A is not too far away from B.

We have not arrived at any precise sense of what "too far away from" means in 27 and we will get only a little closer to a sense of this restriction in the section on The Position of *That,* later in this chapter. This question is certainly among those you might want to explore in a monograph.

The important claim right now is that the trace in Object position in 18 is properly governed because it is lexically governed by the V. But the trace in Subject position in 17 is not lexically governed and its antecedent (the *wh*-phrase) is too far away to antecedent govern it. So this trace is not properly governed. Therefore sentences like 17 (sentences with the *that*-trace effect) constitute violations of the ECP.

The ECP and Empty Categories Other Than Trace

If you think of PRO as an empty category, as we have done up to this point, you will take immediate issue with the ECP as stated in 25. That is, PRO is an ec, yet PRO is not governed. There are two possible ways to handle this. First, we could say that PRO is not empty in the sense relevant to the ECP. Notice that the ECP requires an ec to be properly governed, a requirement that can be satisfied by a certain co-indexation relationship (as in antecedent government). So what matters to the ECP is the feature bundle of an item, not whether it has a phonetic matrix. PRO has no phonetic matrix, but it has a bundle of features (either the feature [+ arb] or the features assigned to it via Control). So PRO is not empty in the sense relevant to the ECP and therefore it is not covered by the ECP.

Alternatively, we could modify 25 to say:

(28)   ECP: Trace must be properly governed.

Which do you think is the better approach on purely theoretical grounds? So far as I can see, there is no *a priori* advantage of one formulation over the other. The choice, then, must be made on empirical grounds. So let us investigate the ramifications of this choice a little farther.

What happens to pro under 25? Is pro always properly governed? If it is, then 25 is the better choice, since 28 would not predict that pro would always be properly governed. But, then, of course, we will have to call the preclusion of PRO from 25 an exception, since pro, like PRO, has a feature bundle (of person, number, and gender—witness agreement facts in sentences with pro in Romance languages). If, on the other hand, pro is not always properly governed, then pro, like PRO, could fall outside 25, since pro, like PRO, will always have a feature bundle and thus not be empty. In that case, either 25 or 28 can handle the facts.

If you look back at the many problem sets we have had that have used pro in various languages (see, in particular, Problem Set 8.6), you will find that when pro appears in Subject position of a clause, the clause has an INFL that is [+Agr]. Now if there really were a co-indexation rule between Agr and its Subject (the rule stated in 10), and if [+Agr] is a governor, then this co-indexation rule would insure that every pro is co-indexed with a governor that is local to it. However, [+Agr] does not c-command Subject position, even though it governs it, so pro is not antecedent governed. Still, one might want to argue that the command relationship relevant to antecedent government is not ordinary c-command, but what has been labeled M-COMMAND, in which a lexical head m-commands everything within its maximal projection. In fact, the notion of government we have been employing since chapter 5 is built on the notion of m-command, not c-command: a head governs everything it m-commands. So this interpretation of antecedent government is welcome.

There are at least two problems, however, with claiming that pro is always antecedent governed. First, this claim means that we must accept 10. But the original motivation for 10 was the notion of accessibility, which we have already rejected. Second, even if we accept 10, claiming that pro is antecedent governed would amount to saying that the indices assigned by 10 are equivalent with respect to the ECP to binding indices. But why should such different sorts of indices be indistinguishable to the ECP? We feel the earth shake under our feet.

If one can accept the two consequences of the claim that pro is antecedent governed outlined in the paragraph preceding this one, then 25 is the best formulation of the ECP. But now, as I mentioned above, we have no motivated way of excluding PRO from 25. That is, pro, like PRO, has a feature bundle. So if pro is to be covered by 25, why isn't PRO also?

It would appear then that 25 is rife with problems, but 28 is not (or, at least, we have not yet addressed problems with 28—but we will below). You will find both 25 and 28 in the literature as statements of the ECP. However, no matter what precise statement of the ECP you find in the literature, every work I know of takes the ECP to apply to trace only, not to pro or PRO. Thus we will now adopt the formulation in 28.

The Position of *That*

The motivation for the ECP and for the very notion of antecedent government came out of trying to account for the *that*-trace effect. These solutions are based on the assumption that *that* is located in specifier of C′ position. But there is reason to propose that *that* is not, in fact, located in this position, but, instead, is in the C slot.

First, *that* shows no indication of being expandable: It does not take a specifier, modifiers, or arguments of its own. Unlike the items moved by *Wh*-Movement, then, it does not appear to be phrasal. But specifier of C′ position is a phrasal slot: *that* does not belong in this slot. C, on the other hand, is a lexical node, so *that* could well be immediately dominated by C.

Second, the presence of a *that*, unlike the presence of a *wh*-phrase, at the start of a clause does not block extraction from that clause:

(29)   Who did you say [that [Sam liked t]]?

(30)   *Who did you wonder [whether [Sam liked t]]?

We know from chapter 9 that 30 is an example in which Subjacency is violated. *Wh*-Movement in 30 moved the *who* from Object position of the V *liked* to specifier of C′ of the matrix clause. Movement into specifier of C′ of the embedded clause was blocked because *whether* already filled that slot (and recall that we cannot have a doubly filled specifier of C'—as discussed in chapters 6 and 8). But 29 is good. This follows if *that* is in the C slot, and it is inconsistent with an analysis in which *that* is in specifier of C' slot.

Third, in Middle English *wh*-phrases and *that* could co-occur, as in the opening line of Chaucer's *The Canterbury Tales*:

(31)   Whan that Aprille with his shoures soote
       when that April   with his showers sweet
       'When April with its sweet showers . . .'

But two *wh*-phrases in initial position of a clause did not co-occur. If *that* is located in the C slot, we can account for this fact by assuming that Middle English has the filter against a doubly filled specifier of C'.

Interestingly, the *that* complementizer is homophonous with the *that* demonstrative (as in *that idea*), which, likewise, is unexpandable. If both *that*s were really two uses of the same lexical item (both certainly have the sense of definiteness that we associate with the [+th] feature), this fact would be explained.

The proper structural analyses for 17 and 18, then, are not 20, 21, and 22–24, but:

(32)   [$_{C''}$Who [$_{C}$did [$_{I'}$Jack say [$_{C'}$[t$_2$] [$_{C}$[$_{C}$that] [$_{I'}$t$_1$ left]]]]]]?

(33)   [$_{C''}$Who [$_{C}$did [$_{I'}$Jack say [$_{C'}$[t$_2$][$_{C'}$ [$_{C}$that] [Bill saw t$_1$]]]]]]?

But now t$_2$, the intermediary trace in the specifier of C' of the embedded clause, does c-command, and, thus, does antecedent govern t$_1$, the trace at the foot of the chain, in both 32 and 33. So why should 32 be ungrammatical when 33 is grammatical?

The intervention of the *that* has to be the key to the question, since if we omit *that* from 32, it becomes grammatical (as we saw above in 17). Thus *that* is preventing antecedent government (in both 32 and 33—recall that 33's grammaticality is assured because the trace at the foot of the chain is lexically governed). It has been proposed that there is a general convention by which *that* will block the antecedent government of the trace at the foot of the chain by the intermediary trace.

(34)   The MINIMALITY CONDITION: Any projection of a head that contains
       that head and a node A prevents a node outside that projection from
       governing A.

That is the head of C''. The C' projection of this C contains t$_1$, the trace that is the foot of the chain, in both 32 and 33, but it does not contain t$_2$, the intermediary trace. Thus t$_2$ cannot antecedent govern t$_1$. As a result, 32 is ungrammatical.

But if *that* is not present, then the Minimality Condition will not apply, and t$_2$ can antecedent govern t$_1$.

The Minimality Condition comes to us as a *deus ex machina* at this point. However, there is independent motivation for it that we will not go into in this book. You will, however, see a principle similar to it appealed to in the next to last text section of this chapter.

One final issue that might be on your mind is whether the intermediary traces (labeled t$_2$) in 32 and 33 are properly governed and whether they need to be. (That is, are they subject to the ECP?)

We learned in chapter 8 that, with regard to extraction from embedded clauses, *Wh*-Movement takes place only out of sentential Objects. That means that the embedded clause will be lexically governed by the matrix verb. But we have repeatedly noted that government by a lexical head often seems to be not just of an X″, but of the specifier position within that X″. So the matrix verb in 32 and 33 can be considered to lexically govern the intermediary trace (which is in the specifier position within the C″ that is the complement of the matrix verb). If this line of reasoning is on the right track, then all intermediary traces of *Wh*-Movement out of sentential Objects will, in fact, be properly governed. So we can adopt 28 above with no added restrictions: all traces must be properly governed.

There is still much that could be explored regarding the ECP and the Minimality Condition, but the length of this book, while it may feel infinite to you at times, is truly finite. Exploration in recent issues of any journal of linguistic theory can lead you quickly to articles that study some of the questions related to these principles. For now, we will turn to other issues.

Strong Crossover

A second major question that arises out of the study of *Wh*-Movement and that we did not address in chapter 8 involves the contrast seen here:

(35)   Who thinks Mary likes him?

(36)   Who does he think Mary likes?

Both of these sentences are grammatical. But their interpretation differs in an important way. In 35 *who* and *him* can be interpreted as coreferential. But in 36 *who* and *he* cannot be interpreted as coreferential. For reasons having to do with the history of the discussion of this phenomenon in the literature, this phenomenon is known as a CROSSOVER effect. We say that 36 exhibits a STRONG CROSSOVER effect. (We will discuss weak crossover later.) You can easily remember that this phenomenon is called a crossover effect by drawing lines connecting the items in the *wh*-chain and seeing where the pronoun falls with respect to these chain lines:

(37)   Who$_i$ [t$_i$ thinks [Mary likes him$_i$]]?

(38)   *Who$_i$ does he$_i$ think [t$_i$ [Mary likes t$_i$]]?

In 37 (= 35) *him* is outside the chain. But in 38 (= 36) the chain lines cross over *he*.

Why should the co-indexing in 37 be acceptable, whereas that in 38 is not? Actually, the answer is quite straightforward. Look carefully at 38. What type of NP is *wh*-trace? We argued in chapter 8 that *wh*-trace is a phonetically empty R-expression. As such, it must conform to condition C of BT. Thus *wh*-trace can never be A-bound. But if *who* and *he* were to be co-indexed as in 38, then *he* and both *wh*-traces would also be co-indexed. That is the problem: Since *he* c-commands both *wh*-traces, we now have bound *wh*-traces. So 38 is a violation of Condition C of BT.

Weak Crossover

There is another phenomenon that is similar to strong crossover but which cannot be accounted for in the same way. It is called WEAK CROSSOVER:

(39)   Who loves his mother?

(40)   Who does his mother love?

Again, both sentences are grammatical, but in 39 we can understand *who* and *his* as coreferential, while in 40 we cannot. Once more, we have a crossover configuration in 40, but not in 39.

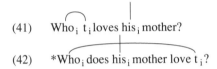

(41)   Who$_i$ t$_i$ loves his$_i$ mother?

(42)   *Who$_i$ does his$_i$ mother love t$_i$?

But this time *his* in 42 does not c-command the *wh*-trace, so we do not have a violation of Condition C of BT (in contrast to 38).

What, then, accounts for the ungrammaticality of 42? Notice that in 41, *who* binds *wh*-trace. Furthermore, both *who* and *wh*-trace bind *his*. But in 42 *who* binds *wh*-trace and *his*, while *wh*-trace binds nothing. Somehow these binding relationships must be the key to the ungrammaticality of 42. What is wrong with *who* binding both *his* and *wh*-trace in 42?

Operators and Logical Form

At this point it is helpful to look back at the discussion in chapter 8. We spoke there of the fact that a *wh*-phrase behaves like an operator, and *wh*-trace behaves like a variable. With those terms in mind, we might ask ourselves whether 42 is well formed. That is, does it make sense for the operator *who* to bind two variables? Certainly one can imagine a complex operator that could take more than one variable (and we will return to this idea later in this chapter). *Wh*-phrases, however, are not complex. They can be represented in Logical Form (LF) in a way that involves only one variable. For example, the question in 43 could be represented in LF as in 44, where we say that the operator "for which x" has SCOPE over the variable x:

(43)   Who left?

(44)   For which x, x left.

(In 44 we say the *wh*-operator "operates over" the variable, which is an argument here, or the *wh*-operator "has scope over" a variable.) In fact, it is by means of LF that we can most easily see a parallel between *wh*-phrases and other one-place operators. (One-place operators are operators that have scope over one variable.) For example, 45 could be represented in LF as in 46, with the universal operator:

(45)   Everyone left.

(46) For all x, x left.

A shorthand for 46 might be:

(47) everyone$_x$ [x left]

How might we represent the existential operator in LF? Consider:

(48) Someone left.

Offer an LF representation of this sentence. It might be something like 49, or the shorthand version in 50:

(49) There exists an x such that x left.

(50) someone$_x$ [x left]

Sentences that have two operators will be represented in LF with both operators in initial position. However, one of them must come first linearly. Linguists have adopted the convention of having the operator which is understood to have WIDER SCOPE appear first. Thus consider:

(51) Everybody loves somebody.

This sentence has two readings. On one reading we are saying that for each person there is somebody that that person loves. The UNIVERSAL OPERATOR (or the "all" operator) has wider scope on this reading, and at LF we represent it with:

(52) For all x, there exists a y such that x loves y. or: everybody$_x$ [somebody$_y$ [x loves y]]

On the other reading we are saying that there is a given person who everybody loves (say Noam Chomsky). The EXISTENTIAL OPERATOR has wider scope on this reading, and in LF we represent it with:

(53) There exists a y such that for all x, x loves y. or: somebody$_y$ [everybody$_x$ [x loves y]]

In the examples in 43–53, we are dealing with quantifiers (or, at least, *wh*-phrases can be argued to be quantifierlike, although we will not go into those arguments here). But quantifiers are not the only kind of operator that we find in natural language. Negation is an operator. Thus 54 could be represented at LF as in 55:

(54) John didn't leave.

(55) Not x, for x = John left.
or: not [John left].

Notice that in the shorthand version of 55 no variable appears. That is because the entire sentence in brackets is the variable that *not* has scope over. In 55 we say *not* operates over an entire proposition—*John left*.

Another type of operator is a modal operator. Thus 56 could be represented at LF as in 57:

(56) John must leave.

(57)   Must x, for x = John leave.
       or: must [John leave].

(Again, *must*, like *not*, operates over an entire proposition.)
   How would you represent the following sentence at LF?

(58)   Someone must leave.

First, ask yourself if this question is ambiguous with regard to scope. It seems to be.
On one reading we are saying that there is a particular person who must leave. On
another reading we are saying that it must be the case that there is someone who
will leave. Try giving an LF representation of these two readings. They might look
something like:

(59)   There exists an x such that it must be the case that x leaves.
       or: There exists an x such that must y, for y = x leave.
       or: someone$_x$ [must [x leave]]

(60)   It must be the case that there exists an x such that x leaves.
       or: must [someone$_x$ [x leave]]

Other potential operators in language include adverbs, tense, and definiteness.
   While we have written LF in a linear form above, all of these representations
could be put into trees that are entirely analogous to syntactic trees. Let me give
some very simplified LF trees here:

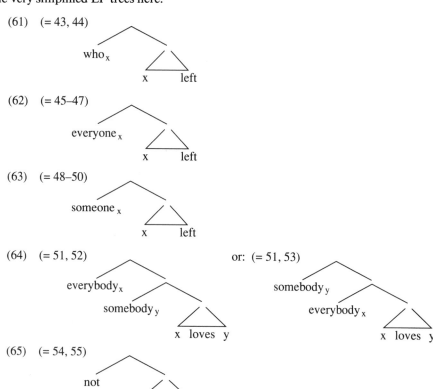

(61)   (= 43, 44)

(62)   (= 45–47)

(63)   (= 48–50)

(64)   (= 51, 52)   or: (= 51, 53)

(65)   (= 54, 55)

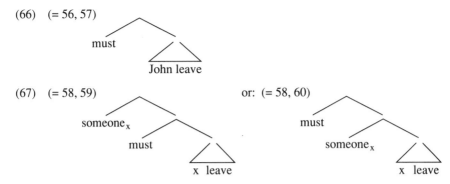

(66)   (= 56, 57)

must

John leave

(67)   (= 58, 59)   or: (= 58, 60)

someone$_x$ must

must   someone$_x$

x leave   x leave

We now see that the operators we have represented in 43–60 c-command all the material that follows them in these particular examples. Furthermore, operators with wider scope can be seen to be hierarchically higher than operators with NAR-ROWER SCOPE. This approach to LF opens the door for asking whether hierarchical relationships that are relevant to syntactic relationships are also relevant to inter-pretive relationships.

Actually, we already have opened that door. BT is a theory that belongs to the LF component of the grammar. When we ask whether one node binds another, we are asking whether, in an LF representation like those above, one node c-com-mands and is co-indexed with the other. When we ask whether the binding takes place within a governing category, we are looking at the LF configuration to deter-mine the governing category. Thus when we say a given head is the governor for some node, we are saying that head m-commands the other node in LF. When we raised such issues in earlier chapters, we looked at syntactic structure only. How-ever, in all instances our LF representation would have been identical to our syn-tactic representation with regard to that material relevant to the issue at hand. Con-trol Theory also belongs to the LF component of the grammar and we have seen how it, also, makes use of the notion of c-command.

The Bijection Principle and Weak Crossover Again

While the above discussion has offered a quick and only very partial look at LF, I hope it has given you some sense of operators in language. With this slight back-ground, can you think of any operators in language that must take two variables? Probably your answer is no. And linguists have claimed that this is no accident. In fact, they claim that this fact follows from a principle of grammar:

(68)   THE BIJECTION PRINCIPLE: Every variable must be bound by exactly one operator and every operator must bind exactly one variable.

If you have a background in logic, you will recognize right away that if the Bijection Principle is correct, natural-language operators are much more restricted than log-ical operators. In logic, there is no theory-imposed limit on the number of variables an operator can take.

The Bijection Principle is certainly not without problems; however, nothing we are going to do in this book will challenge it.

Now look back at our example sentences to demonstrate weak crossover, in 39 and 40, repeated here for convenience:

(69)   Who$_i$ t$_i$ loves his$_i$ mother?

(70)   *Who$_i$ does his$_i$ mother love t$_i$?

If we assume that the Bijection Principle is valid, then *who* must bind exactly one variable. There are two things we need to do before we can proceed in our discussion. First, let me remind you of the definition of *variable* we introduced in chapter 8: *A variable is a node which is locally non-A-bound.*

Second, let us assume that if there are two potential binders for a given node, the closer one (in a hierarchical sense) is, in fact, the binder. This assumption is based on an unstated principle that has similarities to the Minimality Condition in 34. That is, while the Minimality Condition limited us to taking the hierarchically closer governor, we are here invoking a parallel principle that limits us to taking the hierarchically closer binder.

Now in 69 and 70 there are two potential variables: *wh*-trace and *his*. *Who* c-commands both of them, but *who* is restricted to binding only one of them. If *who* binds *his*, then *wh*-trace is left without a binder, which is disallowed by the Bijection Principle.

On the other hand, in 69 another alternative arises. Here both *who* and *wh*-trace c-command *his*. So if *who* binds *wh*-trace, then *wh*-trace can serve as the binder for *his*. And, in fact, since *wh*-trace is closer to *his* hierarchically than *who* is, *wh*-trace is the binder we would want to choose for this possessive anyway. With this account, how is it that we understand *who* and *his* as coreferential in 69? We can understand this coreference by the mathematical principle of transitivity (which is not to be confused with a verb's transitivity or intransitivity). That is, if *wh*-trace is the binder for *his* in 69, then we understand *his* and *who* to be coreferential not because of any direct relationship of binding between the two, but because both are coreferential with the *wh*-trace.

Now what about 70? Here *wh*-trace does not c-command *his,* nor does *his* c-command *wh*-trace. If *who* binds the *wh*-trace, then *his*, which is co-indexed with *who*, is an unbound variable, in violation of the Bijection Principle. On the other hand, if *who* binds *his*, then *wh*-trace is an unbound variable, in violation of the Bijection Principle.

The crucial difference between 69 and 70, then, is that in 69 the *wh*-trace c-commands *his*, so it can serve as the binder for *his* and we need not interpret *his* as a variable. But in 70 neither the *wh*-trace nor *his* c-commands the other, so both are variables co-indexed with *who*.

At this point you may feel awe or distrust—awe if you admire the acrobatic argument above; distrust if you are uncomfortable with it. The further you go with linguistic theory, the more often you will face technical and complex arguments. It is essential that you become comfortable with them. It may help to ask yourself to state in simple terms why a question like 70 is ungrammatical with *his* and *who* co-indexed. The problem with 70 is that the operator would have to help us interpret two positions (that occupied by *his* and that occupied by the trace)—but no operator is allowed to do that. So while the account may seem unreasonably technical, in fact, it is based on a simple and straightforward insight (captured in the Bijection Principle).

Not all acrobatic arguments are insightful. A good habit is to work your way step by step through an argument. Once you understand all its complexities, try to state it in the simplest terms possible. Then ask yourself what insight this argument is based on or is revealing. If you cannot answer that final question, perhaps the argument you just plowed through should be challenged.

Chapter Conclusion

In this chapter we debunked the notion of accessibility on the grounds that it is theoretically unsound and empirically inadequate. We recognized the usefulness of i/i as a condition against referential circularity, but rejected any extension of this condition to indices other than referential and binding indices (and we furthermore questioned the existence of any such additional types of indices).

We adopted the ECP, which requires traces to be properly governed. We allowed proper government to include antecedent and lexical government. And we assumed without argument the Minimality Condition (which allowed us to account for the *that*-trace effect with the ECP while still placing *that* in C).

We accounted for strong crossover effects with Condition C of the BT. We accounted for weak crossover effects by adopting the Bijection Principle and another principle that says of two potential binders of a given node, the hierarchically closer one is the binder (a principle parallel to the Minimality Condition).

We have talked at least as much about semantics as about syntax in this chapter. This is no accident. The further you go with syntax, the more you will find it impossible to talk about syntactic structure without considering semantics. That is why the next step for you to take after finishing this course should be through the doorway into a semantics class.

Problem Set 9.1: English i/i

In this chapter we used the following definition of i/i:

(1)   The i-within-i condition:
       $*[_A \ldots B \ldots]$, where A and B bear the same index.

Part 1

In the text we saw three instances in which i/i correctly ruled out NPs:

(2) $*[a\ picture\ of\ [itself]_i]_i$
       $*[the\ owner\ of\ [his]_i\ boat]_i$
       $*[the\ conclusion\ about\ [it]_i]_i$

Many other examples can be found. Here are some, in which the offending NPs are used in sentences.

(3) *[The proof of [its]ᵢ existence]ᵢ baffled the logicians.
     *[Books about [them]ᵢ]ᵢ bore me.

Find three additional examples of ungrammatical NPs whose ungrammaticality would be accounted for by i/i.

Part 2

In contrast to 2, 3, and the examples you came up with in Part 1, there are other NPs which appear to violate i/i, but are grammatical:

(4) [[John's]ᵢ father's only son]ᵢ isn't here.
     [The mayor who destroyed [her]ᵢ city]ᵢ left town.
     [A man who is in love with [himself]ᵢ]ᵢ isn't interesting to talk to.

Find three additional examples of NPs which violate i/i as stated in 1.

Part 3

In the next three sections I would like you to compare examples like those you discussed in Part 1 to examples like those you discussed in Part 2. The relevant difference may be hard to see, so let me try to lead you through this.

First, consider the NP contained inside the larger NP in all these examples. Now considering anaphors, pronominals, and R-expressions, are all three types of NPs represented in the examples you discussed in Part 1? If not, which type(s) is not represented?

What about in the examples in Part 2? Are all three types of NPs represented or not?

You have now discovered one important difference between the types of examples that i/i correctly rules out (in Part 1) and the types of examples that are problematic for i/i (in Part 2). Hold onto that difference for a moment.

Part 4

Now let us take another tack. Consider the head Ns of the larger NPs in Part 1. What functional relationship does the embedded NP have to this head N?

Now consider the head Ns of the larger NPs in Part 2. What functional relationship does the embedded NP have to this head N?

You have now discovered a second important difference between the types of examples in Parts 1 and 2. Hold onto that difference for a moment.

Part 5

Now consider this NP:

(5) [the artist whoᵢ Ruth prefers tᵢ]ᵢ

Here both *who* and *t* have the same index as the entire NP, yet the NP is acceptable. This is true even if we have no relative pronoun present:

(6)   [the artist (that) Ruth prefers t_i]$_i$

Examples 5 and 6 behave like the examples in Part 2. Did you expect this given your answers to Parts 3 and 4? Explain your answer.

Part 6

Now consider examples like:

(7)   [A man justly proud of [himself]$_i$]$_i$ is usually a bore.
[A man in love with [himself]$_i$]$_i$ isn't interesting to talk to.

The examples in 7 behave like the examples in Part 2. Did you expect this, given your answers to Parts 3 and 4? Explain your answer.

Part 7

Recall that we found in Problem Set 8.7 that movement is involved in relative clauses, both in those that have an overt *wh*-word and in those that do not. That means that all relative clauses will be introduced by an operator (which may be phonetically null) that binds the variable (the *wh*-trace). Thus the SSs for 5 and 6 are:

(8)   [the artist who$_i$ Ruth prefers t_i]$_i$

(9)   [the artist Op$_i$ that Ruth prefers t_i]$_i$

(10)   [the artist Op$_i$ Ruth prefers t_i]$_i$

In 9 and 10, the "Op" represents a phonetically null operator that binds the *wh*-trace.

One could certainly make the argument that all modifiers of a head N, whether they are in relative clauses or not, are inside phrases that can be introduced by phonetically null operators. That is, one could argue that the SS for the Subject NP in the first example of 7 is:

(11)   [A man [Op$_i$ justly proud of [himself]$_i$]]$_i$

Assume for the sake of this problem set that the null operators represented in 9–11 exist.

Now consider all the data and all your discussions thus far and try to come up with a statement that will differentiate those NPs that i/i correctly excludes from those NPs that are problematic for i/i. Be sure not to overlook the fact you discovered in Part 3 in formulating this statement.

Part 8

Certainly i/i is incorrect both as a condition on all indices and as a condition on only referential indices. However, there is a version of it that is needed in order to rule out examples like those in Part 1 above. In light of your statement in Part 7, make a stab at what the correct i/i should be.

Problem Set 9.2: English Accessibility and i/i

This problem set has two short parts which are unrelated to each other.

Part 1

Given i/i as a condition on referential indices only, which analysis of relative clauses is ruled out and why?

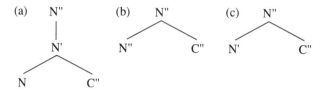

Part 2

Consider the notion of accessibility discussed in the text of this chapter. Can a node be an accessible SUBJECT to itself? In answering this, consider the sentence:

    (1)   John counted on [himself winning].

Recall that in Problem Set 5.5 we learned that the *-ing* in INFL of an embedded clause gives Case to the Subject of its clause. That suggests that this INFL is, in fact, a governor. Use this assumption in your discussion.

Problem Set 9.3: Japanese Relative Clauses

In chapter 8 you learned that relative clauses in English are formed via *Wh*-Movement. You also learned that *Wh*-Movement (and all movement) is restricted by the Subjacency Principle.

    In Japanese, however, we find that Subjacency can apparently be violated in relative clause formation. Assume as you do this problem set that the unmarked word order in Japanese is Subject first, then adjuncts (such as locative PPs), then IO, then DO, then verb. There is, as you know, much variation on this word order in Japanese. But please make this assumption about the unmarked word order here.

    Finally, assume here that Japanese has a VP that contains the IO, DO, and V as well as adverbial-type modifiers. Further assume that Japanese phrases have a similar internal structure to English phrases (although if you did Problem Set 8.2, you may be convinced otherwise). For the sake of this problem set, assume that an NP that contains a relative clause consists of a head N with a sister clause (the relative clause), and the whole NP may or may not have a specifier. You will make use of all these assumptions in Part 5.

Part 1

Consider 1, which has an appositive clause (in brackets) to the head noun *sirase* 'news':

(1) Wareware-wa [[yuuzin-ga   L.A.-ni tuita] -to yuu sirase]-o
    we   -TOP   friend-SUBJ L.A. in arrived-COMP news -OBJ
    kinoo   uketotta.
    yesterday received
    'We received the news yesterday that (our) friend arrived in L.A.'

The sentence in 1 appears as a relative clause embedded in 2:

(2) [[[[L.A.-ni tuita] -to yuu sirase]-o   wareware-ga   kinoo
        L.A. in arrived-COMP news -OBJ we   -SUBJ yesterday
    uketotta] yuuzin]-wa   zitensya-de America oodan   -o
    received friend -TOP bicycle -by America crossing-OBJ
    kokoromita]-no   desu.
    tried   -COMP is
    '(Our) friend of whom we received the news yesterday that (he) arrived
    in L.A. attempted crossing the country in America by bicycle.'

What is the head of the relative clause in 2?
   Where is the position inside the relative clause that is coreferential with the head?
What is the GF of that position within its own clause?
   Is there any word here which seems to be a relative pronoun?
   If relative clause formation involves movement from the position inside the relative clause that is coreferential with the head to a position adjacent to the head, how does that movement in 2 violate Subjacency? (Say which barriers are crossed.)

Part 2

Now consider 3, which has a relative clause modifying the head noun *sensei* ('teacher'):

(3) [[Syoonen-ga   akogarete-ita] sensei] -ga   yamete simatta.
      boy   -SUBJ admiring -was teacher-SUBJ quit
    'The teacher who the boy admired quit.'

The sentence in 3 appears as a relative clause modifying the head noun *syoonen* ('boy') in 4.

(4) [[[[Akogarete-ita] sensei] -ga   yamete simatta] syoonen]-wa
        admiring -was teacher-SUBJ quit   boy   -TOP
    gakkoo-e ikanaku natta.
    school -to go -not became
    'The boy on whom the teacher (he) admired quit stopped going to
    school.'

(In 4 we understand that the teacher that the boy admired quit on him and the boy that this happened to stopped going to school.)

There are two relative clauses in 4. What is the head of each?

Where is the position inside each relative that is coreferential with the head? What is the GF of that position inside its own clause?

Is there any word here which seems to be a relative pronoun?

If movement were involved in relative-clause formation, which movement above would violate Subjacency and how?

At this point do you think relative clauses in Japanese are formed via movement? Why?

Part 3

Now consider 5, which has a relative clause modifying the head noun *gakusei* ('student'):

    (5)   [[Sensei-o   sonkeisite-ita] gakusei]-ga   zisatusita.
           teacher -OBJ respecting was student -SUBJ committed suicide
           'The student who respected the teacher committed suicide.'

(I apologize for such an uncheerful sentence. I am sticking closely to my sources here.) Now we find that if we embed 5 as a relative clause inside another sentence, as in 6, the result is ungrammatical.

    (6)   *[[[[Sonkeisite-ita] gakusei]-ga   zisatusita] sensei]-wa
                respecting-was student-SUBJ com. sui. teacher-TOP
          shokku-o   uketeiru.
          shock   -OBJ receive is
          'The teacher who the student who respected (him) committed suicide is shocked.'

There are two relative clauses in 6. What is the head of each?

Where is the position inside each relative that is coreferential with the head? What is the GF of that position inside its own clause?

Is there any word here which seems to be a relative pronoun?

If movement were involved in relative clause formation, which movement above would violate Subjacency and how?

Part 4

Try to make a generalization that will distinguish the good sentences (2 and 4) from the bad sentence (6), where that generalization has to do with GFs.

Part 5

Draw a tree for 2, 4, and 6.

On every tree, circle the head of every relative clause.

Now put a "t" (for trace) in the position inside every relative clause that is coreferential with the head.

Now draw a line from each t to an empty position (that we are now positing) immediately to the left of the head of the relevant relative clause. (Notice that that is the position that the specifier of C′ would appear in if there was, in fact, movement in relative clauses in Japanese.)

Can you see any difference between the configuration of the lines in the sentences that are good in comparison with the sentence in 6 that is bad?

Part 6

Here are two more examples.

(7) [[[[Nagutta] kodomo]-ga   nakidasita] syoonen]-wa   tomadotta.
       hit   child   -SUBJ cry began   boy   -TOP bewildered
     'The boy on whom the child (he) hit began to cry was bewildered.'

(8) *[[[[Nagutta] syoonen]-ga   huruete-ita]   kodomo]-wa   nakidasita.
        hit   boy   -SUBJ trembling-was child   -TOP cry began
     'The child who the boy who hit (him) was trembling began to cry.'

Example 7 is grammatical and 8 is not. Do these sentences conform in the GFs of the relevant items to the generalization you reached in Part 4? If so, fine. If not, alter that generalization so that it will hold of all the examples thus far.

Do 7 and 8 have trees that conform to the generalization you found at the end of Part 5? If so, tell how.

If not, draw the trees for 7 and 8 and look at all five trees now (2, 4, and 7 [the good ones], versus 5 and 8 [the ungrammatical ones]) and come up with a generalization that will be true of all the sentences thus far. (When you draw the trees for 7 and 8, be sure to circle the heads of the relative clauses, put in the traces, and draw the lines from the traces to the spot in the tree immediately to the left of the head of the relative clause.)

Part 7

Here are some additional examples of ill-formed relative clauses, where the (b) examples below are what you are to concentrate on. The (a) examples (which are grammatical) appear as relative clauses embedded inside the (b) examples. Make sure you keep in mind the unmarked word order in Japanese.

(9) a. [[Syuppansya   -ni hon- o   okutta] sakka]-ga
           publishing company-IO book-DO sent   writer- SUBJ
         totuzen inaku natta.
         suddenly disappeared
         'The writer who sent the book to the publishing company disappeared suddenly.'

   b. *[[[[Hon -o   okutta] sakka]-ga   totuzen inaku natta]
         book-DO   sent   writer -SUBJ suddenly disappeared
      syuppansya]   -ga   komatte iru.
      publishing company-SUBJ in trouble is
      'The publishing company which the writer who sent the book (to it)
      suddenly disappeared is in trouble.'

(10) a. [[Seizika -ni okane -o   watasita] syatyoo] -ga   taihosareta.
          politician-IO money-DO handed   president-SUBJ was arrested
          'The president (of the company) who handed the money to the
          politician was arrested.'

   b. *[[[[Okane-o   watasita] syatyoo] -ga   taihosareta]
          money-DO handed   president-SUBJ was arrested
      seizika] -wa   sono zizitu-o   hiteisita.
      politician-TOP this fact -DO denied
      'The politician who the president who gave the money (to him) was
      arrested denied the fact.'

Do these examples necessitate an alteration in your generalization (in Parts 4 and
6) regarding GFs? If not, explain how these examples are consistent with it. If so,
please do that alteration now.

   Do these examples necessitate an alteration in your generalization (in Parts 5 and
6) regarding trees and the lines you have drawn? If not, explain how these examples
are consistent with it. If so, please do that alteration now.

Part 8

There is one final very important point. For many speakers of Japanese, the generalizations you came up with above do not hold if there is an overt pro-form in the
relative clause. Compare these:

(11) *[[[[Paatii-ni sasotta] dansei]-ga   suteki datta]
           party -to invited man   -SUBJ nice   was
       syoozyo]-wa   ooyorokobi da.
       girl   -TOP very happy is
       'The girl who the man who invited (her) to the party was nice is very
       happy.'

(12) [[[[{Zibun$_i$/ Kanozyo$_i$}-o paatii   ni sasotta] dansei]-ga
           self / she   -DO party to invited man   -SUBJ
       suteki datta] syoozyo$_i$]-wa   ooyorokobi da.
       nice   was girl   -TOP very happy is
       'The girl$_i$ who the man invited {self$_i$/her$_i$} to the party was nice is very
       happy.'

The same contrast is found for these speakers in:

(13) *[[[[Eigo   -o   osiete -ita] gakusei]-ga   ryuugakusuru
       English-DO teaching-was student -SUBJ go abroad
       koto ni natta]   syoonen]-wa   komatte iru.
              became boy   -TOP in trouble is
       'The boy who the student who was teaching (him) English decided to
       go abroad is in trouble.'

(14)   [[[[Kareᵢ-ni eigo -o   osiete-ita]   gakusei]-ga
        he   -IO English-DO teaching was student -SUBJ
       ryuugakusuru koto ni natta]   syoonenᵢ]-wa   komatte iru.
       go abroad   became boy   -TOP in trouble is
       'The boyᵢ who the student who was teaching himᵢ English decided to
       go abroad is in trouble.'

Now describe the phenomena known as strong and weak crossover. Consider the
generalizations you made above regarding GFs and regarding tree structure and the
lines you drew. In light of 11–14, are these generalizations to be taken as examples
of either type of crossover or not? Discuss this issue briefly.

Part 9

Given everything you have done on this homework, do you think relative clause
formation in Japanese involves *Wh*-Movement? Why?

*Problem Set 9.4: English and Italian Binding (with *Ne*)

*At least Parts 1 and 2 of this problem set should be done before going on to the next
chapter.*
This problem set is on Binding Theory and it could be used as an exam.

Use the following definition of *binding*: A binds B iff A c-commands B and is co-
indexed with B.
Use the following definition of *government*: A governs B iff A is a lexical category
or [+ Agr], and B is contained within the maximal projection of A, and every maximal projection that contains B also contains A.

Part 1

Answer with respect to English:
Define the following GFs in terms of government, if possible. If it is not possible,
explain why not and give a definition based on tree-structure relationships.

(A) Subject of a clause

(B) Direct Object (In doing this, set aside the Double-Object construction of
English. That is, give a definition that covers all sentences except those with

Double Objects. Then if your definition also covers Double-Object sentences, fine. If not, explain why it does not.)

(C) Object of a Preposition

Part 2

List all the instances of binding (that is, co-indexation in which one element c-commands the other) in the following sentences, saying what element is bound and what element binds it, in each instance.

(1)   Who did John see?

(2)   Who did you say John saw?

(3)   Jeffrey wanted to leave.

(4)   Jeffrey persuaded Sally to leave.

(5)   Carlos wasn't ignored by anyone.

(6)   Carlos wasn't expected to be ignored by anyone.

(7)   That child just hasn't been talked to enough.

(8)   That bed was slept in by George Washington.

Part 3

Now try to answer the following question about Italian:

What determines whether the perfect-aspect auxiliary verb in Italian will be *essere* 'be' or *avere* 'have'?

Assume that Italian is like English with respect to the definitions of Subject, Direct Object, and Object of a P that you came up with in Part 1. Also assume that binding in Italian is just like binding in English.

I will try to lead you through it, bit by bit, with smaller questions. If you are missing any crucial piece of information (and I hope you are not), state what it is and why it is crucial, assume the missing data fall a particular way (and state exactly what your assumption is), and then continue with the problem set. (Note: Italian verbs are to be taken as having the same relevant semantic and/or syntactic properties that their English counterparts have unless I state explicitly to the contrary.) Please be sure to pay attention to the word-by-word glosses as well as the translations.

Consider these data:

(9)   Luisa ha   visto Carlo.
            have (3s) seen
      'Luisa has seen Carlo.'

(10) Manfredi ha   letto la lettera (a Giulia).
              have (3s) read the letter   to
      'Manfredi has read the letter (to Giulia).'

(11) Ho   pettinato il   cane.
     have(1s) combed   the dog
     'I have combed the dog."

(12) Il   cane è   corso a casa.
     the dog be (3s) run   to home
     'The dog has run home.'

(13) Silvia è   arrivata.
             be (3s) arrived
     'Silvia has arrived.'

(14) Daria è   andata al   mercato.
             be (3s) gone   to-the market
     'Daria has gone to the market.'

(In 14 *al* is a form that means 'to the'. This kind of lexical item has been called a prepositional article, or a PORTMANTEAU. You will see other portmanteaus in 21 and 22.)

Question 1:   On the basis of just 9–14, what determines auxiliary choice?

Now consider:

(15) I   ragazzi hanno   già   mangiato (la carne).
     the boys   have (3p) already eaten   (the meat)
     'The boys have already eaten (the meat).'

(16) Avete   studiato (la lezione)?
     have (2p) studied (the lesson)
     'Have you studied (the lesson)?'

Examples 15 and 16 are representative: all nonreflexive verbs which take an optional DO behave as in 15 and 16 with respect to auxiliary choice.

Question 2:   On the basis of 15 and 16, do you have to modify your answer to Question 1? If so, do it.

Now consider:

(17) Ho   dormito male.
     have (1s) slept   badly
     'I have slept badly.'

(18) Non ha   neanche pianto.
     not have (3s) even   cried
     'He hasn't even cried.'

Question 3:   Do 17 and 18 pose any problem for your hypothesis thus far? (Look back at 12–14.) State precisely what those problems are.

Now consider:

(19)   Maurizio si   è   letto la lettera.
             himself be (3s) read the letter
             'Maurizio has read the letter to himself.'

(20)   Marina si   è   pettinata.
             herself be (3s) combed
             Lit: Marina has combed herself.
             'Marina combed her hair.'

Contrast 19 and 20 to 10 and 11, respectively. *Si* is a reflexive clitic pronoun, homophonous for DO and IO. (This *si* is homophonous with indefinite Subject *si* of Problem Set 8.6. However, it is distinct in meaning and in syntactic behavior. Please assume that reflexive *si*, therefore, is a separate entity from indefinite Subject *si* as you do this problem set.)

Examples 19 and 20 are representative: all sentences in which there is a clitic reflexive behave as in 19 and 20 with respect to auxiliary choice.

Question 4:   Do 19 and 20 pose any problems for your hypothesis so far? (If you did things the way I hope you did, then 17 and 18 posed a problem in light of 12–14, and now 19 and 20 are posing a problem in light of 9–11.)

Question 5:   Do the subjects of 19 and 20 bind anything? If so, what?

Now consider:

(21)   Iole è   ignorata dagli   uomini.
             be (3s) ignored by-the men
             'Iole is ignored by men.'

(22)   Iole è   stata ignorata dal   marito.
             be (3s) been ignored by-the husband
             'Iole has been ignored by her husband.'

In 21 the auxiliary is the passive auxiliary (which happens to be *essere* 'be,' as in English). In 22 there are two auxiliary verbs: the first is the passive; the second is the perfect aspect. *Stata* is a form of the verb *essere*.

Example 22 is representative: all passives in the perfect aspect behave this way with respect to auxiliary choice.

Question 6:   Does the subject of 22 bind anything? If so, what?

Now consider some entirely different data:

(23)   Marcello ha   comprato due chili di frutta.
             have (3s) bought   two kilos of fruit
             'Marcello has bought two kilos of fruit.'

(24)   Marcello ne   ha   comprato due.
             of-them have (3s) bought   two
             'Marcello has bought two of them.'

(25)   Alcune ragazze hanno   comprato frutta.
         A few girls   have (3p) bought   fruit
         'A few girls have bought fruit.'

(26)   *Alcune ne   hanno   comprato frutta.
         A few of-them have (3p) bought   fruit
         'A few of them have bought fruit.'

Ne is a partitive clitic that can appear on the verb when it is associated with a certain type of quantifier.

Examples 23–26 are representative: all transitive verbs allow *ne* cliticization from their DO but not from their Subject. (I do not give the data, but *ne* cliticization is not allowed from objects of prepositions, including the IO, which is always the object of the P *a*).

Now look at intransitive verbs:

(27)   Hanno   dormito alcune ragazze. (a variant on: Alcune ragazze
         have (3p) slept   a few girls   hanno dormito.)
         'A few girls have slept.'

(28)   *Ne   hanno   dormito alcune. (also: *Alcune he hanno
         of-them have (3p) slept   a few   dormito.)
         'A few of them have slept.'

(29)   Sono   venuti molti studenti. (A variant on: Molti studenti sono
         be (3p) come   many students   venuti.)
         'Many student have come.'

(30)   Ne   sono   venuti molti. (but very strange: ??Molti ne sono
         of-them be (3p) come   many   venuti.)
         'Many of them have come.'

(31)   Saranno   invitati molti esperti. (A variant on: Molti esperti
         will-be (3p) invited many experts   saranno invitati.)
         'Many experts will be invited.'

(32)   Ne   saranno   invitati molti. (but very strange: ??Molti ne
         of-them will-be (3p) invited many   saranno invitati.)

Examples 27–30 are representative: those intransitive verbs that take *essere* allow *ne* cliticization from a Subject that follows the verb, but those that take *avere* do not.

And 31 and 32 are representative: *ne* cliticization is allowed from a Subject that follows the verb in a passive sentence.

Question 7: Assume that *molti* in 31 and 32 is a Quantifier Phrase (QP) rather than an NP. (If you need to review what a QP is, look back to chapter 4, particularly Problem Set 4.2.) Is it theoretically necessary (so far as you know) to have had NP movement in 31 and 32? (Hint: consider why NP movement is required in passive sentences where the Object of the verb is an NP—rather than a QP.)

Question 8: Try to give an analysis of the intransitive verbs that take *essere* which will allow a simple statement of the possibilities for *ne* cliticization. In doing this, make sure you note the data in 31 and 32 on passive sentences (those data should help you) and your own answer to Question 7.

Question 9: Now look at all the data again and try to answer the initial question of what determines the choice of perfect auxiliary. You need to find something in common between sentences with those intransitive verbs that take *essere* and sentences with verbs that have reflexive clitics on them (as in 19 and 20).

Problem Set 9.5: Portuguese and Japanese Null Objects

This problem set is conceptually difficult. Work with a group if you can.

Unlike the other Romance languages you have looked at in problem sets in this book, Portuguese allows an empty category in DO position which at first glance does not appear to be bound. Thus in response to a question such as, "Who saw the movie?", it would be more appropriate to answer 1, with an empty DO, than 2, with a clitic DO.

(1)   Eu vi.
      I   saw
      'I saw it.'

(2)   Eu vi -o.
      I   saw-CL
      'I saw it.'

There are many restrictions on this empty category (which I will indicate with "ec" below). Let us explore them.

Part 1

The null DO is disallowed in these constructions:

(3)   *[O Joao enviar [ec]] seria   desastroso.
       the Joao send   would be disastrous
       'For Joao to send (it) would be a disaster.'

(4)   *Eu nao acredito no boato de que [a   pessoa
        I   not believe in story of that the person
       [a quem enviaram [ec]]] nao estava em casa.
        to whom sent   not was   in house
       'I don't believe in the story that the person to whom they sent (it) was not at home.'

Examples 3 and 4 are both grammatical if the clitic *o* (as in 2) is present instead of the ec.
   What is the structure within which the ec finds itself in 3? Consider the GF of the

embedded clause. (Be sure to look closely at the Portuguese example and its word-by-word gloss, rather than its loose English translation.)

What is the structure within which the ec finds itself in 4? Again, consider the function of the lowest clause that contains the ec. Then consider the structure such clauses are part of.

Have you seen the two structures that the ec is found in here pulled together by any principle of grammar anywhere else in this book? (If not, your memory is failing you. Look back to chapter 8 and read about islands and Subjacency.)

Part 2

The ec is also disallowed inside embedded questions and inside adverbial clauses. Put these facts together with the facts you stated in Part 1 above and give a general statement about constructions from which the ec is blocked.

The general statement you just came up with should be surprising to you. Why? What type of phenomenon have we talked about previously that was sensitive to these very same constructions?

Part 3

The following sentences are ungrammatical with an ec:

(5) *Ele$_i$ diz que a   Maria encontrou [ec$_i$].
      he   says that the Maria met
      'He$_i$ says that Maria met (him$_i$).'

(6) ??Os amigos dele$_i$ encontraram [ec$_i$].
      the friends of-him$_i$ met
      'His$_i$ friends met (him$_i$).'

If a clitic is present, again these sentences become grammatical.

The issue in 5 and 6 is one of possible coreference. If we interpret the empty categories here as not being coreferential with the preceding pronominals, then 5 and 6 are grammatical.

This is not the first time you have seen sentences involving empty categories in which grammaticality depended on there not being a coreferential relationship between two elements in the sentence: the other time was in this very chapter in the discussion of strong and weak crossover. Which one of 5 and 6 most closely corresponds to an instance of strong crossover? Which one most closely corresponds to an instance of weak crossover?

Part 4

Assume that *Wh*-Movement has not applied in these Portuguese ec-constructions. Yet, it would appear that the ec here is a variable. Propose an analysis of 1 that will account for all the behavior seen here. Your analysis must include an LF representation of 1.

Part 5

Japanese allows empty categories in DO position which at first glance appear not to be bound, like the Portuguese examples. However, there are several reasons for claiming the Japanese empty Objects are not variables (unlike the Portuguese empty Objects). Give two of those reasons, based on the data in 7 and 8.

(7)   Dare$_i$-ga   [Toshio-ga [ec]$_i$ tasukete-kureta]-to   itta ka.
      who -SUBJ Toshio-SUBJ help   gave   -COMP said-Q
      'Who$_i$ said that Toshio helped (him$_i$)?'

The "Q" below *ka* indicates that this is a question particle. *Ka* appears at the end of most direct questions, as you already know.

Recall from Problem Set 8.2 that Japanese does not employ a syntactic rule of *Wh*-Movement in questions (and you argued that is does not in relative clauses in Problem Set 9.3). Thus *dare* is syntactically in Subject position of the matrix clause in 7. However, Japanese may very well have a rule of *Wh*-Movement in LF, in which case the LF representation of 7 would have *dare* in a position hierarchically superior to the matrix clause. Still, a trace would be left in Subject position in LF. Therefore, this detail should not affect your argument in any crucial way.

One final point: the indices in 7 are possible but not required. Example 7 is also grammatical with the reading in which we are asking who said that Toshio gave the favor of helping some fourth party.

(If you have trouble getting started, look back at our definition of variable in this chapter.)

Your second argument should be based on the grammaticality of:

(8)   Hanako$_i$-ga [[ec$_j$] [ec$_i$] kokoro-kara aisite-kureru] otoko$_j$-o
      Hanako -SUBJ   heart-from love give   man   -DO
      sagasite-iru.
      look for is
      'Hanako$_i$ is looking for a man (who) gives the favor of truly loving (her).'

Here the point is that *Hanako* can be understood as coreferential with the empty DO of the embedded clause.

(If you do not see why 8 is relevant, ask yourself what sort of structure the most inclusive brackets given in 8 enclose.)

Star Problem 9.1

Where does intonation fit into our grammar? Is it available to rules that take place in LF? If so, is it assigned at SS or some earlier point? In answering this, consider the effect on interpretation of scope and on any other aspects of meaning in sentences like those below if an intonation peak is assigned to the words in capitals and then if an intonation peak is not assigned to the words in capitals.

(1)   ALL the boys didn't come.
      All the boys didn't COME.

(2)   I'M not gonna drive to school today.
       I'm NOT gonna drive to school today.
       I'm not gonna DRIVE to school today.

(3)   John doesn't beat his wife because he LOVES her.
       John DOESN'T beat his wife because he loves her.

Star Problem 9.2

It has been proposed that there is a co-indexation rule that takes place between Subjects and predicates, so that a sentence like 1 has the indices shown there:

(1)   John$_i$ is [nice$_i$].

If i/i were to be interpreted as applying to all indices, including indices assigned by the predication relationship, how could we appeal to i/i to rule out 2 on the interpretation in which *John* and *his* are coreferential?

(2)   *John$_i$ is [his$_i$ cook].

Now discuss why examples like 3 call into question the i/i account of the ungrammaticality of 2:

(3)   John$_i$ is [his own$_i$ cook].
       You are [your father's son] all right!

What do you think is the real reason why 2 is out?

Overview

In this chapter we have worked on Binding Theory and Government Theory and made a small addendum to Trace Theory. The descriptions below of the other modules of the grammar, therefore, have not been changed from those found at the end of chapter 8. The new principles we have added to our grammar are:

The Empty-Category Principle
The Minimality Condition
The i-within-i Condition
The Bijacency Principle

Binding Theory

We accounted for the gap in our typology of referring categories: No item with a phonetic matrix may be [+anaphor, +pronominal]. This account depended on the debunking of the notion of accessibility. (See the discussion under Government Theory later.)

We argued in this chapter for the Empty-Category Principle:

(1)   ECP: Trace must be properly governed.

Proper government can be either lexical government or antecedent government, where a node A antecedent governs a node B if A binds B and A is not too far away from B. (And see the remarks on antecedent government under the section on Government that follows.) We never arrived at a precise notion of exactly what counts as "too far away" for the ECP. Our motivation for the ECP came from trying to account for the phenomenon known as the *that*-trace effect.

We generated the complementizer *that* in C position. For that reason we needed to adopt the Minimality Condition in order to be able to appeal to the ECP to account for the *that*-trace effect:

(2)   The Minimality Condition: Any projection of a head that contains that head and a node A prevents a node outside that projection from governing A.

We also discussed the i-within-i Condition:

(3)   i/i: *[$_A$ ... B ...], where A and B bear the same index.

We argued that if we restrict this condition to applying to only binding indices, it is coherent as a principle against semantic circularity. We explored the type of referential circularity it precludes in Problem Set 9.1.

Finally, we discussed the Bijection Principle in this chapter:

(4)   Bijection Principle: Every variable must be bound by exactly one quantifier and every quantifier must bind exactly one variable.

This principle was invoked in accounting for the phenomenon known as weak crossover.

Government Theory

We had developed earlier the following definition of governing category:

(1)   Governing category:
       B is the governing category for E iff B is the minimal N″ or I″ that contains:
       (a) E,
       (b) the governor of E, and
       (c) a SUBJECT accessible to E.

In this chapter we introduced a common definition of accessibility:

(2)   Accessibility:
       A is accessible to B iff B is in the c-command domain of A and assignment to B of the index of A would not violate i/i.

We spent much of this chapter discussing this notion of accessibility and debunking it. We argued that if we restrict i/i to applying to only referential and binding indices, then it is a coherent principle. However, if we extend i/i to apply to all indices and if we allow a proliferation of indices in the grammar (such as indices resulting from a co-indexation rule between Agr and its Subject given in 10 in the text, and the co-indexation rule between a predicate and its Subject discussed in Star Problem 9.2), we lose coherency in this principle. But only if i/i is extended in this way will it be relevant to accessiblity. Thus we rejected the notion of accessibility entirely.

We noted further that there are certain types of structures involving Long-Distance Anaphora that we would expect to be ungrammatical given our notion of accessibility, but which are fine. We promised to address an alternative to accessibility in chapter 10. Thus, for now, we are striking accessibility from our list of notions relevant to the definition of governing category.

We also in this chapter added a new use for the term "government," in the notion of antecedent government:

(3)   A node A antecedent governs a node B iff A binds B and A is not too far away from B.

This is new in that binding nodes are always phrasal so far as we have seen in this book. But ordinary government is by a head (an X, not an X"). Thus antecedent government does not, in fact, use the notion of government at all. The term is a misnomer. Please do not let it confuse you.

Trace Theory

Note that we adopted the ECP, listed earlier under BT, by which trace must be properly governed. Besides the ECP, our Trace Theory has not been changed at all in this chapter.

10

Residual Issues in Binding Theory

Binding Theory and Argument Positions

We have developed many modules of the grammar in this book, and we now have well-motivated and clearly delineated ideas about several areas of Government and Binding Theory. We have developed Case Theory, Theta Theory, Government Theory, Trace Theory, and an outline of some parts of Control Theory, although much more could still be said about all of these areas. However, the one module we set out to handle in chapter 1, Binding Theory (BT), remains as perhaps the most murky. We will now complete the circle we started in chapter 1 by coming back to take a closer look at BT.

We know that in general an anaphor must be bound within its governing category, accounting for the difference in grammaticality between the following two examples.

(1)   John likes himself.

(2)   *John knows the girls like himself.

And, in general, a pronominal must be free within its governing category—all along we have set aside the issue of possessive pronominals and, indeed, we will not discuss the binding of possessives in this book. Thus 3 and 4 contrast:

(3)   John likes her.
       Sally$_i$ knows that John likes her$_i$.

(4)   *Sally$_i$ likes her$_i$.

The problem is that the general case is not the only case. Thus we find anaphors which are not bound within their governing category and we find pronominals which are bound within their governing category: 5 is not a good example for all speakers, but it is for some, and discussions of interpretation of it later (following

24) are based on the judgments of those speakers who accept it. Those speakers who do not accept 5 should substitute in some alternative Long-Distance Anaphora sentence. You might look to Problem Set 7.10, or Problem Set 10.2, or back to example 13 in chapter 9 for examples.

(5) Jill$_i$ knew that nothing could obliterate the memory of those photographs of herself$_i$.

(6) Jill$_i$ took her brother with her$_i$ to the market.

The concept of "Accessible SUBJECT" was developed at least partially to handle instances of Long-Distance Anaphora, but, as we saw in chapter 9, that concept was built on an incoherent interpretation of i/i. Furthermore, we saw in chapter 9 that that concept cannot be appealed to in all the L-D Anaphora cases that it was intended to account for. For example, in 5 *nothing* is the Subject of the embedded clause and serves as an Accessible SUBJECT for the anaphor, yet the antecedent is outside the governing category. We therefore abandoned the concept of Accessible SUBJECT.

Notice further that no principles of GB that we have developed in this book account for 6, although we can account for 6 in our own way. In chapter 4 we came to the conclusion that pronominals that are not arguments and that occur in OP position may be bound within their governing categories (and you might look back at Problem Set 4.6 in this regard). While this statement seems to be a reasonable approximation of the facts, it is *ad hoc* in that it does not follow from any more general principles of the grammar so far as we know at this point. We would like, therefore, to find motivation for this fact. Additionally, this fact brings to mind the general tendency we noted in chapter 5, that anaphors other than the emphatic reflexive and the reflexive that appears in a *by*-phrase are arguments only. These two facts have something in common: they show us that arguments are somehow special to BT with regard to the bindee.

This, then, brings to mind what we learned in chapter 8: Conditions A–C of the BT relate to binders that are in A-positions only, and you will recall that A-positions are positions that can be (but need not be) filled with an argument.

Given this string of facts, we might be tempted to say that Conditions A–C of BT relate to A-positions only. That is, not only are Conditions A–C limited to binders that are in A-positions, but also they are limited to bindees that are arguments. Unfortunately, however, this interpretation of BT is not empirically adequate. In 7 and 8 we see an emphatic reflexive, which is, of course, not an argument. This non-argument anaphor must be bound within its clause:

(7) The president$_i$ announced it himself$_i$ the following day.

(8) *The president$_i$ announced on Tuesday [that the war would begin himself$_i$ the following day].

Furthermore, if Conditions A–C of BT related only to argument bindees, then either "anything goes" in nonargument positions (that is, anaphors, pronominals, and R-expressions should all be able to alternate freely in nonargument positions regardless of what else they might be co-indexed with) or we need to develop a theory of binding for nonargument bindees now. It is easy to show that "anything goes" is not a viable statement of the behavior of nonargument bindees:

(9)   Jack$_i$ did it by {himself$_i$/*him$_i$/*Jack$_i$}.

(10)   Jack$_i$ brought the book with {*himself$_i$/him$_i$/*Jack$_i$}.

In 9 only the anaphor is grammatical. In 10 only the pronominal is grammatical with the indexation indicated. And I have not found any examples in which only an R-expression is grammatical.

So that means we would need to develop a theory of binding relevant to nonargument bindees. This theory would have to incorporate the fact that nonargument R-expressions must be A-free (thereby accounting for the ungrammaticality of 9 and 10 with *Jack* in OP position and for the lack of any sentence parallel to 9 and 10 in which the OP must be an R-expression), just as Condition C of our original BT does. It would have to allow nonargument pronominals to be bound within their governing category (in contrast to Condition B of our original BT), but it would have no immediately obvious account of the contrast between 9 and 10. That is, why is the pronominal excluded from 9? And, finally, this theory would have to account for L-D Anaphora, ruling in L-D Anaphora for 5, where the anaphor is an argument, and ruling out L-D Anaphora for 8, where the anaphor is a nonargument.

The job is formidable and there are no obvious theoretical advantages and some clear disadvantages (such as the fact that Condition C of both theories would be identical, an inexplicable coincidence).

For these reasons we will proceed here with a single BT in which Conditions A–C pertain to all types of bindees but are limited to pertain to binders in A-positions only.

Our task, then, is to come to a better understanding of the exceptions to Conditions A and B. With regard to Condition B, we know that certain pronominals that are nonarguments and that occur in OP position may be bound within their governing category. But the contrast in 9 versus 10 demands an investigation that we will not undertake here. Star Problem 10.1 lays out a direction for beginning research on this question.

Long-Distance Anaphora

We will, however, take a closer look at the phenomenon of L-D Anaphora. We must take into account that we hear instances of anaphors that have no linguistic antecedent in their sentence at all:

(11)   Who's he talking to? This doesn't sound like words to himself.

The context for 11 might be people standing outside a closed door, eavesdropping. From the other side of the door comes a man's voice. I have presented 11 to many speakers, all of whom either accept it without hesitation or feel that it is somehow formal, but still grammatical. When I offered 12 in contrast, everyone preferred 11, saying 12 was clearly unacceptable.

(12) *Who's he₁ talking to? This doesn't sound like words to him₁.

Likewise, when I offered 13 in contrast, saying that the man on the other side of the door's name is John, everyone rejected 13 in favor of 11:

(13) *Who's he₁ talking to? This doesn't sound like words to John₁.

The fact that the man on the other side of the door is talking and that the eaves-droppers are trying to figure out who he is talking to interferes with our interpre-tation of sentences with the form in 14:

(14) This doesn't sound like words to X.

It is as though we are imposing on the LF of such a sentence an argument structure for *words* that includes an agent which binds the object of *to*. Surely such an impo-sition could not be handled by any reasonably constrained theory of LF. So we might try to ask ourselves what element in 14 is open to an expanded interpretation at LF. The demonstrative *this* is the best candidate. And note that if we replace *this* with a semantically expanded NP, we get acceptability judgments that are entirely parallel to 11–13:

(15) [The phrase [that John₁ just said]] doesn't sound like words to {himself₁/ *him₁/*John₁}.

But even if we were to allow 15 as an expanded version of 11–13 at LF, we would not solve the problem for BT: the anaphor is unbound since *John* in the relative clause does not c-command *himself.*

Sentences like 15 raise the whole issue of whether c-command is, in fact, the cru-cial configurational relationship for binding. We will address that issue in the sec-tion after next. For now, we should just note that if *John* does, in fact, bind *himself* in 15, we have a motivated way of accounting for the ungrammaticality of the ver-sion of 15 that contains two instances of *John* (since this would be a violation of Condition C of BT).

Still, 15 does not have the form in 14, and it would take a magical mapping from syntax into LF to claim that 15 is the LF of the second sentence in 11 above. A better alternative might be to follow up on our first idea—that the argument structure of *words* in 11 seems to be behaving as though an agent is present. We would then compare the second sentence in 11 to:

(16) This doesn't sound like [**his** words to himself].

Now the anaphor is bound by the Subject (in boldface in 16) of the larger NP that it is contained within (bracketed in 16). While this is a simple (although absurd) solution, 16 raises serious questions. For one, when are we to interpret ANAR-THROUS NPs (that is, NPs without an article, as the NP *words to himself* is in 11) as having a possessive (phonetically silent, but present at LF, as in 16) and when are we to interpret them as having no possessive (even at LF)? For example, 17 is not synonymous with any of the sentences in 18:

(17) I love words.

(18) I love {my/your/his/her/one's/our/their} words.

How is our grammar to know it must supply a possessive in 11 but not in 17? Another question that arises is: how does our grammar know which possessive to supply?

The answers to these questions are not immediate and the analysis given in 16 is doubtful. But even if one could argue that 16 gave the proper LF for the second sentence of 11, sentences like the second sentence of 11 are not the only types of examples in which anaphors can occur without antecedents. Example 19 is from Ruth Rendell's novel *Make Death Love Me:*

(19)   Christopher had taken the snapshot of himself.

The context makes clear that Christopher had taken the snapshot not of Christopher himself, but of his father, Alan. The sentence is told in a third-person voice, but from the point of view of Alan, and it is this point of view, as we will argue below, that licenses the use of the anaphor. A regular pronominal is also acceptable in 19, however, in contrast to 11.

Certainly not all speakers find 19 acceptable with the interpretation described above (and I am among those who do not). In fact, it is typical of Long-Distance Anaphora sentences that speakers' grammaticality judgments differ, sometimes strongly. We return to this point later. Regarding 19, however, some speakers clearly accept it; witness Rendell (a British author). And, importantly, nowhere in my extensive reading of Ruth Rendell's novels have I found another reflexive without an antecedent in the same sentence. Thus it is likely that the usage in 19 is special for Rendell. So the claim that the particular point of view in this passage of the novel is responsible for the acceptability of a reflexive usage that would otherwise not be grammatical is all the more reasonable.

Another example, here involving a *there*-sentence, is:

(20)   "Why, who are you afraid of?" said Peter. "There's no one here but ourselves."

Example 20 is from C. S. Lewis's *The Lion, The Witch, and the Wardrobe.* Again, the regular pronominal *us* is acceptable in 20 (and preferable for many speakers). The use of the reflexive tends to emphasize a sense of conspiratorial or sympathetic behavior on Peter's part.

Another example involving the reciprocal anaphor was said to a friend of mine by her son, as he explained why he did not want to play football. The boy was thirteen years old.

(21)   Football involves too much bashing into each other.

Example 21 has an intimacy about it. I asked people to compare 21 to 22:

(22)   Football involves too much bashing of (the) players into each other.

Many people felt that if someone wanted to express their own fear of playing the game, 21 was preferable. They found 22 to be a more objective description of the game, even though the same evocative words, *too much bashing*, occur in both sentences.

All these examples depend on context as an aid in interpreting the anaphor. We go searching for an appropriate pragmatic antecedent and if we find one, we sometimes accept the sentence. Still, acceptable examples in which an anaphor lacks a linguistic antecedent are unusual:

(23) *Jack likes myself.

Example 23 is unacceptable, even though it is quite easy for us to see that the speaker of the sentence is the obvious antecedent for the anaphor; 23, of course, is much more the rule than 11 or 19–22. Thus the grammar has a strong restriction on anaphors, which is reflected in condition A of Binding Theory, but it can be broken under certain (not-well-understood) circumstances if an appropriate pragmatic antecedent is available.

Among these circumstances appear to be at least two factors:

I. A situation that we know from linguistic or nonlinguistic information involves identity of two of the role players in a single event (as in 11).

II. A prevailing point of view or perception that makes us interpret an event through the eyes (or ears or any other cognitive mechanism) of a given person, which person serves as the antecedent for the anaphor (as in 19–22).

Factor II has been called the factor of LOGOPHORICITY.

Turning now to instances of L-D Anaphora (that is, of anaphors whose antecedents are not local), we might ask whether either or both of these factors are relevant to binding of an anaphor by an antecedent outside its governing category. Let us begin by looking once more at 5, repeated here:

(24) Jill$_i$ knew that [$_{I'}$nothing could obliterate the memory of those photographs of herself$_i$].

Let us assume that the grammar goes searching in 24 for an appropriate antecedent for the anaphor. Condition A would limit us to the embedded clause in that search, since the embedded I″ is the governing category for the anaphor. (Recall that NPs that do not have Subjects cannot be governing categories. Thus neither the NP headed by *photographs* nor the NP headed by *memory* can be the governing category for *herself*.) No semantically appropriate antecedent is found within the lower I″. Typically, then, the sentence would be rejected. But for some reason, the search extends into the matrix I″ and an appropriate antecedent is found.

Are either of our factors present in 24? I think it is possible to argue that both are. For one, speakers who accept 24, even marginally, tend to interpret it as talking of Jill's memory. That is, Jill cannot forget the photographs. Thus Jill is a participant or role player in the event of memory and so is the photograph of Jill (the inactive participant of theme or patient). So factor I seems to be present. Second, the embedded clause in 24 tells us the perception of Jill; it is a statement about what she knows. So factor II seems to be present.

Are either of these factors truly crucial in 24? If we compare 24 to sentences that do not contain *Jill* (or some other third-person singular potential antecedent for the reflexive), we find ungrammatical sentences.

(25)   *It was known that nothing could obliterate the memory of those pho-
        tographs of herself.
        *Did you think that nothing could obliterate the memory of those pho-
        tographs of herself?

Thus the factors that allow 24 cannot all be located in the embedded clause alone.

So let us test which factors of the matrix clause might be important. First, let us replace the matrix clause in 24 with a clause conjoined to the embedded clause that does not have a verb which expresses the thoughts or feelings or in any other way give away the perception of its Subject. The verb *leave* seems to be such a verb:

(26)   Jill left and nothing could obliterate the memory of those photographs
        of herself.

When native speakers are faced with 26 and told to give it an interpretation, some of them (often reluctantly) agree that *Jill* must be the antecedent for *herself*. Then, most often, they say that the memory spoken of is Jill's, thereby bringing factor I into the event of memory (since Jill is an agent of *memory* and part of the theme of *memory*). That is, they interpret 26 as saying that Jill left and her memory stayed with her. Several informants, in fact, suggested that I replace *and* with *but*, as though Jill left in a failed attempt to get rid of the memory:

(27)   Jill left but nothing could obliterate the memory of those photographs
        of herself.

The very fact that 27 was the substitution suggested to me is important, for in 27, with the connotation that Jill is attempting to rid herself of the memory, the second clause tells us the point of view of Jill. So factor II is present, after all.

Another interpretation that several speakers I have asked assign to 26 is one in which Jill went away and the person left behind cannot stop thinking about the photographs. In that interpretation *herself* is coreferential with the person left behind. And speakers go so far as to suggest that Jill was the photographer or some-how otherwise intimately involved with the memories of the person left behind. Crucially, with this interpretation 26 is told from the point of view of the person left behind—and it is therefore strikingly similar to Ruth Rendell's sentence in 19. For these speakers, 27 has a similar interpretation.

We could go on to discuss many other examples that are similar in structure to 24 and that bring out additional points about L-D Anaphora. But we will not. By now you are able to approach data and pick them apart for yourself with just the lightest guidance. Thus, you will explore issues of semantics and syntax regarding anaphors in Problem Sets 10.1 (on Japanese), 10.2 (primarily on Italian), and in 10.6 (on English). If you like, do those problem sets now before continuing reading the rest of this narrative.

Small Clauses

Now let us turn to a somewhat different type of example that arguably involves L-D Anaphora. Compare:

(28)   Ralph$_i$ considers Mary inferior to himself$_i$.

(29)   *Ralph$_i$ considers Mary fond of himself$_i$.

The adjectives *inferior* and *fond* have their own argument structures. Thus 28 and 29 have two CFCs each (one revolving around the V and one revolving around the adjective). Some linguists have argued that such sentences even have two clauses each, and the embedded clause is a SMALL CLAUSE, in that it lacks a verb—although it has a predicate. (In 28 and 29 the predicate is the adjective.) The arguments for such a claim are based on a wide variety of issues and not solely on issues involving binding. You will find a discussion of some of the motivation for the existence of small clauses and other relevant issues in Problem Set 10.5 of this chapter.

All along we have used the number of verb strings in a sentence as a diagnostic for the number of clauses in that sentence. However, the whole idea of small clauses challenges that diagnostic. In fact, there are many other types of structures for which the determination of clause status is a controversial matter. You will explore some of these in Problem Sets 10.3 (on French and Spanish) and 10.4 (on Italian, French, and Spanish).

Returning to 28 and 29, we need to understand why the issue of whether such sentences contain small clauses is relevant to the binding issues we have been discussing in this chapter. If 28 and 29 involved small clauses, the structures would be:

(30)   Ralph$_i$ considers [Mary inferior to himself$_i$].

(31)   *Ralph$_i$ considers [Mary fond of himself$_i$].

The governor for the anaphor in each sentence is the adjective. If the bracketed material is a clause, *Mary* is the Subject of the clause. But that means that the bracketed material in 30 and 31 is the governing category for the anaphor. We would expect, therefore, that the anaphor would be limited to finding its antecedent within these brackets.

Why is 31 ungrammatical with this account? Because it is a violation of Condition A of the Binding Theory.

Why is 30 grammatical with this account? We have no easy answer: 30 is an instance of L-D Anaphora, and it is as problematic as any other L-D Anaphora example.

We might ask ourselves whether 30 has both factors I and II outlined above. That is, does 30 describe a situation that involves identity of two role players in a single event (factor I)? And in 30 do we find the perceptions of Ralph (factor II)?

Certainly both 30 and 31 have factor II, in that the matrix verb (*consider*) takes as its complement the thoughts of its Subject.

But neither 30 nor 31 has factor I. Ralph is one participant in the event of "inferiority" or "fondness," not two. Furthermore, there is nothing about the pragmatics that forces Ralph to be any participant at all in the events of the small clauses. Ralph could easily consider Mary inferior to or fond of any number of people. Nothing about the pragmatics forces us into coreference between *Ralph* and the anaphor.

However, it is interesting that a semantic restriction on the antecedent of the anaphor is found in 30 that is not found in 31: we do not generally say that one is inferior to oneself, although we can easily say that one is fond of oneself:

(32) ??Mary$_i$ is inferior to herself$_i$.

(33)   Mary$_i$ is fond of herself$_i$.

The predication of inferiority entails a comparison of two unidentical things; hence 32 is semantically ANOMALOUS.

Can we use this fact in accounting for the difference in grammaticality between 30 and 31? In 31 the Subject position of the adjective is a potential slot for an antecedent for the anaphor. But in 30, there is no potential slot for an antecedent for the anaphor within the brackets. The Subject position of the adjective is ruled out (as we see in 32).

It appears that if the structure itself (here for semantic reasons) precludes the possibility of an antecedent for the anaphor occurring within the governing category of the anaphor, the anaphor is allowed to go searching higher in the tree for an antecedent. This searching process may have other restrictions on it, such as that factor II must be present (as it is in 30 and 31). We have possibly identified a third factor, then, for L-D Anaphora:

(III) The absence of a slot for an antecedent within the governing category of the anaphor due to grammatical constraints.

We have seen three factors, then, which, from our brief discussion, appear to be relevant to the possibility of L-D Anaphora. None of these three factors is easily formalized and the judgment of whether any of them is present in a given structure may not be cut and dry. While this situation may not please you, it is actually not unwelcome. If you pick up an article that deals with L-D Anaphora, you will almost assuredly find sentences marked as grammatical that you judge to be ungrammatical. Perhaps you will also find the reverse. Speakers' judgments vary somewhat (and sometimes drastically) on L-D Anaphora sentences (as we noted above and as you undoubtedly know by experience after having considered the examples above of this section). If the factors relevant to L-D Anaphora call for subjective judgments, we would expect native speakers' grammaticality judgments to display some variation. On the other hand, if the factors relevant to L-D Anaphora were purely structural and of a yes/no type, then we would have no explanation for the variation in speakers' judgments.

The statements of the factors we have looked at in this section and in the preceding one are approximations. A closer study of L-D Anaphora may reveal severe inadequacies in these statements. However, these approximations are probably indicative of whatever statements eventually turn out to be adequate. Furthermore, these may not be the only factors on L-D Anaphora. It is quite possible that syntactic factors enter and that other semantic or pragmatic factors enter.

For example, it has been claimed that the antecedent in L-D Anaphora must c-command the anaphor. If you look carefully over all the examples of L-D Anaphora above in which a linguistic antecedent for the reflexive is present, you will notice that in every case the antecedent does c-command the anaphor. Do you agree? Perhaps you are bogged down on 26 and 27, where the antecedent is in a clause coordinated with the clause that contains the anaphor. However, there is evidence that the Subject of one clause c-commands material in a following coordinated clause.

We cannot go into that evidence here since the analysis of coordination is complicated and goes beyond the scope of this book. However, we will look more closely at the claim that the antecedent c-commands the anaphor in L-D Anaphora in Problem Set 10.2. You will also discover a new and surprising structural condition on L-D Anaphora in English in that problem set.

Clearly there is much to be studied. You can be sure that the issue of L-D Anaphora will remain controversial for years to come, since the factors relevant to it are of such an elusive nature.

There is an additional very important point we must make before we leave this section. Our discussion of 28 and 29 above was based on accepting the analysis in 30 and 31, in which these sentences involve small clauses. However, if you eventually decide to reject the notion of small clauses (and I have), the remarks about 30 and 31 still hold, given certain adjustments in the theory.

If we claim that 28 and 29 involve only one clause, then we are going to have to allow the Subject of a predicate not to form a constituent with the predicate phrase. In other words, we will have to say that in:

(34)   Ralph [[considers] [Mary] [inferior to himself]].

(35)   *Ralph [[considers] [Mary] [fond of himself]].

the VP consists of three constituents: the V, the NP *Mary*, and the AP; the NP and the AP do not form a constituent (for if they did, we would have the small clause analysis), yet the AP is understood to be predicated of the NP.

We will then have to admit that the parallel between CFCs and governing categories is not at all perfect. The last two constituents of the VP in 34 and 35 (the NP and the AP) form a CFC, but they do not together form a syntactic constituent, so they cannot be the governing category for anything.

It follows that BT will have to be restated in terms of CFCs. *An anaphor will have to be bound within its CFC. A pronominal will have to be free within its CFC.* So L-D Anaphora will consist of instances in which an anaphor is bound by an antecedent that falls outside its CFC.

These changes are not remarkable, even though they are severe. That is, all along we have recognized that issues of binding are issues of interpretation. Thus BT belongs to the semantic component of the grammar. That BT should, then, be based on semantic notions, such as CFCs, rather than syntactic notions, such as governing categories, is conceptually consistent.

Please, however, be sure to weigh my suggestions here carefully. BT plays a large role in syntax via the ECP (which we studied in chapter 9), which crucially relies on government. Thus many (most?) syntacticians would probably balk at the reframing of BT in terms of CFCs.

C-Command and Linear Precedence

In fact, if we were truly to throw aside the notion of governing category (a hierarchical notion) as a factor in BT, we might want to take a second look at other structurally hierarchical factors claimed to be relevant to BT. The other important claim is that a binder must c-command its bindee. Recall that in order for a node A to c-command a node B, the first branching node that dominates A must also dominate B. One way to state the c-command restriction on binding is to say that the bindee must be within the c-command DOMAIN of the binder.

I am going to do something to you now that I have not done so far in this book. I am going to bombard you with sets of data on six different grammatical phenomena and then draw a conclusion at the end. Typically in this book we have moved step by step, discussing the relevance of each set of data as they have come up. The discussion from here to the end of this chapter, however, may be more similar in style to linguistics articles in the journals. Try not to get frustrated. The point is not for you to understand each specific phenomenon brought up. The point is for you to be able to see generally how these phenomena and their potential analyses come to bear on the issue. Read at a normal pace. Once you have completed this section, you may want to reread, looking more closely at each phenomenon. But remember: the first time through, try to move with the discussion at an ordinary pace. Here we go.

We will discuss six phenomena that have been taken to involve the notion "domain": some of them are instances of binding relationships. That is, in each of them we want to say that one node is within the domain of the other node in order for the phenomenon to be able to occur. It is possible that these six phenomena do not all involve a single notion of domain. However, given that the binding relationship has been claimed to be based on the c-command relationship, it is natural to ask whether the c-command relationship is relevant to other phenomena involving domains. Thus we will do that here.

With respect to these six phenomena, we will look at two constructions for each one. One is the Double-Object construction:

(36)   Double-Object construction
       (as in: I denied [John] [the money].)

The other will be one of the following two constructions:

(37)   double-PP complements with free order
       (as in: I talked [to John] [about Bill].
               I talked [about Bill] [to John].)

(38)   double-PP complements in nominals
       (as in: a gift [from Bill] [to Sue]
               a gift [to Sue] [from Bill])

We will be looking at examples in which there is a domain relationship between two NPs within the VP (in 36 and 37) or within the complements of a nominal (in 38). We will be asking whether grammaticality in these sentences is best accounted for with a notion of domain that is based on c-command or with a notion of domain that is based on some other grammatical relationship.

In instances where two PP complements of a V or N can come in either order, I demonstrate below with only one of the orders. In some of these cases you can easily demonstrate for yourself with the other order. But at other times one of the orders results in ungrammaticality (as in: *I talked about Jim to himself versus I talked to Jim about himself—which pair you might think about as you consider 39 below). The probability is that some extraneous restriction is at play in such cases.

For example, it has been argued that a referential NP cannot be moved across another NP with which it is coreferential. This is known as the CROSSOVER CON-STRAINT (and it is not to be confused with the Crossover effects discussed in chapter 9, which involved the trace of Wh-Movement). Thus if movement is involved in these sentences, the Crossover Constraint would account for the resulting ungrammaticality. (But note that it is not obvious that any movement has applied in the relevant sentences. We would have to analyze these constructions carefully before we could say that the Crossover Constraint was an adequate account of the ungrammaticality.)

Alternatively, it has been argued that theta-roles fall into a THEMATIC HIERAR-CHY in which agent is higher than location, source, and goal, which are all higher than theme. It has been claimed that a reflexive may not be higher on the Thematic Hierarchy than its antecedent, thus accounting for some of the data that the Crossover Constraint was intended to account for.

We will not try to choose between these two accounts or to find others that might be superior. Please just assume that ungrammaticality with these other orders does not present new problems for the issue of what constitutes a domain (although it might pose problems for other issues in the theory of grammar).

We are now ready to look at the six phenomena. The first is very familiar to you: the binding of reflexive anaphors.

(39) Reflexive anaphors:
    a. *Double-Object construction*
       I showed John$_i$ himself$_i$ (in the mirror).
       *I showed himself$_i$ John$_i$ (in the mirror).

    b. *Double-PP complements in nominals*
       gifts from [the boys]$_i$ to themselves$_i$
       *gifts from themselves$_i$ to [the boys]$_i$

(Notice that in 39b we are testing only the relative position of the anaphor and its antecedent, not the variable positions for the PP complements. Thus we are not looking at examples in which the *to*-phrase precedes the *from*-phrase. This point should be kept in mind as you consider the example pairs below.)

The second involves quantified NPs, which we looked at briefly in chapter 4. (See Problem Set 4.2.) When the quantifier is taken to have scope over a pronominal elsewhere in the sentence, questions of domain come up, as demonstrated in:

(40) Quantified NP-bound pronouns:
    a. *Double-Object construction*
       I showed every friend$_i$ of mine his$_i$ photograph.
       *I showed its$_i$ trainer every lion$_i$.

    b. *Double-PP complements*
       I talked to every girl$_i$ about her$_i$ mother.
       ?*I talked to her$_i$ mother about every girl$_i$.

The issue in 40 is whether the pronominal (here a possessive pronominal) can be understood as bound by the quantified NP. For example, the first sentence of 40b is open to an interpretation in which I talked to the mother of each girl. But the second sentence of 40b is not. Instead, the only good reading for this sentence has me talking to precisely one mother about all of the girls. Thus on the reading indicated by the indices, the second sentence of 40b is ungrammatical.

The third phenomenon involves weak crossover, which we discussed briefly in chapter 9.

(41)   *Wh*-Movement and weak crossover:
    a.   *Double-Object construction*
        Who$_i$ did you show [t] his$_i$ reflection in the mirror?
        *Which lion$_i$ did you show its$_i$ trainer [t]?

    b.   *Double-PP complements*
        Which girl$_i$ did you talk to [t] about her$_i$ mother?
        ?*Which mom$_i$ did you talk to her$_i$ daughter about [t]?

In 41 I have indicated the trace left by movement. Here the issue is whether the trace and the possessive pronominal can be understood as entering a binding relationship together. (If you want to understand why that is the issue, you should reread the Weak Crossover section of chapter 9. But I suggest you finish reading this section before you do that.)

The fourth phenomenon is often called the SUPERIORITY EFFECT. We find that when we have two *wh*-phrases within a single clause, we can front one of them, but not the other.

(42)   Superiority:
    a.   *Double-Object construction*
        Who did you give [t] which book?
        *Which book did you give who [t]?
        (OK only with an echo-reading)

    b.   *Double-PP complements*
        Which girl did you talk about to [t] which boy?
        ?*Which boy did you talk about which girl to [t]?

The point to focus on in 42 is the structural relationship between the trace and the *wh*-phrase that is *in situ* (that is, unmoved). This phenomenon is very similar to the preceding one and might be argued to be just another instance of the same issue.

The fifth phenomenon is seen here:

(43)   *Each . . . the other.*
    a.   *Double-Object construction:*
        I gave each man$_i$ the other's$_i$ watch.
        *I gave the other's$_i$ trainer each lion$_i$.

    b.   *Double-PP complements in nominals*
        the gift from each boy$_i$ to the other$_i$
        *the gift from the other$_i$ to each boy$_i$

This instance is similar to the instance in 40, with quantified-NPs. There are reasons for keeping them separate, however. So we will.

The last phenomenon involves the position of the morpheme *any* (which can attach to other roots) in sentences with a semantically negative item (such as *no* or *few*):

(44) Polarity *any*:
    a. *Double-Object construction:*
        I gave no one anything.
        *I gave anyone nothing.

    b. *Double-PP complements in nominals*
        gifts from few of the boys to any of the girls
        *gifts from any of the boys to few of the girls

(Caveat: Be careful to distinguish polarity *any*, which co-occurs with a negative, from the universal quantifier *any* in sentences like *Anyone can do that*. Also, note that the quantifier *few* has different properties from the quantifier *a few*. Here we are considering only *few*.)

Look now at all of 39–44. Circle the two NPs that are relevant to each domain relationship. Now draw a line under the NP that is supposed to have domain over the other NP (the antecedent in 39, the quantified-NP in 40, the trace in 41 and 42, *each* in 43, and the negative in 44). What can you notice about all the good sentences as opposed to all the bad sentences? Probably the first generalization that comes to mind is that *the domain relationship is grammatical when the linearly first NP is taken to have domain over the linearly second NP.*

This generalization is unexpected with a c-command–based notion of domain unless it just happens that in all the good sentences above, the linearly first NP asymmetrically c-commands the linearly second NP (that is, the first c-commands the second, but the second does not c-command the first).

How likely is that?

For each of the six phenomena, the Double-Object construction was used as a demonstration. In that construction both NPs at least superficially appear to c-command each other since both appear to be sisters to the verb. Proponents of the c-command–based notion of domain (including, probably, most generative syntacticians) would have to argue for a very different analysis of the Double-Object construction. We will not look further into what this alternative analysis might be (although we discussed it briefly, with tree analyses, in Tangent 8.2 of chapter 8). We have simply noted this important consequence for our discussion.

The other two constructions used to demonstrate the six phenomena all involve NPs that are inside PPs where the PPs are sisters to a V or an N. At least superficially in these cases it looks like neither NP c-commands the other. A proponent of a definition of domain based on c-command would have to argue that the first NP somehow asymmetrically c-commands the second. That would amount to saying that the P introducing the first relevant NP does not count in the computation of c-command possibilities, but the P introducing the second relevant NP does count (and there are multiple ways one might try to achieve this effect).

While this may be true for some languages (and it has been argued to be true for Modern Irish), it does not immediately appear to be true for English. In fact, it is precisely the effect of the PP node that has been traditionally called upon to establish the role of the notion of c-command in discussions of binding using English data. Thus this response is unmotivated for English. Anyone taking this approach needs to argue strongly for a distinction in types of Ps.

Alternatively, one might argue that the P of the first PP has been incorporated into the preceding verb or noun to form a new V or N node dominating both words. This is the Reanalysis proposal which we discussed in chapter 7. In fact, you saw empirical inadequacies of this proposal as an account for certain facts about controlled PRO in Problem Set 7.8 of chapter 7. After the putative rule of Reanalysis, the first NP is no longer inside a PP but is instead dominated by the V′ or N′ node, and thus c-commands the second NP. If Reanalysis applied to 40b, for example, we would have:

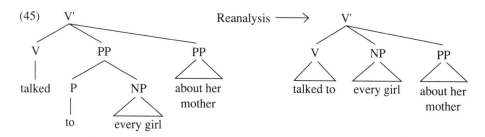

(45)

While there are extensive treatments of Reanalysis in the linguistic literature, we must be particularly careful in appealing to this type of mechanism when it comes to issues of c-command, for *if Reanalysis is not called for on independent grounds, the appeal to Reanalysis robs principles which make use of the notion of c-command of any predictive power.* This is an important point. Please reread it.

In fact, in the case of the double-PP complements of V and N, evidence against Reanalysis exists (and this evidence is parallel to that examined in Problem Set 7.8 of chapter 7 regarding control structures). In 46 we find that a modifier of the head V or N can intervene between the head V or N and a following P, and still the domain asymmetries are observed.

(46) I talked [quietly] to Jim about himself.
      *I talked [quietly] to himself about Jim.
      gifts [long overdue] from the Cub Scouts$_i$ to themselves$_i$
      *gifts [long overdue] from themselves$_i$ to the Cub Scouts$_i$

The presence of such a modifier would require us to allow the operation of Reanalysis to form a new V out of a string of V AP P. That is, the new V would not only consist of multiple lexical items, it would contain a whole phrase (the AP). Reanalysis is a dubious move, at best.

Furthermore, when two PPs follow an NP, and all three nodes are complements or adjuncts of a V, the familiar asymmetry is found again:

(47)   I gave [snapshots] to every boy$_i$ for his$_i$ mother.
       *I gave [snapshots] to his$_i$ mother for every boy$_i$.
       Which boy$_i$ did you give [snapshots] to t$_i$ for his$_i$ mother?
       *Which mother$_i$ did you give [snapshots] to her$_i$ son for t$_i$?
       Which boy$_i$ did you give [snapshots] to$_i$ for which girl?
       *Which girl$_i$ did you give [snapshots] to which boy for t$_i$?
       I gave [snapshots] to each boy$_i$ for the other's$_i$ mother.
       *I gave [snapshots] to the other's$_i$ son for each mother$_i$.
       I gave [snapshots] to no boys for any mothers.
       *I gave [snapshots] to any boys for no mothers.

Here the string *gave snapshots to* would have to be Reanalyzed as a single V. That is, we would now have to allow the operation of Reanalysis to form a new V out of a verb, an NP, and a P. Our Reanalysis operation is becoming more and more suspect.

Finally, there are several types of examples in which one simply would not want to appeal to Reanalysis to account for the ability of an NP inside a PP to have domain over some NP outside the PP. (Not all of these examples may seem lovely to you. Perhaps you can come up with a better group.) Consider:

(48)   I always eat dinner {after/with} each worker$_i$ on his$_i$ birthday.

(49)   Who$_i$ did you eat dinner {after/with} t$_i$ on his$_i$ birthday?

(50)   I ate dinner {after/with} each of the two workers$_i$ on the other's$_i$ birthday.

In LF these sentences have the structures here (and review the Operators and Logical Form section of chapter 9 if you are not comfortable with these representations):

(51)   each worker$_i$ [I always eat dinner {after/with} t$_i$ on his$_i$ birthday]

(52)   who$_i$ [did you eat dinner {after/with} t$_i$ on his$_i$ birthday]

(53)   each of the two workers$_i$ [I ate dinner {after/with} t$_i$ on the other's$_i$ birthday]

Here the trace must be bound by the operator. Given the Bijection Principle (which limits each operator to binding precisely one variable and each variable to being bound by precisely one operator, as we discussed in chapter 9), the possessives cannot also be bound by the operator. Therefore, the trace in each example must be taken to bind the possessive. These traces precede the possessives, but they do not c-command them. Thus such examples offer strong evidence that linear precedence rather than c-command is the relevant structural relationship for determining domain (here, binding domain).

One would not appeal to restructuring in 51–53 for two reasons. The first reason is already exemplified above in 47: an object of the V intervenes between the V and the P. But even if one adopted a version of Reanalysis that could operate on V-NP-P strings, there is still a strong reason for not appealing to restructuring in 51–53: a reason based on the thematic structure of the sentence. The whole effect of restructuring (with the Object of a P becoming a sister to a newly reanalyzed V) is to place an argument of a predicate in sister position to that predicate. There appears to be no motivation in English to appeal to this particular restructuring operation with respect to Ps that introduce an NP that is not an argument of the predicate. But in 48–53, the Object of *after* or *with* is not an argument of the predicate.

Evidence that the Object of *after* or *with* in sentences like 48–53 does not receive a theta-role is forthcoming. First, there is no obvious candidate for a single particular theta-role that could cover all the possible Objects of *after* (as you learned from doing Problem Set 3.3 of chapter 3):

(54)   a. I ate dinner after Bill.
            I ate dinner after the news.
            I ate dinner after dessert.
            I ate dinner after the tub.

       b. I ate dinner with Bill.
            I ate dinner with a spoon.
            I ate dinner with gusto.
            I ate dinner with only a moment's hesitation.

Furthermore, the Object of *after* here cannot serve as the antecedent for a reflexive:

(55)   *I ate after Bill (all) by himself.
        (cf. I ate after Bill (all) by myself.)

(No pragmatically suitable examples using *with* arise here.) Since reflexives require antecedents that are arguments of a predicate, it would appear that 55 is bad because *Bill* is not the argument of a predicate. This proposal is supported by the fact that in examples in which the object of *after* does receive a theta-role from a predicate, like 56, it can serve as the antecedent for a reflexive:

(56)   I'm after Jim for himself, not for his money.

On this basis, we might decide not to appeal to Reanalysis to account for 48–53. Instead, sentences like 48–53 lead us to adopt a definition of domain based on linear precedence.

As we expect, if we reverse the order of the complements in 48–50, the binding fails.

(57)   *I always eat dinner on his$_i$ birthday {after/with} each worker$_i$.
        *Who$_i$ did you eat dinner on his$_i$ birthday {after/with}?
        *I ate dinner on the other's$_i$ birthday {after/with} each of the two workers$_i$.

Here the structures at LF are:

(58)   each worker$_i$ [I always eat dinner on his$_i$ birthday {after/with} t$_i$]
        who$_i$ [did you eat dinner on his$_i$ birthday {after/with} t$_i$]
        each of the two workers$_i$ [I ate dinner on the other's$_i$ birthday
            {after/with} t$_i$]

Again the operator binds the trace. But here the trace is unable to bind the preceding possessive; hence 58 is a violation of the Bijection Principle.

For all these reasons, Reanalysis seems less than promising as an account of binding in these constructions.

There are other possible analyses we could consider here, but each has its own host of complexities and none (to my mind) is of obvious superiority. The bibliography can lead you into reading in these areas.

We conclude not only that linearity is relevant to determining domains but that c-command is not a necessary factor for determining domain in the instances involving two PPs within the VP. Why claim that c-command is a necessary factor for determining domain in any of these instances, then? We have seen no reason. We can conclude that for the six phenomena we have looked at here, in these very restricted structural relationships, linearity is the factor that determines domain.

Notice that our conclusion is crucially based on the rejection of Reanalysis. If one could successfully argue for some version of Reanalysis or for different structural analyses (as in the works cited in the bibliography), a different conclusion might follow.

If you look back now over all the examples in this section, you will find that we limited ourselves to one-clause sentences that had one CFC. Furthermore, both the potential binder and the potential bindee were inside the VP. If we were to look at sentences in which the two relevant NPs stood in different semantic and structural relationships to one another, we would find that a notion of domain based on linear precedence alone is not, after all, adequate. In fact, we would find all the traditional evidence for the original claim that domain should be based on c-command relationships (but wait to make conclusions on this point until after you have done Problem Set 10.2).

If we are correct, it seems that English makes use of two different strategies for determining domain. *Within a single VP and a single CFC, we consider only linear precedence. But in other structures, we seem to consider other factors including c-command and, perhaps, linear precedence, as well.*

Furthermore, we have limited ourselves in this discussion to data from English only. If we were to look at data from Italian, we would find that even within a single VP in a single CFC, the factors relevant to establishing domain are different. Linearity seems not to be relevant. Instead, c-command appears to be.

We will not look into the evidence that we have briefly mentioned earlier in support of c-command being a crucial factor for rules of grammar (in particular, evidence regarding sentences with NPs in different CFCs or not both within the VP, and evidence regarding NPs within a VP in a single CFC in Italian). That is because as you go on with your study of linguistics, you will find article after article in which the relevance of the relationship of c-command to a range of phenomena is shown. You will probably consider it one of the most useful and revered concepts of the theory of grammar.

The point of this section was not to debunk this all-important notion of c-command in general, but to make you aware that you should not assume its relevance to any phenomenon without justification. Other factors, such a linear precedence, may play an important role in linguistic theory.

Book Conclusion

We have come a reasonable distance in our understanding of the various modules and principles of the grammar. The Overview for this chapter summarizes the model we have developed. There is much that we have covered that needs to be challenged and there is much that we have not covered that needs to be explored. That is the job that lies ahead of you. The one skill I hope you will have honed to a sharp point in working your way through this book is the ability to probe. I wish you luck as you probe ahead.

Problem Set 10.1: Japanese *Zibun*

This problem set can be done after reading the second section of this chapter.

In Japanese the word for 'self' is *zibun*. It has two uses in which it can occur without a linguistic antecedent.

One use is when *zibun* refers to the speaker—first-person singular, as in:

   (1)   *Zibun*-wa gakusei desu.
           self-TOP   student be
           'Self be a student.'
           "I am a student."

   (2)   Butyoo-ga   *zibun*-ni soo iimasita.
           captain-SUBJ self-IO   so   said
           'The {captain/division manager} told self so.'
           "The {captain/division manager} told me so."

Here and below I offer two translations: one literal, translating *zibun* as "self," and one that is more natural to English. The other use is when *zibun* refers to the person spoken to—second-person singular only—and this use is rather recent in the spoken language, as in:

   (3)   *Zibun*-ga matigatteru-yo.
           self-TOP wrong
           'Self be wrong.'
           "You are wrong."

   (4)   Taroo-ga *zibun*-o suki-da-to   itte-ita-yo.
           Taro-TOP self-DO like   -Comp saying-was
           'Taro said (he) likes self.'
           "Taro said he likes you."

(Not all speakers accept 4 with the reading here. Note that for all speakers 4 also has the reading in which *zibun* is coreferential with the Subject of its own clause.)

We are going to ignore the uses in 1–4 and concentrate only on the use of *zibun* that has a third-person referent. Let me give you some facts about this *zibun*, which has been claimed to have some properties of anaphors.

Part 1

First, neither 1 nor 3 can be interpreted to mean that some other third person not mentioned elsewhere in the sentence is a student (as in 1) or is wrong (as in 3). The verb is not inflected for person number agreement in Japanese, as you know from doing previous problem sets. Therefore the absence of this reading cannot be due to any problems with verb agreement. Given that, what property does *zibun* with a third-person referent have in common with the vast majority of uses of English anaphors?

Part 2

In some ways *zibun* with a third-person referent is more restricted than English third-person anaphors. Identify one way, given the data here:

    (5)   Taroo$_i$-ga   Michi$_j$-ni zibun$_{i/*j}$-no   koto   nituite hanasita.
           Taro-SUBJ Michi-IO self   -GEN matter about talked
           'Taro$_i$ talked to Michi$_j$ about self's$_{i/*j}$ matter.'
           "Taro talked to Michi about his (only Taro's) matter."

(In 5 the *no* particle is comparable to a genitive marker within an NP, like the *'s* of English.) You will have to make a stab at it, since there are not many sentences I can give you to make the point. If you have no idea after looking at all the Japanese sentences given to you on this problem set, then just skip this question.

Part 3

In other ways *zibun* with a third person referent is less restricted than most uses of English anaphors. Tell me one way, given the data here:

    (6)   Taroo$_i$-ga   Michi$_j$-ni [Hitomi-ga   zibun$_{i/*j}$-o suite-
           Taro -SUBJ Michi-IO Hitomi-SUBJ self   -DO liking-
           iru] -to   itta.
           is   -Comp said
           'Taro$_i$ said to Michi$_j$ [that Hitomi likes self$_{i/*j}$].'
           "Taro told Michi that Hitomi likes him (Taro only)."

Part 4

Still, there is much in common between *zibun* and the English reflexive. One restriction that both share is exemplified in 7. What is it? As you answer this, assume that the initial "because" clause in Japanese is a sister to all the other complements of V. (This would make its attachment within the tree parallel to the attachment for English sentence-final adverbial clauses, as you learned in Problem Set 8.4 of chapter 8.) Also assume that Conditions B and C of the Binding Theory for English hold for Japanese. And be sure to compare instances of L-D Anaphora in Japanese (in which the antecedent for *zibun* is in a separate CFC) to the only structural restriction you know on L-D Anaphora in English.

(7) *Zibun$_i$-ga [[Toshio$_i$-ga horeta] syoozyo]-no koto -o
self -SUBJ Toshio -SUBJ fell in love with girl -GEN matter-DO
katatta.
talked
'Self$_i$ discussed the matter of the girl that Toshio$_i$ fell in love with.'
"He$_i$ discussed the matter of the girl that Toshio$_i$ fell in love with."

As you might expect, 8 contrasts with 7:

(8) Toshio$_i$-ga [[zibun$_i$-ga horeta] syoozyo]-no koto-o katatta.
'Toshio$_i$ discussed the matter of the girl that self$_i$ fell in love with.'
"Toshio$_i$ discussed the matter of the girl that he$_i$ fell in love with."

Another example of the same structural restriction is seen in 9 versus 10:

(9) *Toshio$_i$-ga tabetakatta node, zibun$_i$-wa Misato-ni
Toshio -SUBJ eat wanted because self -TOP Misato-IO
keeki-o tukur-ase-ta.
cake -DO make-caused
'Because Toshio$_i$ wanted to eat, self$_i$ caused Misato to make cake.'
"Because Toshio$_i$ wanted to eat, he$_i$ made Misato make cake."

(10) Zibun$_i$ ga tabetakatta node, Toshio$_i$ wa Misato ni keeki o tukur-ase-ta.
'Because self$_i$ wanted to eat, Toshio$_i$ caused Misato to make cake.'
"Because he$_i$ wanted to eat, Toshio$_i$ made Misato make cake."

Problem Set 10.2: English and Italian Long-Distance Anaphora

This problem set can be done after reading the second section of this chapter.

In the text we looked at L-D Anaphora in English and defined L-D Anaphora as any instance in which an anaphor is grammatical but is not bound within its CFC. An example is:

(1) John knew that there would be a photo of himself hanging in the post office.

We noted that typically in L-D Anaphora cases, the anaphor appeared in a clause that was viewed from the perception of the antecedent—that is, in a logophoric context. Some examples to illustrate this factor are given in 2–6. You may well not find all or even any of these examples grammatical for you. That is to be expected, as we noted in the text. Please feel free to make a short list of good L-D Anaphora sentences in your speech to use instead of these as you do Part 1.

(2) My mother always thinks that photos of herself are ugly.

(3) Those artists actually stood there and insisted that the philanthropist should buy each other's work rather than their own.

(4) Who would want such wrath to be brought down upon himself?

(5) Marie hoped and prayed John would draw a silhouette of no one but herself.

(6) She was older and she couldn't stand what it said about herself.

(Example 6 is an attested example from spontaneous speech.)

Part 1

There appears to be a syntactic restriction on the anaphor in these instances that we did not discuss in the text. Compare 2–6 to 7–11. What is that restriction? In doing this, you might set aside example 3 and answer without considering it. Then add in example 3 and find the minimal way to adjust your answer so as to account for 3, as well.

(7) *My mother always thinks that herself is ugly.

(8) *Those artists actually stood there and insisted that the philanthropist should pay each other.

(9) *Who would want such a terrible fate to destroy himself?

(10) *Marie hoped and prayed that John would draw herself.

(11) *My aunt always feels that there's herself to consider.

(You might want to look back at Problem Set 4.6, in which you discovered a syntactic restriction on pronominals that are bound within their governing category or CFC. There is a strong similarity between the two restrictions. In fact, this similarity could be a starting point for a longer research project.)

Part 2

How does the following example threaten your answer to Part 1?

(12) Sally wouldn't do anything that she thought might get herself hurt.

What sorts of analyses of the *get* construction in 12 would be consistent with your answer to Part 1? What sorts would be inconsistent?

Part 3

Is there any grammatical restriction on the antecedent in L-D Anaphora that falls within the framework of any of the modules of the grammar that we have developed? For example, must it in fact c-command the anaphor? Is it restricted to any particular GF or theta-role? Again, here are some data to help, and please consider all the data above, as well.

(13) John told Mary that there would be a photo of herself hanging in the post office.

(14) John talked to Mary about the fact that there would be a photo of herself hanging in the post office.

(15) John disabused Mary of the idea that there would be photos of herself in every household.

(16) John never understood why there were photos of himself in the post office.

(17) John disabused Mary of the idea that there would be photos of himself in every household.

Part 4

Now let us turn to Italian L-D Anaphora. Assume that the restriction on the anaphor that you discovered in Part 1 for English also holds of Italian. Now consider the antecedent.

Is there any grammatical restriction on the antecedent? For example, must the antecedent c-command the anaphor? Is there any restriction on the GF or the theta-role of the antecedent? Here are the data to base your answer on (and please note that Italian speakers, like English speakers, give varying grammaticality judgments on L-D Anaphora sentences):

(18) La signora era sorpresa che io giacessi   presso di sè.
      the woman was surprised that I   should lie near   herself.
      'The woman was surprised that I should lie near herself.'

(19) *Ha sorpreso la signora che io giacessi   presso di sè.
      has surprised the woman that I should lie near   herself.
      '(It) surprised the woman that I should lie near herself.'

(20) La signora insiste che io giaccia   presso di sè.
      the woman insists that I should lie near   herself
      'The woman insists that I lie near herself.'

(21) *Sarebbe utile per la signora che io giacessi   presso di sè.
      would be useful for the woman that I should lie near   herself.
      'It would be useful for the woman if I should lie near herself.'

(22) Ho ricevuto l'ordine dalla   signora di giacere presso di sè.
      have received the order from-the woman to lie   near   herself
      'I received the order from the woman to lie near herself.'

Recall that Italian allows Subject pronouns to be nonovert (that is, pro can occur in Subject position—and see Problem Set 2.5 of chapter 2). Also, in 21 *dalla* is an inflected preposition (a portmanteau). So the phrase *dalla signora* is a PP, and the nominal within it is the Object of a P.

Part 5

This part of the problem set is open-ended. If you are not particularly interested in the structure of Romance languages, you might want to stop now. However, if you are interested in the structure of Romance, the issue presented here for Italian is important since it has counterparts in many Romance languages.

The word *stesso* in Italian can be used in several ways. One position it appears in is adnominal (that is, to the left of a nominal) to a lexically full N. Another (perhaps indistinguishable, depending on one's analysis) is in an elliptical NP. In both these positions it can be translated as 'same.'

(23) La stessa ragazza di ieri   viene stasera.
      the same girl   as yesterday comes tonight
      'The same girl as yesterday is coming tonight.'

      Ho visto la stessa ragazza.
      have seen the same girl
      'I saw the same girl.'

(24) La stessa di ieri   viene stasera.
      the same as yesterday comes tonight
      'The same (one) as yesterday is coming tonight.'

      Ho visto la stessa.
      have seen the same
      'I saw the same (one).'

(Here *stessa* is the feminine singular form of *stesso*. Do not let the morphology throw you off—it does not change anything structural.)

Another position is with a pronoun or postnominally with a lexically full N to function as an intensifier. In both these uses (which, again, might be indistinguishable from one another and even from the uses in 23 and 24 above, depending on one's analysis) it can be translated as a reflexive (similar to the English emphatic reflexive).

(25) Lui stesso   viene.
      he himself comes
      'He himself is coming.'
      Ho parlato con lui stesso.
      have spoken with him himself
      'I talked with him himself.'

(26) Il presidente stesso   viene.
      the president himself comes
      'The president himself is coming.'

      Ho parlato con il   presidente stesso.
      have spoke with the president   himself
      'I talked with the president himself.'

Keep in mind the uses of *stesso* in 23–26 as you look at the question that follows.

Now let us turn our attention back to anaphors. Some people have claimed there are at least two nominal reflexive anaphors in Italian: *sè* and *se stesso* (and you are familiar with *se stesso* from Problem Set 8.6 of chapter 8). (The fact that *sè* has an accent but *se stesso* does not is due to an orthographic convention. Both *se*s sound the same.) What I want you to figure out is whether there really are two such anaphors or whether *se stesso* is simply a combination of the (one and only) reflexive nominal *sè* plus the *stesso* you saw above in 23–26. Use the data below to help you and you are free to bring up any kind of argument you like.

Sometimes either reflexive can appear in a given position:

(27) Gianni ha ricondotto   Maria a {se stesso/sè} con
      Gianni has brought back Maria to himself   with
      il   suo affetto   paziente.
      the his affection patient
      'Gianni brought Maria back to himself with his patient affection.'

(28) Gianni ha mentito a Maria su di {se stesso/sè}.
      Gianni has lied   to Maria about himself
      'Gianni lied to Maria about himself.'

But if the reflexive is the DO, only *se stesso* can appear:

(29) Gianni ha esaminato {se stesso/*sè} allo specchio.
      Gianni has examined   himself   in-the mirror
      'Gianni examined himself in the mirror.'

And in L-D Anaphora sentences, only *sè* can appear, as in 18–22 above, and in:

(30) Gianni voleva che la signora giacesse   presso di {sè/*se stesso}.
      Gianni wanted that the woman should lie near   himself
      'Gianni wanted (that) the woman should lie near himself.'

(Hint: Ask yourself why the anaphor that shows up in L-D Anaphora should be *sè*, whereas the anaphor that is excluded from L-D Anaphora should be *se stesso*. Can you tie this fact in to the meaning or function of *stesso* in 23–26? Can you tie this fact in to the restrictions you found on anaphors in L-D Anaphora structures in Part 1? Remember that you are to assume that whatever restriction you found for English holds for Italian, as well. It may help to reconsider your answer to the first question from the point of view of whether or not there is any single position in which an anaphor must be locally bound—as opposed to long-distance bound.)

Problem Set 10.3: Italian, French, and Spanish Causatives

This is a hard problem set. Try to work with a group.

In English the verbs *make* and *let* are unusual in that they can occur with an NP following them and an uninflected verb form following that NP, without any *to* preceding the verb form:

(1) Mary {made/let} John leave.

There has been much debate in the literature over what the proper analysis of sentences like 1, CAUSATIVE sentences, really is.

The Romance languages also have causative verbs that occur in structures that have certain peculiarities. I will demonstrate with Italian, but the particular facts given here have a close counterpart in French and Spanish, as well.

(2) Maria ha fatto partire Gianni.
Maria has made leave   Gianni
'Maria made Gianni leave.'
(cf. Gianni parte.
'Gianni leaves.')

(3) Maria ha fatto mangiare la torta a Gianni.
Maria has made eat   the cake to Gianni
'Maria made Gianni eat the cake.'
(cf. Gianni mangia la torta.
'Gianni eats   the cake.')

(4) Maria ha fatto mangiare la torta da Gianni.
                                        by
'Maria made the cake be eaten by Gianni.'
(cf. La torta è (stata)   mangiata da Gianni.
'The cake is (has been) eaten   by Gianni.')

(5) Maria ha fatto scrivere una lettera a Carolina da Gianni.
Maria has made write a letter to Carolina by Gianni
'Maria made Gianni write a letter to Carolina.'
(cf. Gianni scrive una lettera a Carolina.
'Gianni writes a   letter to Carolina.')

Examples 2–5 are representative of certain patterns. When the tenseless verb (which here is in the infinitival form) is intransitive, its sole argument follows it (in 2). When it subcategorizes for a DO only, the DO follows it (appearing in the normal DO position in Romance), and the argument that ordinarily would appear in Subject position shows up in a PP following the DO, and the P is the same P that we expect to introduce IOs (in 3) or the same P that we expect to introduce "apparent" agents in passives (in 4). When it subcategorizes for both a DO and an IO, the DO and IO occur in normal order after the verb (first DO, then IO), but the argument that ordinarily would appear in Subject position shows up in a PP following the IO, and the P is the same P that we expect to introduce "apparent" agents in passives (in 5).

Notice that in both 4 and 5, even though an argument shows up in a passive *da*-phrase (comparable to the English *by*-phrase), the infinitival does not show passive morphology. Furthermore, the causative verb string is not in the passive voice in 4 or 5 nor does this sentence have a passive sense to the causative verb (*fare* 'make') itself.

The facts get even more complex than these, but we will not go into any further facts right now.

One of the major issues in the analysis of Romance causatives is whether they derive from a MONOCLAUSAL or a BICLAUSAL structure. That is, does *fare* 'make' serve as the main V for its own clause, and the infinitival serve as the main V for an embedded clause in DS, as in 6?

(6)

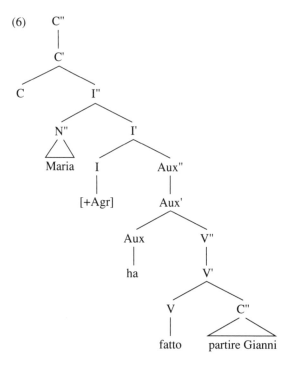

Or is there some rule in the lexicon that lets us create a complex verb from the causative verb *fare* plus any other semantically appropriate verb so that at DS we have a single clause (with a complex V), as in 7?

(7)

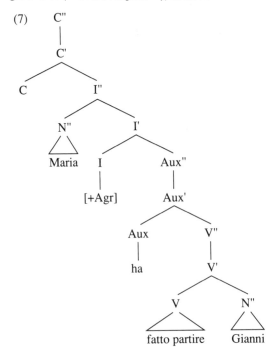

Another major issue is, if we start out with a biclausal structure, as in 6, do we still have a biclausal structure at SS or is there some sort of CLAUSE MERGER that gives us a monoclausal structure at SS, as in 7?

For many years the prevailing view was that causatives started out as biclausal at DS (as in 6) and became monoclausal by SS via a rule of Verb-Raising, which resulted in clause merger. Today that view is regarded as highly questionable.

These issues are particularly important in light of the Projection Principle. That is, we must maintain the lexical information of every predicate that occurs in DS throughout our derivation. How can we do that if we allow a biclausal structure to convert to a monoclausal structure?

We are not going to attempt an analysis of causative structures in Romance in this problem set. Instead, you are presented with three different sets of data and asked to comment on how their potential analyses bear on the issue of the proper analysis of causatives. Thus this problem set is asking for general discussion, rather than the type of clean arguments that you have become accustomed to making in previous problem sets. Nevertheless, not just any discussion is acceptable. Your knowledge of theory up to this point will guide your discussion. (Note: Do not be upset if your discussions in the various parts of this problem set are inconsistent with one another. If the data were open to a single, simple analysis, causatives would not have been the topic of so many books and articles.)

Part 1

Consider the following French sentences:

(8) Il a   menacé   Marie de la laisser.
he has threatened Marie of her leave
'He threatened Marie with leaving her.'

(9) *Il a   menacé   Marie d'être laissée.
he has threatened Marie of be left
'He threatened Marie with being left.'

Examples 8 and 9 show that active-voice *menacer* can have an infinitival complement that is active (in 8), but not passive (in 9). Now consider:

(10) *Marie était menacée   de la laisser.
Marie was threatened of her leave
'Marie was threatened with leaving her.'

(11) Marie était menacée   d'être laissée
Marie was threatened of be left
'Marie was threatened with being left.'

Examples 10 and 11 show that passive-voice *menacer* can have an infinitival complement that is passive (in 11), but not active (in 10). Now consider these causative sentences:

(12) *Il a   fait   *menacer* Marie de la **laisser.**
he has made threaten Marie of her leave
'He made (someone) threaten Marie with leaving her.'

(13)   Il a   fait   *menacer* Marie d'**être laissèe**.
        he has made threaten Marie of be left
        'He made (someone) threaten Marie with being left.'

The matrix verb is active in both 12 and 13. But the verb string of the most deeply embedded infinitival clause in 12 and 13 (in boldface) is active in the ungrammatical 12 and passive in the grammatical 13. What analysis of 13 regarding voice is consistent with the data in 8–11? [You might want to review the data in 2–5 as you think about this question. The issue is the voice of the verb of the intermediate clause, which is italicized in 12 and 13.] How does your answer bear on the issue of whether causative sentences are biclausal or monoclausal at DS and at SS?

Part 2

Spanish has a causative construction which uses *haber* 'have' (comparable to the French *faire* 'make' and the Italian *fare* 'make'). It has been argued that the Subject of the causative infinitive is controlled by the object of the causative verb, as with verbs like *force* in English (as you learned in Problem Set 7.4 of chapter 7). Let us review some facts on *force* first.

(14)   Papi forced Popeye to eat all the spinach.
        [Papi forced Popeye [PRO to eat all the spinach].]

(15)   *Papi forced all the spinach to be eaten by Popeye.
        [Papi forced all the spinach [PRO$_i$ to be eaten t$_i$ by Popeye].]

Contrast these two sentences to:

(16)   Papi expected Popeye to eat all the spinach.
        [Papi expected [Popeye to eat all the spinach].]

(17)   Papi expected all the spinach to be eaten by Popeye.
        [Papi expected [all the spinach$_i$ to be eaten t$_i$ by Popeye].]

Since *force* requires an NP Object as well as a sentential Object, 15 is ungrammatical because *all the spinach* does not satisfy the selectional restrictions that *force* puts on its NP Object. (That is, spinach is not the kind of thing one can force to behave in a certain way.) Only potential agents can be the NP Object of *force*. Example 17, on the other hand, is grammatical, because *expect* takes only a sentential Object, and that Object can be in the active or passive voice.

Now consider these Spanish sentences:

(18)   Los Magos vieron la   estrella.
        the Magi saw   the star
        'The Magi saw the star.'

(19)   La estrella fue vista por los Magos.
        the star   was seen by the Magi
        'The star was seen by the Magi.'

(20) El angel hizo ver la estrella a los Magos.
the angel made see the star to the Magi
'The angel made the Magi see the star.'

(21) *El angel hizo ver la estrella por los Magos.
the angel made see the star by the Magi
'The angel made the star be seen by the Magi.'

What analysis of the causative sentence in 21 would we have to adopt in order to account for the ungrammaticality of 21 in the same way as we account for the ungrammaticality of 15? How does your answer bear on the issue of whether causatives have a monoclausal or biclausal structure?

Part 3

French uses a dummy-*il* in weather and time expressions (like English, although, after Problem Set 7.3 of chapter 7, you know these Subjects are not really dummies, but, rather, pronouns whose referent is underdetermined and which occur with only a handful of weather and time verbs and expressions), whereas Spanish and Italian do not.

(22) Il pleut. (French)
'It's raining.'

(23) Llueve. (Spanish)

(24) Piove. (Italian)

In all these languages (perhaps in every Romance language) you can find weather sentences embedded under causative verbs:

(25) Le magicien a fait pleuvoir. (French)
the magician has made rain
'The magician made it rain.'

(26) El mago hizo llover. (Spanish)

(27) Il mago ha fatto piovere. (Italian)

How does this fact bear on the question of whether causative sentences are biclausal or monoclausal?

Problem Set 10.4: Italian, French, Spanish, and English: Clitic Climbing, *Tous* Movement, and Negatives

This problem set requires you to do work with native-speaker informants of French and/or Spanish. Please be sure to work with informants who learned the language during childhood. Even fluent speakers who acquired the language after childhood are not reliable informants.

In Problem Set 10.3 you were introduced to causative sentences. Causative sentences are special in that there are two verbal forms; each can have its own agent overtly expressed, and yet there is a question as to whether we are dealing with a monoclausal or a biclausal structure. The type of Verb-Raising that has been proposed for causative structures has also been proposed to take place in other kinds of structures. One of the structures is known as CLITIC CLIMBING (CC) sentences, which occur in certain Romance languages. These are Italian examples:

(1) Luigi deve studiarla.
     Luigi must study it
     'Luigi must study it.

(2) Luigi la deve studiare.
     Luigi it must study
     'Luigi must study it.'

In these examples the clitic *la* is an argument of the infinitival verb *studiar(e)* 'study.' In 1 this clitic shows up as an enclitic on the infinitival verb that it is an argument of. But in 2 this clitic shows up as a proclitic on the higher verb *deve* 'must.'

Do not let the English translations of these sentences confuse you. While English has modal auxiliary verbs, Italian does not. All verbs expressing modality in Italian have the syntactic characteristics of main verbs. Thus what we see in 1 and 2 is an instance in which a clitic argument of one verb can appear either on its own verb or on the next higher verb. We say that in 2 we have clitic climbing. (Try not to let the name of this phenomenon lead you into any particular analysis.)

Unlike causatives, the phenomenon here involves sentences with two (or more) verbal forms, but only the tensed one can have its own agent overtly expressed. Thus a sentence like that in 1 is a control sentence or a raising sentence:

(3) [Luigi deve [PRO studiarla]]
     [Luigi$_i$ deve [t$_i$ studiarla]]

As you do this problem set, please do not consider sentences with causative verbs or verbs of perception.

It has been argued that CC (as in 2) is the result of a rule of Restructuring (R) which creates one clause out of two by creating one verb string out of two. The structure of 2 with this analysis would be:

(4) [Luigi la *deve studiare*]

The italicized string, *deve studiare,* is a single verb string, with *deve* presumably filling the Aux slot. This account aims to explain many common properties of CC sentences. Three of those properties are:

(A) Sentences with CC have a higher verb that expresses modality, aspect, or motion.

(B) Sentences with CC generally do not have anything come between the two (or more) verbs.

(C) Sentences with CC cannot have the infinitive moved rightward by Right Node Raising.

Note that within the list types of verbs described in (A) many linguists include verbs translated as "want" under the rubric of modal verbs.

Restructuring could account for (A) because the functions of modality, aspect, and motion are typical functions of auxiliaries in various languages of the world. So such matrix verbs are semantically compatible with a restructuring rule which would change their status from main verbs to auxiliaries. One could take the fact in (A) as either a semantic condition on the rule of Restructuring (a less-than-desirable approach) or as a reflection of how we interpret lexical items that show up at SS in the auxiliary slot.

Restructuring could account for (B) by making one structural condition on the rule be that the string of verbs not be interrupted by any material with a phonetic matrix. (PRO would, then, be overlooked as would trace.)

To understand how Restructuring could account for (C), you need to understand what Right Node Raising is. This is the rule that is taken to operate on a sentence like 5 to give a sentence like 6.

(5) Mary bought the potatoes and Bill cooked the potatoes.

(6) Mary bought and Bill cooked the potatoes.

The claim is that in the two conjoined clauses in 5, the final NP consitutent gets moved out of both clauses to form 6, attaching at some higher level, perhaps as in 7.

(7)

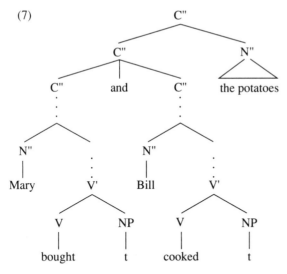

Since it is the final constituent of each of the VPs that gets moved (that is, the rightmost constituent), and since that constituent is moved to some point higher in the tree (that is, Raised), the rule is dubbed Right Node Raising (RNR—and we mentioned it already briefly in chapter 8). RNR is not limited to moving only final NPs. It can move any X″ that is identical (that is, filled with the same lexical items) at the end of two juncts (that is, phrases joined by *and* [conjuncts], *or* [disjuncts], or *but*) and perhaps in other structures as well (as you saw in Star Problem 8.2).

The fact stated in (C) is illustrated in the contrast between 8 and 9, where 8 does not have CC (and, thus, has not been restructured) and can have RNR, but 9 does have CC (and, thus, has been restructured) and cannot have RNR:

(8)   Piero dovrebbe—ma francamente non credo che vorrà—
      Piero should   but frankly   not believe that will want
      parlarne con Gianni.
      speak CL with Gianni
      'Piero should, but frankly I don't believe he wants to, speak with Gianni.'

Here the clitic *ne* (glossed as CL)is attached to the V *parlar-*. The string *parlarne con Gianni* has been right node raised, showing that this string forms a phrasal constituent (a C″ with a PRO for Subject, similar to the structure given in 3).

(9)   *Piero ne dovrebbe—ma francamente non credo che
      Piero CL should   but frankly   not believe that
      ne vorrà— parlare con Gianni.
      CL will want speak   with Gianni

Here the clitic *ne* has climbed onto the higher verb in each junct. But now RNR fails. This shows that the string *parlare con Gianni* does not form a complete phrase. Thus this string is not an X″, but only an X′.

Restructuring can account for the ungrammaticality of 9 because the string that we tried to RNR in 9 would be a V′ after restructuring—not a maximal projection.

Please use (A)–(C) as background as you do the rest of this problem set.

Part 1

In French, clitics do not appear attached to verbs that they are not arguments of except when the higher verb is a causative or a verb of perception. So CC does not occur with the verbs that exhibit it in Italian. However, French has a quantifier *tous* 'all' which can appear in a variety of places. Consider these sentences:

(10) J'ai   voulu les   lire tous.
      I have wanted them read all
      'I wanted to read all of them.'

(11) J'ai voulu tous les lire.

(12) J'ai tous voulu les lire.

Examples 10–12 all mean (very nearly) the same thing. In 10 *tous* sits in ordinary Object position, and it quantifies over the clitic *les*. In 11 *tous* sits to the left of the clitic verb string *les lire*. In 12 *tous* sits to the left of the past participle of the main verb *voulu*.

The phenomenon in 10–12 has been called L-TOUS (for Leftward-tous movement). Like CC sentences in Italian, L-tous sentences are unusual in that *tous* can appear to the left of one verb when it quantifies an argument of another verb (as in 12).

Find an informant and test whether L-tous has the properties of Italian CC sentences listed in (A)–(C). That is, test whether L-tous takes place only when the higher verb expresses modality (including "want"), aspect, or motion. Test whether any items (such as adverbs) can come between the higher verb and the lower infinitive other than clitics. Test whether in conjoined sentences the infinitive can undergo RNR.

If you feel ready for a challenge, continue with the following questions.

First, if L-tous has the properties of CC sentences, will Reanalysis account for this fact? Why or why not?

Second, if L-tous does not have all the properties in (A)–(C) of CC sentences, which one(s) does it have? Why do you think this difference between L-tous and CC occurs?

Part 2

Spanish has CC sentences, just like Italian:

(13) Maria quiere empezar a leerlos.
      Maria wants begin   to read CL
      'Maria wants to begin to read them.'

(14) Maria quiere empezarlos a leer.

(15) Maria los quiere empezar a leer.

Examples 13–15 mean (very nearly) the same thing. (Note: Clitics in Spanish, like in Italian, cliticize to the right of nonfinite verbs—such as infinitives and gerunds—and to the left of finite verbs in all sentences except imperatives, where the facts get complex. Do not worry about that. *Los* is cliticized to a different verb in each of 13, 14, and 15. That is all that matters. Do not worry about the detail of which side of the verb the clitic attaches to.)

Find an informant and test Spanish for whether CC sentences have the same properties CC sentences have in Italian (that is, (A)–(C)). As you test for (B), you will find that some complementizers can come between the matrix verb and the infinitive in Spanish CC sentences and others cannot. Be sure to note those differences. See if you can make a generalization about them.

Part 3

Reread (A). In 16 we find an example of a modal verb in Italian with CC; in 17, of an aspectual verb; in 18, of a verb of motion:

(16) Lo devo mangiare.
      it must eat
      'I must eat it.'

(17) L'ho   finito   di mangiare
      it-have finished to eat
      'I've finished eating it.'

(18)   Lo   vado a   chiamare.
       him go   to call
       'I'm going to call him.'

Example 18 has the sense of "I'm physically going someplace in order to call him."

However, the statement in (A), while covering most cases, is too restrictive. In fact, a wide range of verbs can appear with CC if the context is appropriate. I am not going to give you any contexts. I am simply going to give you a list of some of those verbs. (In the list that follows I have included *volere* 'want,' for those of you who resist classifying it as a modal verb.)

(19)   volere 'want'; sapere 'know' (as in 'I know how to swim'); riuscire 'succeed'; intendere 'intend'; osare 'dare'; sembrare 'seem'; credere 'believe'; prendere 'take to' (as in 'I've taken to playing bridge lately'); usare 'be in the habit of'

Looking at this set of verbs, can you generalize to state some semantic characteristic(s) that all higher verbs in CC sentences must have? Are any of these verbs a surprise to you in that they seem semantically not right for the group? If so, which?

Part 4

This is a very sketchy problem with only suggestions as to a direction for research.
Take sentence pairs with negatives in English, like:

(20)   I didn't think I would leave.

(21)   I thought I wouldn't leave.

Notice that a possible reading of 20 is (at least somewhat) similar to the reading of 21 (and some people have claimed they are synonymous under one reading of 20).

It is not always the case that a negative can appear with either of two verbs without drastically changing the meaning of the sentences. Compare 22 and 23 to 20 and 21:

(22)   I didn't say I would leave.

(23)   I said I wouldn't leave.

Make a list of verbs that behave with respect to negatives and their interpretation like *think* in 20 and 21.

Make a list of verbs that behave with respect to negatives and their interpretation like *say* in 22 and 23.

Now semantically characterize the set of verbs that behave like *think*. Does that set have anything in common with the set of higher verbs in CC sentences in Italian? (I am not saying it does—this is a sincere, not a rhetorical, question.)

Why do you think the effect in 20 and 21 comes about?

*Problem Set 10.5: English Small Clauses

The various parts of this problem set are only loosely related to one another. Thus one can easily select parts to do and parts to skip. However, the issue faced in this problem set is important and you should read through the entire problem set even if you do only some parts.

In the text we talked briefly about one type of sentence for which small clauses have been proposed. The motivation for the proposal that small clauses exist is primarily the following: if we interpret the Projection Principle to mean that all lexical relationships (including predicate-argument structure) must be present at every syntactic level, then even at DS we must indicate which items are Subjects of which predicates. One very straightforward way to do this is to generate Subjects of predicates only as the left branch of clauses, whether clauses are large (that is, contain a verb, so they are C″) or small (that is, do not contain a verb, so let us dub them SC for small clause, where SC is a maximal projection of some sort).

The consequence of this reasoning is that every predicate you find in a sentence will be the main predicate of a clause (large or small) at DS (as well as SS). So sentences like:

(1)   John came in drunk.
      I found Mary a fool. (= I found Mary to be a fool.)

which have two predicates, will have the following DS and SS:

(2)   [John came in [PRO drunk]].
      [I found [Mary a fool]].

In this problem set we are going to look at scattered questions involving the proposal of small clauses. You will find that some of the material may make you doubt the existence of small clauses. Do not be alarmed. It is possible to maintain the Projection Principle without adopting the small-clause proposal as long as we allow a more complex mapping between syntax and semantics. We will not go into the alternatives here, but you can easily follow them up by reading the growing literature in this area once you have done this problem set.

Part 1

Consider the sentence:

(3)   *Workers angry about the pay* is the sort of situation that the ad campaign
      was supposed to avoid.

This kind of sentence has been used as evidence for the existence of small clauses. The claim is that the string *workers angry about the pay* is a small clause. Be careful to recognize the difference in interpretation between this string in 3 and this same string in 4:

(4)   *Workers angry about the pay* stormed the building.

In 4 we have an ordinary NP, whose head is *workers*, and whose modifying phrase is the AP *angry about the pay* (semantically similar to the NP *workers who were angry about the pay*). But in 3 *angry about the pay* is not a modifier, but a predicate, and the whole issue of whether this string forms a constituent is, essentially, equivalent to the question of whether small clauses exist. Do you see the semantic difference between 3 and 4 regarding this string? Keep it in mind as you do the rest of this part of the problem set.

List as many syntactic differences as you can between strings like that in 3 and that in 4. (Consider, for example, Subject-Verb Agreement facts, the choice of the matrix verb, the syntactic positions such strings can appear in in a sentence, Case assignment, and anything else you might notice.)

What issue do strings like the italicized one in 5 raise?

(5)   *Stone drunk* it's hard to make any progress.

Part 2

Consider the data:

(6)   John tried to be happy.
      *John tried happy.

(7)   Fred intends to be quiet.
      *Fred intends quiet.

Try is subcategorized to take certain kinds of complements. One type is propositional. But we see in 6 that while *try* can take an infinitival complement, it cannot take an AP complement. *Intend* shows similar behavior. If bare predicative APs like those in 6 and 7 are small clauses with a PRO Subject (as proponents of the existence of small clauses would claim), then we find the following generalization: *no verb is subcategorized to take a control small clause.* While we have seen only two examples to make our point, if you went through as many other verbs that are subcategorized to take control complements, you would find that absolutely none of them take a control small clause.

The only place we find putative control small clauses is with verbs that are not subcategorized to take a clausal complement. Thus all putative control small clauses are adjuncts, as in:

(8)   Fred left tired.

These kinds of data could be used as evidence against the existence of small clauses. Explain how.

Part 3

Describe the syntactic distribution and any other syntactic and semantic properties you have time to lay out (but you *must* do the syntactic distribution) of putative small clauses in English for one of the following types (these groups may overlap— but examine only one type):

(A) AdjP as predicate: John left *angry*.

(B) PP as predicate: We drove John *to distraction*.

(C) Resultatives: I ironed the shirt *flat*.

(D) Depictives: He drove home *drunk*.

(E) SCs that are controlled by the Subject of the full clause: He ate potatoes *nude*.

(F) SCs that are controlled by the DO of the full clause: He ate potatoes *raw*.

(G) SCs that are controlled by the IO or the Object of any P. One kind of example is in the "absolute *with*-construction": With Mary *sick*, who will defend Sally?

So for example, if you choose depictives, as in (D), ask where linearly they can occur in a sentence.

Once you see the distribution, does this distribution correlate to the distribution of other controlled large clauses (that is, clauses that contain a verb and have PRO as Subject)? If not, point out any differences in distribution.

Now, try to find an explanation for the differences you found between the distribution of putative SCs and the distribution of large PRO clauses.

Part 4

Pick one of the following two constructions and argue whether the underlined string is a SC.

(9) With *the post office on strike*, I guess we'll have to use e-mail.

(10) How could you talk that way, and *your father on his deathbed*!

You might ask: Is the string a syntactic constituent? Does the relevant NP have syntactic properties that only Subjects have? Does the putative Subject slot behave like other syntactic Subjects in allowing dummy-*it* or dummy-*there* to fill it? Can idioms that contain a fixed Subject (such as *The jig's up* or *The penny dropped* or *The earth moved* or *The cat has X's tongue*) occur in these constructions? Can you have Extraposition of a putative sentential Subject from within these types of strings?

Once you have decided whether the construction in question is a SC, discuss the binding properties of this construction.

Part 5

The sentence:

(11) I believed John sober.

is multiply ambiguous. Give all the readings you can find for it. (There are at least three.)

Now account for these readings with a theory that allows SCs.

Now account for these readings with a theory that does not allow SCs.

Problem Set 10.6: English Psych Verbs

This problem set can be done after reading the second section of this chapter.

The sentence:

(1)   Bill frightens me.

can be used if Bill purposely dresses up like Dracula and jumps out at me regularly
or if Bill just is a person who, by his very nature (or appearance or whatever), causes
me fear. In the first instance, we can describe a particular event of fright with:

(2)   I was frightened by Bill.

But 2 is not typically used to describe the second instance. Instead, we might say:

(3)   I was frightened at Bill.

Part 1

List as many verbs as you can think of that behave in a manner parallel to the
behavior of *frighten*.
    Try to characterize their semantic class. (Note: This class of verbs is referred to
as the PSYCH VERBS.)
    List as many syntactic characteristics of this class of verbs as you can think of.

Part 2

Many people have noticed that these verbs allow reflexives properly contained in
their Subject to be co-indexed with some item in the VP:

(4)   (Those) pictures of himself$_i$ frighten Jeffrey$_i$.

Most other types of verbs do not allow this:

(5)   ?*Those recent pictures of herself$_i$ flatter Sally$_i$.
      ?*Those nude pictures of herself$_i$ were lying on Sally's$_i$ bureau.

But some other types of verbs do:

(6)   Those nude pictures of himself$_i$ cost John$_i$ his job.
      Those nude pictures of himself$_i$ left John$_i$ jobless.
      Those nude pictures of himself$_i$ ruined John's$_i$ career.
      Those nude pictures of himself$_i$ made John$_i$ lose his job.
      Nude pictures of themselves$_i$ mean nothing to those thugs$_i$.

Try to come up with other examples like 6 in which a verb that does not fit into the
semantic class with *frighten* can allow a reflexive inside the Subject to be co-indexed
with some NP in the VP.

Part 3

If you think you have some idea as to why verbs like *frighten* can appear in structures like 4, explain and defend that idea. If you have no idea, explain what hypotheses you went through and why you rejected them.

Problem Set 10.7: English Missing Objects

Certain verbs can be used with a reflexive DO or not, where their meaning with and without the DO is quite similar:

(1)   Jack dressed (himself).

(2)   Sally behaved (herself).

Other verbs do a similar thing with reflexives that are Objects of Ps:

(3)   I'm ashamed (of myself).

And many of the verbs that optionally take a reflexive DO also take a particle:

(4)   I dried (myself) off.

(5)   He snuggled (himself) down (under the covers).

Note that:

(6)   I dried.

is not similar in meaning to:

(7)   I dried myself.

Nor is:

(8)   He snuggled.

similar in meaning to:

(9)   He snuggled himself.

In fact, 8 might be ungrammatical for you (as it is for me) and 9 might seem perverse to you (as it does to me). So the particles in 4 and 5 are not trivial.

Come up with a list of verbs that have an optional reflexive of some sort. Subdivide that list into verbs that follow similar syntactic patterns, such as whether the reflexive is a DO (as in 1 and 2), whether the reflexive is the Object of a particular P (as in 3), whether a particle must follow (as in 4 and 5), and any other pattern you might see. For example, consider the verb *prepare* with and without a reflexive, as in:

(10)   I prepared (myself) for bad news.

What syntactic restrictions do we find here?

Now carefully pick pairs with and without reflexives and look at their meanings. Give a few pairs that show clearly that the sentences with and without reflexives are *not* synonymous, after all. Characterize the type of difference in semantics we find between members of the pairs.

Problem Set 10.8: Japanese Passives and Major Subjects

Japanese has passives that seem very similar to English passives, as in:

(1)   Taroo-ga   Hanako-ni sikarareta.
      Taroo-SUBJ Hanako-by was scolded
      'Taroo was scolded by Hanako.'

However, it also has what has been called the complex passive: a nonliteral English translation is very far from the original Japanese in structure (but a literal translation is ungrammatical):

(2)   Taroo-ga   Hanako-ni [kaisha-o   yameta]-to   omowareta.
      Taroo-SUBJ Hanako-by company-DO quit   -COMP was thought
      Lit: 'Taroo was thought by Hanako that (he) quit the job.'
      'It was Taroo that Hanako thought quit the job.'

(Note that in the gloss I indicate past and present by the English agreement morphemes. Recall that Japanese has no Subject-Verb Agreement.) The active counterpart to 2 is:

(3)   Hanako-ga   [Taroo-ga   kaisha-o   yameta]-to   omotta.
      Hanako-SUBJ Taroo-SUBJ company-DO quit   -COMP thought
      'Hanako thought that Taroo quit the job.'

Part 1

Give a brief statement as to why the passive in 2 is called a complex passive.

Part 2

What property of the Subject of the matrix clause of complex passive sentences seems necessary based on 2, 4, and 5?

(4)   Sono maruhijoho   -ga   Sony-no   kenkyuusyatati-ni
      that   top-secret information-SUBJ Sony-GEN researchers-by
      [Tanaka-ga   Hitachi-no   syatyoo-ni   morasita]-to
      Tanaka-SUBJ Hitachi-GEN president-IO leaked   COMP
      omowareteita.
      was thought
      'That top-secret information was thought by researchers at Sony that
      Tanaka leaked (it) to the president of Hitachi.'

(5) Hitachi-no syatyoo- ga Sony-no kenkyuusyatati-ni
Hitachi-GEN president-SUBJ Sony-GEN researchers-by
[Tanaka-ga sono maruhijoho-o morasita]-to
Tanaka-SUBJ that top-secret information-DO leaked COMP
omowareteita.
was thought
'The president of Hitachi$_i$ was thought by researchers at Sony that
Tanaka leaked top-secret information (to him$_i$).'

(Not all speakers accept 5. Please overlook that fact in doing this problem set.) Now
note the following active sentence:

(6) Hanako-ga [Toshio-ga Mariko-to kekkon si-tagatteiru]
Hanako-SUBJ Toshio-SUBJ Mariko-with marry do wants
-to gokaisita.
-COMP suspected/misunderstood

The *to* on *Mariko* is actually a postposition. This particular verb—*kekkon (suru)*—
selects that postposition to introduce one of its arguments (just like our verb *depend*
selects the P *on* to introduce one of its arguments). One of the possible complex
passives corresponding to 6 is given in 7:

(7) Mariko-ga Hanako-ni [Toshio-ga kekkon si- tagatteiru]-to
Mariko-SUBJ Hanako-by Toshio-SUBJ marry do- wants -COMP
gokaisareta.
was suspected/misunderstood
'Mariko was {suspected/misunderstood} by Hanako that Toshio wants to
marry (with her).'

Adjust the statement you made about the matrix Subject of complex passive sentences above to include sentences like 7.

Part 3

Examples 2, 4, 5, and 7 have the grammatical and semantically (close to) identical
counterparts shown in 8–11. What can you say now about the "gap" or "hole" in
a complex passive?

(8) Taroo$_i$-ga Hanako-ni [kare$_i$-ga kaisya- o yameta]-to
Taroo- SUBJ Hanako-by he- SUBJ company-DO quit- COMP
omowareta.
was thought

(9) Sono maruhizyoohoo$_i$ -ga Sony-no kenkyuusyatati-ni
that top-secret information-SUBJ Sony-GEN researchers-by
[Tanaka-ga Hitachi-no syatyoo- ni sore$_i$-o morasita]-
Tanaka-SUBJ Hitachi-GEN president-IO it- DO leaked-
to omowareteita.
COMP was thought

(10) Hitachi-no   syatyoo$_i$- ga   Sony-no   kenkyuusyatati-ni
      Hitachi-GEN president-SUBJ Sony-GEN researchers-by
      [Tanaka-ga   kare$_i$-ni sono maruhizyoohoo-o   morasita]
      Tanaka-SUBJ him- IO that top-secret information-DO leaked
      -to   omowareteita.
      -COMP was thought

(11) Mariko$_i$-ga   Hanako-ni [Toshio-ga   kanozyo$_i$-to kekkon
      Mariko- SUBJ Hanako-by Toshio-SUBJ her-with   marry
      si-tagatteiru]-to   gokaisareta.
      do- wants   -COMP was suspected

(Some speakers find 10 marginal. Please ignore that fact in doing this problem set.)

Part 4

Locate the gap in the example here. What principle of grammar is at stake here if complex passives are formed via movement of an NP from the gap into the Subject position of the matrix clause?

(12) Ano koorudo fyuuzyon nitsuite-no   ronbun$_i$-ga
      That cold   fusion   about -GEN paper-SUBJ
      [$_{NP}$ [$_S$ kaita] gakusha]-ga   kono gakkai-   ni kiteinai] -to
            wrote scholar]-SUBJ this   conference-to come-not -COMP
      sasayakareteiru.
      is murmured
      'That paper about cold fusion is murmured that the scholar who wrote
      (it) did not come to this conference.'

[Hint: The embedded clause in 12 is a relative clause.]

Part 5

Japanese is famous for having what are called multiple-Subject sentences, as in:

(13) Tanaka sensei-ga   musuko san-ga   nakunatta.
      Tanaka prof.-SUBJ son   sir-SUBJ died
      Lit: 'Prof. Tanaka, (his) son died.'
      'It is prof. Tanaka whose son died.'

(14) Yahari natsu- ga   biiru-ga   umai.
      After all summer-SUBJ beer -SUBJ tasty
      Lit: 'After all, the summer, beer is tasty.'
      'After all, it's during the summer that beer tastes good.'

In 13 and 14 there are two NPs that are both marked with the particle that typically goes with the Subject. It has been claimed that the second NP in each of these sentences is the true Subject, whereas the first NP-*ga* is to be distinguished as a *major* Subject. The first NP-*ga* typically receives a stress peak and is followed by a pause. Thus, you might want to insert a comma after each major Subject.

Looking just at 13 and 14, what difference can you see regarding theta-roles between Subjects and major Subjects? In particular, is a major Subject an argument of the predicate?

Part 6

Now compare 15 and 16 to 14:

(15) *Yahari umi-ga   biiru-ga umai.
        sea-SUBJ
      'After all, the sea, beer is tasty.'

(16) *Yahari Taroo-ga biiru-ga umai.
      'After all, Taroo, beer is tasty.'

(Some speakers accept 15 with the reading 'After all, it's at sea that beer tastes good.' Please ignore that variation for the sake of this problem set.) Examples 15 and 16 are semantically anomalous. A native speaker of Japanese is unsure what you might possibly mean by saying them. How do 15 and 16 contrast with 14 semantically? Look particularly at the lexical choice of the major Subject in the context of the overall sentence.

Make a general statement about the semantic relationship between a major Subject and the clause that follows it.

Part 7

There are at least two possible analyses for complex passives. One is that they are generated via movement, so the NP that is the Subject of the passive verb moved there from the position that is a gap in 2, 4 and 5, 7 and 12. At SS the analysis of 2 would then be:

(17) Taroo$_i$-ga   Hanako-ni [t$_i$ kaisya   -o   yameta]-to
      Taroo- SUBJ Hanako-by   company-DO quit   -COMP
      omowareta.
      was thought

The other analysis is that these structures are base generated that way. With this analysis the SS structure of 2 is:

(18) Taroo$_i$-ga   Hanako-ni [e$_i$ kaisya   -o   yameta]-to
      Taroo- SUBJ Hanako-by   company-DO quit   -COMP
      omowareta.
      was thought

The difference between 17 and 18 is that in 17 we have a trace and movement has taken place, while in 18 we have an empty Subject position (something very common in Japanese and other zero-pronoun languages, as you well know) in the embedded clause that is co-indexed with the Subject of the matrix clause.

Give at least one argument in favor of one of these analyses and against the other based on the data in this problem set. If you can give more, great. (Consider all the data in this problem set—particularly those in Part 5.)

Part 8

It has been claimed that complex passives are base generated and that the apparent Subject of the complex passive is really a major Subject. Discuss the viability of that analysis for the data presented in this problem set.

Star Problem 10.1

We have claimed that pronominals that are nonarguments can be bound within their governing categories, as in:

(1) John took the book with him.
These socks have holes in them.

Other examples like this involve optional pronominals:

(2) John had a coat on (him) when he left.

But some nonarguments that are bound within their governing categories must be anaphors:

(3) John did it by himself.

The question is whether 3 contrasts with 1 and 2 because of some difference in the semantic structure of the sentences or because the phrase *by Xself* is listed in the lexicon. In exploring this issue, begin by amassing as long a list as you can of sentences that fit into each of the three groups represented in 1–3.

Star Problem 10.2

Consider *help* with and without a *to* on its complement:

(1) I helped Jack swim.

(2) I helped Jack to swim.

What are the syntactic and semantic differences between them? Try to offer an analysis of each construction that will account for these differences. (To do this properly, you could write a book. For now, if you can come up with a list of differences and suggest some analyses to test, that is fine.)

Star Problem 10.3

In the text the only long-distance phenomenon we paid attention to was L-D Anaphora. However, there are other L-D phenomena. Consider:

(1) They thought I had suggested that [PRO feeding each other] would be difficult.

Do a study of the constraints on L-D control. Ask whether the same factors or ones of similar types come up here to those found for L-D Anaphora.

Star Problem 10.4

The following Italian sentences are grammatical for at least some speakers:

(1) Passando davanti allo specchio, le$_i$ apparve se stessa$_i$.
     passing before-the mirror   CL appeared herself
     'Passing by the mirror, herself appeared to her.

(2) Finalmente, dopo anni di psicoterapia, le$_i$ venne restituita se stessa$_i$.
     finally   after years of psychotherapy CL came restored herself
     'Finally, after years of psychotherapy, herself was restored to her.'

Find native speakers and do a study of this use of *se stesso*. Check to see what restrictions there might be on the verb. Check to see if *se stesso* must always be co-indexed with a c-commanding dative clitic.

Overview: Complete Theory Overview

In this chapter we have worked on Binding Theory. The descriptions below of the other modules of the grammar, therefore, have not been changed from those found at the end of chapter 9.
  The modules of GB are:

1. Binding Theory

2. X-Bar Theory

3. Case Theory

4. Theta Theory

5. Government Theory

6. Trace Theory

7. Control Theory

The major principles of GB that we have worked to understand are:

1. The Case Filter

2. The Theta Criterion

3. The Principle of Full Interpretation

4. The Projection Principle

5. The Extended Projection Principle

6. The PRO Theorem

7. The Subjacency Principle

8. The Principle of Strict Cyclicity

9. The Empty Category Principle

10. The Bijacency Principle

11. The i-within-i Condition

Binding Theory

We have three Conditions to BT.

(A) An anaphor must be A-bound within its governing category.

(B) A pronominal must be A-free within its governing category.

(C) An R-expression must be A-free everywhere.

The definition for *governing category* is given under Government Theory later.

Anaphors generally occur in argument positions.

Pronouns may be locally bound only if they are not arguments and only if they occur in OP position.

We learned in this chapter that if we do not admit small clauses into our theory, these binding conditions must be modified so as to replace "governing category" with "CFC."

We also learned in this chapter that binding across CFCs may well be based on c-command. But binding within a CFC in English (and we noted that this is a language-specific statement) is probably based on linear precedence.

Long-Distance Anaphora seems to be sensitive to a range of syntactic and semantic factors. On the syntactic side, the anaphor cannot be a DO or IO but can be an OP or a genitive. On the semantic side, we gave an approximation of three factors, and we noted that all need refinement. One factor was that if we know from linguistic or nonlinguistic information that there is a required identity of two of the role players in a single event, then we may allow L-D Anaphora. Another was that if the anaphor falls within a logophoric domain of an NP, then that NP may be allowed to be its antecedent even at a distance. And finally, if there is no slot for an antecedent within the CFC of the anaphor due to grammatical constraints, then we might look outside the CFC for an antecedent.

We have a typology of all referring expressions, using the features of [+anaphor] or [−anaphor] and [+pronominal] or [−pronominal], as in this chart. Here the items listed under 1 have a phonetic matrix, while those under 2 are empty categories.

	[+anaphor]	[−anaphor]
[+pronominal]	1. 0 2. PRO	1. pronouns 2. pro
[−pronominal]	1. reflexives, reciprocals 2. NP-trace	1. lexical NPs 2. *wh*-trace

We have the Empty Category Principle:

(1)   Trace must be properly governed.

Our motivation for the ECP came from trying to account for the phenomenon known as the *that*-trace effect. Proper government can be either lexical government or antecedent government, where a node A antecedent governs a node B if A binds B and A is not too far away from B. We never arrived at a precise notion of exactly what counts as "too far away" for the ECP.

We generated the complementizer *that* in C position. For that reason we needed to adopt the Minimality Condition in order to be able to appeal to the ECP to account for the *that*-trace effect:

(2)   The Minimality Condition: Any projection of a head that contains that head and a node A prevents a node outside that projection from governing A.

We also discussed the i-within-i Condition in chapter 9:

(3)   *[$_A$ ... B ...], where A and B bear the same index.

We argued that if we restrict this condition to applying only to binding indices, it is coherent as a principle against semantic circularity. We explored the type of circularity it precludes in Problem Set 9.1.

Finally, we have the Bijection Principle:

(4)   Every variable must be bound by exactly one quantifier and every quantifier must bind exactly one variable.

This principle was invoked in accounting for the phenomenon known as weak crossover. We defined a variable as any node bound by something in a non-A-position.

X-Bar Theory

Phrasal categories have the internal breakdown shown in:

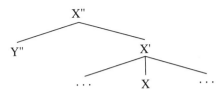

We call X the head of the phrase. It immediately dominates a lexical item or a feature bundle (in the case of I or certain empty categories).

We call X' the X-bar level. It is a phrasal level (but not the maximal phrasal level) and it can have a specifier as its sister.

We call X" the X-double-bar level. It is the maximal projection of the category. (X is the lexical projection. X' is a medial phrasal projection.)

We call the sisters to X the complements. Complements can be arguments or adjuncts. Most adjuncts are modifiers. (Some linguists reserve the term "comple-

ment" only for arguments. So modifiers of a head would not be called complements. We have not made this distinction.)

Some have argued that lexical categories differ from functional categories in their
internal breakdown: lexical categories would head phrases that are never maximal:

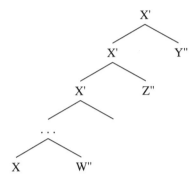

Functional categories would head phrases that are maximal (that is, X″) and would
take only one complement. We have not explored in any depth the ramifications
of this distinction in this book. Instead, we have treated all categories as heading
phrases that are maximal.

There is considerable debate over whether modifiers must all be attached as sisters to an X at DS, or whether some are attached as sisters to X′ or to a variety of
other potential projections of X.

Phrases which are headed by lexical nodes of the same category as the phrasal
node are called endocentric. Most phrases are endocentric. We also realized that
there are some exocentric phrases, such as an NP that branches to specifier and a
verbal phrase:

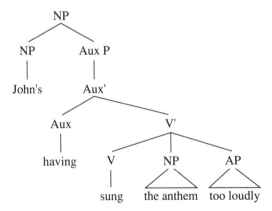

Here the NP *John's* is the specifier of the larger NP. But the head of the larger NP
is a V, not an N. Exocentric phrases fall outside X-Bar Theory.

We did not adopt small clauses in our theory. That is, we did not admit clauses
that do not contain verbs. However, if one were to do so, a major task would be to
figure out exactly what category small clauses belong to.

We adopted movement as a valid test for constituency and we pointed out problems with using the interpretation of pro-forms as a test for syntactic constituency.

We argued that Tense and Agreement are independent features, each heading their own phrase. In English we generated modals under T (which we have identified as I for English), so that they never pass through Agr and thus never show inflection for person/number. *Have* and *be* are generated lower in the tree, heading VPs and taking VPs as their complements. Verb Movement moves the highest auxiliary upward if there are available nodes to move it into. The first auxiliary in the final string, then, will pass through other nodes (such as Agr and T), picking up all the inflectional endings. In a language that has relatively transparent morphology, the order of the morphemes in the final verb form reflects the syntactic derivation. The principle at work here is called the Mirror Principle.

We recognized that the use of the node INFL represents a conflation of the hierarchy of the functional verbal nodes.

Subject-Auxiliary Inversion is an instantiation of Head Movement from I into C.

Case Theory

We have the Case Filter:

(1)   Every NP with a phonetic matrix gets Case.

We also have principles for Structural Case Assignment:

(2)   The Case-Assigners for English are [+AGR], V, and P.

(3)   The Case-Assigner must govern the phrase it gives Case to.

(4)   The Case-Assigners V and P must be adjacent (linearly) to the phrase they give Case to.

In addition to Structural Case Assignment, there are three other rules of Case assignment in English:

(5)   Genitive Rule: An NP in specifier position of NP gets genitive Case.

(6)   Double-Object Rule: The second NP in the Double-Object construction gets Objective Case.

(7)   Exceptional Case-Marking: Certain verbs and prepositions (which are Case-Assigners in other contexts) can assign Case to the Subject of an infinitival clause that is adjacent to them if that infinitival clause is the complement of the V or P.

ECM occurs because in these instances the V or P exceptionally governs the specifier of its complement. Such infinitival clauses are called "ECMs."

All three of the rules in 5–7 are unusual among languages of the world. The Double-Object Rule, in particular, is controversial, and linguists have attempted to make it follow from general principles.

Theta Theory

Predicates may be of a range of categories (V, N, P, A, plus phrases that are indivisible semantically, such as the PP "off his rocker"). Actually, people debate a lot about this. Some people argue that all predicates are phrasal (so VP and not V would be a predicate, for example). But with that notion of predicate, each predicate takes only one role player: its Subject. If we want to allow a way to account for the thematic similarities of the different GFs, we need to allow heads to be predicates. (So V is the predicate—and it can have internal arguments as well as the external argument in GF Subject position.) This is not a matter we can settle in this book. It is just something to be aware of.

We also said that theta-assigners can be made of more than one word and the words need not form a syntactic constituent (such as *take care of* or *look after*).

Theta-assigners set up a set of possible situations in which they can be used, and in each situation they assign theta-roles (player roles, thematic roles) to their arguments (players). The theta-roles we discussed are: agent, theme, benefactee (also known by many other rubrics, including "beneficiary," "recipient," "goal," "benefactive"), instrument, and experiencer. It is an open debate as to how to distinguish between different theta-roles and how many theta-roles any given language makes use of in its grammar, although we did come up with a set of diagnostics for certain theta-roles.

The ability of a lexical item to assign a theta-role is part of the lexical information we know about words. There is a linking mechanism in the lexicon that maps between the predicate-argument structure of a lexical item and its subcategorization frame.

We came up with the following principles:

(1)   Only GFs can have theta-roles, but not all GFs need to.

and 2, which is known as the Theta Criterion:

(2)   Only arguments of a theta-assigner get a theta-role and every argument of a given theta-assigner gets precisely one and a unique theta-role.

and 3, which is known as the Projection Principle:

(3)   All lexical features of a lexical item that appear in DS must appear at every syntactic level.

In talking about theta-roles, we realized that subcategorization is a different thing from theta-roles. Lexical items can be subcategorized according to whether they must, may, or cannot co-occur with certain GFs. Subcategorization frames give structural information, although they clearly have their roots in semantics. Still, there is no obvious mapping from semantics into syntactic subcategorization in all cases.

In all of this discussion we have been assuming a notion of licensing that is termed the Principle of Full Interpretation:

(4)   All nodes in a tree must play a role in the sentence.

Every node must be licensed; many different functions license a node, including being a predicate, an argument, a modifier, and filling a GF.

Government Theory

The notion of government is a configurational one and it is the topic of debate in much literature. We have used the following formulation:
A node A governs another node B iff:

(1) A is a lexical category or [+Agr] and

(2) B is contained within the maximal projection of A (that is, B is contained within A″), and

(3) Every maximal projection that contains B also contains A.

1 allows any head (including I that is marked [+Agr]) to be a governor. 2 says that a governor governs everything within its maximal projection. 3 says that government cannot go across another maximal projection (that is, a maximal projection is a barrier to government.) In ordinary words, this says that a head governs everything inside its maximal projection up to another maximal projection.
Besides the structural notion of government, GT involves four other notions:

(a) Governor: The governor of a node B is the minimal node A that governs it.

(b) Governing category:
B is the governing category for E iff B is the minimal N″ or I″ that contains:
(1) E,
(2) the governor of E, and
(3) a SUBJECT accessible to E.

(c) SUBJECT: A SUBJECT is a Subject for N″ and for I″ that is [−Agr]. But in tensed clauses a SUBJECT is [+Agr].

(d) Accessibility:
A is accessible to B iff B is in the c-command domain of A and assignment to B of the index of A would not violate i/i.

We spent much of chapter 9 discussing the notion of Accessibility. We argued that if we restrict i/i to applying to only binding indices, then it is a coherent principle. However, if we extend i/i to apply to all indices and if we allow a proliferation of indices in the grammar (such as indices resulting from a co-indexation rule between Agr and its Subject), we lose coherency in this principle. But only if i/i is extended in this way will it be relevant to Accessibility. Thus we rejected the notion of Accessibility entirely. We noted further that there are certain types of structures involving Long-Distance Anaphora that we would expect to be ungrammatical given our notion of accessibility, but which are fine. We addressed those structures in chapter

SYNTAX

10. Thus, we should strike (d) from our list of notions relevant to the notion of governing category.

We also added in chapter 9 a new use for the term "government," in the notion of antecedent government:

> Antecedent Government: a node A antecedent governs a node B iff A binds B and A is not too far away from B.

This was new in that binding nodes are always phrasal, but ordinary government is always by a head (an X, not an X″). Thus antecedent government does not, in fact, use the notion of government at all. The term is a misnomer. Please do not let it confuse you.

Government Theory is relevant to other modules of the grammar. Thus far we have seen that:

1. In Case Theory, a Case-Assigner must govern an NP in order to give it Case.

2. In X-Bar Theory, a head governs everything in its maximal projection.

3. Most instances of theta assignment are from a governor to the phrases it governs. (The most prominent exception is Subjects of clauses, which are not governed by the V which assigns them a theta-role, unless we generate these Subjects inside the VP—as in Tangent 10.2 of chapter 8.)

4. In BT, locality is defined in terms of governing categories. However, it is likely that a definition of locality in terms of CFCs is preferable.

Trace Theory

Every movement leaves behind a trace. This must be so in order to fulfill the requirements of the Projection Principle (see Theta Theory above).

NP-movement leaves behind an NP-trace, which is an anaphor. The foot of an NP-movement chain is in a position to which Case cannot be assigned and to which a theta-role may be assigned. NP-movement is always into Subject position. NP-movement is a type of general movement; it is not limited to moving NPs only.

It is important to realize that if we adopt the position that a predicate is generated at DS within the maximal projection that the predicate heads, the specifier position which is the sister to I′ is a non-theta-receiving position automatically. (See Tangent 8.2 of chapter 8.) Thus the fact that Subject position is the only GF that can have movement into it is nicely motivated.

Wh-Movement leaves behind a *wh*-trace, which is a variable and shares binding properties with R-expressions. All variables are locally non-A-bound (by definition). If the foot of a *Wh*-Movement chain is a referring nominal, it is in a position to receive Case and in a position to which a theta-role might or might not be assigned. *Wh*-Movement is always into an empty phrasal position that has the feature [+wh]. Since this feature is limited to specifier of C′, *Wh*-Movement will always be into specifier of C′. A *wh*-phrase can move from one specifier of C′ to the next adjacent specifier of C′ in what is called Comp-to-Comp movement. *Wh*-

Movement is a type of general movement; it is not limited to moving *wh*-phrases only.

Every chain can have at most one theta-role and at most one Case associated with it.

All movement is bounded by the Principle of Subjacency, roughly stated as:

(1) Movement across at most one barrier is fine, but movement becomes more difficult as more barriers are passed.

We said that every primary predicate L-Marks its arguments that fall within the minimal phrase that contains the predicate. We then defined the notion of blocking category as in:

(2) A is a BC for B iff A is not L-Marked and A dominates B, and A is phrasal.

We then defined the notion of barrier as in:

(3) A is a barrier for B iff A is phrasal and:
    (a) A immediately dominates C, where C is a BC for B
    or (b) A is a BC for B and A does not equal I''.

By (a) we see that a phrasal node immediately dominating a BC for a node B becomes a barrier for B. By (b) we see that all BCs are themselves barriers except I''. In other words, I'' can be a barrier for a node B only if it immediately dominates a BC of A—that is, only via (a). We said that barriers defined by (a) inherit barrier-hood (since the BC below them allows them to become barriers).

A phrase of any category that has the GF of Subject, then, is a BC as well as a barrier (assuming Subjects will never be bare I'') to all the elements contained in that Subject. A phrase of any category that functions as a modifier (adverbial modifier or relative-clause modifier) or as an appositive is, likewise, a BC to all the elements contained in that phrase. Only phrases that function as DOs or as OPs where the OP is an argument of the primary predicate are not going to be BCs to the elements contained within them.

We adopted the Principle of Strict Cyclicity:

(4) Strict Cyclicity: No rule may affect only the members of a given cycle once that cycle has already been passed.

Since the only rules we have concerned ourselves with in detail are movement rules, I have placed this principle here under Trace Theory. However, it should apply generally to the entire grammar.

Note that we adopted the ECP, listed above under BT, by which trace must be properly governed.

Control Theory

PRO can be uncontrolled (in which case we have PRO_{arb}) or controlled. If it is controlled, it can be an instance of obligatory control or nonobligatory control. The features that distinguish these two types of control are:

1. PRO does not alternate with a lexical item in obligatory control structures, but it can in nonobligatory control structures.

2. The controller always precedes PRO in obligatory control structures, but not in nonobligatory control structures.

3. If the controller is omitted from an obligatory control structure, the result is an ungrammatical sentence. But in nonobligatory control structures, omission may result in a grammatical sentence, depending on the subcategorization frame of the matrix verb.

We also pointed out that many people take the position that the controller must c-command PRO in obligatory control structures, but not in nonobligatory control structures. However, we found that c-command was not required in either type of control structure.

And, finally, the controller in obligatory control structures always bears a theta-role, but we were unable to determine if this is so in nonobligatory control structures.

PRO is always ungoverned, so far as we know. It therefore has no governing category. We noted, however, that PRO would also fail to have a governing category if it failed to have an accessible SUBJECT. The crucial property of PRO is that it never has a governing category. PRO has both the properties of an anaphor and the properties of a pronominal. It manages not to violate Condition A or B of the Binding Theory by virtue of the fact that it has no governing category. The fact that PRO's status as both an anaphor and a pronominal makes it necessary that PRO be ungoverned (that is, the fact that the distribution of PRO follows from its status as both an anaphor and a pronominal) is known as the PRO Theorem.

A Map Through GB

Our map remains unchanged from the one in chapter 6.

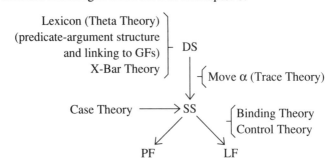

DS = the most underlying level, the first tree in the syntactic derivation. It is sometimes called Deep Structure.

SS = the last syntactic tree. Some people call it the Surface Structure. It is enriched with empty nodes.

PF = Phonetic Form = the sentence as we actually hear it (with all the intonation contour in and all the contractions, etc.) It is SS with the Phonology having applied.

LF = Logical Form = some formal representation of the sentence in which we have every instance of coreference marked, and all the scopes of quantifiers and adverbs and negatives are marked, etc. (as we did in chapter 9). LF is an explicit representation of precisely how we understand the sentence. It is SS with the rules of semantic interpretation having applied.

Bibliography

Below are general references for the main narratives of each chapter. Often in early chapters the discussion is so basic that choosing a particular reference is both arbitrary and difficult. In each case a specific reference is given, but nearly any introductory text in linguistics could have been offered instead.

The references for the theoretical ideas developed in the chapter texts are few and in no sense exhaustive. An exhaustive set of references would be close to endless. The reader desiring to go further into GB should read the following works by Noam Chomsky and follow the references cited in them for further reading in particular areas:

Chomsky, Noam. 1981. *Lectures on Government and Binding.* Dordrecht, Holland: Foris.

———. 1982. *Some Concepts and Consequences of the Theory of Government and Binding.* Cambridge, MA: MIT.

———. 1986. *Barriers.* Cambridge, MA: MIT.

———. 1988. *Language and Problems of Knowledge.* Cambridge, MA: MIT.

———. 1989. "Some Notes on Economy of Derivation and Representation," *MIT Working Papers in Linguistics* 10:43–75. Reprinted in Robert Freidin (ed.) *Principles and Parameters in Comparative Grammar*, Cambridge, MA: MIT, 1991.

Another work that gives an overview of GB theory is:

Lasnik, Howard and Juan Uriagereka. 1988. *A Course in GB Syntax.* Cambridge, MA: MIT.

This book, however, deals with a version of GB theory prior to the proposal of barriers. The reader should also go directly to the many linguistics journals, where not only GB, but other modern theories of grammar, including Lexical-Functional Grammar, Relational Grammar, Head-Driven Grammar, Generalized Phrase Structure Grammar, and others, are represented. Any librarian at a university or college library should be able to help.

Thus the bibliography offered here is a mere suggestion.

I also give references that I have used as sources for information on particular languages and that have served as the basis for various problem sets. Sometimes the information on a given language comes from my own study of the language or is so well known that a specific citation is difficult to make. In those instances I have not given a citation.

Often I have used the data in a given article or book to my own end. Therefore, my citation here does not in any way suggest that the authors of a given work agree with the conclusions that I reach or that I have led the reader to reach. I hereby exonerate them all.

For all of the problem sets, dozens of works could be cited, but sometimes I list none and other times I limit myself to one or just a couple. At times I list several references if I think the problem might be particularly tantalizing (revealing my own inclinations)

CHAPTER 1

Narrative

Department of Linguistics at the Ohio State University. 1991. *Language Files*, fifth edition. Columbus: Ohio State University.

Gleitman, Lila. 1965. "Coordinating Conjunctions in English," *Language* 41:260–93. (for a discussion of examples like 27)

Helke, Michael. 1970. *The Grammar of English Reflexives*, MIT dissertation. Revised and published in 1979, New York: Garland. (for general discussion of reflexives)

Lightfoot, David. 1982. *The Language Lottery: Toward a Biology of Grammars.* Cambridge, MA: MIT.

Tangent 1.1

Wenger, James. 1984. "Variation and Change in Japanese Honorific Forms," in Shigeru Miyagawa and Chisato Kitagawa (eds.), *Studies in Japanese Language Use.* Edmonton, Alberta, Canada: Linguistic Research. 267–302. (for the "o" prefix)

Tangent 1.2

Chase, Alston Hurd and Henry Phillips, Jr. 1966. *A New Introduction to Greek.* Cambridge, MA: Harvard University.

Foley, William A. 1986. *The Papuan Languages of New Guinea.* Cambridge: Cambridge University.

Hale, Kenneth. 1990. "Some Remarks on Agreement and Incorporation," in Joan Mascaro and Marina Nespor (eds.), *Grammar in Progress: GLOW Essays for Henk van Riemsdijk.* Dordrecht: Foris. 279–328. (for Navajo)

———, Laverne Masayesva Jeanne, and Paul M. Pranka. 1991. "On Suppletion, Selection, and Agreement," in George Georgopoulos (ed.), *Interdisciplinary*

Approaches to Language. Dordrecht: Kluwer Academic Publishers. 255–270. (for discussion of some rare types of agreement phenomena in Hopi, Papago, and Uto-Aztecan languages of the American Southwest)

Kispert, Robert J. 1971. *Old English: An Introduction*. New York: Holt, Rinehart and Winston.

Saltarelli, Mario, and Mirin Azkarate, D. Farwell, J. Ortiz de Urbina, and L. Oxederra. 1988. *Basque*. London: Croom Helm.

Tangent 1.5

Chomsky, Noam. 1981. *Lectures on Government and Binding*. Dordrecht, Holland: Foris. (for the idea of abstract Case on NP in English)

Eguzkitza, Andolin. 1987. *Topics on the Syntax of Basque and Romance*. Bloomington: Indiana University Linguistics Club.

Foley, William A. 1986. *The Papuan Languages of New Guinea*. Cambridge: Cambridge University.

Problem Set 1.2

Higgins, F. Roger. 1973. *The Pseudo-cleft Construction in English*. New York: Garland.

Emonds, Joseph. 1972. "Evidence that Indirect Object Movement is a Structure-Preserving Rule," *Foundations of Language* 8:546–561. Reprinted in Maurice Gross, Morris Halle, and M. P. Schutzenberger (eds.), *The Formal Analysis of Natural Languages*, The Hague: Mouton, 1973.

Jackendoff, Ray. 1973. "The Base Rules for Prepositional Phrases," in Stephen R. Anderson and Paul Kiparsky (eds.), *A Festschrift for Morris Halle*. New York: Holt, Rinehart and Winston.345–356. (for the *right* test for PPs)

Problem Set 1.4

Kuno, Susumu. 1973. *The Structure of the Japanese Language*. Cambridge, MA: MIT. (See chapter 1.)

CHAPTER 2

Narrative

Baltin, Mark. 1982. "A Landing Site Theory of Movement Rules," *Linguistic Inquiry* 13:1–38. (for discussion of examples like 55)

Johnson, David. 1977. "On Keenan's Definition of 'Subject Of,'"*Linguistic Inquiry* 8:673–691. (for problems with various definitions of "Subject")

Lakoff, George. 1970. *Irregularity in Syntax*. New York: Holt, Rinehart, and Winston. (See chapter 11, section A for active vs. stative verbs.)

Li, Charles (ed.). 1976. *Subject and Topic*. New York: Academic Press. (for many approaches to the definition of "Subject")

Pica, Pierre. 1986. "On the Nature of the Reflexivization Cycle," *NELS 17*, 2:483–500. (for remarks on Danish)

Stowell, Timothy. 1981. *Origins of Phrase Structure.* MIT dissertation. (for discussion of Case assignment to non-NPs)

Tangent 2.1

Jorden, Eleanor Harz and Mari Noda. 1987. *Japanese: The SpokenLanguage: Part I.* New Haven, CN: Yale University.
Vendler, Zeno. 1967. "Verbs and Times," *Linguistics and Philosophy.* 97–121. Ithaca: Cornell University.

Tangent 2.2

Comrie, Bernard. 1977. "In Defense of Spontaneous Demotion: The Impersonal Passive," in Peter Cole and Jerrold Sadock (eds), *Syntax and Semantics 8: Grammatical Relations.* New York: Academic Press. 47–58. (for impersonal passive examples)
Jaeggli, Osvaldo. 1986. "Passive," *Linguistic Inquiry* 17:587–622. (for impersonal passive examples)
Miyagawa, Shigeru. 1989. *Structure and Case Marking in Japanese, Syntax and Semantics 22.* New York: Academic Press. (See particularly chapter 5 for the passive in Japanese.)
Nagai, Noriko. 1985. *Japanese Passives and Causatives.* Doctoral dissertation. University of Michigan.

Tangent 2.3

Adelaar, Willem. 1977. *Tarma Quechua Grammar, Texts, Dictionary.* Lisse, The Netherlands: Peter De Ridder Press.
Eguzkitza, Andolin. 1987. *Topics on the Syntax of Basque and Romance.* Bloomington: Indiana University Linguistics Club.
Foley, William A. 1986. *The Papuan Languages of New Guinea.* Cambridge: Cambridge University.
Grimshaw, Jane and Ralf-Armin Mester. 1985. "Complex Verb Formation in Eskimo," *Natural Language and Linguistic Theory* 3:1–19 (for Labrador Inuttut)
Hale, Ken. 1990. "Some Remarks on Agreement and Incorporation," in *Studies in Generative Grammar.* Cambridge, MA: MIT Press. 117–144. (for Navajo).
Muysken, Pieter. 1981. "Quechua Word Structure," in Frank Heny (ed.), *Binding and Filtering.* Cambridge, MA: MIT. 279–328.
Sadock, Jerald. 1980. "Noun Incorporation in Greenlandic," *Language* 56:300–319.
Woolford, Ellen. 1986. "The Distribution of Empty Nodes in Navajo: A Mapping Approach," *Linguistic Inquiry* 17:301–330.

Problem Set 2.1

Pope, Emily. 1972. *Questions and Answers in English.* MIT dissertation. Revised and published in 1976, The Hague: Mouton.

Problem Set 2.2

Milsark, Gary. 1974. *Existential Sentences in English.* Doctoral dissertation, MIT. Revised and published in 1979, New York: Garland.

Perlmutter, David and Scott Soames. 1979. *Syntactic Argumentation and the Structure of English.* Berkeley: University of California.

Problem Set 2.3

Perlmutter, David and Scott Soames. 1979. *Syntactic Argumentation and the Structure of English.* Berkeley: University of California.

Postal, Paul. 1964. "Underlying and Superficial Linguistic Structure," *Harvard Educational Review* 34:246–266. Reprinted in David Reibel and Sanford Schane (eds.), *Modern Studies in English.* Englewood Cliffs, NJ: Prentice-Hall. 19–37.

CHAPTER 3

Narrative

Bolinger, Dwight. 1971. *The Phrasal Verb in English.* Cambridge, MA: Harvard University. (for verb-particle combinations)

Carrier-Duncan, Jill. 1985. "Linking of Thematic Roles in Derivational Word Formation," *Linguistic Inquiry* 16:1–34. (for predicate-argument structure)

Cattell, Ray. 1984. *Composite Predicates in English.* North Ryde, New South Wales: Academic Press Australia. (for discussion of predicates consisting of other than a simple verb or verb string)

Davison, Alice. 1980. "Peculiar Passives," *Language* 56:42–66. (for discussion of sentences like example 37)

di Sciullo, Anna Maria and Edwin Williams. 1987. *On the Definition of Word.* Cambridge, MA: MIT. (for discussion of multiple-word predicates)

Fraser, Bruce. 1971. "A Note on the *Spray Paint* Cases," *Linguistic Inquiry* 2:604–607. (for *spray/load* verbs)

———.1976. *The Verb Particle Construction in English.* New York: Academic Press.

Giorgi, Alessandra. 1987. "The Notion of Complete Functional Complex: Some Evidence From Italian," *Linguistic Inquiry* 18:511–518.

Grimshaw, Jane. 1990. *Argument Structure.* Cambridge, MA: MIT.

——— and Armin Mester. 1988. "Light Verbs and Theta-Marking," *Linguistic Inquiry* 19:205–232.

Hoekstra, Teun. 1984. *Transitivity.* Dordrecht: Foris.

Hornstein, Norbert and Amy Weinberg. 1981. "Case Theory and Preposition Stranding," *Linguistic Inquiry* 12:55–92. (for the idea of natural predicate)

Jaeggli, Osvaldo. 1986. "Passive," *Linguistic Inquiry* 17:587–622. (for a range of passive types)

Larson, Richard. 1985. "Bare NP Adverbs," *Linguistic Inquiry* 16:595–622.

Levin, Beth and Malka Rappaport. 1986. "What to Do With Theta-Roles," *Lexicon Working Papers 11*, Cambridge, MA: Center for Cognitive Science,

MIT. Reprinted in Wendy Wilkins (ed.), *Syntax and Semantics 21: Thematic Relations*, San Diego, CA: Academic Press.

Marantz, Alec. 1984. *On the Nature of Grammatical Relations.* Cambridge, MA: MIT. (for theta-roles)

Tenny, Carol. *Grammaticalizing Aspect and Affectedness.* MIT dissertation. Cambridge, MA: MIT. (for the notion of affectedness)

Ziff, Paul. 1966. "The Non-Synonymy of Actives and Passives," *Philosophical Review* 75:226–232.

Problem Set 3.1

Chomsky, Noam. 1970. "Remarks on Nominalization," in Roderick Jacobs and Peter Rosenbaum (eds.), *Readings in English Transformational Grammar.* Waltham, MA: Ginn and Company. 184–221. (for the subcategorization of NPs)

Jackendoff, Ray. 1973. "The Base Rules for Prepositional Phrases," in Stephen R. Anderson and Paul Kiparsky (eds.), *A Festschrift for Morris Halle.* New York: Holt, Rinehart and Winston. 345–356. (for the *right* test for PPs)

Jones, Michael. 1988. "Cognate Objects and the Case Filter," *Journal of Linguistics* 24:89–110. (for exemplification of cognate objects)

McConnell-Ginet, Sally. 1982. "Adverbs and Logical Form," *Language* 58:144–184. (for verbs that require adverbials)

Simpson, Jane. 1983. "Resultatives," in Lori Levin, Malka Rappaport, and Annie Zaenen (eds.), *Papers in Lexical-Functional Grammar*, Bloomington, IN: Indiana University Linguistics Club. 143–157.

Problem Set 3.4

Levin, Beth and Malka Rappaport. 1988. "Non-event *-er* Nominals: a Probe into Argument Structure," *Linguistics* 26:1067–1083.

Problem Set 3.6

Giorgi, Alessandra. 1984. "Toward a Theory of Long Distance Anaphors," *The Linguistic Review* 3:307–361.

———. 1987. "The Notion of Complete Functional Complex: Some Evidence from Italian," *Linguistic Inquiry* 18:511–518.

Problem Set 3.7

Washio, Ryuichi. 1986/87. "The Japanese Passive," *The Linguistic Review* 6:227–264.

Star Problem 3.3

Green, Georgia. 1974. *Semantics and Syntactic Regularity.* Bloomington: Indiana University.

Oehrle, Richard. 1976. *The Grammatical Status of the English Dative Alternation.* Doctoral dissertation, MIT.

Pinker, Steven. 1989. *Learnability and Cognition: The Acquisition of Argument Structure.* Cambridge, MA: MIT. (See chapters 4 and 5 for double-object sentences in comparison to their [V-NP-*to/for*-NP] counterparts.)

Star Problem 3.4

Larson, Richard. 1988. "On the Double Object Construction," *Linguistic Inquiry* 19:335–391.

Star Problem 3.6

Napoli, Donna Jo. 1983. "Comparative Ellipsis: A Phrase Structure Analysis," *Linguistic Inquiry* 14:675–694.

CHAPTER 4

Narrative

Chomsky, Noam. 1970. "Remarks on Nominalization," in Roderick A. Jacobs and Peter S. Rosenbaum (eds.), *Readings in English Transformational Grammar.* Waltham: Ginn and Co. 184–221. (for N subcategorization)

Emonds, Joseph. 1985. *A Unified Theory of Syntactic Categories.* Dordrecht, Holland: Foris.

Giorgi, Alessandra and Giuseppe Longobardi. 1991. *The Syntax of Noun Phrases.* Cambridge: Cambridge University Press. (See chapters 3 and 4 for evidence that the head in Romance is on the left.)

Jackendoff, Ray. 1977. *X Bar Syntax: A Study of Phrase Structure.* Cambridge, MA: MIT.

Kuno, Susumu. 1973. *The Structure of the Japanese Language.* Cambridge, MA: MIT. (for evidence that the head in Japanese is on the right)

McNulty, Elaine. 1988. *The Syntax of Adjunct Predicates.* Doctoral dissertation, University of Connecticut. (for secondary predicates)

Perlmutter, David. 1970. "On the Article in English," in Manfred Bierwisch and Karl Heidolph (eds.), *Progress in Linguistics.* The Hague: Mouton. 233–248 (for the analysis of *a* as a reduced form of *one*)

Speas, Margaret. 1990. *Phrase Structure in Natural Languages*, Dordrecht: Kluwer (for arguments that PS rules are not part of Universal Grammar)

Steele, Susan et al. 1981. *An Encyclopedia of AUX.* Cambridge, MA: MIT. (for a range of auxiliary types across languages)

Stowell, Timothy. 1981. *Origins of Phrase Structure.* MIT dissertation. (for arguments that PS rules are not part of Universal Grammar)

Williams, Edwin. 1983. "Semantic vs. Syntactic Categories," *Linguistics and Philosophy* 6:423–446. (for the distinction between identification and predication)

Tangent 4.1

Soames, Scott and David Perlmutter. 1979. *Syntactic Argumentation and the Structure of English*. Berkeley: University of California.

Tangent 4.2

Abney, Stephen. 1987. *The English Noun Phrase in Its Sentential Aspect*. Doctoral dissertation, MIT. (for the DP analysis)

Bresnan, Joan. 1973. "Syntax of the Comparative Clause Construction in English," *Linguistic Inquiry* 4:275–344. (for evidence that QPs are lexical categories)

Fukui, Naoki. 1986. *A Theory of Category Projection and Its Applications*. Doctoral dissertation. MIT. (for functional-versus-lexical categories, particularly with respect to Japanese)

—— and Margaret Speas. 1986. "Specifiers and Projection," *MIT Working Papers in Linguistics* 8:128–172. (for functional-versus-lexical categories)

Kayne, Richard. 1984. *Connectedness and Binary Branching*. Dordrecht: Foris. (for the theory that all nodes have at most two branches)

Pollock, Jean-Yves. 1989. "Verb Movement, Universal Grammar, and the Structure of IP," *Linguistic Inquiry* 20:365–424. (for a complex analysis of the verbal string that treats auxiliaries as the heads of phrases)

Speas, Margaret. 1990. *Phrase Structure in Natural Languages*. Dordrecht, Holland: Kluwer.

Problem Set 4.6

Napoli, Donna Jo. 1989. *Predication Theory: A Case Study for Indexing Theory*. Cambridge: Cambridge University.

Problem Set 4.7

Bolinger, Dwight. 1943. "The Position of the Adverb in English—A Convenient Analogy to the Position of the Adjective in Spanish," *Hispania* 26:191–192.

——. 1952. "Linear Modification," *Publication of the Modern Language Association* 67:1117–1144.

Waugh, Linda. 1976. "The Semantics and Paradigmatics of Word Order," *Language* 52:82–107.

Problem Set 4.7

Okamoto, Shigeko. 1990. "Reduplicated Verbs in Japanese as Grammatical Constructions," *Berkeley Linguistics Society* 16:248–256.

CHAPTER 5

Narrative

Chomsky, Noam. 1981. *Lectures on Government and Binding*. Dordrecht, Holland: Foris. (for the development of Case Theory and the notion of government)

———. 1986. *Barriers*, Cambridge, MA: MIT. (for the structure of I″)

Hoffman, Mika. 1991. *The Syntax of Argument-Structure-Changing Morphology.* MIT dissertation. (for the Yoruba data on sentences with both a theme and a benefactee argument)

Kayne, Richard. 1984. *Connectedness and Binary Branching.* Dordrecht, Holland: Foris. (for the analysis of the Double-Objection construction in which the second NP is the object of a null P)

Larson, Richard. 1988. "On the Double Object Construction," *Linguistic Inquiry* 19:335–391. (for an example of how the Binary Branching Hypothesis constrains analyses and what sorts of analyses are consistent with it)

Stowell, Timothy. 1981. *Origins of Phrase Structure.* MIT dissertation. (for many of the details of Case assignment)

Problem Set 5.2

Larson, Richard. 1985. "Bare-NP Adverbs," *Linguistic Inquiry* 16:595–622.

Problem Set 5.3

Quicoli, A. Carlos. 1982. *The Structure of Complementation.* Ghent: E. Story-Scientia.

Problem Set 5.4

Wasow, Thomas and Thomas Roeper. 1972. "On the Subject of Gerunds," *Foundations of Language* 8:44–61.

Problem Set 5.5

Reuland, Eric. 1983. "Governing -*ing*," *Linguistic Inquiry* 14:101–136.

Problem Set 5.6

Bonet, Eulalia. 1991. *Morphology After Syntax: Pronominal Clitics in Romance.* Doctoral dissertation, MIT.

Kayne, Richard. 1975. *French Syntax.* Cambridge, MA: MIT.

Problem Set 5.7

Napoli, Donna Jo and Marina Nespor. 1979. "The Syntax of Word-Initial Consonant Gemination in Italian," *Language* 55:812–841.

Problem Set 5.8

Oishi, Hitomi. 1986. *Scope Interpretation of Negation in Japanese.* Doctoral dissertation, University of Michigan.

Star Problem 5.3

Belletti, Adriana. 1981. "Frasi Ridotte Assolute," *Rivista di Grammatica Generativa* 6:3–32.
Rizzi, Luigi. 1982. "Lexical Subjects in Infinitives: Government, Case, and Binding," *Issues in Italian Syntax.* Dordrecht, Holland: Foris. 77–116.

CHAPTER 6

Narrative

Baker, Mark, Kyle Johnson, and Ian Roberts. 1989. "Passive Arguments Raised," *Linguistic Inquiry* 20:219–252.
Baltin, Mark. 1982. "A Landing Site Theory of Movement Rules," *Linguistic Inquiry* 13:1–38. (for restrictions on all kinds of movement)
Hale, Kenneth, Laverne Masayesva Jeanne, and Paul M. Pranka. 1991. "On Suppletion, Selection, and Agreement," in George Georgopoulos (ed.), *Interdisciplinary Approaches to Language.* Dordrecht, Holland: Kluwer Academic Publishers. 255–270. (for evidence that lexical insertion takes place not at DS but at SS, at the input to PF)
Napoli, Donna Jo. 1989. *Predication Theory*, Cambridge: Cambridge University. (for the analysis of the passive *by*-phrase as a modifier)
Riemsdijk, Henk van and Edwin Williams. 1986. *Introduction to the Theory of Grammar.* Cambridge, MA: MIT. (for the idea that theta-assignment takes place identically at DS and SS)
Zubizarreta, Maria-Luisa. 1985. "The Relation Between Morphophonology and Morphosyntax: the Case of Romance Causatives," *Linguistic Inquiry* 16:247–290. (for the analysis of the passive *by*-phrase as a modifier)

Problem Set 6.2

Simon, Mutsuko. 1989. *The Postposing Construction in Japanese.* Doctoral dissertation, University of Michigan.

Problem Set 6.4

Bresnan, Joan. 1982. "Polyadicity," in Joan Bresnan (ed.), *The Mental Representation of Grammatical Relations.* Cambridge, MA: MIT. 149–172.
Hale, Ken and Jay Keyser. 1987. *A View from the Middle, Lexicon Project Working Papers No. 10*, Dept. of Brain and Cognitive Sciences, MIT.
Keyser, Samuel Jay and Thomas Roeper. 1984. "On the Middle and Ergative Constructions in English," *Linguistic Inquiry* 15:381–416.

Problem Set 6.5

Emonds, Joseph. 1979. "Appositive Relatives Have No Properties," *Linguistic Inquiry* 10:211–242. (for an analysis of appositives as not being inside the nominal phrase)

Napoli, Donna Jo. 1989. *Predication Theory*. Cambridge: Cambridge University. (See chapter 5 for an analysis of appositives as not being inside the nominal phrase.)

Rosenbaum, Peter. 1967. *The Grammar of English Predicate Complement Constructions*. Cambridge, MA: MIT.

Soames, Scott and David Perlmutter. 1979. *Syntactic Argumentation and the Structure of English*. Berkeley: University of California.

Problem Set 6.6

Mazuka, Reiko. 1991. "Processing of Center-Embedded Sentences in Japanese," paper presented at the LSA meeting in Chicago, Jan. 5, 1991.

Problem Set 6.7

Burzio, Luigi. 1986. *Italian Syntax: A Government-Binding Approach*. Dordrecht, Holland: D. Reidel.

Chomsky, Noam. 1981. *Lectures on Government and Binding*. Dordrecht: Foris.

Rappaport, Malka and Beth Levin. 1986. "The Formation of Adjectival Passives," *Linguistic Inquiry* 17:623–661.

Wasow, Thomas. 1977. "Transformations and the Lexicon," in Peter Culicover, Thomas Wasow, and Adrian Akmajian (eds.), *Formal Syntax*. New York: Academic Press. 327–360.

Overview

Kayne, Richard. 1984. *Connectedness and Binary Branching*. Dordrecht: Foris. (for the theory that all nodes have a most two branches—which is covered in Tangent 8.2 of chapter 8)

Larson, Richard. 1988. "On the Double Object Construction," *Linguistic Inquiry* 19:335–391. (for a discussion of nonargument complements)

Speas, Margaret. 1990. *Phrase Structure in Natural Languages*. Dordrecht: Kluwer. (for a discussion of where arguments and adjuncts appear within a phrase)

CHAPTER 7

Narrative

Bach, Emmon and Barbara Hall Partee. 1980. "Anaphora and Semantic Structure," *CLS: Papers from the Parasession on Pronouns and Anaphora*. 1–28. (for arguments against reanalysis)

Baker, Mark. 1988. *Incorporation: A Theory of Grammatical Function Changing*. Chicago: University of Chicago Press.

Chomsky, Noam. 1981. *Lectures on Government and Binding*. Dordrecht, Holland: Foris. (for the distribution of PRO and the PRO Theorem)

———. 1982. *Some Concepts and Consequences of the Theory of Government and*

Binding. Cambridge, MA: MIT. (for a typology of NPs and empty categories)

Jackendoff, Ray. 1987. "The Status of Thematic Relations in Linguistic Theory," *Linguistic Inquiry* 18:369–411 (for more on the PRO Theorem)

Manzini, Maria Rita. 1983. "On Control and Control Theory," *Linguistic Inquiry* 14:421–456.

Williams, Edwin. 1980. "Predication," *Linguistic Inquiry* 11:203–238. (for types of PRO)

Problem Set 7.1

Jaeggli, Osvaldo. 1986. "Passive," *Linguistic Inquiry* 17:587–622.

Problem Set 7.2

Quicoli, A. Carlos. 1982. *The Structure of Complementation*. Ghent: E. Story-Scientia.

Rosenbaum, Peter. 1967. *The Grammar of English Predicate Complement Constructions*. Cambridge, MA: MIT.

Soames, Scott and David Perlmutter. 1979. *Syntactic Argumentation and the Structure of English*. Berkeley, CA: University of California.

Problem Set 7.3

Bolinger, Dwight. 1973. "Ambient *It* Is Meaningful Too," *Journal of Linguistics* 9:261–270.

Napoli, Donna Jo. 1988. "Subjects and External Arguments: Clauses and Non-Clauses," *Linguistics and Philosophy* 11:323–354.

Problem Set 7.4

Rosenbaum, Peter. 1967. *The Grammar of English Predicate Complement Constructions*. Cambridge, MA: MIT.

Soames, Scott and David Perlmutter. 1979. *Syntactic Argumentation and the Structure of English*. Berkeley: University of California.

Problem Set 7.5

Williams, Edwin. 1984. "*There* Insertion," *Linguistic Inquiry* 15:131–153.

Problem Set 7.6

Bresnan, Joan. 1982. "Polyadicity," in Joan Bresnan (ed.), *The Mental Representation of Grammatical Relations*. Cambridge, MA: MIT. 149–172.

Chung, Sandra. 1987. "The Syntax of Chamorro Existential Sentences," in Eric Reuland and Alice ter Meulen (eds.), *The Representation of (In)definiteness*. Cambridge, MA: MIT. 191–225.

Phillips, Jean. 1979. "A Typology of Syntactic Strategies for Unspecified Direct Objects," paper presented at the IX Annual meeting of the California Linguistic Association Conference, California State University at Sacramento, May 5–6, 1979.

Woolford, Ellen. 1983/84. "Dative Verbs with Unspecified Objects," *The Linguistic Review* 3:389–409.

Problem Set 7.8

Baker, Mark. 1988. *Incorporation: A Theory of Grammatical Function Changing*, Chicago: University of Chicago Press.

Problem Set 7.11

Stowell, Timothy. 1981. *Origins of Phrase Structure.* MIT dissertation. (for discussion of Case assignment to non-NPs)

Problem Set 7.12

Sells, Peter. 1991. "Raising from Nominal Complements in Japanese," ms. Stanford University.

Problem Set 7.13

Legendre, Geraldine. 1990. "French Impersonal Constructions," *Natural Language and Linguistic Theory* 8:81–128.

CHAPTER 8

Narrative

Chomsky, Noam. 1986. *Barriers.* Cambridge, MA: MIT. (for the category C, for Subjacency, for Strict Cyclicity, for L-Marking, for barriers, for blocking categories, for a typology of NPs)

Maling, Joan. 1972. "On Gapping and the Order of Constituents," *Linguistic Inquiry* 3:101–108. (for Right Node Raising)

Pollock, Jean-Yves. 1989. "Verb Movement, Universal Grammar, and the Structure of IP," *Linguistic Inquiry* 20:365–424. (for the structure of auxiliaries)

Rizzi, Luigi. 1990. *Relativized Minimality.* Cambridge, MA: MIT. (for another account of *wh*-islands)

Ross, John Robert. 1967. *Constraints on Variables in Syntax.* Doctoral dissertation. MIT. Reprinted as *Infinite Syntax*, Norwood, NJ: Ablex, 1986. (for island constraints)

Williams, Edwin. 1977. "Across-the-Board Rule Application," *Linguistic Inquiry* 8:419–423.

Tangent 8.1

Baker, Mark. 1985. "The Mirror Principle and Morphosyntactic Information," *Linguistic Inquiry* 10:533–581.

Chomsky, Noam. 1986. *Barriers.* Cambridge, MA: MIT. (See chapter 11 for a discussion of the Head Movement Constraint.)

———. 1989. "Some Notes on Economy of Derivation and Representation," *MIT Working Papers in Linguistics* Vol. 10. Cambridge, MA: Dept. of Linguistics and Philosophy, MIT. 43–74. (for discussion of the fact that only auxiliaries in English can undergo Verb Movement)

Koopman, Hilda, 1984. *The Syntax of Verbs.* Dordrecht, Holland: Foris Publications.

Pollock, Jean-Yves. 1989. "Verb Movement, Universal Grammar, and the Structure of IP," *Linguistic Inquiry* 20:365–424. (for why lexical verbs in French can undergo Verb Movement but only auxiliaries can in English)

Tangent 8.2

Andrews, Avery. 1982. "A Note on the Constituent Structure of Adverbials and Auxiliaries," *Linguistic Inquiry* 13:313–317.

Jackendoff, Ray. 1977. *X Bar Syntax: A Study of Phrase Structure.* Cambridge, MA: MIT.

Kayne, Richard. 1984. *Connectedness and Binary Branching.* Dordrecht, Holland: Foris. (for the theory that all nodes have at most two branches)

Larson, Richard. 1988. "On the Double Object Construction," *Linguistic Inquiry* 19:335–391. (for one analysis of the Double-Object Construction that maintains only binary branching)

Speas, Margaret. 1990. *Phrase Structure in Natural Languages.* Dordrecht: Kluwer.

Tangent 8.3

Baker, C. L. 1991. "The Syntax of English *Not:* The Limits of Core Grammar," *Linguistic Inquiry* 22:387–429.

Chomsky, Noam. 1986. *Barriers.* Cambridge, MA: MIT. (for head movement)

———. 1989. "Some Notes on Economy of Derivation and Representation," *MIT Working Papers in Linguistics* Vol. 10. Cambridge, MA: Dept. of Linguistics and Philosophy, MIT. 43–74. (for discussion of the fact that only auxiliaries in English can undergo Verb Movement)

Iatridou, Sabine. 1990. "About Agr(P)," *Linguistic Inquiry* 21:551–576.

Pollock, Jean-Yves. 1989. "Verb Movement, Universal Grammar, and the Structure of IP," *Linguistic Inquiry* 20:365–424. (for why lexical verbs in French can undergo Verb Movement but only auxiliaries can in English)

Ross, John Robert. 1967. *Constraints on Variables in Syntax.* Doctoral dissertation, MIT.

Problem Set 8.1

Culicover, Peter and Michael Rochemont. 1990. "Extraposition and the Complement Principle," *Linguistic Inquiry* 21:23–47.

Problem Set 8.2

Fukui, Naoki. 1986. *A Theory of Category Projection and Its Applications.* Doctoral dissertation, MIT.
—— and Margaret Speas. 1986. "Specifiers and Projection," *MIT Working Papers in Linguistics* 8:128–172.
Kuno, Susumu. 1973. *The Structure of the Japanese Language.* Cambridge, MA: MIT. (See chapter 1.)

Problem Set 8.3

Green, Georgia. 1976. "Main Clause Phenomena in Subordinate Clauses," *Language* 52:382–397.

Problem Set 8.5

Hankamer, Jorge. 1973. "Unacceptable Ambiguity," *Linguistic Inquiry* 4:17–68.

Problem Set 8.6

Rizzi, Luigi. 1986. "Null Objects in Italian and the Theory of *pro,*" *Linguistic Inquiry* 17:501–557.
Rosen, Carol. 1981. *The Relational Structure of Reflexive Clauses: Evidence From Italian.* Doctoral dissertation, Harvard University.

Problem Set 8.7

Chomsky, Noam. 1977. "On Wh-Movement," Peter Culicover, Thomas Wasow, and Adrian Akmajian (eds.), *Formal Syntax.* New York: Academic Press. 71–132.

Problem Set 8.8

Talaat, Hala. 1987. *The Verb Phrase in Egyptian Arabic.* Doctoral dissertation, University of Michigan.

Problem Set 8.9

Keenan, Edward and Bernard Comrie. 1977. "Noun Phrase Accessibility and Universal Grammar," *Linguistic Inquiry* 8:63–99.

Problem Set 8.10

Keenan, Edward and Bernard Comrie. 1977. "Noun Phrase Accessibility and Universal Grammar," *Linguistic Inquiry* 8:63–99.

Problem Set 8.11

Andrews, Avery. 1982. "A Note on the Constituent Structure of Adverbials and Auxiliaries," *Linguistic Inquiry* 13:313–317.
Culicover, Peter. 1982. *Though-Attraction.* Bloomington: Indiana University Linguistics Club.

Problem Set 8.12

Schmerling, Susan. 1975. "Asymmetric Conjunction and Rules of Conversation," in Peter Cole and Jerry Morgan (eds.), *Syntax and Semantics* 3. New York: Academic Press. 211–232.

Problem Set 8.13

Gazdar, Gerald, Ewan Klein, Geoffrey Pullum, and Ivan Sag. 1985. *Generalized Phrase Structure Grammar.* Cambridge, MA: Harvard University.
Horn, George. 1983. *Lexical-Functional Grammar.* Amsterdam: Mouton.
Kaplan, Ronald and Joan Bresnan. 1982. "Lexical-Functional Grammar: A Formal System for Grammatical Representation," in Joan Bresnan (ed.), *The Mental Representation of Grammatical Relations.* Cambridge, MA: MIT. 173–281.

Problem Set 8.15

Chomsky, Noam and Howard Lasnik. 1977. "Filters and Control," *Linguistic Inquiry* 8:425–504.
Jaeggli, Osvaldo. 1980. "Remarks on *To* Contraction," *Linguistic Inquiry* 11:239–245.
Lightfoot, David. 1986. "A Brief Response," *Linguistic Inquiry* 17:111–113.
Postal, Paul and Geoffrey Pullum. 1982. "The Contraction Debate," *Linguistic Inquiry* 13:122–138.

Problem Set 8.16

Belletti, Adriana. 1990. *Generalized Verb Movement: Aspects of Verb Syntax.* Torino: Rosenberg & Sellier. (See chapter 1.)
Koopman, Hilda. 1984. *The Syntax of Verbs.* Dordrecht, Holland: Foris Publications.
Iatridou, Sabine 1990. "About Agr(P)," *Linguistic Inquiry* 21:551–577 (for some problems with the breakdown of INFL into many functional nodes)
Pollock, Jean-Yves. 1989. "Verb Movement, Universal Grammar, and the Structure of IP," *Linguistic Inquiry* 20:365–424. (for the breakdown of INFL into various functional nodes)

Star Problem 8.1

Hoeksema, Jack and Donna Jo Napoli. 1991. "Coordinative and Subordinative *So*," unpublished ms. University of Groningen and Swarthmore College.

Star Problem 8.2

Maling, Joan. 1972. "On Gapping and the Order of Constituents," *Linguistic Inquiry* 3:101–108. (for Right Node Raising)

Williams, Edwin. 1977. "Across-the-Board Rule Application," *Linguistic Inquiry* 8:419–423.

Star Problem 8.6

Bresnan, Joan. 1970. "On Complementizers: Toward a Syntactic Theory of Complement Types," *Foundations of Language* 6.

Ernst, Thomas. 1991. "Chinese A-not-A Questions and the ECP," unpublished ms. University of Delaware. (for the distinction between manner/reason and locative/temporal adverbials)

Huang, C.-T. James. 1982. *Logical Relations in Chinese and the Theory of Grammar.* MIT dissertation. (for the distinction between manner/reason and locative/temporal adverbials)

Lasnik, Howard and Mamoru Saito. 1984. "On the Nature of Proper Government," *Linguistic Inquiry* 15:235–289.

CHAPTER 9

Narrative

Chomsky, Noam. 1981. *Lectures on Government and Binding.* Dordrecht, Holland: Foris Publications. (for the original concept of accessibility)

———. 1986. *Barriers.* Cambridge, MA: MIT. (for the Minimality Condition)

Haik, Isabelle. 1984. "Indirect Binding," *Linguistic Inquiry* 15:185–224. (on weak crossover).

Hoeksema, Jack and Donna Jo Napoli. 1990. "A Condition on Circular Chains: A Restatement of i-within-i," *Journal of Linguistics* 26:403–424.

Hornstein, Norbert. 1984. *Logic as Grammar.* Cambridge, MA: MIT. (for scope and quantifiers)

Huang, C.-T. James. 1984. "On the Distribution and Reference of Empty Pronouns," *Linguistic Inquiry* 15:531–574. (on strong crossover)

Koopman, Hilda and Dominique Sportiche. 1982. "Variables and the Bijection Principle," *The Linguistic Review* 2:139–160.

Lasnik, Howard and Mamoru Saito. 1984. "On the Nature of Proper Government," *Linguistic Inquiry* 15:235–290. (on *that*-trace effects and the ECP)

May, Robert. 1985. *Logical Form.* Cambridge, MA: MIT.

Rizzi, Luigi. 1990. *Relativized Minimality.* Cambridge, MA: MIT.

Problem Set 9.1

Hoeksema, Jack and Donna Jo Napoli. 1990. "A Condition on Circular Chains: A Restatement of i-within-i," *Journal of Linguistics* 26:403–424.

Problem Set 9.3

Ue, Noriko. 1982. *A Crossing Constraint in Japanese Syntax.* Doctoral dissertation, University of Michigan.

Problem Set 9.4

Burzio, Luigi. 1986. *Italian Syntax: A Government-Binding Approach.* Dordrecht, Holland: D. Reidel.

Kayne, Richard. 1989. "Null Subjects and Clitic Climbing," in Osvaldo Jaeggli and Ken Safir (eds.), *The Null Subject Parameter.* Dordrecht: Kluwer Academic. 239–261.

Problem Set 9.5

Kameyama, Megumi. 1983. "Topics and Zero Pronouns in Japanese: A Reply to Huang," paper read at the 58th annual LSA meeting, Minneapolis, MN, Dec. 28–30.

Raposo, Eduardo. 1984. "On the Null Object in European Portuguese," in Osvaldo Jaeggli and Carmen Silva-Corvalan (eds.), *Studies in Romance Linguistics.* Dordrecht, Holland: Foris. 373–390.

Star Problem 9.1

Liberman, Mark and Ivan Sag. 1974. "Prosodic Form and Discourse Function," *CLS* 10:416–427.

Star Problem 9.2

Hoeksema, Jack and Donna Jo Napoli. 1990. "A Conditon on Circular Chains: A Restatement of i-within-i," *Journal of Linguistics* 26:403–424.

CHAPTER 10

Narrative

Bach, Emmon and Barbara Hall Partee. 1980. "Anaphora and Semantic Structure," in J. Kreiman and A. Ojeda (eds.), *Papers From the Parassession on Pronouns and Anaphora.* Chicago Linguistic Society, Chicago, 1–28. (for some caveats about reanalysis)

Baker, Mark. 1988. *Incorporation: A Theory of Grammatical Function Changing,* Chicago: University of Chicago.

Barss, Andrew and Howard Lasnik. 1986. "A Note on Anaphora and Double Objects," *Linguistic Inquiry* 17:347–54 (for the six phenomena studied with respect to the Double-Object Construction)

Cantrall, William. 1974. *Viewpoint, Reflexives, and the Nature of Noun Phrases.* The Hague: Mouton. (for the notion of logophoricity)

Carroll, Susanne. 1984. "On Non-Anaphor Reflexives," *Revue quebecoise de linguistique* 15:135–166. (for examples of reflexives that do not have an antecedent in the same sentence)

Chomsky, Noam 1981. *Lectures on Government and Binding.* Dordrecht, Holland: Foris. (for arguments in favor of the existence of small clauses)

Chung, Sandra and James McCloskey. 1987. "Government, Barriers and Small Clauses in Modern Irish," *Linguistic Inquiry* 18:173–237. (for small clauses and for the claim that some Ps do not count in determining c-command in Irish)

den Dikken, Marcel. 1991. "Particles and the Dative Alternation," in *Proceedings of the Second Leiden Conference for Junior Linguists.* 71–86 (for more on the Double-Object Construction)

Giorgi, Alessandra and Giuseppe Longobardi. 1991. *The Syntax of Noun Phrases.* Cambridge: Cambridge University. (for evidence that Italian does not make use of linearity in defining domains for binding)

Jackendoff, Ray. 1972. *Semantic Interpretation in Generative Grammar.* Cambridge, MA: MIT. (for the Thematic Hierarchy and the TH restriction on anaphora)

———. 1990. "On Larson's Treatment of the Double Object Construction," *Linguistic Inquiry* 21:427–455. (for arguments that linearity is important to defining domains)

Larson, Richard. 1988. "On the Double Object Construction," *Linguistic Inquiry* 19:335–391. (for an analysis of the Double-Object Construction in which the first NP asymmetrically c-commands the second)

Napoli, Donna Jo. 1988. "Subjects and External Arguments/Clauses and Nonclauses," *Linguistics and Philosophy* 11:323–354. (for the debate about whether small clauses exist)

———. (forthcoming) "The Double-Object Construction, Domain Asymmetries, and Linear Precedence," *Linguistics.*

Postal, Paul. 1971 *Cross-Over Phenomena.* New York: Holt, Rinehart and Winston. (for the Cross-Over Constraint)

Reinhart, Tanya. 1976. *The Syntactic Domain of Anaphora.* Doctoral dissertation, Cambridge, MA: MIT. (for evidence that c- command is a factor in binding)

Staczek, John. 1988. "Sentential and Discoursal Reflexives in English: A Matter of Variation," *Studia Anglica Posnaniensia*, Vol. XIX. Poznan, Poland: Adam Mickiewicz University. (for examples of reflexives that do not have antecedents within the same sentence)

Stowell, Timothy. 1981. *Origins of Phrase Structure.* Doctoral dissertation, MIT. (for arguments in favor of the existence of small clauses)

Williams, Edwin. 1983. "Against Small Clauses," *Linguistic Inquiry* 14:287–308 (for arguments that small clauses do not exist)

Zribi-Hertz, Anne. 1989. "Anaphor Binding and Narrative Point of View: English Reflexive Pronouns in Sentence and Discourse," *Language* 65:695–727. (for an overview of the literature and for much new evidence on the importance of logophoricity in L-D Anaphora)

Problem Set 10.1

Sells, Peter. 1987. "Aspects of Logophoricity," *Linguistic Inquiry* 18:445–479.
Ue, Noriko. 1982. *A Crossing Constraint in Japanese Syntax*. Doctoral dissertation, University of Michigan.

Problem Set 10.2

Giorgi, Alessandra. 1984. "Toward a Theory of Long Distance Anaphors," *The
Linguistic Review* 3:307–361.
Napoli, Donna Jo. 1979. "Reflexivization Across Clause Boundaries in Italian,"
Journal of Linguistics 15:1–28.
Zribi-Hertz, Anne. 1989. "Anaphor Binding and Narrative Point of View: English
Reflexive Pronouns in Sentence and Discourse," *Language* 65:695–727.

Problem Set 10.3

Bordelois, Ivonne. 1988. "Causatives: From Lexicon to Syntax," *Natural Language and Linguistic Theory* 6:57–93.
Fauconnier, Gilles. 1976. "Complement Subject Deletion and the Analysis of *Menacer*," in Marta Lujan and Fritz Hensey (eds.), *Current Studies in Romance
Linguistics*. Washington, D.C.: Georgetown University. 144–161.
Rosen, Sara. 1989. *Argument Structure and Complex Predicates*. Doctoral dissertation, Brandeis University.

Problem Set 10.4

Napoli, Donna Jo 1974. "Una breve analisi dei verbi modali *potere* e *dovere*," in
Mario Medici and Antonella Sangregorio (eds.), *Fenomeni morfologici e
sintattici nell' italiano contemporaneo*. Rome: Bulzoni. 233–240. (for the
main verb nature of modals in Italia)
Rizzi, Luigi. 1978. "A Restructuring Rule in Italian Syntax," in Samuel J. Keyser
(ed.), *Recent Transformational Studies in European Languages*. Cambridge, MA: MIT. 113–158.
Rosen, Sara. 1989. *Argument Structure and Complex Predicates*. Doctoral dissertation, Brandeis University.

Problem Set 10.5

Safir, Ken. 1983. "On Small Clauses as Constituents," *Linguistic Inquiry* 14:730–
735.

Problem Set 10.6

Belletti, Adriana and Luigi Rizzi. 1988. "Psych-verbs and Theta- Theory," *Natural
Language and Linguistic Theory* 6:291–352.
Grimshaw, Jane. 1990. *Argument Structure*. Cambridge, MA: MIT. (See chapter
2.)

Pesetsky, David. 1991. *Experiencer Predicates and Universal Alignment Principles*, unpublished ms., MIT.

Problem Set 10.8

Nagai, Noriko. 1990. "Complex Passives and Major Subjects in Japanese," unpublished paper, Duke University.

Star Problem 10.3

Chomsky, Noam. 1981. *Lectures on Government and Binding.* Dordrecht, Holland: Foris. (See page 78, in particular.)

Star Problem 10.4

Anonymous. Abstract. "Agreement by Default and Anaphors," given at NELS 21, Fall, 1990

Index